PLATO'S *PHAEDO*

Plato's *Phaedo* is a literary gem that develops many of Plato's most famous ideas. David Ebrey's careful reinterpretation argues that the many debates about the dialogue cannot be resolved so long as we consider its passages in relative isolation from one another, separated from their intellectual background. His book shows how Plato responds to his literary, religious, scientific, and philosophical context, and argues that we can understand the dialogue's central ideas and arguments only in light of its overall structure. This approach yields new interpretations of the dialogue's key ideas, including the nature and existence of "Platonic" forms, the existence of the soul after death, the method of hypothesis, and the contemplative ethical ideal. Moreover, this comprehensive approach shows how the characters play an integral role in the *Phaedo*'s development and how its literary structure complements Socrates' views while making its own distinctive contribution to the dialogue's drama and ideas.

DAVID EBREY is Serra Húnter Fellow at the University of Barcelona. He has co-edited (with Richard Kraut) the *Cambridge Companion to Plato* (2022), edited *Theory and Practice in Aristotle's Natural Science* (2015), and published articles on a variety of topics in Plato and Aristotle.

Plato's *Phaedo*

FORMS, DEATH, AND THE PHILOSOPHICAL LIFE

DAVID EBREY

University of Barcelona

CAMBRIDGE
UNIVERSITY PRESS

Shaftesbury Road, Cambridge CB2 8EA, United Kingdom

One Liberty Plaza, 20th Floor, New York, NY 10006, USA

477 Williamstown Road, Port Melbourne, VIC 3207, Australia

314–321, 3rd Floor, Plot 3, Splendor Forum, Jasola District Centre, New Delhi – 110025, India

103 Penang Road, #05–06/07, Visioncrest Commercial, Singapore 238467

Cambridge University Press is part of Cambridge University Press & Assessment, a department of the University of Cambridge.

We share the University's mission to contribute to society through the pursuit of education, learning and research at the highest international levels of excellence.

www.cambridge.org
Information on this title: www.cambridge.org/9781108790994

DOI: 10.1017/9781108787475

© Cambridge University Press & Assessment 2023

This publication is in copyright. Subject to statutory exception and to the provisions of relevant collective licensing agreements, no reproduction of any part may take place without the written permission of Cambridge University Press & Assessment.

First published 2023
First paperback edition 2024

A catalogue record for this publication is available from the British Library

Library of Congress Cataloging-in-Publication data
NAMES: Ebrey, David, 1978– author.
TITLE: Plato's Phaedo : forms, death, and the philosophical life / David Ebrey, Universitat de Barcelona.
DESCRIPTION: Cambridge ; New York, NY : Cambridge University Press, 2022. | Includes bibliographical references and index.
IDENTIFIERS: LCCN 2022025741 (print) | LCCN 2022025742 (ebook) | ISBN 9781108479943 (hardback) | ISBN 9781108790994 (paperback) | ISBN 9781108787475 (epub)
SUBJECTS: LCSH: Plato. Phaedo. | BISAC: PHILOSOPHY / History & Surveys / Ancient & Classical
CLASSIFICATION: LCC B379 .E27 2022 (print) | LCC B379 (ebook) | DDC 184–dc23/eng/20220708
LC record available at https://lccn.loc.gov/2022025741
LC ebook record available at https://lccn.loc.gov/2022025742

ISBN 978-1-108-47994-3 Hardback
ISBN 978-1-108-79099-4 Paperback

Cambridge University Press & Assessment has no responsibility for the persistence or accuracy of URLs for external or third-party internet websites referred to in this publication and does not guarantee that any content on such websites is, or will remain, accurate or appropriate.

To my parents

Contents

Acknowledgments		*page* xi
	Introduction	1
	A Brief Overview of the Dialogue	8
1	**The Characters**	12
	1.1 Phaedo	13
	1.2 Plato and Other Socratics	15
	1.3 Simmias and Cebes, Philolaus and Pythagoreanism	17
	1.4 Socrates	22
	1.5 Conclusion	27
2	**The *Phaedo* as an Alternative to Tragedy and Socrates as a Poet: 57a–61c**	28
	2.1 The *Phaedo*'s Engagement with Tragedy	29
	2.2 Socrates as a True Hero	35
	2.3 The *Phaedo* as a Story of Gods, Heroes, and the Underworld	38
	2.4 The Action of the Dialogue and Tragic Drama	42
	2.5 An Aesop Fable about Pleasure and Pain: 60b–c	47
	2.6 Socrates as Interpreter of Dreams: 60c–61b	52
	2.7 Conclusion	53
3	**Defense of the Desire to Be Dead: 61c–69e**	54
	3.1 The Argument against Suicide: 61c–63a	55
	3.2 The Aims and Structure of the Defense Speech: 63b–69e	57
	3.3 The Philosopher's Desire to Be Dead	59
	3.4 Itself through Itself (*auto kath' hauto*)	63
	3.5 Bodily Pleasures, Pains, Desires, and Fears	69

	3.6 Forms, Inquiry, and the Soul Itself through Itself	70
	3.7 Acquiring Wisdom while Embodied	75
	3.8 Courage, Temperance, and the Correct Exchange: 68b–69e	77
	3.9 Conclusion	86
4	**Cebes' Challenge and the Cyclical Argument: 69e–72d**	88
	4.1 Cebes' Challenge: 69e–70b	89
	4.2 The Structure of the Cyclical Argument	92
	4.3 Opposites Coming to Be from Opposites	95
	4.4 The Supplemental Argument: 72a–d	98
	4.5 Conclusion	99
5	**The Recollecting Argument: 72e–77d**	100
	5.1 The Place of the Argument in the Dialogue	101
	5.2 Overview of the Argument	103
	5.3 The First Stage – Different Types of Recollecting: 73c–74a	104
	5.4 The Second Stage – Equality, Equal Sticks, and the Source of Our Knowledge: 74a–d	108
	5.5 The Third Stage – Knowing before Sensing, and so before Birth: 74d–75c	118
	5.6 The Fourth Stage – Forgetting the Knowledge We Once Had: 75d–76d	125
	5.7 Coda – The Importance of Forms and the Scope of the Argument: 76d–77d	128
	5.8 Conclusion	128
6	**The Kinship Argument: 77d–80d**	131
	6.1 The Introduction and Conclusion of the Argument: 77d–78a, 80b	132
	6.2 The Structure of the Argument	135
	6.3 The First Half of the Argument – Forms and the Many Things: 78b–79a	136
	6.4 The Second Half of the Argument – The Soul's Kinship with the Unseen: 79a–80b	152
	6.5 The Nature of the Body	157
	6.6 Conclusion	159
7	**The Return to the Defense: 80d–84b**	162
	7.1 Incorporating the Kinship Argument into the Defense: 80d–81a	163
	7.2 The Body's Effects on Impure Souls: 81b–82b	165
	7.3 How the Philosopher's Soul Reasons: 82b–84b	170

	7.4 Is the Body the Subject of Mental States?	180
	7.5 Conclusion	182
8	**Misology and the Soul as a *harmonia*: 84c–86e, 88c–95a**	184
	8.1 Socrates as a Prophet: 84c–85b	186
	8.2 Misology and Motivated Reasoning: 88c–91c	187
	8.3 Simmias' Objection – The Soul as (like) a *harmonia*: 85b–86d	193
	8.4 Socrates' Reply: 91c–95a	199
	8.5 Conclusion	206
9	**Socrates' Autobiography: 95e–102a**	207
	9.1 *Aitia, aition*, and the Aims of Natural Science	208
	9.2 The Background: Ancient Greek Medicine	214
	9.3 Socrates' Initial Inquiry: 96b–97b	216
	9.4 What Socrates Thought Anaxagoras Would Do: 97b–98b	220
	9.5 What Socrates Sees Anaxagoras as Actually Doing: 98b–99c	224
	9.6 Introducing Socrates' Second Sailing: 99c–d	227
	9.7 Forms and *aitiai*	229
	9.8 Socrates' Method of Hypothesis	232
	9.9 Conclusion	246
10	**Cebes' Objection and the Final Argument: 86e–88b, 102a–107b**	248
	10.1 Closely Engaging with Cebes' Objection: 95b–96a	250
	10.2 Cebes' Objection: 86e–88b	251
	10.3 The Final Argument's Response to Cebes' Objection	254
	10.4 The Forms in Us: 102a–103c	255
	10.5 The Bringers: 103c–105c	260
	10.6 The Final Argument Proper: 105c–107a	266
	10.7 The Soul and the Divine as Immortal	271
	10.8 Conclusion	273
11	**The Cosmos and the Afterlife: 107c–115a**	275
	11.1 The First Stage – Socrates' Basic Commitment: 107c–d	276
	11.2 The Second Stage – The Bare Outline of the Journey: 107d–108a	277
	11.3 The Third Stage – The Journey in Light of Earlier Commitments: 108a–c	279
	11.4 The Fourth Stage – Convictions about Cosmology: 108d–110a	280
	11.5 The Fifth Stage – The *muthos* of the Overworld and the Underworld: 110a–114d	285
	11.6 Coda – After the *muthos*: 114d–115a	297
	11.7 Conclusion	297

12	**The Death Scene: 115a–118a**	299
	12.1 Care for the Soul	300
	12.2 Socrates' Temperance, Courage, and Piety	301
	12.3 Socrates' Last Words	303
	12.4 Conclusion	311

Bibliography   313
Index Locorum   325
Index   341

Acknowledgments

This book would not exist without generous institutional support. I was very fortunate to have a one-year Solmsen Fellowship at the Institute for Research in the Humanities at the University of Wisconsin–Madison, and then a three-year research fellowship from the DFG–funded Research Training Group "Philosophy, Science and the Sciences" at the Humboldt University of Berlin. The community of scholars at Humboldt working on ancient philosophy, science, and medicine provided the perfect environment for writing this book. I received valuable feedback on several chapters at Humboldt's weekly ancient philosophy colloquium, led in various semesters by Jonathan Beere, Stephen Menn, and James Wilberding.

I owe a special debt of gratitude to Emily Fletcher and David Sedley, who each read through the entire manuscript, providing detailed comments on each chapter. I am also very grateful to Gábor Betegh, Joseph Bjelde, Sean Coughlin, Sylvain Delcomminette, Matt Duncombe, Tushar Irani, Sean Kelsey, and Franco Trivigno for reading several of the chapters and discussing them with me at length, as well as to Cambridge University Press' readers for their reports. I would also like to thank Rachel Barney, Agnes Callard, Ian Campbell, Willie Costello, Philip van der Eijk, Dhananjay Jagannathan, Gale Justin, Patricia Marechal, Tamer Newar, Suzanne Obdrzalek, Jorge Torres, and John Wynne for comments on individual chapters. In 2018 I organized a week-long reading group on *Phaedo* 88b–103b at Humboldt. I would like to thank the participants; those not already mentioned include Sarah Broadie, Marion Dumont, Nora Kreft, and David Merry. I taught a graduate seminar on the *Phaedo* at Northwestern and two such seminars at Humboldt; in the 2020 seminar at Humboldt the students read through a full draft of the book. I would like to thank the participants in these seminars, including Lukas Apsel, Robert Mordarski, Maribel Ramírez, and Brett Thompson, for their thoughts and suggestions on the chapter drafts. I would also like to thank Kathleen Heil and Manuela Tecusan for their editorial work on the manuscript, Lex Academic for producing the index, and Rosa Matera for reviewing my discussions of the Greek and producing the index locorum.

This book works through the *Phaedo* in order. Most of my essays on the *Phaedo*, by contrast, take up a specific topic and follow it through the dialogue. Hence the content of a single essay typically cuts across several chapters of this book. This is true for "The Asceticism of the *Phaedo*: Pleasure, Purification, and the Soul's Proper Activity," *Archiv für Geschichte der Philosophie* 99 (2017), 1–30, "The *Phaedo*'s Final Argument and the Soul's Kinship with the Divine," *Oxford Studies in Ancient Philosophy* 60 (2021), 25–62, and "The Unfolding Account of Forms in the *Phaedo*," in D. Ebrey and R. Kraut (eds.), *The Cambridge Companion to Plato*, 2nd ed. (Cambridge: Cambridge University Press) (2022), 268–97. "The *Phaedo* as an Alternative to Tragedy," in *Classical Philology* 118 (2023), is the only essay that overlaps with just a single chapter: Chapter 2. I thank the journals for allowing me to use the material from these articles in this book.

In addition to the talks given in support of the published essays (acknowledged in each), I presented parts of this book to audiences at the University of Crete (Rethymno), the University of Tübingen, the University of Oslo, the National Autonomous University of Mexico, the Ancient Medicine Colloquium at Humboldt, and the following conferences: Philosophy in Assos (2019), a keynote address at the 6th Annual Berlin–Munich graduate conference, the 2020 Eastern APA Symposium, the "Plato and Platonism" conference at the University of Oslo, and "Plato's Pleasures: New Perspectives" at King's College London. I would like to thank the organizers and audiences at each of these presentations.

My friends and family have helped me in countless ways through this process. Above all, I thank my parents and my wife, Conni Pätz, for their love and unflagging support.

Introduction

The *Phaedo* is a literary gem that develops many of Plato's most famous ideas and arguments, so it comes as no surprise that there are trenchant debates and deep disagreements about almost every part of the dialogue. This book argues that these debates and disagreements cannot be resolved so long as we consider the dialogue's passages in relative isolation from one another, separated from their intellectual context. Many of the *Phaedo*'s ideas can only be fully understood once one recognizes how Plato is engaging with and responding to ideas in his literary, religious, scientific, and philosophical context. Moreover, the dialogue itself is tightly unified in such a way that one can fully understand its central ideas and arguments only in light of its overall structure. Even arguments that appear to stand on their own rely on claims made elsewhere in the dialogue. Carefully working through the details with an eye to the dialogue's structure and aims, in light of its context, is the best way to understand it. And so, I have written this as a comprehensive treatment of the dialogue. This overall approach yields new interpretations of key ideas in the *Phaedo*, including the nature and existence of "Platonic" forms, the continued existence of the soul after death, the method of hypothesis, and the contemplative ethical ideal. Moreover, this approach shows how the interaction between the characters plays an integral role in the *Phaedo*'s development and how its literary structure complements Socrates' views while making its own distinctive contribution to the dialogue's drama and ideas.

The *Phaedo* is a story of how Socrates, on the last day of his life, faces his death. He does so as a philosopher, and in doing so shows others how to live philosophical lives and philosophize in the face of death. Socrates seems to defend a radical sort of Platonism in the dialogue – although many modern interpreters have denied this in various ways.[1] For example, Socrates claims that the philosopher's only pursuit is

---

[1] In general, references to the secondary literature are found in the following chapters, but here are a few examples of scholarship from the last sixty years that interpret the *Phaedo* in ways that

dying and being dead (64a), that the soul continues to exist after death and reincarnates (e.g. 72a, 81d–e, 107d–e), that the soul is akin to the unchanging forms (79d, 80d, 84a–b), and that, by becoming like the forms, the soul can escape the cycle of reincarnation and be eternally happy (81a).[2] He claims that one should not inquire using the senses (65e–66a, 83a, 99e–100a) and that natural scientists have proposed the entirely wrong sorts of causes (96e–99c); instead he uses forms – things such as largeness, equality, justice, and beauty (100c, 101c) – to specify causes. He holds that forms cannot be seen (65d, 79a) and are superior to ordinary, perceptible objects (74d–75b).

In this book I argue that Socrates' views in the *Phaedo* are every bit as radical as they initially seem – perhaps even more so. They are radical by today's standards as well as by those of his time. Socrates (by which I mean the Socrates of the *Phaedo*, unless otherwise noted) is not trying to seem reasonable and capture ordinary intuitions; instead, he is arguing that we fundamentally misunderstand the nature of reality, how to acquire knowledge, what we are, and how we should live. Scholars sometimes attribute more reasonable-sounding views to Socrates on the basis of charity, thinking that otherwise he would put forward radical views without any explanation, or with laughably poor arguments. This book aims to uncover the explanations for radical ideas widely seen as at the heart of Platonism. One way I do this is by considering all the parts of the dialogue, including the more radical parts that scholars often pass over. I also show that, once we accept that Socrates is genuinely making the radical claims he seems to be making, the details of his account carefully fit together, clarifying what his views are and why he defends them.

Another way in which I develop my reading relies on an important thesis of this book: the *Phaedo* has what I call an "unfolding structure," in which claims are made earlier in the dialogue apparently without being defended, but then are explained and argued for at later stages. Recognizing this structure clarifies the reasons for radical claims that otherwise seem unexplained, allowing me to provide new accounts of forms, the soul, and the good life in the *Phaedo*. These are not three independent topics: Socrates grounds his account of the soul in his account of the forms, and his account of the good life in his accounts of the soul and the forms. Thus, while Socrates' ultimate concern in the dialogue is with how to live, the ultimate basis for his view is found in his account of the forms.

Since these are central topics in the dialogue and important to my overall account, let me provide here a brief overview of this unfolding structure, beginning with the account of the forms. A form is what is picked out by the correct answer to

---

makes it seem less radical than it at first appears: Vlastos 1969, Nehamas 1975, Penner 1987, Most 1993, Woolf 2004, and Lee 2012. For a general overview of secondary literature on the *Phaedo*, see Ebrey 2017a.

[2] Throughout, references to Plato's dialogues are to the most recent OCT editions.

Socrates' "what is *f*-ness?" question. Throughout the dialogue, Socrates repeatedly says that forms are distinct from ordinary, perceptible objects such as sticks, horses, and cloaks. He has no set vocabulary in the *Phaedo* for referring to these ordinary things; instead, he typically introduces them with examples (74a, 78d–e). They are often referred to as "perceptible" or "sensible" things in the secondary literature, following Aristotle, but I will call them "ordinary objects," since I will argue that in the *Phaedo* being perceptible is not one of their most important features.

Scholars often claim that Socrates simply presupposes the existence of so-called Platonic forms in the *Phaedo* – that is, forms that are separate from ordinary objects – or that the recollecting argument provides one of his few arguments for their existence.[3] I argue instead that Socrates introduces the idea that forms are different from ordinary objects near the beginning of the dialogue, but we do not fully understand how and why until the final stages of the unfolding account, well after the recollecting argument. Socrates introduces forms in the defense speech and gets Simmias to agree that they are not perceived (at 65d–e). In the recollecting argument, he draws attention to the fact that ordinary objects change over time, whereas the forms do not (at 74b–c). Moreover, he claims there that ordinary objects are deficient in comparison to the forms (74d–75b), although it is unclear what exactly this deficiency consists in. In the kinship argument (78b–80b, traditionally called the "affinity argument"), Socrates considerably expands his description of how they differ; I argue that he describes forms there as simple and partless and so as having all their features as a whole rather than in virtue of some part or structural feature that they possess. By contrast, not only do ordinary objects change over time, they have opposing features at a single time owing to their complex structure. This clarifies how forms differ from ordinary objects, but does not yet explain why they do so. That is explained in Socrates' account of forms as causes (100b–101e) and in the final argument (102a–107b). Forms, he argues, do a sort of causal–explanatory work that ordinary objects cannot do. The form of *f*-ness is that because of which every *f* thing is *f*. But ordinary objects are by nature receptive of opposites, which, he argues, means that they could not fulfill this role. Thus forms cannot be ordinary objects. For forms to do their explanatory work, they must be simple, be explanatorily prior to ordinary objects, and possess their features owing to their own nature; this is why they must have the features Socrates ascribes to them in the recollecting and kinship arguments.

According to this reading, Socrates distinguishes forms from ordinary objects quite differently from how we might – for example, by distinguishing between universals and particulars, or by thinking that forms are "abstract entities" and that

---

[3] This book presupposes that one has read through the dialogue, ideally several times. If not, I suggest beginning with Sedley and Long 2010's translation. At the end of this introduction there is a brief overview of the dialogue that provides the widely used names for the dialogue's different sections.

such entities, as a conceptual matter, could never be one of the ordinary objects we touch and see. Instead, the idea in the *Phaedo* is that we can learn about the nature of things like justice and largeness by thinking about the sort of causal–explanatory work they do and about what sort of thing is capable of doing this work.

Socrates' unfolding account of the soul builds on his unfolding account of the forms. Despite the *Phaedo*'s lengthy discussion of the soul – in antiquity, it had the alternative title *On the Soul* (DL 3.58) – this topic has not received much scholarly treatment. I argue that Socrates develops a novel account, according to which the soul belongs to the same broad category as the forms (roughly speaking, they share a genus), but, depending on how the soul acts, it can become more or less like the forms. The kinship argument (78b–80b) is the first place where Socrates explicitly turns to the question of the sort of thing the soul is, arguing that it is akin to the forms; this kinship allows the soul to grasp them. Most souls investigate with their bodily senses and are not very form-like (79c), but the philosopher's soul becomes stable like the forms (79d). The soul's ability to be more form-like or less so is crucial for underwriting Socrates' ethical views in the *Phaedo*. But if the soul were able to become less form-like in any and all respects, this would allow it to be destroyed. In Cebes' cloakmaker objection to the kinship argument (86e–88b), he suggests that the soul might ultimately be destroyed by the process of bringing life to the body; he then challenges Socrates to show that the soul is entirely immortal and indestructible. I argue that the final argument directly responds to Cebes' objection by showing that the soul's bringing life to the body, far from leading to its destruction, is precisely what ensures that it is immortal and indestructible. According to this interpretation, the final argument fills out a key part of the kinship argument's account of the soul; taken together, these two arguments present the soul as able to become more form-like or less so in several respects, but fixed in its connection to the form of life, and therefore entirely immortal and indestructible.

In and after the kinship argument (78b–84b), Socrates grounds his ethical account in his account of the soul and forms. But significantly earlier, in the defense speech (63b–69e), he presents his basic ethical account. Socrates says there that the philosopher disdains bodily things, avoids bodily pleasure, pain, desires, and fears, and instead devotes himself entirely to grasping the truth.[4] Again, Socrates makes these claims without fully explaining why they are the case. In and after the kinship

---

[4] I refer to the philosopher as "he" throughout this book, since (unfortunately) Socrates consistently assumes in the *Phaedo* that philosophers are men. Forms of ἀνήρ are used to discuss the actual or aspiring philosopher at 63e9, 67d12, 68b8, 76b5, 78a4, and 85c7. Socrates also refers to the philosophical man (φιλόσοφος ἀνήρ) at 64d2, 84a2–3, and 95c1. Heraclitus, in the first extant occurrence of the word "philosopher," uses the phrase "philosophical men" (B35). Moore 2019, for example, argues that this term was used to refer to Pythagoreans. Perhaps, then, Socrates' use of "philosophical man" is part of his appropriating Pythagorean ideas and language in the *Phaedo*. For a discussion of this appropriation, see Section 1.3.

argument, he explains why we should all live as philosophers and why this means that we should live such an ascetic life. The soul is, by nature, akin to the forms, and so it is able to enter the divine, stable, and unchanging state that they are in. The soul can reach this state by grasping the forms, thereby becoming more like them. We are, most properly, our souls, and so we have a chance to become more like the divine by coming to know the forms. However, bodily pleasures and pains lead us to believe falsehoods, so we do not grasp the stable truth but rather become like the changing ordinary objects. More insidiously, pleasures and pains lead us to desire things other than grasping the truth, so that we do not even attempt to do what will lead to our obtaining wisdom and eternal happiness. When we acquire these bodily desires, our souls become impure, infected with something not proper to the soul. Near the end of the dialogue, Socrates' account of the cosmos and the afterlife (107c–115a) uses his account of the soul's purity and impurity to explain how such souls are benefited or harmed after death. Then in the death scene (115a–118a), Socrates exemplifies the demanding ethical theory he has articulated over the course of the dialogue.

There are several threads running through the *Phaedo*. At its core are the three just mentioned: the unfolding accounts of forms, the soul, and the good life. Another central thread is Socrates' interconnected account of fear, doubt, trust, persuasion, and inquiry.[5] Early in the dialogue, Socrates is happy that Cebes is always scrutinizing arguments and difficult to persuade (63a). In Cebes' challenge (69e–70b), Cebes says that people are fearful that the soul dissipates upon death and so asks Socrates to persuade them not to have such doubts. The cyclical and kinship arguments aim to persuade them not to have this fear. But over the first half of the dialogue, Simmias' and Cebes' rapid-fire acceptance of and objections to arguments leads to the threat of misology that Socrates highlights near the dialogue's midpoint (89c–91c). Socrates says that misology arises from repeatedly trusting a *logos* – here, a theory or argument – and then a little later doubting it; after this has happened several times, one ends up distrusting and hating all *logoi* entirely (90b). I argue that several parts of the second half of the dialogue are designed to show how to avoid misology. Immediately following this discussion, Socrates responds (at 91e–95a) to Simmias' *harmonia* objection to the kinship argument. His response, I argue, displays the method of hypothesis that Socrates later introduces (100a–101e) in the autobiography. This method is part of the skill in argumentation that allows one to avoid misology. Seeing Socrates' response to Simmias as an example of the method of hypothesis helps to clarify the details of this notoriously obscure method. Instead of quickly switching one's allegiance between views, the method involves thoroughly evaluating a view on its own terms before accepting it. It provides a way to cultivate the right sort of trust in *logoi*. Socrates' cosmological and eschatological account, near the end of the dialogue, illustrates another way to avoid misology: by

---

[5] My ideas here are heavily indebted to Sedley 1995, although developed differently.

carefully recognizing the appropriate level of confidence to have in a belief, given the nature and strength of one's reasons.

Another thread running through the dialogue identifies Socrates as a new sort of hero in a new type of story, an alternative to tragedy. The references to epic and tragic drama throughout the dialogue help to establish it as an alternative to tragedy – as Plato conceives of tragedy – with Socrates as a hero responding to the apparently tragic circumstances of his unjust death. Socrates should be admired, not pitied; his happiness is not the result of chance but rather within his control. The *Phaedo*, I argue, is written as a story that meets all the requirements described in *Republic* II–III for a properly told story about heroes, gods, daemons, and the underworld. Socrates not only acts as a hero should in such a story; his philosophical views explain why he can have control over his own happiness and why he, as a philosopher, has courage and the other qualities needed to be a hero. His heroic activities are identified as philosophical, fitting with the dramatic action of the dialogue being driven by arguments and objections, as well as by Socrates' efforts to help his companions avoid misology, the greatest evil (89d). The dialogue shows how a true hero faces death.

There are several other important threads that run through the dialogue and so this book, which I will briefly mention here. The opening of the dialogue introduces the topic of storytelling, which extends through to the end of the dialogue. Another thread is about how to inquire, which is closely connected to Socrates' views on forms and ordinary objects, as well as his account of misology. A third is about the nature of opposites; opposites play a role in each of his arguments that the soul exists before birth or after death. A fourth thread is the way in which Socrates draws on natural philosophy to defend his claims about the soul. Rather than expand on these and other threads here, I will allow them to emerge as we carefully work through the dialogue.

I have begun by introducing these threads because most readers come to the dialogue interested in specific topics, such as the soul or the forms. But ultimately the goal of this book is to understand the progression and development of the dialogue on its own terms, seeing how these various threads are woven into a unified work. At the end of this introduction I describe the overall arc of the dialogue that emerges from my reading.

Another important thesis of this book is that many of the *Phaedo*'s ideas are developments and reinterpretations of ideas from other philosophers or other intellectual and religious groups. The dialogue explicitly and implicitly refers to a large number of such people and groups – beginning with the dialogue's namesake and narrator, Phaedo, himself a writer of Socratic dialogues, who was freed from slavery – perhaps even by Socrates. As noted earlier, there are several allusions to epic and tragedy throughout the dialogue. A number of people connected to Pythagoreanism are mentioned early on, including Philolaus, the most prominent Pythagorean at the dialogue's dramatic date. Socrates goes on to refer to a variety of ideas associated with Philolaus and Pythagoreans, along with related ideas associated with Orphic writings, the Eleusinian mysteries, and initiation practices in general. Later, in the autobiography, Socrates discusses views from the Hippocratic medical tradition and from early Greek cosmologists, explicitly mentioning Anaxagoras and discussing his views at some length. Throughout the dialogue, Plato portrays Socrates as accepting key claims made by these intellectual movements and thinkers, but at the same time reinterpreting and transforming them. In doing so, he provides his own versions of Pythagorean, Orphic, Hippocratic, and Anaxagorean views.[6] Recognizing how Socrates appropriates his predecessors' ideas often clarifies Socrates' own ideas. It also helps avoid the tendency to dismiss parts of the dialogue. In general, the approach of this book is to show how we can develop a richer, more satisfying interpretation of the dialogue by taking seriously all of its many elements, showing how they are carefully integrated into a cohesive whole.

Some parts of the *Phaedo* have been explicitly dismissed for having "religious" arguments and views instead of "philosophical" ones.[7] But the religious language does not signal that Socrates' claims are any less philosophical. Instead, Socrates reinterprets and reimagines terms such as "initiation" and "purification" to express philosophical points. Consider Socrates' account of reincarnation. Pythagoreans (at least typically) believed in reincarnation. Socrates argues that the soul reincarnates, but he provides his own reasons for accepting this; they are initially based on an account of the nature of coming to be (in the cyclical argument), and then further refined with his account of bodily desires (after the kinship argument). Pythagoreans had a distinct way of life, which involved adhering to detailed Pythagorean strictures, the *acousmata*. Socrates argues for a distinctly Socratic form of philosophical life, which involves adhering to different sorts of demanding strictures. Socrates provides an account of how this life allows the soul to be purified and thereby escape reincarnation and obtain eternal happiness. In arguing for this, the *Phaedo* presents a Socratic version of Pythagorean ideas, including a Socratic account of how they are interconnected.

This is not to suggest that Plato intended the dialogue for people with Pythagorean sympathies or, for that matter, for people with Anaxagorean sympathies. We do not know who Plato's intended audience was. He may have thought that the dialogue would be particularly good at convincing people with Pythagorean sympathies, but the arguments do not in fact rely on having them. In any event, Plato could think that it is illuminating to see the best way to defend some Pythagorean ideas, whether or not his audience was antecedently attracted to them. On a similar note, there is no need to suppose that Plato intended the *Phaedo* for those who

---

[6] I am here building on important recent work by scholars. See Section 1.3 for references.
[7] E.g. Hackforth 1955, 44; Dorter 1982, 77; Ebert 2004, passim; and White 2006, esp. 457. Frequently scholars mention that these discussions have a mythical, religious, or Pythagorean overtone and then do not provide a detailed account of them (e.g. Gallop 1975, 88, Bostock 1988, ch. 2).

already accepted central Platonic ideas; on my reading, it contains arguments for them.

More controversially – and not necessary for accepting my other claims in this book – I think that the project of presenting a Platonic version of some Pythagorean, Orphic, Eleusinian, and Anaxagorean ideas can explain some of the discrepancies between the *Phaedo* and other dialogues, including those typically identified as middle-period dialogues. For example, in the *Phaedo* Socrates says that we can never genuinely attain a worthwhile share of wisdom while embodied (66d–e, 68a–b); he develops the idea – found in Orphic religious practices, among others – that if we prepare ourselves properly we can look forward to a better existence after death. By contrast, in the *Republic*, Socrates says that one could acquire genuine wisdom in the correct educational regime and that a philosopher so educated could possess, while embodied, the happiness that comes from true wisdom. Socrates is committed to the same broad principles across the dialogues: knowledge is incredibly difficult to acquire; only philosophers can acquire it; the soul is immortal; and those who live a philosophical life will have a better afterlife. The *Phaedo* provides a version of how Plato's broad commitments could be realized that draws on and develops certain Pythagorean, Orphic, and Eleusinian ideas. I do not see any reason to think that one dialogue or another presents Plato's definitive views on the topic. If Plato thought that he, like Socrates, lacked genuine knowledge regarding the most important matters, he would have reason to explore different ways in which his commitments could be realized.

*

I have not divided the dialogue with an eye toward having roughly equal-sized chapters, but rather toward preserving the structure of Socrates' arguments and allowing readers to turn directly to the parts likely to interest them. While this is a comprehensive book, it is not a commentary, and I do not attempt to resolve every interpretive puzzle or address every interesting issue or bit of reasoning along the way. Doing so would obfuscate the central development of the dialogue, as I see it, and make this book unmanageably long. Instead, I discuss the dialogue's main arguments and ideas – emphasizing those that reoccur across different parts of the dialogue, where a comprehensive approach is particularly fruitful. I also only address topics where I have something new and (I hope) interesting to say.

A BRIEF OVERVIEW OF THE DIALOGUE (WITH THE CORRESPONDING CHAPTERS AND SOME OF MY KEY CLAIMS)

The *Phaedo* is a dialogue within a dialogue, which starts in the outer frame with Echecrates asking Phaedo about the last day of Socrates' life (57a–60a). Phaedo describes who was there – many of Socrates' closest companions – and then begins describing the day, when Socrates had a conversation primarily with Simmias and Cebes. After Socrates sends Xanthippe away, he outlines a myth and then explains why he has been writing poetry (60a–61b). I argue that the opening of the dialogue sets it up as a new sort of story of a hero's death (Chapters 1, "The Characters," and 2, "The *Phaedo* as Alternative to Tragedy and Socrates as a Poet").

Socrates suggests that Evenus, a poet and sophist, follow him as quickly as possible in dying (61b–c). Cebes is shocked by this suggestion, leading Socrates to defend the claim that one should not commit suicide (61c–62c), and then provide what is called his "defense speech" (63b–69e), which explains why the philosopher's true desire is to be dead. In arguing for this, Socrates describes the forms for the first time in the dialogue and draws attention to a variety of problems caused by the body. He ends by arguing that only the philosopher has genuine virtue. This section introduces most of the central philosophical ideas in the dialogue, which are then further developed in later sections (Chapter 3, "Defense of the Desire to be Dead").

The core of the dialogue is structured by four arguments that the soul exists before birth or after death (70c–107b). These come in response to Cebes' challenge that Socrates should convince them that the soul is not destroyed upon death, and that it will have some power and wisdom (69e–70b). Cebes does not ask Socrates here to show that the soul is immortal and, I argue, Socrates' initial arguments are not meant to show this, but rather simply to address the fear that the soul is dispersed upon death. The first argument is Socrates' so-called cyclical argument (70c–72d), which includes a general account of how opposite comes to be from one another. It uses this general account to argue that the soul exists after death and reincarnates (Chapter 4, "Cebes' Challenge and the Cyclical Argument").

The second argument, the recollecting argument (72e–77d), comes in response to a suggestion from Cebes that the same conclusion is also shown by Socrates' view that learning is recollecting. In response, Socrates argues that when we learn, we recollect knowledge acquired before we are born, and so the soul must exist before birth. In arguing for this, Socrates develops views on (among other things) (i) different types of recollecting, (ii) forms and ordinary objects, and (iii) how we cognitively access the forms. I argue that Socrates is thinking of recollecting as an extended process, and that he is focused on a type of recollecting in which someone perceives one thing and brings to mind another, which is the very standard by which we judge the first (Chapter 5, "The Recollecting Argument").

Next comes the kinship argument (77d–80d, traditionally called the "affinity argument"), which argues that the soul is by nature similar and akin to the forms, and so unable to be disintegrated, just like them. I argue that this argument provides a much more careful and detailed account of forms than scholars have appreciated. The aim and structure of the argument has also been misunderstood, obfuscating its interest and strength. In any event, it plays a central role in the structure and development of the dialogue, in part because Simmias and Cebes provide objections to it, which Socrates responds to in the second half of the dialogue (Chapter 6, "The Kinship Argument").

The first thing that the kinship argument sets up is Socrates' return to the ethical claims made earlier in the defense speech, in a discussion I call "the return to the defense" (80d–84b). Socrates here draws on the account of the forms and soul in the kinship argument, as well as the account of reincarnation in the cyclical argument, to provide a basis for almost all of the ethical claims made earlier in the defense speech (Chapter 7, "The Return to the Defense").

After the return to the defense, Simmias and Cebes present their objections to the kinship argument: Simmias' *harmonia* objection and Cebes' cloakmaker objection (84d–88c). These objections lead them to doubt their ability to make any progress on these topics, which prompt the first return to the outer frame discussion, at almost the precise midpoint of the dialogue (88c–89b). After this, Socrates warns the companions to be careful not to become misologues (89c–91c). I argue that Socrates' main argumentative goal in the second half of the dialogue is to respond to Simmias' and Cebes' objections while showing how they can avoid the premature trust in *logoi* that leads to misology. I also argue that Simmias' *harmonia* objection does not present an epiphenomenalist view (Chapter 8, "Misology and the Soul as a *harmonia*").

Socrates says that, in order to address Cebes' cloakmaker objection, they need to thoroughly discuss the cause of coming to be and passing away (95e–96a). This leads to Socrates' so-called intellectual autobiography (95e–102a), in which he describes his early investigation into natural science, including: what he expected from Anaxagoras' claim that *nous* (intelligence) is responsible (*aitios*) for all things, his disappointment with what Anaxagoras in fact did, and his own theory that uses forms to specify causes (*aitiai*), which he supports with his method of hypothesis. I argue that Socrates responds to the project of natural science in just the way one would expect, given his portrayal elsewhere: he has trouble understanding what other people take as obvious, he becomes incredibly excited by the prospect of acquiring knowledge of the good, but when he is unable to acquire this knowledge he finds a way of proceeding that does not require knowledge. I also argue that Socrates' discussion of causes and of hypotheses should be understood in light of the sophisticated Greek medical works that predate the *Phaedo* (Chapter 9, "The Autobiography").

Socrates' intellectual autobiography provides the methodological and metaphysical foundation for the final argument. I argue that this argument is meant to show why Cebes' cloakmaker model of the soul is mistaken: instead of the soul's suffering from its connection to the body, its ability to bring life to the body is precisely what ensures its immortality and indestructability. The soul entirely possesses immortality, a characteristic feature of the divine (Chapter 10, "Cebes' Objection and the Final Argument").

After the final argument, Socrates returns to discussing the afterlife (107c–115a). In the secondary literature this is called "the myth," but Socrates does not refer to all of it as a myth, and doing so obscures the fact that Socrates thinks that different parts of his account have different epistemic statuses: some parts he says he is convinced are true; another part, which he calls a *"muthos,"* he says it would be foolish to insist upon. He provides here an account of the journey that souls take after death – a journey situated within an overall cosmological account of the nature, size, and regions of the earth. I argue that this is a distinctly Platonic account of the cosmos and the afterlife, one that treats the heavens as form-like and the worst parts as the source of flux. Moreover, this eschatology gives no role to divine justice; instead, our souls are harmed or benefited as a natural result of their constitution (Chapter 11, "The Cosmos and the Afterlife").

Socrates turns quickly from the entire cosmos to his own death (115a–118a). He continues to adhere to the philosophical views he has argued for over the course of the day, illustrating how to live in line with his ethical views. Throughout the dialogue Socrates is portrayed as deeply principled, someone who has not changed his approach to living or his basic commitments on the last day of his life. He drinks the poison without trepidation. His companions weep uncontrollably, leading Socrates to chastise them. After regaining their composure, Crito asks if Socrates has any last wishes, leading to Socrates' enigmatic last words: "Crito, we owe a cock to Asclepius. All of you must pay what is owed and not be careless" (118a7–8)[8] (Chapter 12, "The Death Scene").

---

[8] Translations of the *Phaedo* throughout this book are modified from Sedley and Long 2010.

1

The Characters

The first few pages of the *Phaedo* introduce the dialogue's narrator as well as the group of companions present at Socrates' death. Unlike most of Plato's dialogues, the *Phaedo* portrays Socrates in a long discussion with members of his inner circle. Because these interlocutors already accept their own ignorance as well as many basic claims that Socrates makes in other dialogues, and because they share Socrates' devotion to inquiry, the *Phaedo* presents a very different conversation from what is found in most of Plato's other dialogues. Understanding the companions' interests, intellectual characters, and reactions clarifies the dialogue's overall progression. Many scholars do not discuss the dialogue's characters at all, focusing instead entirely on Socrates' individual arguments and on Simmias' and Cebes' objections.[1] To some degree, this is the result of the secondary literature's emphasis on individual arguments and specific passages, where the differences between the characters often seem irrelevant. On the other side, those scholars who do discuss the characters often argue that in the *Phaedo* Socrates adopts the views of these characters – that is, Phaedo's own views, or Simmias' and Cebes' supposedly Pythagorean views.[2] I argue instead that Socrates is appropriating and transforming these views, showing how they in fact express what Socrates takes to be the truth.[3]

The chapter begins by arguing that Plato makes Phaedo the narrator of such a significant event because Phaedo was not only a member of the Socratic circle but also a freed slave, which fits a major theme in the dialogue (Section 1.1). Next, I consider how Plato introduces the *Phaedo* as a dialogue between Socrates and his closest companions (Section 1.2). I argue here that Plato mentions his own absence simply because, as one of Socrates' close companions, he would be expected to be at

---

[1] This is perhaps clearest in Bostock 1986, which says nothing about the first three-and-a-half Stephanus pages of the dialogue.
[2] Examples, discussed in what follows, include Boys-Stones 2004 and Ebert 2004.
[3] In this I follow, in broad outline, the seminal Sedley 1995.

Socrates' death. I then turn to what we know about Socrates' main interlocutors, Simmias and Cebes (Section 1.3). I argue that both are skilled, both make mistakes, and both need to be cautious lest they fall into misology. They are sympathetic to a variety of Pythagorean and Orphic ideas, but are by no means committed followers of the Pythagorean Philolaus. Finally, I turn to Socrates' portrayal in the dialogue (Section 1.4). I note how Socrates encourages his companions to scrutinize arguments on their own rather than to take him as an authority, which makes him an unusual leader figure. Furthermore, while scholars often see a significant discontinuity between Socrates' portrayal here and in the Socratic dialogues, I argue that the *Phaedo* emphasizes how Socrates' questions and views here emerge naturally from his interests in the Socratic dialogues. The *Phaedo*'s distinctive approach to these issues arises in part from the questions that Socrates' interlocutors ask and in part from their already accepting many of Socrates' key views.

1.1 PHAEDO

Why does Plato choose Phaedo to narrate the death of Socrates, even naming the dialogue after him?[4] We have reasonably good evidence for two claims about Phaedo: he was a freed slave; and he wrote several Socratic dialogues, founding some sort of school in Elis.[5] In fact, according to our reports, Phaedo was made a sexual slave and Socrates himself freed him (Diogenes Laertius 2.105). This seems to fit the *Phaedo* almost too well, but, as McQueen and Rowe have argued, the dates suit his being a prisoner of war.[6] There is broad consensus among scholars that he was likely a freed slave, although there is some doubt about whether he was a sexual slave.[7] Phaedo's being a freed slave would at least partially explain why Plato chose to make him the narrator of such a significant event.[8] As Kamen has shown, the language of slavery is prevalent throughout the dialogue; there is a good sort of slavery, to the gods, and a bad sort, to our body.[9] Moreover, Aesop, whose storytelling Socrates says he has been setting to verse (60b–61b), was well known in antiquity as a freed slave.[10] There is clearly strong symbolic value to the dialogue's being narrated by someone whom Socrates released from slavery – perhaps even from a type of slavery dedicated to bodily pleasure – and then led to philosophy. Phaedo's status as

---

[4] Since Aristotle refers to the dialogue as "the *Phaedo*," it seems very likely that this was Plato's name for it.
[5] See Nails 2002 ad loc., Boys-Stones 2004, and especially McQueen and Rowe 1989 and Kamen 2013.
[6] McQueen and Rowe 1989.
[7] Kamen, a historian of ancient slavery, defends the accuracy of this piece of information and notes that "Phaedo's story is much like that of many prostitutes: enslaved in war, forced to sell his body, and finally ransomed by a man, possibly his lover" (Kamen 2013, 95).
[8] Boys-Stones 2004, 2.
[9] See Kamen 2013, 93–4.
[10] For striking similarities between Socrates and our reports on Aesop, see Kurke 2011.

a freed slave fits with a general feature of the opening of the dialogue (discussed in Section 2.1): it refers to ordinary ideas that contrast with Socrates' later extraordinary proposals. Socrates goes on to argue that we face a different sort of slavery, namely to our bodily needs (66c–d); our full freedom from this unworthy master can be had only upon death. Socrates freed Phaedo from ordinary slavery; more importantly, he can help us all escape our enslavement to our bodies.

Phaedo founded a school in his native Elis and – like Simmias, Cebes, and several others mentioned as at Socrates' death (58b–c) – was a writer of Socratic dialogues, none of which survive. One of his best known dialogues, the *Zopyrus*, was concerned with the extent to which features of our bodies determine how we behave and what sort of people we are.[11] While it is impossible to reconstruct most of the details of the dialogue, we can be relatively certain that Zopyrus claims to have been able to tell from physiognomy that Socrates was stupid and dull and somehow sexually immoderate.[12] When Zopyrus says this, the people present laugh; however, Socrates says that it is true, but that philosophy has allowed him to become better than his nature.[13] As Boys-Stones argues, there is ample evidence that Phaedo in general, and the *Zopyrus* in particular, defends the view that philosophy allows us to overcome our nature.

Boys-Stones and Sedley assume that the *Phaedo* could be alluding to the *Zopyrus*;[14] but for all we know the *Zopyrus* could have been written after the *Phaedo*, as a sort of reply to it. However, let us assume that the *Zopyrus* was composed beforehand. Sedley plausibly claims that the *Phaedo* could have been a way to acknowledge philosophical kinship: this dialogue, like Phaedo's own *Zopyrus*, examines our ability to be free from bodily limitations. Boys-Stones argues for more than this: that the *Phaedo* develops a unique psychology, in which the body is the subject of our bodily desires, but the soul can rule over the body. He says that Plato presents in the *Phaedo* "a 'Phaedonian' perspective, not the whole Platonic story."[15] As we will see in Sections 3.5 and 7.4, I do not think that the psychology is unusual in the way Boys-Stones claims. Instead, when a person acts on bodily desires, these desires are in the soul. The body is the source, but not the subject, of these desires.

More importantly, neither Sedley nor Boys-Stones notes the significant differences between the views Phaedo puts forward in the *Zopyrus* and those Plato puts forward in the *Phaedo*. In the *Phaedo*, so long as we are embodied, we cannot acquire a significant share of the wisdom that we seek (66b–67b, discussed in

---

[11] See Sedley 1995, 8–9, and especially Boys-Stones 2004.
[12] As Boys-Stones 2004, 8, says, the reports are that Socrates' "eyes showed him to be either a womanizer (fr. 6, 9 Rossetti; cf. 8), or perhaps a pederast (fr. 11 Rossetti, from Cassian, who is purporting to quote [the *Zopyrus*])."
[13] For references and a fuller description, see Boys-Stones 2004, 8–10.
[14] Sedley 1995, 8–9.
[15] Boys-Stones 2004, 15.

Section 3.7). Socrates simply is the one who has done as much as possible, given bodily limitations. Pleasures and pains are the greatest evils because they force (ἀναγκάζεται, 83c5) the soul to take things to be most true that are not (83b–c, discussed in Section 7.3). Philosophy can liberate us, but – unlike in the *Zopyrus* – not fully until after death. Moreover, the *Phaedo* claims that these problems come from one's body rather than from one's nature, as is claimed in the *Zopyrus*. Thus Socrates is not providing a "Phaedonian" perspective in the *Phaedo*.

In sum, having Phaedo narrate the dialogue fits perfectly with the idea that we are enslaved to our bodies and that philosophy allows us to free ourselves – if not in this life, at least after death. Perhaps the *Phaedo* was written before the *Zopyrus* and the *Zopyrus* is Phaedo's reaction to it, making clear how he wanted to present Socrates. If the *Zopyrus* came first, then Plato may well be picking up and acknowledging a broad topic that Phaedo explored, but developing it in his own way.

1.2 PLATO AND OTHER SOCRATICS

Near the beginning of the dialogue Phaedo lists as present a who's who of people in Socrates' circle (59b–c). Understanding who they were helps us appreciate the sort of conversation Socrates has in the ensuing dialogue. Famously, Phaedo briefly mentions that Plato was not present because he was ill (59b). I argue here that it would have been strange not to mention Plato's absence, so there is no reason to read any larger significance into Phaedo's mentioning this.

One of the first people Phaedo refers to as present is Crito, who appears in several of Plato's dialogues: in a minor role in the *Phaedo*, as the interlocutor in the frame of the *Euthydemus*, in a brief mention in the *Apology*, and as the main interlocutor in the *Crito*. He seems to have been Socrates' closest family friend – present when Socrates takes his final bath and when Socrates speaks with his wife and children for the last time (116a–b). In the *Phaedo*, Crito is associated with worldly affairs (63d–e), revealing at the end that he has not truly appreciated one of Socrates' central philosophical messages (115b–116a). This partially explains why the conversation in the *Crito* is so different from that in the *Phaedo*; Crito is not an intellectual of the sort that Simmias and Cebes are.

Among those listed as present, Phaedo, Crito, Antisthenes, Aeschines, Simmias, and Cebes were all authors of Socratic dialogues.[16] Antisthenes and Aeschines are thought to have been two of the most significant of these writers. Moreover, also mentioned are Euclides and Aristippus, who in some sense founded the Megarian and (perhaps) the Cyrenaic schools, respectively.[17] Other than simply acknowledging their important place in the Socratic circle, mentioning them at the beginning makes

---

[16] For a discussion of the evidence, see Nails 2002.
[17] It is unclear whether this Aristippus or his grandson, Aristippus II, founded the school. For a discussion, see Hackforth 1955, 31, and Nails 2002, 51.

clear that this will be different from the sort of conversation that takes place in most of Plato's other dialogues. Socrates is not speaking to a relatively ordinary person with a claim to knowledge (such as a general or a rhapsode), or to a promising young man, or to an esteemed sophist. He is speaking to his closest companions, serious philosophers who want to learn from him as much as they can. Unsurprisingly, the dialogues with interlocutors most similar to Simmias and Cebes are typically identified as belonging to Plato's "middle period": the *Cratylus*, the *Republic*, and the *Phaedrus*. Of these, only the *Cratylus* has an interlocutor mentioned here: Hermogenes.[18] Glaucon and Adeimantus, the interlocutors in the *Republic*, and Phaedrus were not listed as present at Socrates' death, nor was their absence noted. They are friendly, intellectually curious interlocutors, but are not presented as members of Socrates' inner circle. In Section 1.4 I discuss how Socrates engages with his companions.

For now, let us consider what to make of Plato's illness. Plato is explicitly mentioned in his dialogues only three times, twice in the *Apology* (34a2, 38b7) and once here (59b10). Phaedo is providing a who's who of the Socratic circle. It would have been a strange omission if he had not mentioned Plato at all. He could have had Phaedo and Echecrates discuss his absence or bemoan this misfortune. Instead Plato's absence receives only the briefest of mentions, and the dramatic setting all but requires it. Moreover, Plato is not the only person whose absence is noted; Aristippus and Cleombrotus are also said to be absent but, since they are foreigners, this is explained by their being in Aegina.

It is impossible to know whether Plato would have fabricated his illness for literary effect. If he felt compelled by historical fact, then he found a way to discuss it as briefly as possible. If he did not feel so compelled and had presented himself as present at Socrates' death, he would have either taken part in the discussion or remained silent. Plato does not seem to have wanted to make himself an interlocutor in his dialogues, so he likely would have kept silent. But silence would portray him as someone who did not take an active part in such a discussion. Imagine the books written on Plato as silent witness! All such issues are swiftly removed through his simply being absent.[19] Why illness, in particular? Unlike the absent foreigners, Plato is a native Athenian, so it would be strange for him to be elsewhere when Socrates is about to die. Illness is the most easily understandable explanation. Moreover, disease is later mentioned as a cause of our not having the wisdom that we desire (66c). Enslaved to our bodies, we are unable to devote ourselves to philosophy – even someone as devoted as Plato. In fact, as we will see in the next chapter, in the opening frame luck (*tuchē*) is associated with the ordinary, mortal world. Plato's illness is an example of the ordinary, mortal *tuchē* that lies beyond our control.[20]

---

[18] Apollodorus is also mentioned here in the *Phaedo* and is the narrator of the outer frame of the *Symposium*.
[19] For a similar idea, see Burnet 1911 on 59b10.
[20] Betegh 2020 develops similar views.

In sum, Plato needed to mention himself, and did so about as briefly as possible. If he felt compelled by the historical facts, then clearly we cannot make anything of his illness. If not, then, given that he did not want to be in his dialogues, he needed some explanation for why he was not there, and illness both makes sense and fits with a theme of the dialogue.[21]

If Plato did not feel compelled by historical facts, might his absence be a device for distancing himself from the expectation that the *Phaedo* is a historical record of Socrates' last day?[22] This seems unlikely, since in the first lines of the dialogue Phaedo says that he was there himself at Socrates' death (57a), and then that he will go through every detail as accurately as he can (58d–e). Plato could have left out this emphasis or chosen a narrator who was not there himself (as he does, for example, in the *Symposium*), if he wanted to distance himself from the accuracy of the record. In short, we simply cannot make much of Plato's absence.

1.3 SIMMIAS AND CEBES, PHILOLAUS AND PYTHAGOREANISM

Early in the dialogue Socrates is surprised that Cebes and Simmias have not heard why suicide is impermissible from their association with Philolaus (61d–e). In response, Cebes says twice (61d, 61e) that he has not heard anything clear about suicide from Philolaus. This then leads Socrates to defend a Pythagorean view because the most prominent mathematical Pythagorean of the time, Philolaus, had not done so clearly.[23] This sets the scene for Socrates repeatedly providing his own reasons for accepting Pythagorean views later in the dialogue – including reincarnation, the idea that we can recollect things known before birth, and the need to live a type of ascetic life.[24] Socrates similarly defends religious ideas that are not Pythagorean but are either general features of Greek religion or ideas associated with Orpheus or with the mysteries – for example, the importance of purity in associating with divine things (67a–b, a general feature of Greek religion), the idea that the body is a prison (62b, 82d–e, which Plato associates with Orpheus at *Cratylus* 400c),[25]

---

[21] Most 1993 famously argues that Socrates, on his death bed, is having a vision that Plato has been healed, which is why Socrates tells them to sacrifice a cock to Asclepius. I argue against this reading in Section 12.3.
[22] So e.g. Frede 2005, 2–3.
[23] So Sedley 1995, 11.
[24] For further discussion of these and other Pythagorean views, see Section 4.3, Section 5.1, Section 7.2, and Subsection 11.5.2. In what follows I discuss the possible connection between Simmias' *harmonia* objection and Philolaus' *harmonia* theorizing.
[25] Nightingale 2021, ch. 3, argues that the *Phaedo* is primarily engaging with Orphic religious views. Her chapter presents a fairly traditional account of Orphism, not engaging with the sustained skepticism that Edmonds has argued for in several places (see especially Edmonds 2013). See Betegh 2014 and 2016 for a more moderate skepticism that also raises concerns with key parts of Nightingale's traditional account (for example, its anthropogony). My approach here is to follow this sort of moderate skepticism, in part for methodological reasons: we can appreciate many of the ways in which the *Phaedo* engages with interrelated religious ideas

and the idea that initiation rites draw us closer to the gods, leading us to a better afterlife (69c–d, connected to the mysteries).[26]

Socrates is not simply relying on religious ideas, as is sometimes thought,[27] but rather provides a philosophical defense of them: he aims to show what they get right by showing how they express correct philosophical views.[28] One likely reason for Socrates' charitable approach is that he thinks the gods speak only the truth, and so these ideas must be correct to the extent that they really are from the gods. Socrates famously uses this strategy in the *Apology* when interpreting the Oracle at Delphi (esp. 21a–23b). He holds as fixed that what the Oracle says must be true, and then finds an interpretation according to which it is. Even if it is unclear whether an idea from a poet or a religious authority genuinely is from the gods, if it plausibly might be, it is prudent to see whether there is an interpretation according to which it is correct. Homer calls upon the gods in his poems, and Socrates never directly criticizes Homer in the *Phaedo* (94d–e, 112a). By contrast, he explicitly rejects Aeschylus' account of the path to Hades (107e–108a), as well as the accounts given by Anaxagoras and other natural philosophers (96b–101d). These authors do not claim a divine source for their views, and Socrates uses a different interpretive approach for understanding them.

As modern scholars have emphasized over the past fifty years, the Pythagoreans were not a monolithic group. First, they can be divided into "acousmatic" Pythagoreans – who focused on detailed restrictions (*akousmata*) on how to live (such as the rule not to eat beans) and kept a strict ban on communicating their ideas to others – and "mathematical" Pythagoreans, who may have adhered to detailed restrictions on how to live, but were more philosophical and put their writings into circulation.[29] The mathematical Pythagoreans were a quite varied group, without a single, core set of commitments to distinguish them from others. As noted above, Socrates does not only discuss Philolaus' views in the *Phaedo*, nor does he limit himself to Pythagorean views. He moves smoothly and seamlessly from discussing and reinterpreting Pythagorean views to discussing and reinterpreting other religious views, including those associated with Orpheus and with the Eleusinian mysteries. What ties these together – and to the central topic of the

---

without needing to accept the traditional account. Even if one accepts such moderated skepticism, Nightingale makes a number of insightful observations. For example, she makes a compelling case that the *Phaedo*'s repeated mention of the philosopher's soul's release should be understood as developing the Orphic references to the soul's release (149–51). She also offers a number of insights on the *Phaedo*'s eschatology, some of which I note in Chapter 11.

[26] For this as a general feature of the mystery rites, see Edmonds 2017, Betegh 2022.
[27] See Introduction, n. 7.
[28] For a discussion of this sort of appropriation, see Sedley 1995, Rashed 2009 (esp. 124–5), Morgan 2010, Horky 2013, ch. 5, and Betegh 2022. I also defend the account given here in Ebrey 2017b. By contrast, Dorter 1982, 77, claims that there is only a metaphorical connection between Socrates' views and popular religion, which creates an "illusion of reassurance."
[29] See, e.g. Burkert 1972, Huffman 1993, Horky 2013, Betegh 2014.

dialogue – is that they are all concerned with the afterlife and, typically, with what will lead to a better afterlife.³⁰ An especially clear case of Socrates' switching between different religious views comes at the end of the defense speech, when he refers to the virtues as purifications, to wisdom as a purificatory rite, then to the initiation rites, where he echoes an Orphic reference to the uninitiated "lying in the mud," and finally to the saying that, while many carry the Dionysian fennel wand, few are *bacchoi* (69c–d). The broader idea that one must perform rites and initiations in order to have a good afterlife is common in Greek religion; one finds it for example in the Homeric *Hymn to Demeter* (367–9, 480–2). It is connected to another general idea, namely that so-called initiations (τελεταί, perhaps better translated as "perfections") bring us closer to the divine.³¹ The point Socrates makes with this complex web of religious references is that those who pursue philosophy properly are in fact the only ones to have been properly initiated (i.e., truly perfected), and so only they will live among the gods. He is appropriating and transforming several religious ideas in order to show how they can all be seen as pointing toward his own view.

What should we make of Simmias' and Cebes' connection to Philolaus? Cebes says that they associated (συγγεγονότες, 61d7) with him and that he lived among them (παρ' ἡμῖν διῃτᾶτο, 61e7) for some time. Socrates is surprised that they seem not to have heard anything from Philolaus about suicide. This reaction suggests that they had spent enough time with him to be expected to know his views on prominent topics. Moreover, Simmias later refers to a view that "we" hold, and it seems likely – although not certain – that this is a view that Philolaus held, as I discuss later in this section. This suggests that Simmias saw himself as a member of some group associated with Philolaus. Some interpreters think that Simmias and Cebes themselves are supposed to be close students of Philolaus.³² Others suggest that they are in no sense his students.³³ This might be important to establish if one wished to argue that Socrates' arguments rely on Pythagorean assumptions, which Simmias and Cebes accept because they are themselves Pythagoreans.³⁴ But Socrates is not relying on Pythagorean ideas; he is attempting to show what is correct about them. This is clear, for example, in the cyclical argument. That argument

---

[30] There is no direct evidence that Pythagoreans thought that the way one lives affects one's afterlife, and so some scholars have doubted that they believed this (e.g. Casadesús Bordoy 2013, 168–9; Pellò 2018). In any event, this is certainly an idea associated with Orpheus and mystery religion practices.

The most common view is that Philolaus did not himself accept that the soul exists after death, although he may have thought that there was some other part of us that did (Huffman 1993, 328–32). Huffman 2010, 31–3, suggests that Philolaus allowed the *archē* (principle/origin) of the soul to transmigrate, but not the soul itself.

[31] For a discussion, including on the question of translation, see Edmonds 2017.
[32] E.g. Burnet 1911, Ebert 2004.
[33] E.g. Rowe 1995, 6–7, and note on 59c1.
[34] So Ebert 2004 *passim*.

draws a Pythagorean conclusion, reincarnation, but does not do so using a Pythagorean argument. Similarly, Cebes does not simply accept, on the basis of Philolaus' authority, the view that suicide is not sanctioned; he expects reasons, which Socrates provides. Of course, Simmias and Cebes may be sympathetic to Pythagorean ideas, and this may partially explain why they find some of Socrates' ideas appealing. But this could be true regardless of whether they were, in any strong sense, students of Philolaus.

Our most secure information about Simmias or Cebes' own views, independently of what they agree to in the dialogue, is that Simmias says that Socrates will be aware that "we" hold that the soul is a sort of blend and *harmonia* of hot, cold, dry, wet, and certain other things that make the body taut (86b). The "we" here must be some group of intellectuals that Socrates knows Simmias to belong to. Given that *harmonia* is a central concept for Philolaus – and given that Socrates knows that Simmias spent a considerable amount of time with Philolaus – Sedley, Huffman, and McKirahan have argued that this was one of Philolaus' ideas, although we do not have any direct testimony for this.[35] The important point is that, even if Simmias got this idea from Philolaus, he gives it up very quickly (92a–c) and says that it has come to him "with no proof but with a sort of plausibility and outward appeal" (92d1–2). Moreover, Cebes makes clear from the beginning that he does not accept that the soul is a *harmonia* (87a). As for Cebes' own views, in his cloakmaker objection he claims that it would be reasonable to think that the body is in flux (ῥεῖν) (87d–e). Since Socrates has not used the term "flux" earlier in the dialogue, this portrays Cebes as someone familiar with some type of Heraclitean flux theory. This suggests that he has thought through a variety of different philosophical ideas, not merely Pythagorean ones.

Simmias' and Cebes' strongest commitments seem to be to Socratic ideas. Simmias agrees emphatically when Socrates asks, "do we say that there is such a thing as a just itself, or not?" (65d4–5). Socrates proceeds to clarify (65d–e) that he is talking about the things he is looking for when he asks "what is it?" – that is, what Plato most consistently portrays Socrates as seeking throughout the dialogues. Simmias later says that he has accepted the existence of these things "sufficiently and rightly" (92e1–2), unlike the hypothesis that the soul is a *harmonia*. In fact I argue (in 5.7, 8.4.1, 9.8.4) that Socrates thinks that Simmias is overly enthusiastic about the forms and that they should all use the method of hypothesis to evaluate the forms more thoroughly before accepting them.

---

[35] Sedley 1995, 22–6, Huffman 2010 (changing his mind from Huffman 1993), and McKirahan 2017. Note that *Symposium* 188a and *Laws* X 889b (discussed by Iwata 2020) each describe theories that involve a *harmonia* of hot, cold, wet, and dry, and neither has any clear connection to Philolaus. This suggests that Simmias' "we" need not have gotten this idea from Philolaus; but if they did not get it from Philolaus, it would again be unclear why Simmias would expect Socrates to know that they believe this.

Sedley has argued that Simmias is more credulous than Cebes and methodologically misguided, and that it is Simmias in particular who is in danger of misology.[36] Perhaps Simmias is more credulous overall – as noted, he seems particularly eager to accept the existence of forms – but sometimes Cebes is more credulous and Simmias more cautious. First, it should be noted that at key places in the dialogue the conversation advances because Cebes does not simply accept Socrates' claims. Soon after the discussion of suicide, Cebes presses Socrates to further defend his view, which leads Socrates to praise Cebes for always scrutinizing arguments and not being easily convinced by others (62e–63a). Cebes' challenge (69e–70b) leads to Socrates' cyclical and kinship arguments; his cloakmaker objection (86e–88b) leads to Socrates' final argument. On the other hand, Cebes suggests that recollecting shows the soul's immortality (73a) – something Socrates never claims in the *Phaedo* – and Simmias rightly points out that it only shows the soul's preexistence, not its postexistence (77a–b). Here Simmias is the one who is careful and refuses to be convinced straight away. As for whether Cebes is in danger of misology, at the end of the kinship argument he shows no reservation whatsoever about the conclusion, responding "how could it not be the case?" (80c1). After the return to the defense (80d–84b) and after a long silence (84c), Cebes develops his cloakmaker objection to this argument. It is, of course, not unusual to be initially convinced by an argument and then later develop concerns about it. But, as I discuss in Chapter 8, misology arises from repeatedly putting one's confidence in an argument and then a little later distrusting it (90b–c), which is exactly what Cebes does when he accepts the kinship argument only to doubt it shortly thereafter. Misology is not an easily avoided intellectual vice; instead, all intellectuals need to be vigilant against it, Cebes included.

Let me briefly say something about the other people mentioned in the dialogue who have Pythagorean associations: Echecrates and (perhaps) Evenus.[37] Echecrates is on Aristoxenus' list of the last Pythagoreans, and Phlius, where the dialogue takes place, was a sort of Pythagorean refuge. Echecrates asks Phaedo to give "us" some report about Socrates' last day (58d), which opens the possibility that other Pythagoreans in Phlius are in the audience. Again, this is fitting given the Pythagorean themes of the dialogue, but need not indicate anything substantive about the content. Ebert argues that, when Socrates asks, "isn't Evenus a philosopher?" (61c6), he should be understood to be asking whether Evenus is a Pythagorean; he provides evidence that Evenus may have been a Pythagorean and notes that there is some evidence that "philosopher" was a term Pythagoreans used

---

[36] Sedley 1995, 15–21.
[37] Rashed 2009 argues that we can see in Aristophanes' *Clouds* and *Frogs* signs that the historical Socrates had Pythagorean leanings. I am not entirely convinced, but if so, Plato would be showing how these leanings should be properly understood as fitting into Socrates' overall philosophical commitments and approach.

to identify each other.[38] I find it more likely that Socrates is relying on his own notion of philosopher when asking about Evenus. However, even if Ebert is right, the notion of philosopher that Socrates goes on to develop in the dialogue is not a standard Pythagorean notion, but rather his own distinctive account. At most, Socrates would be appropriating and transforming a Pythagorean idea, not simply relying on it. Recall also that Evenus is mentioned alongside the sophists in the *Apology* as charging five minas as an expert in human and social virtue (20b–c). Socrates distinguishes himself in the *Apology* from such people. When Socrates mentions Evenus in the *Phaedo*, he is about to give a new defense speech, one that will again separate him from such people. While Evenus may have been a Pythagorean, one should not confuse his claim on being a philosopher with Socrates'.

1.4 SOCRATES

Socrates' views and his overall portrayal in the *Phaedo* are, of course, the main topic of this book. As for his "literary" portrayal, in Section 2.2 I discuss how Plato depicts Socrates as a new sort of hero in an alternative to tragedy; in Section 7.5 I consider how Plato presents Socrates as a kind of ascetic; in Section 8.2 I consider Socrates' keen sense of the emotional and psychological state of his companions; and in Chapter 12 I show how he is presented in the death scene as living according to the theories he has articulated over the course of the day. Here I examine how Socrates interacts with his companions and how the views he argues for in this dialogue relate to those in Plato's other dialogues.

For both purposes, it is useful to begin with the *Phaedo*'s close connection to the *Apology*. In the *Phaedo*, Socrates says that he is giving those present a defense speech (*apologia*) that is more persuasive than the one he gave the jury (63b, Chapter 3). Socrates also refers to his decision to stay in prison and so to the *Crito* in his autobiography (98e). Thus the *Apology*, the *Crito*, and the *Phaedo* are not merely a de facto trilogy about Socrates' trial and death; the *Phaedo* refers to these other dialogues, providing further reason for us to read it in light of them. In the *Apology*, Socrates famously says that he has never promised to teach anyone anything and that he has never in fact taught anyone anything (33a–b). He adds that someone would speak falsely if they claimed to have learned anything from him (33b). He mentions that rich young men imitate him (23c), but clearly Socrates did not simply have imitators – he had followers of some sort. How did Socrates relate to these followers, given that he claims not have taught them? The *Phaedo* illustrates exactly this.

First, note that Socrates positively encourages those in his circle to scrutinize his arguments rather than to accept them on his authority. Consider a passage

---

[38] Ebert 2001. For more on the term "philosopher," Moore 2019.

mentioned in the previous section, in response to Cebes' pressing Socrates on his views early in the dialogue:

> When Socrates heard this he seemed to me delighted by Cebes' persistence, and he looked at us and said: "As you can see, Cebes is always scrutinizing arguments, and refuses to be convinced straight away of whatever anyone says." (62e8–63a3)

Being told what delights Socrates reveals what he values: scrutinizing arguments and refusing to be immediately convinced. Socrates' looking at his companions while saying this shows that he wants them to see that he values this and so encourages them to do the same. This is perhaps a simple point, but nonetheless an important one: Socrates wants his companions not to believe things simply because he thinks they are right; instead, they should thoroughly scrutinize his claims and not allow themselves to be easily convinced. They certainly should not be like acousmatic Pythagoreans, who simply accept the *akousmata* as a guide in their life. As we will see, conviction (πίστις) plays a crucial role over the course of the dialogue. For example, Cebes' challenge (Chapter 4) will raise doubts about whether the soul exists after death and will ask for conviction. Socrates will try in his arguments to provide the right sort of conviction rather than letting his companions be prematurely convinced, since this is exactly what can lead to misology (Chapter 8).

Socrates' encouragement not to be easily convinced recurs near the midpoint and end of the dialogue. Near the midpoint, he exhorts the companions not to place any special weight on him, Socrates, but rather to care about the truth (91b–c). He warns them that he might inadvertently deceive them. This adds the idea that his companions need to be *particularly* careful with Socrates, precisely because they may be tempted to trust him, given the high regard they clearly have for him. At the end of the final immortality argument, he tells Simmias that he is right to keep some doubts in his mind and encourages the whole group to go back and further consider the first hypotheses *even if they already find them trustworthy* (107b). The fact that Socrates encourages this even at the end of the climatic final argument shows that he really does want his companions to continue to question what he is saying, to investigate with an eye to the truth, rather than to accept on authority what he says.

Of course, across the dialogues Socrates urges his interlocutors to investigate and search for the truth. What is special in the *Phaedo* is, first, that he explicitly encourages their questioning and investigating his own claims. Second, he points out where they might be tempted to believe him and tells them to make sure that they pursue the truth, since they may be deceived by him. And, third, even if they find his arguments trustworthy, he tells them to examine them further. Perhaps the closest parallel is the point in *Republic* II where, after Glaucon's and Adeimantus' challenges, Socrates says that he admires them (367e–368b). But Socrates says that he admires them for being able to speak so well *despite* not being convinced. The *Phaedo*, by contrast, positively praises Simmias and Cebes for not being too easily convinced. Avoiding premature conviction not only directly helps them discover the truth; as we will see, it will also help them avoid misology (Section 8.2).

Appreciating that Socrates is speaking to interlocutors of a significantly different sort can help us understand the difference between the *Phaedo* and Plato's Socratic or early dialogues. It is often thought that the *Phaedo* presents Socrates radically differently from those dialogues.[39] According to this view, in the *Phaedo*, but not in the Socratic dialogues, Plato presents Socrates as someone who assumes strong metaphysical views, who is interested in a wide variety of metaphysical and epistemological topics, who does not primarily engage in elenchus, and who does not display the sort of Socratic ignorance found in the Socratic dialogues. As noted in the introduction, I argue that Socrates does not assume Platonic views in the *Phaedo*; rather he argues for them. Moreover, as we have seen, Socrates' interlocutors here are quite different from those in the Socratic dialogues. Simmias and Cebes seem to be already convinced of their own ignorance (e.g. 76b, 78a), unlike interlocutors such as Protagoras or Euthyphro, who need to be shown it. In the *Phaedo*, Socrates' closest companions question him about his own views, unlike in the Socratic dialogues, where Socrates is questioning others about theirs. Nothing in the Socratic dialogues suggests that Socrates should not have views, only that he should not think that he knows that they are correct – and he never claims to know that the views he argues for in the *Phaedo* are correct. I argue in what follows that Plato presents Socrates' views and concerns in the *Phaedo* as a natural development from those in the Socratic and so-called transitional dialogues. For almost all purposes, this book stays neutral on when the *Phaedo* was composed and on whether Plato had in mind a particular order in which he thought the dialogues should be read.[40]

In the *Phaedo*'s defense speech, Socrates says early on that they should leave behind what the many think and should speak only among themselves (64c). This difference in audience can explain a variety of differences between the *Phaedo* and the *Apology*. Famously, in the *Phaedo* Socrates is confident that the soul exists after death, whereas in the *Apology* he says that he does not know whether death is good or bad, and so he has no reason to avoid death (29a–b). At the end of the *Apology* he says that those who believe death to be bad are certainly mistaken, because, if it were, his divine sign would have opposed him (40b–c). In the *Phaedo* he does not claim to know that death is a good thing, but he does provide a sophisticated argument that there is good hope for philosophers after death (63b–69e), which he bolsters with his arguments that the soul exists after death (70c–107b). He treats

---

[39] For a classic statement and defense, see Vlastos 1991, chs. 2 and 3.
[40] That said, I accept the strong stylometric evidence that there is a group of late dialogues, and the less strong but still significant evidence that another group comes before them and consists of the *Republic*, the *Phaedrus*, the *Theaetetus*, and the *Parmenides*. See Brandwood 1992 and Kahn 2002. For more on how differences in the characters can explain differences between dialogues, see Ebrey and Kraut 2022a.

these arguments as providing sufficient reason for philosophers to practice for and desire being dead, but he never claims to know that the soul exists after death. Socrates' view in the *Phaedo* is compatible with that in the *Apology*: he does not know that death is a bad thing, and so he has no reason to do something contrary to his divine sign in order to avoid death. Plato avoids having Socrates contradict himself while having Socrates defend new views in the *Phaedo*.

Perhaps the most significant difference between the *Phaedo* and the *Apology* is that in the *Phaedo* Socrates seems confident that he has acquired some degree of wisdom. He says that wisdom is a purifying rite and that only those who are sufficiently purified and initiated can live among the gods (69c). He thinks that there is good hope that he can live among the gods (67b–c), so he must think that there is a reasonable chance that he is sufficiently purified as a result of philosophizing. He says that, if Simmias fully examines the hypotheses that the final immortality argument rests on, then Simmias will follow the argument as well as is humanly possible and will seek nothing further (107b). Again, Socrates is confident that his reasoning is on the right track (cf. his arguments "of iron and adamant" at *Gorgias* 508e–509a). At the same time, Socrates argues in the defense speech that, so long as we are embodied, we cannot acquire even a reasonable share of the wisdom that the philosopher seeks (Section 3.7). Thus, while Socrates thinks there is a good chance that he has enough wisdom to obtain a better afterlife, what he has is very far from the full wisdom he seeks, and hence remains compatible with the Socratic profession of ignorance.

The most famous difference between the *Phaedo* and the Socratic dialogues is the *Phaedo*'s emphasis on the difference between forms and ordinary, perceptible objects. While Socrates does not allude to such a difference in the Socratic or transitional dialogues, he does not deny it either. The question does not arise in them, whereas in the *Phaedo* it is relevant and important for Socrates' arguments. The first three times Socrates mentions the forms in the *Phaedo*, he refers to them as what we seek when we ask the "what is it?" question (65d–e, 75c–d, 78c–d). In the recollecting argument he says that the forms are the things under discussion "when asking our questions and giving our answers" (75d3–4) – a reference to standard Socratic conversations. In the autobiography, Socrates says that what he is hypothesizing is "nothing new, but what I've never stopped talking about, on *any other occasion* or in particular in the argument thus far" (100b1–3, emphasis added). I argue at greater length (Section 3.6) that Socrates is presented throughout the dialogue as interested in the same things he has always been searching for, the forms, but now makes claims about them that were not made (or denied) in the Socratic dialogues.

In general, Socrates presents his "new" interests in the *Phaedo* – topics such as the relationship between forms and ordinary objects, the existence of the soul after death, and how to do natural science – as necessary for answering the ethical questions that arise in the dialogue. Socrates first argues that they, as philosophers, should desire to be dead, and that only philosophers can possess the virtues; he then defends the soul's existence after death as necessary to justify the philosopher's desire to be dead, and describes the forms and natural science in order to explain why the soul exists after death. Plato is showing how Socrates' philosophical mission leads naturally to these other topics. This is similar to the development of the *Meno* and *Republic*, which begin each with a search for an answer to the "what is it?" question about some ethical notion; these searches ultimately lead Socrates to introduce new, non-ethical topics as needed to address his ethical concerns.

The *Phaedo*'s reference to the *Meno* further expands Socrates' characteristic range of interests. Cebes says that Socrates is "accustomed to frequently mention" (72e2–3) that learning is recollecting and, in order to support this view, he provides a description of one argument for it (73a–b) that closely matches Socrates' discussion with the slave in the *Meno* (cf. *Meno* 81a–86a, esp. 82b–c). Here one of Socrates' stronger, more radical views – that learning is recollecting – is presented as something for which he argues in different ways, just as he frequently searches for answers to the "what is it?" question. This reference to the *Meno* makes some of the features of the *Phaedo* seem less unusual. In the *Meno* Socrates argues for the immortality of the soul (*Meno* 85e–86b), just as in the *Phaedo*. He also uses there the phrase "itself through itself," (αὐτὰ καθ' αὑτά, *Meno* 88c6, and αὐτὸ καθ' αὑτό, *Meno* 100b6; discussed in Section 3.4) and he connects intelligence (νοῦς) with doing what is best (*Meno* 88b; see Section 9.4).[41]

None of this is meant to suggest that Socrates' views in the *Phaedo* are all compatible with those in the Socratic dialogues. But, as noted in the introduction, some of his views in the *Phaedo* also seem incompatible with those in the *Republic*. Again, my suggestion is that across the dialogues Plato presents Socrates as developing different views while adhering to the same broad set of commitments. In the *Protagoras*, the *Meno*, and the *Euthydemus*, Socrates argues that virtue is a type of wisdom; he begins his arguments from his interlocutors' acceptance that relatively ordinary things benefit us – things such as pleasure, health, or wealth (*Protagoras* 351b–357e, *Meno* 87c–89a, *Euthydemus* 280b–281e). In the *Phaedo*'s defense speech, Socrates argues that the good life does not involve acquiring these things that are ordinarily conceived of as goods; rather it involves spurning such things and instead pursuing wisdom for its own sake. Wisdom in the *Phaedo* brings about the virtues, instead of the virtues being identical to a type of wisdom (as I argue in Subsection 3.8.2). Socrates may well defend a different view in the *Phaedo* from the sort in the *Protagoras*, *Meno*, and *Euthydemus* because he is speaking to his closest companions rather than trying to convince more or less ordinary people that wisdom is the key to virtue. Whatever the reasons for this difference, Socrates defends broadly similar views in these dialogues: the best life involves knowledge and virtue is very

---

[41] Socrates' description of the so-called temperate person (68e–69a) seems to allude to the *Protagoras*' account of being overcome by pleasures. I discuss this in Chapter 3, n. 49.

closely connected to wisdom, perhaps identical to it. These dialogues show different ways in which Socrates' broad commitments can be developed and defended.

1.5 CONCLUSION

The Socrates presented in the *Phaedo* has the same characteristic interests and the same broad commitments as in other dialogues, but, since he is speaking to philosophically skilled members of his inner circle, he has a very different sort of conversation here from what is found in most other dialogues. Phaedo's, Simmias', and Cebes' views do not constrain or dictate Socrates'. Phaedo is chosen for his symbolic value as a freed slave, and Simmias and Cebes are presented as intellectually curious interlocutors who are sympathetic to a number of ideas, including Pythagorean ones, but not dogmatically committed to any of them. Socrates encourages his companions not to treat him as an authority and he does not claim to know that his own views are right; nevertheless, he is able to present strong, clear reasons for them, unlike Philolaus. The result is a unique Platonic dialogue, in which Socrates explores some of the most famous ideas in the Platonic corpus with sympathetic yet critical and astute interlocutors, thereby providing a model for how his companions – and anyone who would have liked to be his companion – should conduct their search for truth.

2

The *Phaedo* as an Alternative to Tragedy and Socrates as a Poet

57a–61c

To the extent that we view Socrates as a sort of philosophical hero, it is neither because of the details of his arguments nor simply because he is a sort of philosophical martyr. It is in large part because Plato presented Socrates as a moral exemplar, one whose exemplary status comes from his complete dedication to, and excellence in, philosophy. The *Phaedo*, as the story of the last day of Socrates' life, plays a special role in this portrayal of Socrates. I argue here that Plato wrote it so that we would see Socrates as a philosophical hero, a replacement for traditional heroes such as Theseus and Heracles. The dialogue tells a new sort of story of how a hero faces death, providing an alternative to tragedy, as Plato thought that tragedy was actually practiced.[1] The beginning of the dialogue plays an important role in setting it up as an alternative to tragedy; hence I discuss the topic here. But the strength of my case comes from cumulative evidence drawn from across the dialogue, and so I offer an overall reading of the dialogue as an alternative to tragedy. After arguing for this reading, I turn to two other places where storytelling arises at the beginning of the dialogue: in Socrates' Aesop fable and in the dream that tells Socrates to compose poetry.

My approach is to argue in four stages that the *Phaedo* is written as an alternative to tragedy and, in so doing, to fill out this alternative. First I show that the beginning of the dialogue rejects key features of tragedy as understood by Plato: it highlights how pity and lamentation are inappropriate responses and how *tuchē* (chance) does not play an important role in Socrates' happiness (Section 2.1). On its own, rejecting these would be compatible with its simply being written in a completely different genre; instead, like a tragedy, it tells a story about a hero, but a new sort of hero (Section 2.2). Recognizing that Socrates is identified as a hero allows for a new way to think concretely about how Plato has composed an alternative to tragedy: the *Phaedo* meets

---

[1] In this chapter, by "tragedy" I generally mean "tragedy, at least as actually practiced." At the end of Section 2.1 I discuss whether Plato thinks there can be a good type of tragedy. See also n. 7 in this chapter.

each requirement in *Republic* II–III for a properly told story about the heroes, gods, and the underworld – the broad category to which tragedy belongs (Section 2.3). The *Phaedo* is, then, an alternative to tragedy in the sense that it belongs to the same broad category as tragedy, but then rejects key features of it and instead tells a new sort of story about the death of a hero. Once this framework is established, I turn to the story told within it. Rather than dwelling on his own death, Socrates uses philosophical argumentation to help his companions overcome their fear of death and avoid the threat highlighted at the midpoint of the dialogue, the threat of misology (hatred of theories and arguments), which would undermine their ability to be philosophers devoted to truth. In laying out this story, I show how the *Phaedo* can be seen as adopting and adapting formal elements from tragic plays (Section 2.4).

Plato may well have thought that all his dialogues were importantly different from tragedy and thus an alternative to it in a minimal sense. My claim is that the *Phaedo* is an alternative in a much more robust sense: (i) the beginning of the dialogue draws attention to how it rejects tragedy, (ii) it identifies Socrates as a new sort of hero, (iii) it positively meets every requirement presented in *Republic* II–III, and (iv) it adopts and adapts formal elements from tragic plays to tell a new sort of story of a hero's death. Perhaps some other Platonic dialogue is an alternative to tragedy of this sort, but most are not. Recognizing the dialogue's literary structure highlights philosophical views that commentators have passed over. But a reading of the *Phaedo* is not merely valuable insofar as it sheds new light on philosophical ideas within it. Independently of any such benefit, it is worthwhile to understand one of Plato's literary masterpieces on its own terms.

After this account of the overall story of the *Phaedo*, I return to the opening of the dialogue to discuss Socrates' Aesop fable about pleasure and pain (Section 2.5). I argue that this fable can teach us something important about how Socrates composes a certain sort of story, while displaying his sensitivity to different types of stories (*muthoi*). The fable helps us understand something particularly strange: pleasure's relation to pain. Finally (Section 2.6), I briefly turn to Socrates' interpretation of his dream. This again points to the importance of storytelling while giving us a first chance to see how Socrates interprets religious ideas and messages from the gods – a topic of continuing importance throughout the dialogue.

2.1 THE *PHAEDO*'S ENGAGEMENT WITH TRAGEDY

Plato thinks that tragedy, at least as it existed in his time, brings with it a number of commitments that are deeply mistaken. Scholars debate whether Plato completely rejects tragedy or instead attempts to reform it, to create a good kind that avoids its problems.[2] I argue here that the *Phaedo* takes a middle path. It rejects general

---

[2] Nussbaum 2001 (first edition 1986) argues that Plato rejects tragedy, replacing it with what she calls "anti-tragedy." Her critics typically argue that Plato adopts and reworks more features of

features of tragedy to a greater extent than is accepted by those who think that Plato embraces a reformed tragedy. But it adopts the broad framework of tragedy to a greater extent than is recognized by those who think that Socrates simply rejects tragedy.[3] Surprisingly little has been written on the *Phaedo*'s overall relation to tragedy, although commentators have drawn specific connections.[4] Raphael and Halliwell are among the few who have provided overall accounts of the *Phaedo*'s relation to tragedy, and their treatments are rather brief.[5] I agree with them that the dialogue somehow reworks tragedy, but one must examine the details to understand the concrete alternative that the *Phaedo* provides. This is what I do in this chapter.

While Aristotle's *Poetics* provides the first explicit theory of tragedy, Plato has a conception of tragedy that is meant to capture a general outlook on life (e.g. *Cratylus* 408c), as Halliwell has argued at length.[6] This conception of tragedy is not strictly tied to the literary genre; in this respect it is similar to how we can describe it as a tragedy when someone dies in a car accident. Plato understands the literary genre of tragedy partly in terms of this "tragic worldview," as we might call it. In *Republic* X, Socrates describes Homer as the "first of the tragedians" (607a2–3), not because he came first, but because his stories best exemplify this outlook.[7]

In this section I argue that the opening of the *Phaedo* rejects three core features of tragedy identified by Plato in *Republic* X and later by Aristotle and others: pity (ἔλεος, cf. *Republic* 606b–c), lamentation (ὀδυρμός, cf. *Republic* 605d), and chance (τύχη, cf. *Republic* 604d). According to this way of viewing tragedy, it involves horrible events outside a hero's control that lead the hero to pity himself and to lament what has befallen him, bringing the audience to do the same. Plato thinks that the gods would not be responsible for horrible events happening to good people, that the events commonly regarded as horrible are typically not, and that one should avoid pity and lamenting to the extent possible. Tragedy brings with it views of how to live, what is valuable, and how the gods act – views rejected at the beginning of the *Phaedo*.

---

tragedy than Nussbaum accepts (see e.g. Roochnik 1990, Hyland 1993, and Trivigno 2009). Modern interest in Plato's relation to tragedy goes back to Nietzsche's famous 1872 *Birth of Tragedy from the Spirit of Music* (for a modern edition of the German text, see Nietzsche 2015).

[3] In different ways, Halliwell 1984 and 1999 and Nightingale 1995 also take such a middle path.
[4] Dorter 1982, Rowe 1993, and Ebert 2004 draw specific connections. Earlier commentators, such as Burnet 1911 and Hackforth 1955, are much more interested in possible references to Pythagorean and Orphic views.
[5] Raphael 1960, 82–6; Halliwell 1984, 55–8. See also Crotty 2009, ch. 3, and Jansen 2013.
[6] Halliwell 1999.
[7] Similarly, Aristotle says that Euripides is found to be the *most* tragic of the poets (*Poetics* 1453a29–30). The view in the *Cratylus* and *Republic* is apparently in tension with the *Laws*, where the Athenian stranger says that the state they have produced is itself "the truest tragedy" and that they will allow the tragedians' work into the city if it is accepted by the authorities (817a–d). This notion of tragedy does not oppose the tragic to the philosophical and does not associate tragedy with pity and chance. Laks 2010 provides further arguments for thinking the treatment of tragedy in the *Laws* is different from that in the *Republic*. In saying that the *Phaedo* is an alternative to tragedy, I mean the notion of tragedy discussed in the *Republic* and elsewhere, not that of the *Laws*.

2.1 The Phaedo's Engagement with Tragedy

The very first thing Phaedo reports about the last day of Socrates' life is that he did not pity Socrates:

> My own experiences when I was with him were surprising. For pity did not enter me, as you might have expected, from witnessing the death of a friend, since the man seemed to me to be happy, Echecrates, both in his behavior and in what he said, so fearlessly and nobly did he meet his end. (58e1–5)

One might expect pity, that paradigmatic tragic emotion, since Socrates' death seems a misfortune; instead, Phaedo says that Socrates seemed happy and reached his end fearlessly and nobly.[8] Throughout the dialogue, Socrates is portrayed as noble, admirable, and at peace with his death rather than pitiable and distraught – straight through his calmly drinking the poison.[9] Directly after the above passage, Phaedo repeats that he did not feel pity for Socrates and then says that instead he and the others felt a strange mixture of pleasure and pain (59a). This prepares us for a story that will affect us in an unusual way. It is not only that Socrates does not think that what has happened to him is tragic, but also that Phaedo, one of his companions, does not view it this way. Since Phaedo is telling the story, there is reason to expect that we will be similarly affected.[10]

Tragedy involves the hero and the audience not merely pitying, but also being overcome by grief and lamentation (see esp. *Republic* 604b–606c). These responses are also marked as inappropriate in the opening of the *Phaedo*: when Socrates' companions first enter his cell, they hear Xanthippe crying out, bemoaning not her own loss, but rather the fact that this will be Socrates' last chance to speak with his friends (60a). Since Socrates views philosophy as the most valuable activity, if anything is worth lamenting, it would be this. But Socrates immediately tells Crito to take her home; when some of his people do, she cries out again and strikes herself in grief. In three sentences, the *Phaedo* dramatizes lamenting, even using words connected to lamenting in the *Republic* (βοᾶν, 604c; κόπτεσθαι, 605d), and sets it aside as inappropriate. Socrates is in pain from his bonds but, rather than complain, once Xanthippe leaves, he uses his pain as an opportunity for detached reflection on the peculiar nature of pleasure and pain (60b–c), beginning a philosophical conversation that lasts for most of the day. At the end of the dialogue, in the death scene,

---

[8] As noted by Raphael 1960, 84–5, and Nussbaum 2001, 131.
[9] In Plato's dialogues, there is not as close a connection between tragedy and fear as in Aristotle. But Plato may nonetheless have connected them; if so, Socrates' fearlessness would be another way in which he differs from a normal tragic hero.
[10] So Rowe 1993, 111, note on 58e1. Phaedo's reference to laughter alludes to comedy. In my view, the *Phaedo*'s relation to tragedy is more important for understanding the literary structure of the dialogue; I leave for another occasion how the *Phaedo* engages with comedy. According to the end of the *Symposium*, Socrates argued that it belongs to the same person to compose tragedy and comedy (223d). This makes it easier to see how someone could write something that draws on both.

the companions burst into tears and lament, for which Socrates chastises them (117d–e) – a brief reminder that this is an inappropriate response.

As Halliwell and Nussbaum have discussed at length, an important theme of tragedy is that one is at the mercy of events outside one's own control – what Plato calls *"tuchē"* (chance).[11] In the opening of the dialogue, *"tuchē"* and the verb *"tunchanein"* are used several times in succession (twice in 58a6, 58b8, 58c3): it was *tuchē* that it took so long for Socrates to be put to death, *tuchē* that Theseus' ship was sent immediately before Socrates was convicted, and *tuchē* that the ship took a long time to arrive. In the ordinary way of viewing the world, for the ancient Greeks just as for us, much of what is valuable falls outside our control. But in the ensuing dialogue Socrates provides a portrait of how happiness can be within one's control. Socrates is calm, lighthearted, and genuinely happy (*eudaimōn*, 58e3), despite the injustice done to him, straight through his drinking the poison. Moreover, as we shall see, he argues for theories that explain how this is possible.

These passing mentions of *tuchē* in the opening of the dialogue might seem insignificant, but they fit with a broader feature of the opening: it refers to a number of ordinary ideas that contrast with extraordinary alternatives developed later. In explaining why Socrates died long after the trial, Phaedo reports that the Athenians vowed to Apollo that they would send an embassy to Delos every year if the famous "twice seven" were saved – which they were, by Theseus (58a–c). According to Athenian law, while the embassy is away the city must be kept pure, and so no one put to death. Since, by chance, the ship carrying the embassy was delayed, Socrates' execution was too, keeping him in prison. Almost every element of this story contrasts with an extraordinary alternative developed later in the dialogue. Socrates goes on to argue that the prison they should be concerned with is the body, which uses bodily desires to trap us until we are released by philosophy (82d–e, cf. 62b). He argues that death, rather than causing pollution, is our only chance to be pure, a view he defends with his own account of purity (see esp. 67c–d). Rather than trying to avoid death, the true philosopher desires nothing but being dead (64a). Moreover, Socrates describes a very different way to honor Apollo: he says that he is, along with the swans, a slave of Apollo, sacred to the same god, and has a gift of prophecy from his master no less than they do (85b). His prophecy comes from argument: he can tell through reasoning that he will have a good fate after death. He is sacred to Apollo by philosophizing, and thereby preparing for death rather than by avoiding death, like the Athenians. As discussed in the previous chapter (Section 1.1), even the narrator of the dialogue, Phaedo, as a freed slave, fits with this contrast between the ordinary and the extraordinary. Phaedo's ordinary slavery (as well as Aesop's, who is referred to at 60c–61b) contrasts with Socrates' later descriptions of ordinary people's bad slavery to the body as well as with Socrates' own good slavery to Apollo.

---

[11] Halliwell 1984, Nussbaum 2001.

The four references to *tuchē* at the beginning set up a contrast with the extraordinary alternative Socrates argues for later: that chance plays a minor role in living a good life. There is sometimes a tendency to leave out Socrates' philosophical views when considering his literary portrayal. But one of the most striking features of Socrates is how well he lives up to his articulated beliefs.[12] He argues that happiness comes from knowledge (80d–81a), which we acquire on our own, separated from the senses (e.g. 65e–66a, 82e–83b). Companions are useful for this inquiry, but Socrates never suggests that they are necessary. Instead, he repeatedly emphasizes that the soul must inquire on its own. In the recollecting argument (73c–76e), he defends the view that each person has knowledge within oneself that one can recover – which makes us resilient against *tuchē*. Moreover, heroes traditionally have divine lineage. Not to be born with such lineage is, from the beginning, a sort of bad *tuchē* that condemns most people never to achieve true greatness. Socrates argues that one need not be born of special parents to be divine; we all are akin to the divine (78b–80b). A central message of the dialogue is that we have within ourselves the resources needed to fulfill our divine nature and be happy.

This is not to say that Socrates defends the Stoic view that the outside world cannot in any way undermine our wisdom and happiness.[13] He says that the philosopher cannot acquire the knowledge he desires so long as he is embodied (66e–67a, 68a–b).[14] Moreover, intense pleasures and pains are the greatest evil, because they *force* us to believe things to be most true that are not (83c). But even in these cases Socrates emphasizes what we can control. While the philosopher cannot have truth and wisdom so long as he is embodied, he only happens to be in human form at the moment. There is good hope that he can acquire knowledge after death, so long as he properly prepares himself (67e–68b). If he does so, he can escape reincarnation and live in eternal happiness with the gods (81a). Moreover, the true philosopher avoids pleasures and pains to the extent possible, which allows him to prepare properly for death (83b–c). In short, Socrates argues that we have significant control over our situation, which provides good hope (67b–c, 68a–b) that we can spend life after death eternally with the gods.[15]

I have argued that the opening of the dialogue rejects pity and lamentation, and that its several references to ordinary *tuchē* set up a contrast with the extraordinary new role of *tuchē* developed later in the dialogue. We can now see why I claimed in the introduction that the *Phaedo* rejects general features of tragedy to a greater degree than is typically accepted by those who see Plato as reforming tragedy.

---

[12] Indeed, I follow Blondell 2002 in being skeptical that one can cleanly separate the philosophical and literary aspects of the dialogues.
[13] As I argue at greater length in Ebrey 2017b. For further discussion, see Section 7.3.
[14] Recall that I refer to the philosopher as "he" throughout this book, since (unfortunately) Socrates consistently assumes in the *Phaedo* that philosophers are male. See Introduction, n. 4.
[15] For a similar point, see Halliwell 1984, 54.

Consider Trivigno's reading of the *Gorgias*.¹⁶ According to Trivigno, Socrates in the *Gorgias* is committed to the necessity of having conversational partners to make philosophical progress and be happy. Trivigno argues that Socrates is committed to the "fragility of argument": we cannot be certain that our arguments are without fault; they are likely to be shown to be faulty; and, even if they are not shown to be faulty, we cannot verify that they are correct, so we cannot succeed in acquiring wisdom. Socrates' values are substituted for the ordinary values found in a tragedy, but otherwise the dialogue reflects a new sort of tragic worldview: we are dependent on others for our happiness, there is a good chance that things will fall apart, and we cannot acquire what we ultimately seek. On my reading of the *Phaedo*, Socrates does not accept such fragility of argument or the strict need for conversational partners, and so there is much less scope for *tuchē* in the dialogue's outlook. Trivigno may be correct about the *Gorgias* and I about the *Phaedo*. My point is simply that the *Phaedo* is not the sort of reformed tragedy that Trivigno finds in the *Gorgias*.¹⁷

Jansen argues that the *Phaedo* is a sort of tragedy, but one in which the action and the story are about Socrates' companions, not Socrates himself.¹⁸ The companions have to deal with the *tuchē* of losing their leader and guide, Socrates. In my view, the greatest difficulty with this reading is that the *Phaedo* is, first and foremost, a story about Socrates: his arguments, his ideas, how he lived the last day of his life.¹⁹ Socrates is the hero who rises above *tuchē*, happy despite being unjustly put to death. As evidence that the action is about the companions, Jansen notes that, when Socrates drinks the poison, Phaedo says that he cried not for Socrates but for his own *tuchē* – that is, for his own misfortune (117c–d). This is a complicated moment, which I discuss further in the Section 2.3. I understand it as capturing the emotional states of someone who admires Socrates and wants to be like him, but has fallen short of Socrates' own ideals. Phaedo continues to hold on to some elements of the tragic worldview that Socrates shows us how to reject. To the extent that we, as readers, are in Phaedo's position, we can both feel our admiration for Socrates and see if we fall short of his ideals.

Should we consider the *Phaedo* an improved kind of tragedy, or does it reject so many characteristic features of tragedy that it should simply be considered a different

---

¹⁶ Trivigno 2009.
¹⁷ My reading of the *Phaedo* is, in a way, closer to Nightingale 1995's of the *Gorgias* (67–92). She sees the dialogue as criticizing tragedy – in particular by adapting *Antiope* – while imitating its themes and structure, thereby helping to distinguish philosophy from tragedy. Unlike Nightingale's account of the *Gorgias*, my account of the *Phaedo* sees it as positively telling the sort of story that should be told about how a hero faces death.
¹⁸ Jansen 2013. For example, she says that "the 'drama' of the *Phaedo* revolves around the plight of Socrates' companions" (5). Similarly, she argues that we are meant to pity the companions (15).
¹⁹ This said, I agree that the companions' actions are important to the dialogue's overall story. But this story is about how Socrates helps his companions while facing his own death, as described in Section 2.4.

kind of story? In *Republic* X, Plato seems to treat grief, lamenting, and *tuchē* as definitive of tragedy (see esp. 604b–606c). If they are, then the *Phaedo* is not any kind of tragedy. But in *Laws* VII Plato seems to embrace the idea that there could be a good kind of tragedy (817a–d).[20] Determining whether Plato would have thought of the *Phaedo* as a good kind of tragedy would require determining whether (i) Plato has a consistent position on whether there is such a thing, and (ii), if so, whether the *Phaedo* meets the requirements for being such a tragedy. This would take us well beyond the *Phaedo* and so cannot be settled here. Either way, the *Phaedo* rejects what Plato takes to be central features of existing tragedy. The dialogue is written to be a new sort of story, an alternative to existing tragedy.

2.2 SOCRATES AS A TRUE HERO

On its own, the *Phaedo*'s rejecting central features of tragedy would be compatible with its belonging to a very different genre; indeed, Nussbaum has argued that all of Plato's dialogues belong to an entirely different genre.[21] I will argue instead that the *Phaedo* opposes the tragic worldview by telling a story that belongs to the same broad category as tragedy: a story about heroes, gods, and the underworld. My first step in arguing for this thesis is to show that the *Phaedo* identifies Socrates as a hero. This is important for understanding not only the category of story to which the dialogue belongs, but also how Socrates is set up in the *Phaedo* as a new sort of moral exemplar. To identify people as heroes in the ancient Greek world is to identify them as having both human and divine lineage. Clearly this means that they are exceptional; but, for Plato, it also means that they must be good. In the *Republic*, Socrates emphasizes that a hero's actions are sympathized with and praised by those who listen to the story, which means that, if the hero is portrayed as bad, the portrayal will license bad behavior (*Republic* 390c–391e; cf. 605c–e). The *Phaedo* identifies Socrates as a new sort of hero with a new sort of relationship with the divine, and so as a new sort of person to admire.

The *Phaedo* continues the story of the *Apology* (as discussed in Section 1.4), so it is worth briefly recalling that in the *Apology* Socrates compares his disregard for death to that of the heroes who died at Troy, in particular Achilles (28b–d).[22] Socrates is there arguing that his actions are not shameful if they lead to his own death. The beginning of the *Phaedo* reminds us of this attitude, when Phaedo says that Socrates seemed happy, "so fearlessly and nobly did he meet his end" (58e4–5). In the *Apology* there is no need for Socrates to distinguish himself from Achilles to make his point. But, as we will see, Achilles would not fare well by the *Phaedo*'s lights.

---

[20] See n. 7 in this chapter.
[21] Nussbaum 2001.
[22] See Hobbs 2000, 178–86, as well as her discussion of the *Crito*'s reference to fertile Phthia at 186.

As we will see, Socrates is compared to a hero at the beginning, in the middle, and at the end of the *Phaedo*. Moreover, in the first half of the dialogue Socrates defends theories that explain why only a philosopher could be a hero. My case for identifying Socrates as a hero will extend into the next section, where I argue that the dialogue portrays Socrates in a way that meets every requirement in *Republic* III for how to portray heroes.

As noted earlier, in Phaedo's explanation of why Socrates' death was delayed, Phaedo mentions several ordinary ideas that contrast with the extraordinary alternatives developed later in the dialogue. Theseus plays an important role in this explanation: he, traditionally the great Athenian hero, contrasts with Socrates, the extraordinary new one. After Phaedo mentions Theseus and says that he did not pity Socrates, he adds that Socrates likely went to Hades with divine benefaction (58e) – just as one expects of a hero.[23] Then, as Dorter notes, while Phaedo is clear that there were more people at Socrates' death, exactly fourteen people are named, making Socrates someone who leads his own twice seven, just as Theseus did on his mission to Crete.[24] Despite Crito's importance later in the dialogue, he is not named here, only referred to indirectly as Critobulus' father (59c). Unlike Crito, who is roughly Socrates' age, each named companion is significantly younger – the fourteen youths saved by Socrates. But instead of saving them from death, as Theseus did for his twice seven, Socrates prepares them for his own death and provides an exhortation to philosophy, which he says is nothing but practice for dying and for being dead (64a).[25]

Near the middle of the dialogue, at 89b–c, Phaedo compares Socrates to Heracles directly after he says that he had never admired Socrates so much as when Socrates responded to the companions' beginning to lose confidence that *logoi* can help them discover the truth (88c–89a). This comparison of Socrates with Heracles is particularly apt since Heracles is said to have avoided the normal fate after death, instead living eternally with the gods. Socrates has recently argued that he, as a philosopher, will do the same (81a). But Socrates' feats are radically different from Heracles' or any other traditional hero's. Phaedo compares Socrates' "combat to defeat the arguments of Simmias and Cebes" (89c3–4) to Heracles' second labor; Socrates later says that he should come into "close Homeric quarters" (95b7–8, that is, engage in close combat) with Cebes, to test what the latter is saying. Philosophy and argumentation take the place of physical combat as the hero's activity.

---

[23] So Rowe 1993, 111–12, note on 58e3. Perhaps this divine benefaction is the sort described at the end of the *Meno*: true opinions that guide one's actions well but fall short of knowledge (99b–d). Socrates denies having knowledge throughout the *Phaedo*, and yet has reasoned beliefs. These beliefs could be viewed as a divine gift that leads him toward true happiness.

[24] Dorter 1982, 5–9.

[25] Ebert 2004, 99, n. 12, is skeptical that Socrates is supposed to parallel Theseus, since this parallel does not arise later in the dialogue. However, as described in what follows, Socrates is compared to Heracles (89b–c) and, later, to a tragic hero (115a), which strengthens the case that Socrates is being compared to a hero here as well.

Socrates is again compared to a hero at the end of the dialogue (115a). He there jokes that, when he says that he is called by destiny, he is speaking as a hero would in a tragedy. He then takes a bath – the ritual cleansing of a hero about to die – but insists on making it insignificant, saying that he is bathing now in order not to burden the women who would wash the corpse.[26] Socrates is his soul, which will continue to exist after death; the corpse is simply an insignificant vestige of embodied life – in fact his body had been the source of most of his problems. In making fun of himself for speaking like a tragic hero, Socrates punctures the air of solemnity around a hero's death, emphasizing its insignificance. He refuses to delay his execution (116e–117a). He rejects the horribleness of death as represented in tragedy. Plato continues to draw our attention to tragedy while showing that Socrates is not acting as a tragic hero would. Socrates' contrast between himself and a tragic hero marks the beginning of his death scene, one of the most moving scenes in ancient Greek literature. But it does not fill us with anguish. There is no hopelessness and so no despair; there is no suffering and so no pity. Socrates is not at the mercy of horrible forces beyond his control. Instead, while sad, his death is at the same time inspiring – an unusual mixture of pleasure and pain, as Phaedo said at the beginning (59a).

The views that Socrates argues for in the first half of the dialogue help explain why it is appropriate to see him as a new sort of hero. Socrates holds that the non-philosopher's courage is absurd because it overcomes the fear of death through a sort of fear and cowardice (68d); this so-called courage is fit for slaves, a sort of illusory painting (σκιαγραφία) that has nothing sound or true (69b–c). Only philosophers have the heroic virtue of courage, since only they are ruled by wisdom. Socrates explicitly mentions honor lovers as having the absurd non-philosophical courage (68b–c); thus Homeric heroes such as Achilles cannot be true heroes, since they are honor lovers.

Next, a proper hero should be related to the divine. Of course, Socrates does not have divine lineage, as is supposedly true of traditional heroes. Instead, Socrates argues in the affinity argument that every soul is akin to the divine (79a–80b) and so we all can count the divine as our kin. In this way, the *Phaedo* rejects a traditional division between mortals and immortals; indeed, in arguing that our souls are immortal, Socrates argues that every one of us has a mark of the divine.[27] But this does not mean that everyone is equally related to the divine. Another divine mark of heroes like Theseus and Heracles is that they are said to live with the gods after death. Socrates argues that only philosophers are pure enough to do so (69c–e, 80e–81a, 114c). After Heracles died, Zeus supposedly decided that Heracles could live with the gods. The fate of Socrates' soul will not rely on such a decision; instead, if

---

[26] Rowe 1993, 290, note on 115a6. Edmonds 2004, 182–3, argues that this feature of Greek tragedy treats the hero as already among the dead.
[27] See Section 4.1 and Section 10.7.

he can live among the gods, it will be because of how he has lived and how this fits with the nature of the soul (78b–84d).

We know from *Republic* III that Plato thinks there is something wrong with how his fellow Greeks represented heroes. Socrates is not a new version of Theseus, Heracles, or some other traditional hero; he is Socrates, a new hero. In the next section I further fill in this portrayal of Socrates by arguing that he has every feature that, according to *Republic* III, a hero should have.

2.3 THE *PHAEDO* AS A STORY OF GODS, HEROES, AND THE UNDERWORLD

How, according to Plato, should one replace the sort of stories told in tragedy? *Republic* II–III (377d–392c) provides a partial answer, since it presents a number of requirements for any story in the broad category to which tragedy belongs – namely stories about gods, heroes, and the underworld. I argue here that the *Phaedo* is written in a way that meets each requirement in *Republic* II–III for stories of this sort. Stories about gods and heroes are especially important to Plato, since they involve the divine, which people normally – and, Plato thinks, rightly – admire. Socrates says in the *Republic* that misrepresenting gods and heroes is the first and foremost problem with existing stories (377d–e). The *Phaedo* does not simply avoid this misrepresentation; it positively portrays both the gods and its hero as having the features that the *Republic* says that they should have. This interpretation does not require a stance on which dialogue came first; I am simply claiming that these two dialogues reflect the same view about how to tell a story about heroes, gods, and the underworld – as we shall see, down to some very specific details.[28] Of course, many stories could meet the *Republic*'s restrictions without providing an alternative to tragedy. But I have already argued (Section 2.1) that the *Phaedo* draws attention to core features of tragedy and rejects them; moreover, as we have begun to see, it offers a different sort of story of the hero's death (as will be further discussed in Section 2.4). My claim, then, is that the *Phaedo* belongs to the same broad type of story as tragedy, but then rejects tragedy and tells a different sort of story of how a hero faces death. Recognizing this clarifies the sort of story that the *Phaedo* presents, as well as filling in Socrates' portrayal as a hero and providing a new framework for thinking about Socrates' interaction with the gods and his account of the underworld in the *Phaedo*.

I argue here that (i) Socrates' theory in the *Phaedo* and (ii) the way his character is portrayed in the dialogue fit with (iii) the constraints presented in the *Republic*. While any given correlation might be a coincidence, the consistent fit – down to some very specific details – among these three provides strong evidence that the

---

[28] That said, stylometric evidence suggests that the *Republic* is in a second group of dialogues, after the *Phaedo* but before the late dialogues. See Kahn 2002.

Phaedo was written to be the sort of story that meets the *Republic*'s constraints. It also fleshes out Socrates' character by showing how, throughout the dialogue, his actions are in line with his theory.

Before presenting my case, let me address a few reasons why one might think that the *Republic*'s restrictions would not apply to the *Phaedo*. First, most of Socrates' examples of passages to remove are from Homer, and so the restrictions may not seem intended for a story like the *Phaedo*. But Socrates is clear that they apply to any story that involves gods and heroes, and he provides examples from tragic drama as well. Second, these restrictions may seem to be intended only for the young (e.g. 377b), and so not for the audience of the *Phaedo*. However, Socrates is clear that they are valuable for adults as well (e.g. 387b). Third, the *Republic*'s restrictions are intended for the guardians and so, again, may not seem to apply to the audience of the *Phaedo*; however, these restrictions are based on general principles that apply equally to non-guardians. Finally, while one might think that the restrictions are limited to stories told in verse, Socrates never says this.[29] In short, so long as Plato accepts the account in *Republic* II–III, he has every reason to apply these same strictures to composing the *Phaedo*. Of course, the *Phaedo* was written not for a *kallipolis*, but for the Greek world of Plato's time, where tragedy was widespread and well known. This is part of why Plato draws regular contrasts with tragedy in the *Phaedo*.

I will discuss the *Republic*'s restrictions in the order in which they are presented, beginning with Socrates' claims in book II about how to represent the gods. He argues that the gods must not be represented as taking revenge or as doing any serious injustice (377e–378e); that they should be represented as good, hence as responsible only for good things, not for harm (379b–380c); that they do not change their form to deceive us (380c–381e); and, finally, that they are wholly truthful in everything they say and do (381e–383c). These restrictions fit with Socrates' own way of treating the gods in the *Phaedo*. He is confident that his dream is trying to communicate something beneficial to him (60e–61b). He takes it as an obvious interpretive constraint, in interpreting his dream and in discussing Apollo, that the gods never deceive him. He says that he is a servant of Apollo and, as such, speaks the truth about the future (84e–85b). Throughout he treats the gods as good and truthful.

Moreover, Socrates' way of interacting with the gods in the *Phaedo* fits with his theoretical description of them there as well as in the *Republic*. In the *Phaedo*'s defense speech, Socrates says that the gods are good and wise masters and that he will be with them after death (e.g. 69d–e). In the kinship argument (78b–80b) he argues that there are two sorts of things, one seen and mortal, the other unseen and divine. *Republic* II's account of why the gods are good and do not deceive closely matches Socrates' description of the divine in the kinship argument. In the *Republic*

---

[29] So also Jansen 2013, 2–3.

Socrates argues that the nature of the gods is simple; thus they are least likely to depart from their proper form (380d). In *Phaedo*'s kinship argument, the divine things are said to be incomposite and uniform (78c–d, 80b). Both the *Phaedo* and the *Republic* use the same terms to emphasize that the divine does not change: μεταβολή (*Phaedo* 78d4; *Republic* 381b2) and ἀλλοίωσις (*Phaedo* 78d7; *Republic* 380e–381c passim).

Tragedies frequently involve divine forces outside the hero's control that make the hero miserable. One problem, of course, lies with how the heroes react to these forces, and Plato thinks we need a new sort of hero. But another problem lies with how the gods and fate play with the heroes' lives. Socrates' view that the gods are only beneficial, never harmful, is an important part of the *Phaedo*'s overall optimism about our ability to bring about our own wisdom and happiness, both here and in the afterlife.

Republic III turns to the portrayal of heroes. Socrates first claims that the guardians should hear things that make them least afraid of death, in order to cultivate their courage (386a–b). As we have seen, Phaedo reports at the beginning of the dialogue that Socrates was fearless on the day he died. Moreover, Socrates' entire argument over the course of the *Phaedo* is that those who have lived well should not fear death (e.g. 63b–c, 69d–e, 81a, 84b, 114c). Only the wicked should fear it, since they have not taken care of their souls (107c). In the *Republic* Socrates says that, in order for people not to fear death, the storytellers should not disparage unqualifiedly or simply (ἁπλῶς, 386b10) the things in Hades as full of terrors (386b–387b). In the *Phaedo* he argues that he will go on to live among wise masters and that the true Hades is divine, noble, pure, and unseen (80d). In a broader sense of "Hades," everyone who dies goes there, but this too is not to be disparaged unqualifiedly; whether or not it is bad depends on the sort of soul one has when one dies (107c–d). One of the main points of the eschatological account at the end of the *Phaedo* is that the state of one's soul determines where one goes in the afterlife.[30]

Socrates' next topic in the *Republic* is grief and lamentation, which, as discussed in Section 2.1, play an important role in tragedy and are marked as inappropriate at the beginning of the *Phaedo*. The *Republic* gives two reasons for removing passages where famous men grieve and lament. First, "a decent man doesn't think that for a decent man, whose friend he also is, death is a terrible thing" (387d5–6). Socrates' companions in the *Phaedo* meet this requirement: Phaedo says that everyone was

---

[30] In the *Republic* Socrates says that they should also get rid of frightening and dreadful names for such things as "Cocytus" and "Styx" (387b–c). In the myth at the end of the *Phaedo*, Socrates uses the names "Cocytus" and "Styx" (113c) for the places where murderers and the worst of those who are curable go (113d–114b). I suggest that in the *Republic* Socrates is saying that we should not refer to the underworld *simply* (ἁπλῶς) as "Cocytus" or "Styx." Socrates has just quoted passages from Homer where the underworld is presented as an awful place for everyone, or practically everyone (386c–387b). These should be expunged in order not *simply* to disparage the underworld. Similarly, the *Republic*'s myth of Er mentions "Tartarus" – another name that inspires dread – but reserves it for where the incurable tyrants are thrown (616a).

pretty much in the same state that he was in, not pitying or grieving for Socrates (58e, cf. 117c–d). Second, in the *Republic* Socrates says that, because a good person is most self-sufficient and excels beyond all others, he grieves least when any misfortune befalls him, bearing it in the most even-tempered way (387d–e). Socrates is presented as not thinking that a misfortune has befallen him and as being completely even-tempered. But Simmias and Cebes (84d) and Phaedo do view the loss of Socrates as a misfortune, and ultimately do not bear it in the most even-tempered way (117c–d). While the companions meet some of the *Republic*'s requirements for being a hero, Socrates is the one who is truly heroic.

Perhaps most strikingly, in the *Republic* Socrates says that they "will be justified in taking out the scenes where famous men wail, and give them to women, so long as they're not women of a superior sort, along with bad men, so that the people we claim to be bringing up to guard the country will turn up their noses at behaving as people like that do" (387e10–388a3). Xanthippe, as someone who cries out and beats herself in grief rather than philosophizing (60a–b), is represented as a woman not of a superior sort.[31] At the end of the dialogue, when the companions start crying, Socrates says that he sent away the women in order to avoid such behavior (117d–e). Lamenting is brought up in the *Phaedo* only briefly, to show that it is inappropriate to the situation and not something that the best sort of person engages in.

Returning to the *Republic*'s restrictions: after briefly mentioning that young people must not be made overly fond of laughter (388e–389a), Socrates says that they must put a high value on truth (389b–d). In the *Phaedo*, Socrates places the pursuit of truth and philosophy above all else. He spends the last day of his life philosophizing with his companions, admires Cebes for being difficult to convince (63a), says that Simmias and Cebes should challenge his views (84d–85b), and tells them to give little thought to Socrates and much more to the truth (91b–c). And, at a theoretical level, Socrates says that the philosopher's goal is grasping the truth (e.g. 66b) and the greatest evils are those things that bring us to accept falsehoods (83b–c, 89d).

In the *Republic*, Socrates turns next to moderation, saying that the chief features of moderate people are "being obedient to their rulers, and being rulers of themselves in relation to things like drink and sex and the pleasures of food" (389e1–2). Socrates is portrayed in the *Phaedo* as loyal and obedient to the gods (e.g. 61a–b) and to the orders from the Athenian Eleven (e.g. 85b). He argues that he will have good rulers in the afterlife (63b–c, 69e). In the *Republic*, Socrates says that poets should not represent heroes, much less the gods, as having an overwhelming desire for sex, as Homer does with Zeus (390b–c). At the end of the *Phaedo*, Crito suggests that before Socrates drinks the poison he can do what most people do: dine and drink well and have sex with whomever he happens to desire (116e). Socrates responds that these people act this way with good reason – they think that they will benefit from

---

[31] As noted by Nussbaum 1992, 126.

having done them – and that he, too, acts with good reason – he does not see them as beneficial (116e–117a). His behavior, again, fits with his theoretical account: in the defense speech and after the kinship argument he argues that philosophers shun the pleasures of drink, food, and sex (e.g. 64d, 81b) and only they have true moderation (69a–c).

Socrates ends the discussion of heroes in the *Republic* by arguing that good men must be presented neither as corruptible through bribes nor as willing to do the right thing only when offered money; nor can they have a sense of superiority over the gods or act impiously in any way (390e–391e). Socrates is portrayed as a deeply pious person of sterling integrity, actively seeking to understand his dream and to do what he thinks the gods want him to do. He has good hope that after death he will have the gods as his good and wise masters, and views himself as a slave of Apollo (85b). Moreover, he thinks that philosophers in general can hope to have these wise masters (69c–d) and would not be bribable, since they are not money lovers (68c).

At the end of the discussion of gods and heroes in the *Republic*, Socrates briefly turns to how to represent humans (392a–c). He says that the just should be happy and the unjust wretched and, further, that there should be no profit in injustice, not even if concealed (392b). Phaedo says at the beginning that Socrates seemed to be happy (*eudaimōn*, 58e3), and the dialogue ends with him saying that Socrates was the wisest and the most just person they knew (118a). Moreover, Socrates is represented throughout as tranquil and content. He also puts forward the view that only philosophers can have true justice (69b–c) and that only they can become close enough to the divine to live among the gods (69a–e), where they will be eternally happy (81a). Here, too, his character is in harmony with his theory, and both fit with the restrictions in the *Republic*: only the just are truly happy.

In sum, the *Phaedo* has precisely the elements for a properly told story about gods, heroes, and the underworld as described in *Republic* II–III, right down to the detail that lamentation only be given to women not of a superior sort. Socrates is presented not simply as having theoretical views about the gods, but also as interacting with them, interpreting their messages, and viewing himself as their slave. Seemingly offhand comments, such as Socrates saying that he is not interested in food or sex, show that Socrates meets every one of the *Republic*'s requirements for being a proper hero.

2.4 THE ACTION OF THE DIALOGUE AND TRAGIC DRAMA

I have argued that the *Phaedo* presents Socrates as a new sort of hero in a story that belongs to the same broad category as tragedy – one about gods, heroes, and the underworld – but that from the beginning rejects key elements of tragedy, as Plato understands these. Our task now is to understand the dialogue's action within this framework; doing so will involve drawing on many details that were mentioned earlier. I show here how these details contribute to the overall arc of the dialogue, telling a new sort of story of how a hero faces death. I also argue that some elements of this story can be seen as adapting formal elements of tragic drama.

The *Phaedo* is a story of Socrates on the last day of his life, approaching death as a philosopher. The action of the dialogue is driven by Socrates and his companions philosophizing together about the soul and death.[32] One of the most remarkable features of the *Phaedo* is that Socrates does not dwell on his own death, despite being about to die; instead, he spends the day to using philosophical arguments to help his companions cultivate the right attitude toward death. But Socrates does not treat this attitude as the most important thing to develop; he treats it as far more important for his companions to become better philosophers, firmly dedicated to the search for truth. Philosophy's value is far greater than simply as an aid in overcoming the fear of death. The *Phaedo* is the story of Socrates calmly transcending his unjust circumstances to help his companions overcome their fear of death – but, most importantly, to stay committed to philosophy once he is gone.

The opening of the dialogue was discussed at length in Section 2.1, so I will be very brief here. Socrates is presented as an alternative to Theseus, an extraordinary new sort of hero, who is nearly unaffected by *tuchē*. He should not be pitied, nor should one lament his situation despite his being unjustly put to death. He is courageous, noble, and happy, someone who went to Hades with divine dispensation, if anyone has. In interpreting his dream (60d–61b), Socrates shows due humility toward the gods and belief in their beneficence.

Socrates and his companions are quickly engaged in close argumentation. In the defense speech (63c–69e) he argues that being a philosopher involves not merely reasoning well, but taking on an entirely different way of life and approach to death. The true philosopher desires nothing but being dead (64a). In Cebes' challenge (69e–70b), which structures the main arguments of the dialogue, Cebes says that many people fear death because they fear that the soul will disperse upon death and so he asks Socrates to provide some confidence and reassurance not to fear this. Socrates responds with a series of arguments that are meant not merely to show that the soul exists after death but to ensure that their fears are addressed (see e.g. 77d–e), thus providing genuine, trustworthy reassurance.

In arguing that the true philosopher desires to be dead and that the soul is not destroyed upon death, Socrates develops theories that explain why it is appropriate to view the philosopher as the true hero. In the defense speech, he argues that only the philosopher can be courageous (68b–69e). The recollection argument (72e–77d) argues that the philosopher can rely on the resources in his own soul to acquire knowledge; hence, he is much less at the mercy of *tuchē* than one might expect.

---

[32] Nussbaum 2001 says that the action of the dialogue is the "committed pursuit of the truth about the soul"; Nussbaum 1992 says that the drama of the dialogue is the "drama of argumentation, to be pursued by the intellect alone." These formulations overlook the repeated emphasis on how Socrates helps his companions, as described in this section.

The kinship argument (78b–80b) develops the view that all souls are akin to the unchanging and uniform divine; it is how we live – rather than chance features of our birth – that can make us a hero. Socrates' further defense of his ethical views (80d–84b) provides a new account of Hades, explaining why the philosopher, and only the philosopher, will spend the rest of time among the gods (81a) – just as was said of Heracles, to whom Socrates is compared soon thereafter (89b–c).

In the first half of the dialogue, Simmias' and Cebes' questions, objections, and challenges drive the discussion (61d, 62c–e, 69e–70b, 72e–73a, and 77a–78a), creating unexpected twists and turns – as is fitting for a philosophical drama. Providing objections and challenging people's views is at the heart of Socratic philosophizing, and Socrates praises Cebes for always scrutinizing arguments and for refusing to be immediately convinced (63a). Simmias' and Cebes' objections to the kinship argument (85b–86d, 86e–88b) are the culmination of this critical activity, while at the same time setting the main agenda for the second half of the dialogue. Simmias and Cebes raise no further objections or challenges until the end of the final argument (that is, none from 88c to 107b). It is thus apt for Phaedo to treat Socrates' lengthy fight against these objections as a heroic labor (89c).

But what Phaedo describes as most admirable is not how Socrates vanquishes these objections, but how he responds to the companions' incipient misology (88e–89a). Socrates' rapid series of arguments and Simmias' and Cebes' objections had led Simmias and Cebes to change their minds several times (72d, 77c, 80b–c, 85b–88b). After these objections, Phaedo reports that all the companions became dispirited and started to doubt not only Socrates' current *logos*, but also all *logoi* that might be given in the future (88c). This leads Socrates to warn them not to become misologues (89d). Misology, he says, arises when one repeatedly puts one's trust in a *logos* and then loses it, eventually coming to hate *logoi* entirely (90b–c). Misology threatens one's ability to live a philosophical life; this is supposedly why Socrates calls it the greatest evil (89d). Helping his companions avoid misology is Socrates' most heroic deed; if he failed in this task, the arguments he gives, no matter how good, would not benefit his companions. If philosophy is to help these companions overcome their fear of death, they must stay devoted to it. But Socrates says that they should be careful lest he inadvertently deceive them about the soul's existence after death; he says that they should care much more about the truth than about Socrates (90e–91c). Socrates thinks it is most important it to help them become better, more devoted philosophers.

Socrates' discussion of misology occurs immediately after Echecrates breaks into the discussion, returning the reader to the outer frame. The *Phaedo* is unique among Plato's dialogues in having an outer frame that opens the dialogue (57a–59c) and then repeatedly breaks back into the inner dialogue (88c–89a, 102a, 118a).[33]

---

[33] The closest parallel is in the *Euthydemus*, when Crito interrupts Socrates' narration (290e–293b). Unlike in the *Phaedo*, in the *Euthydemus* Socrates is both narrator in the outer frame

2.4 The Action of the Dialogue and Tragic Drama   45

In this outer frame, Phaedo and Echecrates comment on and react to events as they occur in the main dialogue, just as the chorus does in a tragic play.[34] Echecrates breaks in, chorus-like, at crucial moments in the action, thereby emphasizing the significance of what has happened and offering an opportunity to reflect on the events. Moreover, the chorus can function as a sort of ordinary observer of the heroic events that unfold within the play; similarly, Echecrates and Phaedo's discussion responds to significant moments in the dialogue from the standpoint of people outside its central action. Phaedo and Echecrates are "present" as observers during the action of the dialogue – Phaedo literally, Echecrates through the report – whereas the main characters are not present during Phaedo and Echecrates' interludes; again, this is how a chorus functions in tragic drama.[35] In addition to interrupting just before the discussion of misology, Echecrates interrupts again to say how clear Socrates' exposition has been, once Socrates finishes explaining the method of hypothesis (102a). As I argue in Chapter 9, the method of hypothesis is meant to help avoid misology. Echecrates' enthusiastic interruption, then, highlights that Socrates has responded to the problem he drew attention to in his initial interruption, as well as that Socrates has provided a firm foundation for his triumphant final argument (102a–107b).

Of course, the chorus interacts with the main characters in a tragedy, whereas Echecrates and Phaedo cannot, since their conversation happens after the fact. Nonetheless, Phaedo plays a significant role in the inner dialogue as Socrates' main interlocutor in the discussion of misology (89b–91c). Here again Phaedo's involvement is chorus-like, since it is not part of the primary action – the arguments of the dialogue – but rather involves how others, including onlookers such as Echecrates and ourselves, react to it. From Phaedo's opening claim that he did not pity Socrates, through the discussion of misology, all the way up to the final line of the dialogue – where Phaedo says that Socrates was the wisest and most just person they knew – Phaedo provides a guide to how to view the last day of Socrates' life, not from

---

and primary interlocutor in the inner frame. Crito also does not focus on how the argument affected him in the way that Echecrates and Phaedo do. Moreover, there is only one such interruption in the *Euthydemus*, whereas the *Phaedo* has two, in addition to the opening discussion and the final words.

[34] So Raphael 1960, 82–3. Rowe 1993, 1, describes Phaedo and Echecrates as "chorus-like."

[35] It is sometimes claimed that the number of people at Socrates' death is fifteen, the number of members in a standard Greek chorus (Crotty 2009, 66, Jansen 2013, 1). This involves taking the fourteen people mentioned by name in the *Phaedo* and adding Crito, who was simply referred to as the father of Critobulus (59b). However, Phaedo says that there were also "some other locals" (59b9–10). So in fact there were more than fifteen people at Socrates' death. I find it hard to believe that Plato intended for us to remember, at the end of the dialogue, the number of people referred to either by name or indirectly at the beginning and to consider it significant, but to consider insignificant the other locals mentioned. This would also require Plato to set up two different, overlapping groups as replacement choruses: Phaedo and Echecrates on the one hand, and Socrates' companions on the other.

the ideal perspective of someone who would not cry at his death, but from the perspective of someone who admires Socrates and so aspires to be like him.[36]

Again, for Plato tragedy is not specifically tragic plays; my central claim is that the *Phaedo* is an alternative to the broad sort of tragedy that includes Homer. But, once we see Phaedo and Echecrates as chorus-like, it is natural to ask if there are other formal elements of tragic drama mirrored by the dialogue's structure. It takes place within a single circuit of the sun, as Aristotle says that a tragedy should (*Poetics* 1449b12–13). While no Platonic dialogue lasts for more than one day, the *Phaedo* draws attention to how it begins at dawn (59d–e) and ends just before sunset (116e). The servant of the Eleven acts like a messenger, coming in near the end of the action (116b–d). Unlike a play, the main dialogue uses reported speech rather than direct dialogue. But this is natural, given Plato's way of treating Phaedo and Echecrates as a chorus. There is no prologue in the dramatic sense, since the dialogue opens with the chorus. However, the dialogue's opening serves the typical function of a prologue since it sets the scene and establishes the relevant background needed to understand the events before the proper action begins.[37] Simmias' and Cebes' objections, along with the concern about misology, can be seen as a sort of tragic reversal: until they raise these objections, Simmias and Cebes become increasingly convinced of Socrates' claims, and then suddenly the very use of reason to address such questions is thrown into doubt, bringing with it the threat that Socrates' companions will come to hate *logoi*, thereby suffering the greatest evil. The second half responds to this reversal. At the end, Phaedo and Echecrates provide a brief exodus. While any of these parallels could be doubted, it seems likely that the *Phaedo* purposefully alludes to and adapts at least some formal elements of tragic drama.

After highlighting the danger of misology, Socrates shows how reason can provide the sort of persuasion that they can trust. Socrates' response to Simmias' objection convinces both Simmias and Cebes (92c–e, 95a–b) and his response to Cebes' objection ultimately leads to the final immortality argument, which in turn convinces Cebes (107a). Simmias says that he needs more time to remove any lingering doubts in his mind, and Socrates says that Simmias is right to say so – that he should not rush into trusting the argument, but rather analyze the hypotheses further (107b). Socrates' final argument builds upon the method of hypothesis, which he develops in his so-called autobiography (at 100a–102a). As noted earlier, this method can be seen as offering a way to avoid the dangers of misology. Hence, in the face of his own death, Socrates not only argues that none of them should fear death; he also helps his companions approach *logoi* in the right way, thereby helping them pursue philosophy, and so a happy life, rather than letting them head in the opposite direction by becoming misologues.

[36] For a similar idea, see Jansen 2013, 17.
[37] So Raphael 1960, 82.

After the final argument, Socrates properly represents daemons and the underworld, as one should in a story about "gods, heroes, daemons, and things in Hades" (*Republic* 392a4–6).[38] Near the beginning of his account, he argues that Aeschylus has Telephus present the wrong account of the journey to the underworld (107e–108a); he argues instead for an account that fits with the philosophical constraints developed over the course of the dialogue. At the end of his myth, Socrates says that it would be foolish to insist upon its details, but it is worth believing that something like it is right (114d). Socrates' myth fills in a picture of the sort of life he thinks is reasonable to expect after death: one where those who have been unjust pay the penalty, those who are holy are rewarded, and the best possible life is reserved for philosophers.

At the beginning of Socrates' death scene there is another reference to tragedy: Socrates pokes fun at himself for sounding like a tragic hero, then goes off to bathe himself (115a). This sets the scene for a very different sort of heroic death. There is nothing special about his body; no ritual is required for Socrates to journey well into the afterlife, nor is there any reason for him to prolong his life. In the midst of the somber and moving death scene, Socrates reminds us not to lament his death. He dies at peace.

2.5 AN AESOP FABLE ABOUT PLEASURE AND PAIN: 60B–C

We turn now to a different sort of *muthos* mentioned near the beginning of the dialogue. After Socrates asks Crito to have Xanthippe taken home (60a), the mixture of pleasure and pain Socrates feels from being freed from his fetters prompts him to discuss the peculiarity of pleasure.[39] He discusses this by composing a fable of the sort Aesop would compose. As Gábor Betegh notes, this presents a unique opportunity, since Socrates first provides a non-mythical account of pleasure and pain, and then explains how Aesop would put it into the form of a *muthos*.[40] Betegh argues that the fable clarifies the sort of teleological explanation Socrates looks for in his autobiography when he describes Anaxagoras' account of intelligence (*nous*) as a cause. I argue instead that this sort of fable explains only a special sort of explanandum and thus cannot be generalized to all teleological explanations.[41] The value of the story is that it helps us think through the peculiar nature of pleasure and pain and the way in which different sorts of stories (*muthoi*) operate with different norms.

---

[38] Edmonds 2004, ch. 4, argues that this part of the *Phaedo* falls within the genre of a journey to the underworld, which is not only Homeric but also found in tragic plays and Orphic writings.
[39] Here again an ordinary notion, that of fetters, contrasts with Socrates' later extraordinary idea: his body itself is like fetters (67d).
[40] Betegh 2009.
[41] In fact in Chapter 9 I argue that Socrates is not looking for teleological explanations in his autobiography, nor did he expect one from Anaxagoras.

Let us begin with Socrates' non-mythic and mythic accounts of pleasure and pain:

> What a peculiar thing it seems to be, my friends, the thing that people call "pleasant." What a surprising natural relation it has to its apparent opposite, pain. I mean that the two of them refuse to come to a person at the same time, yet if someone chases one and catches it he is pretty much forced always to catch the other one too, as if they were two things but joined by a single tip. And I do believe," he said, "that if Aesop had reflected on them, he would have composed a fable: that they were at war, and that god wanted to reconcile them, and that, when he was unable to do so, he joined their tips together, the result being that if one of them comes to somebody the other too will later follow in its train. That is precisely what seems to be happening to me too. Because pain was in my leg from the fetter, pleasure seems to have come in its train. (60b3–c7)

The key to understanding Socrates' myth, in my view, is that he is explaining the *peculiarity* (or absurdity – ἄτοπον) of pleasure, specifically its surprising relation to its apparent opposite, pain. In calling them "apparent opposites," Socrates may even suggest that, if they were genuine opposites, they might not have this surprising feature, that whenever someone catches the one, that same person will almost inevitably catch the other. In the *Gorgias*, Socrates argues that opposites are acquired successively and that good and bad are opposites, but that pleasure and pain come together and are lost at the same time (495d–497d). He concludes from this that pleasure and pain cannot be the same as good and bad; one could also conclude that they cannot be genuine opposites, since they are not acquired successively.

Some have claimed that this discussion of pleasure and pain anticipates Socrates' cyclical argument.[42] It does introduce the broad topic of opposites, which are important in several parts of the dialogue, as well as the question of when opposites (or apparent opposites) arise, which is important for the cyclical argument. However, the cyclical argument is about the relationship between opposites in general, whereas this myth explains the peculiarity of pleasure and pain – a peculiarity that calls their very status as opposites into question.[43] According to the cyclical argument, opposites come from opposites, and there is a single process from one opposite to the other (70d–71b). But the way in which Socrates describes pleasure and pain is compatible with someone's having one and then acquiring the other without losing the first – precisely the situation described in the *Gorgias*. In fact Socrates is likely still feeling pain from his fetters, which is why he is now rubbing his legs even as he feels the pleasure of the fetters' removal.[44] In this case there is no single process from the one to the other – unlike in the cyclical argument.

Moreover, the cyclical argument does not maintain that every opposite will revert to its opposite. Instead, Socrates claims there that every opposite, when it comes to be, does so from its opposite. So, for example, every hot thing comes to be from a

---

[42] Stemmer 1992, 50.
[43] So Gallop 1975, 77.
[44] So Gallop 1975, 77–8, contra Dorter 1982, 5.

cold thing (71a–b). This does not mean that every cold thing will eventually become hot. Socrates argues there that the living, when they come to be, do so from the dead. He does not need – nor does he argue – that every dead thing will eventually come alive again. (In fact, for his hopes to escape the cycle of reincarnation, it is important that this not be the case.) At the end of the cyclical argument, Socrates provides a supplemental argument that, if the opposites in some group did not balance each other out, then in the end they would all end up with a single form (72a–d). If everything became hotter without some members of this group becoming colder, eventually everything would be hot. This does not require every hot thing to revert to being cold. But, even if Socrates were committed to this view, it is very different from the claim that, whenever one chases and catches pleasure or pain, one will catch the other. Imagine that whenever you tried to get warm you inevitably became cold, or whenever you tried to become stronger you inevitably became weaker. That is how Socrates describes pleasure and pain here. The point of the myth is to explain how pleasure and pain could have this strange nature.

As Betegh notes, this myth seems to be of the same kind as in the *Symposium* and *Protagoras*: a genetic, aetiological myth that uses a divine agent to explain how we ended up with the current state of affairs.[45] I will argue for adding two features to Betegh's account. First, these myths also explain how we arrived at a particularly unusual state of affairs. Second, they explain their peculiar explanandum by providing a complex account of a thing's nature. A defective earlier condition prompts a benevolent divine agent to improve the situation by changing something's nature, leading to the current state of affairs. The following scheme draws on and adds to Betegh's analysis:

(1) The narrative posits an initial state of affairs where things are defective. In the *Phaedo*, pleasure and pain are at war.
(2) A god enters the scene with the power to rectify the situation.
(3) This divine agent analyzes the situation and works out the best practicable solution, given limiting conditions outside his control. In the *Phaedo* the god finds a solution, given the impossibility of reconciling these parties. The solution gives the thing in question a new, unusual nature. In the *Phaedo*, the god joined pleasure and pain's tips together.
(4) The narrative ends with a functional description of the current, unusual state of affairs, without mentioning the divine agent. Here it ends with a description in which pleasure and pain practically always follow each other.[46]

In the *Protagoras*, the peculiar explanandum is that virtue can be taught by everyone, unlike the crafts, in which only a few people are experts (319a–320c).

---

[45] Betegh 2009 also includes the account at the end of the *Gorgias* (523a–524a) of how people ended up being judged without their bodies after death. While I am sympathetic, this account fits this pattern less clearly, so I leave it out here.
[46] Betegh 2009, 84–5.

In Protagoras' myth (320d–322d), at first animals are distinguished by their natural abilities, but humans are defective, with no natural abilities. Thus they are given crafts by Epimetheus, and finally justice and shame by Zeus. This reflects the fact that their natures are fundamentally different from those of other animals: Protagoras says, "it is because humans had a share of the divine dispensation that they alone among animals worshipped the gods, due to their kinship [συγγένειαν] to the god, and erected altars and sacred images" (322a3–5).[47] The arts bestowed upon humans by the gods reveal that they are, by nature, related to the divine. Moreover, the different parts of human nature should be understood differently, depending on who gave them and at what stage. Crafts are different from animals' natural abilities, and justice and shame, which Zeus gave to all humans, are different from crafts. This complex account of human nature explains the unusual phenomenon that virtue can be taught by everyone, unlike crafts.

Similarly, Aristophanes' myth in the *Symposium* (189d–193b) begins by explicitly saying that the strangeness of love is to be understood in terms of human nature (189d). Aristophanes begins with the initial condition in which humans were in the normal situation of being whole animals. But our pride caused a unique problem, leading to a very strange feature of our current nature – that we are halves of what was once whole creatures – which makes our gender quite different from our other features. Again, this strange feature of our nature is marked by its coming from a divine agent at a distinct stage. And it explains the peculiar phenomenon in question: love.

In keeping with this same narrative structure, pleasure and pain have a unique nature, introduced by a divine agent: they now have just one tip, so that they follow each other around. The myth provides an account of the nature of pleasure and pain that captures how they seem on the one hand opposed to each other, but on the other hand bound together.

Thus, *pace* Betegh, it is not clear how this mythical structure could be used in a general account of the natural world, since the structure is not appropriate for ordinary explananda such as "why is the earth a sphere?" (cf. 97d–e). Of course, if there is something especially puzzling about the earth's being a sphere, then perhaps such a structure would be useful; but not every natural explanandum has an unusual nature. Moreover, there is no reason to think that the myth at the end of the *Phaedo* is part of such a myth. Betegh (2009) suggests that this myth provides the final stage (stage (4)) of such a myth and, "as such, it only takes the end-product of a genetic account without explaining from what defective initial conditions, in virtue of what reasoning and calculations and facing what limiting conditions, a divine agent produced this arrangement" (99). But the myth at the end is not, at least on the face of it, attempting to explain why something is especially strange in terms of its unusual nature, unlike the Aesop myth and the

---

[47] Translation modified from Stanley Lombardo and Karen Bell in Cooper and Hutchinson 1997.

myths in the *Protagoras* and *Symposium*. In fact the final *muthos* has no narrative structure at all. In Chapter 11 I tackle the tricky question of why Socrates describes it as a *muthos* (see Subsection 11.5.4).

The simplicity of the *Phaedo*'s Aesop myth helps clarify the structure of the myths in the *Symposium* and the *Gorgias*; but does it have any larger role in the *Phaedo*? As mentioned earlier, it clarifies what makes a certain type of story appropriate – in this case, a type of origin myth. The idea of developing appropriate norms for different sorts of stories is crucial for evaluating the *Phaedo* itself as an alternative to tragedy. More generally, a theme at the beginning of the dialogue is the proper way to tell a story. After Socrates explains how Aesop would tell a story (μῦθος, 60c) about pleasure and pain, he says that he is not someone with the storytelling art (μυθολογικός, 61b),[48] but the gods may have been telling him, through a dream, that he should be engaged in storytelling; shortly thereafter, he says that it may be an appropriate time for him to tell a story (μυθολογεῖν, 61e) about what the afterlife is like. Later Socrates asks, in responding to Cebes' worry that the soul may be destroyed upon death, whether they should thoroughly tell a story (διαμυθολογεῖν, 70b) about whether or not it is likely that the soul is destroyed. At the end of the dialogue, Socrates provides his eschatological and cosmological *muthos* (see Chapter 11, esp. Subsection 11.5.4). We are given many opportunities to reflect on what it is to tell a story, how to tell different sorts of stories, when they are appropriate, and who can and should tell them.

The Aesop myth also introduces the idea that, contrary to most people's beliefs, it is not clear that pleasure is good.[49] Socrates raises several concerns about pleasure and pain in the dialogue, as discussed in Chapters 3 and 7. But at this stage we already see reason for caution, similar to that found in the leaky jar metaphor in the *Gorgias* (493a–d): even if one supposed that pleasure is worth acquiring, it generally cannot be acquired without pain.

Socrates uses here the phrase "what people call the 'pleasant'"; this seems to be picked up a few pages later, when Socrates mentions "the sorts of things called pleasures" (64d3). It is sometimes thought that Socrates' emphasizing that these are *called* pleasures indicates that they are not genuine pleasures, in line with what Socrates says in *Republic* IX and the *Philebus*.[50] The typical translation of τὰς ἡδονὰς καλουμένας at 64d3 as "so-called pleasures" reinforces such an interpretation. However, nothing else in the *Phaedo* casts doubt on the reality of these pleasures.

---

[48] The ending *-ikos* indicates that this is some sort of *technē*. Socrates denies that he has any expertise in composing *muthoi*, but he does provide the outlines of the Aesop fable and says, on the next page, that it is appropriate to tell a *muthos* about the afterlife. His lack of art leads him to versify Aesop's tales, but it has not stopped him from telling stories altogether. Hence his claims are not in tension, contra e.g. Gallop 1975, 78.

[49] For a related idea, see Frede 2005, 12–13.

[50] Hackforth 1955, 33, n. 2. Gosling and Taylor 1982, 86, suggest this view without fully endorsing it.

Later, when he speaks of "this time that we call 'living'" (107c2–3), he is not referring to a time of "so-called" living; rather the point is that we call this time living, although in fact the term "living" also applies to us before we are born and after we have died. I suggest, similarly, that Socrates, in using the phrase "the things called pleasures," is referring only to what most people identify as pleasures, leaving open the possibility that there are other pleasures (such as those of learning, mentioned at 114e).

2.6 SOCRATES AS INTERPRETER OF DREAMS: 60C–61B

After telling his Aesop fable, Socrates explains why he has recently composed poetry: he is considering a new interpretation of a dream that has frequently visited him in the past, which tells him to compose and to work at music. Socrates had been interpreting this dream as an exhortation to continue doing philosophy, but now is considering the possibility that it is telling him to practice the arts as conventionally conceived. This introduces the topic of how Socrates interprets ideas from the gods and, more generally, religious ideas.

Note that Socrates assumes here that the gods are benevolent. One or more of them are trying to send him a message, which will help him if he properly interprets it. Socrates feels a religious duty to do what the gods ask, but he does not see this duty as conflicting with his own interests. Appreciating the gods' benevolence clarifies Socrates' initial interpretation of the dream. The obvious interpretation of "compose music and work at it" is not to keep doing philosophy. However, Socrates thinks that the gods are benevolent and thus telling him something true and good for him to hear. He thinks it is true that he should keep doing philosophy. This constraint changes what interpretations are likely. Socrates' approach to religious claims in the *Phaedo* is similar to his approach to the Oracle in the *Apology*.[51] The right way to interpret the Oracle is not the most obvious one, but rather the way that fits with what Socrates thinks is true. This interpretive strategy will reappear throughout the *Phaedo*, especially in the defense speech, the return to the defense, and the eschatological account.

Socrates' new interpretation is that his dream is telling him to compose poetry in the conventional sense. Why would Plato provide this new interpretation at the beginning of the dialogue? It emphasizes Socrates' unique form of piety and humility: while he may not have a conventional approach to religion, he is quite serious about doing what he thinks the gods want, and is ready to acknowledge that he may have misunderstood them. Also, Plato may well want us to consider which of Socrates' interpretations is correct. Socrates was already doing philosophy and working at it; he hardly needed to be cheered on like a runner (60e–61a). If the dream is supposed to benefit him, that is some reason to prefer his new

---

[51] So Morgan 2010.

interpretation. Socrates' engagement with storytelling has already shown some rewards in his Aesop fable. Stories continue to play an important role later in the dialogue. There is Socrates' account of why swans sing when they are about to die (84e–85b), his autobiography – a story about his own intellectual development – and his final eschatological account. There is also the *Phaedo* itself, which I have argued is written as a specific sort of story. My suggestion, then, is that composing stories is not a diversion from Socrates' goal of grasping the truth and living a philosophical life; instead, it is supposed to complement this goal in a variety of ways, as presented over the course of the dialogue.

2.7 CONCLUSION

Storytelling dominates the opening of the dialogue. The *Phaedo* begins by laying out the foundation for a properly told story of gods, heroes, and the underworld, a story that describes a hero, in the face of death, using philosophical argumentation to remove his companions' fear of death while helping them avoid the perils of misology. Socrates illustrates how the philosophical life is admirable by calmly transcending his unjust circumstances while dedicated to the search for the truth. Understanding the *Phaedo*'s framework and story sheds new light on Socrates' philosophical views in the dialogue, but its greatest value lies in helping us appreciate this literary masterpiece on its own terms.

Within this new story, Socrates' first activity is to describe a different sort of story, an origin myth of the same sort as in the *Protagoras* and *Symposium*. Considering these different types of stories helps us reflect on how to tell such stories appropriately. Socrates' dream suggests that storytelling may itself be an important complement to his philosophical activity.

The opening of the dialogue also introduces a number of key ideas that are developed later in the dialogue. Several ordinary things are mentioned that contrast with the extraordinary proposals to come: purification, prison, dedication to Apollo, Hades, and slavery. Phaedo and Echecrates are introduced, along with the rest of the inner circle of Socratics who were there on the last day of Socrates' life. Socrates' Aesop fable provides the first step toward undermining the value of pleasure. Socrates' interpretation of his dream begins to illustrate how he interprets ideas from the gods. In just over four Stephanus pages, Plato has carefully laid the groundwork for the main theme of the *Phaedo*, which will determine its structure until the end: the philosopher's desire to be dead.

3

Defense of the Desire to Be Dead

61c–69e

Socrates defends here the claim that the sole pursuit of philosophers is dying and being dead (64a). In arguing for this and related claims, he introduces most of the key topics in the dialogue, including forms, inquiry, the soul, and the philosophical life. Nonetheless, there has been relatively little discussion of this long section of the dialogue, aside from the famous exchange passage (69a–d). Perhaps one reason for this is that many of Socrates' claims here are put in religious language. However, as I argued in Section 1.3, Socrates systematically reinterprets religious ideas in a way that fits with his philosophical theory; thus, the religious language need not make his views any less philosophical. This section of the dialogue may also be overlooked because it seems simply to assert some of its claims rather than argue for them. As we will see, Socrates does provide reasons for them but, as part of the *Phaedo*'s unfolding structure, we sometimes must wait until later in the dialogue to fully appreciate them. Once we take this section seriously, we can appreciate its tight and careful argumentative structure, which (to my knowledge) has not been carefully laid out before. Moreover, Socrates' accounts here, in particular his ethical account, are sophisticated theories in their own right, with many of the key claims not further elaborated later in the dialogue. The section also introduces some unusual and important terminology that Plato uses both in the *Phaedo* and in other dialogues, such as *auto kath' hauto* (which I argue should be translated "itself through itself") and terminology for identifying the forms.

While we might be tempted to discuss separately this section's ethics, psychology, epistemology, and metaphysics, Socrates carefully interrelates them, and so I do the same. The chapter begins (Section 3.1) with Socrates' argument that suicide is prohibited (61d–62c). I argue that his reasoning relies on a tentative suggestion that is incompatible with his broader theological views, but that he points toward a more satisfying reason not to commit suicide that he develops later in the dialogue. Then I turn to Socrates' defense speech (63b–69d), starting with what its aims are, what its main parts are, and how they fit together (Section 3.2). In the remainder of the chapter I go through these parts roughly in order. First (Section 3.3) I argue that Socrates' claim that the philosopher desires to be dead is based on a technical sense of the term "dead," which uses Socrates' obscure phrase "itself *kata* itself" (αὐτὸ καθ' αὑτό). I draw on pre-Platonic texts to provide a new general account of what this phrase means (Section 3.4), which explains why the *Phaedo* connects it closely with purity. The philosopher desires to be dead because of the problems caused by the body. I begin with the different ways in which bodily pleasure, pain, fear, and desire make it more difficult to search for wisdom (Section 3.5). Then I consider why inquiry through the senses does not lead to the truth (Section 3.6). Examining this topic involves a long discussion of what Socrates is introducing when he introduces the forms. Next I argue that Socrates allows that we might acquire some knowledge while embodied but that, even if we do, it would fall far short of the wisdom that the philosopher seeks (Section 3.7). This completes my account of why the philosopher desires to be dead.

Socrates next turns to why the philosopher will have a better afterlife. He argues that philosophers have genuine virtue and thus can live with the gods after death, whereas non-philosophers do not and thus cannot (Section 3.8). First he argues that non-philosophers cannot even meet their own criteria for courage and temperance (Subsection 3.8.1); then he suggests an alternative way to think of the virtues in the famous "exchange passage" (Subsection 3.8.2). I argue that non-philosophers' so-called virtue involves their being ruled by their bodies without even realizing it. By contrast, to the extent that the philosopher possesses wisdom, he is ruled by his soul, which provides him with genuine virtue.[1]

3.1 THE ARGUMENT AGAINST SUICIDE: 61C–63A

Socrates' argument that suicide is not sanctioned has a few puzzling features that, to my knowledge, have not been discussed in the secondary literature. He begins by saying that "what is said in secret accounts of these matters, that we human beings are in a sort of prison and that one must not release oneself from it or run away, seems to me a weighty saying and one that is not easy to penetrate" (62b2–6). Socrates does not endorse this claim or use it in what follows. Why mention this idea that we are in a sort of prison only to set it aside?[2] The second strange feature is that Socrates' argument seems to go against broad principles of Socratic theology found both in the *Phaedo* and elsewhere in Plato's corpus. Socrates asks whether Cebes would be angry at one of his possessions if it killed itself and whether he

---

[1] On Socrates' (unfortunate) presupposition in the *Phaedo* that the philosopher is a man, see Introduction, fn. 4.
[2] In Cooper 1989's, Warren 2001's, Tuominen 2014's, and Long 2019's discussions of suicide in the *Phaedo*, this secret account is treated as a first argument. But Socrates simply contrasts this weighty and difficult-to-penetrate saying with what strikes him as well said: that the gods take care of us and we humans are one of their possessions (62b).

would punish it (τιμωρεῖν) if he could – suggesting that the gods would similarly be angry and vengeful if we killed ourselves, since we are their possessions (62c). Socrates generally thinks that the gods are not vengeful; for example, he earlier treated it as obvious that his divine dream was trying to benefit him (60e–61b) – and in this very argument (62b) and afterwards (63b–c, 69d–e, 80d–81a) he says that the gods will care for and benefit us, which is why we wish to be with them in the afterlife. A vengeful god is about as un-Socratic and un-Platonic as possible (*Republic* 379b–c; cf. *Euthyphro* 6a–c, 14e–15a, *Timaeus* 29e–30b).[3]

One might think, then, that Socrates means that the gods would punish people in a way that improves them. But in this case not only would the anger be irrelevant, but anyone should gladly receive the punishment, since it would be beneficial (cf. *Grg.* 480a–b). Instead Socrates seems to treat the anger and punishment as themselves worth avoiding. Why would Socrates suggest such an un-Socratic reason for not killing oneself? My suggestion is that he first points toward the real reason, but Cebes is not yet in a position to appreciate it, so – without actually endorsing it – Socrates suggests this weaker, un-Socratic reason. He only says that "perhaps" (ἴσως, 62c6) this reasoning about the gods' anger and vengeance means that one should not kill oneself.[4]

As for the real reason not to kill oneself, after saying here that the idea of the body as a prison is "weighty" and "difficult to penetrate" (62b), Socrates goes on to explain what it means later (82d–e), in the ethical discussion that I call "the return to the defense" (80d–84b).[5] As we will see in Section 7.3, Socrates argues there that the body imprisons us with bodily desires, which hinder the soul from pursuing its genuine end, wisdom. The insidiousness of this prison is that we desire being in it rather than freeing ourselves to pursue our own proper end. In fact most souls reincarnate because their desire for the bodily pulls them into a new body after death (81d–e); only the philosopher's soul is able to avoid this, instead living eternally with the divine where it can acquire acquiring what it truly desires: wisdom (81a).

Thus the real reason why most people should not commit suicide is that they will simply end up in another body, probably a worse one. Socrates argues in the cyclical argument that the soul reincarnates and then, in the return to the defense, that most people will be reincarnated into a new body worse than our current one (81d–82b). Thus, for most people death is not a good thing, and so benevolent gods would not want us to commit suicide. As we will see, Socrates thinks that a soul must be

---

[3] For a similar thought, see Damascius I, 19.
[4] Warren 2001 and Tuominen 2014 similarly emphasize that Socrates does not clearly endorse this argument.
[5] In the later passage, Socrates uses the term εἱργμός for prison (82e); at the opening of the dialogue he uses δεσμωτήριον (58c and 59d); here at 62b he uses φρουρά. On the question of whether φρουρά means watchtower or prison, see Loriaux 1969 ad loc. Plato may be purposefully leaving this ambiguous; it is, after all, supposed to be a difficult saying to penetrate. Then, at 82e, Socrates clarifies in what sense the body is a φρουρά: it is a εἱργμός.

sufficiently purified to have a better afterlife, but since there is no clear way to know whether we are suitably prepared, we should allow ourselves to die only if the gods "send some necessity" (62c7) – which is precisely what Socrates thinks the gods have done for him. Later in the defense speech, Socrates makes clear that only a philosopher could be properly benefited by the gods' release:

> And in the time when we are alive, it seems that we will be closest to knowledge if, so far as possible, we do not consort with the body nor associate with it, except when absolutely necessary, and are not infected with its nature, but instead keep pure from it, until god himself releases us; and being thus pure, through release from the body's folly, we will likely be in similar company, and will know through our very selves all that is unalloyed, which is, equally, the truth. (67a2–b2)

Socrates' initial point is that philosophers must consort with the body as little as possible until the god releases them. But he then describes a reward that only philosophers can reap, since it requires a purity that only they can achieve. Thus suicide would not benefit most people. If we simply sever our connection with the body, the problems it causes will not go away. The gods can be genuine benefactors – rather than vengeful – if they release us at the best time. Hence, there would never be any reason to commit suicide: as soon as we are ready, the gods will release us.

Cebes is innocent of all of this when he asks Socrates why suicide is not sanctioned. He thinks that Socrates wants ordinary death; and, given this, why not simply kill oneself? Socrates will soon say that ordinary people do not understand the way in which the philosopher desires to be dead (64b–c). Socrates has not yet given his account of purifying, of reincarnation, or of our different possible lives after death. So he points to the real reason, that the body is a prison, while giving another reason, which does not fit with his view of the gods but can be appreciated from an ordinary perspective.

3.2 THE AIMS AND STRUCTURE OF THE DEFENSE SPEECH: 63B–69E

Cebes responds to Socrates' argument against suicide by asking why Socrates would want to leave the care of the gods, given that they are our wise masters. Socrates replies that he will defend himself against these charges as if in court (63b) and that those present are his jurors (63e), leading to the ensuing discussion (63b–69e) being called his "defense speech."[6]

Socrates provides two descriptions of what he will argue for in this defense. Initially (63b–c) he says that his strongest affirmation is that (Ia) he will enter the presence of wise and good gods, and hence he does not resent death but rather is

---

[6] Section 1.4 discusses this connection to the *Apology*.

hopeful. He also says here that (Ib) he will be in the presence of good men, although he would not insist on this; at the end, he adds that (Ic) for these reasons he is hopeful that death is far better for the good than for the wicked. After Crito interrupts (63d–e), Socrates describes differently his goals for the speech (63e–64a). Rather than focusing only on his own case, he claims that (IIa) anyone who truly spends his life in philosophy has good reason to be confident when he is about to die, and that (IIb) there is good hope that such a person will win very great benefits in the other world. Socrates here does not mention the gods, nor does he say that the good will fare better than the wicked, but rather that philosophers will have great benefit. (IIb) fits well with what he does for most of the speech: he barely mentions the gods again until the very end of the defense speech, the sole exception being the passage quoted in the previous section (67a–b). The heart of his argument is that the philosopher desires to be dead because only then can he have what he truly desires: wisdom and truth. Cebes' challenge, which comes directly after the defense speech, effectively concedes that, if the soul exists after death, this would benefit the philosopher (IIb), but asks whether the soul does exist and so whether we should accept (IIa).

Does the defense speech fail, then, to defend the main claim that Socrates originally said he would defend (Ia), namely that he will enter the presence of wise and good masters?[7] At the end of the defense (69c–d), Socrates provides his interpretation of the claim that those who come to Hades purified and initiated will dwell among the gods. Since he has argued that the philosopher alone will have a purified soul (66e–67d), in keeping with his general interpretive strategy (see Section 1.3), he takes this to mean that only those who have pursued philosophy correctly will dwell among the gods. But Socrates does not argue here for the general religious view that purification is needed to interact with the gods. At this stage, he shows how his account fits with these religious views without giving independent reasons for accepting them. The return to the defense (Section 7.1) offers a fuller explanation for why the philosophers will live among the gods, one that relies on the kinship argument's account of the soul's relation to the divine. In short, the defense speech focuses on the final goal that Socrates articulates: to show that (IIb) the philosopher will win very great benefits after death (namely truth and wisdom). At the end, Socrates outlines a defense of his original primary goal (Ia), which he further defends in the return to the defense.

We can divide the defense speech into the following parts:

(1) description of the philosophers' practice for and desire to be dead; definitions of death and being dead (64a–c);
(2) observations that the philosophical man does not value bodily things, and arguments that he does not use the senses to inquire (64c–66a);

---

[7] As White 2006 maintains.

(3) description of how genuine philosophers would speak to one another about how the body prevents them from acquiring what they truly desire, wisdom (66b–67b);
(4) interim conclusion: Socrates, and in general philosophers, should have good hope and look forward to the time after death (67b–68b);
(5) distinction between philosophers and non-philosophers in terms of whether they can have genuine virtues and the sort of "exchange" they make when acting; this distinction is used to argue that only philosophers should have good hope about the afterlife (68b–69e).

The basic argument is that philosophers can acquire the wisdom that they desire only by being dead, hence they desire to be dead. (1) explains what is being argued for; (2) provides initial reasons for this conclusion that Simmias happily agrees to; and (3) provides stronger reasons that philosophers would provide to one another, which allows the conclusion (IIb) to be reached in (4); (5) then uses the conclusion that only the philosopher can have genuine virtues to support Socrates' claims that after death the philosophers will dwell among the gods (Ia) and with other good people (Ib), resulting in the afterlife being far better for the good than that for the wicked (Ic).

In the remainder of this chapter I go through the defense speech roughly in order, explaining how Socrates reaches his conclusion while laying out the ethical, epistemological, and metaphysical picture that emerges from his arguments.

3.3 THE PHILOSOPHER'S DESIRE TO BE DEAD[8]

Socrates says that the sole pursuit of those who correctly engage in philosophy is dying and being dead (64a). This might seem overwrought, or simply an overstatement. I argue here instead that Socrates means exactly what he says – but in a technical sense of being dead, that, given Socrates' other commitments, has the following consequence: the pursuit of wisdom, for those who are embodied, simply is the pursuit of being dead. An initial sign that Socrates means this claim in a special sense is that Simmias initially laughs and say that most people would think it well said that those who pursue philosophy really want to be dead (64b). Socrates responds that they have not realized this because they have not realized the sense in which true philosophers desire to be dead and deserve death, nor what that death is like (64b–c). Clearly, most people must misunderstand something about being a philosopher or about being dead – or, as it turns out, something about each.

In order to understand what the philosopher's death is like and in what sense the philosopher desires and deserves to be dead, we need to consider carefully Socrates' definitions of death and of being dead:

---

[8] The following three sections draw heavily on Ebrey 2017b. The material is rearranged, new arguments are provided, and some old arguments modified.

"Do we believe that there is such a thing as death (θάνατον)?"

"Certainly," replies Simmias.

"And [do we suppose] that it is anything other than the release (ἀπαλλαγήν) of the soul from the body? And that being dead (τὸ τεθνάναι) is this: the body has come to be itself through itself (αὐτὸ καθ' αὑτό), separate (χωρίς), released (ἀπαλλαγέν) from the soul, and the soul is itself through itself, separate, released from the body? Can death be anything other than that?" (64c2–8)

Notice that, at least on the face of it, Socrates provides two different definitions in this passage, one for death – which requires nothing but release of the body from the soul and another for being dead, which requires (i) the body and soul to each be separate and released and from one another and (ii) that each is itself through itself.[9] It is the second part of the definition, the "itself through itself," that has been overlooked. According to this definition, being dead requires more than death.[10] That said, the passage's final sentence seems to suggest that Socrates is offering only one definition here – of death – and thus is not distinguishing death from being dead. As we will see, over the next two pages Socrates relies on these being distinct definitions; and later, in the return to the defense, he again treats them as distinct, referring there to the philosopher as preparing "really to be dead" (τῷ ὄντι τεθνάναι, 81a1). The cumulative evidence suggests that he is indeed providing two definitions here, which is why he uses two clearly distinct formulations in the above passage. Moreover, viewing them as distinct clarifies why being dead is supposed to be an accomplishment, something that requires practice. Everyone must suffer death, but only a few are truly able to be dead. My suggestion is that Socrates carefully provides distinct formulations here that he later relies on, but he realizes that Simmias may not have immediately grasped these subtle differences. And so, at the end of the above passage, he asks Simmias only about the simpler definition, that of death.[11]

---

[9] The perfective aspect of "being dead" (τεθνάναι) suggests an end state rather than a process. In the *Phaedo*, Socrates consistently uses ἀποθνήσκειν for the process of dying and τεθνάναι for its result, being dead. "Death" (θάνατος), by contrast, could refer to a final state or to the process that leads up to this state. When "death" refers to the resulting state, it is still easier to achieve than being dead (τεθνάναι) according to this definition, since it does not require the soul or the body to be itself through itself.

On a separate point, note that Socrates introduces the soul into the dialogue through these accounts of death and being dead. In Homer, the terms "soul" and "body" are used only for after death – they are, as it were, what results from death. Unfortunately, it is far too large a topic to discuss here how Socrates' treatment of the soul in the *Phaedo* relates to that in other dialogues and in pre-Platonic authors.

[10] None of the major English translations preserves this distinction in the argument that follows, which makes it impossible to follow Socrates' reasoning; in various places, τεθνάναι is translated with "death" instead of "being dead," or translate a demonstrative with "death" although it refers back to τεθνάναι.

[11] That said, the important point for my argument is that Socrates presents two separate notions here, not that his words "death" (θάνατος) and "being dead" (τὸ τεθνάναι) track these two notions. One notion involves the soul's simply separating or releasing from the body. This is

3.3 *The Philosopher's Desire to Be Dead*

I offer an account of the unusual phrase "itself through itself" (αὐτὸ καθ' αὑτό) in the next section. For now, let us leave it uninterpreted. First, a preliminary consideration: one Stephanus page after Socrates provides his definition of being dead, he says that the soul reasons best when it is itself through itself – which it is so long as it does not associate with the body (65c). It would be a surprising coincidence for Socrates to (i) say that the philosopher desires to be dead, (ii) define being dead in terms of the soul being itself through itself, and then (iii) just happen to say, a page later, that philosophy requires the soul to become itself through itself. I suggest that, rather than this being a coincidence, the philosopher desires to be dead because he desires wisdom, which requires reasoning in the best way, and this requires being dead in the technical sense. Most souls are never themselves through themselves, and thus never really dead.

Two Stephanus pages after his definition of being dead, Socrates relies on this definition when describing how philosophers would explain to each other why they desire to be dead:

> The time, so it seems, when we will have that which we desire and whose lovers we claim to be, namely wisdom, will be when we reach our end, as the argument indicates, and not while we are alive. For if it is impossible to have pure knowledge of anything when we are in the company of the body, then one of two things: either knowledge cannot be acquired anywhere, or it can be acquired when we reach our end. For at that time the soul will be itself through itself, separate from the body, whereas before then it will not (66e1–67a1).

Socrates explains with two "for" (γάρ) clauses why the philosopher will have what he desires – wisdom – only when he has reached his end (i.e. when he dies). The philosopher desires wisdom. But this requires the soul to be itself through itself, which in turn requires separation from the body, and hence the soul must be, by definition, dead: separated from the body and itself through itself.[12] Mere separation (death) would not be enough, since that would be compatible with the soul's not being itself through itself, and so with its not being able to acquire wisdom. Immediately before this passage, Socrates explains why the soul cannot be itself through itself until it is genuinely released from the body (66c–e): the body makes it impossible to successfully acquire genuine wisdom (as discussed in Sections 3.5–3.7). One might have hoped that the soul could simply ignore the body and

---

what we ordinarily think of as death. The other, which only the philosopher can achieve, involves the soul's also being itself through itself.

[12] Socrates does not address what is needed for the body to be itself through itself. I discuss the nature of the body in Section 6.5. It seems that, when the body and the soul are joined, each becomes more like the other, so that neither is purely in line with its own nature. After the soul leaves the body, the soul typically continues to have the body's nature mixed into it, which (as I discuss in the next section), makes it unable to be itself *kata* itself. But the soul's nature does not stay mixed in the body after death, and so it is easier for the body to be itself *kata* itself.

become itself through itself while still conjoined to the body, but unfortunately it must be released from the body, thereby meeting the definition of being dead.

Near the beginning of the return to the defense, Socrates says that when an impure soul is released from the body it is not itself through itself (81b1–2 and 81c1–2). Hence, by Socrates' definitions, this soul has gone through death (separation from the body) but is not, strictly speaking, dead – separate from the body and itself through itself. This impure soul is contrasted with the philosopher's, which prepares for "really being dead" (τῷ ὄντι τεθνάναι, 81a1); this allows it to spend the rest of time with the gods, eternally separated from the body (81a). The other souls, by contrast, are drawn back to another body by their impurity(81c–e), thereby reincarnating.

Sometimes Socrates' talk of the soul as "separate" (χωρίς) or its "release" (ἀπαλλαγή) from the body is taken to mean that the soul could be separated or released from the body while the person is still alive in the ordinary sense.[13] The idea is that the philosopher separates his soul from the body through his philosophical practice, and so could be dead while still embodied. But this does not fit with Socrates' usage in the dialogue. At 80e–81a Socrates speaks of a philosopher who, through constant practice, has kept his soul so pure that he will be able to be eternally with the gods; however, it is only when this soul is "released" that he can be eternally with the divine. Here, clearly, "release" is death in the ordinary sense. Similarly, Cebes' challenge (69e–70b), which launches Socrates' arguments for the existence of the soul after death, is put in terms of what happens once the soul is "released" from the body. Cebes is worried about the soul's being destroyed by ordinary death, not about its being destroyed by philosophical purification. Socrates repeats this language of "release" in recapping the kinship argument (84b) and the final immortality argument (107c), to describe the event in which one might think the soul is destroyed – that is, ordinary death. As I argue in Section 3.7, Socrates thinks that philosophers cannot come close to the wisdom that they desire so long as they are embodied. This is why he says that only after genuine release from the body (if ever) can they have what they desire (68a–b, cf. 67b–c).

There are two passages where Socrates uses "release" and "separation" in a way that does not suggest literal death. At 65e–66a, he says that the one who comes to know each thing most purely is the one who is released (ἀπαλλάττειν) as much as possible (ὅτι μάλιστα) from his eyes, ears, and virtually his entire body. And at 67c–d, Socrates says that purifying involves separating (χωρίζειν) the soul from the body as much as possible (ὅτι μάλιστα), both now and afterwards (i.e. after death). The phrase "as much as possible" in each case signals that Socrates is using these terms in a way that allows them to come in degrees. By contrast, he does not use similar modifiers in his definition of death and being dead, or in the many places described

---

[13] E.g. Pakaluk 2003, 99, and Woolf 2004, 97.

earlier where he and Cebes invoke these definitions and are clearly talking about ordinary death.

Scholars want to explain how the philosopher, while embodied, can become closer to being dead. On my account, this happens through the soul's becoming more through itself (καθ' αὑτήν), which involves not associating with the body to the extent possible. But the soul cannot become entirely itself through itself so long as it is connected to the body, which is why the philosopher desires to be separated and released from it, which requires death in the ordinary sense.

Let me turn to two concerns frequently raised about Socrates' definition of death.[14] First, it seems to presuppose that the soul will continue to exist after death, when this is something that Socrates should show.[15] However, Cebes' challenge assumes that the soul is released from the body, but not that it continues to exist once this happens (70a). For all this definition says, the soul could be destroyed immediately upon its release. The second concern about the definition is that it applies only to a combination of soul and body. This seems to pose a problem for Socrates' final immortality argument, since he there discusses whether the soul itself can receive death.[16] I suggest that Socrates' definition of death in the defense speech can naturally be generalized to apply to the soul as well. In short, the basic notion of death is the destruction of a living thing through separation. At this stage, Socrates has not yet described the soul as alive; Cebes is the first to do so, in his cloakmaker objection (87d), and Socrates provides a theoretical defense of this in his final argument (Section 10.6).[17] Once they describe the soul itself as alive, the question arises whether it too can receive death – that is, be destroyed through separation.

After discussing the meaning of "itself through itself" in the next section, the following three sections discuss the various ways in which the body prevents the soul from being itself through itself.

3.4 ITSELF THROUGH ITSELF (AUTO KATH' HAUTO)

The phrase "itself *kata* itself" – which I translate as "itself through itself," for reasons given further down – is famously applied to the forms in the *Phaedo* (first at 66a). This phrase is important for understanding not only Socrates' description of forms and his definition of being dead (64c), but also his account of the soul's nature and how the philosopher acquires wisdom (first at 65c). Scholars often connect the phrase to the notion of separation, perhaps because Aristotle describes Plato's forms as separate (*Metaphysics* M.4, 1078b30–1, M.9, 1086a32–b5; *Eudemian Ethics* I.8, 1217b15–16). Aristotle gives a technical meaning to being "separate" (χωριστός), and

---

[14] So e.g. Gallop 1975, 86–7.
[15] E.g. Sedley 1995, 15.
[16] So O'Brien 1968, 98.
[17] See also Ebrey 2022b.

its exact meaning in Aristotle is a matter of dispute. But, whatever Aristotle may have meant by it, I argue that the ordinary meaning of the word "separate" does not capture the meaning of "itself *kata* itself," since something that is itself *kata* itself can be with many other things, not separated from them.[18] We can better understand the *Phaedo*'s use of this phrase by considering some important pre-Platonic precedents. This will take some time but sheds light on Socrates' description of the soul, the forms, and being dead – and so is well worth the philological detour.

While "itself *kata* itself" can seem like Platonic jargon, it was used before Plato in both non-technical and medical contexts. I have found nine occurrences in extant treatises that are certainly or likely pre-Platonic: Aeschylus *Prometheus Bound* (1013), Euripides *Ion* (610), Antiphon the Orator, *On the murder of Herodes* (21, 8),[19] Thucydides (VII 28, 3, 7), Aristophanes *Clouds* (193–4), and the Hippocratic *On Fractures* (2.7), *Prognostic* (12.30), *On Diseases* (3.17.19), and *On Acute Diseases* (4.27).[20] There are five further occurrences in Hippocratic treatises that are typically dated to either the late fifth or the early forth century.[21]

In the *Clouds*, Aristophanes seems to make fun of Socrates' student for using this expression, and the Hippocratic uses might be viewed as a sort of specialized terminology, but the first four occurrences listed above seem to be non-technical Greek. In these passages, "itself *kata* itself" modifies a noun, agreeing with it in number and gender (and so is not adverbial, but rather a further specification of the noun). Here the phrase seems to mean "on its own" and could be translated this way, but it does not seem to imply being "all alone" but rather to have the sense of "relying only on itself," or "not receiving aid or help from others," or "not being part of a larger group." In Antiphon, the defendant says that he was on a ship himself *kata* himself, for his own business, instead of having convinced Herodes to accompany him. He is not saying that he was on the ship all alone, or separated from others. He simply is saying that he was not on the ship as part of a group. Aeschylus says that, for the one who does not think well, stubbornness itself *kata* itself is not strong at all. Aeschylus, of course, is not asking us to engage in a bizarre thought experiment of taking stubbornness all alone, without any thoughts, desires, and

---

[18] Plato describes the forms as "separate" (χωρίς) in the *Parmenides* (first at 129d), though it is at least unclear whether he means by it what Aristotle means. See e.g. Fine 1984 and Meinwald 2016, 301–6. My goal here is simply to understand what "itself *kata* itself" means in the *Phaedo*.

[19] The manuscripts of Antiphon (emended by Stephanus and followed by later editors) and some of the manuscripts of Aeschylus have κατ' αὐτ* (smooth breathing) instead of the standard rough breathing, thus meaning "*kata* it" instead of "*kata* itself." While unusual, this, I assume, would not substantively change the meaning.

[20] This list is drawn from TLG searches, checked against the occurrences noted in Schiefsky 2005, 268–70, and El Murr 2014. Note that, aside from *On Diseases*, the Hippocratic treatises use the Ionic καθ' ἑωυτ* rather than the Attic καθ' αὐτ*. The dating of Hippocratic treatises is far from certain. Craik 2014 dates *On Diseases* III and *On Fractures* to the second half of the fifth century, *Prognostic* to the late fifth century, and *On Acute Diseases* to the end of the fifth century. Jouanna 1999 thinks that *On Fractures* may be early forth century.

[21] *Epidemics* 6.8.10.1 and 8.10.4, *On Regimen* 37.7, *Diseases of Women* 192.11, 205.21.

other psychic states, and then trying to evaluate whether this stubbornness would be strong. Instead, his point is that stubbornness itself contributes nothing to a person's strength. We might say that, for the one who does not think well, stubbornness "in and of itself" is not strong at all. In short, when used in this way, "itself *kata* itself" modifies a subject and says that the verb applies to it on its own, although the subject may, of course, be with other things when this happens.

As Dimitri El Murr points out, drawing on Festugière's analysis, the use of "*kata*" in "itself *kata* itself" seems to be a distributive one, the kind of use involved in counting or classifying "by clan" or "by head."[22] Hence we can think of the first "itself" (*auto*) as referring to the thing and of "*kata* itself" as demarcating it using itself rather than as being part of some other grouping. "Itself by itself" would be a reasonable translation if the "by" could be heard as similar to its use in "by clan" or "by head." However, in English "by itself" means "all alone," which I have argued is not what it means. This is why I do not follow most translators in translate it as "by itself" (Grube) or "alone by itself" (Gallop, Sedley and Long). The Cambridge Greek Lexicon (CGL) suggests "independently" for this distributive use of "*kata* itself" (D 2). Someone can, of course, travel on a ship independently even if the ship is crowded, and so that person is not at all separated from others.

Before considering further pre-Platonic evidence, note that in the *Meno* there is a use of "itself *kata* itself" very similar to Aeschylus'. The phrase is not used in the so-called Socratic dialogues but does occur in the *Meno*, to which the *Phaedo* refers at 73a–b (see Section 1.4). Socrates says in the *Meno* that all the attributes of the soul, such as boldness and speed of learning, are beneficial when guided by wisdom and harmful when guided by ignorance; from this he concludes that they are "themselves *kata* themselves" (αὐτὰ καθ' αὐτά) neither beneficial nor harmful, only becoming so when wisdom or folly is added (88c–d; cf. *Euthydemus* 281d–e). There is no reason to see Socrates here as divorcing boldness from all other thoughts, desires, or other psychic attributes associated with it and simply considering it in the void. Instead, the expression isolates the level of benefit that boldness itself provides in a psyche. Again, we could say that boldness "in and of itself" is neither beneficial nor harmful.

To survey the relevant pre-Platonic evidence, we should consider not only the expression "itself *kata* itself," but also the use, by Anaxagoras and by various authors in the Hippocratic corpus, of the very similar phrase "itself *epi* (upon) itself" (αὐτὸ ἐφ' ἑαυτοῦ/ἑωυτοῦ).[23] Examining this use, I will argue, clarifies why the *Phaedo* connects "itself *kata* itself" with being pure. "Itself *epi* itself" seems to be used as a

---

[22] El Murr 2014, 40.
[23] The expression is found in Anaxagoras B12 and in the Hippocratic corpus in *On Diseases*, 2.29.4 (second half of the fifth century), *On Ancient Medicine*, 14.4 and 15.1 (last quarter of the fifth century), and *On the Nature of Man*, 2.21 (end of the fifth century). These dates come from Craik 2014 in consultation with Jouanna 1999. Another occurrence of the phrase is in *On Affections*, at 58.2; Craik dates this treatise to the late fifth or early fourth century, whereas

quasi-technical phrase in these treatises. But Aristophanes' joke about Socrates' student's asshole pointed to the sky – "itself *kata* itself it is being taught to do astronomy" (*Clouds* 193–4) – suggests that intellectuals, and perhaps even Socrates himself, also used "itself *kata* itself" as a sort of jargon, one that Aristophanes lampoons.[24] Plato seems to belong in a tradition that used the phrase in an apparently technical way.

Anaxagoras describes *nous* (reason, intelligence) as "itself *epi* itself" in B12.[25] He says there that, if *nous* were not *epi* itself, it would have things mixed in it that would thwart it, but in fact it controls all things, and so has nothing mixed in it, since it is *epi* itself. Anaxagoras connects this with *nous* being the purest (καθαρώτατον) and knowing all things. *On Ancient Medicine* (*VM*) also associates "itself *epi* itself" with being unmixed; according to its author, in a human being there are "salty and bitter and sweet and acid and astringent and insipid and myriad other things," which when mixed and blended with one another do not cause pain, but pain a human when one of them "separates off and comes to be itself *epi* itself" (*VM* 14.4; translation from Schiefsky 2005, modified).[26] Note that the separation would not result in the salty's becoming all alone, but rather in the salty's being separated *out* from the mixture. This need not mean that the separated salty would be completely and absolutely unmixed; however, it would at least no longer be mixed with the bitter, the sweet, and myriad other things mentioned. "Itself *epi* itself" is also used to describe *VM*'s opponents' views at 15.1: they have not discovered a hot, a cold, a dry, or a wet "itself *epi* itself" (αὐτό ἐφ' ἑωυτοῦ) that is "common to no other form" (μηδενὶ ἄλλῳ εἴδει κοινωνέον). The author says that his opponents want to prescribe such a thing to their patients, but that instead they, like everyone else, must suggest foods that are not only hot but also astringent, for example. Here having some form in common with hot, such as astringent, means that a thing is not itself *epi* itself. At the first occurrence in the *VM*, "itself *epi* itself" is connected with not being mixed; at the second, with not being combined. But not every fifth-century use of "itself *epi* itself" involves a contrast with mixture or combination. For example, in *On Diseases* 2.29.4 the uvula's swelling along with the jaw is contrasted with the uvula's swelling "itself *epi* itself." This seems to mean simply "the uvula's swelling on its own." Furthermore, some fifth-century uses of "itself *kata* itself" seem connected to purity (e.g. *On Diseases* 3.17.19, "pure rain water"). The two expressions are indeed very similar; it is simply that "itself *epi* itself" is more frequently connected to being uncombined or unmixed.

Jouanna places it around 380 BCE. The expression is also used once in Thucydides (VI 40, 2, 6).

[24] For a discussion of this passage as evidence about the historical Socrates, see Broackes 2009.
[25] For a general discussion, see Curd 2007, 57–58.
[26] For discussions, including of how the usage in *VM* fits in with that of other Hippocratic works, see Schiefsky 2005, 258–60, and El Murr 2014.

I suggest we understand this connection to being uncombined or unmixed as follows. If x does an activity along with something else, then x does not do this activity itself *kata/epi* itself: recall that, if I travel with someone else, then I am not traveling myself *kata* myself. But if x is combined with something else (through mixture or by some other means), then x cannot do this activity itself *kata/epi* itself; x will always do it along with this other thing. Something that is mixed or combined cannot genuinely act on its own, and thus cannot be itself *kata/epi* itself. What counts as being relevantly "on its own," of course, is determined by context and so complete purity is not always required.

Note that in Anaxagoras and in the *VM* "itself *epi* itself" is used in a different grammatical construction from that of the early, non-technical occurrences of "itself *kata* itself," where it modifies a noun. In Anaxagoras and in the *VM*, "itself *epi* itself" is used with the verb "to be" or "to become": *nous is* itself *epi* itself; the salty *becomes* itself *epi* itself. "Itself *epi* itself" again agrees in gender and number with the subject, but now serves as a predicate complement. I will call the first the "modifier use" and the second the "predicative use." In Anaxagoras and in the *VM*, this predicative use is connected with being uncombined or unmixed. It is a delicate question how exactly to understand the predicative use in these authors; rather than provide a general account, I will provide an account of the use in the *Phaedo*.

In the *Phaedo*'s use of "itself *kata* itself," we see the sort of idea found in Anaxagoras and in the *VM*: something that is itself *epi/kata* itself is unmixed and pure. The language of being pure in the defense speech has generally been connected to religious concerns; my suggestion is that it is also connected to Anaxagoras and the medical tradition. Socrates' repeated use of "unalloyed" (εἰλικρινής) alongside "pure" (beginning at 66a) suggests a more physical sense of unmixed. In the defense speech, Socrates describes the body as "filling" (ἐμπίμπλησιν, 66c4) us up with loves, desires, fears, and fantasies of every kind, and later he speaks of us getting filled up (ἀναπιμπλώμεθα, 67a4) with the body's nature (that is, infected with it). It is precisely when these things are mixed into the soul that it is not itself *kata* itself and not pure.

How should we understand the *Phaedo*'s predicative use of "itself *kata* itself"? One might be tempted to think that it simply means that the thing exists in and of itself. But this has no obvious connection to being unmixed or pure, and Socrates suggests that a soul that is itself *kata* itself will behave in certain ways (e.g. it will reason well, 65c), which have nothing to do with something's existing in and of itself. So I suggest that, if x is itself *kata* itself, then x itself *kata* itself engages in all its activities and itself *kata* itself has all its properties. This means that x must have nothing mixed into it, since any admixture would hinder these activities or properties. It is like Anaxagoras' *nous*, which, since it is itself *epi* itself, can properly do its characteristic activities, ruling and knowing. Since the soul has nothing mixed into it, everything it does and everything it is, it does and is simply on its own. This way of understanding the predicative use makes sense of Socrates' claim in the *Phaedo* that the soul itself *kata* itself is *with* (μετά) what always is and is immortal (79d). This cannot literally or conceptually mean "all alone," since the whole point is that it is with something else.[27] Instead, the idea is that, when the soul becomes entirely pure, it acts in the way that is natural to it, and thus is drawn to its kin – what always is and is immortal (see Section 6.4).

The overall model, apparently Anaxagorean, seems to be that, if something is not acting itself *kata* itself, then there is something *in it* that makes it act differently. It is as if a lump of copper were not melting at copper's normal temperature, despite being in normal conditions. In that case, there must be some impurity mixed into the copper to make it behave differently. Analogously, if the soul is acting in a way that is not natural for a soul, it must not be itself *kata* itself and must have something mixed into it to make it act differently. In my discussion of the return to the defense, Section 7.2, I argue that this model explains Socrates' claims there about what is mixed into the soul.

While the connection between "itself *kata* itself" and being pure is not a distinct meaning of this expression, it is worth acknowledging that, once this connection is recognized, two other meanings of *"kata"* with the accusative are also relevant: itself *throughout* itself (CGL A 5, B 11, C 5); and itself *as the basis* for itself (CGL G). When a thing is entirely itself throughout itself, it is pure: there is nothing else mixed into it. This pure subject, taken on its own, is the basis for the actions and properties attributed to it. I translate "itself *kata* itself" as "itself through itself" to capture these aspects of Plato's use of "itself *kata* itself" while avoiding the meaning of "all alone." "Through" here is to be understood both in a spatial sense – through(out) itself – and in a non-spatial sense, to indicate the basis: speed of learning may be beneficial, but it is not beneficial through itself. The soul investigates properly when it does so itself through itself: the basis for its investigation is itself. The forms have all their features through themselves. In my discussion of the kinship argument (Section 6.3), I complete my account of "itself *kata* itself" by discussing at length the preposition *"kata"* in this expression, connecting it to some of Socrates' other uses of *"kata"* and further filling in and defending the idea that *"kata"* in "itself *kata* itself" identifies the basis for attributing a predicate to the subject.

What are the ramifications, given this account, for the *Phaedo*'s definition of being dead, account of the soul, and description of forms? First, according to that definition, the body must become itself *kata* itself and the soul must be itself *kata* itself. In other words, each must come to be on its own; the soul and the body cannot remain in one another. But it turns out to be very difficult for the soul to be on its own, even after death, because of the bodily impurities that are mixed into

---

[27] In several places in Plato's corpus something is described as αὐτὸ καθ' αὑτό that is not all alone. For example, at the beginning of *Republic* II, Glaucon wants to know what justice and injustice are and what power each has αὐτὸ καθ' αὑτό when in the soul (358b). Glaucon does not want to know their power when they are all alone in the soul.

it. In the end, only the philosopher's soul can come to be truly on its own – that is, itself *kata* itself. This is why it is difficult to be truly dead, something for which one must practice. The philosopher wants to be dead because the soul reasons and investigates best when it is itself through itself, and so the philosopher purifies his soul of these impurities that hinder its proper activity.

Socrates' description of each form as "itself through itself" can be seen as fitting with the early, ordinary use of this expression, where it serves to isolate, for example, what is true simply of stubbornness, leaving aside anything that might accompany stubbornness. But when Socrates applies it predicatively rather than as a modifier, he asserts that justice, largeness, and such things have all their features in and of themselves – that they have nothing mixed into them that would give them features that are not their own. Forms' being this way allows them to provide a type of intellectual clarity: when we examine justice itself, all the features it has are properly its own, because it is itself *kata* itself. There is no concern that it possesses a feature only because it happens to be mixed or combined with something else. This need not bring with it strong "metaphysical" commitments, but it does pave the way for them – as part of the dialogue's unfolding structure.

3.5 BODILY PLEASURES, PAINS, DESIRES, AND FEARS

Philosophers desire to be dead because only then can they truly acquire wisdom. Bodily pleasures, pains, desires, and fears pose two sorts of problems for aquiring wisdom: (1) they lead us to desire something other than wisdom; and (2) they make it difficult to discover the truth, even when we seek it. These problems are introduced in the defense speech and then considerably expanded upon in the return to the defense (Section 7.2 and Subsection 7.3.1).

Over the course of the defense speech Socrates makes increasingly strong claims about the philosopher's relationship to these bodily affections. He starts with Simmias' impression of philosophers, asking whether it seems characteristic of a philosophical man to be eager for the things called pleasures, such as those of food and drink (64d).[28] Once Socrates turns to the acquisition of wisdom, he notes that pain and pleasure distract us, leading us to reason poorly (65c). This is not a mere report on the philosopher's attitude but a positive reason to avoid pain and pleasure. Then, in Socrates' description of how genuine philosophers speak to one another, he says that the body fills us up with loves, desires, fears, and fantasies of every kind, which make it impossible for us to be wise (φρονῆσαι), leading us into wars, uprisings, and conflicts (66c–d). The body enslaves us to its service (66d). These bodily affections cannot be easily avoided; instead, the body puts desires and fears into us, changing which goals we pursue, thereby altering the course of our lives (as well as others'), making us its slaves. The body's mechanism for ruling the soul

---

[28] For the translation "the things called pleasures," see Section 2.5.

seems to be these loves, desires, fears, and fantasies that it puts into it. As we will see in Subsection 3.8.2, the philosopher at least partially avoids letting these affections into the soul by being ruled by wisdom, which purifies the soul, to the extent possible, of these bodily affections. Of course, the mere presence of a desire or fear does not ensure that one will act on it, but it is likely to change our behavior, unless we exert mental strength to resist it. In the return to the defense, Socrates discusses the need for such strength (Subsection 7.3.2).

As noted in Section 1.1, scholars disagree about whether the body is the subject of bodily desires in the *Phaedo*.[29] While I argue in Section 7.4 that they are not, the important point for understanding the *Phaedo*'s moral psychology is that people act only on desires in their souls.[30] If, as some think, a person's body is a subject of some desires, these are motivationally inert until they are in the soul. Socrates says that the body infects us (i.e. our souls) with bodily desires, fears, and the like. The philosopher wants to purify his soul of these bodily affections precisely because their presence leads him away from philosophy (66c–67b). If people acted on desires that had only the body as a subject, there would be no need to purify the soul of them. These desires can be described as an infection because they are not proper to the soul but rather come from outside, having been put there by the body.

The philosopher is the focus of the defense speech, so Socrates does not discuss here how bodily pleasures and desires affect ordinary people. In the return to the defense, he describes the effects of bodily affections on non-philosophers (81b–84a), thereby explaining (1) how the body creates desires in us, (2) the effects of pleasures and pains on us, and (3) the way in which bodily pleasures and pains change our values, so that we think that we are pursuing the right things when in fact we are pursuing things contrary to our wisdom and happiness. Already in the defense speech Socrates is committed to the idea that bodily pleasures and desires set people's goals, leading them to pursue things other than the truth. I argue in Section 3.8 that non-philosophers' slavery to the body makes them blind to how their bodily desires undermine their chance for true virtue.

3.6 FORMS, INQUIRY, AND THE SOUL ITSELF THROUGH ITSELF

The philosopher's goal is to acquire wisdom, which his soul does through inquiry. But, Socrates argues, the body only hinders inquiry and so, given the problems caused by the body, the soul would be far better off without it. Socrates' arguments

---

[29] Those who think that the body is the subject of bodily desires in the *Phaedo* include Bobonich 2002, 26–7; Boys-Stones 2004; Lorenz 2008; and Johansen 2017. For further arguments against making the body the subject of bodily desires, see Tenkku 1956, 105–7; Gallop 1975, 89; Bostock 1986, 26–7 and 31–3; Woolf 2004, 107–8; Beere 2010, 261–4; and Reed 2021.

[30] *Pace* Bobonich 2002, 26–7, who reconstructs the moral psychology of the *Phaedo* around desires that are endorsed or unendorsed.

3.6 Forms, Inquiry, and the Soul Itself through Itself

for this conclusion introduce two of the central themes of the dialogue: inquiry and forms. After the defense speech, inquiry returns as a topic in the recollecting argument, in the kinship argument, in the return to the defense, in the discussion of misology, and in the autobiography. Here in the defense speech, Socrates repeatedly says that only a soul that is itself through itself can successfully inquire, thereby acquiring genuine knowledge (65c, 66a, 66e–67c, 67e–68b).

Socrates presents three reasons for thinking that the body hinders inquiry. First, even the poets keep telling us that nothing we hear or see is accurate – and the other senses are inferior to hearing and sight (65b). Just as Socrates began with the commonly accepted idea that the philosopher does not care about pleasures, so here he begins by noting that conventional views support his view of inquiry. Socrates' claims fit with conventional views, even if he takes his conclusions much further than most people would. On the the basis of poets' testimony about the senses' lack of reliability, Socrates concludes that the soul grasps (ἅπτεται) the truth not when together with the body, but rather in reasoning (λογίζεσθαι), if anywhere (65b–c). His second reason for thinking that the body hinders inquiry is that the senses can "trouble" us, as do pleasure and pain (65c). The body distracts the soul from properly engaging in its own activity, which it does itself through itself.

Socrates mentions forms for the first time in the dialogue when he provides his third reason for thinking that the body hinders the soul's inquiry. How one understands the forms in the rest of the dialogue is partially determined by what one thinks Socrates is introducing here, so it is worth discussing the passage in depth.

> Well now, what do we say about things like the following, Simmias? Do we say that there is such a thing as a just itself, or not?
> Indeed we do!
> Yes, and a beautiful, and a good?
> Of course.
> Now have you ever actually seen with your eyes any of the things of this kind?
> Not at all, he said.
> Or have you grasped them with one of the other senses that are through the body? I'm talking about all of them, such as largeness, health, and strength and, to sum up, about the being of all the rest – what each one turns out to be. (65d4–e1)

Note that Socrates does not refer to these as "forms" here. It is not until the fifth and final stage of the *Phaedo*'s unfolding account of forms, at the beginning of the final argument (102b1), that he first uses the term "form" (εἶδος) as a name for the thing referred to by the correct answer to a "what is it?" question. Instead, he refers here to each of them as "an *f* itself," then with an abstract noun (*f*-ness), then as the "being" (οὐσία) of all other such things, and, finally, as "what each one turns out to be."

Is Socrates, at the beginning of the passage, simply asking whether there are those things that he is always searching for when he asks his "what is it?" question – the sort of thing sought in the *Charmides, Laches, Euthyphro,* and *Meno*? Or is he rather asking Simmias for a stronger commitment – not simply to there being such things, but to these having a number of other features that would make them "transcendent" or "Platonic" forms? I will argue that Socrates here is only asking for the weaker commitment; over the course of the *Phaedo* he will explain why they should accept much stronger claims about the forms.[31] This is why Socrates separates the question of whether there is a just itself from the question of whether Simmias has ever seen such a thing. The latter is a new question about those things that Socrates is always interested in.

Socrates often asks whether there are the things sought by his "what is it?" question. In the *Euthyphro* (5d), *Meno* (71e–73a), *Protagoras* (329d, 330c, 330d), and *Hippias Major* (287c–d, 289d), Socrates explicitly asks his interlocutors whether they agree that there are such things as holiness, virtue, justice, and the fine. In the *Euthyphro*, *Meno*, and *Hippias Major*, he does so when introducing his "what is it?" question. In the *Phaedo*, just one page earlier, Socrates similarly asks whether there is such a thing as death, and then gives an account of what death is (64c). He does not seem to be asking there about a transcendent form of death, nor does he seem to be asking about a transcendent form in any of the other dialogues just mentioned. When Socrates first mentions a given form he asks whether there is such a thing because he recognizes that this is a substantive commitment. The *Meno* provides an example of how someone could deny this commitment: Meno suggests that there are a variety of things called "virtue," with no single account that unifies them (71e–73a).

Does any of the language in the *Phaedo* passage refer specifically to transcendent forms? In the *Euthyphro*, *Meno*, and *Hippias Major*, Socrates calls the thing referred to by the answer to the "what is it?" question a "form" (ἰδέα and εἶδος) and a "being" (οὐσία),[32] so these terms need not refer to transcendent forms. The most likely candidate for a quasi-technical phrase for "transcendent" or "Platonic" forms is Socrates' expression "an *f* itself."[33] However, he also uses this expression or closely related ones in the *Protagoras*, *Hippias Major*, and *Euthyphro*. In the *Protagoras*, after agreeing that justice is "some thing" (πρᾶγμά τι, 330c1), Protagoras agrees that "this [thing] itself" (αὐτὸ τοῦτο, 330c4–5) is just. Later he agrees that holiness is something (πρᾶγμά τι, 330d4) and that "holiness itself" (αὐτὴ ἡ ὁσιότης, 330d9–e1) is holy, if anything is. Similarly, in the *Hippias Major*, after Hippias attempts to

---

[31] I argue over the course of this book that Socrates presents reasons for accepting his radical claims about the forms. So, even if he were assuming transcendent forms here in the defense speech, they would not be *merely* assumed in the dialogue.

[32] ἰδέα: *Euthyphro*, 5d4, 6e1; εἶδος: *Euthyphro*, 6d11, *Meno* 72c7, 72d8, 72e5, *Hippias Major*, 289d4; οὐσία, *Euthyphro*, 11a8, *Meno*, 72b1, *Hippias Major* 302c5. As noted in Chapter 10, I accept the widely held view that Socrates in the *Phaedo* reserves the term ἰδέα for the forms in us.

[33] So Sedley 2007, 27, who says that "the 'F itself' is *de facto* Plato's most favored, even if not his most technical locution for [transcendent] Forms. Its mere occurrence here does not yet guarantee that the reference is to a [transcendent] Form." Sedley's further adduced evidence is discussed in notes 35 and 37.

3.6 Forms, Inquiry, and the Soul Itself through Itself

answer "what is the fine (τὸ καλόν)?" by identifying particular fine things (287e–289b), Socrates rephrases his question as "what is the fine itself?" (αὐτὸ τὸ καλόν, 289c3, 289d2). And in the *Euthyphro* he says, "bear in mind then that I did not bid you tell me one or two of the many holy actions but that form itself (ἐκεῖνο αὐτὸ τὸ εἶδος) by which all the holy things are holy" (6d10–11), and "teach me what this form itself (αὐτὴν τὴν ἰδέαν) is, so I may look upon it and using it as a model, say that any action of yours or another's that is of that sort is holy, and if it is not that it is not" (6e4–7). The addition of 'itself' seems to help ensure that one focuses only on *f*-ness, not on individual instances or a subclass of *f*-ness.

Socrates and his companions seem to use "x itself" as a quasi-technical expression for what Socrates has always been searching for, across all Plato's dialogues, rather than as an expression that bundles this with a variety of other commitments. In fact Socrates seems to introduce "x itself" as such an expression in the *Cratylus* when speaking to Hermogenes, who does not show any prior familiarity with "transcendent" forms. Early in that dialogue, well before he has discussed Heraclitean flux, Socrates asks Hermogenes whether the carpenter will look to a broken shuttle or to the form of the shuttle when making a new shuttle (389b).[34] After introducing the form of the shuttle in the *Cratylus*, Socrates says, "then it would be absolutely right to call that 'what a shuttle itself is'" (389b5–6). He seems to introduce this "x itself" expression as a sort of quasi-technical piece of vocabulary: he then uses it to say that the name giver must look to what a "name itself" is (389d).[35] At this stage in the *Cratylus*, Socrates seems to be assuming no more about forms than in the *Euthyphro* or *Meno*. Since he wishes to refer to the forms frequently and to be sure that his audience knows what he is talking about, it makes sense for him to use a distinctive vocabulary for them. Soon after the *Phaedo* passage under discussion (65d4–e1), Socrates describes each form as "unalloyed and itself *kata* itself" (66a). As explained in Section 3.4, since each form is "itself *kata* itself," it has all its features in its own right, not because of anything else that is combined or mixed into it. This means that, when we investigate the form and learn its features, we can be sure that these features hold properly of it.

Socrates' later references to the forms in the *Phaedo* continue to highlight that he is talking about those things that have always interested him. In the recollecting argument, he refers to them as "everything to which we attach this label (ἐπισφραγιζόμεθα), 'what such and such is,' both when asking our questions and when giving our answers" (75d2–4). Again, in saying that they attach this expression as a label, Socrates seems to be establishing a sort of technical vocabulary. But the language of asking questions and giving answers clearly emphasizes continuity with

---

[34] In the *Gorgias* – another dialogue that does not refer to transcendent forms – Socrates likewise says that a craftsman looks to a form (503e).

[35] Sedley 2007, 72, notes that this passage introduces terminology, but he takes it that this terminology is specifically for transcendent forms.

Socratic dialectic. The fact that it is a fixed terminology does not mean that it refers specifically to transcendent forms.[36] Similarly, in his autobiography Socrates introduces his hypothesis that there are forms by saying that he is talking about "nothing new, but what I've never stopped talking about, on any other occasion or in particular in the argument thus far" (100b1–3). It is difficult to know how Plato could have been clearer that he does not want us to see Socrates as introducing something new.

Let us return to our passage from the defense speech: Simmias agrees that one does not grasp with the bodily senses anything of this sort. Taken on its own, the idea of using the senses to perceive a form might seem like a sort of category mistake. I suspect that Plato is thinking something along these lines; but we should be careful not to assume that he puts largeness in the same category as we might – for example, of abstract entities. Plato seems to be the first Greek author to think, in general, about such things as largeness and holiness. It is not clear that we have a clear notion of such things but, to the extent that we do, we should not assume that he conceives of them the way we do. Moreover, Socrates does not explain here why forms are not the sort of things to be perceived. If one merely wanted an argument that forms are different from ordinary, perceptible objects, Socrates all but gives such an argument here: forms are never perceived; hence they are not ordinary, perceptible objects. This, I think, is the most intuitively gripping argument the dialogue has to offer: justice itself simply is not the kind of thing we see or touch. But this leaves open whether being perceptible is a fundamental difference between forms and ordinary things, reflected in their natures, or rather a relatively superficial difference. In general, one should ask what the goal of an argument is. To start from premises that seem obviously true? Or to provide an underlying explanation of why the conclusion is the case? There is no reason to expect that an argument could do both. Here, in the first stage of the unfolding account of forms, Socrates presents an argument with premises that are easy to accept.[37] But I will argue (in Chapters 6, 9, and 10) that perceptibility is not one of the fundamental differences between forms and ordinary objects.

Aristotle might agree with Socrates' claim that we cannot grasp forms with the senses; after all, Aristotle at least often thinks of forms as universals and of knowledge as of universals, whereas perception is of particulars (e.g. *De anima* II.5, 417b23; *Posterior Analytics* I.31, 87b37–88a7). However, Aristotle thinks that we can come to know universals in part through perception. By contrast, Socrates says that we must not use our senses at all in investigating the forms (65e–66a). He does not here explain why the senses could not provide relevant evidence for grasping the

---

[36] Pace Sedley 2007, 72, who takes this as a "guarantee" that Socrates is referring to transcendent forms.

[37] By contrast, Dancy 2004, 250, looks for an explanatory argument and suggests that one must be operating here but that Socrates does not make it explicit.

forms, as Aristotle thinks. Socrates says that the body does not allow the soul to grasp the truth (65a–c) – but, again, he does not explain why here. These questions are addressed in the recollecting and kinship arguments, fitting with the dialogue's unfolding structure. The basic reason why perception cannot play a role is that the nature of ordinary, perceptible objects is deficient in a way that does not allow one to acquire knowledge of the forms from them. Similarly, Socrates does not explain here how the soul could acquire knowledge without the senses. Again, the recollecting and kinship arguments provide the basic answer: the knowledge has been within us all along and the soul's kinship with the forms allows it to grasp them.

One can see why some interpreters think that Socrates assumes the existence of "Platonic Forms" in the dialogue. My suggestion is that Socrates raises questions not found in the Socratic dialogues about the things he is always looking for.[38] Moreover, he provides the answer to these new questions: you cannot see forms and you cannot investigate them with the senses. But we must wait to understand fully why these are his answers.

3.7 ACQUIRING WISDOM WHILE EMBODIED

The body hinders philosophers in their search for wisdom, which is why they want to be released from it. Socrates imagines a conversation (66b–67b) in which philosophers explain why, so long as they are embodied, they can never sufficiently have what they desire: wisdom and truth. Rashed has argued that Socrates himself is not endorsing this view attributed to philosophers;[39] however, Socrates endorses it repeatedly after he finishes reporting the conversation (67b–c, 67e–68b). And we would expect him to endorse it, since he considers himself a philosopher, and it is needed in order to explain why the philosopher desires to be dead.

How skeptical is Socrates in the *Phaedo* of our ability to acquire wisdom while embodied?[40] This is important for understanding not only the defense speech but also passages later in the dialogue. The philosophers say to one another that they will never *sufficiently* acquire what they desire, the truth (66b6–7, 67b8), and that, if they are ever to have *pure* knowledge of something, they must be separated from the body (66d7–8, 66e4–67a1). This suggests that they can have impure knowledge and acquire truth while embodied, albeit insufficiently. On the other hand, Socrates twice mentions the embodied philosopher's coming "closest to knowledge" (65e4, 67a2–3), which suggests that he never arrives there. Socrates says that the body makes us *unable* to keep the truth in sight (66d6–7). While the strength of these claims varies, they consistently suggest that one cannot fully acquire wisdom while

---

[38] So also e.g. Irwin 1999, 144.
[39] Rashed 2009, 109–17.
[40] A question raised by Trabattoni 2011 and 2016, who sees Plato's Socrates as being more skeptical than many other scholars do.

embodied. Socrates' final statement (in his own voice) seems a good guide to his overall view. He says that the philosopher thinks that "nowhere but in Hades will he have a worthwhile encounter with it [wisdom]" (68a9–b1). Perhaps we can acquire some knowledge and wisdom while embodied, but whatever is acquired will fall far short of what the philosopher desires.

Throughout the rest of the dialogue Socrates never suggests otherwise. In the recollecting argument he says that if people have knowledge they can provide an account, and Simmias implies that, after Socrates dies, no one may be able to do this (76b). While Simmias suggests that Socrates has acquired some knowledge before death, he never says that Socrates has acquired full wisdom. Socrates never claims to know that the soul exists after death. He never says that his method of hypothesis results in knowledge. At the end of the final argument, he tells Simmias that, if they analyze the hypotheses well enough, they will follow the argument as far as a human being can and not seek anything further (107b). This suggests that the soul's immortality may not be something humans can know while embodied. Of course, they could have good reasons for their views and might hit upon the truth despite lacking knowledge. This does not mean that Plato is, in general, skeptical of our ability to acquire wisdom. First of all, we are our souls, which simply happen to be in human form at the moment. We could acquire wisdom after this temporary period is over. Moreover, as mentioned in the introduction, in the *Republic* Plato develops the view that someone could acquire comprehensive knowledge of the forms, including the form of the good, while embodied – at least a philosopher in the kallipolis could. Neither the *Phaedo* nor the *Republic* need provide Plato's definitive views on whether one can acquire genuine wisdom while embodied; he could be seriously exploring different possibilities in each dialogue. The *Phaedo* is Plato's dialogue about the last day of Socrates' life, a dialogue in which Socrates is set up as a hero. It is fitting that Plato here suggests that genuine wisdom is not possible while embodied, so that Socrates can be the one who, while embodied, has come as close as possible to the divine.

I discussed in Section 3.5 one of the main reasons why we cannot have a worthwhile encounter with wisdom while embodied: the body fills us up with desiderative states (loves, desires, fears), which lead us to war and, in general, lead us to pursue things other than the truth. Socrates presents this problem at 66b–d, alongside two others. First, the soul must look after the body's needs, which can make investigation impossible: the body requires sustenance, and diseases can impede inquiry. Second, if we somehow find ourselves in a position to pursue the truth, the body causes confusion, turmoil, and shock (θόρυβον παρέχει καὶ ταραχὴν καὶ ἐκπλήττει, 66d5–6). The confusion it causes is presumably not that caused by trying to inquire using the senses, since philosophers are describing this to one another and know not to inquire using the senses. Instead, to translate the terms differently, the body creates a sort of loud clamor (θόρυβον) and disorder (ταραχήν) and strikes the soul with fear-panic (ἐκπλήττει), making it impossible for us to succeed in our inquiry. This may well be connected to Socrates' earlier claim that the senses – along with pleasure and pain – trouble reasoning (65c). When these problems are taken together, the net result is that we will never have a worthwhile encounter with wisdom so long as we are embodied.

Given these problems, Socrates reaches the final conclusion of his main argumentative line in the defense speech:

> If all this is true, my friend, for someone who reaches the place to which I am journeying, there is much hope that there, if anywhere, he will sufficiently acquire that for the sake of which we have worked hard in our past life. Hence the travel assigned to me comes with good hope, as it does for any other man who considers his thought to have been purified, as it were, and so ready. (67b7–c3)

What should we make of the role of good hope here? This hope is the result of Socrates' reasoning. The point of calling it a "good hope," I suggest, is that it is neither irrational nor unreasonable. Socrates is not certain what the afterlife is like, but, given his considerations, it is reasonable to think that he can find in the afterlife what he has been seeking his entire life. It is a good hope not merely in the sense of being likely, but also well grounded. One of Socrates' goals in his defense speech (IIa) was to show that it is reasonable (εἰκότως, 63e9) for a man who has genuinely spent his life in philosophy to be in good hope about his imminent death.

3.8 COURAGE, TEMPERANCE, AND THE CORRECT EXCHANGE: 68B–69E

As discussed in 3.2, Socrates articulates two different sets of goals for the defense speech. We have seen a single argumentative line from 64a to 68b that explains why the philosopher desires to be dead, supporting Socrates' second set of goals (IIa and IIb). However, there remain the primary goal he initially articulated (Ia) – showing that he will enter the company of the gods after death (63b) – and the secondary goals – showing that he will have good human companions after death (63c, Ib) and that the outcome is better for the good than for the bad (63c, Ic). The end of the defense speech addresses these goals by arguing that philosophers alone are genuinely good, and so after death they alone will live among the gods and with one another. This part of the defense speech is divided into two. First Socrates argues that, even using ordinary people's notions of courage and temperance, the philosopher is courageous and temperate, whereas the non-philosophers' courage and temperance are absurd by their own standards (68b–69a). Then, in the famous "exchange passage" (69a–d), Socrates turns from showing how non-philosophers do not meet their own standards to a positive alternative, according to which the philosophers' values are completely different from ordinary people's, allowing philosophers to have genuine virtue, which comes from wisdom. This, in turn, is what ensures that they alone can live among the gods.

The exchange passage has generated a substantial literature, in large part because it tantalizingly suggests a different way to think about moral psychology and the relation between the virtues, while at the same time raising a number of interpretive difficulties. I defend the following view: directly before the exchange passage, Socrates argues that ordinary people's conception of virtue requires courage and temperance to oppose the body but, because ordinary people are ruled by their bodies, they cannot meet their own requirements for these virtues. In the exchange passage, Socrates then says that the philosopher is not guided by values that come from the body, but instead by wisdom. Wisdom provides the genuine virtues, which oppose the body's means of ruling the soul.[41]

I argue that Socrates provides an appealing way to think about the relationship between wisdom on the one hand and courage, temperance, and justice on the other. Unlike in the *Protagoras* and *Meno*, where (in my view) he argues that these virtues are identical to wisdom (e.g. 360d and 361b; 89a), here in the *Phaedo* he treats these virtues as distinct from wisdom, but as both resulting from wisdom and serving it. In those dialogues Socrates argues that anything that lacks wisdom could be harmful (357b–e, 88b–e; cf. *Euthydemus* 281c–e). Here in the *Phaedo* Socrates accepts that these other virtues do not exist without wisdom and are a result of wisdom, and thus are never harmful. Nonetheless, they are distinct from wisdom, since they result from it.

3.8.1 The Non-philosophers' Courage and Temperance: 68b–69a

The goal of Socrates' first arguments is to show that the philosopher has "that which is called 'courage'" (68c5) and "that which even the many call 'temperance'" (68c8–9), whereas ordinary people's courage and temperance are absurd. As with the discussion of "what are called pleasures" (Section 2.5), Socrates leaves it open whether ordinary people wrongly use the term "courage"; he simply argues that they never meet their own requirements for what they call "courage." The case is slightly different with temperance: Socrates refers to it as "what *even* (καί) the many call 'temperance,'" which suggests that he, too, calls it temperance. Nonetheless, he may think that temperance extends more widely than they think. Socrates' argument show that, even by ordinary people's own standards, the philosopher has courage and temperance whereas ordinary people do not. In the return to the defense, Socrates comes back to temperance and courage (82c and 83e). I argue in Subsection 7.3.2 that he provides an account of courage there different from the one attributed to the many here.

Socrates offers fairly straightforward arguments for thinking that the philosopher has that which is called "courage" and "temperance." First, courage: since it would be irrational for the philosopher to fear death, and since the philosopher does not

---

[41] My closest ally is Sedley 2014, who also connects the exchange passage to opposing the body.

3.8 Courage, Temperance, and the Correct Exchange: 68b–69e

resent death, he most of all possesses what is called "courage" (68c). Turning to temperance: since only philosophers genuinely disdain the body, only they are truly not in a flutter about their desires, but rather disdainful of them while staying composed (68c).

Socrates further argues that *only* the philosopher meets these criteria by arguing that in fact the non-philosophers' courage and their temperance are absurd. His arguments here, as we will see, illustrate how even the best among non-philosophers are ruled by the body. Socrates says that ordinary people's courage is due to fear, a fear of something greater than death – presumably loss of honor (68d; cf. 82c, where this idea is explicit). Once Simmias agrees that ordinary people's courage is due to fear, Socrates adds that it is due to cowardice (68d). Why think that their courage is due to fear rather than being despite fear, due to love of honor or another such desire? He does not explain, but we can make progress by considering his more detailed account of why the non-philosophers' temperance is absurd:

> Because they fear being denied other pleasures, which they desire, they abstain from some pleasures because they are overcome by others. Yet although they call being ruled by their pleasures "intemperance," what happens is that they overcome some pleasures because they are overcome by other pleasures. And this is like what we were just now talking about – that it is in a way because of intemperance that they have become temperate. (68e5–69a4)

Intemperance is a way of being ruled by pleasure – as opposed to temperance, which (as we have seen) even ordinary people agree involves being disdainful of our desires for pleasure and staying composed, not allowing these desires to rule us. But non-philosophers' so-called temperance actually involves being ruled by pleasure rather than being genuinely unaffected. It is in fact a type of intemperance.[42] They deceive themselves, thinking that they are in control, when they are actually being ruled by pleasure. To be ruled by these pleasure is, of course, a way of being ruled by the body. As we saw, the body enslaves us (66d), in part, by filling us with loves, desires, fears, and fantasies of every kind (66c–d).

---

[42] A separate interpretive puzzle is why it is supposed to be absurd to be temperate by intemperance or courageous by cowardice. Gallop 1975, 100, and Sedley 1998, 117, suggest that the absurdity results from a general causal principle Socrates accepts in the autobiography: that one thing cannot cause its opposite. But Socrates argues for this causal requirement in the autobiography (esp. 97a–b), so it is not clear why he would simply rely on it here. In any event, I think another solution is more likely: the problem is with the very same thing's being one opposite *by being* the other opposite. Socrates seems to allow a single thing to suffer the compresence of opposites, but in those cases it is not precisely by being *f* that something is the opposite of *f*, for example it is not by being beautiful that something is ugly. The absurdity is in the non-philosophers' being courageous by being cowardly, or in their being temperate by being intemperate.

Socrates says that the problem with non-philosophers' temperance is similar to the problem with their courage (69a).[43] Indeed, just as the non-philosopher does not oppose pleasure, so he does not oppose the fear of death. Instead, as a body lover, he accepts the fear of death and so, in order to overcome it, he must be ruled by something else, which he considers to be greater. If this case is like the temperance case, this person is deceived, thinking that he is in control of his fear of death when he is not. Given this, we can understand Socrates' argument against ordinary people's so-called courage in the following way. Courage involves ruling over one's fears, whereas cowardice involves being ruled by them. But ordinary people do not genuinely rule over their fear of death; instead, they overcome it only when it is outweighed by something else. Perhaps Cebes should not have accepted that the fear of greater evils is what outweighs non-philosophers' fear of death; perhaps non-philosophers' courage comes from a love of honor. I am not sure whether Socrates would accept this,[44] but either way he would still have his larger point that such so-called courage does not actually involve controlling the fear of death; another value simply outweighs it. Since according to Socrates being an honor lover is a way of being a body lover (68b–c), such a person would still be ruled by his body rather than genuinely controlling it. This, in turn clarifies why in the exchange passage Socrates says that, when exchanges are done without wisdom, all that sort of virtue is fit for slaves (ἀνδραποδώδης, 69b7–8): it involves subjugation to the body. According to Socrates' alternative, true courage and temperance are a type of purifying of the bodily affections; the philosopher avoids enslavement to the body by directly resisting and removing the bodily affections – including the fear of death.

This explains not only why ordinary people's virtues are described as fit for slaves but also why Socrates describes these virtues as a sort of illusory painting (σκιαγραφία, 69b6–7).[45] The courageous non-philosopher thinks he is ruling over his fear, when in fact he is being ruled by it until something more fearful comes

---

[43] Reed 2020, 121 argues that non-philosophers can perform virtuous actions with their absurd virtue, although they lack virtue itself. I do not see evidence that Socrates is using a category of "virtuous action" here. To support his view, Reed mentions that Socrates speaks of "the courageous among" non-philosophers. I suggest that we take these people as either "those among the non-philosophers with the best claim to being courageous" or "those whom the non-philosophers think of as courageous."

[44] To use the language of the exchange passage, this would involve trading fears for loves instead of trading fears for fears. This is not imagined in the exchange passage, presumably because such exchanges requires a common currency. Perhaps, then, one must overcome the fear of death with another fear because otherwise one cannot determine which is greater, and so which is to be followed. Since the philosopher rejects the value of pleasures, fears, and the like, he can oppose them without using their currency, instead measuring them with wisdom.

[45] Vasiliou 2012 argues that Socrates allows for different sorts of non-ideal virtue in the *Phaedo* – in particular, that the habituated virtue described in the return to the defense (82a–b) is better than the so-called virtue described here. But Socrates is clear in the exchange passage that *any* virtue kept apart from wisdom is a kind of illusion fit for slaves, containing nothing sound or true.

along. The temperate non-philosopher thinks he is opposing the pleasures, but is ruled by them. The idea that non-philosophers are under the illusion of control, unaware of what genuinely motivates them, comes back in the return to the defense, with the idea that the body's desires and pleasures are bewitching (81b) and that we are accomplices to our own imprisonment in the body, without even realizing it (82e; discussed in Section 7.2 and Subsection 7.3.1).

3.8.2 *The Correct Exchange: 69a–e*

I have argued that directly before the exchange passage Socrates draws on and develops the idea that non-philosophers do not meet their own criteria for courage or temperance because, unbeknownst to themselves, they are ruled by their bodies rather than ruling over them. With this in mind, we can approach the famous exchange passage in a new light:

> For I suspect, my good Simmias, that this is not the correct exchange for virtue, the exchanging of pleasures for pleasures, pains for pains, and fear for fear, greater for less, like currencies, but that just one thing is the correct currency, in return for which one must exchange all these, namely wisdom, and that all things' being bought and sold for this and with this[46] – with wisdom – really is, I suspect, courage, temperance, justice, and, in sum, true virtue, regardless of whether

---

[46] The translation of καὶ τούτου μὲν πάντα καὶ μετὰ τούτου ὠνούμενά τε καὶ πιπρασκόμενα τῷ ὄντι ᾖ... (69b1–2) is quite difficult. I know of four serious possibilities, each with significant drawbacks. (1) Sedley and Long take ὠνούμενά τε καὶ πιπρασκόμενα as modifying "all things": "when all things are bought and sold for this and with this – with wisdom – they really are, I suspect, courage..." This is the most natural reading of the Greek, but has a quite problematic meaning. It makes the things bought and sold courage, temperance, and in sum true virtue. But directly before and after this clause, "all things" (πάντα) refers to pleasures, pains, fears, and the like. Thus, if this were right, courage, temperance, and in sum true virtue would be the same thing as the pleasures, pains, and fears that we gain *and lose* in taking our actions. Nothing Socrates says elsewhere in the *Phaedo* fits with such an extraordinarily strange view. (2) The reading I give here is the one suggested by Bluck 1955 and followed by Verdenius, Gallop, and Rowe. Bluck lists Euripides, *Iphigenia in Aulis* 988–9 for a similar use of the participle: it functions like an articular infinitive, serving as the subject of a verb and picking out an action (here, being bought and sold), rather than as the subject that performs that action. According to this reading, the buying and selling (for and with wisdom) are true virtue. As long as one is willing to accept this rather unusual use of the participle, this seems to me the most elegant solution. (3) Sean Kelsey suggested to me that we could supply καταλλάττεσθαι from the previous clause as the subject of this one, so that together they would read "but that just one thing is the correct currency, wisdom, in return for which one must exchange [καταλλάττεσθαι] all these; <exchanging> all things, when bought and sold, for this and with this is courage, temperance..." This proposal does not require an unusual reading of the participles. One disadvantage is that in the previous clause καταλλάττεσθαι is the complement of δεῖ, whereas here it would be the subject. Also, the previous καταλλάττεσθαι referred to an exchange between currencies, whereas here the exchange is of the normal sort, using a single currency. (4) After considering the problem with (1), David Sedley suggested to me a new reading of this difficult part of the passage. It involves repunctuating (to create two clauses) and lightly emending the text, thus:

pleasures, fears, and everything else like that are added or removed, but that when they are kept apart from wisdom and exchanged in return for one another, that sort of virtue is a kind of illusory painting, really fit for slaves, and contains nothing sound or true, whereas the reality is that temperance, justice, and courage are a kind of purifying from everything like this, and that wisdom itself is a kind of rite to purify us. (69a6–c2)

This is an incredibly rich and difficult passage, which poses significant philological difficulties (see n. 46). In what follows I consider the currency metaphor itself and then turn to the relationship between wisdom and the virtues.

The currency metaphor has been accused of being inapt and confusing, since wisdom does not seem to function at all like a coin. Kathryn Morgan has shown in detail that wisdom or virtue as the genuine currency is a common metaphor in Greek literature from Hesiod onward.[47] This metaphor fits with the common concern in the late fifth and early fourth centuries that many coins in circulation were counterfeit, not containing the precious metals they should. At one point the Athenians even wanted their currency to be considered the only legitimate one in the empire – quite an unusual idea for that time. The metaphor works because money is naturally understood to hold and measure value; yet at the same time there is a widespread concern that money is replacing virtue as the genuine value. Plato's original readers would recognize this passage as his version of this common metaphor. Of course, the idea of wisdom as a currency would not work if one thought of currency fundamentally as a tool for acquiring other things rather than as itself the goal of one's actions.[48] However, just half a page earlier Socrates referred to money-lovers (68c), who presumably pursue money for its own sake. Such a person enjoys a vivid description in *Republic* VIII (553a–555a) in the portrait of the oligarchic man, who is said to value money above everything else (554a–b). While Socrates thinks that it is a mistake to value ordinary money above all else, he does not consider it psychologically impossible.

Nonetheless, it is strange to think of wisdom as a currency. This, I take it, is part of the point: it is a sign of how unusual wisdom is as a measure and possessor of value.

> καὶ τούτου μὲν πάντα καὶ μετὰ τούτου ὠνούμενά τε καὶ πιπρασκόμενα τῷ ὄντι ᾖ, καὶ ἀνδρεία καὶ σωφροσύνη καὶ δικαιοσύνη καὶ συλλήβδην ἀληθὴς ἀρετὴ <ᾖ> μετὰ φρονήσεως, καὶ προσγιγνομένων καὶ ἀπογιγνομένων καὶ ἡδονῶν καὶ φόβων καὶ τῶν ἄλλων πάντων τῶν τοιούτων· (69b1–5)
>
> and all things are in reality both bought and sold for this and with this [sc. wisdom], and courage, temperance, justice, and true virtue as a whole are with wisdom, regardless of whether pleasures, fears, and everything else like that is added or removed;
>
> Sedley notes that this use of "with wisdom" (μετὰ φρονήσεως) fits with that at *Meno* 88b–c. Note that, on this reading, unlike in (2) and (3), Socrates is not claiming that the virtues themselves are a type of exchange. For purposes of my claims in this chapter, readings (2), (3), or (4) will work.

[47] Morgan 2021.
[48] So Gosling and Taylor 1982, 92.

3.8 Courage, Temperance, and the Correct Exchange: 68b–69e

Ordinary currency – just like most other things that we ordinarily value – is given up when we acquire something else: one has to spend money to make money, and one has to give up some pleasures to acquire others. But this is not the case with wisdom. One trades pleasures for pleasures, pains for pains, but there is no mention of trading wisdom for wisdom. Instead, one buys and sells all things – in other words, does all of one's actions – using wisdom, for the sake of wisdom, thereby increasing one's currency without giving any of it away. How can you act with wisdom, if at the same time you are trying to acquire it and so do not have it? I argued earlier (Section 3.7) that Socrates thinks of wisdom as something that we can completely possess only once we are dead, but that we can have a share of while embodied. Thus one uses wisdom to maintain what one has, or to acquire more wisdom. Wisdom allows us to recognize what is genuinely good. As we acquire wisdom, we recognize that acquiring more wisdom would be good (ultimately leading to our eternal happiness, 81a); hence we make it our goal. By contrast, the *Protagoras* works from the assumption that pleasure is the good (353c–354e), and so when one is guided by knowledge, one tries to maximize not wisdom but rather pleasure.[49]

Socrates rejects the sort of exchange involved in the non-philosophers' courage and temperance and replaces it with one in which things are bought "for and with" wisdom. In the first clause of the exchange passage, pleasure is compared to a currency that one exchanges to acquire further pleasures; this exchange is analogous to investing dollars to acquire more dollars. In the next clause, Socrates says that pleasure and all other such currencies must be exchanged in return for (*anti*) wisdom. This is a different sort of exchange, analogous to exchanging all one's dollars, yen, and other currencies for euros. Returning to the first clause: recall that the many think that one is temperate when trading pleasures for more pleasures. Two things are supposedly gained in this exchange: additional pleasure and temperance. The first clause captures this by saying that this exchange is "for" (πρός) both virtue and pleasure. But when we switch to the currency of wisdom, there are not two different things with analogous roles; instead, this exchange is said to be both "for and with" wisdom. The "with" (μετά), I take it, tracks the currency used in the exchange, and the "for" (a genitive of value) what one acquires from this transaction.[50] Unlike the many – who think that they can go on valuing ordinary things

---

[49] Socrates' discussion of the non-philosopher's temperance is likely a reference to the famous discussion of being overcome by pleasures in the *Protagoras* (351b–357e; so Sedley 2014). Whether or not it is, comparing the two accounts is illuminating. In the *Protagoras*, Socrates adopts the view (dialectically, in my view) that pleasure is the good, and thus the art of measurement measures pleasure. In the *Protagoras*, someone who maximizes pleasures has wisdom, whereas in the *Phaedo* such a person has intemperance. In the *Phaedo* wisdom is the good, and so this is what the wise person maximizes. In the *Phaedo*, someone who had the art of measuring pleasures and pains and pursued pleasure would still have only illusory temperance and would in fact be ruled by the body. Even if such a person acts with knowledge, they do not act for knowledge, but rather for one of the body's ends.

[50] See Sedley 2014, 70, for a discussion of Plato's use of μετά here.

such as pleasure and the avoidance of fear, and at the same time have virtue – Socrates is saying that one's actions must be entirely for wisdom.

Non-philosophers value a variety of bodily things, such as pleasure and the avoidance of fear, and use these currencies to increase their store of them. Philosophers exchange this swarm of different currencies for just one: wisdom. Philosopher also try to maximize their currency, as is clear from the "for wisdom" part of buying "for and with" wisdom. This fits with Socrates' characterization, earlier in the defense speech, of the philosopher as entirely dedicated to the pursuit of wisdom, desiring nothing else (66e, 67d, 68a–b).[51] This interpretation is sometimes rejected by those who would have Socrates say that we do virtuous actions for their own sake rather than for the sake of wisdom.[52] But there is no indication of this in the text, and throughout the defense speech Socrates has emphasized that the philosopher's goal is wisdom, as he will continue to emphasize and elaborate in the return to the defense (80e–81a, 82c, 84a–b).

Once we change our currency to wisdom, what is the status of pleasures, pains, and, in general, the old currencies? In particular, how do we reconcile (1) the idea that true virtue is with wisdom "regardless of whether pleasures, fears, and everything else like that are added or removed" (69b1–5) with (2) the idea, found earlier in the defense speech, that pleasures and pains distract us (65c) and lead us away from the pursuit of philosophy (66c–d)? In the return to the defense, Socrates is even more emphatic that we should avoid all bodily pleasures and pains, saying that we suffer the greatest evil when we suffer intense pleasures and pains (83b–c). It seems, then, that the addition of pleasures could switch an action from wise to unwise, from temperate to intemperate. Weiss has argued that this clause provides evidence that we are not literally supposed to avoid pleasures and pains but simply to devalue them, since Socrates says that something counts as wisdom regardless of whether pleasures or pains are added or removed.[53] However, the passage need not be read this way and, given the evidence just mentioned, should not be. Socrates' point is that, so long as one acts with wisdom, one will possess virtue regardless of whether one's amount of pleasure or fear increases or decreases as a result of the action. This does not mean that the wise person will ignore how much pleasure or pain an action would involve. For example, an action may at first seem wise but turn out not to be, since it involves walking over hot coals. Similarly, a person may choose to eat, and thus experience the unavoidable pleasure of eating, in part because she recognizes that this will help her avoid the greater pain of hunger, as well as to keep her body healthy. The wise person will consider pleasure and pain, but the worth of the

---

[51] So Bobonich 2002, 16.
[52] Irwin 1977a. Similarly, Vasiliou 2012, 18–19, argues that the philosopher is aiming at nothing above virtue.
[53] Weiss 1987, 58–9.

action is not determined by the amount of pleasure or pain, only by whether or not it is wise (cf. *Gorgias* 497d–500a, *Philebus* 55b).[54]

Let us turn to Socrates' account of true courage, temperance, and justice. He provides two different descriptions of them in the passage; taken together, these suggest that wisdom is prior to and responsible for courage, temperance, and justice. This is clearest in Socrates' second claim: that the virtues are a type of purifying of bodily affections and wisdom is the purifying rite.[55] A purifying rite is what brings about purifying, and so wisdom brings about the virtues. This is confirmed by Socrates' other description of the virtues in the passage: "all things' being bought and sold for this and with this – with wisdom – really is, I suspect, courage, temperance, justice, and, in sum, true virtue" (69b1–4). In the *Meno*, "with" is used to identify what guides an action (88b–c). In the metaphor of exchange, buying and selling things corresponds to actions; buying and selling all things with wisdom as your currency, then, means doing all one's actions guided by wisdom. Given that the virtues are here identified with this exchange and the exchange is guided by wisdom, wisdom again seems prior to and responsible for the virtues. The rest of the exchange passage, as well as Socrates' account of the virtues in the return to the defense (Subsection 7.3.2), is consistent if we interpret wisdom, courage, and temperance in this way.

What does it mean for courage and temperance to be a purifying of bodily affections and for wisdom to be a purifying rite (69b9–c3)? Earlier in the defense speech, Socrates described at length the problems caused by bodily desires, fears, pleasures, and pains. They are a pollution that infects the soul (67a, cf. 81b), leading the soul to pursue things other than wisdom. They deceive us, leading us to think that we are temperate and courageous when we are in fact intemperate and cowardly. The wise person sees the problems they cause and so wishes to be purified of them. Wisdom, as a purifying rite, brings about this purifying – to the soul's separating and habituating itself to be alone through itself (cf. 67c–d). Consider how this would work with what even ordinary people call temperance: "not being in a flutter about one's desires, but rather being disdainful of them and staying composed" (68c9–10). A temperate soul will disdain bodily desires, and thus habituate itself to being on its own, to acting according to its own desires, and to living by itself, freed from the body's fetters. It will thereby stay composed. Wisdom brings this about by getting one to recognize that bodily desires undermine one's happiness and so should not be allowed into the soul. Hence wisdom guides our response to bodily desires and other affections. This involves selling things like bodily pleasures and buying other things in their place – perhaps philosophical conversation, or inquiry on one's own. Courage, too, can be seen, at least in part, as removing the fear of

---

[54] Subsection 7.3.1 further discusses how and why the wise soul avoids pleasure and pain.
[55] I translate κάθαρσις as "purifying" rather than "purification" because κάθαρσις typically refers to a process, whereas "purification" is normally understood as the completion of a process.

death that comes from the body. Normally one thinks of courage in terms of facing external difficulties: enemies on the battlefield, dangers at sea, perhaps also diseases. But here courage *is* a purifying of the bodily affections.

Let me summarize the account thus far. Earlier in the defense, Socrates focused on why the philosopher desires to be dead, noting problems caused by the body that make it impossible for philosophers to acquire full wisdom so long as they are embodied. Socrates then distinguishes philosophers from non-philosophers by whether they are slaves to their bodily affections – in which case they do not even meet their own standards for virtue – or are instead guided by an entirely different value, wisdom, which genuinely opposes the bodily affections, thereby purifying the soul of them. Courage, temperance, and justice are types of purifying that are brought about by wisdom and serve to further it. In the return to the defense (Chapter 7) and in Socrates' reply to Simmias' *harmonia* objection (Chapter 8) we will learn more about how the philosopher opposes these affections.

After claiming that wisdom is the purificatory rite and the virtues are a purifying of the bodily affections, Socrates says that those who pursue philosophy correctly are the ones who can live among the gods, whereas those who are uninitiated will lie in the mud (69c–d) – an Orphic reference.[56] In *Republic* II Adeimantus refers to fraudulent priests and prophets who claim to use the books by Musaeus and Orpheus to initiate and purify, allegedly helping people secure a good afterlife (364b–365a). In the *Phaedo* Socrates describes the genuine version of what these fraudsters claim to do: the philosopher is genuinely purified and initiated, thereby genuinely securing a good afterlife. In general, Greek mystery initiation rituals aim at bringing initiates into a kind of direct experience with a god that will lead to their having a better afterlife.[57] Hence Socrates, in claiming that philosophers are the true initiates, is saying that they are the ones who genuinely have a direct experience with the divine and so can genuinely live among the gods after death. It is a general feature of Greek religion that one must be pure in order to interact with the gods (see 67b); specifically, one needs to be purified before being initiated. By identifying the virtues with purifying and wisdom with the purificatory rite, Socrates has identified the philosopher as the only one who can interact with the gods, thereby earning a good afterlife.

3.9 CONCLUSION

The defense speech is a carefully crafted argument that the philosopher desires to be dead, in a technical sense. In order for the embodied philosopher to acquire wisdom, his life must end, in the ordinary sense, but he must also make his soul itself through itself, so that he can be really dead. In presenting this argument,

---

[56] I discussed this passage in 1.3 and 3.2.
[57] See Edmonds 2017 and Betegh 2022.

Socrates introduces some of the most important ideas in the dialogue: the dangers of bodily pleasures and desires, the distinction between forms and ordinary objects, the proper activities of the soul, and the need to inquire without the senses. The exchange passage at the end should be understood in light of this earlier discussion of the body's malign influences on us. The philosopher resists these influences by using wisdom to purify his soul. Over the course of the defense speech, Socrates introduces most of the central topics of the dialogue, but offers full explanations for only a few of them, allowing others to come later in the dialogue's unfolding structure.

4

Cebes' Challenge and the Cyclical Argument

69e–72d

After Socrates' defense speech, Cebes lays out a challenge (69e–70b) that structures most of the remainder of the dialogue.[1] Cebes accepts the other claims Socrates has made in the defense speech, but says that Socrates should address the fear many people have that the soul disperses and thus is destroyed when a person dies. Cebes then says that Socrates should convince them that the soul will continue to exist after death and retain some power and wisdom. This challenge leads to what is typically called Socrates' four "immortality arguments," which structure the core of the dialogue: the cyclical argument (70c–72d), the recollecting argument (72e–77d), the kinship argument (77d–80b), and the final argument (102a–107b). In the first half of this chapter I examine how Cebes' challenge sets the expectations for Socrates' subsequent arguments. His arguments are designed to help remove the fear that the soul is dispersed at death by rationally persuading his interlocutors that it will continue to exist. Cebes' challenge does not ask Socrates to show that the soul is immortal or indestructible, and Socrates' first three arguments do not purport to show either of these claims. Only the final argument aims to do so.

The second half of the chapter discusses the cyclical argument. I provide a new account of its basic structure: it rests on an agreement between Socrates and Cebes to count an argument for one conclusion as sufficient evidence for reaching another conclusion. Given the details of this agreement, the argument need not address the nature of the soul. At best, it establishes that the soul exists after death and that there is reincarnation, without explaining why either of these is the case. Nonetheless, the argument is important for its attempt to establish reincarnation and for how it argues for this. It aims to show that this Pythagorean view is correct by understanding death

---

[1] Throughout this book, I refer to this as "Cebes' challenge" and to Cebes' objection to the kinship argument (86e–88b) as "Cebes' cloakmaker objection."

and rebirth as part of a much larger phenomenon: the coming to be and passing away of opposite things. In doing so, it shows why one might need to understand the nature of reality quite broadly to defend a prerequisite of Socrates' ethical views, namely the existence of the soul after death. Moreover, the cyclical argument includes an important discussion of opposites, which play a crucial role in each of Socrates' subsequent arguments.

4.1 CEBES' CHALLENGE: 69E–70B

Let us begin with the challenge:

> Socrates, the other things you say seem to me well said, but the matter of the soul causes people to have great doubt, fearing that once released from the body it no longer exists anywhere, but is destroyed and perishes on the day when the human being dies, immediately as it is released from the body, and that as it comes out it is dissipated like breath or smoke, flies away in all directions, and isn't anything anywhere. Since if it really would be somewhere itself through itself, gathered together and released from the evils you just described, then there would be much hope, and a noble hope at that, Socrates, that what you say is true. But this very point requires no little reassurance and conviction, that the soul exists when the human has died, and has some power and wisdom. (69e6–70b4)

Note that Cebes does not mention "immortality"; instead, he puts his challenge in terms of being convinced that the soul does not dissipate upon death but rather continues to exist.

The term "immortality" arises in a very specific context in the *Phaedo*: all of Socrates' mentions of the soul's immortality can be traced back to Cebes' cloak-maker objection. Before this, Cebes uses the term "immortal" once, at the beginning of the recollecting argument. He claims there that the view that learning is recollecting shows that the soul existed before birth, and so "in this way too" (καὶ ταύτῃ, 73a2) it seems to be immortal. Socrates never claims in the *Phaedo* that the recollecting argument shows immortality, only that it shows that the soul existed before birth (76d–e). In fact Socrates never claims that the recollecting argument responds to Cebes' challenge. Instead, it is an additional argument that Socrates provides when Cebes claims that it is relevant (72e–73b), as discussed in Section 5.1. In the kinship argument, Socrates attributes immortality to the group he calls "the unseen," whose members always hold *kata* the same things (at 79d2, 80b1, cf. 81a5, 86b1). He never says that the soul is a member of this group – as I argue in Chapter 6, it cannot be a member of this group, since no soul *always* holds *kata* the same things. Instead he says that the soul is similar and akin to the immortal unseen, whose only identified members are the forms and the gods. Traditionally, immortality is a feature of the gods. As Alex Long points out, in Homer the souls of humans continue to exist in the underworld after death, but humans are still called mortals; in Homer only the gods and their possessions are immortal.[2] I argue in Chapter 10 that the final argument, in defending the claim that the soul is immortal, attributes to the soul one of the features of the divine.

At the end of his cloakmaker objection, Cebes says for the first time that no one should be confident in the face of death unless he can show that the soul is "entirely immortal and indestructible" (παντάπασιν ἀθάνατόν τε καὶ ἀνώλεθρον, 88b5–6). One way to understand his objection is as saying that the soul should not merely be more like and akin to the things that are immortal and indestructible – as the kinship argument claims – but in fact one of them. All of Socrates' subsequent mentions of the soul's immortality are either part of summarizing Cebes' cloakmaker objection (95c1, d1, and e1), or part of Socrates' final argument, which responds to this objection (100b9, 105c–107e passim, 114d4).

What, then, is Cebes' original challenge, if not to show that the soul is immortal or indestructible? We should start with the important and rarely noted epistemic and psychological dimension to Cebes' challenge. Cebes says that matters concerning the soul provide people with great doubt (ἀπιστία), and so he asks Socrates to provide them with some reassurance (παραμυθία) and conviction (πίστις) that the soul is not destroyed upon death (70a–b).[3] Cebes is challenging Socrates' claim, from the beginning of the defense speech, that it is reasonable for the philosopher to be confident (θαρρεῖν, 63e10) about his impending death and have good hope (see Sections 3.2 and 3.7). Connected to this is Cebes' request that Socrates address the *fear* that the soul is destroyed upon death. In general, an argument that we should not fear something (e.g. a boat's sinking) need not show that it is impossible for the feared event to happen; you can convince someone to be confident that something will happen without needing to convince them that it must happen. I will argue that this is especially important for recognizing how the kinship argument addresses Cebes' challenge (Section 6.1).

The interrelated psychological and epistemic terms in Cebes' challenge – fear, doubt, confidence, and conviction – recur throughout the dialogue. Earlier, Socrates was delighted that Cebes is always scrutinizing arguments and refuses to be convinced straightaway by them (63a). Before the kinship argument, Socrates says that, while the continued existence of the soul has been shown by combining the cyclical and recollecting arguments, Simmias and Cebes still fear what children fear, namely that the soul will be dissipated (77c–e). Cebes asks Socrates to convince them as if they had that fear, or rather as if a child within them had this fear (77e). Socrates then identifies the alternatives as being confident or fearful of death (78b). But Cebes, in his cloakmaker objection, ends by saying that this would be an

---

[2] Long 2019, 11–14.
[3] For a general discussion of πίστις in the *Phaedo*, see Miller 2015, 146–52. It is not easy to translate πίστις uniformly in the *Phaedo*; in my discussions of misology (Section 8.2) and of the method of hypothesis (Section 9.8), I translate it as "trust" rather than "conviction." Throughout, it is worth bearing in mind that its semantic range covers both meanings.

unintelligent confidence (ἀνοήτως θαρρεῖν, 88b4). Cebes phrases his cloakmaker objection by imagining that Socrates' personified argument asks Cebes why he is doubtful (ἀπιστεῖς, 87a8). In the misology section, Socrates says that misology results when people repeatedly put their conviction in *logoi* and then change their minds (90b). He wants to convince them that the soul exists after death, but does not want them to become convinced too quickly, since this is what he says can lead to misology. At the same time, the true philosopher, being courageous, will not fear death. Thus, becoming convinced in the right way not to fear death is an important part of becoming a true philosopher with genuine virtue.

I argue that Socrates' method of hypothesis, which he presents in his autobiography, is designed to help avoid misology, providing a way to acquire rational confidence in *logoi* before accepting them (Subsection 9.8.2). Socrates' application of the method of hypothesis to the existence of forms is meant to show his companions how they can gain the right sort of confidence in the final argument. Cebes' response to the final argument is that he cannot doubt it in any way (107a), whereas Simmias says that he is compelled to still keep some doubt in his mind, to which Socrates' response is that Simmias should go back and further analyze the hypotheses (107b) – the opposite of telling Simmias that he should immediately be convinced. As we will see in chapter 12, this focus on conviction and doubt continues into the final eschatological account. In short, throughout the dialogue Socrates addresses the interconnected psychological and epistemic aspect of Cebes' challenge.

Let us turn to the specific concern that Cebes wants addressed. He says that people fear that after death the soul is "dissipated like breath (πνεῦμα) or smoke, flying away in all directions, and isn't anything anywhere" (70a5–7). Cebes contrasts the option of dispersal with the possibility that the soul exists somewhere "gathered together" (συνηθροισμένη, 70a7); however, Socrates' own alternative, in the kinship argument, is that the soul is something "incomposite" (ἀσύνθετον, 78c3). The soul does not avoid dispersal by simply happening to be gathered together; instead, its nature would not allow it to disperse.

Cebes says twice in his challenge that people fear that the soul is not *anywhere*, contrasting this with its really being somewhere. This explains Socrates' discussion, in several subsequent arguments, of *where* the soul is after death.[4] The cyclical argument and the final argument both claim that it is in Hades. After the return to the defense, Socrates clarifies that the true philosopher goes to Hades as it truly is, which is divine, pure, and unseen (80d). Non-philosophers, before they are reincarnated, first wander around monuments, tombs, and such places (81c–d) or, if their souls are better, go to other, unspecified places (82a–b). These differences in where souls go after death set up Socrates' long discussion near the end of the

---

[4] As Lukas Apsel pointed out to me.

dialogue of the true structure of the earth, including its different places for souls of different levels of purity (107c–114c).

At the end of his challenge, Cebes asks to be convinced that the soul not only exists after death but also has some power and wisdom (70b). The cyclical argument does not address this, but it is addressed in different ways in the other three arguments. The recollecting argument aims to establish that every soul has within it knowledge of all of the forms, which it can recollect – thus telling us something about both the soul's power and its wisdom. Similarly, the kinship argument aims to establish that our soul's kinship with the forms allows the soul to grasp them; this state of grasping the forms is identified as wisdom (79d). This argument also highlights the soul's power to rule over the body (79e–80a). The final argument does not touch on the soul's wisdom but does provide an account of its power to bring life to the body, as well as to ensure its own life.

4.2 THE STRUCTURE OF THE CYCLICAL ARGUMENT

In order to understand how the cyclical argument works, it is important to recognize that it is based on an agreement to take an argument for one conclusion as a sufficient sign for a different conclusion. To my knowledge, the significance of this agreement has not been appreciated in the secondary literature. Socrates says to Cebes:

> If this is so – that living people come to be again from those who have died – surely our souls would exist there [Hades]? For, I take it, the souls would not come to be again, if they did not exist. And so it would be sufficient evidence of the truth of this, should it really come to be clear that the living come to be from nowhere other than the dead. (70c8–d4)

Cebes agrees to take an argument that the living come to be from the dead as evidence that the souls exist in Hades after they have died and then come back to life again. Thus in the remainder Socrates simply argues that the living come to be from the dead, just as the dead come from the living.

In the passage just quoted, Socrates justifies the claim that this is sufficient evidence by saying that he takes it that the souls would not come to be again if they did not exist after death. Perhaps the implicit idea is that the souls must continue to exist after death for there to be any reason to think that the living are coming to be from the dead rather than from somewhere else or from nowhere at all. If this is the idea, it relies on some substantive commitments, including (1) that something must continue to exist from A to B in order for B to come to be from A and (2) that only the soul could be this continuant.[5] And even this would not justify the claim that souls exist in Hades after death, as opposed to existing somewhere else or going directly into a new body. In any

---

[5] Huffman 2010, 31–3, suggests that for Philolaus the *archē* (principle/origin) of the soul transmigrates, but not the soul itself. This would be one alternative continuant.

event, whatever ideas might be implicit, Cebes simply accepts that Socrates only needs to show that the living come to be from the dead. This agreement allows them to focus on what is likely the most contentious issue.

Once Cebes agrees to take this as a sufficient sign, Socrates does not mention the soul again except when drawing his conclusions. There is something dissatisfying about such an argument: it provides no underlying explanation for why the soul is this way. But it is worth remembering that Cebes' challenge asks Socrates for conviction, and at the end of the cyclical argument he seems quite convinced. It ends with Cebes saying, "I think that would be inevitable, Socrates, and in my opinion what you're saying is completely true" (72d4–5). Arguments based on agreeing to such conditionals ("if x is shown, that is a sufficient sign for y") can be especially good with a specific interlocutor with specific doubts. At the same time, Socrates later says that Cebes and Simmias still seem to fear death (77d–e). Perhaps Cebes is not thoroughly persuaded precisely because this argument has not identified what it is about the nature of the soul that makes it exist after death. The kinship argument and the final argument aim to show this. But only the cyclical argument aims to establish reincarnation, something that Socrates is committed to throughout the remainder of the dialogue (81c–82b, 107d–e, 113a). Each argument makes an important contribution to Socrates' overall account; none is completely superseded.

In fact Socrates seems to view the cyclical argument as having a different status precisely because it is based on this sort of agreement. At the end of the recollecting argument, Simmias says that, while they have been convinced of the pre-existence of the soul, its post-existence has not yet been shown (ἀποδεδεῖχθαι, 77b3). Cebes had recently enthusiastically accepted the cyclical argument, but nonetheless he and Socrates agree that this has not been shown. Instead, Socrates says that the existence of the soul after death "has already been shown ... if you're prepared to combine this argument with the one we agreed to before it – that everything living comes to be from what is dead" (77c6–9). Why does Socrates think that combining these arguments does anything at all? After all, the recollecting argument does not address what happens to the soul after death, whereas the cyclical argument does this on its own.[6]

The way in which Socrates combines the two arguments removes the part of the cyclical argument that involves agreeing to take one claim – that the living come to be from the dead – as sufficient evidence for another – that the soul exists after death and reincarnates. My suggestion is that removing this agreement is what makes the argument *shown* (ἀποδεδεῖχθαι). This is the verb that Aristotle uses for the highest form of scientific proof in the *Posterior Analytics*; it is normally translated in Aristotle as "to have been demonstrated" and I would translate it that way in the *Phaedo*, were it not for its Aristotelian connotations. While I do not think that Socrates is using it

---

[6] For the question, see Gallop 1975 ad loc. For other answers, see Hackforth 1955, 79–80, Osborne 1995, 212–14, and Ebert 2004, 251.

in Aristotle's technical sense, I do think that he is using it for an argument that meets a higher standard. An argument that relies on agreeing that one thing is a sufficient sign for another might convince a specific interlocutor, but it does not show why the conclusion holds.[7]

Consider how Socrates combines the two arguments, after the recollecting argument:

> For if the soul exists before as well, and it is necessary, when the soul enters upon living and is born, that it [the soul] come to be from nowhere other than from death and being dead, how could it not also be necessary to exist when it has died, given that it must come to be again? (77c9–d4)

Note that there is no role played here by the cyclical argument's agreement that, if the living come to be from the dead, then this is a sufficient sign that the soul exists in Hades. Instead, Socrates here combines the conclusion of the recollecting argument, that the soul exists before birth, and the sub-conclusion directly argued for in the cyclical argument, that the living come from the dead. His reasoning is very terse, but we can unpack it. Start with someone born now; call her "Sarah." Sarah's soul must pre-exist, by the recollecting argument. But Sarah must come to be from the dead, by the cyclical argument. Put together, this means that Sarah's soul must have been among the dead. Now the dead, of course, come to be from the (previously) living. Hence Sarah's soul must have come from the (previously) living. What applies to Sarah applies to everyone else, including those born in the future. So the souls of the currently living must continue to exist after death, so that the souls born in the future can come to be from them.

Let me turn to a different aspect of the cyclical argument's structure: it draws its conclusion twice, in two different ways. Socrates first argues that, (i) in general, opposite things come to be from opposites (71a), and then, setting up his second conclusion, that (ii) there are processes that go from one opposite to the other and from the other to the one (71a–b). Cebes agrees that (iii) living and dead are opposites (71d). From (i) and (iii) Socrates concludes that (iv) the living come to be from the dead and the dead from the living (71d) and then draws the conclusion, using their sufficient-sign agreement, that (v) the soul exists in Hades (71d–e). Then Socrates points out that (vi) there is a process of dying (71e), and concludes from this and (ii) that (vii) there must be a process of coming back to life along with it, and so "in this way too" (καὶ ταύτῃ, 72a4) it is shown that (iv) the living come to be from the dead and the dead from the living. When he draws the conclusion this second time,

---

[7] In *Prior Analytics* I.23, I.29, and I.44, and *Posterior Analytics* II.6, Aristotle discusses arguments that involve an agreement to take one conclusion to suffice for another; he calls these "syllogisms from a hypothesis." I argue in Ebrey 2015, §2 that Aristotle does not count these as genuine syllogisms; rather they simply include syllogisms for the directly argued-for sub-conclusions. Socrates, Simmias, and Cebes seem to be using "show" in a similar way here, not allowing something to count as "shown" if it involves such an agreement.

he explicitly refers back to their agreement that this would be "sufficient evidence" (ἱκανόν ... τεκμήριον, 72a6) for the claim that the souls exist somewhere after death.

What is the point of drawing the conclusion a second time, using processes? Gallop says that, if the living comes to be from the dead, clearly there must be a process by which they do so. But it is not clear that there must be *a* process. Socrates is arguing that, just as there is a single process, dying, so there needs to be a single process, coming back to life. One might object to the first argument that in some sense the living may come to be from the dead, but only through a string of complex processes: decomposition, propagation of seeds, fertilization, growth of plants, plants being eaten, and so on. There being a single process of coming back alive, parallel to that of death, blocks this sort of objection.

4.3 OPPOSITES COMING TO BE FROM OPPOSITES

The heart of the cyclical argument is a general account of coming to be from opposites. Socrates claims that, whenever something that has an opposite comes to be, it does so from nothing other than its opposite (70e–71a = my (i)). David Sedley has provided strong arguments for what, in any event, seems the natural reading: that Socrates means "opposite" in a robust sense, so that opposites are a restricted group, identified by predicates that come in pairs (like hot and cold, light and dark), rather than every predicate and its contradictory (such as table and non-table, blue and non-blue).[8] Socrates' claim in the cyclical argument is only about things that have opposites: they always come to be from their opposite.[9]

It is tricky to understand how Socrates conceives of opposites here, in part because he lists as examples not only pairs such as large and small, but also comparative opposites such as larger and smaller. This larger class, which is referred to with both simple (grammatically "positive") and comparative adjectives, Sedley calls "converse contraries." It seems to me that Sedley's analysis is correct:

f and *g* are converse contraries if and only if

(1) *f* and *g* are contraries (i.e. incompatible features that lie on a single range), and
(2) x is *f* compared with y if and only if y is *g* compared with x.[10]

---

[8] Sedley 2012, 153–4, denied by Barnes 1978, 397–419; Bostock 1986, 43–51, and Pakaluk 2003.
[9] When an animal first becomes alive, it is awake. Should we say that it comes to be awake? If so, it would have to do so from previously having been asleep. As far as I can tell, Socrates need not say that when an animal comes to be alive it also comes to be awake. It is coming to be alive, and so is awake or asleep, but not coming to be awake.
[10] Sedley 2012, 155. Justin 2020 nicely brings out the strength of Sedley's position, though she holds a different account of the opposites in question. In particular, she argues that Socrates treats evaluative opposites (such as good and bad, or just and unjust) differently from non-evaluative opposites. I am skeptical; but even if this is right, it is not crucial for reconstructing the argument, since the relevant opposites here are alive and dead.

"Small" and "average-sized" are not converse contraries, even though they are incompatible features that lie on a single range (size), because, if x is small compared to y, then y is not average-sized compared with x. However, "small" and "large" are converse contraries, as are the comparative contraries "smaller" and "larger." Consider the latter: smaller and larger are incompatible descriptions on a single range – the comparative size of something – and if x is smaller than y, then y is larger than x. So, if something larger comes to be, it does so from something smaller, and if something large comes to be, it does so from something small (at least in comparison to its current size).

Why include comparative contraries such as larger and smaller in the theory? As Sedley suggests, it provides a more general account of change, since not every change is between polar opposites, and any change along a continuous range must go through intermediate stages. For example, when something goes from very hot to very cold, it must become lukewarm as it moves between these two extremes. This can be understood as the colder coming to be from the warmer. Socrates may also include comparative contraries because in the defense speech being dead seems to come in degrees: the philosopher is closer to dead than others, and one is only truly dead once one's soul is itself according to itself. The point of the comparative analysis, then, would be that, even if being dead comes in degrees, it still has an opposite, and so the living can still come to be from the dead and the dead from the living.

To clarify this account of coming to be from opposites, it helps to consider an objection (made by someone whom Phaedo says he cannot remember) in the final immortality argument (103a). The objection is that, according to Socrates' account in the final argument, the large in us is never willing to admit the small, whereas in the cyclical argument Socrates said that the larger comes to be only from the smaller. Socrates clarifies that in the cyclical argument he was talking about opposite things coming to be from opposite things, whereas in the final argument he is talking about the opposite itself: the opposites themselves never admit their opposites, whereas opposite things come only from opposites (103b–c). Hence the cyclical argument is arguing that hot things come to be only from cold things. In the case of the living and the dead, the "thing" characterized by these opposites seems to be the animal that is alive or dead. Given Socrates' earlier account of death and being dead, the animal is alive when its soul and body are together and dead (at least in a loose sense of the term) when they are apart. Socrates may give detaching and combining (διακρίνεσθαι καὶ συγκρίνεσθαι, 71b6) as examples of processes before being alive and dead precisely because he thinks of living and dying as specific types of detaching and combining.[11] The end of the recollecting argument strongly suggests that the soul becomes connected to a body when we are born (76c–d); hence a body and a soul exist separately before birth, at which point they are

---

[11] So Sedley 2012, 161.

connected, and at death they separate. When the soul is reborn, it is joined to a new body.

One might worry that Socrates' argument simply assumes that living and being dead are opposites.[12] However, Socrates is sensitive to the possibility that apparent opposites are not actually opposites – for example, in sketching his Aesop fable, Socrates suggests that pleasure and pain are only apparent opposites (60b). So we should take him as asking a real question when he twice asks Cebes whether living and dead are opposites (71c, 71d). Cebes apparently thinks that they are and so agrees. Since Socrates and Cebes seem to be thinking of death as a certain type of separation and of life as a certain type of combination, we can see why Cebes would agree. And Socrates' primary goal, of course, is to convince Cebes.

Finally, let me suggest that Socrates may be not only appropriating and transforming the Pythagorean view of reincarnation but also doing so from appropriated and transformed Pythagorean premises. According to Aristotle's report, some Pythagoreans tried to explain everything in the universe using ten pairs of opposites as principles (*Met.* A.5, 986a22–b2). Given the many ways Socrates is appropriating and transforming Pythagorean commitments in the *Phaedo* (see esp. Section 1.3), he may be appropriating this as well. This begins with his needing to provide his own account of why suicide is not sanctioned; in the next chapter (Section 5.1) I argue that the recollecting argument and the kinship argument also seem to provide Platonic versions of Pythagorean ideas. Here in the cyclical argument the idea would be that Pythagoreans were right to think that opposites are crucial for understanding the natural world, but were wrong to choose ten specific pairs of opposites: this led them not to understand the proper role of opposites in change. We could, even more speculatively, further specify which Pythagoreans Socrates is appropriating. Many scholars have questioned whether Philolaus accepted reincarnation.[13] Schofield argues that the opposite theorists Aristotle describes are likely to be earlier Pythagoreans, precisely the ones who most clearly accepted reincarnation.[14] The cyclical argument, then, may well be showing how to appropriate and reinterpret an older, more traditional Pythagorean view (explaining the world in terms of opposites) in order to argue for another traditional Pythagorean view (reincarnation). Nonetheless, the argument is Socrates' own. He starts from opposites in general – not the specific Pythagorean ten pairs – and uses them in an entirely new argument. Moreover, the way he describes reincarnation in the return to the defense (81c–82b) and in the eschatological account at the end of the dialogue (107d–108c) fits with his own accounts of the nature of the soul, of moral psychology, and of the soul's impurities – not with Pythagorean views. The *Phaedo* presents a version of these Pythagorean ideas that fits with Socrates' basic commitments.

---

[12] For concerns of this sort, see Hackforth 1955, 63–4, and Gallop 1975, 107–8.
[13] See Huffman 1993, 328–32. As noted in n. 5, Huffman 2010, 31–3 suggests that Philolaus allowed the *archē* (principle/origin) of the soul to transmigrate, but not the soul itself.
[14] Schofield 2012, 156.

4.4 THE SUPPLEMENTAL ARGUMENT: 72A–D

Socrates introduces his final consideration in favor of cyclical coming to be and passing away as a way of seeing "that we have not agreed wrongly" (72a11–12). Gallop interprets this as meaning that what follows is supposed to support one of the premises of the argument, thereby showing that they were right to agree to it. However, Socrates' final consideration does not seem to support any of the premises. More importantly, Socrates and Cebes have each agreed that the living come to be from the dead and the dead from the living (72a); this directly argued-for conclusion certainly seems to be what Socrates thinks they have not wrongly agreed to. Hence Socrates offers here a supplemental consideration in favor of a cyclical relationship between living and dying. This supplemental argument is the target of special derision among commentators. Interestingly, it is what seems to lead Cebes to being completely convinced (72d). Perhaps he sees it as yet another sign pointing in the same direction.

Socrates' basic argument is that, if there were a process of dying but no process of coming back to life to balance it out, then in the end everything would be dead and nothing alive (72c–d). One might object that there is no problem with this result: perhaps life in the universe is finite and will eventually end.[15] While this seems possible, it is fair to point out this consequence, which someone might not want to accept – for example, if one is committed to the possibility of never-ending life or thinks that such a possibility should not be closed off. Moreover, the possibility that in the end everything would be dead may seem incompatible with divine beneficence. A different sort of objection to this argument is that it leaves out the possibility that the living turn into the dead, and the dead decompose and then become new living things. But in that case coming to be does happen in a circle; the whole point of the supplemental argument is to deny that it happens in a circle (72a–b), then see what the results would be.

Anaxagoras, who will play an important role in Socrates' autobiography, is mentioned for the first time in this supplemental argument. Socrates says that, if there were only combining without detaching, Anaxagoras' saying "all things together" would come true (72c4–5). This highlights that the cyclical argument, like the autobiography, shows Socrates engaging in a form of natural philosophy, providing broad accounts of how to understand a wide range of natural phenomena. Directly before the cyclical argument, when Socrates first responds to Cebes' challenge, he says: "I really don't think that anyone who heard us now, even if he were a comic poet, would say that I'm prattling on (ἀδολεσχῶ) and talking about irrelevant things" (70b10–c2) – a reference to Aristophanes' characterization of Socrates in the *Clouds* as a "prattler" (ἀδολεσχῶν, 1485).[16] In the *Apology* Socrates

---

[15] Cf. Gallop 1975, 112–13.
[16] For a discussion, see Rashed 2009, 118. Other references to Aristophanes in the *Phaedo* are noted in chapter 8, n. 10.

denies this characterization by arguing that he is not the sort of person to discuss things "above the sky and below the earth," that is, he is not one of the natural philosophers (19b–d). Later he says that Meletus is acting as if he were prosecuting Anaxagoras (26d–e). In the *Phaedo* he avoids the accusation in a different way. No one could accuse him of prattling on about topics of no importance when, on the last day of his life, he discusses whether the soul continues to exist after death. Yet doing so requires examining precisely the sort of issues discussed by people like Anaxagoras.[17] Socrates' brief reference to Anaxagoras here paves the way for his much more thorough engagement with natural science in the autobiography, where again he shows that discussing these issues is not to prattle on about topics of no importance; instead, the autobiography is part of his response to Cebes' cloakmaker objection, which ultimately aims to show why the soul is immortal and indestructible, and so why the philosopher really should practice for being dead.

4.5 CONCLUSION

Cebes' challenge asks Socrates to provide conviction, because people fear that the soul is dispersed and thereby destroyed upon death. He does not ask here to be shown that it is immortal or indestructible. Moreover, Cebes wants to be shown that the soul exists somewhere after death, with some power and wisdom. Socrates responds to different parts of this challenge in different ways in his four subsequent arguments – to the fear and request for conviction, to the concern with dispersal and destruction, to identifying where it exists, and to identifying its power and wisdom. In the cyclical argument, using an agreement to take an argument for one conclusion as sufficient evidence for a different conclusion, he convinces Cebes that the soul continues to exist and reincarnates. Once they make this agreement, Socrates argues that the living come from the dead, just as the dead come from the living; he leaves the subsequent arguments to explain why the soul continues and what power and wisdom it has. Nonetheless, the cyclical argument is important in several ways. Unlike the recollecting argument, it argues for the existence of the soul after death. Moreover, as in Socrates' account of suicide, Socrates provides a new argument for a Pythagorean view, reincarnation, thereby putting it on sounder footing. He does so by drawing on broad considerations of how all change works, a topic within natural philosophy. Later, in the second defense (81c–e and 83d–e) and again at the beginning of his final eschatological account (108a–c), Socrates provides a mechanism by which reincarnation happens. But only the cyclical argument aims to establish that it takes place.

---

[17] For other references to Anaxagoras in the *Phaedo*, see Section 9.4.

5

The Recollecting Argument

72e–77d

Perhaps no other argument in ancient philosophy has received as much attention in the past seventy years as the "recollection argument" in the *Phaedo*. Many scholars have viewed it as one of Plato's few arguments for the existence of "Platonic" forms, or even his only one.[1] It is also one of Plato's most thoroughly developed accounts of the mental processes involved in acquiring knowledge. Moreover, it vies with the final argument as the longest continuous argument in the *Phaedo* and is arguably the most complex, giving rise to a seemingly limitless number of questions about how exactly it works. Unfortunately there is no simple way to understand the argument; one must work carefully through its many details while keeping an eye on how it fits into the dialogue as a whole.

Socrates draws a contrast between forms and ordinary objects in the argument. However, in my view, Socrates does not argue here for accepting "Platonic" forms, where these are understood as including all of Plato's central commitments about the forms. Instead, the argument highlights one key difference between ordinary objects and forms: that the latter do not change over time, whereas the former do. This is important for the dialogue's unfolding account of ordinary objects and forms, but there is still much left to be said later in the dialogue about how they differ from one another.

One of my central interpretive claims in this chapter is that Socrates treats recollecting as an extended process that begins when we first perceive something and continues until we acquire knowledge of the relevant form. This is why I translate "*anamnēsis*" as "recollecting" rather than "recollection": the latter naturally is understood as the result of a process, whereas Socrates is discussing the process itself. Moreover, I argue that Socrates is specifically interested in a type of

---

[1] Penner 1987, White 1992, Irwin 1999, Kelsey 2000, Dimas 2003, and Tuozzo 2018. White 1992, 280, claims that this is perhaps the only argument we find in the corpus for thinking there are forms.

recollecting which begins when we perceive one thing and another thing comes to mind, which is the very standard by which we judge the first. A number of interpretive difficulties are resolved once we recognize that Socrates is considering the extended process of recollecting the standard by which something is judged.

While the recollecting argument discusses important topics and advances our understanding of inquiry and the forms, I argue in the next chapter that the kinship argument – which has received far less attention – is more important for understanding the *Phaedo*'s account of the forms and the soul, as well as more important to the overall structure of the dialogue.

5.1 THE PLACE OF THE ARGUMENT IN THE DIALOGUE

Before diving into the details, we should situate the argument in the dialogue. As noted in the previous chapter (Section 4.2), Socrates never says that the recollecting argument shows that the soul exists after death, only that it exists before we are born (76d–e). It is Cebes who first mentions recollecting and who says that, if learning is recollecting, it seems that the soul is immortal (72e–73a). Cebes says that Socrates has the habit of discussing recollecting (73a–b); Cebes describes these discussions exactly like Socrates' conversation with the slave in the *Meno*.[2] In response to Cebes, Socrates says that he will show in a different way that what is called "learning" can be recollecting (73b). From Socrates' dramatic perspective, we can see why he follows Cebes' suggestion that they discuss learning as recollecting. Cebes has enthusiastically endorsed the cyclical argument (72d). Socrates has no reason to think that he needs to give another argument that the soul exists after death, and so happily discusses another, related topic – one where he has something new to say. But why does Plato choose to have Socrates argue for something that does not directly address Cebes' challenge (69e–70b), given that after the argument Simmias will press Socrates to show that the soul is not destroyed upon death (77a–b)? While the argument adds to our understanding of forms and ordinary objects, it is easy to imagine that a different argument could have allowed Socrates to make the same points.

Let me highlight four more specific things that the argument accomplishes. First, it addresses how we can acquire knowledge at all, which is pressing given Socrates' account of inquiry in the defense speech. He argued there that the senses deceive us when we use them to inquire, and so the philosopher's only chance to discover the truth is by reasoning on his own, using his soul, itself through itself (65a–66a, Section 3.6). Socrates reaffirms his commitment to this in the return to the defense (82e–83b, Chapter 7), and in his autobiography he says that his method of inquiry does not involve using the senses (99d–e, Section 9.8). The recollecting argument explains how you can discover something new without interacting with the outside world: the knowledge is already in your soul, and so

---

[2] See section 1.4 for this connection to the *Meno*.

you can inquire entirely using your own inner resources.³ One must perceive in order to trigger recollecting – but, I shall argue, this is not a proper part of inquiry itself.

The argument also begins to provide a positive account of the soul. At the end of Cebes' challenge, Cebes asks to be persuaded that the soul has "some power and wisdom" (70b4) after death. The cyclical argument does not address this. By contrast, Socrates here argues that the soul has knowledge of all of the forms within it and the power to recover this knowledge. In the conclusion he draws attention to this, saying that he has shown that the soul had *wisdom* before birth (76c). Of course, this is not yet to say that it has wisdom after death. But, when the argument is combined with the cyclical argument, we can conclude that it must not entirely lose its power and wisdom after death since it needs to retain them to be able to recollect in the next life.

As discussed in the previous chapter (Section 4.2), the recollecting argument's most direct contribution to the argumentative structure of the dialogue is to strengthen the conclusion of the cyclical argument by replacing the part of the argument that was a mere agreement. They agreed there to accept one conclusion (that the living come to be from the dead) as a sufficient sign of the other (that the soul exists before birth and after death, reincarnating). Once Socrates combines the two arguments, removing this mere agreement, he says that it has been shown (ἀποδέδεικται, 77d5) that the soul exists after death.

The recollecting argument is also part of Socrates' transforming and appropriating Pythagorean ideas in the dialogue. Pythagoreans (including Empedocles) claimed to remember things from past lives, thereby obtaining insights not possessed by ordinary people.⁴ As Betegh has noted, the recollecting argument similarly identifies a way in which knowledge from before birth provides an epistemic advantage. Thus this argument, like the cyclical argument, adapts a Pythagorean view.⁵ But Socrates, unlike the Pythagoreans, argues for this epistemic advantage independently of reincarnation. Thus Socrates defends two Pythagorean views in succession – reincarnation and recollecting from before birth – but does so independently of one another, unlike the Pythagoreans. This continues in the next argument, as Betegh also notes. The Pythagoreans (including Empedocles) connect reincarnation and memory to a recognition of divine lineage: in the same fragments and testimony, Empedocles claims to be a *daimōn* who was once with the gods and will be reborn among them, and Pythagoras is reported to claim that he remembered that he was the son of Hermes. In the kinship argument, Socrates argues that we are akin to the divine — that is, belong

---

³ Bedu-Addo 1991 (esp. 27–30) is structured around how this is possible. See also Gentzler 1994.
⁴ For a discussion see Pellò 2018 and Betegh 2022. For Pythagoras evidence includes Diogenes Laertius 8.4 and for Empedocles B111, B126, B146, and B147.
⁵ Betegh 2022.

to the same *genos* (kin, kind) as it. But the notion of the divine and kinship are quite different from what we find in Pythagorean sources, and Socrates' argument for this conclusion does not rely on either reincarnation or recollection. Hence these three arguments (70b–80b) defend Pythagorean views, but reinterpret and provide new, independent arguments for each.

5.2 OVERVIEW OF THE ARGUMENT

We turn now to the argument,[6] which can be divided into four stages. First, Socrates uses ordinary examples of recollecting to describe various necessary or sufficient conditions for different types of recollecting (73c–74a). Next, he provides the much-discussed argument that equality itself is not the same as equal sticks and uses this conclusion to argue that Simmias recollects equality when seeing equal sticks (74a–d). Third, he argues that they must have gained knowledge of equality itself – and indeed of the rest of the forms – before they used their senses, and so before they were born (74d–75c). Finally, he argues that we must have forgotten this knowledge, so learning must be recollecting and the soul must exist before birth (75c–76e). After finishing the argument, Socrates emphasizes that the conclusion depends on the existence of forms, and Simmias then notes that the argument has not ruled out the possibility that the soul is destroyed upon death (76e–77d).

One surprising feature of the overall argument is that Socrates draws the conclusion that Simmias has recollected at the end of the second stage (74c–d). Ebert and others have wanted to excise this claim, but it is in our manuscripts and does in fact follow from what has come before.[7] But, of course, the simple fact that Simmias has recollected does not mean that his soul existed before birth, or that he recollected all the forms, or that learning is recollecting.[8] I will argue that Socrates' strategy is to establish, in the second stage, that Simmias has recollected equality, and then in the following two stages to use this, along with his interim conclusions from stage one, to draw his final conclusions. In particular, Socrates draws a distinction in this first stage between recollecting from similar things and doing so from dissimilar things, and makes a strong claim about what happens in cases of recollecting from similar things. I argue that in the third stage he relies on Simmias' recollecting from similar things to argue that Simmias must have possessed knowledge of the forms before birth. Moreover, Socrates says in the first stage that, when the knowledge is forgotten, this is "especially" recollecting. In the fourth stage Socrates argues that indeed we must have forgotten our knowledge of the forms, and so this is one of the especially clear cases of recollecting.

---

[6] Unfortunately there is no space to quote long sections of the argument here. I suggest reading it alongside my account.
[7] Ebert 2004, 213–15.
[8] Sedley 2006 emphasizes this often neglected feature of the argument.

5.3 THE FIRST STAGE – DIFFERENT TYPES OF RECOLLECTING: 73C–74A

Socrates here uses ordinary examples to make a number of claims about different types of recollecting, including the distinction between recollecting from dissimilar things and recollecting from similar things. (It is worth bearing in mind that the Greek word translated as "recollecting," *anamnēsis*, also covers cases that we would call "being reminded of something," that is, cases in which something might not be forgotten but simply brought back to mind by a prompt.) Many of Socrates' claims in this stage seem irrelevant to the ensuing argument, and interpreters have generally treated them as such.[9] I will argue, by contrast, that each is crucial for the later stages.

Throughout the argument, it is important to carefully consider the different epistemic terms that Socrates uses and how they are related. Let us begin by examining these terms in a passage that will be important in several ways for the subsequent argument:

> [The sufficient conditions passage] Now do we also agree that whenever (i) knowledge (ἐπιστήμη) comes in the following sort of way, there is recollecting? What do I mean? I'll tell you. Suppose someone (ii) sees or hears or has some other perception of one thing, and not only recognizes that thing, but also (iii) comes to have in mind (ἐννοεῖν) something else, (iv) which is the object not of the same knowledge but of a different one; aren't we to say that he recollected this second thing, the one which he had in mind? (73c5–d1)

First note that Socrates begins by saying that (i) he is considering cases where *knowledge* comes about in a certain way. This eliminates potential counterexamples where seeing one thing leads to fabricating something imaginary: in those cases, knowledge does not come about. In particular, Socrates considers cases where knowledge comes about from someone's (ii) perceiving something and recognizing it, and (iii) coming to have something else in mind, (iv) which is the object not of the same knowledge but of a different one (more literally: "of which the knowledge is not the same but different"). In general, it is easier to have something in mind (ἐννοεῖν) than to possess knowledge (ἐπιστήμη). Hence this description allows for the following possibility: I see Simmias, and that puts Cebes in mind; but I have not yet regained my knowledge of Cebes. At first my recollection is dim, and it takes a while to jog my memory and so properly know him again. All this is part of the process of recollecting. The standard translation of *anamnēsis* as "recollection" is potentially misleading, since recollection is normally thought of as the result of a process. But, in general, -*sis* endings indicate processes in Greek, and Socrates says here that, when knowledge *comes* (or *arises*, παραγίγνηται, 73c5–6) in a certain way, it is *anamnēsis* – drawing

---

[9] Bostock 1986, 62–3, is perhaps the most extreme version of such a view; he says that Plato's own presentation of the argument is confused.

attention to the process.¹⁰ Throughout the argument, Socrates normally uses the verb "recollect" in the present tense, allowing it to refer to an ongoing activity. There are two noteworthy exceptions. First, in the passage just quoted he uses the aorist to say that, when someone meets all of the conditions listed there, this person recollect*ed* something. This makes sense, since one of those conditions is that knowledge arises – the culmination of this process. Similarly, in the conclusion of stage two, Socrates says that, in Simmias' case, "recollecting has come about" (ἀνάμνησιν γεγονέναι, 74d2), using the perfect (i.e. completed) tense. Again this is appropriate, since Simmias already has knowledge of equality, and as such is no longer in the process of acquiring it. I will argue over the course of this chapter that recollecting is a process that begins when we first see equal things and have equality come to mind, and continues until we acquire knowledge of what equality is.

The remainder of my discussion of the first stage is structured by a new proposal that resolves a number of puzzles and makes it significantly easier to understand the third stage of the argument. Let me set up my proposal by asking why, in the passage quoted above, Socrates includes condition (iv) – that the thing recollected is the object not of the same knowledge, but of a different one. Condition (iv) is added to (iii) – that what is brought to mind is something else. This suggests that Socrates thinks that in some cases different things are the objects of the same knowledge, since otherwise (iv) would be redundant. This passage is often taken to offer a general account of recollecting, although it presents only sufficient conditions: Socrates says that, whenever (i)–(iv) happen, the person is recollecting – not that, whenever someone recollects, (i)–(iv) happen.¹¹ This is why I call it the "sufficient conditions" passage. Socrates goes on to say simply that this is "one sort of recollecting" (73e1). Although many scholars acknowledge that this is just one sort of recollecting, as far as I can tell all of them have thought that it is the relevant sort for Socrates' argument.

I propose that the sufficient conditions passage does not describe the sort of recollecting that is ultimately relevant; instead, it only describes what Socrates calls later in the first stage "recollecting from dissimilar things." In particular, I propose that condition (iv) – that what one has in mind is the object of a different knowledge – is required only in cases of recollecting from dissimilar things. When one recollects from similar things, the thing known is an object of the same knowledge as the thing perceived; this is the sort of recollecting relevant in the later stages of the argument. Before providing my evidence for this view, let me explain it.

If someone knows Simmias, Simmias is the primary object of knowledge, but this knowledge also allows one to judge accurately whether a poem about Simmias captures his spirit, whether something is a picture of Simmias, and, if it is, whether it is a good picture of him. But this knowledge does not provide any ability to judge

---

¹⁰ On the -*sis* ending, see e.g. *The Cambridge Grammar of Classical Greek*, 23.27.
¹¹ As is noted by Ackrill 1973, 182, Gallop 1975, ad loc., and Bostock 1986, 63.

whether someone is Cebes. Hence, Simmias is the object of one knowledge and Cebes of another, but Simmias and a picture of Simmias are objects of the same knowledge. In general, for Plato, the one who can judge an imitation well is the one who has knowledge of what it is imitating (*Cratylus* 439a–b; cf. *Ion* 536e–541e). My suggestion is that the sort of knowledge Socrates is discussing here in the *Phaedo* has a standard as its primary object; it can be used to judge accurately other things related to this standard – and, according to Socrates' terminology here, these things, too, will be objects of this same knowledge. Someone who knows Simmias has knowledge of a standard that can be used to judge properly poems about and pictures of Simmias, and so these are objects of this same knowledge. Socrates says that, when one sees Simmias and recalls Cebes, this is a case of recollecting from dissimilar things, whereas when one sees a picture of Simmias and recalls Simmias, this is a case of recollecting from similar things (73d–e). Obviously, by "similar" Socrates does not mean "has the most features in common," since Simmias and Cebes have more features in common than Simmias and his portrait – any two humans share more features than any person and a picture. My suggestion is that two things count as similar in the relevant sense if they are related to a single standard, and hence are objects of the same knowledge. Simmias and Cebes provide distinct standards, and so are objects of different knowledges.

It is sometimes considered an objection to Socrates' view that, in describing the painting as "of Simmias," Socrates is presupposing that one judge the picture in light of one's knowledge of Simmias, which would mean that it does not meet condition (iv): that what one has in mind is the object of a different knowledge.[12] Rather than being an objection, this is exactly Socrates' point: when one recollects from similar things, they are objects of the same knowledge. The mistake is assuming that (iv) applies to all cases of recollecting.

Socrates illustrates the "type of recollecting" described in the sufficient conditions passage entirely with examples of dissimilar things (73d). My suggestion is that, when he turns to recollecting from similar things (73e–74a), he is turning to a new type of recollecting.[13] Given that the same knowledge is needed to know Simmias and a picture of Simmias, Socrates expected Simmias to realize that what distinguishes these types of recollecting is whether or not they are objects of the same knowledge. Socrates began with recollecting from dissimilar things as a way to make clearer, through contrast, the sort of recollecting that ultimately interests him: that from similar things. While Socrates could have been clearer on this point, we can certainly make sense of the text this way, and there are good reasons to accept this reading: (a) it helps us understand the distinction between the two types of

---

[12] E.g. Ackrill 1973, Gallop 1975 at 73c4–d11.
[13] These need not be the only two types of recollecting or being reminded. As Gallop 1975 notes at 73c1–3, at the beginning of the argument Cebes jokingly asks to be *reminded* (73b) of Socrates' theory. This sort of being reminded does not involve directly perceiving anything – words can remind us of things, too.

5.3 The First Stage – Different Types of Recollecting: 73c–74a

recollecting, as I just described; (b) there is direct textual evidence for it; and (c) it helps us understand the principles Socrates goes on to articulate.

The direct evidence for this interpretation comes in the next stage, in Socrates' argument that Simmias has recollected equality. Socrates carefully gets Simmias to agree that they have knowledge of equality (74b, meeting condition (i) in the sufficient conditions passage), that they acquired this knowledge from seeing equal things (74b, meeting condition (ii)), and that these equal things are different from equality (74c, meeting condition (iii)). Socrates' last step in the argument is the following:

> "Yes, but it makes no difference," he said. "So long as upon seeing one thing you come from this sight to have in mind something else, whether similar or dissimilar, it is necessary that," he said, "recollecting has come about." (74c13–d2)

On the standard interpretation, Socrates thinks that the different knowledge condition (iv) applies to both types of recollecting. However, he never claims that equality and the equal sticks are objects of different knowledges (condition (iv)). On the standard interpretation, in stage one Socrates carefully sets up the conditions needed for recollecting and then, in stage two, shows that Simmias meets all but one of them. On my interpretation, condition (iv) only applies to recollecting from dissimilar things, and so he should not mention it here. Instead, if someone meets the other conditions mentioned in the sufficient conditions passage (i–iii), they have recollected, although this does not determine whether it is from similar or dissimilar things – which is exactly what Socrates says in the passage just quoted.

I have argued that, in cases of recollecting from similar things, the thing seen and the thing recollected are objects of the same knowledge. This knowledge has a primary object (e.g. Simmias), which serves as a standard that allows one to know other things (e.g. portraits of Simmias). This interpretation makes it much easier to understand the principle that Socrates articulates at the end of the first stage:

> [The falling short principle] But whenever it is from similar things that one recollects something, is it not necessary to have the following experience as well: that of having in mind whether or not in its similarity it in some way falls short of the thing one has recollected? (74a5–7)

It has puzzled interpreters why Socrates would be committed to such a strong claim: that one *necessarily* compares the thing perceived to the thing recollected.[14] However, once we recognize that similar things are grasped by the same knowledge, which has a single standard for judging, we can see why this necessarily happens. In recognizing each thing, one cannot help but judge how each relates to this standard: by setting the standard, by meeting the standard, or by falling short of it. Of course, when we see a picture of someone, we normally do not consciously ask ourselves whether or not the picture falls short of the person depicted. But Socrates need not think of this as a conscious thought; he simply needs that one in fact does form this

---

[14] E.g. Sedley 2006. Franklin 2005 faces significant difficulties explaining this passage.

judgment.¹⁵ When we see something as a picture of Simmias, we apply the standard one knows when one knows Simmias; given that we are doing this, we cannot help but have in mind whether or not it falls short of this standard.

What counts as "falling short" in this principle? Is it the ordinary way a portrait can be inaccurate? Or is it the way in which any representation could be thought of as necessarily falling short of what it represents – because, for example, a portrait of a person is not itself alive? If, as I argued, the falling short principle derives from the way in which knowledge brings with it a single standard, then Socrates need not choose between these options. In context, it is natural to think first of inaccurate portrayals. But there is no reason why the principle could not extend to all the ways in which something could fall short of a standard. This will turn out to be the relevant type of falling short in the third stage.

In sum, this interpretation clarifies recollecting from similar things, makes better sense of the argumentative structure at the end of stage two, and clarifies the falling short principle, which is not only puzzling in its own right, but also (I will argue) crucial in the third stage. This interpretation will prove fruitful in other ways in stage three.

On a separate note, I take Socrates' examples of knowledge here not to meet his own full requirements for knowledge that he articulates later. He is employing here an ordinary, intuitive notion of knowledge, according to which we know people and things such as Simmias and lyres. He uses such ordinary examples to illustrate the different types of recollecting. However, he provides no reason to think that everyone who knows Simmias can give an account of Simmias – which he says, in stage four, that knowledge requires (76b). Moreover, Socrates thinks that the philosopher loves and searches for *all* wisdom and truth, but only seeks knowledge of the forms; this strongly suggests that, if there is any genuine knowledge that is not of the forms, it depends on knowledge of them. But knowing Simmias does not require knowledge of the forms. I discuss this issue further in Section 5.6.

5.4 THE SECOND STAGE – EQUALITY, EQUAL STICKS, AND THE SOURCE OF OUR KNOWLEDGE: 74A–D

This stage has received the lion's share of scholarly attention, since it has been taken to provide the crux of an argument for the existence of Platonic forms.¹⁶ Socrates

---

¹⁵ For the idea that this is not a conscious thought, see Kelsey 2000, 96 ff. While I disagree with Kelsey on many details of how the argument works, our overall accounts are similar. Woolf 2000, 128–9, and Sedley 2006, 313–14, ask why Socrates says that one must judge whether *or not* the thing falls short. On my account, recollecting from similar things involves perceiving one thing and thinking of another of the same knowledge. Thus seeing Simmias and being reminded of his portrait would be a case of recollecting from similar things where the thing seen (Simmias) does not fall short of the thing recollected (his portrait).

¹⁶ See n. 1 above and Tuozzo 2018 for an extensive bibliography.

begins by asking Simmias whether there is an equal besides (*para*) the equal things, the equal itself. After Simmias says that there is and he knows what this is, Socrates asks where he got knowledge of it from, building toward the conclusion that Simmias meets conditions (i)–(iii) from the sufficient conditions passage. But then Socrates interrupts this line of questioning to consider the possibility that the equal sticks do not seem to Simmias different from equality; to address this possibility, Socrates argues that these equal things are not the same as the equal itself. Once this is finished, he resumes his argument that Simmias meets conditions (i)–(iii).

In what follows I first discuss the famous sub-argument that equality is different from equal things, then the argument that Simmias has recollected.

5.4.1 These Equal Things and the Equal Itself Are Different: 74a–c

Aristotle lies in the background of any discussion of why and how Plato distinguishes forms from ordinary objects. Before turning to the details of this sub-argument, it is worth reflecting on how Aristotle's concerns have led to a search for arguments for the existence of Platonic forms. Aristotle's discussions of Plato's forms are sometimes quite useful for understanding Plato's dialogues; for example, he frequently notes (*Metaphysics* A.6, M.4, M.9) that Plato's unusual commitments about perceptible objects are part of the reason why he thinks that forms are distinct from them – an observation that I think is basically right.[17] But we can also be easily misled by Aristotle if we rely on him to understand Plato's dialogues. Aristotle frequently distinguishes his own view of forms from Plato's by saying that Plato "separates" forms from perceptible things, whereas he does not (*Met.* A.6, A.9, M.4–5, M.9, and the *Peri ideōn*). Socrates does not use the term "separate" in connection with the forms in the *Phaedo*.[18] This idea, I contend, plays no role in the *Phaedo*'s reasons for viewing forms as different from ordinary objects.[19] Moreover, Aristotle focuses on what arguments there are for the existence of Platonic forms – that is, for the existence not simply of forms, but of forms that are separate from ordinary objects (*Met.* A.9, M.4, and the *Peri ideōn*). Throughout the *Phaedo*, Socrates treats the question of whether there are forms as distinct from the questions of why and how they are different from ordinary objects. In the first instance, he thinks that there are forms because he thinks that there are answers to "what is it?" questions (as argued in Section 3.6). But he does not ultimately rely on his (and his interlocutors')

---

[17] So also e.g. Irwin 1999, Kelsey 2000, Dancy 2004. As noted in the Introduction, Socrates tends to refer to ordinary objects using examples in the *Phaedo*; he does not refer to them as "perceptible things." Such terminology risks overemphasizing this feature of them.
[18] Plato uses the term "separation" in the *Parmenides*, though it is at least unclear whether he means by it what Aristotle means. See e.g. Fine 1984 and Meinwald 2016, 301–6.
[19] One might think that the forms are separate in the *Phaedo* because each is described as *auto kath' hauto*. But I argued (in Section 3.4) and will continue to argue (in Section 6.3) that this phrase does not refer to, or require, separation.

commitment to there being forms. In the autobiography, he famously lays out his method of hypothesis and adopts the hypotheses that there are forms, which serve as the causes of things (Section 9.8). This method provides a way to rationally defend the existence of forms, but is not a deductive argument for their existence.

Unlike the sort of arguments Aristotle is interested in, the recollecting argument does not contain an argument for forms having all of the features that make them "Platonic" or "transcendent;" instead, it draws attention to one feature that differentiates forms from ordinary objects: they do not change over time. But there are several other features – indeed, in my view, more fundamental ones – that differentiate forms and ordinary objects in the *Phaedo*, features that are not referred to here explicitly or implicitly. These come in the kinship argument, in the autobiography, and at the beginning of the final argument.

Let us return to the details of the argument. On the face of it, Socrates gets Simmias to agree to something – that equality is something else, besides these equal things (74a) – and then proceeds to argue for this same conclusion (74b–c). To explain why Socrates would do this, some scholars take him to be starting simply from an agreement to the existence of the things referred to by a correct answer to Socrates' "what is it?" question – that is, the existence of so-called "Socratic" forms – and then using this to argue for the existence of transcendent "Platonic" forms.[20] Socrates' language for forms here mirrors the language he used in the defense speech; as I argued in Section 3.6, this is the language that he also uses in the *Euthyphro*, *Protagoras*, and *Meno*, which are not committed to any sort of "transcendent" or "Platonic" forms. In the defense speech, Socrates asked Simmias whether forms are perceived by the senses, rather than assuming that they are not perceived (65d). From the defense speech, we can expect Simmias to think that forms are not perceived by the senses, in addition to their being the things referred to by correct answers to the "what is it?" question. But we should not expect Simmias to think significantly more about them than this. Thus I agree with those who think that we are starting with "Socratic" forms – or at least something close to them.

What, then, is Socrates trying to establish, given that Simmias has agreed to the existence of Socratic forms? I suggest a relatively modest explanation. Socrates begins by simply clarifying what he means when talking about "an equal" (τι... ἴσον, 74a9–10): he does not simply mean something that is equal (a very natural way to understand the Greek) but rather the thing one is searching for when asking, "what is the equal?" (cf. 65d–e). Simmias agrees that this equal is different from ordinary equal things, but in doing so he simply clarifies what Socrates is referring to. But in order for Simmias to be recollecting, it is crucial that he meet condition (iii) in the sufficient conditions passage: that the thing perceived is different from what is in mind. Socrates does not want simply to rely on Simmias' naïve

---

[20] So Kelsey 2000 and Dimas 2003. Penner 1987 thinks that Socrates is starting from Socratic forms but not going to Platonic ones.

5.4 The Second Stage – The Source of Our Knowledge: 74a–d

acceptance of this, and so argues for it. This makes sense of how Socrates introduces this sub-argument: "Or doesn't it seem different to you? Consider it in this way *as well* (καί)" (74b6–7, emphasis added). Socrates is providing an additional way of considering it, one that confirms that they are different.[21] This interpretation allows that, in providing this argument, Socrates is setting up claims that he will need in the next stage of the argument, even if they are not part of his explicit conclusion. In particular, when Socrates says in the next stage that the equal sticks and stones are inferior to, fall short of, and want to be like equality itself (74d–75b), it is reasonable to think that this stage can help us understand this claim, even if its explicit goal is not to argue for it.

We turn, then, to the key step in Socrates' argument that they are different. Unfortunately our manuscript traditions divide here, offering two different texts. Almost all English translations follow the text of the OCT edition, which can be translated as follows:

> Don't equal stones and sticks sometimes, while being the same ones, seem equal *to one*, but not *to another*? (74b7–9, emphasis added)
> ἆρ' οὐ λίθοι μὲν ἴσοι καὶ ξύλα ἐνίοτε ταὐτὰ ὄντα τῷ μὲν ἴσα φαίνεται, τῷ δ' οὔ;

However, there are good reasons to accept the other main manuscript reading, which is adopted by recent French, German, and Italian translations:

> Don't equal stones and sticks sometimes, while being the same ones, seem *at one time* equal, *at another time* not? (74b7–9, emphasis added)
> ἆρ' οὐ λίθοι μὲν ἴσοι καὶ ξύλα ἐνίοτε ταὐτὰ ὄντα *τότε* μὲν ἴσα φαίνεται, *τότε* δ' οὔ;

David Sedley has recently argued at length in favor of this latter reading, as Verdenius had earlier in his textual notes; it is the reading followed in the recent Sedley and Long translation.[22] It has somewhat better support among the manuscripts (being supported by two families of manuscript, instead of one).[23] I will offer here a brief version of Sedley's argument, which I accept. The first reading requires one to ask what it means for equal sticks and stones to seem equal "to one" (τῷ μέν) but not "to another" (τῷ δέ). Three different ways are typically considered. These expressions are sometimes understood as meaning equal in one respect, but not in another respect. However, the use of the expression "to one" or "to another" (in the neuter) to indicate a respect seems to have no parallel elsewhere in Greek literature. The second option is that the phrase means equal to one thing (e.g. another stick), but not to another (e.g. a stone). But it is difficult to see how this is relevant.

---

[21] So Franklin 2005, 304.
[22] Verdenius 1958, Sedley 2007, followed by Tuozzo 2018. Verdenius 1958 (the most extensive textual notes on the dialogue) argues that this is the *lectio difficilior*. Such a reading is also found in Dixsaut 1991, Ebert 2004, and Trabattoni 2011 ad loc.
[23] Sedley 2007, n. 25. It is in the group of manuscripts Duke et al. 1995 identify as T and δ, whereas the other reading is in their β manuscripts.

Socrates' next step is to contrast these equal stones and sticks with equality itself, but he does not say what equality itself is equal to. For an appropriate contrast between the equal sticks and equality itself, such a reading would seem to require that, unlike the equal sticks, equality itself is, somehow, not unequal to anything – a strange idea, and not a topic that the dialogue examines. The final – and most likely – option is that it would mean "seems equal to one person, but not to another person." But then the next step in Socrates' argument does not work: he asks whether it seems *to Simmias* that equality is ever not inequality. But, if the point were about whether equal sticks seem different to different people, he should ask whether equality seems *to anyone* to be inequality. By contrast, if we follow the other manuscript tradition, then Socrates' next step draws an appropriate contrast, involving time: unlike a pair of equal sticks, which *sometimes* seem equal and at *other times* seem the opposite, equality *never* seems to be the opposite of what it is.[24]

In what follows, I take this to be the correct manuscript tradition to follow, and turn to how the argument works. On the face of it, Socrates infers from its seeming (φαίνεται) that two things are different to their being different – which in general, of course, is a faulty inference. It would be analogous to the following:

A. The highest mountain has seemed at one time to be Everest, at another time not to be.
B. But Everest has never seemed not to be Everest.
C. Therefore, the highest mountain is not Everest.[25]

There are three basic strategies for responding to this objection:

(1) Simply accept that Socrates is making an invalid inference, but note that it is a subtle point and an easy mistake to make.[26]
(2) Argue that the language of "seeming" is crucial to the argument, but that Socrates is talking about a special sort of seeming or about objects being of a sort to seem in a certain way, so the objection does not apply.[27]
(3) Argue that when Socrates asks Simmias how things seem to him, this is a way of asking him how things in fact are, and so the language of "seeming" is not crucial to the argument.[28]

---

[24] I have nothing new to say about Socrates' mention of "the equals themselves" at 74c1. Given that he immediately draws his conclusions only about equality itself and never mentions the equals themselves again, I agree with most interpreters that this must be a variant way to refer to equality itself. For a reasonable discussion, see Sedley 2007, 82–4. If the phrase is a variant way of referring to equality itself, the equals themselves may never seem unequal because they are entirely equal. For self-predication in this argument, see Subsection 5.5.2.
[25] Example from Sedley 2007. I discuss the translation of φαίνεται in what follows.
[26] E.g. Penner 1987, Sedley 2007.
[27] E.g. White 1992, Tuozzo 2018.
[28] This is the most common sort of interpretation. E.g. Irwin 1999, Kelsey 2000.

5.4 The Second Stage – The Source of Our Knowledge: 74a–d

Both type (1) and (2) interpretations have a significant problem explaining the specific way in which Socrates introduces the language of "seeming" into the argument. Immediately before the famous sentence about the sticks' seeming different, Socrates says:

> Upon seeing that either sticks or stones or some other things were equal, wasn't it from them that we came to have it [equality] in mind, different as it is from them? Or doesn't it seem different to you? Consider it this way as well. (74b5–7)

Socrates clearly means "Or doesn't it seem different to you?" as an alternative to their *being* different. But if "seems" added something substantive to the claim, these would not be genuine alternatives. Moreover, Socrates concludes that these equal things and the equal itself are not the same (74c), which clearly is supposed to answer the question he asks here, whether they *seem* different. Also revealing is Simmias' response to Socrates' conclusion that they are not the same: "not at all, it seems to me" (οὐδαμῶς μοι φαίνεται, 74c6). After Socrates has simply asserted the conclusion, Simmias adds that it seems so to him. Socrates goes on to rely on their actually being different, not merely seeming so. Socrates' and Simmias' adding and dropping the language of "seeming" raises a significant problem for the type (1) and type (2) interpretations. Rather than engage further with the details of such accounts, my strategy will be to develop a type (3) interpretation and allow it to be evaluated on its own merits. On such readings, Socrates' argument works entirely with the equal sticks' in fact being one way, whereas equality itself is relevantly different.

But why, then, put the argument in terms of how things seem (φαίνεται) to Simmias? First, note that, if I ask you whether it seems to you that it is going to rain, you typically consult the sky (or your weather app), not your internal mental states. Asking whether it seems to you that x is often simply a way of asking you to form a judgment about x.[29] Suppose that I ask you if it seems that *p*, and you agree, and if it seems that if *p* then *q*, and you agree, and then I conclude that *q*. It would be perverse to take this as a non-sequitur; we see perfectly well the valid inference, although of course *q* does not follow from the seemings, but rather from the propositions themselves. By putting his questions in terms of how things seem, Socrates asks Simmias to form his own judgments. This may be to ensure that Simmias is not simply accepting on Socrates' authority that equality is different from equal sticks or equal stones. Moreover, doing this gets Simmias to reflect on how equal things and equality manifest themselves to him, which will be important in the third stage, where Socrates asks Simmias whether he has had certain experiences of them.

More importantly, the type (3) interpretation simply makes good sense of Socrates' claim about the sticks. The key point is that when we call a pair of sticks

---

[29] For a similar idea, see Kelsey 2000, 104, n. 24. It is inspired, of course, by Wittgenstein's reflections on transparency.

"equal" we are not saying that they are eternally equal, we are simply saying that right now they are equal. Hence it is sometimes the case – indeed, it is typically the case – that sticks that are equal at one time are unequal at another. We could take the initial "sometimes" in the sentence ("Don't equal stones and sticks sometimes...") to mean "in some cases." Alternatively, it could refer to actual temporal stretches; it would then be within these stretches that at one time the sticks are equal and at another time unequal. Either way, it is not that sticks merely seem this way. When, for example, one of the sticks gets worn away, it is no longer equal to the other. It would be strange for Socrates to ask whether they merely appear this way without also thinking that they genuinely are so.

When we take the other manuscript reading and interpret Socrates as making a point about different observers, it makes sense to understand him as asking how things merely seem to these observers. But, when we take the temporal manuscript reading, it is a straightforward fact that sometimes sticks that are now equal have been, or will be, unequal.[30] Tuozzo is the only scholar I am aware of who has discussed this interpretation, having received this suggestion from an anonymous reviewer.[31] He rejects it on the grounds that it cannot explain why Socrates says that "sometimes the equal sticks, *while being the same things* (ταὐτὰ ὄντα), seem equal to one..." (emphasis added). Tuozzo seems to think that this is naturally understood as meaning that the sticks continue to be equal. But for equal sticks to be the same things is for them to continue to be sticks, not equal. If you take two equal sticks and sand one of them down a bit, they are not thereby different things. Socrates includes the phrase "while being the same sticks" (ταὐτὰ ὄντα) – two short words in Greek – to clarify that he is not considering different sets of sticks or destroyed sticks, but rather the very same sticks, changed with respect to whether they are equal.

Type (3) interpretations are sometimes thought to gain some further plausibility, given an ambiguity in the Greek term that I have translated as "seems" (*phainetai*). When *phainetai* takes a participle as a complement, it normally means something like "manifestly is the case," whereas with an infinitive as complement it simply means "appears" (whether correctly or incorrectly). In our passage the complement is left off, leaving it ambiguous. Moreover, in the lover of sights and sounds argument in the *Republic*, this same verb again is used without a complement, and there Socrates describes the same things as seeming both beautiful and ugly, or as doubles and halves, or as big and small, and then drops the "seeming" language and moves directly to saying that they are both beautiful and ugly, doubles and halves, and so on and are no more one than the other (479a–b). At a minimum, this

---

[30] Hence I do not understand why Sedley 2007 accepts the temporal manuscript tradition and rejects a type (3) reading on the grounds that, in describing the sticks as "equal sticks," Socrates is attributing "straightforward equality" to them. At most, calling them "equal sticks" attributes straightforward equality to them *right now*.

[31] Tuozzo 2018, 5, n. 12. (I was not the reviewer.)

5.4 The Second Stage – The Source of Our Knowledge: 74a–d

shows that sometimes Plato has Socrates move from claims about how things seem (*phainesthai*) to claims about how they are.

In thinking through the lack of a verb to complement *phainetai* in our argument, it is important to note that in the next stage of the argument *phainetai* is used with an infinitive.

> "Well then," he said, "do we experience something like the following concerning what happens in the case of sticks and, more generally, the equal things we just mentioned? Do they seem to us to be equal in this way, just as the what-is-equal itself? (ἆρα φαίνεται ἡμῖν οὕτως ἴσα εἶναι ὥσπερ αὐτὸ τὸ ὃ ἔστιν ἴσον) Or do they in some way fall short of it in being like the equal? (ἢ ἐνδεῖ τι ἐκείνου τῷ τοιοῦτον εἶναι οἷον τὸ ἴσον) Or in no way?' (ἢ οὐδέν;) (74d4–7)

Note, first, that Socrates asks Simmias about whether they have had a certain experience, and then he asks Simmias whether things seem a certain way to them. This fits with my suggestion that at least part of the reason Socrates asks about how things *seem* is in order to draw attention to the experience of judging the sticks as falling short. Second, note that Socrates is asking a new question here, about the *way* in which these two things are equal; perhaps in the previous stage "*phainesthai*" was meant as if with a participle, although it takes an infinitive here. But, more importantly, it is difficult to understand Socrates in the passage just quoted as asking about how things *merely* seem to Simmias. If he were, Socrates would again be offering a false choice, since the sticks could *merely seem* equal in the same way as the equal itself while at the same time in fact falling short in how they are equal. The broader context makes clear that Socrates and Simmias think the sticks genuinely fall short, not merely that they seem to do so. So, even with the infinitive, Socrates is asking Simmias about what, in Simmias' judgment, is in fact the case, not for a report on Simmias' mental state. Of course, defenders of type (1) or (2) interpretations could claim that merely appearing unequal *is* a way of falling short in how something is like the equal, but I have yet to see a satisfying account of why that would be.[32] It is, at a minimum, much easier to understand Socrates' question in this passage if he is simply asking Simmias how he thinks things are.

If (as I have argued) the manuscript reading with temporal markers is correct, there is an interesting progression over the dialogue. In the next argument – the kinship argument – Socrates says that the many equal things never hold *kata* the same things (κατὰ ταὐτὰ ἔχει, 78e2). I will argue that this means that each ordinary equal thing is equal *kata* some things and unequal *kata* other things. (The meaning of "*kata*" here will turn out to be a very tricky issue, but is not crucial for my present point.[33]) Then

---

[32] Svavarsson 2009, 70, offers such an account of how they fall short, but does not explain why the sticks are not the same as equality *in the way in which they are equal*. I discuss this aspect of the passage further in Subsection 5.5.2.

[33] In brief, I argue in Chapter 6 that, if x is *f kata* y, then y is internal to or belongs to x and y determines the manner in which x is *f*.

in the lead-up to the final argument Socrates describes how the same person can be large *pros* (in relation to) one thing while small *pros* another (102b–d). Thus – to put it in modern scholarly language – ordinary things suffer three different types of "compresence of opposites" in the *Phaedo*: at different times (recollecting argument), *kata* different things (kinship argument), and *pros* different things (final argument). And this fits perfectly with a principle that Socrates famously articulates in the *Republic*: "It is clear that the same thing will not be willing to do or undergo opposites, at least *kata* the same thing, in relation to the same thing, and at the same time" (436b8–9). Ordinary objects are not willing to do this, but they will undergo opposites *kata* different things, or *pros* different things, or at different times, as the *Phaedo* illustrates. By contrast, forms do not suffer opposites in any of these three ways.

Thus the many interpreters who have seen here an important argument about the difference between forms and ordinary objects are right. But Socrates has already distinguished forms from ordinary objects earlier, in the defense speech, and will continue to bring out their differences – and, I will argue, their more fundamental differences – in later parts of the dialogue. The mistake is thinking that Socrates is either talking about Platonic forms – with all of Plato's commitments about them taken together – or not. Instead, Socrates builds up several claims about the forms over the course of the dialogue.

What I have said thus far is compatible with a claim made by Gosling 1965 and widely accepted since then: that, since Socrates describes the sticks as "equal sticks," he must think of them as genuinely equal rather than somehow deficiently equal. My account can allow that they are equal when he calls them equal, but at some other time they are not equal, and so they are equal at one time, but not at another. However, it is worth noting that, in the other two places where compresence of opposites arises in the *Phaedo*, Socrates provides an account of what it means to attribute a predicate such as "equal" to an ordinary object, and this account allows that such things are simultaneously equal and unequal or large and small. This suggests that they can be deficiently equal, *pace* Gosling. The relevant passage in the kinship argument (78d–e) is difficult, but the passage at the beginning of the final argument is easier and suffices for our purposes. Socrates says there that the things other than the forms are "named after" the forms (102b); then he explains how Simmias can be called both "small" and "large" at the same time, because he is large in relation to one thing and small in relation to another (102b–c). Socrates says that "large thing" is appropriately applied to Simmias, although he is also, at the same time, a small thing. In retrospect, then, in describing the sticks or stones as "equal" in the recollecting argument, Socrates could allow that they are also unequal, even though they are rightly called equal.

This will need to suffice for this most famous part of the recollecting argument. One could reject my reading of this subsection and accept my overall reading of the argument, since, for the purposes of the overall argument, Socrates needs only to establish here that equality is different from the equal things that prompted their recollecting.

5.4.2 *Simmias Has Recollected: 74b–d*

I discussed at the end of Section 5.3 how the second stage aims to show that Simmias meets conditions (i)–(iii) in the sufficient conditions passage and thus that recollecting has come about. Before Socrates introduced the sub-argument that equal sticks are different from equality itself, Simmias said that he and Socrates know equality itself (74b), thus meeting condition (i). Socrates then began asking Simmias whether his knowledge of equality came from seeing sticks and stones, but he interrupted this line of questioning to ask whether Simmias thought the equal sticks are different from equality itself, so that they would meet condition (ii). After finishing this sub-argument, Simmias agrees that his knowledge came to be from seeing such things (74c), meeting condition (iii). Socrates then draws the conclusion that Simmias is recollecting, regardless of whether these things are similar. Again, simply concluding that Simmias has recollected is not yet to conclude that he has knowledge of the forms from before birth, or that this knowledge has been forgotten, or that learning is recollecting.

In the second stage, as in the first, Socrates treats the state of having "knowledge" (*epistēmē*) as a more difficult state to be in than that of simply "having [something] in mind" (*ennoein*). Simmias' knowledge ultimately arises from an initial event of seeing equal sticks and having equality come to mind. This process of seeing equal things and having equality come to mind seems immediate, like seeing a lyre and immediately having this bring to mind one's lover.[34] For Socrates, learning – that is, acquiring genuine knowledge – is a long process. Since his goal is to show that learning is recollecting, he must think that recollecting is a long process. Thus there are two interrelated mental processes here: (a) upon seeing one thing, having another thing in mind; and (b) the final acquisition of knowledge, which is the culmination of recollecting.[35] As noted earlier, it is important for maintaining consistency with Socrates' claims, both earlier and later in the dialogue, that one cannot acquire knowledge using the senses. These claims are consistent so long as the time when one first sees equal things is precisely when one is put in mind of equality, but this initial putting in mind is not part of the inquiry proper.[36] Once one has it in mind, one can inquire into it. As Socrates says in the defense speech (65c–66a), in the kinship argument (79c), and in the return to the defense (83a–b),

---

[34] Indeed, in the case of first seeing equal things, equality must be in mind in order to judge these things as equal. Thus, equality comes to mind exactly when one first sees the equal things as equal.
[35] Similarly, in the *Meno* the slave is said to be recollecting in order (82e), supposedly because he is engaged in a process that would ultimately lead to knowledge (85c–e).
[36] So Osborne 1995, 231, Franklin 2005.

inquiry through the senses confuses, harms reasoning, and does not lead to truth; only investigating with the soul itself through itself (αὐτὴν καθ' αὑτήν), making no use of the senses, leads to truth and wisdom.

5.5 THE THIRD STAGE – KNOWING BEFORE SENSING, AND SO BEFORE BIRTH: 74D–75C

This is the heart of the argument. Socrates argues here that they must have had their knowledge of equality since before birth. Before diving into the details, we should take stock. In stage one, Socrates distinguished recollecting from similar things from recollecting from dissimilar things and articulated the falling short principle, which applies to recollecting from similar things. In stage two, he argued that Simmias meets sufficient conditions for recollecting equality. We certainly should expect Socrates to use these claims – if not directly, at least indirectly. Nonetheless, almost no reconstructions of the argument rely on both the falling short principle and Simmias' having recollected; many rely on neither of them.[37] I will argue that in the third stage Socrates relies on Simmias' recollecting – specifically, on his recollecting a similar thing – in order to apply the falling short principle.

I again divide my discussion into two subsections. First, I work through the steps of the argument without discussing why Socrates and Simmias think that the equal sticks fall short of equality in how they are equal; afterwards I address this tricky question, which requires discussing so-called self-predication.

5.5.1 *The Overall Argument of the Third Stage*

Once again, understanding the argument requires addressing a much-disputed question: who is the "we" referred to in the crucial first step of stage three?

> "Do we experience something like the following concerning what happens in the case of sticks and, more generally, the equal things we just mentioned? Do they seem to us to be equal in this way, just as the what-is-equal itself? Or do they in some way fall short of it in being like the equal? Or in no way?"
> "They fall *far* short," said Simmias. (74d4–8)

One option is to understand the "we" as only designating a select group, and then to argue that only these people – for example, philosophers – recollect.[38] Another is that the "we" includes everyone and describes a universal human phenomenon.[39] It certainly is easier to understand Socrates' claim if he means to ascribe it only to a select group, since this is not an idea that most people would articulate. Given the

---

[37] Sedley 2006 is an important exception.
[38] This view is most famously defended by Scott 1995. Bedu-Addo 1991 offers a very different defense for it. Sedley 2006 offers a "moderate" form of such a view.
[39] So e.g. Gulley 1963, Ackrill 1973, and Kelsey 2000.

5.5 The Third Stage – Knowing before Sensing, and so before Birth: 74d–75c

desideratum that Socrates' argument rely on the results of the first two stages, I think the "we" must refer to the "we" that came earlier, in the second stage: the "we" who know what equality is. That Simmias knows equality is crucial for the stage-two argument that he has recollected (since it shows that he meets condition (i) in the sufficient conditions passage). The stage-two argument would work equally well for anyone with knowledge of equality, and so, given their agreement that Socrates also has knowledge, Socrates too has recollected. Hence Socrates can say here, in stage three, that "we" have had this experience – meaning Socrates and Simmias.

Nonetheless, Socrates' ultimate conclusion is not restricted to philosophers or some other select subgroup. In the fourth stage, after Simmias says that perhaps no one knows any of the forms, Socrates asks Simmias if *everyone* recollects what they once learned, and Simmias says "necessarily" (76c5). This has been thought to be a problematic claim for Socrates to make, since most people do not have knowledge. But, once we recognize that recollecting is an extended process, it becomes clear that everyone can be recollect*ing* even if few people have successfully recollect*ed*. Hence, by the end of the argument, recollecting is not limited to a select group.[40] This explains why Socrates thinks it is a straightforward conclusion that the soul exists before birth; there is no reason to worry that he has only shown that some subgroup's souls preexist.

Thus we need to explain why, at the beginning of stage three, Socrates' claims are restricted to a limited "us" – the ones shown in stage two to recollect – but later are broadened to include everyone. In the first step, quoted at the beginning of this subsection, Simmias agrees that they experience the sticks as falling short. I discuss this step in the next subsection. Soon after, Simmias agrees that equal things resemble equality itself (74e). Resemblance is a type of similarity, the type found in Socrates' example of recollecting Simmias when seeing a painting of him (73e). We can understand why they think that the equal sticks are similar to equality itself if we accept my account of recollecting from similar things (see Section 5.3). According to this account, things are (relevantly) similar when they are objects of the same knowledge; such things are judged by a single standard. The knowledge needed to identify something as a picture of Simmias simply is the knowledge of Simmias. The same is true for equal things and equality.[41] When we study equality, we are studying what it would be for things to be equal – that is, the standard things must meet to be equal. The knowledge of a form of *f*-ness is the knowledge that allows one to judge accurately whether a given thing is *f* or not (cf. *Euthyphro* 6d–e).

---

[40] Scott 1995, 64–5, argues that whatever Socrates means by saying that everyone recollects at 76c, it must be equivalent to the second option at 76a: that learning is recollecting. But Socrates articulates that option at 76a because this is the thesis he has explicitly set out to show (73b). The fact that he does not mention at 76a that everyone recollects does not mean that he is not committed to this. At 76c he is building to a different conclusion, that everyone's soul exists before birth. This is why he claims there that everyone recollects.

[41] For a similar view, see Dimas 2003, 210.

More generally, there is not a separate type of knowledge specific to the perceptible world – the forms are the standard for making good judgments about ordinary, perceptible objects. Hence the knowledge needed to judge properly that ordinary things are equal is the knowledge of equality. In getting Simmias to see that he experiences the equal sticks as falling short of equality, Socrates is getting Simmias to see that he applies the standard of equality to the equal sticks, and so has recollected from similar things.

Socrates goes on to replace the term "falling short" with "inferior to," "seeking to be like," and "yearning to be like" (74d–75b). I suspect one reason for this varied vocabulary is to clarify what sort of relationship is meant – one in which the sticks are naturally judged by the standard of equality, even though they fall short of it. But another point, I take it, is that there is no existing terminology for what Socrates is trying to describe: this experience of seeing something and judging that it does not fully meet the standard by which it should be judged.

The other crucial step in stage three is the following:

> [The prior knowledge principle] Now do we agree that whenever someone, upon seeing something, has in mind, "What I am now seeing wants to be like something else among the things that are, but falls short and can't be like it, and instead is inferior," the person who has this in mind must presumably have actually known beforehand the thing that he says it resembles but falls short of? (74d9–e4)

In order to recognize that this picture of Simmias falls short of Simmias, I must have at some point known who he is. And in order to recognize that these equal things fall short of equality, I must have previously known equality. Note that Socrates does not say that, as soon as one has this thing in mind, one's knowledge comes back. Instead, the principle can allow for cases analogous to seeing a picture of someone you had not seen in a long time and thinking: "somehow this picture isn't quite right." Forming such a judgment is a sign that you previously knew the person. Your dim recollection allows you to judge that the picture is flawed.[42] Similarly, you must at one point have had an accurate understanding of equality, given your ability to judge that equal sticks are not equal in the way in which equality itself is, but at first it could be a dim recollection.

I noted earlier that having something in mind (*ennoein*) requires less than knowing something. But can I have something in mind that turns out to be false? If so, there would be good reason to doubt the prior knowledge principle: to doubt that, if you have in mind that x falls short of y, you must have previously known y. I might think that a painting falls short of a Rembrandt and simply be wrong, since I'm no Rembrandt expert. I suggest, then, that "having in mind" is a way of accurately grasping how things are (i.e. it is factive), although it does not require

---

[42] For a similar view, see Dimas 2003, 209–10. For a similar idea for recollection in the *Meno*, see Ebrey 2014a, 17–20.

an account of why they are this way. Socrates, then, is saying that, when I accurately grasp that x falls short of y, I must have previously known y.

Socrates concludes that they must have known the equal "before we first had in mind, upon seeing equal things, that all these are seeking to be like the equal, but fall short of it" (74e9–75a2). This follows from combining two claims from the third stage: (i) the prior knowledge principle and (ii) Simmias' agreement that they have experienced the equal things as falling short. But this says nothing about when they first brought this to mind. The next steps in Socrates' argument are meant to pull back when one must have first had knowledge to the time before birth (75a–c). He notes that we have been perceiving since birth. But how exactly does that deliver the conclusion that we knew the equal before birth? Socrates has two principles that could help: the falling short principle, articulated at the end of stage one, and the prior knowledge principle, articulated earlier in the current, third stage. But, on most interpretations, it is difficult to see why they are applicable when someone first perceives something. The prior knowledge principle applies only when someone judges that "what I am now seeing wants to be like something else among the things that are." The falling short principle applies only when someone is recollecting from similar things.

Once we recognize that recollecting is an extended process and that recollecting equality upon seeing equal sticks is a case of recollecting from similar things, we can see how these principles are applicable. When Simmias first, upon seeing ordinary equal objects, has equality in mind, he is beginning to recollect from similar things. Since this is a case of recollecting from similar things, we can apply the falling short principle. By this principle, he will judge whether the sticks fall short. Since they do fall short (as explained in the next subsection), by the prior knowledge principle, he must have had knowledge of equality before having them in mind.[43] To draw the conclusion that Simmias had knowledge before birth, we do not need to answer when Simmias first had equality in mind. Suppose that it was not until he was twenty; nonetheless, by this argument, he must have had knowledge of equality before he first had it in mind. Given that he had not even had equality in mind between birth and the age of twenty, he clearly could not have had knowledge of it during this time. But, by this argument, he did know about it some time before the age of twenty. Hence he must have known it before he was born.

While the argument works even if Simmias first had equality in mind as an adult, there are good reasons to doubt that this is what Socrates is thinking, and recognizing this strengthens his argument. I argued in stage two that, when Socrates refers to equality, he is not speaking specifically about "Platonic" forms. Instead, as he says

---

[43] Scott 1995, 63, also relies on the falling short principle to argue that everyone has knowledge before birth. However, as Dimas 2003, 192, points out, this principle applies only to people who are recollecting, and the main idea behind Scott's interpretation is that only philosophers recollect.

here in stage three, he is speaking about what one is searching for when one asks the "what is it?" question about equality (75c–d). This is the question he asks about courage, virtue, and such things. It would be very strange to think that Socrates' interlocutors had never even had a thought about courage or virtue until he asked them about it. Instead, I take it that, for Socrates, when one thinks that someone is courageous, this is simply to think that this person has courage – and so, whenever one thinks that someone is courageous, one is thinking of courage. If this is right, upon seeng sticks as equal, one will have equality in mind. This means that we can run the argument as soon as Simmias first sees sticks as equal. As soon as he does so, he must have judged whether or not they fall short of the standard set by equality; since they do, he must have known equality before having had this in mind. Supposedly Socrates does not think that Simmias judged this consciously. But, of course, most people do not judge consciously that portraits fall short of their subjects, but Socrates nonetheless thinks that they necessarily judge this. Again, we need not decide when this first happens. Suppose that a baby first sees two objects as equal when she is six months old and so she first has equality in mind then. Then, by the prior knowledge principle, this baby must have had this knowledge before she first had equality in mind. Given that she did not even have equality in mind for the first six months of her life, she certainly did not know it then. And so she must have had knowledge of it before she was born.

Once we recognize that having equality in mind is a perfectly normal thing that people do from a young age and that Simmias has been recollecting since that age, it is hard to deny that everyone else is recollecting too, even if they have not yet acquired knowledge, and so have not yet recollect*ed*. Suppose that Apollodorus does not know what equality is, and thus does not meet sufficient condition (i) for having recollected. If he were to learn what it is – given that recollecting is an extended process that starts with his perceiving equal things – it would turn out that he had been recollecting ever since he first saw equal things at a young age and had equality in mind. Given this, it is natural to think he has been in the process of recollecting the whole time, even if he never acquires knowledge. This interpretation explains why Socrates says in the fourth stage that everyone is recollecting what they once knew (76c), which in turn explains why the argument is supposed to show that *all* souls exist before birth.

At the end of the third stage, Socrates says that his "present argument" is not simply about the equal but about all the forms. As in the defense speech and in stage two of the argument, Socrates does not use the term "form" here but rather expressions he used earlier: "the f" and "the f itself" (see Section 3.6). In the defense speech, he identified these with what each thing is (65d–e); here he uses the metalinguistic expression "everything to which we attach the label 'what it is' both when asking our questions and when giving our answers" (75d2–4). This terminology is perhaps an innovation, but it clearly describes what Socrates seeks in the Socratic dialogues. Similarly, at the end of the argument he refers to the forms as "those things that we always talk about" (76d7–8) – another clear sign that Socrates does not mean to refer to anything new. In the recollecting argument, he draws attention to features of the forms that are not discussed in the Socratic dialogues: they do not change over time and are brought to mind whenever we perceive things. Similarly, in the defense speech Socrates asks Simmias whether he has ever seen things like beauty and the good (65d) – a type of question he does not ask in the Socratic dialogues. The recollecting argument makes clear that, while they are not perceptible, forms are crucially involved in perception; indeed, in this life it is because of perception that we first have them in mind. Once they are in mind, we can begin to inquire into them.

5.5.2 Self-Predication and the Equal Sticks Falling Very Short

Let us return to the first step of the stage-three argument and examine why, when Socrates and Simmias compare the equal sticks to equality itself, they experience the sticks as falling short. Addressing this requires stepping into the thorny issue that scholars typically call "self-predication," that is, how to understand sentences in Plato of the form "equality is equal" or "justice is just." Consider again Socrates' initial question about whether the equal sticks fall short:

> Do they seem to us to be equal in this way, just as the what-is-equal itself (αὐτὸ τὸ ὅ ἔστιν ἴσον)? Or do they in some way fall short of it in being like the equal? Or in no way? (74d5–7)

The first question presupposes that there is a way in which equality is equal. The second presupposes that we can compare the way in which equality is equal with the way in which equal things are equal. Both presuppositions are typically overlooked in the secondary literature, which tends to talk simply of the equal sticks as "falling short." Given these presuppositions, not only is it the case that "equality is equal," but also "is equal" here cannot have the sort of ambiguity "is a bank" has. It makes no sense to ask whether the northern shore of the Thames is a bigger bank than J. P. Morgan, since "bank" means two entirely different things here, and so there is no way to compare them. Even when different meanings of a term are related to one another, in most cases such comparisons do not make sense: which is healthier, an apple or my brother? Socrates thinks that we can compare how equal equality is with how equal the equal sticks are, and that one of them is clearly inferior to the other.[44]

---

[44] I do not see how several interpretations of self-predication can explain this comparison. For example, Nehamas in several articles (e.g. Nehamas 1975, 1979) suggests that, when Socrates says that "equality is equal," "is equal" means "is what it is to be equal." But he also accepts Gosling's thought that ordinary equal things are genuinely equal. What, then, on this account, does it mean to compare equality's way of being equal (namely: equality is what it is to be equal) to the equal sticks' way of being equal? This seems like comparing how an apple is healthy to how my brother is.

As for why Socrates thinks that self-predication is obvious, this is, in my view, beyond the scope of this book.[45] But that he not only is committed to it but takes it to be obvious that *f*-ness is most clearly *f* is well attested across the dialogues, including some that are standardly taken to have been written before the *Phaedo* and that make no reference to "Platonic" forms, such as the *Protagoras* (330c–e). Note that "the equal," "the equal itself," and "an equal itself" are particularly apt names for equality given self-predication, since then equality is in fact equal.[46]

How do Socrates and Simmias use equality to judge whether sticks are equal? Given that equality is equal and that the sticks fall short of equality in how they are equal, it seems likely that, when one uses equality to judge sticks as equal, one compares how the sticks are equal with how equality itself is equal. Equality is the yardstick for judging whether things are equal. This would explain why Socrates assumes that Simmias has compared the way the sticks are equal with the way equality itself is – because this is exactly the comparison involved in judging the sticks to be equal in the first place. This also fits with the idea that forms are paradigms that we look to in judging whether something is *f* or in judging whether something is a good *f* (e.g. *Euthyphro* 6e, *Gorgias* 503d–504a, *Cratylus* 389b, *Republic* 484c–d, *Timaeus* 28a–b). Evidence that equality serves as the standard by being (perfectly) equal is that, after saying that the equal sticks yearn to be like "the equal" (75a2), Socrates says that they "yearn to be that which is equal" (ὀρέγεται τοῦ ὃ ἔστιν ἴσον, 75b1–2). In other words, they yearn to be equal the way that equality is equal, but they fall short of this.

If this is correct, it identifies one reason why the recollecting argument has been difficult for modern interpreters to understand. When we think about "equality," it does not seem (at all) obvious to us that it is equal, and so, *a fortiori*, we do not think of ourselves as judging whether things are equal by comparing how they are equal to how equality is. There is a tendency among modern scholars to assume that Plato thinks about equality, justice, and so forth in basically the same way as we do, and then to be puzzled about the things he says are obviously true of them. For us, the meaning of so-called abstract nouns such as "justice" is somewhat fixed, even if many philosophical debates remain unresolved. But in the fifth and fourth centuries BCE the use of these nouns in Greek was on the rise.[47] And while earlier philosophers, poets, historians, medical writers, and other intellectuals used these

---

[45] Frede 1988 and 1992 has a suggestion, taken up by Meinwald 1991 and Mann 2000. I offer a different suggestion in Ebrey (unpublished).

[46] In fact self-predication seems to arise as soon as forms are mentioned in the recollecting argument, in stage two. He introduces the form of equality by saying "there is an equal… the equal itself" (74a). "An equal" is not a mere name; it describes something as, in fact, equal. For a similar thought, see Svavarsson 2009, 61–3.

[47] See Denniston 1960, ch. 2, and especially Long 1968, ch. 2, for the pre-Platonic use of abstract nouns. Both works make clear that, in the fifth century, there was a rise both in abstract nouns formed from adjectives accompanied by the definite article and in newly coined abstract nouns formed from verbs and adjectives (with endings such as -ια).

words, Plato may have been the first to reflect quite generally on what sort of thing these are. My suggestion is that how he is thinking about them makes it obvious that f-ness is f.

Let us return to why Socrates and Simmias think that equal things are equal in a way that falls short of how equality is equal. The only claim Socrates has made in the dialogue thus far that might explain this is that sometimes sticks are equal at one time and at other times not, whereas equality never is its opposite, inequality. Why would this count as the equal things' not being equal *in the way in which* equality is equal? Plato seems to be thinking that, if something is truly f, then it is always f (this is similar to, but distinct from, Parmenides' suggestion in B8).[48] If something is not f for some time, then it would not simply be f. This said, Socrates does not specify in what ways the equal things fall short of equality itself. And so, when we read a few more pages and learn that equal things are practically never *kata* the same things as themselves (78e), we can see this as a further way in which they fall short of equality itself. There will be, I take it, as many ways for them to fall short as there are ways for ordinary equal things to be somehow unequal.

My account, then, of this first step of the third stage is the following. When Simmias sees sticks as equal, he judges them using equality as his standard, and thus must have equality in mind. He does this by comparing the way the sticks are equal with how equality itself is equal. Equality is unqualifiedly equal, and so eternally or atemporally equal, whereas the sticks are sometimes equal, other times not. Hence the way in which the sticks are equal falls short of the way in which equality is.

5.6 THE FOURTH STAGE – FORGETTING THE KNOWLEDGE WE ONCE HAD: 75D–76D

In this final stage, Socrates argues that our knowledge of equality and other such things is forgotten, and so this is a case of what was identified in stage one as "especially" a case of recollecting (73e). This stage of the argument is sometimes treated as more or less dispensable, since Socrates has already concluded at the end of stage three that they possessed knowledge of the forms before they were born (75c).[49] But the main thesis that Socrates set out to show is that learning is recollecting (73b). If we possessed all knowledge and never lost it, we would not learn at all. Moreover, in order to argue that we had this knowledge before birth, Socrates needs to argue that it was forgotten at birth, as opposed to our being born with it (76c–d).

His argument in this stage is (finally!) fairly straightforward. The basic idea is that, in order to have knowledge, one must be able to give an account. But most people

---

[48] For this connection, see Owen 1966. Parmenides denies that what-is was or will be. By contrast, Socrates seems to think that what-is always was, is, and will be.
[49] E.g. Gallop 1975 ad loc. and Rowe 1993 ad loc.

cannot give an account, and so do not have knowledge. Therefore we must have had knowledge before we were born, but forgotten it. Learning is a process of reacquiring this knowledge. We cannot have acquired it for the first time at the moment when we were born, since this (they agree) is when we lost it, and those two opposite processes could not happen at the same time. Thus we must have had such knowledge before then.

There are two topics I would like to discuss in this final stage. First, Simmias initially reports that he cannot say whether or not they have forgotten this knowledge. It seems to be a presupposition of Socratic elenchus that, if one had knowledge, one would be able to explain what one knows (e.g. *Apology* 22a–c, *Euthyphro* 5c–d, *Gorgias* 449c–d; cf. *Gorgias* 465a). Moreover, in the *Laches* Socrates explicitly states this principle (190c). Simmias agrees to it as soon as Socrates mentions it. Simmias, as one of Socrates' close companions, seems broadly familiar with Socrates' main views. Why, then, did Simmias need to be reminded of this requirement? One reason, I suspect, is that Socrates started with ordinary examples, such as seeing Simmias and recollecting Cebes, which Socrates called "knowledge of a person" (73d3). These cases of so-called knowledge by acquaintance do not normally seem to require the ability to give an account. Moreover, Socrates' focus on how things *seem* to Simmias kept his focus on his acquaintance with the forms, as it were, rather than on his ability to properly articulate an account of them. We can see how Simmias could have lost track of the Socratic requirement that one must be able to give an account of what one knows.[50]

Socrates' argument in stage two relied on Simmias' having knowledge of equality. It is difficult to say what Simmias thinks he is agreeing to when he agrees to this, given that (i) later he cannot say whether or not we all have knowledge of the forms, and that (ii) Socrates had just been using a lower standard for knowledge in stage one, in order to illustrate his claims about recollecting. Perhaps, then, Simmias should not really count as knowing equality. But this may not pose a serious problem to the argument. When Socrates asks, "Do you really think that everyone can give an account of the things we just mentioned?" (76b8–9), Simmias replies that he is afraid that tomorrow no single human could do this properly. According to some interpreters, Simmias is claiming only that, once Socrates has died, no human can give an account of *all* the things mentioned.[51] This would mean that Simmias thinks that Socrates can give an account of *all* the things, including the beautiful, the good, the just, the holy, despite Socrates' near constant claims to the contrary, including recently in the defense speech (67b–c, 68a–b). It seems much more likely that Simmias means that, once Socrates dies, no one will be able to give an account of *any* of the forms. Sedley argues that Socrates thinks of equality as a form for which they have succeeded in finding an

---

[50] Sedley 2006 and 2007 argues that Simmias is supposed to be able to give a proper account of equality, and so know it in that sense.

[51] Rowe 1993, 168; Scott 1995, 67–8; Sedley 2007, 75.

5.6 The Fourth Stage – Forgetting the Knowledge We Once Had: 75d–76d

account, something like "neither exceeding nor being exceeded," and that Simmias could be expected to grasp this account.[52] However, even if Simmias grasps this form, Socrates does not think it sufficient for knowledge to simply have the correct account; one must be able to properly articulate it and defend it against objections.[53] There is no reason to think that Simmias can do this.

Perhaps Socrates does not clarify this point because it is not crucial for his argument that Simmias has knowledge, only that *someone* has knowledge, so he can establish that someone has recollected equality. Socrates' question in the second stage is whether "*we* have knowledge of it [equality], what it is" (74b2, emphasis added). Perhaps the point of Simmias' suggesting that no one may have knowledge *after Socrates has died* is that Socrates, at least, has knowledge of equality – even if Simmias himself does not. So long as Socrates knows equality, the argument goes through: Socrates has recollected, and this started as soon as he first saw equal things. And, if he was recollecting from a young age, we all must be too, even if we have not yet acquired knowledge.

Let me turn to the second topic, which is connected to the argument's conclusion: "our souls existed earlier as well, separate from bodies, before they were in human form, and they had wisdom" (76c11–12). Why does Socrates think that he can conclude that our souls not only existed before death, but also were separate from bodies? His argument does not seem to exclude the possibility that souls might sometimes go directly from one body to another. But his conclusion also does not say *when* they existed without bodies. And, if his argument is right, then either our souls have always existed or there must have been some time before we were first in human form when we acquired knowledge of equality. To see why, suppose that there is a first time when a soul is embodied and that this soul sees something equal and so has equality in mind. By Socrates' argument, this soul would need to have previously known equality. This knowledge could only have come before it was first embodied.[54] Hence this soul must have existed without any body. Could our souls eternally have had previous embodiments? I am not sure whether Plato would imagine such a possibility but, even if he did, it is not clear that it would help. For it to help, every piece of knowledge we could acquire must have been possessed by an infinite number of past lives. (If it were a finite number, consider the first one. Where did its knowledge come from?) Given how difficult it is to acquire knowledge, it seems unlikely that Socrates would think that every potential object of knowledge had been acquired by an infinite number of past lives. It seems at least reasonable to suppose, then, that the soul existed at some time without a body, and this is when it acquired its knowledge. In any event, whether justified or not, this

---

[52] Sedley 2007.
[53] So Kelsey 2000.
[54] Similarly, the *Timaeus* says that souls go on a tour of the cosmos before embodiment (41e); Timaeus' account of reincarnation makes no reference to a disembodied state between embodied states.

conclusion means that the soul can exist without a body and that, when it does, it can acquire knowledge of the forms.[55] This possibility is, of course, crucial for Socrates' good hope about the afterlife.

5.7 CODA – THE IMPORTANCE OF FORMS AND THE SCOPE OF THE ARGUMENT: 76D–77D

After the argument, Socrates draws out the importance of the existence of forms for drawing its conclusion (76d–e) without insisting that they do exist. Simmias is consistently the most enthusiastic person in the dialogue about the existence of forms (in the defense speech at 65d, here, and in Socrates' reply to Simmias' *harmonia* objection at 92d–e), whereas Socrates is always careful to ask Simmias and Cebes whether they agree that there are such things, and highlights that his arguments rely on them. Simmias, at the end of this argument, claims that they have been sufficiently proved (77a, cf. 92e), but Socrates never claims this. As we will see, this is crucial for understanding Socrates' method of hypothesis. This method is supposed to help establish that we are right to accept the existence of forms. But one should go through its procedure before accepting their existence rather than doing so prematurely, as Simmias does here. At the end of the final argument, Socrates says that Simmias is right to express his doubts about the conclusion and that they should consider the first hypotheses most clearly (107b). The only things Socrates has clearly flagged as hypotheses are the individual claims about each form, that each exists. I take it, then, that all the way up to the end of the final argument Socrates thinks that they should be careful not to accept too quickly their existence. This is further reason to doubt that Socrates thinks that he has proved the existence of forms here in the recollecting argument.[56]

The discussion ends with Simmias' making the point that, for all that has been said in the recollecting argument, there is no reason to think that the soul might not be destroyed upon death (77b), and so the argument does not address Cebes' challenge (articulated at 69e–70b). Cebes agrees with Simmias and says that only half of what is needed has been shown (77c). Socrates responds by suggesting that the conclusion is shown if they combine the cyclical and the recollecting arguments, as discussed in Section 4.2.

5.8 CONCLUSION

With so many details, it is important to step back and pull together the overall account. I have argued that each stage and indeed each step of the argument is crucial for reaching the conclusion.

---

[55] As is widely noted, e.g. Gallop 1975 at 76c11–13. This is important to the overall view in Osborne 1995.

[56] As e.g. White 1992, Kelsey 2000, and Dimas 2003 maintain.

5.8 Conclusion

In the first stage, Socrates provides sufficient conditions for different types of recollecting and provides two different distinctions between different objects of recollecting: between forgotten things and things not forgotten, and between similar things and dissimilar things. Recollecting from similar things happens when the thing seen and the thing recollected are objects of the same knowledge, which allows one to judge by a single standard; recollecting from different things happens when the thing seen and the thing recollected are objects of different knowledges, judged using different standards. In describing recollecting from similar things, Socrates articulates the falling short principle, which is crucial in the third stage: that when one recollects from similar things, one must judge whether or not the thing perceived falls short of the thing recollected. This principle holds because, in the case of similar things, either one is comparing two things judged by the same standard or one of the two things simply is the standard; either way, the recollector will judge, perhaps unconsciously, how well each measures up to the standard.

In the second stage Socrates begins presenting an argument that Simmias has recollected equality itself. He interrupts this argument to ask Simmias whether, in his judgment, sometimes equal sticks are at one time equal and other times not, by contrast with equality itself, which is never its opposite, inequality. Simmias agrees that the equal sticks differ from equality itself in this way, and thus that equality must be different from the equal sticks. But it is from such equal things that Simmias has in mind, and ultimately acquired knowledge of, equality; and so, Socrates concludes that Simmias is recollecting when he, upon seeing the equal sticks, has equality in mind.

Socrates then says, at the beginning of the third stage, that, when he and Simmias see the equal sticks, they judge them to be equal in a way that falls short of the way in which equality itself is equal. The sticks fall short of their standard, equality; at least one reason for this is that they are equal sometimes but not at others, whereas equality itself is always equal. Socrates then articulates the prior knowledge principle: in order to judge the sticks to have fallen short in how they are equal, one must have had prior knowledge of equality. Seeing equal things brings equality to mind. The first time this happened to Socrates marked the beginning of his recollecting, and so, by the falling short principle, when he saw equal things and had equality in mind, he must have judged whether or not the equal things fell short of equality. But then, by the prior knowledge principle, he must have known equality before he first saw equal things and had equality in mind. Since this knowledge came before he first had equality in mind, he must have had this knowledge since before birth. But if Socrates and Simmias were recollecting equality as soon as they first judged that things were equal, the same must be true of everyone else, too. The same holds for the other forms.

In the fourth stage Socrates argues that, since most people cannot now articulate this knowledge, everyone must have forgotten it upon birth; those people who have since learned recollected what we all once knew. Our souls must have existed before they were first embodied in order to have acquired knowledge and then forgotten it upon birth, allowing us to recollect.

The argument advances our understanding of both forms and ordinary things. Ordinary things change over time, unlike the forms; this is one way in which they fall short in how they are equal. When we see ordinary things, we (perhaps unconsciously) judge them by the standards set by the forms. We need the forms to make perceptual judgments, but perception is not needed for grasping the forms. Moreover, the argument clarifies how the soul can perform one of its central activities, inquiry, on its own: by relying on wisdom the soul once possessed, disembodied. It clarifies three central topics of the *Phaedo* – the soul, inquiry, and the forms – in a way that reimagines the Pythagorean idea that we can gain superior knowledge from before birth. Finally, Socrates thinks that combining this argument with the directly argued for sub-conclusion of the cyclical argument (that the living come to be from the dead) shows that the soul continues to exist after death.

6

The Kinship Argument

77d–80d

The kinship argument (typically called the "affinity argument," as discussed below) is central to the structure of the *Phaedo*, setting up much of the remainder of the dialogue. Directly after it, the return to the defense (80d–84b) uses the account of the soul argued for here to provide further defense of ethical claims made earlier in the defense speech (63b–69e). Simmias and Cebes then raise their *harmonia* and cloakmaker objections against the kinship argument (85b–88b). Socrates responds to these objections first by warning them not to become misologues (89c–91c), and then presents several counterarguments to Simmias' objection (91e–95a). In presenting these counterarguments, I argue (in Section 8.4), Socrates defends and clarifies the account of the soul laid out in the kinship argument. To respond to Cebes' cloakmaker objection, Socrates says that they must thoroughly study the causes of coming to be and ceasing to be, leading to Socrates' autobiography (95e–102a) and then to his final immortality argument (102a–107b). The final argument, I argue (in Chapter 10), responds to the details of Cebes' objection, an objection targeted specifically to the kinship argument. In doing so, the final argument fills in a crucial part of the account of the soul laid out here. Even the eschatological account (107c–115a) and the death scene draw on the return to the defense, and so are only one step removed from the kinship argument.

In addition to being central to the structure of the dialogue, the kinship argument also further develops several of its fundamental ideas. It provides the dialogue's most detailed account of the forms and of ordinary objects. It argues for an innovative and important account of the nature of the soul, according to which it is broadly of the same kind as the divine (a category that includes the forms) and able to become, in crucial respects, more like the divine. This theory is the basis for Socrates' ethical account in the return to the defense. Moreover, Plato explores the view that the soul is akin to divine entities (either the forms or the gods) in many dialogues that stylometry suggests are later than the *Phaedo*, including the *Republic* (e.g. 490a–b,

494d–e, 611e), *Phaedrus* (246d–e), and *Timaeus* (90a).[1] The idea that the soul is situated between ordinary objects and the forms is also important in the battle of the gods and giants in the *Sophist* (246e–249d) and in Timaeus' account of the construction of the world soul in the *Timaeus* (35a–b).[2] Far from being an account of the soul superseded by that in the final argument (or in *Republic*), the broad idea behind this account is explored in many of Plato's later dialogues.

Despite the central role the argument plays in the structure of dialogue, the fundamental topics it discusses, and the way its ideas are developed in later dialogues, it has received very little scholarly attention. The basic reason for this, I take it, is that scholars widely view it as an especially bad argument, and so of little interest.[3] I argue here that this reputation is undeserved; one goal of this chapter is to show that the argument is much more precise and stronger than has been appreciated. Even the standard name – the "affinity argument" – gives the impression that it is a loose and weak argument. Since the argument does not rely on any mere "affinity" between the soul and the unseen, I call it the "kinship argument," given the crucial role of kinship in it. The soul's kinship with the divine is supposed to reveal something about the nature of the soul by identifying what its kin are. This argument goes further than the previous two in explaining why the nature of the soul means that it will not be destroyed upon death.

Perhaps because the kinship argument has received little attention, scholars have not recognized that Socrates describes here a new, fundamental feature of the forms: they are simple in a way that makes them partless, and so each has its characteristics as a whole – in strong contrast to ordinary objects, whose complex structure allows them to simultaneously have opposing features at the same time. In other words, Socrates argues that, because the forms are not composite, they cannot suffer a type of compresence of opposites suffered by ordinary objects. Appreciating this feature of forms and ordinary objects, in turn, sheds new light on Socrates' infamously difficult expression "itself through itself" (*auto kath' hauto*).

6.1 THE INTRODUCTION AND CONCLUSION OF THE ARGUMENT: 77D–78A, 80B

The way in which the kinship argument is introduced has led some to think that it is not meant as a rational argument, but rather as appealing primarily to our emotions.[4] The conclusion, too, is often taken to show that the argument is loose or

---

[1] The general consensus is that the *Phaedo* is in the first stylometric group, the *Republic* and *Phaedrus* in the second, and the *Timaeus* in the third. See Kahn 2002.
[2] For a discussion of this in the construction of the world soul, see Betegh 2021a.
[3] For the claim that it is a weak argument, see e.g. Dorter 1982, 71–2 and 75–6, Gallop 1975 on 79a1–b17, Bostock 1896, 119–20, Rowe 1993 on 80b9–10, Elton 1997, 313, Ebert 2004, 252, and Iwata 2020.
[4] E.g. Dorter 1982, 71–2, Elton 1997, 316, Ebert 2004, 252. Rejected by Woolf 2004, 111, n. 18.

6.1 The Introduction and Conclusion of the Argument: 77d–78a, 80b

inadequate. I argue here that neither provides evidence that the argument is suboptimal, so we should approach it with the working assumption that it is serious. In arguing for this, I clarify the argument's aims.

After Socrates says that combining the recollecting argument with the cyclical argument shows that the soul exists after death, he says to Cebes that he thinks that "you fear what children fear – namely that what really happens is that when the soul leaves the body the wind blows it apart and dissipates it, especially when someone happens to die not in calm weather but in a strong wind" (77d7–e3). Socrates' humor is, of course, important to lightening the mood, but no sign of a lack of seriousness (cf. 101b, 115c for humor with a serious point). His mention of fearing dissipation alludes back to Cebes' challenge (69e–70b), where Cebes says that people have great doubts and fear that the soul is dissipated like breath or smoke. As noted in Section 4.1, Cebes asks in this challenge to be convinced (70b), thereby assuaging these fears. Socrates is now saying (at 77d–e) that, despite having just given a good argument (the recollecting argument), the fears seem to remain.

Cebes' response, however, seems to turn the discussion in a less rational direction: "Or rather, not as if we have the fear – maybe there's a child actually inside us who's afraid of things like that" (77e5–7). Socrates' response, that they must chant spells over the child every day to remove this fear, has suggested to some that the kinship argument is not supposed to be primarily rationally persuasive, but rather to appeal to them at a more childlike, emotional level.[5] But the exchange that follows makes clear that Cebes and Socrates both think they should seek philosophical persuasion. Cebes asks who a good enchanter would be, given that Socrates is leaving them (78a). Socrates is a powerful reasoner, but has no special abilities in appealing to people at a more childlike level. Furthermore, Socrates says that when he is gone they should spare neither money nor effort to find such an enchanter who can dispel their fear of death (78a).[6] Surely Socrates is suggesting that they search far and wide for a proper philosopher who can help them, not that they spend all of their effort finding someone to non-rationally soothe them. Socrates' search for an enchanter (ἐπῳδός) has a parallel in the *Charmides*, where Socrates says that he has an enchantment (or charm, ἐπῳδή) that will cure Charmides' headache (155e –158c).[7] This enchantment turns out to be nothing other than the rational discussion that ensues. Why does Cebes mention a child inside him, if he wants to be rationally persuaded by Socrates? Perhaps he is persuaded by Socrates' earlier arguments, but at the same time some part of him is not convinced. This part might

---

[5] See n. 4 for references.
[6] One might wonder whether Socrates is being serious, since he is famously suspicious of self-proclaimed teachers of virtue who accept money. But in the *Laches* Socrates says that they should spare neither money nor anything else to find a teacher, now that they have seen that they do not know what courage is (201a). The money need not be used to pay the teacher; it could be used for the costs incurred in searching.
[7] So Hackforth 1955, 79, n. 1, Gallop 1975 on 77e8, Rowe 1993 on 78a2.

not feel rational to Cebes, but even if the fear is irrational, that hardly means that the therapy should be.[8]

Recall that Socrates argued in the defense speech that, because non-philosophers view death as a great evil, their courage is absurd (68d). It would be very odd if shortly thereafter Socrates were suggesting that they spare no effort to find someone to overcome the fear of death in a non-philosophical way. Instead, Socrates' discussion of enchanting playfully picks up on Cebes' mention of a child inside him and Simmias, but at the same time Socrates aims to help them overcome their fear of death appropriately, through reason. In doing so, he is, as he says, "persevering with the *logos* even more thoroughly" (77d6–7).

Let us jump, then, to the argument's conclusion, since scholars have also taken it as a sign that this is not a rigorous, serious argument:

> If all this is the case, isn't the body the sort of thing to be quickly disintegrated, but the soul, on the other hand, the sort to be altogether incapable of being disintegrated, or nearly so? (80b9–11)

Scholars have viewed the "or nearly so" as showing that Socrates does not view the argument as reaching the desired conclusion.[9] But Cebes did not ask Socrates to show that the soul cannot be destroyed; instead, Cebes' challenge asked Socrates to offer reassurance against the fear that the soul is destroyed upon death, to persuade him not to have this fear (69e–70b, Section 4.1). He ends his challenge by saying that he wants no small amount of reassurance and conviction that the soul exists when the human has died (70b). Rational persuasion not to fear an event typically does not involve arguing that the event cannot possibly happen. Suppose that someone is afraid to cross bridges, thinking that they will collapse. Of course, if you could show that it is impossible for bridges to collapse, that would offer rational reassurance. But so would providing data about the unlikelihood of bridges falling, and, in a different way, so does explaining the principles of engineering that keep them up. The kinship argument, I will suggest, is analogous to the principles of engineering: it explains why the nature of the soul makes it very unlikely that it is destroyed. This offers a type of reassurance and conviction that a non-explanatory argument does not provide, even if such an argument were to conclude that it is absolutely impossible that the feared event could occur. Given the subsequent history of philosophy, we expect an argument for the continued existence of the soul to argue that it *must* continue to exist. But Cebes has asked Socrates to respond to the fear that the soul will be dispersed upon death; it would be a very strong response to show that this is either impossible or nearly so.

Of course, once Socrates concludes that the soul is at least nearly incapable of being disintegrated, someone might then hope that Socrates would argue for the

---

[8] See Young 1988 for another explanation for why Cebes mentions a child inside them, one that also does not suggest that Cebes wants to be irrationally soothed.

[9] E.g. Hackforth 1955, 85–6, Bostock 1986, 119–20.

stronger claim, that the soul simply is incapable of being disintegrated. However, it takes a while before anyone asks Socrates to show something like this. Cebes happily accepts the conclusion of the kinship argument without reservation (80c). It is only after Socrates' subsequent ethical discussion (80d–84b) and after a long silence (84c) that Simmias and Cebes develop objections. And Cebes, at the end of his cloak-maker objection, asks Socrates something that he had not requested earlier: to show that the soul is altogether immortal and indestructible (88b). As noted in Section 4.1 and argued for at length in Chapter 10, Socrates' final argument addresses this new request, which the kinship argument is not designed to meet.

It is sometimes said that Socrates' argument here is only meant to establish that the philosopher's soul continues to exist after death.[10] But he never says this, and it is difficult to reconcile with the soul's nearly being indestructible, since most souls do not belong to philosophers. I will argue that the structure of the argument is that the soul in general – and so every soul in particular – is akin to the unseen, and so we should expect the soul in general to share with it the feature of being indestructible.

6.2 THE STRUCTURE OF THE ARGUMENT

The kinship argument is an investigation into what sort of thing (ποῖον) the soul is (78b), the sort to be destroyed or not. It is often said that Socrates' strategy is to show that the soul is a member of the unseen, and as such, we should expect it to be indestructible.[11] Instead, Socrates argues that the soul is akin and similar to the unseen, but he never says or argues that it is a member of this group. The soul's kinship with the unseen reveals that it does not simply share some features with the unseen, but that its nature is related to that of the unseen, and so there is good reason to expect it to be indestructible, as the unseen is.[12]

Let me note now the main evidence that the soul is not a member of the unseen; further evidence will arise as we work through the details. Halfway through the argument, Socrates refers to the class of things that includes the forms as "the unseen" (79a7). He does not treat this as a class whose extension is anything that is not seen; instead, "*the* unseen" is the name of a group whose members have a number of characteristic features, including being unseen, and whose only identified members are the forms (78c–d) and the gods (implicit at 80a; explicit after the argument, at 80d–81a).[13] (Similarly, "*the* Eleven" at 59e6 is the name of a group of

---

[10] So Woolf 2004, 111–16, and Obdrzalek 2021, 71–4.
[11] E.g. Hackforth 1955, 84, Gallop 1975 on 78b4–10, Apolloni 1996, and Obdrzalek 2021, 68–71.
[12] Most scholars take Socrates to be saying that the soul simply shares features with the unseen – e.g. Gallop 1975, Rowe 1993 on 80b9–10. By contrast, Apolloni 1996, 11–12, says that these are "definitive" features of the soul.
[13] So Gallop 1975 on 79a1–b17 and Sedley 2018, 212, n. 2; by contrast, Hackforth 1955, 84–6, Bostock 1986, 118–19, Rowe 1993 on 79b4–5, and Apolloni 1996, 10–13, all take it as a class whose extension includes anything unseen. Nightingale 2021, 51 argues that the unseen includes only the forms, not the gods, on the grounds that the unseen is unchanging. But

officers who enforce Athenian court decisions, not the extension of all the things that add up to eleven.) One characteristic feature of *the* unseen is that its members *always* hold "*kata* the same things" (an expression whose meaning we will examine in the next subsection) (78d, 79a, 80b). By contrast, most souls do not hold *kata* the same things, since they investigate through the senses (79c). In fact only the rare soul with genuine wisdom reaches a state where it eventually comes to hold *kata* the same things (79d), but this takes work and so it was not *always kata* the same things, and so not a member of *the* unseen. This is why throughout the argument Socrates never says that the soul is a member of the unseen; instead, he says that it is unseen, and then takes this as a sign that it is akin and similar to *the* unseen (79b).[14] The contrasting group, the visible, also has a number of characteristic features, including being visible. Because the two groups are characterized by several features and a thing can have some features without having all, they do not provide a mutually exclusive and exhaustive division of things; hence the soul need not belong to either group.

In the first half of the argument Socrates introduces the question of whether the soul is the sort of thing to be destroyed, and quickly connects this to the question of whether it is composite. This leads to his discussion of the two different classes of things: the unseen and the visible. He provides here his detailed account of the forms and the many beautiful things. In the second half, Socrates returns to the soul, asking which of the two classes the soul (and which of the two classes the body) is more similar and akin to.

6.3 THE FIRST HALF OF THE ARGUMENT – FORMS AND THE MANY THINGS: 78B–79A

Cebes' challenge raised the concern that the soul dissipates (ἐκβαίνειν) and is scattered (διασκεδασθῆναι) upon death (70a); Socrates used these exact terms to redescribe Cebes' fear directly before the kinship argument (77d). Socrates' first step in the argument is to address this directly by asking what sort of thing dissipates (78b). He says that it belongs to composite things to do so – supposedly because they could decompose into their parts. By contrast, it belongs to something incomposite – if anything – not to dissipate (78b). The next step raises a few very important puzzles, which I use to develop my overall interpretation of the forms and ordinary objects in the kinship argument. This turns out to be a difficult set of interconnected issues, which take up almost half of this chapter. The payoff for this long, difficult discussion is that it will reveal an overlooked fundamental feature of the forms and a

---

Plato sometimes thinks of the gods as unchanging (e.g. *Republic* 380d–381e) and the evidence cited clearly includes the gods among the unseen.

[14] Apolloni 1996, 9–10, rightly emphasizes this, but nonetheless goes on to interpret Socrates as arguing that the soul is a member of the unseen.

6.3 The First Half – Forms and the Many Things: 78b–79a

contrasting feature of ordinary objects, as well as allowing us to better understand Socrates' famously obscure expression "itself through itself" (*auto kath' hauto*). My discussion here is more detailed than in any other part of the book. Some readers will want exactly this; others will wish to skip to my summary in Subsection 6.3.3.

6.3.1 *Holding* kata *the Same Things*

For the next step in the argument, I begin with a standard translation – that of Sedley and Long:

> Now isn't it true that the things that are always in the same state and same condition are most likely to be the incomposite ones, whereas those that are in different conditions at different times and are never in the same state are most likely to be composite? (78c6–8)
>
> Οὐκοῦν ἅπερ ἀεὶ κατὰ ταὐτὰ καὶ ὡσαύτως ἔχει, ταῦτα μάλιστα εἰκός εἶναι τὰ ἀσύνθετα, τὰ δὲ ἄλλοτ' ἄλλως καὶ μηδέποτε κατὰ ταὐτά, ταῦτα δὲ σύνθετα;

The first puzzle is what is supposed to connect being "always in the same state and same condition" with being incomposite, and similarly what is supposed to connect being "in different conditions at different times and ... never in the same state" with being composite. Socrates might seem to be presupposing a very substantive theory here: that any change in state requires an internal change in parts, so that incomposite things could not change.[15] But why would he reject ahead of time the possibility of a small, incomposite atom that can move around or change some other condition without changing its parts? Moreover, if all composite things eventually lose their parts, then these parts themselves clearly undergo motion, which seems to involve a change of state. If this change requires a change in parts, then every part would need to be divisible into further parts, so that Socrates would be commiting himself here to there being no atoms. At best, on the standard translation of this passage, Socrates is either claiming that a very rough empirical generalization is "most likely" or presupposing a robust theory of change without explaining or arguing for it.

The second puzzle has to do with how Socrates opposes the two groups mentioned in the passage. Socrates describes one set of things as *always* in the same state and same condition. You might expect Socrates to oppose this to a set of things that are *never* in the same state or same condition, or perhaps to a group that is *sometimes* in the same state or condition. But instead he contrasts "are in the same state" (κατὰ ταὐτὰ ... ἔχει) differently from how he contrasts "are in the same condition" (ὡσαύτως ἔχει): he contrasts the latter with "are in different conditions at different times" (τὰ δὲ ἄλλοτ' ἄλλως) and the former with "never in the same state" (μηδέποτε κατὰ ταὐτά). Of course, if one begins thinking that the kinship argument is weak, it is easy to think that Socrates is simply being loose here. But before

---

[15] So Gallop 1975 ad loc.

deciding that Socrates is relying on rough generalizations and loose connections, we should consider the possibility that he is making more precise claims.

My solution to both puzzles relies on the same idea: "in the same state" is the wrong translation for κατὰ ταὐτά . . . ἔχει. It is not more or less synonymous with "in the same condition" (ὡσαύτως ἔχει), as it is normally taken to be.[16] The fact that Socrates opposes these two expressions differently there ("are in different conditions at different times and never in the same state") provides some initial evidence that they mean different things. The meaning of this expression, in my view, cuts to the heart of Socrates' descriptions of forms and ordinary objects here. Understanding it turns out to be difficult and connected to other central questions about the kinship argument.

The expression "hold *kata* the same things" is not found in any author before Plato[17] or in any of the Socratic dialogues. This suggests that it was not ordinary Greek, but rather a phrase that Plato coined for a specific philosophical purpose. The expression "*kata* the same things" is used in a famous discussion in the *Republic*, where it clearly does not mean "unvarying" or "in the same state." I suggest we take our lead from it. There Socrates is clarifying his famous principle of non-opposition: "It is clear that the same thing will not be willing to do or undergo opposites, at least *kata* the same thing, in relation to the same thing, and at the same time" (Δῆλον ὅτι ταὐτὸν τἀναντία ποιεῖν ἢ πάσχειν κατὰ ταὐτόν γε καὶ πρὸς ταὐτὸν οὐκ ἐθελήσει ἅμα, 436b8–9; cf. *Sophist* 230b4–8). Before giving an example of the qualification "*kata* the same thing," Socrates says that someone whose hands and head are moving but who is otherwise still does not count as moving and standing still. Instead one should say that one thing (supposedly the hands and head) is moving and another (the rest of the body) standing still (436c–d). By contrast, he says that tops that are spinning in a circle but not wobbling can be said to be both moving and standing still. But they are not moving and standing still *kata* the same things (οὐ κατὰ ταὐτά, 436d8). Instead, he says that the tops have a circle in them (i.e. their perimeter) and a straight in them (i.e. their axis). Each top is moving *kata* the circle in them and standing still *kata* the straight in them (436d–e). Minimally, this shows that Socrates uses the phrase "not *kata* the same things" to indicate a qualification on how something has a feature ascribed to it (in this case, moving or standing still). There is a heated interpretive debate about how the *kata* qualification fits into the *Republic*'s tripartition argument, but happily there is no need to settle this for the present purposes.[18]

---

[16] E.g. Burnet 1911, Gallop 1975, Rowe 1993 on 78c, and Ademollo 2018, 37–8.

[17] According to a TLG search, the only exception is a case in Herodotus where "*kata*" has a very different meaning, indicating location: "Even in my day Persians had (ἔχειν) guard posts in the same places (κατὰ ταὐτά), as was the case in the time of King Psammetichus" (2.30.12–13, trans. after Waterfield).

[18] See Bobonich 2002, 229–31, and Lorenz 2006, 24, who are each responding to Price 1995, as well as the view implicit in many translations. Price provides a revised version of his view in Price 2009; Brown 2012, 58–62, takes something of a middle path.

6.3 The First Half – Forms and the Many Things: 78b–79a

Setting aside the details, my basic proposal is that in the *Phaedo* to say that the forms always hold *kata* the same things is to say that they do not have some feature *kata* one thing but another feature *kata* something else. Hence forms, unlike the spinning tops, do not manifest the compresence of opposites that occurs via the *kata* relation. Similarly, they do not manifest the compresence of opposites that occurs over time. In the recollecting argument, Socrates noted how ordinary equal things manifest opposite features over time (see Subsection 5.4.1), and I take Socrates to refer to that here with his talk of things holding differently at different times (ἄλλοτ' ἄλλως). At the beginning of the final argument, Socrates describes how the same thing can, at the same time, be large in relation to (*pros*) one thing and small in relation to another, whereas largeness itself cannot receive both of these (102b–103a) (Section 10.4). Hence, as the account of the forms and of ordinary objects unfolds across the dialogue, Socrates attributes all three types of compresence of opposites (referred to in the principle of non-opposition) to the many *f* things, and denies of each of these types that it applies to the forms.

To understand the meaning of "hold *kata* the same things," we first need to understand its grammar. In the *Republic*'s principle of opposition and in its spinning-tops example, the expression "*kata* the same things" functions adverbially, modifying the way in which something has a feature or activity attributed to it, such as moving. My suggestion is that "*kata*" is doing the same thing in the expression "hold *kata* the same things." This is clearest when Socrates does not put an "and" between "in the same way" (ὡσαύτως) and "*kata* the same things" (κατὰ ταὐτά), but rather simply says, "holds in the same way *kata* the same things" (ὡσαύτως ἔχει κατὰ ταὐτά, 78d2–3, 78d6, 79d5–6). In Greek, one can use the verb "to have/hold" (ἔχειν) with an adverb to mean more or less the same thing as the verb "to be" with an adjective, and so " to hold in the same way" (ὡσαύτως ἔχειν) is very close to "to be the same."[19] My suggestion is that, when "*kata* the same things" is added to this, it adverbially modifies the way in which this thing is the same, just as when "*kata* the circle" is added to "the top is moving" it modifies the way in which it is moving. I take it to continue to be used adverbially when Socrates simply says that something "holds *kata* the same things," leaving out "in the same way" (ὡσαύτως). In particular, if x "holds *kata* the same things," I take this to mean that, *whatever* features x has, it has/holds them *kata* the same things.[20] Of course, this is very difficult to understand in the abstract, so let us turn to the meaning of "*kata* the same things."

---

[19] In general, such constructions with "to have" indicate a longer lasting feature of the thing – so, in this case, it would mean something like "to be the same for an extended period of time."

[20] The LSJ treats the use of ἔχειν with an adverb as subordinate to the basic use of ἔχειν as meaning to be. Two examples it lists are ἑκὰς εἶχον (being far off), *Odyssey* 12.435, and εἶχε κατὰ οἴκους (he was at home), Herodotus 6.39. I take it that it is used in this absolute way when Socrates says κατὰ ταὐτὰ ἔχει, without ὡσαύτως. Note that in the *Timaeus* Timaeus uses the expression τὸ κατὰ ταὐτὰ εἶδος ἔχον (52a1). Here it is clear that εἶδος refers to the thing possessed and κατὰ ταὐτά modifies *how* it is possessed.

It is a subtle and difficult question how to understand this *kata* relation, one that cannot be answered in a simple word or phrase. Part of the problem is that, aside from the spinning-tops example, there are no other undisputed examples of this use of "*kata*."[21] In the *Republic* Socrates clearly does not mean to use "*kata*" in a way that covers every possible use of this preposition; instead, he is interested in a philosophically important relation that he uses "*kata*" to pick out, one that allows the same thing to manifest opposites.[22] As noted earlier, the expression "hold *kata* the same things" is used in the *Phaedo* perhaps for the first time in Greek literature. In fact, the kinship argument and return to the defense (immediately afterwards) have at least three apparently newly coined terms, as discussed in the next subsection (6.3.2). Plato's contemporary readers may well have been puzzled by these expressions, just as we are. The *Phaedo* is a conversation between Socrates and his closest companions, who perhaps are supposed to understand these terms. We can see Socrates as now turning to a deeper explanation for why the soul exists after death, one that requires (or at least is helped by) new terminology.

This said, I think we can make good sense of this relation, and in doing so understand the language of not only "holding *kata* the same things" but also "itself *kata* itself." Recall that before the spinning-tops example in the *Republic kata* is contrasted with *pros* – they offer two different ways in which something can, at the same time, suffer from opposites. Normally "*pros*" is translated as "in relation to," and the relevant use of "*pros*," at least typically, relates two distinct things. In the spinning-tops example, Socrates says that the round and straight are *in* and *of* the tops (436d–e). They belong to the tops. They are not parts of the tops, but they reflect that each top has a sort of spatial complexity.[23] This spatial complexity allows the top to be moving *kata* one thing while being at rest *kata* another thing.[24] This suggests that, when x is *f kata* y, y relates to the structure of x, and x is *f* due to its relation to y.

---

[21] According to some readings of the *Republic*'s argument (see Price 2009), the soul thirsts *kata* one of its parts and opposes drink *kata* another part. If correct, this would be another very important example of how something can possess features *kata* one part but not *kata* another. This dispute is beyond the scope of this book. I will argue that the uses of "*auto kath' hauto*" provide us with further examples of *kata*, but again, this is not uncontroversial.

[22] The *Euthydemus* uses the expression once (293c–d) and in the *Republic* it is associated with eristic puzzles (436d). Aristotle refers to the three *Republic* qualifications as among the things needed to avoid eristic puzzles (*SE* 167a21–35, discussed later in this subsection). This leads Campbell 2019 to argue that Plato's and Aristotle's use of the *kata* qualification is motivated, at least in part, by their efforts to provide solutions to eristic puzzles.

[23] So Lorenz 2006, 24, n. 14. Bobonich 2002 and Lorenz 2006 argue that these are not parts. They are arguing against earlier interpreters who see the strategy of the tripartition argument as showing that the soul is thirsty *kata* one thing and opposes thirst *kata* something else, and so must have different parts. However, even if Bobonich and Lorenz are correct about the strategy of the argument, I see no reason why parts could not be among the things "*kata*" ranges over, so long as the predicate applies to the whole object, not simply to this part. I provide such an example later in this subsection.

[24] Bobonich 2002, 529, n. 19, agrees that the circular motion needs to be with respect to *the top*'s perimeter.

In fact I think that *"kata"* picks out a more specific sort of relation than this. In the spinning-tops example, Socrates says that, if a top wobbles instead of standing still *kata* something, it "in no manner" (οὐδαμῇ) stands still (436e5); as discussed in the next subsection (6.3.2), Socrates' description of the forms also contrasts *kata* with "in no manner" (78d7). This suggests that, if x is *f kata* y, x is *f* in some specific manner determined by y. Simmias is larger than his hand – that is a relation between him and one of his internal things – but I doubt that he is large *kata* his hand, because his hand does not determine some specific manner in which he is large. By contrast, if someone asks, "in what manner is the top moving?," we could answer, "with respect to its circumference," thereby specifying a manner of moving. The question "in what manner is he large?" is not answered with "with respect to his hand," but rather with "with respect to his height." Simmias could be large in relation to (*pros*) Socrates with respect to (*kata*) his height, but small in relation to (*pros*) Socrates with respect to (*kata*) his width. In one manner Simmias is larger, in another Socrates is. The proposal is that *"kata"* picks out something related to the internal structure of the subject that determines some manner in which a predicate applies to it. This explains Socrates' connection between *kata* and manner.[25] Moreover, it fits perfectly with what Aristotle says in the *Sophistical Refutations* (167a21–35), which draws on the language of the *Republic* and provides us with another example.[26] Aristotle, using the language of the principle of non-opposition in the *Republic*, gives the example that x could be double *pros* (in relation to) y *kata* length but not be double *pros* y *kata* breadth.

If the *Republic*'s principle of non-opposition is correct, then in any case where something is, as a whole, both *f* and the opposite of *f* (un-*f*) at the same time and not in relation to (*pros*) different things, it must be *f* and the opposite of *f* (un-*f*) *kata* different things. The account offered makes sense of such cases. Suppose that a painting is both beautiful and ugly – and not merely some part of it, or merely at different times, or merely in relation to different things. Then, the suggestion is, it must have some internal structure that allows it to be beautiful *kata* one thing and ugly *kata* another thing. It will then in one manner be beautiful and in another ugly. This might have to do with its parts, so long as the beauty or ugliness applies to the whole painting, not merely its parts. Perhaps the painting is beautiful *kata* the figure's eyes. The eyes themselves may not be beautiful, but the whole painting is beautiful in virtue of them – perhaps the color perfectly complements the skin tone

---

[25] In the *Symposium*, Socrates says the form of the beautiful "is not beautiful in this respect (τῇ μέν) but ugly in that respect (τῇ δ(έ)), or beautiful at one time but not at another, or beautiful in relation to this but ugly in relation to that" (211a2–4). Here we get the *Republic* trio, but with "in this respect" (τῇ μέν) replacing *"kata"*; this fits with the idea that *"kata"* determines a specific manner in which something holds.

[26] I thank Ian Campbell for the reference and for many valuable discussions about the meaning of *"kata."*

as well as picking up a color in the background. At the same time, the painting could be ugly in virtue of the figure's posture.[27]

Note how this account of "holding *kata* the same things" solves the two puzzles about the second step in the argument. As a reminder, that step is:

> "Now isn't it true that the things that hold always *kata* the same things and in the same way are most likely to be the incomposite ones, whereas those that hold differently at different times and never *kata* the same things are most likely to be composite?" (78c6–8)
>
> Οὐκοῦν ἅπερ ἀεὶ κατὰ ταὐτὰ καὶ ὡσαύτως ἔχει, ταῦτα μάλιστα εἰκὸς εἶναι τὰ ἀσύνθετα, τὰ δὲ ἄλλοτ' ἄλλως καὶ μηδέποτε κατὰ ταὐτά, ταῦτα δὲ σύνθετα;

The first puzzle was, if Socrates is saying that a group of things simply never change their features, why would this be connected to their being incomposite? I have argued that Socrates is not merely talking about staying unchanged. Instead, if something does not hold *kata* the same things, it must have some sort of internal complexity. Some of its features will be *kata* one internal thing and others *kata* other internal things. As Socrates says here, such a thing would most likely be composite. We can now understand why, given that it has some sort of internal structure. If, by contrast, all of a thing's features are *kata* the same things, it most likely does not have any such internal structure, and so is incomposite.[28] Socrates is pointing to an important feature of composite things that allows them to suffer from a distinct type of compresence of opposites, which incomposite things are very unlikely to suffer from.[29] On this reading, the distinction between composite and incomposite things is not tenuously related to Socrates' primary contrast between forms and ordinary objects, but rather crucial to this contrast: being composite is what allows ordinary objects to suffer from this sort of compresence.

In the spinning-tops example, when x is *f kata* y, y is some structural feature of x. I have suggested that in the kinship argument y is also such a structural feature. One might worry that this overextrapolates from our limited examples and that y could also be some aspect of x.[30] An aspect of x is also internal to it but need not be

---

[27] This example is inspired by *Hippias Major* 290a–d, although Socrates there uses the language of "making" (*poiein*) rather than "*kata*." Another similar example is at *Republic* 420c–d.

[28] Why are these connections "most likely," as opposed to certain? Perhaps because Socrates has not ruled out the possibility of, for example, an atom that has internal complexity – distinct height, width, shape – but is nonetheless incomposite. Similarly, he has not ruled out the possibility that something is composite, and so has an internal structure, and yet has all of its features *kata* the same structural feature, instead of some *kata* some structural features and others *kata* others.

[29] Ademollo 2018, 37–8, says that Socrates here attributes only change over time to sensible things, not anything like Irwin 1977b's "aspect change." I agree that Socrates does not describe this compresence of opposites as a type of change, but I disagree that Socrates here describes only change. For further discussion of Irwin's aspect change, see n. 44.

[30] E.g. Price 2009, 8 and 14, takes "*kata*" to range over aspects.

thought of as related to x's structure. However, this would then not help us understand the connection between (i) being incomposite and (ii) holding *kata* the same things. According to my account, holding *kata* different things requires structural complexity; something with such complexity would likely be composite, so that it could be destroyed through its parts dispersing. By contrast, something incomposite could have different aspects, and so, if *kata* ranged over aspects, an incomposite thing could hold *kata* different things. In the next subsection I will argue that the aspect interpretation faces further difficulties explaining why forms always hold *kata* the same things.

The second puzzle was why Socrates opposes the composite things with the incomposite things using two different temporal modifiers: the composite things hold "differently at different times and never *kata* the same things." I have argued that, if something never holds *kata* the same things, then it must always have an internal structure that makes it have some features *kata* some internal things, and others *kata* others. If Socrates had instead said that these things "hold *kata* different things at different times," then at a given time a thing might have all of its features *kata* the same things. Instead, at any given time it is beautiful *kata* some things, ugly *kata* others, large *kata* some things, and small *kata* others. Hence they literally at no time have their features *kata* the same things. Anything that both changes over time and has such internal complexity is, as Socrates says, very likely to be composite.

The point is that, because incomposite things lack internal complexity, there is only one thing for them to be *kata*. Whatever features they have, they have *kata* the same things. Why does Socrates use the plural, saying that they hold *kata* the same things? I take this to mean, "*kata* the same thing or things." This helps create a clear contrast: what is always *kata* the same things versus what is never *kata* the same things. But it is also worth noting that, while the expression "*hold kata* the same things" is very unusual Greek, the expression "*kata* the same things" is ordinary Greek, and the force of the plural is often hard to detect. It is often translated simply "in the same way" (compare to the English "along the same lines"). On the other hand, "*kata* the same thing" (κατὰ ταὐτόν) is much more unusual. The only clear occurrence that might come before Plato's corpus is Isocrates' *Against the Sophists* (12) and it only occurs seven times in Plato. Once in the *Cratylus* (436c), once in the *Republic* (in the principle of non-opposition), and the remainder in late dialogues. Given this, it is not surprising if Socrates uses "*kata* the same things" to mean "*kata* the same thing or things."

This ends my basic account of what it means to "hold *kata* the same things." My evidence for this view continues into the next subsection, where I argue that it clarifies Socrates' description of the forms and the many ordinary things. I am only claiming that it describes the meaning in the *Phaedo*. Perhaps it means something else elsewhere in Plato's corpus. That said, having surveyed Plato's 111 uses of "*kata* the same things," I have found no case in which the "same things" refer to something external to or not belonging to the subject.³¹ The unfortunate fact is that the *Republic* is the only place where Plato clearly offers an explanation of this *kata* relation and the *Phaedo* is the only place where Plato contrasts forms with sensible things in terms of whether they are composite. The *Phaedo* contains one of Plato's most detailed descriptions of the forms, so it is not surprising that this does not come up elsewhere, but this does mean that we have limited evidence.

6.3.2 *The Contrast between Forms and the Many Things*

This interpretation of "hold *kata* the same things" presents the kinship argument's next step, its descriptions of forms, in a new light:

> "Then let's turn," he said, "to the same things as in the previous argument. Take the being itself which is the object of our account when in our questions and answers we give an account of what it is. Does each of them always hold in the same way *kata* the same things or in different ways at different times? The equal itself, the beautiful itself, what each thing itself is, that which is – does that ever admit of change of any kind at all? Or does what each of them is always, since it is uniform itself *kata* itself, hold the same way *kata* the same things, and at no time, in no way, in no manner admit of any difference?"³² (78c10–d7)

This is a complicated description of the forms. Socrates' basic goal is to determine where to put the forms: in the group of things that always hold in the same way and *kata* the same things, or in those that hold different ways at different times and never *kata* the same things. If the forms are different at different times, they clearly are not in the former group. The reason he gives at the end of the passage for them not admitting of any difference, temporal or otherwise, is quite compressed:

> Or does what each of them is (i) always, since it is uniform itself *kata* itself, hold (ii) in the same way (ὡσαύτως) (iii) *kata* the same things, and (a) at no time, (b) in no way (οὐδαμῇ), (c) in no manner (οὐδαμῶς) admit (ἐνδέχεται) of any difference? (78d5–7)

---

³¹ "*Kata* the same things" is frequently used simply to mean "in the same way." For example, it is often used in the *Laws* to say that, just as a law applies to one sort of person, it applies *in the same way* to another sort (e.g. 765d). In this idiomatic Greek, we are not really supposed to think about the "things" in "*kata* the same things." In addition to this more idiomatic use of "*kata* the same things," sometimes the expression seems to be used in a more technical way. Just as forms are said to "hold *kata* the same things" in the *Phaedo*, so they are also described elsewhere in the corpus (in dialogues that, according to stylometry, come after the *Phaedo*): e.g. *Republic* 479e, *Sophist* 252a, *Timaeus* 28a, 52a, *Philebus* 61b. Another frequent use for this expression is to describe the rotation of the cosmos as *kata* the same things: e.g. *Statesman* 269e, *Timaeus* 34a, and *Laws* 898 a–b. I take this to mean that the rotation is always *kata* the same circle(s) within the cosmos.

³² At *Republic* 454c, ἀλλοίωσις clearly means difference, not alteration (as noted in LSJ). I translate it that way here, since alteration is a sort of difference over time, whereas Socrates is saying that the forms do not admit ἀλλοίωσις in way, manner, or time.

6.3 The First Half – Forms and the Many Things: 78b–79a

At first, let us set aside "since it is uniform *auto kath' hauto*." Note that this is not simply a claim about how the forms in fact are, but one about how they admit of being. They do not admit of any difference in time, way, or manner.[33] This is a strong claim about the nature of forms, and one that is paired with them always holding in the same way and *kata* the same things. Since (i) and (ii) clearly contrast with (a) and (c), it seems that (iii) – holding *kata* the same things – must contrast with (b), in no manner (οὐδαμῇ)[34] admitting of difference. As we saw, in the *Republic* Socrates also said that, if the top ceased staying still *kata* the straight in it, then it would in no manner (οὐδαμῇ) stay still. This is why I suggest that, when x is *f kata* y, x is *f* in a manner determined by y.

How should we understand the participial phrase, "being uniform itself *kata* itself" (μονοειδὲς ὂν αὐτὸ καθ' αὑτό)? I have translated it as an explanatory use of the participle ("since it is uniform itself *kata* itself"), because Socrates' goal is to show that the forms are in the group of things that always hold in the same way and *kata* the same things, and so it makes sense for this phrase to support this; moreover, it seems to do a good job of doing so.[35] Let us begin with "itself *kata* itself." First note that each form's being itself *kata* itself explains why each holds *kata* the same things: it is *kata* itself, and so not *kata* anything else, but rather *kata* the same thing(s). Most translators translate the "*kata*" differently in "itself *kata* itself" and "hold *kata* the same things," completely obscuring even the possibility of this inference.

If Socrates is indeed making such an inference, then he is using "*kata*" in "itself *kata* itself" the same way as he uses it in "hold *kata* the same things." This makes sense and helps us better understand "itself *kata* itself." I provided a detailed account of this expression in Section 3.4, which I will very briefly summarize here. Plato, like earlier authors, sometimes uses "itself *kata* itself" simply with "to be" (predicative use); other times he uses it along with a different verb or a predicate, such as when he says that the soul itself *kata* itself investigates (modifier use). The "*kata* itself" in "itself *kata* itself" is often taken to mean "by itself" in the sense of "all alone." But Socrates and earlier authors use the expression for things that are not on their own. For example, later in the kinship argument Socrates says that, when the soul comes to be itself *kata* itself, it comes to be *with* the unseen (79d). I argued that the expression, instead of meaning all alone, means that something is not identified as part of a larger group or mixture, but rather is acting independently, and so in this sense "on its own," even if with other things. In the defense speech, Socrates connects each form's being itself *kata* itself with its being pure (66a, 66e–67b) – just as Anaxagoras and *On Ancient Medicine* do with the closely related phrase "itself *epi* (upon) itself." Socrates says that the soul is alloyed and impure when it has the

---

[33] As I discuss in Section 10.4 (on the final argument), ordinary things, by contrast, admit of (δέχεσθαι) opposites like large and small at the same time (102e).
[34] I do not translate οὐδαμῇ as "in no way" because this is already being used for οὐδαμῶς. Socrates is carefully using different terms whose normal meanings are very similar.
[35] So Mann 2000, 107–8, n. 50.

body's nature mixed into it (67a); an impure soul, he says in the return to the defense, is not itself *kata* itself (81b–c). I argued in Section 3.4 that the expression is connected to purity because, if something is combined or mixed with something else, then it does not really act on its own, but rather along with this admixture. I suggested the translation "itself through itself" to capture the sense that it is pure, and so has only itself through(out) itself, as well as the idea that its own features and activities come "through" itself, in a way that determines how it has these features and performs these activities. When a soul is itself *kata* itself, it only has "itself" throughout it, and so is pure. The word "itself" here refers to what it truly is, once all impurities are removed – only it is throughout itself, determining its features.

My account of "*kata*" further clarifies how Plato is thinking of "itself *kata* itself." I have argued that, when x is *f kata* y, (i) y is not outside of x, but rather in some sense "belongs to" the structure of x, and (ii) y determines the manner in which x is *f*. With "itself *kata* itself," the x and y are the same, and so one is not outside the other; instead, y simply is the whole of x. When the soul itself *kata* itself investigates (modifier use), it investigates, not *kata* some part or narrowly understood structural feature of itself, nor *kata* some impurity within it, but rather *kata* its whole, true self. Its nature is what determines the manner in which it investigates. When Socrates says that a form or the soul simply is itself *kata* itself (predicative use), he is saying that all of its features are determined by its (whole) self, rather than having features in a manner determined by some part, structural feature, or impurity. The philosopher's soul must work hard to become itself *kata* itself, since most souls are polluted by the body, acting and investigating in a manner determined by the body, possessing desires that are *kata* the body. Each form, by contrast, is *always* itself *kata* itself. As noted in Section 3.4, this means that justice, largeness, and the other forms have nothing mixed into them that would give them any other features. This allows forms to provide a sort of intellectual clarity: considering justice itself *kata* itself allows us to examine only the features that belong strictly to justice.

Later in the kinship argument, Socrates contrasts the soul investigating itself *kata* itself (79d) with its investigating *dia* the senses (*dia* with the genitive, 79c). This use of "*dia*" is typically translated "through"; unlike the use of "*kata*," the senses are not internal or proper to the soul, but rather outside them, used as something like a tool for investigating. By contrast, when the soul itself *kata* itself investigates, it investigates using itself in accordance with its own nature.[36]

Can we consistently use "through" as a translation of the kinship argument's use of "*kata*," recognizing that it is somewhat different from what is meant by "*dia*"? Recall that, in the *Republic*, each top is moving *kata* its circumference and standing still *kata* the straight in it. To say that the top is moving "through" its circumference –

---

[36] I draw on this account of "itself *kata* itself" in Section 7.2, to explain Socrates' claim in the return to the defense that a pure soul is itself *kata* itself, whereas an impure soul is not, but rather has the body-like interspersed in it.

if this is understood as passing through the circumference – is not wrong, but does not capture the way in which the circumference determines the manner of the movement. Here it might be better to say that the top is moving "in line with" the circumference, but that translation does not capture the connection to purity (as "itself through itself" does), and it certainly makes the other expressions harder to parse: "itself in line with itself" and "holding in line with the same things" hardly roll off the tongue. Ideally there would be a uniform, easily readable translation of this use of *"kata,"* but I have not yet found something satisfactory. In any event, *"kata"* does not mean "because of" or "by virtue of," since the top is not spinning either because of or by virtue of the circumference; instead it is moving in relation to, or in line with, its circumference. "With respect to" does not capture that *"kata"* determines a manner in which something performs an action or has a feature, which is suggested by "through" and "in line with."

The last step in understanding Socrates' account of forms in the kinship argument is to consider his description of each as "uniform" (*monoeides*). Socrates later says that the visible things are each, by contrast, "multiform" (*polueides*, 80b4). This word "uniform" may even be used in the *Phaedo* for the first time in Greek literature.[37] As noted earlier, using a standard chronology of Plato's dialogues, Socrates is coining a number of terms and expressions in this stretch of text. In the return to the defense, Plato will go on to (apparently) coin two other words with the same *-eides* ending: bodily (literally "body form") (*sōmatoeides*, 81b5) and earthy ("earth form") (*geōdes*, 81c9).[38]

The evidence I describe in what follows suggests that "uniform" means here that the forms are simple in such a way that they have no (even non-spatial) parts with independent functions or roles.[39] In saying that forms are "uniform," Socrates is thus saying that anything attributable to a form is not attributed to some part or structural feature of it (since it has no internal complexity), but rather to the entire form. Being uniform does not require having only one feature – Socrates describes them as having many features, including being immortal, divine, and unchanging – but rather being simple in a sense that makes them partless, so they do not have any of these features *kata* some part or structural feature. The primary evidence for this

---

[37] It is also used in the *Symposium*, as discussed later in this subsection, which many people think is earlier than the *Phaedo*. What is testified before Plato, in some texts of Parmenides' B8 fragment (line 4), is μουνογενές. I suspect that the similarity is not an accident. The vocabulary used here to describe forms is close to that used by Parmenides in B8, esp. lines 3–4, 29–30, but at the same time differs in important ways. (The same is true of Anaxagoras B12.) Plato seems to me to be alluding to Parmenides (and Anaxagoras) while purposefully putting things slightly differently. In the *Timaeus*, Timaeus uses Parmenides' term μονογενές to describe the world soul as being one of a kind (31b, 92c). Socrates, I take it, does not think that the forms are one of a kind – to the contrary, he thinks they are *sungeneis* with each other and souls are *sungeneis* with them. While they are not of single *genos*, each is of a single form, and so *monoeides*.
[38] I owe this observation about σωματοειδές and γεῶδες to Gábor Betegh.
[39] For a similar idea, see Hackforth 1955, 81, n. 2.

interpretation comes from passages in the *Republic*, *Phaedrus*, and *Symposium*. Near the end of *Republic* X, Socrates asks whether or not the true nature of the pure soul includes several parts. He does so by asking whether the soul in its pure state is "uniform" or " multiform" (611b–612a). Similarly, in the *Phaedrus* Socrates asks whether the soul is "simple" or "multiform," where this is determined by whether or not it has different parts with different functions (270e–271a). In considering the possibility that the soul is uniform in the *Republic* or simple in the *Phaedrus*, Socrates is not doubting that it could have several things attributed to it; instead, he is considering the possibility that anything attributed to it is attributed to the whole soul. The term "uniform" is applied twice to the form of the beautiful in the *Symposium*. The first time (211b1) is part of such a long description of the form that it is difficult to know what its force is supposed to be. The second time, though, beauty itself being "uniform" is closely connected to seeing it as "unalloyed, pure, unmixed, and not contaminated with things like human flesh, color, and much other mortal nonsense" (211e1–3, in Rowe's translation). Having something mixed into beauty itself would give it a sort of complexity that Socrates rejects. An alloy is complex, even if the metals in it are thought of as thoroughly mixed in such a way that they are not in spatially different locations. Each form is one simple thing with no parts or admixtures, spatial or otherwise.[40] The forms, being uniform, are always pure.[41]

In Section 3.4 we saw that Socrates treats something that is "itself *kata* itself" as pure, just as he treats something that is uniform as pure. The two notions are closely related but make distinct claims. To describe something as "itself *kata* itself" is to say that its features hold in a manner that is determined by itself. Something that is truly uniform has no internal structure or impurities; its features could only hold *kata* itself – hence, it will be itself *kata* itself. Hence each form's being uniform ensures that it is itself *kata* itself, and that, in turn, ensures that it always holds the same way *kata* the same thing(s).

I have argued that "*kata*" here picks out a subtle relation where, if x is *f* kata y, y is connected to the internal structure of x. Let me return to an alternative raised in the previous subsection: that y could also be an aspect of x. It is difficult to see on what basis one could deny that forms have distinct aspects – for example, a divine aspect and a stable aspect. But then it would seem that a given form does not always

---

[40] Mann 2000, 81, says it is "natural" to suppose the form of x is uniform just in case the form of x is *only* x, having no other features. However, Socrates includes "uniform" in a list of several other features that all the forms have: unseen, immortal, indestructible, always in the same state, and so forth (80b). Silverman 2002, 91, suggests that *monoeides* means that each form is its essence, which he interprets as a single property. Silverman allows that a form could have other properties. But if this interepretation were right, the participial phrase in question would then only explain why a form's essence does not differ in time or manner, whereas it should explain why forms do not differ *in any way*.

[41] In the *Republic* (611b–612a) Socrates asks about the true nature of the soul once it has become "pure" (611c2), whether it is uniform or multiform. This allows that the impure soul might be multiform because it is polluted, even if its true nature is uniform.

hold in the same way *kata* the same things, because it would hold in some ways *kata* some aspects and other ways *kata* other aspects. But Socrates explicitly says that they hold in the same way *kata* the same things. This provides further reason to think that "*kata*" does not range over aspects.

To finish this long account of "hold *kata* the same things," "itself *kata* itself," and "uniform," we should consider the contrasting case of the many beautiful and equal things.

> What about the many beautiful things, such as people or horses or cloaks or anything else whatsoever that are of that sort? Or again, equal things, and so on for all the things that share the names of those things? Do they hold *kata* the same things, or – entirely the opposite to those things – do they hold at no time, virtually in no way *kata* the same things, either as themselves or as one another? (78d10–e4)

Each of the many beautiful things share the same name as the beautiful itself – in Greek, each can be referred to as "the beautiful" – but they differ from the beautiful itself in whether they always hold *kata* the same things. I have argued that, if something holds *kata* the same things, it has whatever features it has *kata* the same things. The forms *always* hold *in the same way* (ὡσαύτως) *kata* the same things. To consider the contrast with the many beautiful things, begin by setting aside the "virtually" (ὡς ἔπος εἰπεῖν). The many beautiful things hold *at no time* virtually *in no way* (οὐδαμῶς) *kata* the same things. In particular, they – and the many equal things, and so forth – at no time, in no way hold *kata* the same things *either as themselves or one another*. Compare: we do not like the same kinds of ice cream either as ourselves or as one another. It is easy to understand the idea that we do not like the same kinds of ice cream as one another. But for us not to like the same kinds as ourselves, each of us must like and not like the same kinds of ice cream, for example simultaneously liking and not liking chocolate. Similarly, for the many beautiful things not to hold *kata* the same things as *one another* is for one to hold *kata* one thing, another to hold *kata* another thing. Perhaps one horse is beautiful *kata* its mane but not its shape, another *kata* its shape but not its mane. What does it mean for each thing not to hold in some way *kata* the same things as *itself*? This requires it to have some feature *kata* one thing, but not have this feature *kata* another thing.[42] Although Socrates softens the claim with "virtually," he says that the beautiful things *in no way* hold *kata* the same things as themselves; thus, for *any* given feature, each beautiful thing will both have this feature *kata* one thing and not have it *kata* another thing. This is the compresence of opposites that the many ordinary objects have *kata* different things.

The phrase translated here "virtually" (ὡς ἔπος εἰπεῖν) softens a claim. Ademollo argues, I think rightly, that in this passage it softens the word that comes directly after

---

[42] In the conclusion to the kinship argument, Socrates puts his description in the singular, referring to a single thing that "never holds the same way *kata* the same things as *itself*" (80b4–5). This confirms the account of "themselves" given here.

it: "in no way" (οὐδαμῶς). He notes that Socrates makes each of the other claims about the many ordinary objects elsewhere in the kinship argument without softening these claims (see esp. 80a–b).[43] Moreover, if Socrates is softening this, the many beautiful things can still be in the group specified at the beginning of the argument – the things that "hold in different ways at different times and never hold *kata* the same things." To be a member of this group, it is not necessary to *never* hold in the same way; they just need to sometimes hold one way and at other times another way. But to be a member of this group, it is necessary to *never* hold *kata* the same things. Thus the many beautiful things will always have some feature *kata* one thing and an opposing feature *kata* something else. Socrates is embracing a very strong version of the compresence of opposites.[44]

6.3.3 *Summary and the Final Contrast between Forms and Ordinary Objects*

Socrates begins the argument by claiming that, if something is composite, it is most likely to be the sort to be dissipated or divided, and, if it is incomposite, then it, if anything, avoids any such division. Then he notes that the things that always have the same features and hold *kata* the same things are most likely to be incomposite. I have argued that, if x is *f kata* y, y is related to the structure of x and y determines the manner in which x is *f*. For example, if something is large *kata* its width, then width is a structural feature of this thing and the manner in which it is large is determined by its width. The forms, Socrates argues, belong to this group of incomposite things that do not change over time and have all their features *kata* the same thing. They belong to this group because each form is uniform and itself *kata* itself. Being "uniform" means that each is simple in a way that involves it having no parts or impurities. Thus, since forms are uniform, they do not have any features in a manner determined by some part or impurity. Being uniform in fact ensures that each form is itself *kata* itself; there is nothing else for it to be *kata* other than itself. Because each form is itself *kata* itself, it always holds *kata* the same thing(s) – namely itself. Each form has all its features in a manner determined by itself, as a whole. By contrast, things that both change over time and are never *kata* the same things are most likely to be composite: they both have internal structure and change, and so are very likely to have parts. Ordinary objects belong to this

---

[43] Ademollo 2018, 38–40.
[44] There is some similarity between this account and Irwin 1977b's idea of "aspect change," but also important differences. According to Irwin, in addition to the ordinary sort of change, Plato is committed to there being "aspect change," which does not involve change in an ordinary sense, but rather being *f* in one aspect and not *f* in another. Unlike Irwin, I am not claiming that Socrates refers to this sort of compresence of opposites as a "change." Moreover, unlike Irwin's talk of "aspects," I have argued that *"kata"* relates something to its internal structure. Finally, Irwin thinks that the compresence of opposites applies because opposites exist within a kind such as horse, whereas I've argued that the opposites exist within individuals such as a particular beautiful horse.

group, since they nearly constantly change their features and the features that they have are always *kata* a variety of different parts or internal structural features.

Fitting with the unfolding structure of the dialogue, this is a much fuller description of the forms and of ordinary objects than Socrates provided in the recollecting argument. There he said nothing about each being uniform, being itself *kata* itself, always holding *kata* the same things, or being incomposite – or the many *f*-things having the opposite features. I argued that the main contrast in the recollecting argument has to do with time: the many equal things are sometimes equal, other times not, whereas equality itself is never inequality. That returns here with the idea that many beautiful things sometimes are one way, other times another way, whereas the forms always hold in the same way. The one feature of ordinary objects and the forms that is thematized in the recollecting argument, but not here, is that ordinary *f*-things are deficient and want to be like the form of *f*-ness, but fall short and are not *f* in the way the form of *f*-ness is. The only resource in the recollecting argument for understanding this deficiency is that ordinary things change over time. The kinship argument adds that the ordinary *f*-things are never *kata* the same things as themselves or as one another, and so are both *f* and not *f* at the same time. This likely should be seen as another way in which the ordinary *f*-objects fall short of the form of *f*-ness. Similarly, it seems fair to describe as deficiently *f* anything that is simultaneously *f* and not *f*. Much has been clarified, but we do not yet know why forms are uniform and themselves *kata* themselves. This, I will argue, is explained over the final two stages of Socrates' unfolding account of the forms (namely forms as causes and the final argument, Sections 9.7, 10.4, and 10.5). Socrates also clarifies in the final stage why the many *f* things are, by contrast, multiform.

Despite having learned much about the forms and ordinary objects, so far nothing has been said in the kinship argument about being visible or invisible. That is the next step:

> Now isn't it true that these you could touch, see, and perceive with the other senses, but that when it comes to those that hold *kata* the same things, you could never get hold of them with anything other than the reasoning of your thought, such things being unseen and not visible? (79a1–4)

The language here is almost identical to that used in the defense speech (65c–66a) and alludes to a central idea Socrates articulates there: that we do not perceive the forms. In Section 3.6 I noted that he seems to be suggesting a category difference between forms and visible things, without saying what these categories are. We now have a basic account of the categories. The difference between them is not, in the first instance, in terms of the perceptible–non-perceptible divide, but in terms of the forms' being uniform, always *kata* themselves, and unchanging – unlike the many *f*-things. He does not explain why being unseen is connected to these other, systematically interconnected features of the forms. Perhaps being tangible or visible requires spatial extension, which in turn requires a level of structural complexity – at least length, breadth, and depth. But Socrates does not explicitly draw any such connection and may not be thinking in these terms.[45] Section 3.6 noted that the defense speech provides the dialogue's most intuitive argument that forms are distinct from ordinary objects: forms are not seen, whereas ordinary objects are. But while this provides a reason to think *that* they are distinct, it does not explain why they are. Being visible or invisible is the most salient feature for us and so Socrates first distinguishes them using this distinction in the defense speech. But these are features that relate to us, unlike the independent features of forms and ordinary objects that were identified earlier in the kinship argument: ordinary objects change over time, whereas forms do not; forms always hold *kata* the same things, whereas ordinary objects never do.

Socrates uses "visible" and "unseen" to name these two groups, but his basic description of each group is in terms of whether it is *kata* the same things: "the unseen always holds *kata* the same things, the visible never holds *kata* the same things" (79a9–10). The term "unseen" is associated with the divine, setting up Socrates' later connection between "Hades" and the things that are unseen (80d) – a connection that is crucial in the return to the defense. As we will see, over the course of the second half of the argument Socrates associates more and more features of the divine with the "unseen." But he does not mention "unseen," or anything to do with being imperceptible, in his final, lengthy summary of this group's features (80b). This, again, suggests that the perceptible–imperceptible divide is not one of the fundamental differences between forms and ordinary things, even if this is one of their most noticeable differences.

6.4 THE SECOND HALF OF THE ARGUMENT – THE SOUL'S KINSHIP WITH THE UNSEEN: 79A–80B

We have finished examining one of the argument's major contributions to the dialogue – its description of forms and ordinary objects – and turn now to its other major contribution – its account of the soul. (I discuss its account of the body separately, in the next section.) Once Socraters has provided an initial characterization of these two kinds – the unseen and the visible – his strategy is to argue that the

---

[45] Betegh (unpublished) notes that the *Phaedo* is the first place in extant Greek literature where a non-organic thing is called a "body": Simmias claims that the lyre itself and its strings are bodies (85e–86a). Betegh notes that, in the *Phaedo*'s return to the defense, Socrates introduces the term "body-like" (*sōmatoeides*), apparently using this also for the first time in Greek literature (as discussed in Section 7.2). Before Plato, "body" always belongs to something living or previously living. By the *Sophist*, such a notion of a non-organic body is treated as obvious (246a–b). Aristotle is the first extant author to clearly lay out the idea that a body involves spatial extension (*de Caelo* 1.1), although in the *Timaeus* (53c) there is at least the notion that body involves depth. So perhaps Socrates does not provide a clear connection between being perceptible and being composite because he has not yet developed the relevant category that combines these: body.

soul is more similar and akin to the unseen than to the visible, whereas the body is more similar and akin to the visible. His descriptions of the unseen and the visible are not held fixed here; instead, as he relates the soul and the body to these two kinds, he further describes each kind until the unseen is identified with the divine and the visible with the mortal.

In the basic sense of the word, to claim that the soul is "akin" (*sungenes*) to the unseen is to say that it belongs to the same kin as the unseen and so is related to it. In this broader sense, we can roughly think of them as sharing a genus but being different species.[46] Confirmation of this comes directly after the kinship argument, where Socrates treats it as a result of the argument that the soul is naturally of the same sort (ἡ τοιαύτη καὶ οὕτω πεφυκυῖα, 80d8–9) as the unseen. The kinship argument argues for this conclusion by pointing to three features that indicate the soul's similarity and kinship with the unseen: (i) the soul is itself unseen, (ii) it becomes like the unseen when it itself *kata* itself investigates, (iii) and it is by nature a ruler, just as the unseen is.[47] Note that the latter two relate the soul to its ability (ii) to know and (iii) to rule. Socrates is arguing that, for the soul to possess these basic abilities, its nature must be like that of the divine unseen. I consider each of these three features in what follows, but my focus will be on (ii), since it is both the most difficult description and also, in my view, the most important.

Socrates begins by asking whether the soul is seen, and Cebes says that it is not seen by human beings, at any rate. Supposedly Cebes is suggesting that perhaps something with different eyes could see it. Socrates responds: "But what we were talking about was what is and what isn't visible (τὰ ὁρατὰ καὶ τὰ μή) to human nature" (79b9–10). This clarifies that the visible–unseen distinction is fundamentally understood in terms of how *we* relate to the soul and the unseen, unlike the other two features, which are not defined in terms of us. Socrates may also be leaving open a different sense in which the soul is visible.[48] In the return to the defense, Socrates says that the soul *sees* (ὁρᾶν, 83b) what is intelligible and unseen; he also speaks there of what is unseen *to the eyes* (81b). Perhaps, just as the forms can be seen by the soul, so too our souls can be seen by other souls. Socrates is clarifying that in any event the soul is not visible using our human, bodily senses.

Having secured agreement that the soul is unseen and the body visible, Socrates then concludes that the soul is more similar to *the* unseen and the body more similar to *the* visible. In the return to the defense, Socrates says that some impure souls present apparitions that can be seen; he says that such souls are seen (81c–d). This is

---

[46] The term "akin" is sometimes used this way in the late dialogues, when describing collection and division. In fact the Visitor in the *Sophist* describes a core part of his method of collection and division as determining what is and is not akin (227a–b).
[47] So Olympiodorus 2009 ad loc.
[48] So Burnet 1911 ad loc.

sometimes treated as undermining the kinship argument.[49] But Socrates is claiming only that the soul is more similar to the unseen than to the visible, not that the soul is a member of the class "the unseen." If some souls are occasionally seen, that does not undermine his claim that they are similar and akin to *the* unseen. Note also that Socrates does not directly infer that the soul's being unseen makes it *akin to* the unseen, nor does he say that it indicates something about the soul's nature – he only says that it shows that they are similar (79b). By contrast, he claims that the next feature (ii) indicates kinship with the unseen and that the following one (iii) shows that the soul's nature resembles the unseen.

I take the next set of contrasting features to be the most important for the kinship argument's account of the nature of the soul. Socrates begins by saying that, when the soul investigates with the body, it is dragged into the things that never hold *kata* the same things and wanders, is disturbed, and is giddy as if drunk, because it is grasping things of this sort (79c).[50] Unfortunately Socrates' contrasting description – of what happens when the soul itself *kata* itself investigates – is one of the most difficult sentences in the dialogue:

> But (I) whenever [the soul] itself *kata* itself investigates, it departs into that which is pure, always is, is immortal, and holds in the same way; and (II), because it [the soul] is akin to this, it always comes to be with this whenever it comes to be itself *kata* itself and is able to do so; and (III) it then ceases from its wandering, and around (περί) those things always holds the same way *kata* the same things, because it is grasping things of this sort; and (IV) this condition (πάθημα) of the soul is called "wisdom"? (79d1–d7)

From the first half of the kinship argument, we can understand why Socrates says in (I) that the things investigated, the forms, always are and hold in the same way. But why are they pure and immortal? I argued in the previous section that, since each form is itself *kata* itself and uniform, it is pure. It is not as easy to explain why they are immortal. The first half of the argument has given us reason to think they are indestructible, since they are incomposite. But in the ancient Greek context to call something immortal is not simply to make a claim about its ability to be destroyed; it is to put it among the divine by giving it a key characteristic of the gods.[51] The reason to think that the unseen is immortal is that it (a) always is, (b) is unseen, and (c) is pure – all characteristics of the divine. This extension to immortality is crucial for the overall structure of the dialogue, since, at the end of his cloakmaker objection,

---

[49] So e.g. Dorter 1982, 79; Woolf 2004 takes it as a sign that the argument is not meant to show that all souls are indestructible.

[50] Socrates' talk of the soul as "wandering" should be understood alongside his later claim that ordinary people's souls do not take the same journey as philosophers, but rather are unaware of where they are going (82d). They move aimlessly. By contrast, the philosopher heads in the direction in which philosophy leads (82d; cf. Section 9.3 and 11.3).

[51] Long 2019 examines this throughout ancient Greek and Roman philosophy. Woolf 2004, 113 makes this point about the kinship argument.

Cebes asks Socrates to show that the soul is immortal and indestructible (88b), apparently generalizing Socrates' description of the unseen here as immortal and unable to disintegrate (as I discuss in Section 10.2). This, in turn, is what leads Socrates to argue for the soul's immortality in the final argument. In doing so, he argues that the soul has a characteristic feature of the divine unseen.

Socrates' next claim, (II), is especially difficult. It helps to reverse the order of the clauses and to fill in the references of some of its pronouns. Doing so yields: "whenever the soul comes to be itself *kata* itself, it always comes to be with the unseen, since it is akin to the unseen." I argued in the last section (building on my discussion in Section 3.4) that when the soul is itself *kata* itself, all its features and activities are *kata* itself – that is, in a manner determined by its true self. Socrates is saying that, when the soul acts in the way determined by its true self, it comes to be with the unseen, because the soul is akin to this. Why would being akin to the unseen mean that it comes to be with it? This would not make sense if being akin simply meant sharing a genus: cats and dogs share a genus but are not drawn to one another. Socrates seems to be suggesting that things are, in a basic way, drawn to their kin, much as, in the *Timaeus*, the hot is said to move to what is akin to it (79d). In the *Republic*, the soul is said to long (ἐφίεται) to be with what is divine and immortal and always is *because* it is akin to this (611d–e); this kinship provides it with an impulse (ὁρμή) to be with what is. I suggest that here, too, the soul is drawn to its kin; one's kin are one's own, and things have a basic impulse to be with their own. In Section 7.2, I argue that the same mechanism draws infected souls to the visible, since the pollution within them is akin to the visible.

In (II) Socrates uses the soul's kinship to explain why it acts as it does. But is this not begging the question, given that the kinship argument is trying to show that the soul is akin to the unseen?[52] I take Socrates to be starting from the phenomenon and working back to what explains it. According to (I), when the soul itself *kata* itself investigates, it comes to be with the unseen. And so, *a fortiori*, (II) when the soul becomes itself *kata* itself – and so does all its activities *kata* itself – it comes to be with the unseen. Why is our soul brought to the forms, rather than away from them, when it investigates through its own nature? The soul's kinship with the forms explains the phenomenon that both Socrates and Cebes agree takes place: (I) the soul is drawn to forms when it investigates *kata* itself. One could imagine the soul as having an unfortunate nature that meant that, when it investigates on its own, it is led away from the truth. But then it would not be drawn to what is when it inquires on its own. Since it is so drawn, we can infer that it is akin to what is.

Socrates' reasoning here is similar to that of some Presocratic philosophers, who identify the soul either as a mixture of elements or as some key element. They seem to think that the nature of the soul must have something in common with what it cognizes: in order to cognize fire, it must be composed of fire, or at least of

---

[52] A question Rowe 1993 notes ad loc.

something related to fire.[53] Socrates thinks that the ultimate objects of knowledge are not fire or air, but the forms; hence the nature of the soul must accordingly be quite different from what these Presocratics identify – Socrates thinks the soul must be akin to the forms to grasp them.

Socrates next says that (III), since the soul is grasping things that always hold *kata* the same things, it comes to a rest, like them. Here we see a way in which the soul's nature is fixed, but at the same time can vary within fixed constraints. The soul's kinship with the forms means that it always is broadly similar to them; the soul then becomes specifically more like them as it grasps them – in particular, it comes to hold the same way *kata* the same things, just like them. In doing so, the soul comes close to acquiring the central defining feature of the unseen – always holding *kata* the same things – although of course the soul previously did not hold *kata* the same things, and so does not *always* hold *kata* the same things.[54] It is sometimes thought that Socrates is only showing that the philosopher's soul is like the forms. But Socrates' claim is that all souls are akin to the unseen: every soul would come to be with the forms, if it truly became itself *kata* itself. This shared kinship makes all our souls form-like, even if in specific respects the philosopher's soul becomes more like the forms.

At the end of this difficult sentence, Socrates says (IV) "and this is wisdom." Recall that Cebes' challenge asks to be shown not only that the soul exists after death, but also that it has power and wisdom (70b). Socrates has now said what wisdom is, which allows him to argue more precisely, in the return to the defense, that the philosopher will have wisdom after death. This may be the most specific account of wisdom in the Platonic corpus. It is the state of the soul where it has become itself *kata* itself and at rest, since it is grasping the unseen. In the return to the defense, Socrates connects this to the philosophical soul's being happy after death (81a). Socrates might seem to be providing something like a function argument here (similar to Socrates' in *Republic* I, at 352d–354a, or Aristotle's in *Nicomachean Ethics* I.7): the nature of the soul determines its virtue (wisdom) and so happiness. But is this life a good, happy life *because* it fits with the soul's nature?[55] I suspect instead that this life is good because it is divine, and we are

---

[53] Aristotle makes a similar claim in *De anima* I.2; see also Theophrastus, *De sensibus* 1–2. For modern discussions of such a principle, see Lescher 1999, Betegh 2006, and Sassi 2018, ch. 4. According to Betegh 2013's account of Heraclitus, the soul is an exhalation that can become wetter or dryer; the wiser soul is dryer, making it more like fire, the key cosmic principle. This is analogous to how the soul in the kinship argument is broadly like the forms and becomes more like them as it becomes wiser.

[54] Socrates says that "it then ceases from its wandering, and around (περί) those things always holds the same way *kata* the same things." The "always" here is limited by what has come before. Compare: "I'm normally tired, but when I am around my beloved I always have lots of energy." One cannot infer from this that, in general, I always have lots of energy.

[55] *Pace* the last two sentences of Ebrey 2017b, where I suggested that the nature of the soul determines what it should do.

fortunate because our souls allow us to live a divine life. Socrates' description of the body in the kinship argument, which I have so far delayed discussing, is relevant here. He says that the body is more similar and akin to the visible; however, the body should *not* become more like the visible. Instead, the soul should rule over the body, opposing the body's desires and affections by getting the body to do gymnastics, take medicine, and so on (see esp. 94b–e). Hence simple kinship does not determine what is good for something. If our own souls were akin to the visible, we would have every reason to fight against becoming more like it. Fortunately we are akin to the divine, and so when our soul acts *kata* itself, it becomes more like what is independently worth emulating.

This ends my account of how the soul's kinship with the forms is revealed by the way the soul properly investigates. It highlights the basic feature of the soul that allows us to become wise, divine, and so happy.

Let us turn to the last sign that the soul is similar and akin to the unseen: nature instructs the soul to rule the body and the body to be a slave (79e–80a). In the defense speech, Socrates says that we are enslaved to the body's service (66d). By contrast, here his claim is not that the soul (in fact) rules the body, but that it does do so by nature.[56] Again, the soul's nature is fixed in one respect, but able to vary in another: every soul's nature is to rule, but few act in accordance with their nature. Socrates describes the unseen here for the first time as "the divine," befitting its status as ruler. He has built up to this description by naming this group "the unseen" and then describing it as pure and immortal. This description means that the forms – as the only explicitly identified members of the unseen thus far – rule. I will argue in Section 9.7 that they rule by being what is responsible (*aition*) for things' being the way they are. At the same time, since the unseen is identified as ruling, this suggests that the gods are members of the unseen, as Socrates confirms soon after the argument (80d and 81a).

Preparing for his conclusion, Socrates gathers together the features that the soul is most similar to and those that the body is most similar to. He then asks if Cebes can think of any way in which the soul and body do not fit this description, and Cebes says no (80b). This is an underappreciated step in the argument. Socrates is not simply relying on these three characteristics of the soul; Cebes also cannot identify any features that would point in the other direction. It is only after this agreement that Socrates draws the conclusion that it belongs to the soul to be indestructible, or nearly so.

6.5 THE NATURE OF THE BODY

The *Phaedo*'s most famous reference to the body comes near the end of the dialogue, when Socrates quips to Crito that he can be buried "however you want,

---

[56] So e.g. Gallop 1975 ad loc.

as long as you can catch me and I don't escape you" (115c4–5). Socrates then says that Crito will be burying his body, not him. Early in the dialogue he already suggests that we are our souls, for example when he says that the body fills *us* up with "loves, desires, fears, and fantasies of every kind, and a great deal of nonsense," (66c2–4) and then says that "we" must be separated from the body if we are going to acquire pure knowledge (66c–d). This might suggest that Socrates simply identifies himself with his soul. The situation, however, is more complex.

In the second half of the kinship argument, Socrates says that "we are ourselves part body, part soul" (ἡμῶν αὐτῶν τὸ μὲν σῶμά ἐστι, τὸ δὲ ψυχή, 79b1–2; cf. 106e). Similarly, at the beginning of the final immortality argument, Socrates says that *properly speaking* Simmias exceeds Socrates because Socrates has smallness relative to Simmias' largeness (102c). Simmias, not merely his body, is *properly* said to exceed. Socrates further says, "I admit and withstand smallness and, while still being just who I am, am small" (102e3–5). This only makes sense if, as Socrates says in the kinship argument, his body is a part of him. But how is this compatible with Socrates' identifying himself with his soul rather than his body?

My proposal is that Socrates thinks that our bodies are temporarily a part of us, so long as we are embodied, but an inessential part. The body is like a limb that one can lose without one's ceasing to be what one is. And it is more like a diseased limb than a healthy one (cf. *Symposium* 205e), and so the philosopher would rather be without the body, and awaits release from the body by the gods (Section 3.1). When Socrates speaks of the body's filling "us" with desires, he is speaking about us *qua* our essential element, our soul. By contrast, when he speaks of himself as admitting smallness, he is including his non-essential part, the body. This fits with Socrates' speaking of the time before the soul was in human form (εἶδος, 76c12), or of when the soul arrives in the human kind or form (γένος, 82b7; εἶδος, 92b6). We are our souls, and these souls occasionally take on human form, and other times become other animals, when they reincarnate. When they do so, they temporarily have a body.

What, then, is the body? First note that throughout the dialogue, including in the kinship argument, Socrates uses the term "body" to pick out the organic body of the living (or once living) person – except in Simmias' *harmonia* objection, where "body" seems to be applied to something non-organic for the first time in Greek literature: the lyre and its strings are referred to as "bodies."[57] Socrates' description of the body in the kinship argument walks a delicate line. The first, and perhaps strangest, thing to recognize is that he says that the body is more similar and akin (79b, 79e, 80b) to the visible, but does not say that it is a member of the visible. Just as "*the* unseen" is a name for a specific group that the soul is not a member of, so also "*the* visible" is the name for a specific group and Socrates never says that the body is a member of this group. Of course, the body is visible, but there is more to

---

[57] See n. 45 in this chapter.

being a member of this group than simply being visible. One could maintain that Socrates thinks that the body is a member of this group and simply does not mention it. However, one would not normally say, for example, that someone is akin to the gods if they were a god. Rather than resist attributing a counterintuitive view to Socrates, it is worth considering why he might not think the body is a member of the visible. What features does the body have that make it not entirely like the visible things?

My suggestion is that the body does in a distorted and imperfect way what the soul does properly; this gives the body's nature something of what is found in the unseen, even if it is still more similar and akin to the visible. Recall that the soul is more similar and akin to the unseen than to the visible because (1) the soul is unseen, (2) it is drawn to the unseen when it inquires itself *kata* itself, and (3) it naturally rules the body. I argued that (2) and (3) identify something about the nature of the soul. Let me start with (3). While the soul naturally rules the body, for most people the body in fact rules over the soul. The body has the capacity to rule, even if it is not the rightful ruler. Turning to (2), while the soul should inquire itself *kata* itself, the body offers a (faulty) means of inquiry: the senses. Moreover, as Socrates will emphasize in the return to the defense, the body can produce views in the soul about what is true and what is false, through the bewitching (81b) and riveting (83b–d) effects of bodily desires, fears, pleasures, and pains. And so the body, like the soul, provides a way of forming beliefs. By contrast, the many beautiful and equal things make some claim on being beautiful and being equal, but no claim on ruling or arriving at the truth. Hence, by the criteria identified in the kinship argument, the soul is more similar and akin to the unseen than the body is, but that still allows the body to have some similarity to the unseen. All this could explain why Socrates does not commit himself to the body's being a member of the visible.[58]

Why would Socrates adopt such a notion of the body? At a theoretical level, it makes sense within a picture in which the soul and the body deeply influence each other. While the body influences the soul much more than we would like, the soul's influence on the body is even greater. As Socrates notes in the final argument, the body would not be alive without the soul. Perhaps in bringing life to the body, the soul brings with it other characteristics – an impulse toward rule and an influence on forming judgements.

6.6 CONCLUSION

Let me pull the argument together, highlighting the resulting account of forms, ordinary objects, and souls. The kinship argument examines whether or not the soul is the sort of thing to be dispersed. Socrates first notes that it belongs to composite

---

[58] Section 7.2 examines Socrates' notion of the body-like (τὸ σωματοειδές), connecting it to this account of the body and the body's kinship with the visible.

things to be dispersed and to incomposite things not to be. Then he claims that things that always hold in the same way and *kata* the same things are most likely to be incomposite. This is because to hold *kata* different things would require an internal structure that allows some features to hold *kata* some parts (or structural features) and other features *kata* other parts (or structural features). When x is *f kata* y, y is related to the internal structure of x and y determines the manner in which x is *f*. For example, when the top moves *kata* the circle in it, the circle is connected to the structure of the top, and the circle determines the manner in which the top is moving (namely, by spinning). I argued that Socrates uses the "*kata*" in "itself *kata* itself" the same way, so that, when he says that the soul itself *kata* itself investigates, he is describing a manner in which the soul is investigating, a manner determined by its entire self rather than by some foreign impurity within it or some part of it. Forms have all their characteristics by virtue of their entire self, since each is itself *kata* itself. Being "uniform" (*monoeides*) means that forms are simple in a way that involves having no impurity or parts. This is why forms must be *kata* the same thing (s) – namely themselves. By contrast, the many beautiful things not only change over time, but also have one feature *kata* one thing and an opposing feature *kata* something else. They will, for example, at the same time be both beautiful and ugly, but *kata* different things. Socrates identifies the forms as members of "the unseen," a group that always holds *kata* the same things. By contrast, ordinary objects belong to "the visible," which never holds *kata* the same things.

In the second half of the argument, Socrates argues that the soul is more similar and akin to the unseen things. He never says, nor does he argue, that the soul is a member of the unseen. Socrates identifies three features that make the soul more similar and akin to the unseen; while doing so, he identifies new features of the unseen, ultimately identifying it with the divine. The three features are: (1) soul is not seen; (2) it comes to be with the unseen when it itself *kata* itself investigates; and (3) it is by nature a ruler. In describing the second characteristic, Socrates says that wisdom is the state in which the soul has become itself *kata* itself through its kinship with the unseen. Thus, if the soul follows its nature, it will become wise. At the end of the argument, Cebes cannot identify any way in which the soul is more similar to the visible than to the unseen. And so Socrates takes the cumulative result of this to be that it belongs to the soul not to disintegrated at all, or something very near to this.

The kinship argument identifies fixed features of the soul's nature that are supposed to show that all souls are by nature related to the divine; at the same time, it identifies ways in which the soul's nature is flexible within this fixity. The soul has fixed abilities to acquire knowledge and rule over the body, but is flexible as to whether it exercises these abilities. This flexibility is crucial for Socrates' ethical account in the return to the defense. The kinship argument does a better job than the previous arguments of explaining what sort of thing the soul is and why we would expect something of this sort not to disperse; however, the features of the soul that it points to – being unseen, drawn to the forms when it inquires, and a natural ruler – do not identify *in virtue of what* the soul is not destroyed. By contrast, the final argument identifies the relevant feature of the soul that is supposed to be the basis for its not being destroyed: it is a bringer of life. The final argument does not provide a basis for the dialogue's ethical account or the soul's other psychic abilities, but it clarifies the soul's relationship to life and, in doing so, more precisely identifies a reason to think that the soul will not be destroyed upon death – and, indeed, that it is immortal and indestructible.

7

The Return to the Defense

80d–84b

This section of the *Phaedo* is, along with the defense speech, one of the two major ethical discussions in the dialogue and, arguably, the most important, since Socrates explains here in greater detail the ethical threat posed by the body.[1] Discussions of the ethics of the *Phaedo* tend to draw from both of these parts of the dialogue without differentiation; however, the return to the defense is importantly different: it draws on the cyclical and kinship arguments to revisit and further defend nearly every claim in the defense speech, thereby clarifying the theoretical basis for many of them.[2] Just like the defense speech, the return to the defense has received relatively little attention, likely for the same reasons: (i) its religious language is taken as a sign that this is not philosophically serious and (ii) most people find off-putting the radical asceticism that Socrates seems to endorse. My approach, as usual, is to show that Socrates is making serious philosophical points while defending radical claims that we are not likely to find antecedently appealing.

Socrates provides here an interconnected account of virtue, happiness, moral psychology, reincarnation, and soul–body interaction. In the kinship argument, Socrates argued that, because of the soul's kinship with the divine unseen, when the soul becomes itself through itself, it comes to know the divine and thereby becomes more like it (79d; see Section 6.4). Here we learn that this will ultimately

---

[1] In addition to chapter 3 (on the defense speech), readers primarily interested in ethics may also wish to read Sections 6.4 and 6.5 (on soul, wisdom, and the body), Section 8.4 (on how Simmias' theory of the soul cannot explain basic ethical facts), Chapter 11 (on justice, benefits and harms to the soul, and the problem of evil in the afterlife) and Chapter 12 (on how Socrates exemplifies his ethical ideal in the death scene).

[2] Socrates returns to the claims that the body is a prison (82e, cf. 62b), that philosophy provides a purifying rite (82d, cf. 69c), that non-philosophers display something that they call "temperance" (82a–b, cf. 68c–69a), and that the philosopher will go to Hades and be with the gods (80d–81a, cf. 63b–c, 70c), desires to be dead (80e–81a, cf. 64a), does not use the senses to investigate (82e–83b, cf. 65a–67b), avoids bodily pleasures and pains (81b, 82e–84b, cf. 65c, 66b–67b), and possesses genuine courage (83e, cf. 69a–c).

allow the philosopher's soul to spend the afterlife eternally with the gods, and so be eternally happy. By contrast, non-philosophers reincarnate because their desire for the body-like pulls them into a new body after death. Thinking through how this works will involve clarifying how Socrates understands the impurities in non-philosophers' souls. It is not easy to avoid the body's effects on the soul, because of the way in which the body deceives the soul into desiring things that are in fact not good for it. Socrates develops the account of true courage and temperance from the exchange passage (69a–c) in order to explain how the philosopher avoids and resists these insidious effects, allowing the soul to pursue wisdom and so be eternally happy.

Just as in the kinship argument, Socrates coins here new terminology and, as in the defense speech, he pushes words well beyond their standard meaning. We will need to consider carefully Socrates' newly coined terminology to understand the bold theories he advances.

7.1 INCORPORATING THE KINSHIP ARGUMENT INTO THE DEFENSE: 80D–81A

Cebes' challenge asked Socrates to show not merely that the soul exists after death but also that it will have wisdom (70b). The kinship argument provides a definition of wisdom (79d); Socrates draws on this definition here to explain why the purified soul will possess wisdom after death. In doing so, he responds to this part of Cebes' challenge.

Socrates begins with the idea that after death the philosopher's soul will meet the good and wise god (80d). Recall (63b–c; Section 3.2) that Socrates said in the defense speech that his strongest affirmation is that (Ia) he will enter the presence of wise and good gods, and hence he does not resent death but rather is hopeful. He also said that (Ib) he will be in the presence of good men, although he would not insist on this, and that (Ic) for these reasons he is hopeful that death is far better for the good than for the wicked. After Crito interrupts (63d–e), Socrates redescribes his aims. Rather than focusing on his own case, he claims that (IIa) any man who truly spends his life in philosophy has good reason to be confident when about to die, and that he is confident that (IIb) such a person will win very great benefits in the other world (63e–64a). In Section 3.2 I argued that the defense speech focused on addressing this second set of goals (IIa and IIb); only at the end does Socrates briefly argue for his original set of claims. Here, at the beginning of the return to the defense, Socrates uses the kinship argument to explain further his strongest affirmation, that (Ia) pursuing philosophy will bring him to the gods after death, as well as to further explain why (IIb) those who pursue philosophy will win very great benefits in the other world. The kinship argument provided a fuller understanding of what the divine is that Socrates hopes to be with and what kind of benefit comes from being with it. When combined with the next discussion, about those who are not pure, Socrates also clarifies why (Ic) death is far better for the good than for the wicked.

The defense speech's main argument explained why the true philosopher desires nothing other than being dead – a claim that Socrates refers back to here (80e–81a). By providing reasons for Ia–Ic and IIb, the return to the defense strengthens Socrates' explanation of why the philosopher desires to be dead. Socrates' definition of being dead requires the soul to be released from the body and to be itself through itself (64c; Section 3.3). Socrates here says that the philosopher is preparing for really (τῷ ὄντι, 81a1) being dead; by contrast, an impure soul is not itself through itself when released from the body (81b–c) and so does not meet Socrates' definition of being dead. In fact, as we will see in the next section, it reincarnates precisely because it is impure. This provides a new reason to say that such people are not truly dead – they are only temporarily released from a body.

Socrates' first step is to connect the kinship argument's account of the unseen to the defense speech's claim that, after death, the philosopher's soul will go to Hades and be with the gods:

> But as for the soul, his unseen (*aides*) part, which departs to a different sort of place, one which is noble, pure, and unseen, Hades (*haidēs*) as it truly is, where it will meet the good and wise god, the place to which, god willing, my soul too must go imminently... (80d5–8)

Socrates claims here that "Hades as it truly is" is unseen, suggesting an etymological connection between "Hades" (*haidēs*) and "unseen" (*aidēs*).[3] But this etymological connection is not his only reason for thinking that Hades is unseen; it also fits with the kinship argument's identification of *the* unseen with the divine (80a; Section 6.4). In the kinship argument Socrates used the same phrase, "departs to" (οἴχεται εἰς): when the soul inquires itself through itself, it departs to that which is pure and immortal when it comes to be with the things that always are (79d).[4] Once we are dead, no longer inhibited by the body, we can depart to the unseen divine, coming to grasp it in a way we could not when embodied (cf. Section 3.7). Hades, then, as the place where we come to be with the divine unseen, will itself be unseen.

According to Cebes' challenge (69e–70b), people fear that the soul dissipates and is not anything *anywhere*; if it really were *somewhere*, gathered together, there would be much hope that what Socrates is saying is true. Socrates addresses where the soul will go by describing Hades in the passage just quoted as a place (τόπος) that the soul departs to. This is perhaps the best evidence in the *Phaedo* for thinking that there is some sort of "realm" of the forms. But just as the soul does a type of "grasping" and "looking" that is very different from the bodily sort, so the sort of "place" it departs to is also very different. The forms, as uniform (*monoeidē*), could not have any width, length, and breadth (so Subsections 6.3.2 and 6.3.3). Thus this

---

[3] At *Cratylus* 404b, Socrates says that it is unlikely that the god Hades' name comes from "unseen," suggesting instead that it comes from his knowing (*eidenai*) everything fine and beautiful.

[4] Noted by Rowe 1993 ad loc.

Hades could not be a place in a sense that we would find recognizable. Similarly, our departure to there will not involve an ordinary change of location. Socrates could have rejected Cebes' request to show that the soul exists somewhere after death. Instead he argues that even the purified soul is somewhere, but this place is not like the ones we know. Socrates has repeatedly made this interpretive move in the *Phaedo*, especially with religious claims: in cases where we might expect him to deny that something exists, Socrates instead accepts that it exists, but interprets it radically differently from how it is normally understood.

Having identified Hades as the place where the unseen things are and reintroduced the idea that the philosopher is practicing for being dead, Socrates connects this practice to the pure soul's happiness after death, thereby explaining why (IIb) those who pursue philosophy will win very great benefits in the other world:

> So does a soul in this condition go off into what is similar to it, the unseen, the divine, immortal, and wise, where after its arrival it can be happy, separated from wandering, unintelligence, fears, savage sorts of love and other human evils, and just as is said of the initiates, does it truly spend the rest of time with gods? (81a4–10)

This is the first time Socrates has mentioned happiness in the dialogue and, as one would expect, it arises only once the philosopher is truly wise – after death. Socrates says that the soul spends the rest of time with the gods and so escapes the cycle of reincarnation. As discussed in the next section, the desire for the body-like pulls impure souls back into new bodies. Since the philosopher's soul has weakened and restrained such desires to the extent possible, it can avoid this fate. The soul itself through itself has no desire for the body-like and instead is drawn to what it is akin to – the unseen – thereby remaining eternally happy.

In this passage Socrates does not rely on what people say of the initiates; instead, his account explains why what is said of them is true. As noted in Subsection 3.8.2, Greek mystery initiation rituals, in general, aim at bringing initiates into a closer relationship with the divine, which in turn helps them have a better afterlife. Socrates here explains why the philosopher is the true initiate (cf. 69c–d), that is, why his purifying rite (wisdom) allows him to come into closer contact with the divine, both now (through inquiry) and after death.

7.2 THE BODY'S EFFECTS ON IMPURE SOULS: 81B–82B[5]

The defense speech focused on philosophers; the return to the defense discusses in greater detail the problems that the body brings to non-philosophers, thereby clarifying why philosophers avoid, to the extent possible, letting their bodies affect

---

[5] This section and Subsection 7.3.1 draw on Ebrey 2017b while adding significant new material. Ebrey 2017b engages more with rival interpretations of these passages, especially those of Woolf 2004 and Russell 2005.

their souls. Socrates articulates here an important idea for his ethical account: that the body deceives the soul using pleasures and desires. He then connects this to how the soul is reincarnated. Understanding this account requires thinking carefully through the impurities in an impure soul.

This section begins with a key passage for understanding the problems caused by the body:

> But now, I mean, take a case where a soul has been defiled and is impure (μεμιασμένη καὶ ἀκάθαρτος) when it is separated from the body, because it has always been coupled with the body, waited on it, loved it and been bewitched by it – by its desires and pleasures – so that the soul thinks nothing is true except the body-like (σωματοειδές), what one can touch, see, drink, eat, and enjoy sexually. By contrast, it has come always to hate, dread, and avoid what is murky and unseen to the eyes, but is intelligible and grasped with philosophy. Do you suppose that a soul in this condition will be unalloyed, itself through itself when released? (81b1–c2)

Let us begin with the idea that the impure soul has been bewitched by the body. The idea of bewitching suggests that these desires and pleasures make the soul a willing partner, but not for good reasons. Plato uses forms of the verb "to bewitch" (γοητεύειν) alongside "pleasure" (ἡδονή) in three other places in his corpus (*Republic* 413b–d and 584a and *Philebus* 44c). These passages make clear that pleasure, in bewitching us, changes our beliefs and desires without good reason and without our realizing it. This idea was already suggested in the defense speech, when Socrates says that the body enslaves us to its service, in part by filling us up with loves, desires, fears, and fantasies of every kind that lead us into wars, uprisings, and conflicts (66c–d). Supposedly people engaged in such conflicts do not think that they are enslaved to the body's service. Similarly, non-philosophers think that they are temperate, but in fact are intemperate (68e–69a), and so are deluding themselves (Section 3.5 and Subsection 3.8.1). Here, in the return to the defense, Socrates highlights what brings about this deception – desires and pleasures – and makes clear that it happens to all non-philosophers. If we reject Socrates' disapproval of bodily pleasures and desires – thinking that Socrates has removed part of what makes living worthwhile – this is, of course, precisely how his theory predicts that we will react, on the grounds that pleasures and desires have bewitched us.

Note that Socrates says that desires and pleasures change beliefs about what is true or real (ἀληθές). One might have thought that pleasure and desire would affect only what things are thought to be good. But instead we become so subservient to the body that we do not count anything as real unless it has some connection to bodily desires and pleasures – that is, to the things one is able to touch, see, drink, eat, or enjoy sexually. The body does not simply provide a (bad) means for inquiry; bodily pleasures and desires directly affect what we believe, as Socrates further discusses in the next section.

Socrates calls what one is able to touch, see, drink, eat, or enjoy sexually "the body-like" (τὸ σωματοειδές), a word normally translated "the corporeal." This word does not occur before Plato in extant Greek literature, nor does it occur in any of the Socratic dialogues; it seems to be used here for the first time.[6] By Plato's late dialogues, it seems connected to a notion of the body that counts any physical object as a body; but in the passage under discussion he connects it specifically to the objects of bodily desires and pleasures, as is appropriate, since "body" in the *Phaedo* up to this point has always referred to a living or once-living body. "The body-like," as Socrates glosses it here, is intimately related to our bodies, since the things identified as body-like are the objects of bodily pleasures and desires. Socrates' next two uses of the term "body-like" seem rather different from this one. Thinking through them is difficult, but important for understanding Socrates' account of soul–body interaction.

After Socrates and Cebes agree that an impure soul will not be unalloyed and itself through itself when it is released (that is, after death), Socrates says that instead it will be intermingled with the body-like (81c). Before considering what exactly it is intermingled with, note that impure souls need to be mixed with something or other. I argued in the previous chapter (Section 6.3) that the relevant use of "*kata*" in "itself through (*kata*) itself" identifies something *in* the subject that determines how an activity or a feature – or all of a thing's activities and features – apply to that subject. I argued that, when a soul is (simply) itself *kata* itself, it does all its activities and possesses all its features in a manner determined by its (true) self. If the soul is not itself *kata* itself, then some of its activities or features must be *kata* something else that is in it. This – however it is to be understood – is the impurity in the soul. In Section 3.4 I argued that this is analogous to a case where some copper does not melt at copper's normal temperature, despite being in normal conditions. In that case, there must be something mixed into the copper to make it behave differently, some impurity. Similarly, if the soul is not acting in the way natural for it, something must be mixed into it. As noted in Section 3.4, this is an Anaxagorean explanatory model: a thing's features are determined by what is mixed into it. In fact Socrates even uses Anaxagoras' vocabulary shortly after this passage, saying that after death some impure souls present a shadowy apparition that *"has a share* of the visible" (τοῦ ὁρατοῦ μετέχουσαι, 81d4, emphasis added; cf. Anaxagoras B12).[7]

I suspect Socrates' real commitment is to something's being interspersed with the soul, not to what this is. Whatever it is, the soul should be purified of it, since it undermines its eternal happiness. In the defense speech, Socrates says that the body pours loves, desires, fears, and fantasies into the soul (66c) and that, so long as we are

---

[6] I have learned much on this from Betegh (unpublished).
[7] See Furley 1976 and 2002 for the idea that in the autobiography Socrates is drawing on Anaxagoras' language of "having a share." I discuss a different Anaxagorean explanatory model in Section 10.4.

with the body, our soul can never become pure, itself through itself, but instead is infected by the body's "nature" (67a5). Here in the return to the defense, he identifies the thing that is in the soul as "the body-like." A few sentences earlier, Socrates glossed the body-like as "what one can touch, see, drink, eat, and enjoy sexually" (81b5–6). Supposedly things like wine and lentils – things one can drink and eat – are not being interspersed with the soul. (If nothing else, they are no more in the soul of the impure than in the soul of the pure, since everyone eats and drinks.) Perhaps "body-like" here means having a similar nature to the body's. This fits with the defense speech's idea that the soul is infected with the body's nature. In Section 6.5, I argued that the body's nature is connected to its attempt to rule and to its providing a faulty means for forming beliefs. Thus we could think of being interspersed with the body-like as (i) letting the body rule and (ii) forming beliefs in the body's way. In support of this interpretation, Socrates says, a few Stephanus pages later, that pleasures and pains make the *soul* body-like, "since it believes to be true the very things that the body says are true" (83d6–7). Simply believing things in a way that is influenced by the body is sufficient for making the soul body-like.

On the face of it, after Socrates says that the soul is interspersed with the body-like, he suggests a more physical interpretation of "body-like" than the one just outlined:

> And one must suppose, my friend, that the body-like is burdensome, heavy, earth-like and visible. That's what this sort of soul actually has, and so it is heavy and drawn back into the visible place by fear of the unseen and of Hades, drifting, as is said, around monuments and tombs, the very places where certain shadowy apparitions of souls indeed have been seen. Such apparitions are presented by souls like these, those that have not been released in a pure way but have a share of the visible – which is why they are seen. (81c8–d4)

Describing the body-like and the soul as "heavy" suggests that they are drawn downward, toward the center of the earth.[8] But, of course, the area above is no less visible than that below. Moreover, this passage seems to explain the soul's return to the visible in two different ways: (1) it is heavy, and (2) it is afraid of the unseen and Hades.[9] How are these related to each other?

We might be tempted to think that Socrates is speaking metaphorically. But the *Timaeus* gives accounts of the terms "heavy" (βαρύ) and "earth-like" (γεῶδες) (63c–d) that allow us to understand them here in a non-metaphorical way. "Earth-like" – alongside "uniform" and "body-like" – is a term with the "-*eides*" ending that Plato seems to have coined in the *Phaedo*. Timaeus says "the path toward what is akin (συγγενές) [to the earth and the earth-like, 63c] is what makes a thing moving along it 'heavy' and the region into which it moves 'below'" (63e4–6). If Socrates in

---

[8] In standard translations, the verb βαρύνεται is translated as "is weighed down," which makes this directional interpretation seem all the more natural. But it is simply the verb for being heavy.

[9] So also, Dorter 1982, 79–80.

the *Phaedo* is thinking of heavy and earth-like similarly, then something that is akin to and moving toward the earth is thereby heavy, regardless of where it is moving from. Typically, this movement comes from what we would consider to be above, but in this case the movement is from a disembodied state. (In the same part of the *Timaeus*, Timaeus defines light and above in terms of air (63d–e); the disembodied soul is neither in the air nor drawn to it, so is not above.) According to this reading, Socrates is saying in the passage under discussion that the impure soul is drawn back to the visible because the body-like is akin to the earth and so drawn to it. This does not require the soul to have something we would consider mass or bulk; it simply needs to have in it something that draws it back to the earth.

How does this *Timaeus*-inspired account fit with the idea that the soul is drawn back to the visible by its fear of the unseen and of Hades? Fear is *how* the body-like draws the soul away from the unseen and toward the visible. In the same way, Socrates says that impure souls, having paid their penalty by wandering around, are then "bound again into a body *by their desire* for that which follows them around, the body-like" (81e1–2, emphasis added; cf. 83d–e, 108a–c). These souls are interspersed with the body-like, so it follows them around, leading them to desire to be more body-like, drawing them back into another body. Fear and desire are the means by which the body-like's kinship to the visible pushes the impure soul away from the unseen and toward a new body. As noted in Section 6.4, in the *Republic* the pure soul is said to "long to (ἐφίεται) to be with what is divine and immortal and always is because it is akin to this" (611e1–2); this kinship provides it with an impulse (ὁρμή, 611e3) to be with what is. My suggestion is that the same sort of mechanism is in an impure soul: kinship between the impurity and the visible gives rise to a desire that draws the soul to the visible.

This fits with Socrates' subsequent discussion of different types of reincarnation (81e–82b). Impure souls retain their desires and fears after death (cf. 107d), which is why "in all likelihood" people are drawn into the bodies of animals that resemble them in character (gluttons into donkeys, tyrants into wolves, etc., 81e–82a). People with a tyrannical character have certain desires, which can be more easily realized in wolves, those with a gluttonous character have other desires, more easily realized in donkeys, and so on. This is not a punishment – Socrates says that such souls have already "paid the penalty" by wandering (81d–e) – but rather a natural consequence (to use Kamtekar's expression) of the soul's character.[10] These views about who reincarnates into which animal fit naturally with the views he has argued for, but are hardly required by them, which is supposedly why Socrates describes them merely as likely.

---

[10] Kamtekar 2016 argues that it is generally true across Plato's dialogues, including the *Phaedo*, that punishment in the afterlife happens before reincarnation, whereas reincarnation is a natural consequence of the soul's character. I argue in Chapter 11 that the penalty paid (i.e. justice served) need not be thought of as a punishment.

In sum, Socrates' use of "itself through itself" and "pure" requires that, when the soul is not acting in the way appropriate for a soul, it has something mixed into it. Whatever this thing is, it is akin to the visible, just as the body is, and so draws the soul to the visible and pushes it away from the unseen. It does this by giving rise to a fear of the unseen and a desire for the body-like. The soul should resist this, since it leads the soul away from the divine and happy life.

Just as pure souls depart to Hades as it truly is, the impure souls spend time somewhere before they are reincarnated. Some impure souls wander around monuments and tombs (81c–d); those who have pursued non-philosophical virtue go to the "best place" (82a12) (among the places of those who have not pursued philosophy). This also sets up an important idea in the final eschatological account: that souls with different levels of purity go to different places (108b–c) – which leads Socrates to describe at length the various regions of the earth (108d–114c).

The last group of non-philosophers that Socrates discusses consists of those who pursue what "they call 'temperance' and 'justice,' which has come about from habit and practice without philosophy and intelligence" (82b1–3). Socrates says that such people are the happiest of the impure, and so he might seem to be describing a more positive form of non-philosophical virtue here than he did in the exchange passage.[11] However, they are the happiest "because it's likely that they come back into a civic and tame species like themselves, that of bees, I suppose, or wasps or ants, or even back into the very same one, the human race, and that decent men are born from them" (82b5–8). In their current embodiment, these souls have the possibility to gain enough wisdom to escape the cycle of reincarnation. In the next, the most they can hope for is to be reincarnated again as humans, in which case there is no reason to expect their chances to be better than now. Saying that these people have what "they call 'temperance'" alludes back to the exchange passage (68c). Socrates says there that, when courage, temperance, and justice are kept apart from wisdom, that sort of virtue is fit for slaves and contains nothing sound or true (69b–c). Such people are the happiest of the non-philosophers, but they do not have genuine virtue or happiness.[12]

7.3 HOW THE PHILOSOPHER'S SOUL REASONS: 82B–84B

I have argued that in the first half of the return to the defense Socrates further defends his main conclusion of the defense speech (63b–68b), namely that the philosopher desires to be dead, explaining why the nature of the soul makes it so that the philosopher will be among the gods after death and will fare better than the non-philosophers, whose impure souls will pull them into new bodies. In the second half, Socrates further defends his claims about the virtues that come at the end of the

---

[11] So Vasiliou 2012.
[12] So also Reed 2020, esp. 125 and 128.

defense speech (68b–69e), and in doing so provides the dialogue's most detailed account of the body's effects on the soul. This account explains the problems that the true virtues help us avoid and resist. I begin with the problems caused by the body, and then turn to how the true virtues help address them.

7.3.1 The Problems from the Body: 82d–83e

Socrates begins his description of the problems that come from the body by returning to and reinterpreting an idea Plato associates with Orphic views (*Cratylus* 400c): that the body is a prison. Socrates had mentioned this idea in his argument against suicide (62b; Section 3.1). His account here builds on the idea that we are bewitched by bodily pleasures and desires – in particular, that these affect us without our realizing it (81b; Section 7.2):

> "Lovers of learning," he said, "recognize that when philosophy takes control of their soul it has been really bound in the body and glued to it, forced to examine the things that are through (*dia*) this, as if through (*dia*) a prison, rather than itself through (*dia*) itself, and it wallows in utter ignorance. And philosophy discerns the cunning of the prison, that it imprisons through desire, so that the prisoner himself may most of all be an accomplice in his imprisonment." (82d9–83e7)

Philosophy allows the lover of learning to see something.[13] The prisoner – that is, the soul bound to the body – is imprisoned in the body by desires. Why do these desires make the soul an accomplice in its own imprisonment? These desires are, supposedly, for things like food and sex; Socrates has suggested earlier that the body's ends include its nourishment (τροφή, 66c1), its care (θεραπεία, 66d1), and bodily pleasure (68e–69a). Such desires lead one to want to stay in the prison of the body, because they lead one to see the body as something good. This is what makes the prison so insidious: without realizing it, the prisoner – the soul – desires something that leads to its continued imprisonment. Most souls do not view bodily desires as foreign; instead, they take them as their very own, bewitched by them. This is why most people's souls do not struggle against their bodies' desires. Philosophers, by contrast, see the cunning of the prison and so – as we shall see – do everything they can to avoid and resist it.

How do bodily pleasures and desires change our beliefs and our values? After the prison passage, Socrates explains that philosophy tries to persuade the soul not to inquire with the senses and to distance itself from them, except to the extent they are necessary. Instead, the soul should trust nothing but itself concerning what is true (ἀληθής) (83a–b). This leads to Socrates' fullest explanation of why philosophers avoid bodily pleasures, desires, pains, and fears to the extent possible:

---

[13] Socrates seems to use the term "lover of learning" (*philomathēs*) interchangeably with "philosopher" in the *Phaedo*, perhaps with an emphasis on being a philosopher in progress, not someone with perfect wisdom.

"Now the soul of the true philosopher thinks that it should not oppose this release and for this reason avoids pleasures, desires, pains, and fears to the extent possible, reckoning that when someone feels intense pleasure, pain, fear, or desire, he in no way suffers so great an evil from the things one might think (for example, falling ill or wasting money because of his desires) but that he suffers the greatest and most extreme of all evils, without even reckoning it."

"What is that, Socrates?" said Cebes.

"It's that the soul of every human being, at the same time as it experiences intense pleasure or pain at something, is forced to think that this thing, about which it most of all feels pleasure or pain, is most manifest and most true,[14] when it isn't. Those are above all visible things, aren't they?"

"Certainly."

"Isn't it, then, in this feeling that soul is most of all bound tight by body?"

"How so?"

"Because each pleasure and pain nails it to the body, as if with a nail, and pins it and makes it body-like, since it believes to be true the very things that the body says are true. For, from its having the same beliefs as the body and enjoying the same things, it is forced, I think, to come to have the same way of life and the same nourishment, and to be the sort of soul never to enter Hades purely, but every time to depart infected by the body, and so to fall quickly back again into another body and, as it were, be sown and implanted, and because of this be deprived of the company of the divine and pure and uniform." (83b4–e3)

Intense pleasures and pains force (ἀναγκάζειν) us to think certain things are most true that are not, without even realizing that we are doing so. We can see why Socrates says that this is the greatest and most extreme of all evils, since it directly undermines our chance to be divine, which requires grasping the truth. The passage also mentions a second, related problem that arises from pleasures and pains: they lead the soul to believe and enjoy the same things as the body, which in turn changes the soul's way of life.[15]

---

[14] I translate ἀληθέστατον as "most true" rather than "most real" to keep a consistent translation for the philosopher's goal.

[15] The passage also includes the surprising claim that the soul takes on the same nourishment as the body (is ὁμότροφος with it). In addition to "nourishment," τροφή can mean nurture, rearing, or way of life, so one might want to translate the adjective ὁμότροφος as "having the same way of life." However, ὁμότροφος picks up on claims made elsewhere in the dialogue, where Socrates is referring to nourishment or nurture, not way of life (e.g. τροφή at 66c1). And shortly after the passage quoted, Socrates says that the soul is nourished (τρέφεσθαι) by "following its reasoning and being always engaged in reasoning, viewing what is true, divine, and not an object of opinion" (84a8–9). τρέφειν does not normally refer to a way of life (cf. LSJ); rather, it refers to something's growth, rearing, or nourishment. I think best to view Socrates as contrasting the philosopher's nurture and nourishment with ordinary people's. In general, nurture and nourishment are what lead to something's developing into and being sustained in a good condition. The soul is put into a good condition by reasoning and ultimately grasping the forms, and so this is its nourishment. Thus this passage is saying that, when the soul experiences bodily pleasures, pains, desires, and fears, it becomes confused about what truly puts it into a good condition.

Before we consider how the soul comes to believe and enjoy the same things as the body, we should consider the scope of Socrates' claims. Woolf says that this passage makes claims only about intense pleasures and pains, leaving us free to have other such pleasures and pains.[16] However, the passage starts with the claim that the philosopher refrains from pleasures, desires, pain, and fears "to the extent it is possible" (καθ' ὅσον δύναται, 83b7) without restricting the claim to intense pleasures and pains. Socrates then reckons that intense pleasure and pain is "the greatest and most extreme of evils" (83c2). They are the greatest evil because they actually *force* (ἀναγκάζειν) us to think something "is most manifest and most true" (83c7–8) that is not.[17] Socrates then says that these "most of all" (83d1) bind us tight to the body. When Cebes asks how so, Socrates responds that in fact *each* pleasure and pain nails and pins the soul to the body, making it bodily. Each one leads us to think that these things are to some degree true. The intense ones are, indeed, our greatest evils. They force us to believe that these are most true, directly undermining our wisdom and happiness.

Let us turn to Socrates' claim that pleasure and pain lead the soul to believe and enjoy the same things as the body, which in turn changes its ways. In Section 7.4 I discuss whether the body literally says these things, has beliefs, enjoys things, and has a way of life. For now, my question is how the beliefs caused by pleasure and pain change our way of life. Simply believing "this piece of cake is most real" would not change one's way of life. We must be brought to believe that the cake is genuinely good or worth enjoying. That is why believing the same things as the body goes along with enjoying the same things as it: you acquire beliefs about what to pursue. Socrates seems to be operating with the idea, typically thought of as Socratic, that, if you believe that something is good, then you desire it.[18] The interesting twist in the *Phaedo* is the thought that experiences can force us to change our beliefs, changing what we desire and how we act. We can avoid this, though, if we do our best to avoid having these experiences in the first place.[19] Socrates is

---

[16] Woolf 2004, 103; Russell 2005 also thinks the passage is only about a certain subgroup of pleasures. He says, "Socrates' focus is on pleasures that come to dominate a person" (89).

[17] Marechal 2021, 9–10, notes that sometimes ἀναγκάζειν in Plato means to make something compelling, in the sense of persuasive, without anything's being literally forced. But if we read it that way here, why would these be the greatest and most extreme of evils? Also, non-intense pleasures and pains seem like they would be "compelling" in this weaker sense, but Socrates does not use ἀναγκάζειν with them.

[18] This idea is emphasized in Bobonich 2002, 13–40 (*passim*). See also Gosling and Taylor 1982, 85. Beere 2010, 269–70, emphasizes the other direction: that if you desire something, then you think it is good. For a general discussion of how Plato thinks that pleasure deceives us into seeing things as good, see Moss 2006.

[19] Why are not only intense pleasures but also intense pains the greatest evil, given that intense pains force us to think that things are bad that, according to Socrates, are in fact bad? Pain forces us to think that things are most true that are not, and it leads us to change our way of life. It makes us think that painful things are worth avoiding for their own sake, when in fact there is nothing intrinsically bad about them. What is bad about pain is not what pain makes us think is bad about it.

providing reasons truly to avoid bodily pleasures and desires, not merely to evaluate them as worthless, since when we have such desires they subvert our soul's ends, changing our values so that we perpetuate our imprisonment.[20] Hence Socrates goes on to say that the philosopher's soul avoids pleasure and pain because it realizes that otherwise it would undertake Penelope's endless task in reverse (84a–b). The philosopher's soul would not hope for philosophy to free it and then put itself back in harm's way, since this would unravel the work already done.

Crucial here is Socrates' qualification "to the extent it is possible" (καθ' ὅσον δύναται). We cannot avoid eating and drinking, and putting them off for too long will only lead to more pain. Moreover, in the *Republic* sex is listed as a necessary desire (559c), so perhaps "to the extent it is possible" is not complete abstinence.[21] Socrates is also clear that one should avoid not only pleasures and pains but also desires and fears. If abstaining only made one's desire grow, one would clearly not gain a rest from such things. But Socrates seems to think – quite reasonably – that in general pleasure increases desire and pain increases fear. Avoiding pleasures and pains, then, typically helps one avoid desires and fears. Socrates is also clear that the philosopher avoids these in order to grasp the truth and acquire wisdom. If avoiding them became an end in itself – if one started to make a fetish of avoiding them, as Woolf puts it – this would simply be a different way of having the body rule over you.[22] The philosopher's goal is to not let them distract him or change his beliefs or desires, so that he can focus on acquiring wisdom. But one cannot entirely avoid these bodily affections so long as one is embodied. This is part of why the philosopher can never have a worthwhile encounter with wisdom so long as he is embodied (66b–68b; cf. Section 3.7). The body will always cause problems; best, by far, simply to be rid of it.

While the philosopher avoids pleasures and pains to the extent possible, feeling a single pleasure will not ruin a philosopher's chance at happiness. It is not that we should avoid pleasures, pains, and bodily desires because we are powerless to resist them – on the contrary, I will argue that courage's role is precisely to resist them. Instead, we should avoid them because they push us away from the truth and change our values unless we exert ourselves resisting them. Much better to obtain a rest from such things, so we can devote our energies to grasping the truth. Socrates is advocating a radical view, which we can describe as a form of asceticism. But we can see why he thinks it is necessary, given his plausible claims about how bodily pleasures and desires affect us and given what he thinks will lead to our eternal happiness.

It is worth stepping back and taking stock of the problems caused by the body. Over the course of the dialogue, Socrates describes problems that fall under two

---

[20] Woolf 2004, Russell 2005, and Marechal 2021, in different ways, argue that Socrates thinks we should simply take the right evaluative attitude toward such bodily affections. I argue against the first two views in Ebrey 2017b.
[21] For a discussion of this, see Jones and Marechal 2018.
[22] Woolf 2004, 104.

7.3 How the Philosopher's Soul Reasons: 82b–84b

broad categories: (1) the body can make us not succeed when we try to grasp the truth; and (2) it can make us not even try to grasp the truth, because we value and desire something else. There are three ways in which the body can (1) make us not succeed in grasping the truth. Both pleasures and the senses can (1a) distract the soul so it does not reason well (65c). A person can also try to inquire using the senses. And Socrates is quite clear that (1b) inquiry through the senses is deceptive (e.g. 65a–b, 65e–66a, 83a–b). The recollecting argument clarified why: the true objects of knowledge, the forms, cannot be sensed, and what can be sensed is inferior to, and wants to be like, the forms. Hence we cannot simply reach the forms by abstracting from perception. We can only come to know them using the soul itself through itself (79c–d). Pleasures and pains also lead to a distinct problem: (1c) even if we are not inquiring or reasoning, pleasures and pains make us think that things are true and real that are not, as described in the above passage (83b–e).

Thus Socrates treats the senses and bodily desires as presenting overlapping but distinct problems. In order for the philosopher to achieve his goals he must not use the senses to investigate (addressing 1b), and he must avoid and resist bodily pleasures, desires, pains, and fears, so that he is not distracted by them (addressing 1a), or led to believe falsehoods (addressing 1c), or led to value the wrong things (addressing 2). While the senses are sometimes distracting, Socrates never suggests that we must always avoid using them; in fact he explicitly says that philosophy permits their use to the extent necessary (83a).

7.3.2 *True Courage and Temperance*

In Subsection 3.8.2 I argued that in the exchange passage (69a–c) true courage, temperance, and justice are guided by wisdom and aim to further it. Socrates describes courage, temperance, and justice there as true virtue; he says that they are a purifying of bodily affections and that wisdom is the purifying rite. But that passage does not explain how courage, temperance, and justice differ from one another and how they purify the soul of bodily affections. Socrates argues that the many do not meet their own criteria for courage and temperance; but he does not give a positive account there of what the criteria are for true courage or temperance. I argue that Socrates provides a positive account of courage and temperance here: both courage and temperance are involved in different ways in reducing bodily affections, which is why each is a purifying of such affections.[23]

Before the exchange passage, Socrates says that the philosopher meets the non-philosopher's requirements for courage, because the philosopher does not fear death

---

[23] As for justice, I suspect that when Socrates describes the true philosophers as the "proper (i.e. just, δικαίως) lovers of learning" (83e5) – in a sentence also describing them as courageous and temperate – this is supposed to identify the philosophers as just. But I do not see how this would fit into an overall account of justice. I discuss justice in the afterlife in Chapter 11 (esp. Subsection 11.5.3) and Socrates' care for the soul as a type of justice in Section 12.1.

(68b–d). Does Socrates think that true courage – not merely what non-philosophers consider courageous – is partly constituted by not fearing death? Socrates has argued that the true philosopher desires to be dead (64a–68b). Moreover, he thinks that we are our souls (most memorably at 115c–e, but already implicitly at 66c), our souls are immortal, and we merely happen to be in a human form at the moment (e.g. 76c, 82b; as discussed in Section 6.5). Intuitively, at least, there does not seem to be anything courageous in the philosopher's not fearing death. It certainly does not seem to involve persevering in the face of adversity for the sake of some good cause.

Socrates never says that non-philosophers are right to call not fearing death "courage." I argue here that Socrates has a very different account of the philosopher's true courage, one that involves persevering against genuine evils. But these evils are not death, enemies on the battlefield, or any such thing. Instead, they are in our souls: the bodily pleasures, pains, fears, and desires that our body fills our souls with, resulting in our being ruled by the body (66c–d). The fear of death is one of these evils, not because death itself is bad, but because this fear leads the body to rule over us. Courage is an active resistance against these psychic enemies, a resistance that results in the soul not surrendering.

The first step in developing this interpretation is to consider what Socrates says after his long discussion of the problems caused by the body (the last passage quoted in the previous Subsection, 7.3.1). After explaining how pleasure and pain nail the soul to the body, depriving it of the company of the divine and pure and uniform, he says:

> [The first passage] So, Cebes, for the sake of these things [being with the divine, pure, and uniform[24]] the proper lovers of learning are composed and courageous, not for the sake of those things which most people say.[25] (83e5–7)

---

[24] Sedley and Long 2010 translate τούτων... ἕνεκα as "for these reasons" instead of "for the sake of these things." However, given the close parallel to the next passage I quote (82b10–c8), I think the second is the better translation, where the "things" are company of the divine, pure, and uniform, which he has just mentioned. My overall reading works equally well if we take Sedley and Long's translation and take the reasons to be the problems caused by the body.

[25] I follow Burnet 1911 here rather than the recent OCT (Strachan in Duke et al. 1995). Burnet prints φασιν, which is found in all manuscripts and in Iamblichus. It is omitted in one papyrus fragment; Verdenius 1958, in his textual notes on the *Phaedo*, suggests omitting it, saying that "the motives ascribed by the multitude to the philosophers are irrelevant in this context, and with regard to the conduct of the multitude it is equally irrelevant that they should be alleged by the multitude itself" (219). If omitted, the end of the passage would be translated: "not for the sake of which most people are [courageous and composed]." Strachan follows Verdenius' suggestion, as does Sedley and Long's translation. This overlooks that Socrates is referring back to the end of the defense speech (as Rowe 1993 notes ad loc.), where the motives alleged by the many for being courageous and composed are precisely what is at issue and are contrasted with the philosophers' motives. The many desire some pleasure and so abstain from others (68e); they think they can exchange pleasure for pleasure and at the same time have their actions be for virtue (69a). An advantage of the manuscript reading is that it does not claim that the many are courageous and composed, whereas to discuss the "that for the sake of which most people are courageous" implies that they *are* courageous, which Socrates denies. The many make a

After Socrates' long account of how the body causes problems for the soul, he here draws the surprising conclusion that the proper lovers of learning are courageous for the sake of being with the divine and pure. How does courage help one be with the divine and pure? And what does this have to do with the problems caused by the body, which he has just gone through at length? Recall that the term paired with courage in this passage, "composed" (κόσμιος), is described in the defense speech as part of what *even* ordinary people call "temperance."[26] Moreover, just as in the defense speech, in this passage Socrates contrasts that for the sake of which philosophers are courageous and composed with that for the sake of which the many say that they are.

In light of this first passage, it becomes clear that at the very beginning of this section of the return to the defense Socrates is also referring to genuine courage and temperance. This second passage (which comes earlier in the dialogue) clarifies how he is thinking of these two virtues. The passage comes directly after he says that those with so-called temperance and justice are reincarnated as social animals.

> [The second passage] Yes, but coming into the race of gods isn't sanctioned for anyone who did not pursue philosophy and has not departed in a perfectly pure condition, but only for one who loves learning. For the sake of these things, my dear Simmias and Cebes, those who properly love wisdom avoid all bodily desires, remain steadfast, and do not surrender themselves to these desires, and not at all because they fear poverty and loss of property, as the money-loving majority do. Nor do they avoid such desires because they fear dishonor and a reputation for immorality, as the lovers of power and honor do. (82b10–c8)

The division of non-philosophers into money-lovers and honor-lovers refers back to the discussion of courage and temperance in the defense speech (68c). Recall that even the many agree that temperance involves being disdainful of one's desires and staying composed (68c). But the many's temperance involves abstaining from pleasures in order to acquire further pleasures, and so turns out to be a type of intemperance (68e–69a). Socrates says in the passage just quoted that the lover of learning avoids bodily desires for a very different reason from the money-lovers and the honor-lovers: not to satisfy other desires, but to depart in a perfectly pure condition and come into the race of the gods. Nonetheless, what they do fits with what even the many call temperance: they disdain desires and stay composed. The philosopher genuinely does this, rather than deluding himself into thinking that he is temperate, and he does so to purify himself and come to be with the divine.

In this second passage Socrates says that the lovers of learning "remain steadfast, and do not surrender themselves to these desires." My proposal is that courage is this

---

claim about that for the sake of which people are courageous, which differs from what in fact is the goal of those who are genuinely courageous.

[26] As Rowe 1993 notes ad loc. He briefly offers a similar suggestion to the one developed here.

active resistance against the bodily desires – and more generally bodily affections – when they arise in us.[27] True courage may result in actions on the battlefield, but it is primarily a struggle within the soul against our true enemies, bodily affections. Note that, in the *Laches*, Laches' first (genuine) account of courage is that it is a type of steadfastness (καρτερία) of the soul (192b–c). The ensuing discussion in the *Laches* uses finite forms and participles of the verb καρτερεῖν, the verb that Socrates uses here in the *Phaedo* to say that the lover of learning is steadfast. Variations of Laches' proposal are rejected because they would include those who are foolishly steadfast or who wisely calculate that they have the upper hand (192c–193e). To avoid including such people, one needs to ensure that the one with courage has knowledge of which things are worth fighting for. By the end of the *Laches*, Nikias has moved the focus entirely to knowledge (194d ff.), so that steadfastness has fallen away. By having the steadfastness guided by wisdom in the *Phaedo*, Socrates avoids the pitfalls of Laches' proposals while retaining what is appealing about it. Courage is a type of mental fortitude, but crucially a type guided by wisdom. It is engaged when the soul fights against the difficult-to-resist affections that the body pours into the soul.

Socrates' language in the second passage closely parallels that in the first, but with the first passage (which comes later in the dialogue) phrased as a conclusion. I suggest, then, that the structure of this whole section, from 82b to 83e, is the following: Socrates starts by asserting (in the second passage) that the lovers of learning are temperate (avoiding all bodily desire) and courageous (steadfast and not surrendering) for the sake of being in a pure condition among the divine (the gods); he then explains the problems caused by the body that require courage and temperance and that keep us from acquiring the truth needed to be with the divine (as described in the previous Subsection, 7.3.1); finally, he draws the conclusion (in the first passage) that indeed courage and being temperate (composed) are needed to be in a pure condition with the divine.

This account of courage garners further support from what Socrates says after the first passage:

> But this is how a philosophical man's soul would reckon. It would not suppose that, its own release being a job for philosophy, while philosophy is doing this releasing, the soul should of its own accord surrender itself for the pleasures and pains to bind it back inside again, and should undertake something like Penelope's interminable task by working at a sort of web in reverse. (84a2–7)

Given that Socrates connects not surrendering to being steadfast in the second passage, I take the soul's reckoning that it should not surrender (mentioned in the passage just quoted) to explain why the philosopher's soul is courageous: because

---

[27] Marechal 2021 nicely brings out the importance of this active resistance, given that we cannot entirely avoid these bodily affections. She sees temperance as doing this, whereas my claim is that it is courage.

otherwise pleasures and pains will bind it back inside the body again, requiring it endlessly to undertake the task of releasing itself again and again from the body, rather than allowing it to be with the divine. The soul reasons that this is an enemy worth fighting against and so acts courageously, not surrendering. This ultimately helps it secure a rest (γαλήνη) from these things, so it can view the truth and the divine that it is akin to, thereby entering what it is akin to upon death, separated from human evils (84a–b). Again, the philosopher does not fetishize this fight, just as the guardians in the *Republic* do not fetishize war while nonetheless remaining ready to fight to protect what is valuable.

This account of courage helps explain the puzzling conclusion of the return to the defense:

> So, given that sort of nourishment [reasoning and viewing what is true and divine], and since it practiced these things, there is no risk of its fearing, Simmias and Cebes, that it may be torn apart during its separation from the body and blown apart by the winds, and then fly away in all directions and no longer be anything anywhere. (84b3–7)

This refers back to Cebes' challenge (69e–70b), which says that most people worry that the soul will be blown away, and so Socrates should reassure and convince them that it exists after death. But Socrates does not provide them with such reassurance or conviction here; instead, he says that *the soul of the true philosopher* will not fear destruction. Why mention this soul's fear at all? Because it is connected to the philosopher's courage, which he has just been discussing. This courage is primarily a kind of resistance against bodily affections, such as desires and fears. Socrates is noting that the philosopher's soul will not fear its own destruction – which it will recognize is impossible – and so will be courageous in this way as well.[28]

Note how this account of courage and temperance fits with Socrates' account of the virtues in the exchange passage, according to which they come from wisdom and are for the sake of wisdom (Subsection 3.8.2). Socrates in the return to the defense personifies philosophy – which, I take it, reflects wisdom – saying that it shows philosophers the cunning of the prison; this cunning is why they should not surrender to pleasures and pains, since it would stop them from acquiring wisdom. The body seeks to rule us, but we must avoid this to live happily with the gods. Hence Socrates explains the sort of insight that wisdom provides that leads philosophers to be courageous and temperate for the sake of wisdom. This is how courage and temperance can come from wisdom, the purifying rite, and also be for the sake of wisdom. Moreover, this account clarifies the way in which courage, alongside temperance, purifies the soul of bodily affections. Temperance purifies by disdaining bodily desires, avoiding them, and keeping the soul in a composed state. It seeks

---

[28] See Subsection 8.2.3 for a further example of courage that arises in Socrates' discussion of misology.

to rise above them. Ideally such gentle methods would suffice. But we cannot avoid the body's effects so long as we are embodied. Hence the embodied philosopher will always need courage, as part of the ongoing struggle between the soul and the body described throughout the *Phaedo*, in which each vies to rule the other.

Courage, like justice, is ordinarily thought of in terms of our other-regarding behavior. In the *Republic* Socrates argues that individuals' justice is internal to their souls (443c–e), that conventionally just behaviors result from having such a soul, but that one should not identify justice with this behavior (442d–443e). In the *Phaedo*, the courageous philosopher will fight against the body's rule, and so not allow in the fear of death, which the body attempts to fill his soul with. This seems like it might lead to conventionally courageous behavior, but one might worry that, if philosophers literally avoid pain, viewing intense pain as the greatest and most extreme evil, they would not engage in conventionally courageous actions that would likely lead to pain.[29] To address this concern, recall from the exchange passage that wisdom, not pleasure or pain, is the value we should use to guide our actions. Philosophers will not allow themselves to be ruled by pain; if they did, they might be dissuaded from going into dangerous situations. Instead, they will actively fight the affections that cause people to be cowardly. Wisdom will take the badness of pain into consideration, but it will not treat avoiding it as what is most important (Subsection 3.8.2). At the end of the dialogue, Socrates says that, if people care for themselves, they will care for others as well (115b–c; Section 12.1). Caring for oneself involves cultivating one's own wisdom. This suggests that wisdom will direct philosophers to care for others, and so display conventional courage, even while the real struggle happens in their souls.

7.4 IS THE BODY THE SUBJECT OF MENTAL STATES?

Let us reconsider whether the body has (what we would identify as) mental states, a topic mentioned in Sections 1.1 and 3.5. It is sometimes maintained that in the *Phaedo* the body is the subject of some mental states and the soul the subject of others.[30] I do not see support for this in the text. The body fills the soul with bodily affections, but the soul then has these bodily affections, which is why it should be purified of them. Socrates describes these as desires and affections that are *kata* the body (αἱ κατὰ τὸ σῶμα ἐπιθυμίαι, 82c, τὰ κατὰ τὸ σῶμα πάθη, 94b), but that need not mean that the body is the proper subject of them. These desires are connected to the body's attempt to rule us, but that does not mean that the body is doing the desiring.[31]

---

[29] A concern rightly pressed by Marechal 2021, 18–19, who takes this as a reason to think that the philosopher need not avoid painful situations to count as "avoiding pain."
[30] See Chapter 3, n. 29 for lists of scholars who accept or reject this.
[31] It is unclear to me whether this is the use of "*kata*" identified in Subsections 6.3.1 and 6.3.2. That use picks out something internal to a subject that determines the manner in which the subject performs some activity. If Socrates is using "*kata*" the same way here, what is the

7.4 Is the Body the Subject of Mental States?

The only passage in the *Phaedo* that clearly says that the body has beliefs and affections is the last passage quoted in Subsection 7.3.1.[32] Socrates says there that the soul can have the very *same* beliefs and affections as the body, so this passage certainly does not support the view that the body is the subject of some mental states and the soul of different ones. It is worth quoting the relevant part again:

> [E]ach pleasure and pain nails it to the body, as if with a nail, and pins it and makes it body-like, since it believes to be true the very things that the body says are true. For, from its having the same beliefs as the body and enjoying the same things, it is forced, I think, to come to have the same way of life and the same nourishment, and to be the sort of soul never to enter Hades purely, but every time to depart infected by the body. (83d4–10)

Socrates says here that the body has beliefs, that the body says that certain things are true, that it enjoys things, and that it has a distinctive way of life. The body's having this way of life is not identified as problematic; the problem is when the soul comes to believe and enjoy the same things as the body, and so comes to have the same way of life and nourishment. The soul then comes to take on the body's ends and promote its goals. Socrates uses here a metaphor of the soul's being nailed and pinned to the body. Should we also take it as a metaphor when he says that the body "says" (φῇ) things that the soul then believes? We frequently talk of our body "telling us" things without thinking that it literally speaks to us. In any event, the body does not seem like it could have a way of life independently of the soul. Its way of life is closely connected to its beliefs and the things that it enjoys. Perhaps, then, Socrates is simply saying that the soul is influenced by the body to have various beliefs and is enjoying various things (cf. *Tim.* 87e–88b). If not, then the soul and the body each have beliefs and other mental states, but these only influence a person's actions once the soul comes to have the same mental states as the body.

As far as I can tell, there is no conflict with Socrates' broader commitments if we think that the body literally says things, has beliefs, enjoys things, and has a way of living. But given that this is the only passage in the *Phaedo* where Socrates clearly makes such claims and given that at least part of the passage is metaphorical – the part about nailing and pinning – and given how natural it is to speak this way without meaning it literally, I suspect that we should not attribute to Socrates the view that the body has its own mental states. In any event, they do not have an important role in his overall theory. The important thing is that the body deeply

---

subject? If it is the soul, then the body would be internal to the soul. In the next chapter (Subsection 8.4.3) I argue that the bodily affections mentioned at 94b should be thought of as inside the person, not the body or the soul. We could understand the bodily desires mentioned at 82c the same way. The idea then would be that a person sometimes desires *kata* their body, which is internal to them.

[32] 94b–c is sometimes taken to say that the body has beliefs. He says there that thirst and hunger are in something, but I argue in Subsection 8.4.3 that there is good reason to take this something to be the whole human, not the body.

influences the soul, unless the soul is kept pure through courage and temperance, and even then it cannot entirely resist the body's influences so long as it is embodied.

7.5 CONCLUSION

The return to the defense uses an account of the nature of the soul to explain what leads to better or worse afterlives. We have a chance to live eternally with the divine, contemplating the forms, which our souls are akin to. However, our soul can be manipulated by the body into pursuing other ends: without our realizing it, pleasure and pain profoundly impact what we value and how we live. What is more, our view of what is true is influenced by our desires, pleasures, fears, and pains. This epistemological effect has important ethical ramifications, since the best life is one of grasping the truth. We need the purificatory virtues of moderation and courage to avoid these effects and fight against them when they inevitably arise, allowing us to live eternally with the divine. If we do not, the impurities in our souls will lead us to desire the body-like after death, drawing us into a new body.

Even if one does not accept Socrates' view that we will be able to live with the gods in the afterlife, he poses an interesting ethical challenge here. The things we value may well be the result of our body being hardwired to value things, even if not they are not in fact good. If grasping the truth genuinely is the route to a good life and experiencing bodily pleasures and pains leads us to form false beliefs and value things other than the truth, then we do have reason to avoid and resist bodily pleasures, pains, desires, and fears to the extent we can.

One source of resistance to this sort of interpretation is the idea that Plato does not portray Socrates as an ascetic.[33] The first thing to note is that Socrates never claims to be a perfect philosopher; in fact he thinks that, so long as he is embodied, he will desire food and sex just like everyone else. Socrates also never suggests that avoiding pleasure or pain is good for its own sake, nor does he prefer pain to pleasure. He is not advocating a self-flagellating asceticism. Instead, the idea is to gently distance ourselves from bodily affections to the extent we can, in order to focus on what will bring true happiness. Note also that, while Socrates is famously attracted to young men, Plato does not portray him as sexually pursuing them. In the *Symposium* he is portrayed as calm and collected in battle (220d–221b, alluded to at *Laches* 181b) and as regularly standing motionless in thought for long periods of time (174d–175b). The *Phaedo*'s approach seems to me very similar to the *Symposium*'s: it is recognizably the same person as is portrayed in the Socratic dialogues, but a portrait that emphasizes his incredible courage and temperance in a way that distances Socrates from bodily pleasures and desires. When Socrates is in bed with Alcibiades, he does not fight against himself, punishing himself – he is calmly in control of himself and

[33] See e.g. Woolf 2004, 104–6.

goes to sleep (*Symposium* 219c–d). Alcibiades says that this made him admire Socrates for his temperance and courage, that Socrates was a person with wisdom and steadfastness of a sort he thought he would never encounter (219d). I argue in Chapter 12 that Socrates' death scene also provides a portrait of Socrates as calmly following his wisdom, thereby showing us how to exemplify the sort of temperance and courage described here. Socrates turns down the chance to have sex, to have a great meal, or to delay his death in any way (116e–117a). He calmly goes to his own death, showing how the fear of death can be purified from one's soul.

8

Misology and the Soul as a *harmonia*

84c–86e, 88c–95a

The eleven pages between the return to the defense and the autobiography (84c–95a) have received scant scholarly attention, despite playing an important role in the structure of the dialogue and being of considerable interest in their own right. Simmias and Cebes raise objections here to Socrates' kinship argument, Socrates warns them to avoid misology, and then he responds to Simmias' objection. These objections and this warning simultaneously serve as the climax of the first half of the dialogue and set the agenda for the second. This pivotal role is highlighted by Echecrates' breaking into the discussion, returning us to the outer dialogue, and by Phaedo's then comparing Socrates to Heracles.[1] In the first half of the dialogue, Simmias' and Cebes' questions, objections, and proposals (61c, 61d, 62c–e, 69e–70b, 72e–73a, and 77b–c) drive the course of the discussion, culminating in Simmias and Cebes' *harmonia* and cloakmaker objections to the kinship argument (85b–88b). After presenting these objections, they provide no further objections or major questions until after the final argument – for twenty pages, from 88b to 108c.[2] Socrates main task in these pages is to respond to their two objections, and so Phaedo's comparison of this response to Heracles' second labor (89c) turns out to be apt – a lengthy, heroic endeavor. I argue that Socrates' responses to these objections clarify and fill in the kinship argument's account of the soul, in part by thinking through why he rejects Simmias' and Cebes' alternative accounts.

But the second half of the dialogue is not only driven by the content of Simmias' and Cebes' objections but also by the threat of misology that they raise. As we will see, over the first half of the dialogue the threat of misology has been building, while

---

[1] Further discussed in Section 2.4.
[2] The most substantive objection comes at 103a. Phaedo says that he cannot remember who asked this, and at the end of Socrates' response (103c) Cebes says that he was not disturbed by the objection. Having an unnamed objector means that neither Simmias nor Cebes interrupts Socrates' heroic feat.

at the same time Simmias and Cebes were becoming more and more convinced of Socrates' view that the soul exists after death. But then, as a result of their objections, the whole group of companions suddenly doubt whether they will ever be able to judge such matters (88c). As I argued in Section 2.4, this serves as a sort of tragic reversal, where what had seemed like progress threatens to leave them in a much worse situation than when they began. Scholars often call this discussion an "interlude,"[3] suggesting that it contrasts with what comes before and after rather than playing an integral role in the overall development of the dialogue. But Cebes' challenge (69e–70b) asks Socrates to *convince* them that the soul exists after death because people have *doubts*. The problem of misology, as we will see, is that an alternating pattern of conviction and doubt can lead one to hate *logoi* entirely, so that one is no longer convinced by any *logos*. Thus, avoiding misology is necessary for addressing Cebes' challenge, and so we should expect Socrates to address it in the second half of the dialogue, not to treat it as a mere interlude. In the next chapter I argue that one of the central goals of the method of hypothesis is to help avoid misology by developing the right sort of trust in a *logos*. Furthermore, I argue there that Socrates applies this method earlier, when he responds to Simmias' *harmonia* objection. The eschatological account near the end of the dialogue shows a different way to avoid misology, by carefully lowering one's confidence in some claims. Thus, over the course of the second half of the dialogue, Socrates not only responds to the details of Simmias and Cebes' objections but also develops and illustrates different ways to avoid misology.

I discuss the text out of order here, since it is useful to consider Simmias' *harmonia* objection (85b–86d) alongside Socrates' response to it (91c–95a), and similarly with Cebes' cloakmaker objection (86e–88b). I discuss the latter in Chapter 10 in order to show how the final argument carefully responds to the details of Cebes' objection. In this chapter, after a brief discussion of Socrates as a prophet (Section 8.1), I turn to his discussion of misology (Section 8.2). I argue that it is a more specific problem than it is typically taken to be, a problem that aspiring philosophers (such as Socrates' companions) are especially at risk of suffering, one that involves not merely becoming cynical about arguments but positively hating them. I then discuss Simmias' objection (Section 8.3) and Socrates' response to it (Section 8.4). I argue for a new account of Simmias' theory that the soul is a *harmonia*. As Socrates interprets Simmias' theory, it makes the soul a properly fitted together composite thing, not the formal structure possessed by such a composite. This means that Socrates is not arguing against a type of supervenience theory or epiphenomenalism, as is frequently claimed. Socrates' arguments against this theory highlight how it cannot explain basic ethical features of the soul that the kinship argument's account can explain.

---

[3] So Bluck 1955, Hackforth 1955, and Rowe 1993.

8.1 SOCRATES AS A PROPHET: 84C–85B

After the return to the defense, Cebes and Simmias speak quietly with each other and then report that they have not wanted to say anything to Socrates lest it be "irksome to you because of your present plight" (84d7–8). As Socrates notes (84d–e), this reveals that not only has Socrates failed to convince them that his present situation is not bad, he has not even convinced them that he does not himself view it as bad. Before Simmias and Cebes provide their objections, Socrates responds to their not wanting to be irksome. This (genuine) interlude clarifies how radical Socrates' claims are in the return to the defense, as well as clarifying his interpretive procedure. Socrates begins:

> You seem to think that I'm worse at prophecy than the swans: though they sing at earlier times too, it is when they realize they must die that they sing longest and most of all, overjoyed that they are about to depart to meet the god whose servants they are. (84e3–85a3)

Socrates goes on to say that people wrongly think that the swans are singing in distress; and that he is a fellow slave of Apollo, just as the swans are. This is an example of Socrates' typical interpretive procedure (as discussed in Sections 1.3 and 2.6): he takes a phenomenon (servants to Apollo singing before dying), considers a standard interpretation (they are distressed), rejects it because it does not fit with the larger views he has argued for (death is not bad), and offers an alternative that fits with his own view (they are overjoyed).

After Socrates has provided so many revisionary religious views in the return to the defense, one might think that he has completely abandoned anything identifiable as traditional Greek religious belief. Here we see that, despite his unorthodox views, Socrates continues to view himself as a pious slave of Apollo. This is important for the portrait of Socrates as a new sort of hero (as discussed in Sections 2.2 and 2.3) as well as for maintaining continuity with the portrait of Socrates in the *Apology* (as discussed in Section 1.4). Nonetheless, he offers a radical reinterpretation of what counts as a prophet. He is saying that Simmias and Cebes clearly think that Socrates is a poor prophet because the conclusions of his arguments will turn out to be incorrect.[4] Socrates has argued that the soul exists after death, which supports his good hope about the afterlife. Since prophecy makes claims about the future, Socrates is saying that he too, as a philosopher, practices a type of prophecy, which connects him to Apollo. But this is an entirely new form of prophecy. Yet again, we see Socrates appropriating and reinterpreting traditional religious ideas, in a way similar to how he identified the true initiate as a philosopher (69c–d and 81a; cf. Section 3.2, Subsection 3.8.2, and Section 7.1).

---

[4] Pace Hackforth 1955, 96.

In Section 12.3 I argue that there are good reasons to see Socrates' last words as a type of prophecy; if so, this discussion also serves to expand the notion of prophecy and introduce an idea important for the end of the dialogue.

8.2 MISOLOGY AND MOTIVATED REASONING: 88C–91C

Often, in thinking about arguments, we tend to abstract from the psychological processes involved in engaging with them – of being convinced or skeptical of them, of the frustrations they cause, and of the excitement they bring about. Plato's dialogues frequently illustrate that, if you want to convince somebody, you need to be sensitive to how they are reacting, not simply to their counter-arguments. Socrates' discussion of misology brings these issues squarely into focus.[5] He highlights two specific problems that aspiring philosophers, in particular, are in danger of experiencing. I argue that the key to understanding misology is to pay close attention to what spurs the discussion as well as to how it is analogous to misanthropy. After discussing misology, Socrates points to a different problem he does not name (91a–c), which he says that he himself is in danger of suffering. I argue that it is a type of motivated reasoning.

8.2.1 *The Warning Signs of Misology: 88c–89c*

Socrates discusses misology after everyone becomes very dispirited from hearing Simmias' and Cebes' objections to the kinship argument:

> [Phaedo:] Now when we all heard them say this, our mood took an unpleasant turn, as we later told each other, because we had been utterly persuaded (πεπεισμένους) by the earlier *logos*, but then they [Simmias and Cebes] seemed to have disturbed us all over again and sent us plummeting into doubt (εἰς ἀπιστίαν), not just about the *logoi* given before, but also about what would be said later. We were worried that we might be worthless judges, or even that the very facts of the matter might merit doubt (ἄπιστα).
>
> Echecrates: Heavens, Phaedo, I quite sympathize with you. Now that I too have heard you, it makes me, too, say something like this to myself: "What *logos* will we still trust (πιστεύσομεν) now? How utterly persuasive (πιθανός) the argument that Socrates was giving, yet now it has been plunged into doubt (εἰς ἀπιστίαν)!" (88c1–d3)

This is Echecrates' first interruption of the narrative. It highlights, chorus-like, that this is a problem not just affecting those there, but also those (like us) responding to the events. Phaedo then becomes Socrates' conversational partner in what follows,

---

[5] The topic has received little scholarly attention. Woolf 2007 and Miller 2015 are rare articles on the topic. Delcomminette 2018 also has a substantive discussion of it. It is unmentioned by Bostock 1986; Gallop 1975 discusses it briefly, calling it a "preface" to Socrates' reply to Simmias, and Ebert 2004 devotes five pages to it in his 515-page translation and commentary.

allowing Phaedo to respond to the events of the dialogue, like a chorus in Greek tragic drama (as discussed in Section 2.4).

Phaedo and Echecrates emphasize that they first were persuaded and then thrown into doubt, not knowing what *logos* to trust. Note that the word translated "doubt" (ἀπιστία) is the opposite of "trust" (πίστις) in Greek. Phaedo and Echecrates connect doubt with not being persuaded in the passage just quoted. The word translated "persuade" (πείθειν) is also etymologically connected to "trust" (πίστις), and Plato elsewhere treats the two as closely connected: for example, persuasion leads to trust, according to the *Gorgias* (454c–455a).[6] These interrelated topics of persuasion, trust, and doubt have arisen at crucial points earlier in the dialogue, as discussed in Sections 1.3 and 1.4 and at greater length in Section 4.1. As a brief reminder: after providing his argument against suicide, Socrates praises Cebes for refusing to be immediately persuaded but rather always scrutinizing arguments (63a). Cebes then phrases his challenge – which launches Socrates' arguments for the existence of the soul after death – in terms of people having doubts that the soul survives death; these doubts lead them to fear, and so Cebes is looking for trust (πίστις) – there typically translated as "conviction," or even "proof" (Sedley and Long 2010) – that the soul continues to exist after death (69e–70b). After the recollecting argument, Cebes asks Socrates to try to *persuade* the child within them not to fear (77e). Thus the explicit goal of Socrates' last three arguments was to persuade Simmias and Cebes, so that they trust the conclusion. But now they are worried that they might be worthless judges or that the facts of the matter might merit doubt; either way, they may never be able to be rightly persuaded.

Being persuaded and then plunged into doubt is not a failing of the stupid or uneducated, but rather an easy mistake even for those talented and with good intellectual dispositions. Although Cebes is supposed to be difficult to convince, he enthusiastically endorses the cyclical argument (72d). Cebes also shows no reservations at the end of the kinship argument, strongly endorsing it (80b–c); it is only later, after a long pause, that he raises his cloakmaker objection (87b–88b). Thus even someone as smart, difficult to persuade, and philosophically inclined as Cebes is liable to be convinced and later doubt a conclusion. Simmias' *harmonia* objection and Cebes' cloakmaker objection, as we will see, each provide an alternative model of the soul, creating competing conceptions of the soul. This provides further reason for their oscillating conviction, leading the companions, in the passage under discussion, to question their ability to judge at all.

Socrates cannot simply give more arguments to help them avoid this fate. Instead, Phaedo says:

---

[6] For how I translate πίστις, see Chapter 4, n. 3. Miller 2015, 146–52, provides a useful discussion of trust (πίστις) and related terms in the *Phaedo* and elsewhere. However, he repeatedly suggests that trust in the *Phaedo* is associated with the *merely* persuasive. Yet, as he himself notes (150–1, n. 15), Socrates says that the soul *should* trust itself when investigating each thing that is *auto kath' hauto* (83a–b). In the *Phaedo* trust can be rightly placed.

> I particularly admired in him [Socrates], first how pleasantly, genially and respectfully he took in the young men's argument, then how discerningly he noticed the effect the arguments had had on us, and next how well he cured us and rallied us when we'd taken to our heels in defeat, so to speak, and spurred us on to follow at his side and consider the argument with him. (89a2–8)

The companions' problem comes from being on a sort of emotional rollercoaster, repeatedly feeling confident and then having their hopes dashed. Socrates displays the sort of even-keeled approach that they need while identifying the problem they must avoid. Socrates is soon compared to Heracles (89c); his even-keeled, emotionally sensitive, and kind approach is part of Plato's new portrait of how a true hero acts (cf. Section 2.2).

8.2.2 *Misology Proper: 89d–90e*

Misology is sometimes treated as a rather general problem – for example, the problem of abandoning the search for truth because one has been taken in by a sophist or orator.[7] I will argue that Socrates is highlighting a more specific problem, one that fits precisely with the companions' and Echecrates' worries: the problem of putting one's trust in *logoi*, losing this trust, and having this happen repeatedly, so that one ultimately hates *logoi*, thinking that there is nothing sound or true in them. This pattern of gaining and losing trust in *logoi* has happened to Simmias and Cebes a few times now, and (according to Phaedo's report) to Socrates' other companions as well. Socrates is saying that, if it continues, they could end up hating argumentation altogether.

The word "misology" seems to have been coined by Plato.[8] In the *Phaedo*, Socrates introduces misology by analogy with misanthropy:

> Misology and misanthropy come about in the same way. For misanthropy sets in as a result of putting all one's trust in someone, doing so without expertise, and taking the person to be entirely truthful (ἀληθής), sound (ὑγιής), and trustworthy (πιστός), and then a little later finding him to be wicked and worthy of doubt (ἄπιστος) – and then again with someone else. When this happens to someone many times, particularly with those whom he would take to be his very closest friends, and he has been falling out with people again and again, he ends up hating everyone and thinking that there is nothing sound in anyone at all. (89d3–e3)

The first sentence is crucial: misanthropy and misology *come about* in the same way. It is sometimes suggested that there is something strange about the analogy between misology and misanthropy, since Socrates goes on to mention a way in which

---

[7] So Hackforth 1955 and Dorter 1982 ad loc.
[8] In Plato's corpus, the μισολογ- stem is found only here, in the *Laches* (188c and e), and in the *Republic* (411d). It seems to be used in a more specific way here than in those dialogues, where it is not analyzed or elaborated upon.

misology does not resemble misanthropy (89e–90b).⁹ But Socrates only says that they are analogous in their formation.

Socrates' account of how misology arises closely parallels that of misanthropy:

> *logoi* do not resemble people in that way (I was following your lead just now), but in the following way: when someone without expertise in *logoi* trusts (πιστεύειν) a *logos* to be true (ἀληθής), and then a little later thinks that it is false, sometimes when it is, sometimes when it isn't, and when he does the same again with one *logos* after another. This happens especially to those who have wasted their time dealing with the contrary *logoi* used in disputation. As you know, they end up thinking they have become very wise, and that they alone have understood that there is nothing sound (ὑγιής) or firm in any thing or in any *logos*, but that all things turn back and forth, exactly as if in the Euripus, and do not stay put for any time. (90b4–c6)

Like misanthropy, misology arises from putting your trust into something without expertise – taking it to be true – and finding this trust betrayed, and then having this happen repeatedly until you end up thinking that no people, or no *logoi*, are true or sound at all. It is caused by repeatedly doing what Phaedo says they have done once: put their trust in a *logos*, taking it to be true, and then come to doubt it. In this passage Socrates says that frequent oscillation in this trust happens especially to those who waste time with the arguments used in disputations. Those who give these arguments used in disputation (the *antilogikoi*) may never have valued truth and so never placed their trust in them. But those who waste their time with such arguments may well have begun intellectually curious, drawn in by these arguments used in disputation.¹⁰ If they spend enough time with these arguments, they end up hating all *logoi* and thinking that there is nothing sound or true in any thing or *logos*.

Socrates' account of how misanthropy arises explains how a person comes to genuinely hate people by feeling betrayed by them – as one would expect, since "misanthropy" means hatred of people. You could imagine someone who likes people but is cynical about them thinking that there is nothing sound or trustworthy in them. Such a person might enjoy the company of people, seeing them as useful tools to achieving their own aims. This person may be a cynical narcissist, but they are not a misanthrope. Similarly, Socrates' parallel account of how misology arises explains why someone would come to hate *logoi*, not merely distrust them. Misology

---

⁹ For example, Miller 2015, 154 and 158, Gonzales 2018, 91.

¹⁰ Balla 2021, 3, notes that this adjective, *antilogikos*, is used in Aristophanes' *Clouds* to describe Pheidippides, supposedly as a result of his spending time in Socrates' school (*Clouds* 1173). Given the clear earlier allusion to the *Clouds* (70c, cf. *Clouds* 1485; see Section 4.4) and the likely later allusion to the *Clouds* (99b, cf. *Clouds* 264; see Section 9.5), I am inclined to take this use of *antilogikos* also as a reference to the *Clouds*. The allusion yet again shows why Aristophanes' description of Socrates is not apt: Socrates, in fact, is highly sensitive to the dangers of *antilogikoi logoi* and helps his followers avoid them, rather than making his followers *antilogikoi*, as Aristophanes suggests.

means "hatred of *logoi*," and we can see how this sort of betrayal could lead to hatred. Misology arises when someone begins by valuing *logoi* and so puts their trust in them – as Delcomminette puts it, it is a danger for the philosophically disposed.[11] This is why the mood of Socrates' companions took an unpleasant turn, and why it is an apt problem for Plato to highlight in Socrates' conversation with his closest companions.

At its broadest, the term *"logos"* can refer to anything spoken or written, but clearly Socrates is not imagining people who come to hate all utterances. Referring to *logoi* as true or false seems to suggest that they are theories rather than arguments, but the reference to the *antilogikoi logoi* is certainly to the *antilogikoi*'s arguments. Shortly after the misology section, Socrates will ask Simmias which *logos* he chooses: that learning is recollecting or that the soul is a *harmonia* (92c). One could translate this as either "argument" or "theory," although no argument is given for the view that the soul is a *harmonia*. All in all, *logoi* are probably best thought of as theories (and hence capable of being true or false), but the sort of theories that are supported by arguments or put forward in an argumentative context.[12] This is what one comes to hate.

Note how this can happen to you, even if it is perfectly understandable why you put your trust in a *logos* to begin with – it seems like a strong argument – and even if you are right to later reject the *logos*, since you rightly notice a flaw in it. Given the severity of the problem, and given that Socrates thinks that the greatest good is for us to grasp the truth, we can appreciate why he says that there is no greater evil than misology (89d).[13] Misology arises when someone begins by rightly caring about the truth; this care could lead to wisdom and so to eternal happiness, but instead this care is part of what leads to their hating the very *logoi* needed to arrive at the truth.

How do we avoid misology? Socrates says that it arises when one does not blame oneself or one's lack of expertise but instead transfers the blame to the *logoi* (90d). This leads to his recommendation: "so first let's make sure we avoid this, and let's not allow into our soul the notion that there's probably nothing sound in *logoi*. It will be much better to assume that we are not sound yet, but must make a courageous effort to be sound" (90d9–e3). This is sometimes thought of as the entirety of Socrates' suggestion for how to avoid misology. But he only says that this is the *first* step; it offers immediate assistance when we have repeatedly put our trust in *logoi* only to change our mind about them later. Clearly the best way to avoid the problem would be to acquire expertise in *logoi*, which would prevent us from too

---

[11] Delcomminette 2018, 45.
[12] So Woolf 2007, 2–3.
[13] To this extent, I agree with Woolf 2007 that Socrates' own conception of what is true – in particular, his ethical account – provides him with an account of the value of truth. But, unlike Woolf, I do not think that he values his own conception of truth over truth itself, whatever that may turn out to be. I argue for this in the next subsection.

quickly putting our trust in *logoi* in the first place. I argue in Section 9.8 that the method of hypothesis does exactly this, by providing a way thoroughly to evaluate a *logos* before trusting it.[14] Moreover, I argue there that Socrates applies this method when he replies to Simmias' objection. In applying and then articulating the method of hypothesis, Socrates is identifying at least part of the expertise in *logoi* that would allow one to avoid the threat of misology.

8.2.3 *Self-deception and Motivated Reasoning: 90e–91c*

After describing misology and the first line of defense needed to avoid it, Socrates describes a separate problem, which has neither the same causes as misology (repeatedly trusting) nor the same effect (hating argument). His description of the problem is remarkably subtle and complicated. I will argue that it is a specific sort of motivated reasoning.

> [1] It will be much better to assume that *we* are not sound yet, but must make a courageous effort to be sound. [2] You and the others should do this for the sake of your whole life to come, but I for the sake of my death considered in its own right, because concerning that very thing I'm now in danger of desiring not wisdom but victory, like those who are utterly uneducated. [3] For when they are at odds about something, they do not care about the facts of the matter they are arguing about, but strive to make what they themselves have proposed seem true to those who are present. [4] And I think that now I will differ from them only to this extent: I won't strive to make what I say seem true to those who are present, except as a byproduct, but instead to make it seem so as much as possible to myself. [5] For I reckon, my dear friend – see how ambitious I'm being – that if what I'm saying is actually true, then it's quite right to be convinced; if, on the other hand, there is nothing in store for one who has died, at least in this period before I die I will be less of a mournful burden to those who are with me, and this folly won't stay with me – that would have been an evil – but will perish shortly. (90e2–91b7)

Note that Socrates says in [2] that he is *in danger* of desiring victory over wisdom, not that he is doing so.[15] Similarly, in [4] he says that he thinks that he *will* differ from them, not that he does differ from them. This is the standard use of the future tense to indicate what happens if some condition is met – in this case, if he truly is desiring victory over wisdom. Soon after the passage, he says that Simmias and Cebes should make sure that he does not deceive himself and them, too (91c); Socrates is not confident that he is deceiving himself, but he sees that it is a danger. Socrates has maintained from the defense speech through the return to the defense that only the lover of wisdom will have a chance to have genuine virtue and to live eternally

---

[14] For a similar idea, see Burger 1984, 10–11.
[15] *Pace* Dorter 1982, 94, Ebert 2004, 305, and Miller 2015, 164, who claim that Socrates says that he desires victory.

among the gods. The possibility that Socrates loves victory instead of wisdom would undermine his good hope for the afterlife, and so, as Socrates says (sentences [1] and [2]), he must courageously fight against it (cf. Subsection 7.3.2, for courage as a fight against psychic evils).

Why would Socrates be motivated to desire victory rather than wisdom? The basic idea, I will argue, is that he would be motivated to believe something because it would be advantageous to believe it, independently of its truth. If he succumbs to this motivation, he will desire victory rather than wisdom. This is because to desire wisdom is to desire what is in fact true, whereas to desire victory, in this case, is to desire something specific that is advantageous for you (here a belief), independently of truth [3]. Socrates believes that there is something in store for the one who has died. The danger is that he is defending his view about the afterlife not because it is true, but because he has incentives to believe it. The incentives are that [5] he can reckon, as well as anyone can, that, if his arguments are right, then it is good to be convinced, but if not, then he will not be a burden on those around him and will soon lose this ignorance. The reasoning is similar to Pascal's wager: dominance reasoning explains why it would be better to believe something, independently of its truth. But, unlike in Pascal's wager, the idea is not that Socrates would consciously decide on these grounds; instead, he runs the risk of deceiving himself, [4] convincing himself that the soul exists after death, not because this is where his search for wisdom leads him, but influenced by the usefulness of this belief. If he did so deceive himself, he could end up deceiving others as well – as he goes on to say (91c).

This is perhaps the most insidious form of self-deception described in the dialogue. Until now, self-deception has been confined to clearly identifiable body lovers – for example those who think that they are temperate when in fact they are only trying to maximize their pleasures (68e–69a), or the non-philosophers who are accomplices to their own imprisonment without even realizing it (82d–e). It turns out that one can also deceive oneself by thinking that one is desiring wisdom, when in fact one is desiring some specific belief. Socrates thinks he must be courageous in fighting against this. But his companions should not assume that he will succeed, so they should "give little thought to Socrates and much more to the truth" (91c1–2). This is one reason for his companions to carefully scrutinize his arguments, not merely to accept them on his authority (as discussed in Section 1.4). Socrates' companions do not need him; they need philosophy, which they will still have after he departs.

8.3 SIMMIAS' OBJECTION – THE SOUL AS (LIKE) A *HARMONIA*: 85B–86D

We now turn back in the text to Simmias' challenge. Simmias first briefly articulates a methodology for inquiry (Subsection 8.3.1). Then he provides an argument allegedly parallel to kinship argument, according to which the soul is like a *harmonia*, and afterwards says that in fact he belongs to a group that believes that the soul is a *harmonia* (Subsection 8.3.2).

8.3.1 *Simmias' Methodology: 85c–d*

Simmias' methodology here is sometimes taken to be the same as Socrates' method of hypothesis, although Sedley has argued that they are significantly different.[16] I agree that they differ but I offer a new account of how. Let us begin with the passage:

> Well, I think, Socrates, as perhaps you do too, that knowing the clear truth about things like this in our present life is either impossible or something extremely difficult, but that all the same not testing in every way what is said about them, refusing to give up until one is exhausted from considering it in every manner, is the mark of an extremely feeble sort of man. Because concerning them one ought surely to achieve one of the following: either learn or discover how things are, or, if it is impossible to do that, at least to take the best human *logos* – the hardest one to disprove – and ride on that as if one were taking one's chances on a raft, and to sail through life in that way, unless one could get through the journey with more safety and less precariousness on a more solid vehicle, some divine *logos*. (85c1–d4)

Socrates has expressed in the defense speech Simmias' view that "knowing the clear truth about things like this in our present life is either impossible or something extremely difficult." While Socrates and Simmias may have knowledge of what equality is (as they claim in the recollecting argument, 74a–b), the philosopher will not have a "worthwhile encounter" (68a9) with the wisdom that he seeks so long as he is embodied, which is why he desires to be dead (66b–68b; Section 3.7). On the other hand, Socrates will deny that one should test *logoi* in every way – unless one sets a very high bar for what counts as a "way of testing." The *antilogikoi*, in arguing against every position, test *logoi* in ways that Socrates will go on to criticize: not carefully separating starting points from what comes from them (101e). Moreover, the method of hypothesis pointedly does not involve testing a theory by seeing how well it fits with other theories. Instead, I will argue, this method involves testing a theory on its own merits by seeing whether its consequences are harmonious with one another.

The next difference between Simmias' method and Socrates' is that Simmias suggests two possibilities: either learn and discover how things are, or take the human *logos* that is hardest to disprove and ride through life on that. He contrasts this latter option with finding a "divine" *logos*, which would provide further safety.

---

[16] For example, Rowe 1993 takes them to be the same. See Sedley 1995, 18–20.

Socrates' method of hypothesis is also presented with a sailing metaphor: it is part of his "second sailing" (99d1). He says that safety is found not in some divine hypothesis but in always replying using one's hypothesis (100e, 101d; cf. Subsection 9.8.2). Thus, Simmias wrongly suggests that safety is found only in a special sort of *logos*. Socrates claims that any *logos* can be safe as long as one does not accept it until it has been thoroughly tested.

At the end of the final argument, Socrates says that they should analyze the hypotheses more clearly; if they do, they will "follow the argument, I imagine, as far as a human can follow it. Should this itself become clear, then you won't seek anything further" (107b7–9). For this topic, at least, we cannot reach the best epistemic state so long as we are human. Thus Socrates' contrast between the human and the divine does not apply directly to the *logoi*, but rather to our epistemic relation to them: while there may be a divine way to grasp certain *logoi*, as we currently are we must grasp them in a human way.

In sum, Socrates' method, unlike Simmias', suggests specific sorts of testing and it allows any *logos* to be a safe, but so long as we are human there are some *logoi* that we will not be able to know.

8.3.2 *Simmias' Parallel Argument and His Theory*

Simmias' objection has two parts: (1) his argument that is supposedly parallel to the kinship argument, and (2) his description of what "we" believe, namely that the soul is a *harmonia*. I argue here that these two parts are more different from each other than is generally appreciated.[17] In particular, *harmonia* means rather different things in these two parts – or at least Socrates interprets them as meaning different things, and Simmias happily accepts Socrates' interpretation. This means that Simmias is not putting forward a supervenience or epiphenomenal theory of the soul, as is often claimed.

Simmias begins by saying that one could use the same reasoning as in the kinship argument to justify an obviously false conclusion:

> One might, he said, say the same thing about a *harmonia* too, and a lyre and strings: that the *harmonia* is something invisible, un-body-like, and utterly beautiful and divine in the tuned lyre, whereas the lyre itself and its strings are bodies, body-like, composite and earthy, and akin to the mortal. So when someone either smashes the lyre or cuts and snaps its strings, what if one were to insist with the same *logos* as yours, that the *harmonia* must still exist and not have perished? (85e3–86a6)

Simmias does not suggest here that the soul is a *harmonia*; he only says that Socrates' argument would be analogous to saying that a lyre's *harmonia* could not be

---

[17] My main ally is Young 2013, as I discuss later in this subsection. Dorter 1982, 108–9, and Iwata 2020 also briefly accept similar accounts.

destroyed.[18] In its basic sense, a *harmonia* is a fitting or fastening together. In music, it refers to how strings are fastened together, and hence to the method of stringing. By extension, it can refer to the musical mode – that is, the key that the instrument is tuned to; the lyre can then be heard to be in this key. Sedley and Long (2010) translate *harmonia* as "attunement," and this seems appropriate here, given Simmias' claim that it is invisible, which is not true of the way the strings are fastened together.

Recall that in the kinship argument Socrates pointed to three features of the soul that indicate that it is most similar and akin to the unseen: (1) it is invisible, (2) it comes to be with the unseen when it inquires itself through itself, and (3) it is by nature a ruler, just as the divine is. In his objection, Simmias claims to identify something that is invisible and divine, but which is clearly destroyed. I argued that Socrates does not claim that the soul's invisibility, (1), indicates anything about the soul's kinship or nature, and so is the least important of the three features (Section 6.4). Simmias' analogy, of course, says nothing about inquiry or the lyre being a ruler. In fact, Socrates' final objection to Simmias' position (94b–95a) argues that a *harmonia* cannot be a ruler; he concludes that argument by saying that the soul is "much more divine" (94e5) than a *harmonia*. Hence this argument is not actually parallel to the kinship argument.

But Socrates' reply does not address this supposedly parallel argument, but rather the second part of Simmias' objection, the alternative view that the soul *is* a *harmonia*:

> In actual fact, Socrates, I think that you yourself are well aware that we take the soul to be this sort of thing [a *harmonia*] most of all, since our body is made taut, so to speak, and held together by hot, cold, dry, wet and some other such things, and our soul is a *krasis* and *harmonia* of those very things, when they are blended properly and proportionately with one another. (86b5–c3)

As noted in Section 1.3, it is difficult to say who this "we" is; it may refer to some group connected with Philolaus, but this sort of idea seems to have had wide currency at the time, so Simmias may be a member of some other group that holds this view – another group that Simmias thinks Socrates would know that Simmias belongs to. According to this view, the soul is a *krasis* (proportionate-blend or tempering) and *harmonia* of hot, cold, dry, wet, and other such things. Later, Simmias simply says that the soul is a *krasis* of the things in the body (86d), making clear that he takes "*harmonia*" and "*krasis*" to be interchangeable here. A *krasis* is a

---

[18] Betegh (unpublished) notes that the plural "bodies," referring to the lyre and the strings, is the first extant use in Greek literature of "body" (*soma*) to refer to something that is not alive or formerly alive. Perhaps it arises here first because this is supposed to be an analogous argument, with the lyre and strings standing in for the living body; it is in in the plural because they are multiple things. Being in the plural also highlights that they can be dispersed and so destroyed.

sort of blend that tempers extremes, bringing things into balance.[19] A *harmonia* is a sort of fitting together, so that things are in dynamic tension, like the strings of a lyre. Both are ways of balancing opposites, rather than averaging them out in a way that neutralizes them.

In general, a blend of perceptible things is a composite thing with perceptible qualities – a blend of hot, cold, dry, and wet will have tactile qualities, and supposedly visual ones as well.[20] But on the basis of Simmias' earlier analogy, which claimed that the lyre's *harmonia* is invisible and un-body-like, scholars have taken Simmias' notion of soul as something like a ratio, rather than the blend that has tactile properties and is in a certain ratio.[21] The word "*harmonia*" can refer either to something's structure or to the thing that exhibits this structure.[22] Given that the soul is also referred to as *krasis*, it is fairly natural to understand it as having a structure, but given that the earlier parody argument said that it is invisible, it is natural to understand it as the structure possessed. Simmias may, of course, himself be unclear about what he means by "*harmonia*," and perhaps the "we" who have this theory are unclear about this too. Simmias will go on to say that he accepted the theory "without proof, but with a sort of likelihood and outward appeal" (92d1–2, discussed in Subsection 8.4.1), which fits with his not having a determinate idea. Perhaps Simmias' statements were supposed to mean that the soul is a *harmonia* in the sense of a ratio or in the sense of a topological arrangement among various parts.[23]

But this is not how Socrates understands Simmias' view, and Simmias happily accepts Socrates' characterization of it. Socrates attributes to Simmias the view "that *harmonia* is a composite thing (σύνθετον πρᾶγμα), and that soul is composed, as a *harmonia*, of those bodily things that are held taut" (τὸ ἁρμονίαν μὲν εἶναι σύνθετον πρᾶγμα, ψυχὴν δὲ ἁρμονίαν τινὰ ἐκ τῶν κατὰ τὸ σῶμα ἐντεταμένων συγκεῖσθαι, 92a7–9). According to this description, the *harmonia is* the composite thing. One might think of a formal structure as a composite thing, composed out of more basic formal components, but Socrates says that the soul, on this view, is composed of "bodily things that are held taut," and formal or abstract components are neither bodily nor the sort of things that can be held taut. In each of his objections, Socrates treats the *harmonia* as a composed object. This fits nicely with the soul being a mixture (*krasis*) of things such as the hot, cold, wet, and dry; the soul is a

---

[19] Caston 1997.
[20] As Young 2013 notes.
[21] So Hackforth 1955, Gallop 1975, Taylor 1983, Bostock 1986, and Ebert 2004.
[22] It can also refer to the concrete thing, such as a joint, that holds a composite object together, but I take that to be irrelevant here, since Socrates says that the hot, cold, wet, and dry are themselves blended properly and proportionately.
[23] If the theory is Philolaus', Philolaus may have had a clear idea of what sort of *harmonia* he meant, which Simmias did not understand. In F6a (Huffman 1993) Philolaus says that an octave is a *harmonia* and a *logos*. In F6 he says that unlike things are "bonded together" and "held in order" by *harmonia*. Socrates thinks that a *harmonia* cannot "bond together" or "hold together" its components (in either sense of *harmonia*), as discussed in Subsection 8.4.3.

composition of these bodily things when they are held taut. According to this interpretation, the soul is the properly blended hot, cold, wet, and dry. This is, then, a type of reductivist account, since it reduces the soul to something simpler (the blend of hot, cold, wet, and dry), but it is not an epiphenomenalist account.

How does this blend relate to the body? Simmias says that "the soul is a blend of *the* things in the body" (86d2, emphasis added). The definite article here makes clear that "hot, cold, dry, wet, and some other such things" are supposed to exhaust the things in the body, since taken together these are "*the* things in the body."[24] This is not an unusual account of the constituents of a human or indeed of the cosmos. It is the sort presented in the Hippocratic *Diseases* 1 and *Nature of the Human Being* and the sort attacked in *On Ancient Medicine* (cf. *Symposium* 188a and *Laws* X 889b). Moreover, Philolaus seems to have thought that the human body's true nature was the hot in its origin, but needs to be tempered by the cold, drawn in from breath, to survive, thereby forming a sort of mixture of hot and cold (A27).[25] In any event, if this interpretation is correct, then the soul is the mixture of the things in the body and so has the very same basic ingredients as the body. These ingredients count as the soul to the extent that they are properly blended and attuned. This properly blended and attuned mixture is said to "make taut, so to speak," and hold together the body. I take the idea to be that the soul is the hot, cold, wet, and dry's being in the right sort of dynamic tension, and this is what keeps the body held together and so alive. It is a tricky question how to understand the relationship between, on the one hand, the hot, cold, wet, and dry and, on the other hand, the body. But most early medical theories, like Philolaus', will face this question of how the body can be composed of some basic elements (like the hot) and at the same time of ordinary bodily parts.

Commentators have resisted the idea that for Simmias the soul is a composite of physical things,[26] but as long as we carefully distinguish Simmias' parody argument from the theory that he says "we" believe, this fits the text better. Whoever this "we" is, they did not develop their theory of the soul by analogy with the kinship argument, so they have no reason to think of a *harmonia* as something invisible. It is true that, when Simmias transitions from the analogous argument to his own theory, he says that they take the soul to be "this sort of thing" (τοιοῦτον, 86b7), meaning a *harmonia*. On my proposed reading, this is not precisely the same sort of *harmonia* as what the lyre has, which was something un-body-like, incomposite, and invisible. But any interpretation must accept that these are somewhat different sorts of *harmoniai*, since Socrates does not interpret Simmias' own theory as involving an incomposite *harmonia* – each of his counter-arguments rely on this *harmonia* being composite.

---

[24] Salles 2018 helped me see the importance of this.
[25] So Huffman 1993, 289–297.
[26] E.g. Hackforth 1955, 113, n. 1, Taylor 1983, 76, Rowe 1993 ad loc. Young 2013 and Iwata 2020 accept that it is the composite thing.

Part of the appeal of the idea that the *soul* is a *harmonia* – however one understands *harmonia* – is that it provides an account of the soul in terms of something that seems easier to understand: either a structured whole, or the structure possessed by this whole. Modern scholars have typically been interested in the theory that the soul is some sort of structure that supervenes on some more basic parts.[27] But there are several advantages to thinking of the soul instead as a composite object. The soul is what knows, desires, and believes things. It is difficult to understand what it means for a structure to desire or believe, but not for a structured thing to do so. Given that Socrates describes the soul as a composite of bodily things, we can see why he never points to such a difficulty.[28] Similarly, if the soul simply were the structure and this structure were composed of formal or abstract parts, one would want to know why these formal or abstract parts and the resulting structure could not exist before the animal came into existence and why they could not exist afterwards. By contrast, if the soul is composed of physical stuffs in the right tension, then when these stuffs are not yet together or disperse the soul must not exist. This explains why Socrates and Simmias take it as obvious that a *harmonia* cannot exist before its components (92a–b). Moreover, as we will see (Subsection 8.4.3), Socrates' last argument against Simmias' view avoids a common objection once we understand the view this way.

When "*harmonia*" refers to a composite object, the translation "attunement" is misleading. Young suggests instead "arrangement" and "structure" as translations.[29] "Structure" seems particularly apt, since "a structure" can refer not only to the overall abstract form that something has, but also to a concrete object that has that form (such as a playground structure, a Lego structure, or a structure as a building). In general, a *harmonia* is the result of fitting together; it is either the structure that is built or the structure that this built object possesses.

8.4 SOCRATES' REPLY: 91C–95A

Socrates first points out that Simmias cannot be committed both to the recollecting argument and to the soul's being a *harmonia*, since according to the recollecting argument the soul must exist before the body, but a *harmonia* cannot exist before the things from which it is composed (91e–92c). When Socrates then asks Simmias to choose between the *logos* that learning is recollecting and the *logos* that the soul is a

---

[27] See especially Dorter 1982 and Caston 1997.
[28] While Socrates says that a *harmonia* is a σύνθετον πρᾶγμα, Aristotle, in considering the idea that the soul is a *harmonia*, says that the primary sense of "*harmonia*" is as a σύνθεσις (*De anima* 408a7) – roughly, a *composition* rather than a composite thing. Aristotle objects that a *harmonia* cannot initiate motion and that it is difficult to attribute to it the affections and actions of soul (407b34–408a5) – an apt objection for a composition, but not for a composite thing. For a discussion of Aristotle's argument, see Betegh 2021b.
[29] Young 2013.

harmonia, Simmias chooses the first, giving a damning appraisal of his own reasons for accepting the view that the soul is a *harmonia* (92c–e).

Why does Socrates spend more than two pages (92e–95a) providing two further lengthy and complicated arguments against the view that the soul is a *harmonia* after Simmias abandons the view about as forcefully and dramatically as possible? This does not seem to have puzzled commentators, but it is an unusual thing to do. Simmias abandons his view immediately after Socrates' warning to avoid misology, a problem that arises from repeatedly putting one's trust in a *logos* and shortly thereafter deciding that it is false. Simmias advances his view that the soul is a *harmonia* and then within a Stephanus page dramatically abandons it. This is a grave danger, given the cause of misology. Suppose that soon thereafter Simmias decided that there was a problem with the recollecting argument – whether rightly or wrongly. He might then put his trust again into the view that the soul is a *harmonia*. Socrates' subsequent arguments evaluate the view that the soul is a *harmonia* on its own terms. I will argue in the next chapter (Subsection 9.8.3) that, in retrospect, we can see that Socrates evaluates Simmias' account by applying the autobiography's so-called method of hypothesis. I argue that this method allows one to evaluate a theory on its own terms, which is part of how it helps people avoid misology.

In addition to illustrating the method of hypothesis, these two objections each highlight a different feature of the soul that the kinship argument's account accommodates but Simmias' theory cannot. According to the first, the *harmonia* theory cannot account for there being better and worse souls. By contrast, the kinship argument makes room for some souls to be wiser and more like the divine unseen, and so better than others. According to the second objection, the *harmonia* theory cannot account for the soul's ability to rule over the body. This was precisely one of the features of soul that the kinship argument uses to point toward its kinship with the unseen (79e–80a). Together, these objections highlight how Socrates' account provides a solid basis for the soul's ethical features, which Cebes' does not.

8.4.1 *Quickly Abandoning Simmias'* logos: *92c–e*

When Simmias explains why he chooses the *logos* that learning is recollecting instead of the *logos* that the soul is a *harmonia*, he says that he had accepted the later "without proof but with a sort of likelihood and outward appeal" (ἄνευ ἀποδείξεως μετὰ εἰκότος τινὸς καὶ εὐπρεπείας) (92d1–2). If this is Philolaus' view, then Simmias is harshly critical of Philolaus here, much as Cebes said earlier that Philolaus told them nothing clear about why suicide is not sanctioned (61d–e). It raises the question of how one should provide proofs that do not rely on likelihood and outward appeal. Simmias goes on to say that the *logos* about learning and recollecting was provided by a hypothesis "worthy of acceptance" (92d7) – namely the existence of forms. Simmias says that he has accepted this hypothesis "both sufficiently and correctly" (92e1–2) and so he must not allow himself or anyone else to say that the soul is a *harmonia*.

Simmias does not say what makes his acceptance of forms sufficient and correct. Just as at the end of the recollecting argument – when Simmias enthusiastically accepts the existence of forms (76e–77a) – so here too Socrates does *not* say that Simmias is right to accept their existence. Instead, Socrates consistently notes when his argument relies on the existence of forms and ensures that his interlocutor agrees to them before proceeding. I will argue in Sections 9.7 and 9.8 that Socrates thinks that, before accepting forms' existence, they should carefully evaluate their existence using the method of hypothesis – which Simmias has not yet done. As noted earlier, at the end of the final argument Socrates tells Simmias that he is right to keep some doubt in his mind about what has been said and that they should consider the first hypotheses more clearly, which will allow them to follow the argument as far as a human being can (107b). This clearly suggests that Simmias needs to consider the hypotheses about each of the forms that each exists. Thus, contrary to what Simmias claims here, he has not yet accepted them "sufficiently and correctly." But before turning to those hypotheses, Socrates thinks that they should thoroughly evaluate Simmias' hypothesis (identified as such at 94b) that the soul is a *harmonia*.

8.4.2 *The Argument that Souls Would All Be Equally Good: 93a–94b*

Socrates provides the premises for these final two counter-arguments in an unusual order. He begins by providing some premises for the last counter-argument – in particular, the premises about what is true of a *harmonia*, in general (92e–93a).[30] But he then switches to his other counter-argument, that if the soul were a *harmonia*, souls would all be equally good, again beginning with the general premises about *harmonia*. After giving that argument in full (93a–94b), he provides the final counter-argument's premises about soul and then finishes arguing that, if the soul were a *harmonia*, it could not rule (94b–e). Why divide up the premises in this way? Simmias says he accepted the view that the soul is a *harmonia* on the basis of its plausibility and superficial appeal. Perhaps, in order to counteract this, Socrates wants Simmias to think carefully through the features of a *harmonia* before turning to whether these are compatible with the features a soul can possess.

There are many delicate points for understanding Socrates' argument that souls would all be equally good if the soul were a *harmonia*. Since this argument is not crucial for my main claims in this chapter, let alone this book, I simply provide a

---

[30] Gallop 1975 and Rowe 1993 ad loc. say that Socrates provides all of the premises for the second argument before the first. Taylor 1983 and Bostock 1986 rightly say that only some of the premises are provided.

basic interpretation of the argument here without defending the details.[31] First, Socrates and Simmias agree that, if a *harmonia* could come in degrees – if one *harmonia* could be more *harmonized* (fitted together) than another – then it would be more of a *harmonia*, and if less *harmonized*, then it would be less of a *harmonia* (93a–b). Socrates then turns to souls and asks whether one soul is any more of a soul than another (93b). Simmias says that none is. So far, their claims are not in conflict: perhaps some *harmoniai* come in degrees, but souls are *harmoniai* that do not. Socrates' other major question about souls is whether some have intelligence (*nous*), virtue, and are good, whereas others have ignorance, vice, and are bad (93b–c). After Simmias agrees, Socrates asks how those who have proposed that the soul is a *harmonia* will describe virtue and vice. Will virtue be a further kind of *harmonia* and a good soul be further harmonized (fitted together), whereas vice a sort of non-*harmonia* and a bad soul less harmonized (93c)? Simmias says that clearly the one hypothesizing this would say some such thing.[32] To understand the idea of being further harmonized, we could think here of a lyre that is better or worse tuned (fitted together). Virtue would be a sort of tuning to become properly fit together. Socrates next notes that, since the soul does not come in degrees, the *harmonia* that the soul is (by hypothesis) must not come in degrees (93d). But this would mean that the soul could not be more or less of a *harmonia* and so could not be more or less harmonized (fitted together) (93e). The soul is like a lyre with fixed strings, unable to have its tuning changed. But this means that all souls would have to have the same level of virtue and vice, since they would each be equally harmonized, which contradicts some souls being better than others (93e). At the end of the argument, Socrates suggests that, in fact, a *harmonia* can never be any less of a *harmonia*, so no *harmonia* could have a share of vice (94a). Each one is like a perfectly tuned lyre. All souls would then be completely good – an even more absurd consequence. But either way, if the soul is a *harmonia*, there is a problem explaining how some souls can be better than others.

8.4.3 *The Argument that the Soul Would Not Rule: 92e–93a, 94b–e*

Socrates' second argument is that the soul, especially the wise soul, commands in a way that involves opposing its alleged bodily components, but a *harmonia* cannot oppose its components. Hence, the soul is not a *harmonia*. This argument is often

---

[31] Gallop 1975 and Taylor 1983 provide elaborate accounts and raise a number of difficulties. My account is meant to avoid these difficulties. Dorter's 1982, 100–5, Trabattoni's 1988, and Young's 2013 accounts are the best I am aware of. Mine is closest to Dorter's and Trabattoni's.

[32] Perhaps "the one hypothesizing" this would give such an account because the appeal of a *harmonia* theory is that it can explain complex things like souls in terms of a *harmonia*. Philolaus identifies everything in the world as a limiter, unlimited, or a *harmonia*. In fact, *harmonia* may be the only normative feature available to Philolaus (so Huffman 1993, 44–5), in which case virtue, as normative, would need to be a *harmonia*.

discussed in connection with epiphenomenalism about the soul – that is, the view that the soul is not itself causally efficacious.[33] I have already described in Subsection 8.3.2 why I think this is not apt. Socrates' argument here assumes that the *harmonia* is the compound (93a). The compound is causally efficacious – for example it walks, talks, and so forth. Socrates simply argues here that it cannot be causally prior to its components.

Socrates begins from the claim that a compound cannot be different from how its components are (92e–93a). Next, Socrates draws the straightforward consequence that, since a *harmonia* is a compound and a compound cannot be different from how its components are, a *harmonia* cannot act on or be affected in a way different from its components (93a). The third step is that "a *harmonia* is not the sort of thing to lead its components, but rather to follow them" (93a6–7). Why say this, rather than that they have an equal claim on both leading and following? It is useful to see how Socrates uses this claim in the fourth step: "there's no chance that a *harmonia* move contrary to its own parts or to make a sound or in some way oppose them" (93a8–9). The point, then, is that, if a *harmonia* is acting, then so are its parts; if the *harmonia* is being affected, then so are the parts. Hence, if the *harmonia* were to move contrary to its own parts, its parts would be moving contrary to themselves, since anything that the *harmonia* does, its parts also do. Thus Socrates only needs that the *harmonia* and its parts co-vary; it is not crucial for his argument that the whole follow the components.[34]

The basic way in which Socrates' argument works from here is clear, but the details are tricky. The argument is that the soul rules its alleged components in a way that involves opposing them. But if it were a *harmonia*, it could not do so. It is often claimed (1) that in this argument Socrates makes the body the subject of (what we would call) psychological states and (2) that the argument only shows that the soul cannot be composed of bodily affections, but leaves open that the soul is composed of bodily parts. I will argue against each of these claims.

Let me begin with whether Socrates is committed here to the body's being the subject of some (of what we would call) psychological states.[35] Instead, Socrates seems very careful not to attribute the psychological states to any particular part of us:

> "Next," he said, "of all the things in a human (ἐν ἀνθρώπῳ), is there any other than soul that you would say rules, and especially a wise soul?"
> "No, I wouldn't."
> "Does soul do so by surrendering to the affections that are according to (κατά) the body or by actually opposing them? What I mean is something like the

---

[33] See especially Dorter 1982 and Caston 1997.
[34] So Caston 1997, 324.
[35] As claimed by Caston 1997, 324; Lorenz 2006. For my general discussion of this question, see Section 7.4.

following. When heat and thirst are there inside (ἐνόν), the soul pulls toward the opposite, not drinking, and when hunger is there inside, the soul pulls toward not eating. And there are surely countless other ways in which we see the soul opposing the things that are according to (κατά) the body, aren't there?" (94b4–c1)

Socrates says that heat and thirst are inside, but he does not say what they are in. It might be the body, but it might also be the human – which Socrates says at the beginning of the passage that the soul is *in*. The claim that these are affections according to (*kata*) the body need not mean that they have the body as their subject. It simply means that they are in line with the body's aim of ruling us (so Section 7.4). Socrates should describe the situation in a way compatible with how the *harmonia* theory would treat psychological states. According to this theory, if something is "inside" the human, then it is inside both the soul and its components. Socrates is carefully describing the phenomenon without prejudging which theory is right. If, on such a theory, the ultimate constituents of the soul are the hot, cold, wet, and dry, then thirst could be understood as an excess of hot and dry in both soul and body.

This argument is also regularly criticized for making the bodily affections components of the soul rather than the body's parts themselves.[36] I take Socrates' view instead to be that the soul opposes its bodily components *by* opposing the body's affections. Here is the key passage, which comes shortly after the previous one:

> Well then, don't we discover that in reality it does quite the opposite, directing all its alleged components, and opposing them almost everywhere through its entire life, and playing the master in every way, correcting some of them – those to which gymnastics and medicine are appropriate – more ruthlessly and with certain hardships, but others more gently, some with threats, others with reprimands, conversing with the desires, rages, and fears as if it were one thing and they another? Homer himself has, I think, represented this sort of thing in the *Odyssey*, when he says of Odysseus:
>
> He struck his chest and spoke reproachfully to his heart:
> "Endure, my heart. You once endured something even more shameful."
>
> Now do you suppose that when Homer composed this he thought that soul is a *harmonia* and the sort of thing to be led by the body's affections? (94c9–e4)

Note, first, that Odysseus is reproaching his *heart*, one of his parts, not one of his bodily affections. The question, then, turning to the earlier part of the passage, is what components the soul is correcting. Socrates starts with the idea that it corrects more ruthlessly and with certain hardships those to which gymnastics and medicine are appropriate, but others more gently. One might think that these are the bodily parts: exercising the legs, taking medicine for the kidney, and so on. But what, then, should we make of "some with threats, others with reprimands, conversing with the desires, rages, and fears as if it were one thing and they another"? Socrates does not

---

[36] Gallop 1975, Taylor 1983, Bostock 1986, Young 2013.

say that the desires, rages, and fears *are* the parts. In addressing his heart, Odysseus is clearly conversing with his desire for revenge. My suggestion, then, is that we can oppose our parts *by* opposing these desires, rages, and so forth.[37] This allows Socrates to do what he should be doing: explain how the soul can oppose its components. We can put the idea this way: the body gives rise to desires, rages, and fears, and the soul genuinely opposes these bodily affections and thereby opposes the body.

By analogy with the heart, I suggested that one might think of the components as the legs, kidneys, and so on. But according to Simmias' theory, the soul's components are the hot, cold, wet, dry, and such things, rather than ordinary bodily parts. And the Odyssey passage was only supposed to illustrate the same *sort of* thing. In the Hippocratic *On Regimen*, for example, animals are said to be made up of water and fire (3) and exercise can help promote balance in people (67), evidently by getting the balance of their components right. So perhaps it is best to think that the components here continue to be the hot, cold, and so on, not the bodily parts. We might imagine that there is an excess of hot in the body, leading to desire for drink in the person, but the wise soul rules over its components, conversing with this desire as if it were something else, thereby opposing the hot, if that is best.

Interpreters often claim that a defender of a *harmonia* theory could reply to Socrates that in such cases of conflict one part of the body is opposing another part instead of the soul opposing the body.[38] While that may be a possible reply for some types of epiphenomenalism, it would not help save the view that the soul is a properly fitted together composite thing. Suppose that we analyze Odysseus' inner conflict as one part, his brain, opposing another part, his heart. Then Odysseus' parts are not properly fitted together. In the *Republic* it is the soul whose parts do not oppose one another that has *harmonia* (443d–e); if bodily parts opposed each other, they too would supposedly lack *harmonia*. And in the previous argument in the *Phaedo*, Socrates says that every *harmonia*, to the extent that it is a *harmonia*, is entirely harmonized (94a). The *harmonia* theory thus would not allow either a conflict between body and soul or a conflict within the parts of the body or within the parts of the soul. This explains why Simmias does not pursue the idea of one bodily part opposing another.

Socrates' description of how the soul opposes bodily affections is compatible with his account in the defense speech and in the return to the defense, but does not require it. In the defense speech, he says that the body fills us with loves, desires, fears, and fantasies of every kind (66c). Here the bodily affections are like agents of the body in the soul that further the body's aims. By opposing these agents, one opposes the body's aims, and so the body. Socrates' argument against the *harmonia* theory does not presuppose his own account, which is why these details are not

---

[37] Cf. *Timaeus* 69c–71e for specific psychological states' being associated with specific parts of the body.
[38] E.g. Gallop 1975, Dorter 1982, Taylor 1983, and Bostock 1986.

spelled out. Socrates thinks that any theory of the soul should be able to explain the fact that soul can genuinely oppose bodily affections.

8.5 CONCLUSION

Misology is not a mere palate cleanser at the middle of the dialogue before returning to the "serious" argumentation. Instead, it identifies a serious threat, which has been building over the course of the dialogue: that the very people who are philosophically disposed might in their enthusiasm put their trust into theories and arguments too quickly and then find themselves burned too many times, turning them into haters of theorizing who do not trust any theory. Socrates must ensure that the companions avoid this problem if he is to meet Cebes' challenge, which asked him to *persuade* them that the soul exists after death. While Socrates' companions are in danger of misology, Socrates himself is in danger of deceiving himself, thinking that he is desiring wisdom when he is in fact desiring victory in argumentation. Both of these dangers need to be avoided for them to be true lovers of wisdom and so have a chance for eternal happiness.

Simmias' objection comes in two parts: first, a parody of the kinship argument; then a rival theory of the soul as a *harmonia*. Socrates only replies to the latter. As he interprets this theory, the soul is something composite, rather than the structure that this composite possesses. Socrates' counter-arguments are designed to show that, unlike his own theory, this one is incompatible with basic ethical features of the soul: that some souls can be wiser and better than others, and that the soul can rule over the body.

9

Socrates' Autobiography

95e–102a

Socrates' (alleged) autobiography is, alongside the recollecting argument, one of the most discussed parts of the *Phaedo* and indeed the entire Platonic corpus. It may also be the most influential part of the dialogue, since it (1) is perhaps the first Greek philosophical reflection on how to do natural science, (2) provides a classic account of a method for inquiry – the *Phaedo*'s so-called method of hypothesis – and (3) includes an important discussion of forms. These three are interconnected: Socrates says that natural science aims to identify *aitiai* (standardly translated as "causes"); he rejects the sort of things natural scientists had identified as *aitiai*; and then he uses the method of hypothesis to put forward the existence of forms, which he relies on to specify *aitiai*.[1]

Precisely because this discussion has been so influential, it is typically read in light of its ancient reception (especially by Aristotle and the Stoics) and Plato's later dialogues, rather than its own intellectual background. Of course, reading it in light of these texts can be insightful, but to understand the autobiography's distinctive claims and contributions we should first carefully consider how it fits into the dialogue as a whole and its intellectual background. Ancient philosophy scholars frequently overlook the sophisticated discussion of *aitiai* and hypotheses in fifth-century medical treatises. I argue that Socrates is critically engaging with claims about *aitiai* and hypotheses in this tradition. I further argue that the autobiography shows how Socrates – as portrayed throughout Plato's dialogues – would engage with the natural scientific tradition: he shows his hallmark profession of ignorance; he becomes excited by the prospect of acquiring knowledge of the good; since he is unable to learn this from Anaxagoras or others, he proceeds in a way that does not require knowledge; instead, it requires him to hypothesize the existence of the things that he is always searching for, the things sought by his "what is it?" question.

---

[1] I argue that a form is not strictly speaking an *aitia*, but rather the *aitia* of x's being f is the following: x's having a share of f-ness.

Whether or not the historical Socrates ever had the sort of intellectual journey described here, Plato presents a distinctively Socratic response to the natural scientific tradition. The autobiography is typically thought of as providing a classic statement of Platonic teleology. I argue that, when it is not read in light of later texts, it is not clear that Socrates is interested specifically in teleology here, as opposed to simply being interested in knowledge of the good.

Scholarship on the autobiography often treats it as a stand-alone discussion. Situating it within the dialogue helps resolve several disputes, but is especially important for understanding the method of hypothesis. I argue that this method is supposed to help one avoid prematurely putting trust in a theory, but rather slowly build rational trust in one, thereby avoiding the cycle of trust and doubt that brings about misology. Furthermore, we can clarify the method by recognizing that Socrates applied it earlier, when arguing against Simmias' *harmonia* theory.

The autobiography falls into three parts. In the first, Socrates describes the aims of natural science (Section 9.1), which I argue should be understood against the background of ancient medicine (9.2). After Socrates describes his initial inquiry, he considers and rejects ordinary ways of explaining why something is larger or becomes larger, beginning to reveal his criterion for something's being an *aitia* (9.3). In the second part, he turns to Anaxagoras' proposal that intelligence (*nous*) is responsible (*aitios*) for everything, which he was excited about (9.4), but which he says Anaxagoras did not actually develop, instead identifying other things as responsible, which Socrates says cannot be (9.5). In the third part of the autobiography, Socrates turns to his alternative, using forms to specify causes (*aitiai*), which he introduces as a second sailing (9.6). I first discuss how Socrates uses forms to specify *aitiai* (9.7) and then the method of hypothesis that he uses to put forward this theory (9.8). I argue that, when he hypothesizes forms, he is hypothesizing nothing more than what he is searching for in the Socratic dialogues, showing how these can be used to specify *aitiai*. His method is meant to ensure that one does not accept the existence of forms prematurely, but rather thoroughly examine them first.

This is the longest chapter in the book because of the many interrelated questions and topics that need to be addressed. One could think of it as two shorter chapters – one on the first two parts, describing Socrates' earlier investigation and disappointment (Sections 9.1–5), and another on the final part, his own positive theory (Sections 9.6–8).

9.1 AITIA, AITION, AND THE AIMS OF NATURAL SCIENCE

Socrates says that research into nature (περὶ φύσεως ἱστορία) involves knowing the *aitiai* of each thing (96a). His autobiography then describes his search for *aitiai*. It is unclear what an *aitia* is supposed to be, and so what Socrates is searching for. Clarifying this is crucial for understanding why he rejects some proposed accounts and accepts others. Indeed, divergent accounts of the autobiography frequently hinge on divergent accounts of what an *aitia* is supposed to be.[2] I argue here that to understand this we need to distinguish his use of the noun "*aitia*" (plural: *aitiai*) from that of the adjective "*aitios/-a/-on*."[3] (To avoid ambiguity and aid the Greekless reader, I only use the neuter and masculine singular forms "*aition*" and "*aitios*" for the adjective.)[4]

Socrates describes the search for *aitiai* as the search for "that because of which each comes to be, that because of which it passes away, and that because of which it is" (96a8–9). In his examples, Socrates always fills out "comes to be" or "is" with a predicate complement: because of what something is *larger* (96d–e, 100e–101b), or because of what it comes to be *two* (96e–97a, 101b–c) or because of what it is *in the center* (97e–98a).[5] Typically, the explanandum is taken as obvious – for example, that one person is larger than another – and the question is what its *aitia* is. But if the explanandum is not obvious, one first states the fact – e.g. the earth is a sphere – and then the *aitia* because of which this is the case (97d–98a).

Michael Frede has noted that, in the Greek legal context as well as in ordinary Greek, the adjective "*aitios-/a/-on*" is applied to the person or thing responsible for a crime.[6] The noun "*aitia*" can simply mean responsibility, but in a legal context it is the accusation, that is, it describes what someone allegedly is responsible for doing. Frede suggests that Socrates distinguishes between these two expressions in the *Phaedo*, with "*aitios*" referring to what is responsible, and (according to Frede) "*aitia*" referring to a propositional item that identifies this as responsible.[7] Lennox and Mueller agree that these terms differ here, but Mueller doubts that the *aitia* should be seen as propositional.[8] However, Irwin, Sedley, Ledbetter, and Wolfsdorf have raised doubts that these words are clearly distinguished in the *Phaedo*,[9] and, in general, no distinction is observed in more recent secondary literature or translations – both are typically translated as "cause."

---

[2] For example, Kelsey 2004, Sharma 2009, and Bailey 2014 offer different accounts of what Socrates is looking for in an *aitia*, which is part of why they provide substantively different interpretations (i) of Socrates' criticisms of rival accounts and (ii) of what he sees as promising in his own account.

[3] He also uses the verb "*aitiasthai*" (to assign responsibility) twice (98c2, 98d8), as discussed in Section 9.5.

[4] The Greekless reader might otherwise find it difficult to distinguish the various *aiti*-stem words in this chapter. In the case of the feminine adjective and neuter plural, it also helps disambiguate the adjective from the noun.

[5] For a discussion of the relation between so-called complete and incomplete uses of "to be" in Greek, see Brown 1999, Kahn 2004.

[6] Frede 1980; see also Sedley 1998. Darbo-Peschanski 1999 discusses earlier, especially Homeric, uses of these terms. Pelling 2019, ch. 1 discusses these terms in Herodotus.

[7] Frede 1980, Lennox 1985; Mueller 1998, 86 and Johansen 2004, 70, n. 4 think this distinction is also observed in the *Timaeus*.

[8] Mueller 1998, 83–5.

[9] Irwin 1983, Sedley 1998, n. 1, Ledbetter 1999, Wolfsdorf 2005.

"*Aitia*" is Socrates' favored term in the autobiography. While it is sometimes ambiguous which term is used (whether the noun or the feminine adjective),[10] by my count he uses the noun "*aitia*" twenty-seven times in this part of the dialogue (95e–102a) – at least twice on each page from 96 to 101. He uses the adjective eight times, five of them in a single cluster when he distinguishes the *aition* thing from that without which something would never be *aition* (99a–b).[11] On its own, "*aitios*" normally means responsible. Two of the eight occurrences of "*aitios/-a/-on*" are with a neuter article (both at 99b3), forming a noun (as one can in Greek). An adjective with the neuter article is sometimes equivalent to the abstract noun in Greek; for example, "the just" (*to dikaion*) can refer to justice – or it can refer to a just thing. Using this construction, "the *aition*" in Greek is sometimes equivalent to "*aitia*." But these two occurrences of "*to aition*" clearly refer to a responsible (*aition*) thing; they are not simply equivalent to "*aitia*."

In Socrates' description of Anaxagoras' theory, he clearly uses "*aitios*" in a significantly differently way from "*aitia*." Socrates reports that according to Anaxagoras intelligence (*nous*) orders and is *aitios* (responsible) for everything. Socrates then says that if this is so, then the *aitia* concerning each thing *is* its being best for it to be the way it is (97c–d). So, for example, the *aitia* of the earth's being spherical would be its being best for it to be spherical. Describing this *aitia* would require explaining why it is better for the earth to be this way (97d–98b), which would require knowing what is better and what worse. So, as Socrates describes this theory, only one thing, intelligence, is *aitios* for everything, but the *aitia* of each is different. The *aitia* of the earth's being in the center of the universe (assuming it is) would describe why it is best for it to be there; this is different from the *aitia* of why the earth is a sphere. Moreover, Socrates says that, if intelligence is *aitios*, then one still needs to work to discover the *aitia* of how each thing comes to be (97c–d). Hence Socrates clearly uses the adjective "*aitios/-a/-on*" differently from the noun "*aitia*"; the difficult question is exactly how.

To answer this, it is useful to briefly consider how these terms were used in fifth century treatises (and so before the *Phaedo*). As noted earlier, in the Greek legal context the *aitia* is the accusation, which describes what the accused (the one *aitios*) has done. Thus, in the *Encomium of Helen*, Gorgias considers four accusations (*aitiai*) against Helen and argues that in each case she is not to blame. Each accusation (*aitia*) states *by what* (causal dative) she came to Troy: (i) by the wishes of Chance and the purposes of the gods and the decree of necessity, or (ii) by force, or (iii) persuaded by speeches, or (iv) captivated by love (*Encomium* §6 and §15). In the *Histories*, Herodotus offers a several pages account of "the *aitia*" (3.139.1) of how

---

[10] I use "*aitia*" to refer to the noun, never the adjective, unless otherwise specified.
[11] The eight occurrences are: 97c2, 97c4, 99a4, 99b3 (twice), b4, b6, 101b10. For some ambiguous cases, see n. 33 and 40 in this chapter.

King Darius captured Samos (3.139–49).[12] In this case it is clear who is responsible, King Darius, but a question remains: how it happened. The *aitia* clarifies this.

This also seems to be the use of "*aitia*" in Herodotus' famous opening of the *Histories*. He says that he is presenting his research (*historia*) which will discuss the *aitia* of the hostilities between Greeks and non-Greeks. He quickly reports the Persian view that the Phoenicians are *aitioi* (plural of *aitios*, 1.1) and that the Greeks are also *aitioi* (1.4). Here again the adjective (*aitios/-a/-on*) is used for the simple attribution of responsibility to some specific person (or group), whereas the noun (*aitia*) refers to what research seeks to understand, a more complicated description of how an agent is responsible. Similarly, in the fifth-century Hippocratic *On Ancient Medicine*, the author says that correctly grasping medical knowledge in its entirety would be the following research (*historia*): "knowing what a human is and because of what sort of *aitiai* it comes to be and other such things with precision" (20.2; text and translation Schiefsky). Socrates is clearly echoing this way of thinking when he says that research into nature (*peri phuseōs historia*) involves knowing the *aitiai* of each thing (96a). In these earlier works, specifying the *aitia* involves describing in detail – sometimes in great detail – how the *aition* thing is *aition*.[13] Knowledge comes from properly grasping this – not merely who or what is responsible. Once you grasp the *aitia*, you understand why the explanandum is the way it is: why Helen is in Troy, why there are these hostilities, and why a human comes to be. My suggestion is that the *Phaedo* is distinguishing "*aitios/-a/-on*" and "*aitia*" in this way.

What's unusual about Socrates' description of the *aitiai* he expected Anaxagoras to provide, if intelligence were *aitios*, is that they do not mention intelligence at all – as if you made an accusation without mentioning the perpetrator. The reason for this, I think, is twofold. First, according to this proposal, intelligence is responsible for *everything*. Normally a number of different people are candidates for being responsible; seeing how this person is responsible helps show their responsibility. If intelligence is responsible for everything, there is no need to mention it. Second, Socrates thinks that if intelligence is responsible (*aitios*), we know, in general, how it would be responsible: it would arrange each thing in the way that is (actually) best (97c). Thus, if we determine what is in fact best, we know how intelligence arranged things. It's as if a perfect alphabetizer alphabetizes every file in a catalogue. If someone then asks why this file comes before that one, you can simply point to the fact about alphabetical order – there is no need to point to facts about the alphabetizer. By contrast, according to Socrates' own view, the *aitia* of x's being *f* is that x has a share in the form of *f*-ness (100c). The form of *f*-ness seems to be what is responsible (*aition*). The *aitia* describes how this form is responsible for a thing's being beautiful: by that thing's having a share of the form. According to this theory,

---

[12] For a nuanced discussion of *aitia* and *aition* in Herodotus, see Pelling 2019, esp. 5–8.
[13] So Frede 1980.

unlike the intelligence theory, the specification of the *aitia* mentions what is *aition*. This is necessary because there is not only one thing responsible for everything, but rather different forms are responsible for different things.

Let us return to the idea that research into nature involves grasping the *aitia*. Simply recognizing what is responsible (*aition*) is not sufficient for understanding this thing's responsibility. By contrast, once one grasps the *aitia*, one has reached the goal of research, because one can see in virtue of what it is responsible. Understanding why it is best for the earth to be a sphere allows one to understand in virtue of what intelligence is responsible for this. It is sometimes suggested that in the *Phaedo* there is a sort of transparency or intelligible connection between a cause and an explanandum.[14] This does not hold between an *aition* thing and the explanandum: simply grasping that intelligence is responsible does not transparently explain or make intelligible why the earth is in the center, nor does grasping the form of largeness transparently explain why Simmias is larger than Socrates. But there is a sort of transparency between the *aitia* and the explanandum: if Simmias has a share of largeness with respect to Socrates, it is clear why Simmias is larger than Socrates. If intelligence is *aitios* and it is better for the earth to be in the center, it is clear why the earth is in the center. This interpretation makes clear why the goal of research is to come to know an *aitia*: doing so makes the explanandum intelligible.

It is sometimes claimed that in the *Phaedo* a cause is necessary and sufficient for the explanandum.[15] This does not seem true for what is *aition*: the form of largeness is not sufficient for Simmias to be larger than Socrates – after all, he could be smaller. In fact Socrates goes on to suggest that his decision to stay in prison is a reasonable candidate for what is responsible for his being in prison (99b), although such a decision is neither necessary nor sufficient for being in prison – there are many other explanations for why he might be there (hence not necessary) and Socrates could decide to stay in prison but be dragged away by his friends (hence not sufficient).[16] But the two major theories of *aitiai* that Socrates considers – involving intelligence and forms – do seem to each specify *aitiai* that are necessary and sufficient. Suppose that intelligence is *aitios*; then, its being best for the earth to be a sphere is necessary and sufficient for its being a sphere. Similarly, if Socrates' forms theory is right, then Simmias' having a share of largeness is necessary and sufficient for his being large. I do not see clear evidence that Socrates is thinking of *aitiai* in general as necessary and sufficient, but perhaps he is in these cases.

---

[14] E.g. Kelsey 2004, 22, Sharma 2009, 165.
[15] See esp. Bailey 2014.
[16] In describing why he is in prison, Socrates says that the "real *aitiai*" are that, "since the Athenians have decided that it was better to condemn me, on account of that I too have also decided that it is better to sit here" (98e1–3). It is difficult to say exactly what the distinct *aitiai* are here – I take one to involve the Athenians' initial decision and the other Socrates' decision in response – but none of the candidates seem necessary or sufficient for Socrates' being in prison.

Socrates does not only use the terms *"aition"* and *"aitia"* when describing what he is looking for; he also uses the causal dative ("by") and the preposition *"dia"* with the accusative ("because of").[17] The causal dative seems to always be used with a noun that is purportedly *aition*. By contrast, *"dia"* (+ acc.) typically is used with a larger fact – the *aitia*. For example, the causal dative is used to say that one person is larger than another *by a head* (96d–e). *"Dia"* (+ acc.) is used to say that that ten is more numerous than eight *because of* "there being two added to it" (96e3). But Socrates also uses *"dia"* (+ acc.) with something that is purportedly *aition*: for example, he says that something is larger both *by* and *because of* (*dia* +acc.) largeness (101a) or smaller *by* and *because of* smallness (101a) or numerous *by* and *because of* numerousness (101b).

I am not claiming (or denying) that Plato uses *"aition"* and *"aitia"* differently in other dialogues – simply that he uses them differently here.[18] It is not unusual for Socrates to distinguish words in one dialogue that he does not in others, and we can understand why he would distinguish them here, since it is a somewhat technical discussion.[19] I maintain that in the autobiography an *aitia* consistently explains in virtue of what the *aition* thing is *aition*. But if there is an exception to this, that would not undermine there being an important conceptual distinction, which in the *Phaedo* he generally expresses using these terms.

A topic of considerable debate since Vlastos' 1969 article – particularly in the 1970s and 1980s – was whether to translate *"aition"* and *"aitia"* as "cause," or instead as something like "reason" or "explanation." I think we should translate *"aition"* as "responsible," and will do so for the remainder of the chapter. "*Aitia*" is significantly trickier. Ideally one would retain its close linguistic connection to *"aition."* At the same time, as described in the next section, Socrates is working within a rich scientific tradition in which *"aitia"* is a technical term – neither "accusation" nor "responsibility" capture this meaning. "Causal description" perhaps fits this quasi-technical sense, but it has no linguistic connection to "responsible" and a description is a linguistic item, whereas the *aitia* is what is described. I will leave *"aitia"* untranslated in this chapter, but have found no better translation than "cause."[20]

However *"aitia"* is translated, Socrates is operating with a concept that some have thought does not line up with our ordinary notion of cause. An *aitia* need not be an

---

[17] Noted by Sedley 1998. Sedley also mentions *"poiein"* ("to make"), which Socrates uses once to describe an *aitia*'s relation to the explanandum (100d5): the beautiful's presence, or however one understands this relationship, *makes* each beautiful thing beautiful.
[18] This avoids the main objections in Ledbetter 1999 and Wolfsdorf 2005. On the *Timaeus*, see n. 7.
[19] Similarly, in the final argument Socrates distinguishes between *"eidos"* and *"idea"* in a way he does not in most other dialogues (see Section 10.5).
[20] "Reasons" suggests something psychological, and *aitiai* are not, in general, psychological. Similarly, "explanation" suggests a linguistic utterance of some sort, which an *aitia* is not. However, we sometimes say, for example, that the air in the radiator explains the loud noise you are hearing – and in this sense the *aition* thing "explains" something.

event, need not be temporally prior to what it causes, nor need it have several other features some contemporary philosophers require of causes – though contemporary philosophical views of causation are also fairly different from what they were from the 1960s to 1980s, when Vlastos' position was developed and most thoroughly discussed.[21] While we might expect all causes to belong to some broad category – such as event, object, or power – Socrates treats anything that could answer the "because of what?" question as a candidate for being *aition* or an *aitia*. The candidates he puts forward include: food, a head, division, intelligence (*nous*), and the form of beauty. He does not reject any on the grounds that they belong to the wrong category.[22]

Socrates does not lay down at the beginning the general requirements he thinks something must meet to be *aition*. Instead, he slowly reveals implicit requirements by criticizing other accounts. When he provides his own account, he repeatedly points out how it avoids problems that the initial accounts face (100e–101c). I will argue that Socrates consistently rejects candidates for failing to identify something that makes the explanandum intelligible. Socrates' two main requirements that involve opposites – the same thing cannot be responsible for opposites and opposites cannot have an equal claim on being an *aitia* for something – are supposed to signal that we have not identified something that makes the explanandum intelligible.[23]

9.2 THE BACKGROUND: ANCIENT GREEK MEDICINE

Reflections on early Greek natural philosophy tend to focus on the early Greek cosmologists, such as Anaxagoras. These cosmologists do not use "*aition*," "*aitia*," or any other words with the *aiti-* stem in our fragments, aside from (i) a few fragments from Democritus, which keep the original sense of "person responsible" (B83, B159)[24] and (ii) the report that Democritus said that "he would rather discover a single causal account (*aitiologian*) than acquire the kingdom of the Persians" (B118). The compound word "*aitiologia*" ("causal account") is not in any other fifth century source.[25] By contrast, *aiti*-stem words are used frequently in fifth-century works by Greek medical writers (most of whose works come down to us under the name "Hippocrates"). Ancient Greek medicine often presents itself as a craft (*technē*) that draws on and contributes to research into nature – sometimes in a way that includes

---

[21] Vlastos 1969, followed for example by Gallop 1975, Frede 1980, and Bostock 1986. Humean accounts of causation were frequently taken to be obvious from the 1960s through the 1980s. Schaffer 2016 makes clear the deep disagreements in the contemporary debate about causation.
[22] So Sedley 1998.
[23] At 101a–b, after presenting one reason to doubt that something is large because of a head, Socrates presents a second: it would be bizarre if a person were large because of something small. Unlike his other reasons, this one is presented as a *further* reason, and unlike his others, it arises nowhere else. Hence I leave it aside here.
[24] See Vegetti 1999.
[25] Vegetti 1999 doubts that it is verbatim.

cosmology, sometimes in a way that rejects the role of cosmology in medicine (see *On Ancient Medicine* 1 and 20). When Socrates describes the questions addressed by research into nature (96b–c), he begins with and focuses on questions and views in this medical tradition. "Is it when the hot and the cold start to decompose... that living things grow together?" (96b2–3) is answered affirmatively in *On Fleshes*, which gives an account of how the putrefaction of heat, along with cold, gives rise to the basic parts of the body (§3). As for the questions "is it by blood that we think (φρονοῦμεν), or air, or fire? Or is it none of these, but is it rather the brain that..." (96b3–5), *On Regimen* (1.35) claims we think (or are intelligent, φρονεῖν) with a mixture of the right sort of water and fire, whereas *On the Sacred Disease* (16) claims that air provides the brain with wisdom (*phronēsis*) and it is with the brain that we think.[26] Thus, in thinking about "research into nature," Socrates is clearly thinking about the medical tradition, although we cannot know which works he has in mind. It is important to recognize the sophistication of Hippocratic treatments of *aitia* and *aition* to appreciate what is, and is not, innovative in Socrates' approach in the *Phaedo*, as well as how he is developing and appropriating ideas from his predecessors.[27]

On Ancient Medicine (VM) has a good claim on providing the most sophisticated treatment of *aitia* and *aition* in a fifth-century Greek medical text.[28] It begins by attacking the hypothesizing of *aitiai* in medicine; it then puts in its place the author's preferred procedure and *aitiai*. Later, in Subsection 9.8.1, I argue that Socrates' method of hypothesis is meant to avoid the sort of attack on the use of hypotheses found in VM. VM frequently rejects a hypothesis by arguing that the things hypothesized as responsible are present and yet the explanandum is not there, or the explanandum is present but the things hypothesized as responsible are not. Its most nuanced treatment of causation is the argument in 19.3 that the things responsible for certain diseases are specific fluxes (discharges of salty, moist, and acrid from the body):

> One must of course consider these [fluxes] to be responsible (αἴτια) for each condition, since their presence is necessarily accompanied by that condition in a certain form, while when they change into another blend it ceases. (19.3, text and trans. Schiefsky)

---

[26] Discussed in Menn 2010, 57–61.
[27] It is beyond the scope of this book to consider fifth-century Hippocratic treatises' uses of "*aitia*" and "*aition*." For a brief discussion, see Vegetti 1999, 280–2. The fifth-century Hippocratic treatises I have examined (e.g. *On Ancient Medicine, On Breaths, On the Sacred Disease* and *Airs, Waters and Places*) fit with the broad outlines of the account given in the previous section. "*To aition*" is sometimes used as equivalent to "*aitia*" in these works and sometimes "*aitia*" simply means responsibility, as elsewhere.
[28] So Vegetti 1999 and Schiefsky 2005, 288. See also Hankinson 1998, ch. 2. Schiefsky 2005 is the best translation and commentary on VM, which is too often overlooked by ancient philosophy scholars. For a discussion of VM's use of the expression "*auto epi heautou*," see Section 3.4. For a discussion of the theory of the hot, cold, wet, and dry that it attacks, see Subsection 8.3.2. *Sacred Disease, On the Art,* and *Airs, Waters, Places* are some of the other fifth-century Hippocratic works with sophisticated uses of "*aition*" and "*aitia*."

This seems to be the earliest extant articulation of the idea, roughly put, that a cause must be necessary and sufficient for its effect.[29] Socrates never makes such a claim in the *Phaedo*; indeed, as noted in the previous section, Socrates does not seem to think that what is responsible need be necessary or sufficient. Instead, Socrates famously emphasizes in the *Phaedo* that being necessary does not ensure being responsible – that it is compatible with merely being that without which the responsible thing could never be responsible (99a–b).

At the end of the Hippocratic *On Breaths*,[30] after arguing that *pneuma* is responsible for a variety of different diseases, the author at least partially anticipates this famous distinction in the *Phaedo*, by distinguishing what is responsible from something less than fully responsible:

> It is clear, then, that breaths are the most active factor in all diseases, all other things are concomitantly and secondarily responsible (συναίτια καὶ μεταίτια), but I have shown that this is the thing responsible for diseases. I promised to declare the thing responsible for diseases, and I have shown that *pneuma* has the greatest power both in other things and in the body of living creatures. I have let my discourse dwell on familiar ailments in which the hypothesis has shown itself correct. (*On Breaths* § 15)

Of course, Socrates would not accept the author's claim that breaths in fact are what is responsible. The point is simply that this text, like the *Phaedo*, distinguishes what is genuinely responsible from other things that fall short of being genuinely responsible. The *Phaedo* does not use the language of "concomitantly and secondarily responsible," but this is nonetheless similar to the *Phaedo*'s distinction between what is responsible and that without which it could not be responsible.

In sum, Socrates in the *Phaedo* is engaged in a tradition of natural science, which – on the medical side – involves sophisticated criteria for being responsible, criteria that can be used to criticize one's predecessors, to put forward rival alternatives, and to distinguish what is responsible from something less than responsible. These are not innovative features of Socrates' approach; what is innovative is the specific ways he criticizes other accounts, the conditions he thinks something must meet to be responsible, and the rival theory he advances.

9.3 SOCRATES' INITIAL INQUIRY: 96B–97B

Socrates begins by describing his own initial inquiry, which ended in failure. Understanding why this failed clarifies his own approach and his criteria for being an *aitia*.

The way Socrates describes his initial inquiry is typically treated as innocuous; however, he introduces it in a way that suggests he was in significant danger. After

---

[29] See Herodotus 2.20.2–3 for the idea that, if something is not necessary, it must not be *aition*.
[30] This work seems to be from the last quarter of the fifth century; see Craik 2014.

Socrates describes natural science's aim, he says: "frequently I would turn up and down, investigating first these sorts of things:..." (96a9–b1). Plato associates the phrase "up and down" (ἄνω κάτω) with the view that there is no stability in the world (*Cratylus* 386d–e, cf. *Parmenides* 129c) or everything is in flux (*Philebus* 43a) or things move in a disorderly way (*Timaeus* 43b and *Phaedo* 112b, discussed in Subsection 11.5.1). Plato's use of the phrase ultimately derives from Heraclitus B60: "The way up and down (ἄνω κάτω) are one and the same."[31] Socrates used the expression earlier in the *Phaedo* when describing misology: those who waste their time with the arguments used in disputations end up thinking that there is nothing sound or firm in any thing or *logos*, but rather all things turn *up and down* (90c; cf. *Protagoras* 356d, *Republic* 508d). Thus here in the autobiography Socrates is effectively saying that he was himself in flux. The kinship argument explains why this would be: when the soul investigates things through the senses it wanders, just like them (79c); in the same way, when investigating things at rest it comes to a rest (79d). Socrates initial interest in natural science involved pursuing *aitiai* that wander (ordinary, sensible things), leading his soul to turn up and down; Socrates then settled on his hypothesis of forms – and his soul came to a rest.

Socrates reacts to his initial natural scientific investigation just as one would expect, given how he is portrayed across Plato's dialogues – especially the Socratic dialogues. After listing the sort of questions he had become interested in, Socrates says:

> And in the end I myself came to think that I was uniquely unqualified for this inquiry. I'll give you ample evidence for this: I was so utterly blinded by that inquiry with regard to the very things that, at least as I and others supposed, I had previously known clearly that I unlearned those very things that earlier I had thought I knew, on many subjects and in particular because of what a human grows. (96c1–8)

Note the standard Socratic procedure: everyone else takes certain things to be obvious (e.g. what virtue is in the *Meno*, what we want to instill in our sons in the *Laches*) and asks fairly sophisticated questions (is virtue teachable? Should the sons learn fighting in armor?). But Socrates is having so much trouble with the topic that he cannot even understand the simplest thing about it. And, just as in the Socratic dialogues, the problems that Socrates presents as his own turn out to be difficulties for everyone – Socrates proceeds to argue, in quite general terms, that these accounts face insuperable difficulties. Scholars debate whether Socrates sincerely believes that he has special difficulty understanding the topics he discusses in the Socratic dialogues; the fact that we could ask the same question here – whether he really believes he is uniquely unqualified – shows the parallelism. Socrates' advantage in the autobiography, just as in the *Apology*, is that he recognizes his ignorance.

---

[31] In extant texts before Plato (aside from this Heraclitus fragment), the phrase is used only for physically moving up and down, or for, as we say, turning everything "upside down" – wrecking it in some way (e.g. Herodotus 3.3).

He argues that his account, which uses forms, requires no substantive knowledge (as discussed in Section 9.7) while at the same time being superior to the natural philosophers' accounts. We are seeing Socrates approach research into nature as he would an ethical or political topic. Just as people have not carefully thought through the consequences of the view that virtue is beneficial, or that good things bring happiness, so too they have not carefully thought through the notion of being responsible, and so failed to recognize that even the prosaic things ordinary people identify as responsible cannot be – let alone the more sophisticated options natural philosophers offer.

After Socrates' general description of (i) research into nature and (ii) his failure to succeed at it, he identifies a number of concrete accounts that he found dissatisfying (96c–97b). At this stage he only explains what is dissatisfying with one of them, waiting until the third stage to explain the other cases (100e–101c). Each proposal identifies something as responsible for a thing's being or becoming larger. Vlastos says that they present the modern reader with a sort of "meta-puzzle": why would Socrates find these explanations puzzling at all?[32] But not only the modern reader is puzzled: Cebes also does not see what is wrong with them (96e). Socrates is questioning ordinary explanations in a way that would also be surprising then. I will argue that Socrates here provides a neutral criterion for evaluating whether something is a genuine *aitia*.

Socrates begins by asking: "because of what does a human grow?" (96c7–8). He thought it was obvious to everyone that (I) it was because of flesh being added to flesh, and bone to bone, and so too in other cases. Then he considers (II) the option that one person is larger than another *by* a head (96d–e) and then that (IIIa) ten is more numerous than eight because of two being added to it (96e) and that (IIIb) two cubits is larger than one because of its exceeding by half (96e). (I) and (IIIa) are purported explanations of *coming to be*: a human coming to be larger, ten coming to be from eight. (II) and (IIIb) purport to be explanation of *being*: one person's being larger than another or two cubits' being larger than one.

Socrates' final example explains what is wrong with at least one such account:

> I am a long way indeed from thinking that I know the *aitia* of any of these. I don't allow myself to say even that, when somebody adds one to one, either the one it was added to has become two, <[Wyttenbach's conjecture:] or the one that was added has become two>, or the one that was added and the one it was added to became two, because of (διά + acc.) the addition of the first to the second. For I find it astonishing that when each of them was apart from the other, each turned out to be one, and that they weren't two at that time, but when they came near each other, this supposedly became an *aitia*[33] for their coming to be two, namely

---

[32] Vlastos 1969, 310.
[33] The passage uses αἰτία four times, which (as far as the form of the word is concerned) could be a noun or the feminine adjective. The first instance clearly seems to be the noun and is universally translated as such. In the final case, it needs to be the noun so that the adjective

the union that is their being put near each other. No, nor can I still persuade myself that if somebody divides one, this, the division, has now become an *aitia* for its coming to be two. For then there comes to be an *aitia* of coming to be two that is opposite of the earlier one. Back then, you see, it was because (ὅτι) they were brought together into proximity with each other, and one was added to the other, but now it is because (ὅτι) they are brought apart, and one is separated from the other. (96e6–97b3)

I think we should reject Wyttenbach's conjecture.[34] However, even if we accept it, the point of this whole phrase ("either the one it was added to..."), is not to choose between these possibilities precisely because Socrates wishes to highlight a problem that applies regardless of what becomes two. The problem is introduced in the next sentence with "for" (γάρ): Socrates is astounded that the union could be an *aitia* for such a thing.[35] To explain why this is astounding, he points out that division would have an equal claim to being an *aitia* for the same effect. One thing (addition) cannot be an *aitia* since its opposite (division) has an equal claim to being an *aitia*. This reason to reject a candidate has nothing to do with *becoming*, in particular, and so could equally well be used to reject a candidate that is supposedly responsible for being.

Socrates is often taken as relying in this passage on a "principle" or "law" about opposites: that, if x is the *aitia* for y, then the opposite of x cannot have an equal

---

ἐναντία can agree with it – again, it is universally translated as such. In the second and third occurrences, Socrates could be using the adjective, saying the union or division is responsible, but given that he is using the noun beforehand and afterwards, the progression of the reasoning suggests he is doing so there as well.

[34] Burnet 1911 and Strachan (in Duke et al. 1995) print the conjecture, but it is rejected by Hackforth 1955, Verdenius 1958, Gallop 1975, and Sedley and Long 2010. Accepting it is important to Menn 2010; see next footnote. The reason for accepting the conjecture is that it is found in a passage from Plotinus (6.6.14, 13–29), where Plotinus quotes a short phrase from the *Phaedo* (without saying that he is doing so). Plotinus says, "[f]or the one did not become two, neither the one that was added to nor the one that was added" (6.6.14-15, οὐ γὰρ τὸ ἓν ἐγένετο δύο, οὔτε ᾧ προσετέθη οὔτε τὸ προστεθέν). Note that the beginning of this sentence and the end of the sentence are not in the *Phaedo*. Furthermore, Plotinus does not include the *Phaedo*'s option that both of them become two. The question is whether Plotinus was quoting the *Phaedo* when he said, "nor the one that was added" (οὔτε τὸ προστεθέν). Plotinus is arguing that if that which is one does not undergo change, it will not cease being one. For his purposes, it is important that *neither* one could become two – neither the one that was added to nor the one that was added. Socrates is arguing for a different conclusion in the *Phaedo*, so we can see why Plotinus would add these words to Socrates' phrase. Joseph Bjelde pointed out to me that, in addition to these words not being in any of our manuscripts, they are also not in the papyrus fragment for this part of the text, PSI XIV 1393a (= CPF 251 = OCT Π₅), which is dated no later than the second century CE (and so before Plotinus).

[35] *Pace* Menn 2010, 40–50. Menn accepts Wyttenbach's conjecture and sees Socrates as pointing to a puzzle about growth: which should we say becomes two, the first one or the second one? Menn ultimately says that Socrates' reasoning is hard to follow here because of the way Socrates alternates between cases of becoming and being (46). The account I offer explains why Socrates' problem applies equally to both types of cases.

claim to being the *aitia* for y.³⁶ But in the passage Socrates does not treat this as a basic principle or law. Instead, he begins by first describing a problem with addition without mentioning any opposite, and then brings in the opposite, division, to clarify and sharpen the problem. The initial problem is that Socrates cannot see why bringing these together would be an *aitia* of their coming to be two. Why were they not already two when they were apart? To sharpen and clarify the problem, he then points out that in other circumstances we could just as easily use the opposite thing, division, to explain why things came to be two. This is meant to show that the purported *aitia* does not really help us understand the explanandum – that there is no transparent or intelligible connection between bringing together two disparate things and becoming two. After all, drawing apart has as much of a claim on explaining why things become two. Hence, grasping that things have come together does not seem to help us understand why they have become two. Of course – to use Socrates' later distinction – it might be that in some cases addition is that without which the *aition* thing could never be *aition* (99b), but that is not sufficient for it to be the *aitia*. Rather than being archaic or simplistic, opposites are mentioned here to bring out an extreme case, since this make it especially clear that they have not identified the genuine explanation.

9.4 WHAT SOCRATES THOUGHT ANAXAGORAS WOULD DO: 97B–98B

We come now to a stretch of text that is extremely difficult to read uncolored by Plato's and Aristotle's subsequent works – in particular, *Republic* VI–VII, the *Timaeus*, and Aristotle's natural teleology (for example, *Physics* II.1–3 and II.7–8, *Parts of Animals* I.1). We should approach the passage on its own terms before deciding how well it lines up with those texts. I argue here that Socrates is primarily interested in and excited about Anaxagoras' proposal because he thinks that it offers the possibility of acquiring knowledge of the good, not because of any special insight that it would offer into the natural world. I further argue that there is no clear sign that he expects Anaxagoras' account to be teleological.

Before beginning, recall that Socrates drew on Anaxagoras at the end of the cyclical argument (72c; Section 4.4). I also argued that Socrates adopted and modified Anaxagorean ideas in connecting something's being *auto kath' hauto* with its being pure (Sections 3.4 and 7.2; see also Chapter 6, n. 37). As Furley has pointed out, Socrates' language of "having a share" of the forms later in the autobiography (100c) seems to draw on Anaxagoras; I argue in the next chapter that Socrates'

---

³⁶ For example, Sedley 1998, 121. I thank Axel Barcelo and Edgar González pushing me to develop the new account in this paragraph.

language of forms "in us" also draws on an Anaxagorean mixture model.[37] As Sedley points out, Socrates seems to refer back to Anaxagoras in the cosmological account at the end of the dialogue (as discussed in Chapter 11).[38] In short, Socrates engages with Anaxagoras throughout the dialogue; this is simply the most sustained place.

Socrates begins with what he thought when someone, reading from a book by Anaxagoras, said that it turns out that *nous* (intelligence) both orders things and is responsible for everything.[39] Socrates reports:

> I was pleased with this *aitia*,[40] and it struck me that in a way it is good that *nous* should be responsible for everything, and I supposed that, if this is the case, when *nous* is doing the ordering it orders everything and places each thing in whatever way is best. (97c2–6)

Socrates is clear in the passage that he is providing *his* account of what it would mean for *nous* to order all things and be responsible for everything: *he* supposed that, if this were the case, then *nous* would place each thing in whatever way is best. Socrates develops this expectation before he has read Anaxagoras' books (98b). In several Socratic dialogues, Socrates says that, to the extent that people are guided by knowledge or wisdom, they are benefited (e.g. *Apology* 25b–e, *Gorgias* 464b–465d, *Protagoras* 356d–357b). In the *Meno* he specifically says about *nous* that it benefits and that what is done without it harms (88b). It is natural, then, that Socrates would interpret the idea that *nous* is responsible as meaning that it does things in the best way. I will argue that Socrates does not hold that, in general, any *aitia* would need to be related to the good. Instead, this is a result of supposing that *nous*, in particular, is responsible. A further sign that Socrates is interpreting Anaxagoras' claim in a distinctly Socratic way is that he immediately goes on to mention the idea that there is a single knowledge that will encompass both the best and the worse (97d), which is closely connected to his idea that the knowledge of good is the same as that of bad (*Crito* 44d, *Hippias Minor* 376a–b, *Laches* 199c–d, *Republic* 332d–334a).

Socrates thinks that, if *nous* is responsible, then identifying the *aitia* of each thing would require an account of what is best, which would require substantive knowledge of the good. Socrates shows exactly the enthusiasm one would expect from his encountering the chance to acquire this knowledge: "I got hold of his books with real excitement and started reading them as quickly as I could, so that I might know

---

[37] Furley 1976 and 2002.
[38] Sedley 1990.
[39] For *nous* as something like a virtue of rationality or reason, see Menn 1995.
[40] This use of "*aitia*" is unlike the ones that follow. First, consider why he does not instead say "the one *aitios*": that would mean that he was pleased with this thing, intelligence. Instead, he was pleased by assigning responsibility to intelligence – in particular, with the idea that intelligence is responsible by being what orders. While Socrates immediately grasps this (general) *aitia* – this general assignment of responsibility – he expected Anaxagoras to tell him the "*aitia* concerning each thing, how it comes to be, is destroyed, or is" (97c6–7). Anaxagoras failed to provide these more specific *aitiai*.

as quickly as possible the best and the worse" (98b4–6). Socrates does not say he was excited to know as quickly as possible the shape of the earth or its *aitia*, nor does he say that he was excited to read an account in which everything in the cosmos is explained by the good. Instead, he was excited to learn about the best and the worse. Throughout the dialogues, this is the knowledge Socrates is most eager to find, the knowledge that would allow him to acquire virtue and so be happy. There is no indication that he is excited about an approach to the study of nature.

It is frequently said that Socrates, in discussing Anaxagoras' view, is describing a sort of "teleological" cause.[41] It is not normally clarified what is meant by "teleology."[42] If *nous* is responsible, it seems likely that there is some *telos* that it aims at – that is, some goal or end. Thus *nous* would be an agent or something agent-like and there would be an end. But typically teleology does not simply involve the idea that there is an agent and an end; instead, it crucially involves the idea that this end explains certain other, subordinate facts about (i) what other things exist, or (ii) what features other things have, with particular emphasis on (iii) what other things are good.[43] Put simply, in a teleological account, an end somehow explains other things' existence or features. For example, a teleological account could explain the existence of leaves in terms of the flourishing of a plant. Or it might explain why stirrups are good in terms of the end of horse riding. The *Timaeus* offers teleological accounts of many things in the cosmos. For example, the good of reasoning explains why humans have necks separating their heads from their bodies (69d–e). The shape of the neck is subordinate to and explained by the good that it promotes. Of course, someone could decide to use the word "teleology" to describe any explanatory structure that involves an end, even if nothing exists for the sake of anything else and there are no other similar subordinate structures. But this is not how the term is typically used.

The question, then, is whether, when Socrates describes *nous* in the *Phaedo*, he uses *nous*'s end to explain why something other than this end exists, has some feature, or is good. I see no clear evidence for this. First, there is no "for the sake of" language in Socrates' description of cosmic *nous*. Given what Socrates says, this *nous* could be responsible for each thing directly, without there being a subordinate

---

[41] E.g. Vlastos 1969, 297; Bedu-Addo 1979, Annas 1982, Lennox 1985, Bostock 1986, Wiggins 1986, Hankinson 1998, Johansen 2004, Sharma 2009, 142; Menn 2010, and Johansen 2020.

[42] For the eighteenth-century origins of the term, see Brisson 2019.

[43] I mean this to include the option that these other "things" are parts of some whole, which is the *telos*. McDonough 2020, 1 says that teleology's "central idea is that some things happen, or exist, for the sake of other things." Johansen 2004, 2, says: "A teleological explanation, understood very broadly, explains something by reference to its end or goal. In Plato's natural philosophy, however, teleology takes the more specific form of explaining phenomena by reference to ends considered as good or beautiful." Notice the difference between (i) the "some things" (McDonough) or the "phenomena" (Johansen) and (ii) the end. The end explains something distinct from that end. Brisson 2019 understands teleology in terms of Aristotle's final cause and then argues that there is no teleology in the *Timaeus*. On Platonic teleology, see also Lennox 1985 and Johansen 2020.

structure of other things that exist or are good because of this end. Perhaps *nous* directly makes (or eternally sustains) things the way it would be best for each of them to be. Consider how Socrates describes what he expected from Anaxagoras:

> I supposed that he would tell me first whether the earth was flat or round, and, when he had done so, would also explain the *aitia* and its necessity, saying what was better – better, that is, that the earth should be like that. And if he said that it was in the center, he would also explain, I thought, that it was better that it should be in the center. If he showed me these things, I was ready to stop wishing for any other kind of *aitia*. (97d8–98a2)

Given what Socrates says, he would have been satisfied if Anaxagoras had said first that the earth is round, and then that it is round because goodness is unity, explaining why goodness is unity and why round things are more unified than flat things. Such an account would not need to be teleological – it would not need to use an end to explain why other things are the way they are – but it would meet Socrates' expectations.[44] Of course, Socrates also could have provided a teleological account, explaining why the earth was round by explaining how its roundness is subordinate to some further end – perhaps the overall symmetry of the cosmos. Socrates simply does not seem to commit himself one way or another on whether there is any such subordinate structure. Note that, even if in some cases things are good because of how they contribute to some further good, that is a far cry from thinking that *aitiai* in general are teleological, or that Socrates' interest is specifically in teleological *aitiai*.

There are two features of Socrates' account that might seem to suggest that Socrates is expecting a teleological account. First, he says that *nous* orders things. Perhaps *nous* aims at some good end (or ends) and orders everything else to promote that end (or ends). But another possibility is that everything has a way that it is good for it to be and *nous* arranges things so that each thing is in the way best for it; thus, *nous*' ordering is putting each thing in its own best place – like in an ordered, tidy room. In this case, there need not be any subordinate structure. Another feature that might seem to support a teleological reading is that Socrates says that he expected to learn from Anaxagoras both (i) the *aitia* for each thing – what is best for each – and (ii) the *aitia* that is in common for all things – the good common for all (98a–b). A single, unified cosmological teleology would ensure that the individual good is not in conflict with the common good. But that does not mean that Socrates is committed to such a teleological structure here; instead, he might think it incumbent on anyone, like Anaxagoras, who wants to develop such a theory to explain why they are not in conflict or to explain why such a conflict is not problematic.[45]

---

[44] Thomas Johansen suggested to me that the roundness of the sphere could be seen as for the sake of its unity. I agree that it could be seen that way, but I do not see evidence that Socrates is thinking of it that way here.

[45] Perhaps the individual good and the common good simply are in tension: Fletcher 2022 argues that there is a tension between the cosmic good and the individual good in the *Timaeus* – a dialogue that clearly has teleological explanations.

My defense of the claim that Socrates does not seem specifically interested in teleology will only be complete once we consider, in the next two sections, passages that have been taken to support a teleological reading. In any event, the key point is that Socrates was excited because he thought that, for Anaxagoras to make the claims he made, he must have knowledge of the good.

9.5 WHAT SOCRATES SEES ANAXAGORAS AS ACTUALLY DOING: 98B–99C

Socrates supposed that any theory that made *nous* responsible would explain everything in terms of the best; however, Socrates complains that Anaxagoras in fact assigned responsibility to air, aether, water, and other such absurdities (98b–c). One might expect Socrates to make an internal critique of Anaxagoras, since he did not make *nous* responsible despite claiming that he would. Instead, Socrates objects to Anaxagoras' de facto account using a neutral criterion for being responsible that has nothing to do with *nous* or the best.

Socrates objects using an analogy. He says that Anaxagoras' theory is just as if someone said that it is because of *nous* that Socrates does everything that he does, but then says that he is sitting in prison because his body is composed of bones and sinews, and then provides an account of how the bones and sinews allow him to be bent here in the sitting position (98c–d). This person would also assign responsibility to voices, airs, and ears, failing to identify the real *aitiai*, namely that, "since the Athenians have decided that it was better to condemn me, on account of that I too have also decided that it is better to sit here, and more just to stay put and suffer whatever punishment they decree" (98e1–5). Socrates explains why these are the real *aitiai*, not the bones and sinews, as follows:

> For, by the Dog, I think these sinews and bones would long have been in Megara or Boeotia, transported by an opinion as to what is best, if I didn't think it more just and honorable to suffer whatever punishment the city imposes, rather than to escape and run away. (98e5–99a4)

The problem with assigning responsibility to the bones and sinews is that they are no more responsible for his staying than for his going.[46] By contrast, Socrates' decision is responsible for his staying in a way that it would not be for his going. If he left – perhaps bound and carried away by his companions – it would be despite his decision, not because of it.

The problem with the bones and sinews is analogous to that with addition and division. In that case, Socrates threw out a candidate (addition) whose opposite would have an equal claim to being an *aitia* for the same explanandum. By contrast, in this case, the same candidate is equally responsible for staying in prison and being

---

[46] So Sedley 1998, Johansen 2020.

in Megara or Boeotia. If one thought that Socrates is operating with strict *principles* about opposites, it would be important to determine whether being in Megara or Boeotia is truly opposite to staying in prison.[47] I have suggested that the key point is not about opposites per se but about whether something offers a genuine explanation. The bones and sinews do not make a difference to whether Socrates is in prison or in the very different and incompatible situation that he is in Megara or Boeotia. They do not help explain why he is in one place rather than another. By contrast, Socrates' opinion explains his being in prison, but would not explain his leaving.

There are several signs that Socrates thinks the problem is not identifying what, strictly speaking, is responsible. He says that "to call such things [the bones and sinews] 'responsible' is very absurd" (99a4–5). A few lines later, Socrates says that people are fumbling in the dark who call something "responsible" when instead it is that without which the responsible thing would never be responsible; he says that such people are using the name "responsible" for something that applies to something else (99b). This attention to correct "calling" and "naming," as well as the idea that people are failing to make a distinction, suggests that Socrates thinks that people are not clearly thinking through the meaning of "responsible." Socrates also uses the verb "to assign responsibility" (*aitiasthai*, 98c2, 98d8) here. Socrates is carefully thinking through the notion of being responsible by considering human agency, its core application. He uses this to argue that natural scientists have not identified what is genuinely responsible.

How would Anaxagoras' intelligence avoid the problem that the bones and sinews fall into: being no more responsible for one thing than its opposite? After all, if intelligence is responsible for everything, it would seem to be responsible for opposite things.[48] One question is the scope of "everything." Socrates says that he expected an account from Anaxagoras about the sun, moon, and other celestial bodies (98a) and he only discusses these. I suspect we are supposed to understand "everything" as the main elements of the cosmos, not questions such as why this leaf is smaller than that one. Moreover, and more importantly, Socrates seems to expect Anaxagoras to settle questions about opposites. Socrates wanted to know from Anaxagoras why it is better for the earth to be round or flat, in the center (rather than, for example, in orbit), and other such things (97d–98a). If *nous* is responsible, identifying an *aitia* would require knowing which is better; this *aitia* would explain why the earth is spherical rather than flat. What if it is, in fact, no better for the earth to be spherical than it is for it to be flat? Then *nous* would be like the bones and sinews: no more responsible for its being a sphere than for its being flat. It is incumbent on someone defending Anaxagoras' account to explain not only what goodness is, but also how this can be responsible for everything in the cosmos. By contrast, one great advantage of Socrates' form theory is that it does not require this

---

[47] Sedley 1998 and Johansen 2020 assumes that they are.
[48] A question Joseph Bjelde has repeatedly pressed on me.

sort of knowledge – without knowing what justice is or which things are just and which unjust, you can tell that the form of justice will never be responsible for injustice.

After discussing the failure to distinguish the thing responsible from that without which it could not be responsible, Socrates says that the people who fail to make this distinction put forward rival theories of why the earth is held up, such as a vortex theory or that the earth is a flat kneading-trough propped up by air (99b). Socrates' discussion of these theorists provides the strongest evidence for thinking that any account of an *aitia* must somehow involve the good.[49] I will argue instead that Socrates' claims here are restricted to cosmology. The key passage is the following:

> That is why one individual puts a vortex around the earth and thus makes the earth actually be kept stationary by the heaven, while another compares it to a flat kneading-trough and props it up with air. But as for these things' ability to be positioned now in the best possible way for them to be placed, they neither seek it nor suppose that it has any daemonic might; instead, they believe that one day they might find an Atlas that is mightier and more immortal and keeps everything together more than this one does, and they do not suppose for a moment that what is good and binding truly does bind and keep anything together. (99b6–c6)

In saying that these theorists are trying to replace Atlas with something more immortal, Socrates is suggesting that they are trying to replace the divinities. Socrates is distancing himself from such atheism; recall that in the *Apology* Meletus says that, according to Socrates, the sun is not a god but rather a stone (26d). He is characterized as such an atheist in Aristophanes' *Clouds*, and so Plato has particular reason to defend Socrates against this accusation. In fact, in the *Clouds*, Aristophanes' Socrates says that air keeps the earth suspended (264), one of the views that Socrates dismisses here in the *Phaedo*; he also says that the vortex, not Zeus, moves the clouds (379–81).[50] In contrast to such theories, Socrates is suggesting that gods do hold the cosmos together. He only explicitly mentions the earth as having an ability with the daemonic power to be positioned in the best possible way – but supposedly other heavenly bodies have such abilities as well.[51] Socrates accepts the role of the divine in cosmology. I will argue in Chapter 11 that Socrates' cosmology at the end of the dialogue presents the heavens as pure, divine,

---

[49] Noted, for example, by Bedu-Addo 1979, 105.
[50] For a discussion of this allusion and of how the *Phaedo* may also be alluding to the views Aristophanes is alluding to, see Vázquez 2022. See Section 4.4 and Chapter 8, n. 10, for other allusions to the *Clouds*.
[51] Note that the daemonic might is possessed by the (passive) ability to be positioned now in the best possible way. In the *Symposium*, Socrates says that a daemon is in between the mortal and the immortal (202d–203a) and that "being in the middle of the two, they [daemons] round out the whole and so bind fast the all to all" (202e6–7, trans. Rowe, slightly modified). Here too, in the *Phaedo*, the daemonic plays an important role in binding. Divine Atlas actively keeps the cosmos together; the earth has a daemonic ability that this divine being can interact with, which in turn keeps us mortals supported.

and form-like, whereas the place where we live and the underworld are in flux. He identifies there the *aitia* of flux, which turns out to be in no way divine or good (112b; Subsection 11.5.1). This fits with his suggesting here that only the celestial bodies are connected to the divine.

9.6 INTRODUCING SOCRATES' SECOND SAILING: 99C–D

In this final part of the autobiography, Socrates uses his method of hypothesis to put forward a theory that uses forms to specify *aitiai*. This theory is important for the dialogue's unfolding account of forms and for the final argument. I argue that this method provides a way to avoid misology and to put the final argument on firmer epistemic footing – while responding to earlier criticisms of the use of hypotheses, of the sort found in *On Ancient Medicine* (VM).

Socrates famously describes his account here as a "second sailing" (99d1). I agree with the scholarly consensus that this means that it is a second best.[52] But it means more than this, and it is important to see exactly what it means. The expression "second sailing" is a proverb, which seems to allude to a situation where a first sea voyage was attempted with sails, but failed, and so a new one is made with oars.[53] There are no extant occurrences of the expression before Plato; it occurs two other times in Plato and twice in Aristotle.[54] In these four cases, one supposes that the ideal situation does not obtain; the second sailing is the best thing to do in the non-ideal circumstances. For example, in the *Statesman* the ideal situation is to do without written laws and have a statesman; the second sailing "for those who establish laws and written rules about anything whatever, is to allow neither individual nor mass ever to do anything contrary to these – anything whatsoever" (300c1–3, trans. Rowe). In the *Philebus*, Protarchus says that, "while it is a great thing for the wise man to know everything, the second sailing is not to be mistaken about oneself, it seems to me" (19c1–3, trans. Frede, in Cooper and Hutchinson 1997). In these cases, the second sailing achieves considerably less than the first option, while still being the best among suboptimal possibilities. The same is true of Aristotle's usage (*Nicomachian Ethics* 1109a34–35, *Politics* 1284b19–20), and, according to Martinelli Tempesta's survey, of later authors as well.

What is the ideal in *Phaedo*, then, from which the "second sailing" falls short? It is easy to project almost any interpretation back on to the text here: whatever one thinks is good about what Socrates was hoping to find earlier, treat this as what is missing from his new account. Following Martinelli Tempesta, I think we should understand the phrase in light of the immediate context where he uses it:

---

[52] So e.g. Bluck 1955; Hackforth 1955, 127n5; Vlastos 1969, 279; Lennox 1985, Martinelli Tempesta 2003.
[53] For a thorough discussion, see Martinelli Tempesta 2003.
[54] There are seventy-four other occurrences, mostly in much later authors. The next occurrence after Aristotle is in Polybius (second century BCE). See Martinelli Tempesta 2003.

> Now I would gladly become anyone's pupil to learn just what the truth is about that sort of *aitia*. But since I was denied it and was not able either to find it myself or to learn it from someone else, would you like me to give you a demonstration, Cebes, of how I've pursued my second sailing in search of the *aitia*? (99c6–d2)

Socrates' basic claim here is that he has been unable to acquire knowledge of this sort of cause and so has come up with something else. He does not claim to have acquired knowledge using this other method; in fact, as we will see, Socrates emphasizes that his alternative procedure does not require knowledge, but instead offers ignorant answers. Thus I suggest that this second sailing is non-ideal because it proceeds without knowledge. The same is true of the other two second sailings in Plato: both are suboptimal because of a lack of knowledge – either the lack of a knowledgeable ruler (in the *Statesman*) or the lack of knowledge of everything (in the *Philebus*). Socrates' theory is the best available, given the non-ideal situation of lacking knowledge, and so a second sailing.

Simmias' methodology is also presented in a sailing metaphor (85c–d) that contrasts (i) "either learning or discovering how things are" (85c8) with (ii) a different procedure if that is impossible. We can thus see Socrates' own sailing metaphor as agreeing with Simmias' that knowledge would be the best but that we may need to pursue a second best. I argued in the previous chapter (Subsection 8.3.1) that Socrates' second-best method is different from Simmias' – Socrates is here saying what he thinks the true second sailing is.[55]

One might instead think that Socrates' second sailing is suboptimal because it is not the same "sort of *aitia*" as Anaxagoras proposed. This would fit with interpreting Socrates as wanting *aitiai* to be in terms of the good, but instead providing a second-best theory not in terms of the good. I do not think that such a reading is ruled out on the basis of this passage alone. But the immediate context suggests a contrast with having knowledge rather than with an account in terms of the good. I have argued that Socrates never requires *aitia* to be related to the good; instead, he has a content-neutral criterion for evaluating proposed accounts: they must identify what is genuinely responsible, which they cannot if they fail either of the requirements involving opposites. This passage on its own does not provide any evidence to the contrary. Ideally, Socrates would have learned from Anaxagoras or some other natural philosopher, or found such knowledge on his own. Since Socrates could not do this, he heads to the same destination – the cause – but without knowledge.[56]

Before introducing the method of hypothesis, Socrates says that he was worried that he would be utterly blinded in his soul by seeking things with his senses (99d–e). Earlier, Socrates said that he was utterly blinded by the inquiry involved

---

[55] For a similar thought, Benson 2015, 107.
[56] Note that Socrates uses forms to provide *aitiai* both for things' *being* as they are as well as their *coming to be* (101b–c) – as he should, if he is showing how to reach the destination sought by natural science.

in natural science (96c). This fits with Socrates' repeated claims in the defense speech and return to the defense that inquiry through the senses is full of deceit (65a–68b, 82e–83b).[57] Recollecting explains how it is even possible to inquire without using the senses. The method of hypothesis provides steps one can take to inquire without using them.

9.7 FORMS AND *AITIAI*

I argue here that Socrates, in hypothesizing forms, is hypothesizing nothing more than the existence of the things that he searches for across the dialogues – including the Socratic dialogues – when he asks, "what is it?" In general, one can also use the answer to these questions to answer, "because of what?" questions, thereby identifying what is responsible. This is why hypothesizing forms is useful for reaching the destination sought by natural scientists. One crucial feature of Socrates' account is that it does not require substantive knowledge, fitting with Socrates' profession of ignorance. It does this partly by using hypotheses, partly from the "thinness" of the theory, and partly due to basic features of forms.

In introducing the hypotheses that there is a form of the beautiful, that there is a form of the good, and so on, Socrates says that what he is talking about "isn't anything new, but what I've never stopped talking about, on any other occasion or in particular in the argument thus far" (100b1–3).[58] Emphasizing that he has *always* been searching for them fits with these things' being what, across the dialogues, he is looking for when he asks, "what is it?" I argued in Section 3.6 that in the defense speech Socrates is starting from a commitment to nothing more than these. The main reason why some think that he is referring specifically to something like "transcendent" forms is that he goes on to speak of "a beautiful itself *kata* itself" (100b6).[59] But, as noted in Section 3.6, Socrates uses the language of "*f*-ness *itself*" in the *Protagoras* (330d–e) and asks "what on earth, itself *kata* itself, virtue is" in the *Meno* (100b6); neither of these dialogues seems committed to transcendent forms. Similarly, when Glaucon wants to hear justice praised "itself *kata* itself" in the *Republic* (358d3; cf. 358b), he does not seem to want transcendent justice in particular to be praised. It is difficult to see how a reader, simply from the term "itself *kata* itself," would know that Socrates is referring to transcendent forms. Section 3.4 also examined the pre-Platonic use of "itself *kata* itself" and argued that

---

[57] So also Kanayama 2000.
[58] Palmer 2021, 8, claims that Socrates is referring back to his method of hypothesis as "what he never stops talking about on any other occasion." But "what" is in the plural (ἅπερ), which could refer to the several forms, but not to a single method. Moreover, even if Socrates sometimes mentions this method, it is difficult to see it as what he "never stops talking about," whereas he *is* constantly going on about his "what is it?" question. Lastly, as Palmer 2021, 8, n. 16 concedes, Socrates description in the next sentence of forms as "the oft-mentioned entities" (100b5) seems to confirm that these are what he is always talking about.
[59] For the meaning of "itself *kata* itself," see Sections 3.4 and 6.3.

it involves picking something out precisely – without any impurities – but that it need not indicate that something is separated, in the sense of being all alone.

Moreover, it is unclear what Socrates would gain by hypothesizing transcendent forms. Socrates shows in his second sailing how, if there are forms, these can be used to specify *aitiai*. For this purpose, forms do not require any of the features that would make them count as transcendent. Socrates hypothesizes that the form of beautiful exists and then says that, if this is the case, all beautiful things are beautiful because of nothing other than it.[60] He identifies the *aitia* as having a share of the beautiful (100b); hence my suggestion in Section 9.1 that the form of *f*-ness is what is responsible (*aition*) for every *f*-thing's being *f*; and the *aitia* of each *f*-thing's being *f* is that it has a share of *f*-ness. While Socrates may be connecting forms to *aitiai* for the first time in the *Phaedo* (see also *Hippias Major* 296e–297d), both the *Euthyphro* and the *Meno* use the term "form" and say that the form of *f*-ness is that because of which (*dia* + acc.) and by which (dat.) some group of *f* thing is *f* (*Euthyphro* 6d–e, *Meno* 72c–e, cf. *Hippias Major* 289c–d, 294a–e, and 296e–297d). Admittedly, in those dialogues the form is only said to explain the features of some subgroup of the *f*-things: the form of holiness is that by which all holy *actions* are holy; in the *Meno* the form of virtue explains what is in common to all *people* who have virtue. But the *Phaedo* generalizes this in a very natural way: the form of *f*-ness explains why *any f* thing is *f*.

Why would Socrates need to hypothesize the existence of these things he has always sought? While their existence might seem obvious, Socrates typically does not assume in the Socratic dialogues that they exist.[61] For example, he asks whether Euthyphro thinks that everything that is unholy has some one form (5c–d). He asks whether Meno thinks that there is a single form in all cases of virtue (72c–d; cf. *Hippias Major* 287c, *Protagoras* 330c–d, 332c). Part of this commitment, for Socrates, is to there being a *single* thing in common. Meno denies that there is a

---

[60] See Benson 2015, 193–204, for convincing arguments that the hypothesis is that a particular form exists, for example that the form of the beautiful exists, and that it is an (immediate) consequence of this hypothesis that it is because of the form that all beautiful things are beautiful. So also Gallop 1975, 222.

When Socrates presents his own form theory, he is emphatic that it is because of nothing other than the form of *f*-ness that *f*-things are *f* (or more *f*), as I discuss at greater length in Ebrey 2014b. See also Sharma 2009, 148, Bailey 2014, 20, and Johansen 2020. He uses this "nothing other than" locution in describing his own theory six different times (100c4–6, 100d3–6, 101a1–4, 101a4–5, 101c2–4, and 101c4–5). Sedley 2021, n. 12. has noted that the expression "nothing other than" in Greek can be a way of saying "precisely," without literally meaning only one thing. But "precisely" does not fit with 100e–101a, where he treats as incompatible alternatives one person being larger than another "by a head," and everything being larger by *nothing other than* largeness. Socrates also treats Anaxagoras as giving only one *aitia* for each explanandum without using the "nothing other than language." For example, Socrates says of Anaxagoras, "I never thought that... he would introduce an *aitia* for them other than its being best that they should be as they are" (98a7–9; cf. 98a1–2, 97d1–4).

[61] As I argued in Section 3.6.

single form of virtue on the grounds that the virtue of a child is different from that of an adult, that of a man from that of a woman, and so forth (73a, cf. 71e–72a) – thereby illustrating why this is a substantive commitment. In the *Phaedo*, the first two times Socrates mentions forms he asks Simmias and Cebes whether they accept that they exist (65d, 74a–b) and afterwards he highlights that his conclusions continue to rely on this acceptance (76d–e, 78c–d). Simmias has been especially enthusiastic in accepting their existence (76e–77b and 92d–e) but Socrates continues to highlight that his arguments rely on this acceptance (as discussed in Section 5.7 and in Subsection 8.4.1).

Unlike Socrates' approach in the Socratic dialogues, the method of hypothesis does not require some particular interlocutor to accept the hypothesis – one could use the method to investigate alone. More importantly, the method offers a way to evaluate the hypothesis that a form exists before accepting that it does. The *Phaedo* also, unlike the Socratic dialogues, has a sustained discussion of *aitiai*, which allows it to draw important consequences from their existence.[62]

Readers often note that Socrates' hypotheses seem vacuous. As noted above, it is a substantive claim that there is a single thing by which all beautiful things are beautiful. Nonetheless, it is a thin proposal. The advantage of Socrates' theory is precisely that it does not require substantive knowledge while meeting the requirements about opposites – unlike the naïve candidates and Anaxagoras' de facto theory. In hypothesizing a form, one is hypothesizing something that, simply by virtue of what it is, must meet the requirements about opposites.[63] One does not need to know what the form of largeness is, or how this form relates to large things, to know that it is by largeness (never smallness) that each large thing is large and by smallness (never largeness) that small things are small (100b–e). Of course, one might worry that there is something incoherent or otherwise problematic with hypothesizing forms. This is exactly what the method of hypothesis is meant to address. Again, this is a very Socratic position: while he may not have substantive knowledge, he has thoroughly tested his theory to see whether it is coherent. By contrast, I noted in Section 9.5 that explaining how *nous* could be responsible would require substantive knowledge of what the good is and why certain cosmological configurations are better than others. It is also worth noting that, if Socrates were to learn the answer to the "what is *f*-ness?" questions, his account would become much more substantive.

The autobiography plays an important role in the dialogue's unfolding account of forms. Socrates made many claims about the forms in the defense speech, recollecting argument, and kinship argument, but until now has not said that the form of

---

[62] In the *Euthyphro* and *Meno* Socrates says that *f*-things have (*echein*) the form of *f*-ness in them and are *f* (5d and 72c–73a). In the *Phaedo* Socrates does not commit himself to what the relation is between forms and ordinary things, and instead of saying that the ordinary things have – *echein* – the form, he says that they have a share of – *met-echein* – them.
[63] This is similar to the central idea in Bailey 2014, although we differ on most of the details.

f-ness is that because of which *f*-things are *f*. Identifying this role clarifies the idea in the recollection argument that forms are superior to ordinary objects. At least one way they are superior is by being explanatorily prior: equal things are equal because of the form of equality, not the other way around.[64] Turning to the kinship argument, we now have a positive characterization of what forms do, which clarifies why each is uniform (*monoeides*). I argued that being uniform means being simple in a way that involves not having separate parts with separate functions or groups of characteristics (Subsection 6.3.2). We see now that each form has just one role, being (for example) that because of which large things are large. If the form of *f*-ness had a part that were irrelevant to explaining why something is *f*, the relevant part of the form would have a better claim on being what explains why things are *f*. Since what it is to be the form of *f*-ness simply is to be that because of which *f*-things are *f*, forms have no such irrelevant parts. In short, rather than assuming something like "transcendent" forms, Socrates' characterization of the forms here helps clarify his claims from the previous two stages. This clarification continues at the beginning of the final argument (102b–103c; Section 10.4), the last stage of Socrates' unfolding account of forms and ordinary objects.

9.8 SOCRATES' METHOD OF HYPOTHESIS

Socrates describes here a method that is notoriously difficult to interpret, one that involves putting forward and evaluating a hypothesis.[65] I argue that we can make progress in understanding the method by situating it in its broader intellectual context and drawing on earlier and later parts off the dialogue. This is a complicated set of evidence, and so a lengthy discussion. I argue that the method slowly builds one's rational trust in a hypothesized theory by getting one to think through what would be true and what would be false if the theory were right. Its safety is found in not accepting it or its results until they have been thoroughly examined. Socrates is describing a process we frequently go through when we think through theories: we examine not merely their logical consequences but, more broadly, what anyone accepting the theory would accept or deny. It is often thought that Socrates dogmatically holds on to views about the forms in the *Phaedo* and other "middle period" dialogues. The opposite is the case if I am right: the point of applying this method to the forms is to avoid putting one's trust in them too quickly, but instead first to evaluate thoroughly what one would be committed to, if they exist.

My discussion is divided into four subsections. First, I argue that the method should be seen as avoiding some of the criticisms of the use of hypotheses in *On Ancient Medicine* (VM). It avoids these criticisms by thoroughly evaluating

---

[64] I suspect that another part of their superiority is related to the so-called compresence of opposites that belongs to ordinary things. The form of *f*-ness is entirely what it is and in no way its opposite, unlike ordinary things.
[65] The fullest bibliography on the method is in Benson 2015; he discusses it in chs. 4, 5, and 7.

hypotheses before accepting them (9.8.1). I then consider the basic passages that describe the method and argue that the method's aim is to develop trust, thereby avoiding the cause of misology (9.8.2). Next, I draw on Socrates' arguments against Simmias' *harmonia* theory to give a detailed account of how the method works (9.8.3). Finally, I address how the procedure comes to an end, arguing that the method is supposed to provide the best epistemic state humanly available, which in some cases will fall short of genuine knowledge (9.8.4).

9.8.1 On Ancient Medicine, *Mathematics, the Use of Hypotheses*

The first extant uses of the noun translated as "hypothesis" (*hupothesis*) are in the Hippocratic *VM* and *On Breaths*, which date to the second half of the fifth century BCE;[66] it is not used in other works until the fourth century BCE. Both use the word "hypothesis" specifically to discuss hypothesizing something as *aition* or as an *aitia*. (See Section 9.2 for the relevant passage from *On Breaths* 15.) The verb "hypothesize" was more widely used in the fifth century (not only by medical authors), but not in any fragments from early Greek cosmologists. The fifth-century Hippocratic *On Fleshes* prominently uses this verb to discuss hypothesizing an *aitia*. In general, to "hypothesize" something, in this original Greek sense, is to put it forward as a starting point. As Robinson, Wolfsdorf, and others have noted, a *hupothesis* is typically not put forward tentatively, and so does not exactly match the English "hypothesis."[67]

VM attacks the practice of putting forward certain hypotheses to identify *aitiai* in medicine; the *Phaedo* defends this practice in a context that includes medicine (as discussed in Section 9.2). We cannot know whether Plato specifically read *VM* or whether there were other, similar attacks in circulation. My claim is that the *Phaedo* responds to the sort of attack found in *VM*, if not to *VM* itself. *VM* seems to have been written as a type of public lecture, meant to persuade the public of the legitimacy of medicine while attacking recent attempts to give medicine a basis in cosmology.[68] This makes it more likely that Plato was familiar with the work, or at least the ideas in it.

Nonetheless, Schiefsky, in his impressive commentary on the work, denies that Plato's discussion of hypotheses closely engages with medicine, let alone with the sort of attack in *VM*.[69] Schiefsky thinks that Plato's use of the term "hypothesis"

---

[66] See Jouanna 1999 [1992], Schiefsky 2005, Craik 2014.
[67] Robinson 1953, ch. 7, provides a useful general discussion of the term; see also Schiefsky 2005, 111–26. Wolfsdorf 2008 presents a survey of the term "*hupothesis*," but does not seem to me to give enough consideration to the uses in Hippocratic texts, which, I think, undercut his claim that a *hupothesis* is generally "cognitively secure" and a "solid foundation." The author of *VM* certainly does not think that his opponents' *hupothesis* is cognitively secure or a solid foundation. It is, however, put forward as a starting point.
[68] So Schiefsky 2005.
[69] Schiefsky 2005, 123–5. Similarly, Cooper 2004.

draws on the mathematical rather than the medical tradition. He considers the use of "hypothesis" in the *Meno* and the *Republic* and argues that it does not correspond to that in VM, and from this concludes that Plato in general is not responding to VM. He seems to be thinking that Socrates has just one "method of hypothesis" across the dialogues, and so, if what the VM says about hypotheses is inconsistent with what we find in the *Meno* and *Republic*, then Plato's views about hypothesis must not involve a close interaction with medicine. In my view, the *Meno* and the *Phaedo* offer substantively different ways to use hypotheses in inquiry; the *Republic* is closer to the *Phaedo*, but in a way that is compatible with Socrates responding to the VM in the *Phaedo*. These three dialogues do not refer to their procedures the same way; none of them uses the name "method of hypothesis." I have argued at length elsewhere that the method described in the *Phaedo* is quite different from the use of hypotheses in the *Meno* (86e–87c).[70] In the *Meno*, Socrates describes the process of reducing one geometrical problem to another, which it is hoped will be easier to solve. He then uses this sort of process to reduce the question of whether or not virtue is teachable to the question of whether or not it is knowledge. That technique does not involve tentatively or otherwise putting forward a view. By contrast, in the *Phaedo* he does not discuss problem reduction. The method in the *Phaedo* is a way of evaluating whether to accept or reject a *logos*, which is not the goal of the *Meno*'s technique.

The *Meno* and the *Republic* both discuss hypotheses in the context of geometry, whereas the *Phaedo* does so in the context of natural science, including medicine. My proposal is that the use of hypotheses in Hippocratic medicine is the relevant background for understanding the *Phaedo*. The *Meno* is sometimes cited as evidence that in Plato's time mathematicians used the term "*hupothesis*," which otherwise is not attested in Greek mathematics until Euclid's *Elements*, roughly fifty years after Plato's death.[71] However, if anything, the *Meno* suggests that the term was not used by mathematicians at the time. The relevant passage from the *Meno* begins as follows:

> By "on a hypothesis" I mean the following. Take the way in which geometers often consider some question someone asks them; for example, whether it is possible for this area to be inscribed as a triangle in this circle. One of them might say, "I don't know yet whether this is such that it can be inscribed, but I think that I have, as it were, a sort of hypothesis which is useful for the question, as follows... (86e4–87a3, trans. Sedley and Long).

Socrates supposes that a geometer *might* say that that he has "as it were, a sort of hypothesis." The use of "as it were" (ὥσπερ) along with "a sort of" (τινα) strongly suggests that this usage is seen as somehow metaphorical or extended. *Supposing*

---

[70] Ebrey 2013, 2016.
[71] For example, Robinson 1953, 99–100; Bluck 1955, 92; Szabó 1978; Huffman 1993, 91; Schiefsky 2005, 124.

that a geometer *might* speak this way strongly suggests that geometers did not typically do so.[72] In any event, the passage certainly does not provide positive evidence that geometers in Plato's time spoke in terms of hypotheses, whereas there are many examples of authors in the early Greek medical tradition doing so.[73]

Let us return to VM as the relevant background. It is arguably the first extant Greek work to discuss epistemic methodology in general. VM objects, in general, to using hypotheses to identify *aitiai*. Consider the beginning of the treatise:

> All those who have undertaken to speak or write about medicine, having laid down as a hypothesis for their account hot or cold or wet or dry or anything else they want, narrowing down the starting point of the *aitia* (τὴν ἀρχὴν τῆς αἰτίης) of diseases and death for human beings and laying down the same one or two things in all cases, clearly go wrong in much that they say. (VM 1.1, trans. Schiefsky, slightly modified)

The author might seem to be objecting in general to identifying the same one or two things as the starting points of *aitiai*. But the author only says that there is a problem with those who *lay down as a hypothesis* hot, cold, wet, dry, or anything else they want. Over the course of the treatise, the main target is this theory involving hot, cold, wet, and dry, but the author's objection to this theory is more general, as is clear from "or anything else that they want" and the generic description of this method as narrowing things down to "the same one or two things in all cases." Laying down a hypothesis, in the VM, seems to involve specifying beforehand the starting point for all of one's explanations. Throughout the treatise, the author develops his own theory by first considering the phenomena and *then* coming to an explanation.[74] For example, chapter 3 begins with a discussion of how people noticed that they are unable to digest raw, unprocessed foods, and this led to the discovery of the need to process foods so that they are not too strong. The VM never describes its own view as a hypothesis, and later criticizes anyone who proceeds from a hypothesis in medicine (13.1, 15.1). Its objection is to the way in which the view is arrived at, not to the formal features of the view itself. The author argues that all the things responsible for human suffering can be reduced to the same thing: ingesting strong foods (VM, ch. 6). So the VM is not against reducing explanations for very diverse explananda down to a single thing – only against doing so by means of a hypothesis.

---

[72] In the divided line passage in *Republic* VI (509d–511e), Socrates introduces the term "hypothesis" when initially providing the divided line (510b), before mentioning mathematics (510c). Then he uses the terms "hypothesizing" and "hypothesis" to describe what they do without making any claim about how they speak.

[73] "Hupothesis" occurs twice in Euclid's *Elements*. Both are in book 10 (44 and 47), where it is used for a claim considered for *reductio*. This is very different from the sort of usage considered in the *Phaedo*, where one hypothesizes whatever *logos* seems strongest. Henry Mendell pointed out to me that ὑπόκειμαι functions as the passive of ὑποτίθημι and is used frequently in Euclid, so there is effectively a verb form of "hypothesize" in the *Elements*.

[74] So Cooper 2004, 41–2.

Cooper claims that the VM does not criticize the use of hypotheses in other fields, only medicine.[75] On this reading, hypotheses are perfectly acceptable for a field like cosmology, given the limitations of that field. If so, VM would be of limited relevance to the *Phaedo*, given its more general character. However, this seems to me to misread the final part of the first chapter:

> For this reason I have deemed that medicine has no need of a newfangled hypothesis, as do obscure and dubious matters. Concerning these things it is necessary to make use of a hypothesis if one undertakes to say anything at all about them – for example, about things in the sky or under the earth. If anyone should recognize and state how these things are, it would be clear neither to the speaker himself nor to his listeners whether what he says is true or not, for there is nothing by referring to which one would necessarily attain clear knowledge. (VM 1.3)

Schiefsky's translation ("newfangled" for καινῆς, "dubious matters" for ἀπορεόμενα) captures the abusive tone.[76] The key here is the phrase "if one undertakes to say anything at all about them." The author's suggestion, surely, is that it is better not to say anything at all when one cannot attain clear knowledge on a topic – supposedly because one cannot employ the sort of bottom-up methodology that the author embraces. Recall also that the opening sentence of the work says that people can hypothesize *anything* that they want. They can do so because they have no way of verifying that they have it right. There is "nothing by referring to which one would necessarily attain clear knowledge," as he says in the passage just quoted. One can verify, by contrast, when it comes to medical matters. A good portion of the VM attempts to do just this, arguing against the view that hot and cold are responsible by looking at specific examples and seeing whether hot and cold, in fact, are responsible. It is in this context that VM deploys necessary and sufficient criteria described in Section 9.2: that fluxes are a good candidate for being responsible, since they are present when the effect is there and absent when it is not.

In the *Phaedo*, Socrates does exactly what the VM argues one should not do: put forward a hypothesis that identifies an *aitia* before considering the phenomena. He says that his method involves not investigating with the senses, but rather in *logos* (99e–100a). But crucially, Socrates' method allows him to check the hypothesis for adequacy, so that if someone hypothesized whatever they wanted, their hypothesis would likely fail. Schiefsky notes that the evaluation of hypotheses plays an important role in the *Phaedo* and agrees with Robinson that this is not found in earlier works such as VM.[77] I agree, but think that this is because Plato is *responding* to the sort of attack on hypothesizing *aitiai* found in VM. Of course, given the VM's

---

[75] Cooper 2004, 35–8; Schiefsky 2005, 118, mostly agrees.
[76] Jorge Torres pointed out to me that the M manuscript reads κενῆς ("empty") – an equally abusive term – for the A manuscript's καινῆς.
[77] Schiefsky 2005, 124; Robinson, 1953, 112.

preferred method of starting from the phenomenon and working to what is responsible, the author would almost certainly be unhappy with Socrates' method. But earlier in the autobiography Socrates has given reasons to think that the kind of *aitiai* that the VM favors could not possibly be adequate. If these empirically identified candidates are bound to fail, we need to put something forward without empirical verification. Socrates' method shows how one can do so while addressing the VM's basic concern that one can hypothesize whatever one wants without any way to check whether it is correct. Instead, Socrates describes a way to thoroughly evaluate the consequences of a hypothesis to see if they harmonize before accepting the hypothesis.

9.8.2 *The Aims of the Method – And How It Responds to Misology*

I discuss here the main passages that describe the method and consider a puzzle that arises from the second passage; in resolving this puzzle, I argue that the goal of the method is to develop the right sort of trust in a theory, thereby avoiding misology. Once the goal of the method is clear, the next subsection examines the details of how to apply it.

The crucial passages for understanding the method come at the beginning and end of Socrates' discussion of how he uses forms to specify *aitiai*. The first is the following:

> In any case, this is how I started out: on every occasion I hypothesize whatever *logos* I judge most robust, and then I set down as true whatever seems to me to harmonize[78] with it – both about *aitia* and about everything else – and as not true whatever doesn't. I want, though, to tell you more clearly what I'm talking about. I think that at the moment you don't understand. (100a3–8)

Socrates phrases the method in general terms: on every occasion he hypothesizes *whatever* logos seems strongest to him. Cebes, however, has trouble understanding this general description, and so Socrates turns to the relevant application of the method: hypothesizing a form of the beautiful, of the good, and the like (100b). Note that Socrates counts as true whatever *seems to him* to harmonize with the *logos*. He does not claim to know for certain which things harmonize with which. Following this part of the procedure, he should count as true whatever seems to him to harmonize with the hypothesis that there is a form of the beautiful, and as false whatever seems not to.[79]

---

[78] A note to the Greekless reader: the word translated as "harmonizing" is not "*harmonia*" but rather "*sumphōnein.*"

[79] Following Gentzler 1991, 269–70, I take Socrates to count as false only those things that seem positively disharmonious, rather anything that is not harmonious. Thus, anything irrelevant to the hypothesis is not put down as true or false.

The other main passage that describes the method is the following:

> As for those divisions and additions and other such ingenuities, you'd ignore them and leave them for those wiser than yourself to answer with. If you should at some time fear your own shadow and inexperience, as the saying goes, you'd hold on to the safety of the hypothesis and reply accordingly. But if someone were to hold on to the hypothesis itself, you would ignore him and not reply until you had managed to consider its consequences and see whether or not you found them harmonizing with each other.[80] (101c7–d6)

I follow most scholars in thinking that the method proceeds in two stages. According to the first passage, one considers as true whatever harmonizes with the hypothesized *logos* and as false whatever is disharmonious. According to the second, one then takes the results from the first stage and checks whether they harmonize with each other or are disharmonious.[81] In the next subsection I discuss the thorny question of what it means for claims to harmonize.

Before addressing this, let us consider a different puzzle, since its resolution will clarify the method's aims. In back-to-back sentences in the second passage, Socrates says that you should hold on to the safety of your hypothesis, but that if someone should hold on to the hypothesis itself, you would ignore them. Why is it good to hold on to the safety of the hypothesis, but bad to hold on to the hypothesis itself? This puzzle led Grube, among others, to translate *echein* as "cling" in the first sentence, but then as "attack" in the next.[82] However, as David Blank and others have forcefully argued, the sentences come directly after each other and have a parallel structure that is clearly meant to contrast holding on to the safety of the hypothesis with holding on to the hypothesis itself.[83] Moreover, the verb rarely if ever means "attack," making it extremely difficult to believe that its meaning is supposed to switch completely.

My solution begins from a suggestion by David Sedley, but we develop our ideas in different directions.[84] Let me begin with a summary of my view. Socrates means "hold on to" or "cling to" in both places. You ignore someone who holds on to your own hypothesis because you do not want simple agreement with your interlocutor; you want to check that your hypothesis is worth accepting. The concern is not that someone is attacking your hypothesis, but rather that someone prematurely accepts it. The hypothesis itself is some *logos*. Examples that Socrates gives of hypotheses include that the form of the beautiful exists (100b) and that the soul is a *harmonia*

---

[80] Subsection 9.8.4 quotes and discusses the continuation of this passage.
[81] Along with most interpreters, I think that the "consequences" in the second passage are the things set down as true or false in the first passage. For a different reading, see Benson 2015, chs. 5–8.
[82] See Benson 2015, 141, n. 78, for a list of many scholars who reject "attack" and a few scholars who accept it.
[83] Blank 1986. See previous footnote.
[84] Sedley 2021.

(94a–b, discussed in the next subsection). To hold on to a hypothesis itself, then, is to hold on to a specific theory. You ignore those who hold on to your hypothesis itself because their doing so carries a significant danger for both of you: that you put your trust in this *logos* prematurely. When someone agrees with you, it is easy to simply work from this shared agreement, rather than ensure that this *logos* is worth accepting. This is dangerous because misology arises from repeatedly putting one's trust in a *logos* and then a little later deciding it is wrong (90b; Section 8.2).[85] The solution to misanthropy is to be more discerning about whom to trust, evaluating people before putting your trust into them. The solution for misology, I suggest, is the same: evaluate *logoi* before trusting them. Indeed, I will argue that Simmias and Cebes have clung to Socrates' forms hypothesis itself, and Socrates then ignored them and proceeded to evaluate his hypothesis, just as he says he should.

Let me begin with evidence that the method is related to misology. Socrates said that misology arises especially among those who have spent time with the *logoi* used in disputation (*hoi antilogikoi logoi*) (90c); immediately after the second method of hypothesis passage, he describes how those who practice disputation (the *antilogikoi*) argue (101e). These are the only two occurrences of words with the *antilogik-* (disputation) stem in the dialogue. According to the misology passage, the people who waste their time with these *logoi* take themselves to be most wise, thinking that they can show that there is nothing sound or firm in any argument. After the second method of hypothesis passage, Socrates says that "thanks to their wisdom" the *antilogikoi* mix together starting point and result (101e), which seems to explain how they try to show that no argument is sound or firm. Socrates' slow process of carefully choosing a starting point as one's hypothesis and then thoroughly evaluating it offers a way to find something real rather than the quick, empty wisdom offered by the *antilogikoi*, which leads one to think that no *logos* is trustworthy.

More revealing evidence for misology's connection to the method of hypothesis comes at the end of the final immortality argument. Earlier Socrates said that, if Cebes grants him his hypothesis that the beautiful exists, and all the rest, then he will use this to show that the soul is immortal (100b), creating the expectation that the hypotheses will be used in the final immortality argument. The final argument then ends with the following exchange:

> "Well," said Simmias, "given what's been said I too no longer have any room for doubt. All the same, because of the magnitude of the issues in our *logoi*, and because of my low regard for human weakness, I'm compelled still to keep some doubt in my mind about what has been said."
>
> "Yes, not only that, Simmias," said Socrates, "but you're right to say so, and besides, even if you all find the first hypotheses trustworthy, nonetheless they should

---

[85] The connection to misology is noted in Sedley 1995, followed by Jansen 2013, Delcomminette 2018, and Sedley 2021. The detailed case over the next several paragraphs is my own.

be considered more clearly. And if you all analyze (διέλητε) them fully/fittingly (ἱκανῶς), you'll follow the *logos*, I suppose, as far as a human being can follow it up. Should this itself become clear, then you won't seek anything further." (107a8–b9)

The issue of doubt and trust, central to the account of misology, is here connected to the use of hypotheses. Socrates' account of misology makes clear that coming to trust a theory is dangerous, because this trust may later be betrayed, leading one ultimately to hate *logoi* altogether. And so, as we'd expect, Socrates says in the passage just quoted that Simmias is right to keep some doubts in his mind and that they should consider the first hypotheses more clearly, even if they find them trustworthy.[86] This suggests that the method aims to build the right kind of rational trust in a hypothesis, avoiding the premature trust that leads to misology. It addresses doubt while providing the most secure views a human can reach.

Recall that these interrelated topics of persuasion, trust, and doubt have arisen throughout the dialogue, as discussed in Section 4.1 and Subsection 8.2.1. Cebes phrases his challenge – which structures most of the dialogue – in terms of people having doubts that the soul survives death, and so he is looking for trust that the soul continues to exist after death (69e–70b). Thus the goal of Socrates' previous three arguments was not simply to establish his conclusion, but rather to address doubts so that they trust the conclusion. Socrates' method of hypothesis directly addresses this, helping them gain rational trust in the final argument.

To finish resolving the second puzzle, we need an account of what it means to hold on to the safety of the hypothesis (literally, "that safe thing of the hypothesis").[87] The key, in my view, is that Socrates says in the second method of hypothesis passage that you will "hold on to to the safety of your hypothesis *and reply accordingly*" (ἐχόμενος ἐκείνου τοῦ ἀσφαλοῦς τῆς ὑποθέσεως, οὕτως ἀποκρίναιο ἄν, 101d2–3, emphasis added to translation). What is safe about the hypothesis is that it provides a way to reply that does not require accepting the hypothesis itself. You reply on the basis of the things that you "set down as true" in the first stage of the method. The point of setting these down as true, rather than simply believing them, is that this gives you a way of evaluating a theory before putting your trust in it.

Socrates connects safety to replying in a passage where he describes what it is safe to "hold on to":

> For I don't go so far as to insist on this, but only that it is because of the beautiful that all beautiful things are beautiful. For it seems to me safest to give this reply both to myself and to another, and I believe that if I hold on to this I could never fall, but that it is safe to reply both to myself and to anyone else that it is because of the beautiful that beautiful things come to be beautiful. (100d6–e3)

---

[86] Subsection 9.8.4 discusses how to understand "analyzing" here.
[87] Sedley 2021 argues that we should translate this phrase (ἐκείνου τοῦ ἀσφαλοῦς τῆς ὑποθέσεως) as "the safe part of the hypothesis." His account involves distinguishing between the safe part of the hypothesis, that forms exist, and the hypothesis itself, that transcendent forms are causes. I argued in Section 9.7 that Socrates is not referring specifically to transcendent forms here.

What Socrates describes as safest here is *giving a reply*. He does not insist on the existence of the beautiful; instead, having adopted his hypothesis, he insists on this answer to why things are beautiful.[88] In other words, he replies to questions using the things set down as true if this hypothesis is correct. In the final sentence Socrates says that he believes that "if I *hold on to* this" (emphasis added) I could never fall. The "this" is "to give this reply both to myself and to another." This is the safety of the hypothesis that he, a page later, says that he *holds on to*. In other words, the safety of the hypothesis is to be found in treating it as put forward provisionally without yet having been accepted.[89] This is the point of setting down the consequences *as true*, rather than immediately believing these consequences.

Let us turn to the places where Socrates ignores Simmias and Cebes when they hold on to his hypothesis. Consider the first use of the term "hypothesis" in the dialogue. Simmias uses the term when he abandons his *harmonia* theory in response to Socrates' noting that it is incompatible with the recollecting argument:

> The *logos* about recollecting and learning, on the other hand [that is, in contrast to the *logos* that the soul is a *harmonia*], has been provided by means of a hypothesis worthy of acceptance. Because it was said, I think, that our soul also existed before it entered a body just as much as the being itself exists that bears the label "what it is." And I have accepted that hypothesis, or so I convince myself, both fittingly (ἱκανῶς) and correctly. So for these reasons, it seems, I mustn't allow myself or anyone else to say that soul is a *harmonia*. (92d6–e4)

Simmias claims that he convinced himself of the hypothesis that the forms exist fittingly and correctly. However, as we have seen, Socrates makes clear at the end of the final argument that Simmias has not fittingly analyzed the hypotheses and that, once he does so, he will have as good of an account as is humanly possible (107b). So, despite Simmias' claims to the contrary, he seems not to have convinced himself of the hypothesis that forms exist fittingly and correctly. Moreover, his acceptance of this theory is, from the standpoint of misology, quite dangerous: in just over a page he goes from accepting that the soul is a *harmonia* (91c–d) to completely rejecting it and holding on to a new *logos* (92d). Socrates' response is to ignore Simmias' acceptance of the form theory and instead use the method of hypothesis to evaluate Simmias' theory that the soul is a *harmonia* – as I discuss in the next subsection.

---

[88] Sedley 2021, n. 11, provides an alternative translation for Sedley and Long's 2010: "For I don't go so far as to insist on this" (οὐ γὰρ ἔτι τοῦτο διισχυρίζομαι), namely: "I no longer insist upon this." The Sedley and Long translation seems good to me, but if one wishes to use this other translation, perhaps Socrates has in mind the following. In the *Euthyphro*, for example, Socrates says that the form of unholiness is *in* every unholy action. This seems to be an account of how unholiness accrues to unholy things. Socrates in the *Phaedo* "no longer" insists on such a manner of accruing.

[89] See Subsection 8.3.1 for how Socrates' mention of the safety of the hypothesis, as well as his reference to never falling, implicitly responds to Simmias' earlier methodology, which he provided with his own sailing metaphor.

Only afterwards does he put forward his hypotheses about the forms and evaluate them before using them in the final argument.

Similarly, after Socrates first hypothesizes that there is such a thing as a good itself and all the rest, Cebes responds, "yes, I do grant you that, so proceed as quickly as you can" (100c1–2). Socrates ignores Cebes' request to proceed quickly and instead evaluates the hypothesis, showing how it avoids the problems that the earlier accounts fell into (100d–101c). In short, Simmias and Cebes quickly accept the existence of forms and want Socrates to move ahead. Socrates thinks that they should thoroughly vet the theory before accepting it, so they can gain a firm grip on the starting points he will use to show the immortality of the soul.

9.8.3 How to Apply the Method

Having clarified the method's aims and overall approach, let us turn to how it works, beginning with what it means for something to harmonize with a *logos*. Robinson influentially claimed that Socrates' use of the term "harmonize" is incoherent on the grounds that the two options are "is a logical consequence of" or "is consistent with" and neither works.[90] Here is one way to see why neither would work: "harmonize" could be understood as "is a logical consequence" in the first stage, where you count as true what harmonizes with a *logos*, but then we could not make sense of the second stage, where you check whether the consequences of a *logos* harmonize with one another – surely the consequences of a hypothesis need not be consequences of each other. In the second stage, "logically consistent" seems to fit the meaning of "harmonize" better, but we would not want in the first stage to count as true everything that is consistent with a hypothesis – many things that are consistent with a hypothesis are inconsistent with one another.[91]

"Fit together" seems a better way to understand the meaning of "harmonize": count as true the things that fit together with a *logos* and then see whether the consequences of the *logos* fit with one another. But "fit together" is still a metaphor, even if a clearer one than "harmonize." In determining what claims fit with one another, one will need to rely on more than simple logical relations. But it seems that one should not use any and all of one's beliefs to determine which claims fit together and which do not. Suppose that you independently accept the theory that souls are composed of fine particles. It does not seem that you should find that "the soul is a *harmonia*" has disharmonious consequences simply because it is incompatible with the soul's being composed of fine particles. Somehow the method seems to evaluate a *logos* on its own, but it is not restricted to formal, logical features of the *logos*.

We can understand how the method evaluates a *logos* on its own by recognizing that Socrates applies the method when he argues against Simmias' *harmonia* theory.

---

[90] Robinson 1953 (first edition 1941).
[91] This explanation of the problem draws on Gentzler 1991 and Bailey 2005.

Robinson already proposed in 1941 that Socrates is applying the method of hypothesis when replying to Simmias – and several have mentioned this idea since.[92] But to my knowledge no commentator has used this to help fill in how the method works, which is what I do here.[93] Note that, if (as I have argued) Simmias is here especially in danger of misology and the method of hypothesis helps one avoid this, then Socrates has good reason to use this method when replying to Simmias.

Let me begin with the evidence that Socrates applies the method of hypothesis in replying to Simmias. The metaphor of *logoi* being musically complementary begins with Socrates asking whether the *logos* that the soul is a *harmonia* will "sing with" (συνᾴσεται, 92c3; συνῳδός, 92c6 and 92c8) the *logos* that learning is recollecting. They agree that it does not, supposedly because they cannot both be true. Simmias then forcefully and at length abandons the view that the *soul* is a *harmonia* (92c–e, partially quoted in the previous subsection). So why, then, does Socrates proceed to argue against this view for two more pages (92e–95a)? Socrates' initial argument depended on Simmias' accepting the recollecting argument. If Simmias changed his mind later about that argument, he might again find appealing the view that the soul is a *harmonia*. Immediately after Simmias uses the term "hypothesis" for the first time in the dialogue (92d7, quoted in the previous Subsection, 9.8.2), Socrates' second and third arguments against Simmias' theory evaluate it on its own merits, not in terms of how well it fits with the recollecting argument or any other theory he accepts. Simmias speaks about "someone who hypothesizes" (93c10) that the soul is a *harmonia* and Socrates later refers to this view as a hypothesis (94b1). At the end of Socrates' arguments against this hypothesis, he says that they should not say that the soul is a *harmonia* since "we'd be agreeing neither with Homer, a divine poet, nor with ourselves" (95a1–2). The method of hypothesis involves checking whether, when adopting a hypothesis, one agrees with oneself.

After the term "hypothesis" is first used, Socrates' two arguments against Simmias' hypothesis each fit with his description of the method, as presented in the autobiography. In these arguments (discussed in Section 8.4) Socrates asks Simmias what features a *harmonia* seems to him to have and what features a soul seems to him to have (93a–c, 94b–c). He then argues that these features are incompatible with one another (93d–94b, 94c–e), and so Simmias should reject the view that a soul is a *harmonia*. Considering what features a *harmonia* seems to have and what features a soul seems to have corresponds to the first stage of the method: counting as true the things that seem to harmonize with the *logos* that a soul is a *harmonia*. And checking whether these features are compatible with one another corresponds to the second stage: checking whether the consequences harmonize with one another. It is especially clear that Simmias is meant to think

---

[92] Robinson 1953 (the second edition), 142; Gallop 1975, 166; Dorter 1982, 99–100; Sedley 1995.
[93] Sedley 2021 claims this as evidence confirming his interpretation; I am indebted to an earlier draft of his paper for spurring my ideas here.

through the hypothesis on its own terms when Socrates asks him what someone who hypothesizes that the soul is an attunement will think about virtue (93c). Simmias replies, "I for one can't say ... but clearly someone who adopted this hypothesis would say some such thing" (93c9–10). Although Simmias has already said that he no longer accepts the hypothesis, he thinks through what someone who accepted it would be committed to.

Recognizing that this is an example of the method clarifies what it means for claims to harmonize. Again, harmonizing must involve more than logical relations between *logoi*, but if one brought to bear all of one's beliefs, a theory could be rejected because it is incompatible with a completely different substantive theory. My suggestion is that, when someone considers whether a claim harmonizes with a *logos*, they consider whether this claim makes sense as part of a larger theory based on this *logos*; similarly, when someone considers whether two claims harmonize with one another (where each of these claims derive from a single *logos*), they consider whether these claims can both be part of a larger theory based on this *logos*.[94] Anyone should accept that souls can be good or bad and anyone should accept that souls can rule over the body, and so these claims harmonize with the claim that something is a soul, although neither logically follow from them. Similarly, anyone should accept that one *harmonia*, insofar as it is a *harmonia*, cannot be better or worse than another, and anyone should accept that a *harmonia* cannot rule over that of which it is a *harmonia*. These claims about souls and *harmoniai* harmonize with the hypothesis that the soul is a *harmonia*, but they do not harmonize with one another. Hence we should reject this hypothesis. To put it differently: when we think through this hypothesis, we see that it cannot be worked out in a coherent way.

Once we recognize this as an application of the method, we can also recognize Socrates applying the method to his hypotheses of forms (100b–101d).[95] He considers what would be the case if each form existed. If the form of the beautiful existed, it would be because of it that every beautiful thing is beautiful. This harmonizes with this *logos*, although it does not logically follow. As we have seen, there are minimal requirements that any proposed *aitia* should meet: what it identifies as responsible should not be responsible for opposites, and the *aitia*'s own opposite should not have an equal claim on explaining the explanandum. Socrates notes that the forms meet these requirements, whereas his initial candidates do not (100e–101c). He is considering what harmonizes with the hypothesis that a form exists and seeing whether these consequences harmonize with each other. He does not say that he has considered all the consequences of a given form's existing, or that this is a full examination of whether its consequences harmonize. But it illustrates what is

---

[94] For a similar idea, see Bailey 2005 and Sedley 2021, 55–6.
[95] So also e.g. Blank 1986, 151, and Sedley 2021.

9.8.4 Completing the Method

How does the method come to an end? Consider the continuation of the second method of hypothesis passage:

> And when you should have to give an account of your hypothesis itself, you would do so in the same way, giving in turn another hypothesis, whichever higher one seemed best, until you came to something fitting (ἱκανόν). (101d6–8)

It is often thought that one necessarily will move to a higher hypothesis, in part because in the *Republic* Socrates says that the power of dialectic uses hypotheses to reach the unhypothetical first principle of everything (511b). The word "unhypothetical" seems to be coined in the *Republic*.[96] It is worth recalling that in general a *hupothesis* is a proposed starting point that need not be provisional. There is no general reason to expect a *hupothesis* always to require further defense. Moreover, since Socrates says that the new hypothesis will be defended "in the same way," there would be an infinite regress if a *hupothesis* always needed to be further defended with a further *hupothesis*. I will argue that Socrates is saying that theoretically one might need a higher hypothesis, but he does not think that in fact the hypotheses that forms exist will need to be defended with further hypotheses.

The claim quoted above need not commit Socrates to there being a time when you need to reach a higher hypothesis.[97] First, to speak of "when" something would happen brings with it a mild presupposition that it will happen, but it need not be necessary. The sentence "when you need a lawyer, call me," need not mean that you necessarily will need a lawyer.[98] Next, recall that at the end of the final argument Socrates says of the first hypotheses that "if you all analyze (διέλητε) them fully/fittingly (ἱκανῶς), you'll follow the *logos*, I suppose, as far as a human being can follow it up. Should this itself become clear, then you won't seek anything further"

---

[96] As discussed in Wolfsdorf 2008.
[97] So also Blank 1986, 155–63.
[98] The use of ἐπειδή with the optative is very unusual. Perhaps Socrates uses it here because he wants to be clear that he is talking about a mere possibility – that it is effectively a temporal version of a future less vivid conditional: "if, at some time, you should have to give an account of the hypothesis itself, you would..." This fits well with the interpretation developed below but is not necessary for it. Plato sometimes uses the optative when he had used an optative in a previous sentence to set up a hypothetical possibility (e.g. *Republic* 515e–516a). This is how Blank 1986, 155, n. 30, understands this sentence. If that were right, then the sentence would only make claims within the hypothetical scenario described in the previous sentence, namely *that someone has held on to your hypothesis*. It would only claim that in this case you have to give an account of the hypothesis itself. It is not clear why Socrates would restrict his claims to this hypothetical scenario, but if he does, then he is certainly not claiming here that everyone will need to move to a higher hypothesis.

(107b6–9). The only hypotheses Socrates has mentioned are those for the existence of the individual forms. This suggests that Socrates thinks that when it comes to the hypotheses that each of the forms exist, they will *not* need higher hypotheses – they simply need to further analyze them. While it is unclear what "analyze" means here, there is nothing in the notion of analyzing that involves moving to something different – instead, it involves working carefully through what one already has. Perhaps analyzing here is simply the method: seeing what harmonizes with a hypothesis and what is disharmonious with it, and then seeing if these results harmonize with one another. In any event, Socrates thinks they need to consider more thoroughly the hypotheses they have, not find new ones.

If Socrates thinks that, while embodied, one cannot do better than analyzing the hypotheses that forms exist, then he must not think that there is a humanly graspable higher hypothesis – since if there were one, grasping it would improve our understanding of the final argument (cf. *Republic* 511b–d). It should not be surprising that Socrates thinks this is the best grasp humanly available, since he claimed in the defense speech that the philosopher cannot acquire a significant share of wisdom so long as he is embodied (as discussed in Section 3.7). By contrast, Socrates argues in the *Republic* that, at least in the kallipolis, it is possible to acquire the highest form of knowledge while embodied. The *Phaedo*'s method of hypothesis can be seen as providing the best results possible while embodied, given that we cannot acquire full wisdom.[99] In the *Phaedo* Socrates allows that people could acquire some knowledge while embodied; nonetheless, the philosopher will fall far short of the wisdom he seeks (see Section 3.7). Socrates does say that Cebes should follow Socrates' method if he wants to *discover* (εὑρεῖν, 101e3) something of the things that are, so the method can at least sometimes lead to genuine knowledge. But in the case of the soul's immortality, it seems that the best humanly available is less than knowledge. Taken together, the evidence suggests that the method will lead to the best epistemic state that humans can hope for – which for some topics will fall short of knowledge, but not for all.

9.9 CONCLUSION

At the end of Socrates' long discussion of *aitiai* – the subject of so much controversy – Echecrates brings the reader back to the outer frame to marvel at how clearly Socrates has put everything, even for someone with little intelligence (102a). Scholars have noted the irony, from our perspective, of Echecrates' claim, while also noting that it almost certainly is not meant ironically.[100] But what, then, is the point of this interruption into the outer frame? As noted in Section 2.4, the *Phaedo* is unique among Plato's dialogues in having an outer frame that repeatedly breaks

---

[99] For a similar thought, see Benson 2015, 110–12.
[100] E.g. Rowe 1993 ad loc, Sedley 2021.

back into the inner dialogue. I suggested that Plato is treating Phaedo and Echecrates like the chorus of a play, one of whose functions is to serve as an ordinary observer on the extraordinary events taking place, offering a guide to how to react to them. Echecrates' first interruption marked the beginning of the misology section, where he noted how confused and doubtful he felt. Now he emphasizes how clear Socrates has made everything, showing that Socrates has turned things around, addressing the cause of misology while creating a firm foundation for his triumphant final argument.

In the autobiography, Socrates draws on and engages with a medical tradition of searching for *aitiai*. He considers alternate theories of what, for a given explanandum, the *aitia* is. One might identify something as responsible (*aition*) for an explanandum without recognizing in virtue of what it is. Specifying an *aitia* requires describing in virtue of what this thing is responsible. Grasping this allows one to understand the explanandum. Just as in the medical tradition, Socrates develops criteria for being responsible or for being an *aitia* and criticizes accounts for not meeting these criteria; similarly, he distinguishes what is genuinely responsible from what falls short of this. In general, Socrates approaches the natural scientific project exactly as one would expect, given our portrait of him in Plato's other dialogues: he cannot understand claims others take as obvious, he emphasizes his ignorance, he values a theory that he can consistently maintain, he is incredibly excited about the prospect of learning about the good, and he relies heavily on those things he is searching for when he asks his "what is it?" question – the forms.

Socrates puts forward his ignorant forms theory using a method that aims to avoid the sort of concerns about hypotheses found in *VM*. This method involves thinking through what anyone should accept who accepts a given theory and seeing whether these results cohere with one another. By thoroughly evaluating a theory before placing one's trust in it, one can avoid the premature trust that leads to misology. This process of slowly building rational trust in a theory is the best possible method in our current, embodied state.

10

Cebes' Objection and the Final Argument

86e–88b, 102a–107b

The *Phaedo*, in a sense, has three conclusions. First, the final argument (102a–107b) finishes the main argumentative thread of the dialogue, which began with Cebes' challenge (69e–70b). Then Socrates' eschatological account (107c–115a) finishes discussing the idea that those who properly care for their souls will fare better after death than who do not – a claim that Socrates said in his defense speech that he would defend (at 63b–64a). Finally, in the death scene, prosaic concerns of the sort mentioned at the opening of the dialogue, along with Socrates' family and his full group of companions, come back into focus, and Phaedo addresses Echecrates' initial request to be told how Socrates met his end (57a). The dialogue, thus, has a ring composition with the opening of the dialogue matched by the death scene and the defense speech by the final eschatological account. After the defense speech, Cebes' challenge leads to his first three arguments that the soul exists after death or before birth (69e–80b). In the middle of the dialogue, Simmias' and Cebes' objections and the threat of misology are the pivots that turn us toward the autobiography and the final argument.[1]

I call this the "final" argument rather than the "final immortality" argument because, as we have seen, the earlier arguments did not claim to show that the soul is immortal (see Section 4.1 and Chapters 5 and 6).[2] This is the only immortality argument. While one could consider the autobiography part of the final argument, after Echecrates breaks back into the outer frame (102a) Socrates takes a more focused approach of establishing exactly what is needed for his conclusion; hence I treat the argument as beginning here. There are short arguments that come later in the dialogue (e.g. 107e–108a, 108e–109a, 115c–116a), but this is the argumentative

---

[1] See Section 2.4 for the idea that the threat of misology is a sort of tragic reversal in the middle of the dialogue.
[2] As mentioned in Section 4.1, all of Socrates' mentions of the soul's immortality in the dialogue are either part of summarizing Cebes' cloakmaker objection (95c1, d1, and e1) or part of Socrates' final argument, which responds to this objection (100b9, 105e–107c *passim*, 114d4).

climax of the dialogue, Socrates' heroic feat (see Section 2.2), and so can reasonably be called the dialogue's "final argument." It not only completes the dialogue's unfolding account of the soul but also its account of how and why forms are different from ordinary objects.

I argue in this chapter that the final argument's account of the soul further fills in Socrates' account in the kinship argument by responding to Cebes' cloakmaker objection.[3] This objection presents an alternative model of the soul – compatible with the features of the soul identified in the premises of the kinship argument – according to which the soul provides life to the body by "constantly reweaving" it (87d9–e1), but the soul is ultimately destroyed in this process. Socrates' final argument rejects this model by showing why the soul's bringing life to the body, rather than destroying the soul, ensures that it must be immortal and indestructible. The final argument thus does not simply argue that the soul is immortal and indestructible; it shows what is wrong with Cebes' alternative model. In doing so, it identifies a way in which the soul has a characteristic of the divine – immortality – thereby specifying one way in which it is akin to the divine.

I begin the chapter (Section 10.1) by considering Socrates' claim, which leads into his autobiography (95b–96a), that he will engage closely with Cebes' objection – not merely provide a new, independent argument. Then (Section 10.2) I examine this objection (86e–88b) to consider exactly what Socrates is responding to. After giving an overview of how the argument responds to Cebes' challenge (Section 10.3), I turn to its first step (Section 10.4), which involves distinguishing between the forms in us (which I sometimes call "immanent forms") and the forms themselves (which up until now I have simply called "forms"). I provide an account of these immanent forms and then argue that this part of the dialogue identifies the fundamental reason why forms cannot be ordinary, perceptible things: the latter are receptive of opposites, whereas forms cannot be. Socrates' next step is to introduce a class of things that he does not name, but that I call "bringers," since they always bring one member of a pair of opposites to whatever they occupy (Section 10.5). Scholars sometimes treat bringers simply as things that essentially have some feature; instead, they are a much more specific category than this: they each bring, to whatever they occupy, one of the immanent forms that Socrates described in the previous stage. With this background in place, Socrates turns to what I call "the final argument proper" (Section 10.6). I argue that it relies on his account of forms and bringers, and that, given his account of these and given that the soul is a bringer of life, his conclusion follows. Finally, I consider how this account fills in the model of the soul laid out in the kinship argument (Section 10.7).

---

[3] This chapter overlaps considerably with Ebrey 2021; Sections 10.4 and 10.5 also include a discussion of forms that overlaps with Ebrey 2022a.

10.1 CLOSELY ENGAGING WITH CEBES' OBJECTION: 95B–96A

What is the relationship between Cebes' objection and the final argument? A few commentators do not address this question.[4] However, most say that the final argument responds to Cebes' objection simply by providing a new, independent argument that the soul is completely immortal and indestructible.[5] Sometimes, this is explicitly connected to the idea that Cebes' objection has pointed to a serious problem with Socrates' kinship argument, which is what prompts the need for a new argument.[6] According to all such interpretations, Socrates is providing a better argument than the kinship argument, but there is no suggestion that he is responding to anything specific in Cebes' objection.[7] But there are good reasons to think that Socrates aims to do just this.

After Socrates restates Cebes' objection at length (95b–e), before beginning his autobiography, he says:

> What you're seeking is no small matter, Cebes; we must altogether study thoroughly the *aitia* of coming to be and ceasing to be. So, if you like, I'll recount my experiences concerning them; then, if you see something useful in what I say, you'll use it to convince yourself concerning the very things you are discussing. (95e9–96a3)

Socrates says that Cebes will be able to use Socrates' response to convince himself concerning the very things he discusses in his targeted objection to the kinship argument. It is unclear how an entirely new argument for the soul's continued existence would help convince Cebes about the very things in his targeted objection. Moreover, immediately before restating Cebes' objection, Socrates says, "let us come to close quarters in Homeric style and see if there is something in what you are saying" (95b7–8). And at the end of summarizing Cebes' objection (95b–e), Socrates says that he is deliberately going over this to make sure that "nothing escapes them" (95e3). According to the standard interpretation, Socrates does not engage with the objection at close quarters and so it should not matter whether anything escapes them, since Socrates simply provides a new argument.

In addition, the standard interpretation goes against our broader philosophical expectations of how to respond to an objection to an argument. We expect a response to speak specifically to that objection, not simply to bypass it and provide a new argument. Occasionally this is appropriate, but it has the disadvantage that the

---

[4] For example Damascius 2009, Burnet 1911, Bluck 1955, Bostock 1986, and Denyer 2007.
[5] See Hackforth 1955, 104; Gallop 1975, 153; Dorter 1982, 87; Rowe 1993 on 88b5–6; Apolloni 1996, 8; Kanayama 2000, 86–6; Ebert 2004, 335; Sedley 2009, 146; Bailey 2014, 15; see also next footnote.
[6] E.g. Frede 1978, 36; Frede 2011, 143; see also Menn 2010 (next note).
[7] Menn 2010 (see esp. 62–3) agrees that the final argument responds to the substance of Cebes' objection. O'Brien 1968 emphasizes how the final argument responds to Cebes' demands at the end of his objection.

objector typically does not learn what, if anything, is wrong with the objection. If Socrates is addressing the specifics of Cebes' objection, he provides a more satisfying response. I suspect that many commentators would agree that we would expect Socrates' response to engage with Cebes' objection; however, it simply seems to them that he does not do so. I will argue that close attention to Cebes' objection, Socrates' restatement of it, and Socrates' final argument shows that he is responding to its details. The next section examines Cebes' objection and the following one provides an overview of Socrates' response.

10.2 CEBES' OBJECTION: 86E–88B

Cebes' cloakmaker objection responds to the kinship argument in three phases. The secondary literature has not distinguished these phases; as we will see, doing so is crucial for understanding how Cebes objects to the kinship argument, which in turn clarifies the final argument's strategy and goals. In the first phase, Cebes puts forward an argument allegedly parallel to the kinship argument (cf. Simmias' objection at 85e–86b). The second phase uses this parody argument to suggest an alternative model of the soul according to which it is destroyed upon death (cf. Simmias' objection at 86b–d). In the third phase (unparalleled in Simmias' objection), Cebes fills out his model and concedes that the soul might survive death, reincarnating several times before inevitably being destroyed. This phase ends with a new, stricter demand than Cebes' original challenge: to show that the soul is altogether immortal and indestructible. Socrates' final argument is designed to meet this new, stricter demand while showing what is wrong with Cebes' alternative model.

The first phase presents an argument whose structure is supposedly parallel to the kinship argument, but with a conclusion that clearly does not follow (87b–d). In brief, the argument is as follows: a cloakmaker is longer lasting than the cloaks he weaves for himself and the final cloak he weaves for himself does not perish; hence the cloakmaker must himself not perish. Cebes concludes this first phase by saying that everyone would describe this argument as "simpleminded" (εὔηθες, 87c7) and then pointing out that, despite being superior to the cloaks and lasting longer than many of them, the cloakmaker perished before his last one (87c–d). Cebes appears to be referring to a supplemental consideration Socrates gives *after* drawing the conclusion of the kinship argument (at 80b): that after death the corpse tends to last for a long time (80c–d). In response, Socrates could simply say that being longer-lasting was never one of the three key features used to indicate that the soul is akin to the unseen: (1) invisible, (2) such as to become like the unseen when it inquires itself through itself, and (3) by nature a ruler (see Section 6.4). It is weak, then, as a parallel argument. However, just as Socrates ignores Simmias' supposedly parallel argument and instead addressed Simmias' model of the soul (according to which the soul *is* a *harmonia*), so too he ignores Cebes' supposedly parallel argument and addresses Cebes' alternative model – which offers a much more serious challenge.

Cebes' parallel argument makes no claims about the soul, only about the structure of Socrates' reasoning. By contrast, the second phase (87d–88a) offers a rival account of the soul's relation to the body, according to which the soul's activity is fundamentally similar to a cloakmaker's. Cebes marks this new stage by saying that soul's relation to body warrants "this same image" (τὴν αὐτὴν ταύτην ... εἰκόνα, 87d3) – the same as is in his parallel argument. He does not himself endorse this rival way to view the relation between soul and body, but he says someone might reasonably endorse it. He describes it as follows:

> Nonetheless, he [the imagined proponent] would say, although each soul wears out many bodies, especially if it lives for many years (because if the body is in flux and perishing when the human being is still alive, the soul still always reweaves what is being worn out), all the same, when the soul perishes it must at that moment have its last piece of weaving and perish before that one alone. And, after the soul perishes, only then does the body show its natural weakness and quickly rot and disappear. (87d6–e5)

According to this model, the soul is constantly "reweaving" the falling apart body. This model makes the soul at least in some ways superior to the body, since it keeps the body in a good condition. In fact, this model is compatible with the soul having each of the features Socrates used to identify the soul as akin to the unseen – (1) invisible, (2) such as to become more like the unseen when it inquires itself through itself, and (3) by nature a ruler. By contrast, recall that Socrates' final counterargument to Simmias' *harmonia* theory showed how it was incompatible with the soul being a ruler (Subsection 8.4.3). Hence, Cebes' model shows how something could have the features identified in the kinship argument and yet not be close to unable to disintegrate. Cebes ends this second phase by saying that it is not right to put one's trust in (πιστεύσαντα, 87e6) this *logos* and be confident that the soul exists somewhere after death (87e–88a). This alludes back to Cebes' original challenge, which asked for some reason not to doubt (ἀπιστίαν, 70a1) but rather trust (πίστεως, 70b3) that the soul will exist somewhere after death. Cebes is saying that Socrates has not yet adequately addressed this fear, despite his having said that the kinship argument would do so (77d–e).

Whereas the second phase argues that Socrates has not met Cebes' original challenge, the third phase introduces a new demand while introducing a mechanism that explains why the soul is destroyed while reweaving the body. First, Cebes grants that the soul might be tough enough to endure being born several times (88a). But then he imagines that someone,

> having granted these things, refused to concede the further point that the soul does not suffer in its many births and at the end perishes completely during one of those deaths, and that he said that no one knows which death and which parting from the body make the soul perish. Because, he would say, none of us can observe that. Now, if this is so, nobody who is confident in the face of death can fail to be

displaying unintelligent confidence, unless he can prove the soul is altogether immortal and indestructible. (88a8–b6)

The second phase did not explain why the soul is destroyed along with the body. Here Cebes offers a mechanism: coming into, being in, and leaving a body wears on the soul. Since Cebes now concedes that the soul may reincarnate several times, he can no longer expect Socrates to address the earlier fear that the soul simply dissipates upon death. Hence, he asks Socrates to show something new: that the soul is altogether immortal and indestructible. Before Plato, the term "immortal" is almost exclusively applied the gods and their possessions, and prior to this point in the *Phaedo* Socrates has never applied it to the soul. However, he did apply it to the the unseen, which he also calls "the divine."[8] Cebes is now asking Socrates to show that the soul has features of the divine; his language of "immortal and indestructible" (ἀθάνατόν τε καὶ ἀνώλεθρον) seems to simply generalize the kinship argument's description of the divine as immortal (ἀθάνατος) and unable to be disintegrated (ἀδιάλυτος) (80a–b).[9] Cebes seems to be asking Socrates to show that the soul is not merely most like and akin to these unseen, divine things, but in fact one of them. Socrates does not think that the soul is a member of this class, but Cebes' request pushes him, in the final argument, to explain why the soul completely possesses at least these two characteristic features of the divine.

It is not obvious that one needs to show that the soul is immortal and indestructible to address the fear that it is destroyed upon death. Socrates could have rejected Cebes' claim (in the previous block quotation) that one would display "unintelligent confidence" unless one showed the soul to be altogether immortal and indestructible. If Socrates held different views, he could have argued, for example, that the soul is so extremely strong that while it may not be indestructible, the chances of its being destroyed are so slim that it would be irrational to worry about it. Or again, if he held different views, he could have argued that the only thing that could destroy the soul is vice, and so as long as one lives a good life, there is nothing to fear (cf. *Republic* 608d–611b). Instead, Socrates accepts the new demand to show that the soul is altogether immortal and indestructible – supposedly because he in fact believes this to be the case and thinks he can show this in his final argument.

In several ways, Cebes' alternative model of the soul poses a more serious challenge than Simmias' (discussed in Section 8.3). Both models purport to explain why the soul will (at least eventually) be destroyed upon death. Socrates' first

---

[8] See Long 2019, ch. 1, for a discussion of pre-Platonic uses of the term "immortal." I discuss Long's account in Ebrey 2022b.

[9] Cebes' challenge raises the fear that the soul dissipates upon death (70a); this fear is reiterated at the beginning of the kinship argument (77d–e). Hence Socrates argues in the kinship argument that the soul, like the unseen, cannot be disintegrated (78b, 80a–b). At the end of the cloakmaker objection, Cebes steps back from the specific fear of dissipation to the general concern that it perishes in some way or other and so now asks Socrates to show that it is indestructible.

objection to Simmias (91e–92c) is that his account is incompatible with the recollection argument. Cebes introduces his own account by saying that he found that argument convincing and so is not doubting that the soul existed before it came into human form (87a). Socrates' other two objections to Simmias' account (discussed in Section 8.4) point out how it cannot explain how some souls are better than others (93a–94b), and how the soul can rule over the body (94b–e). Precisely because Cebes provides a less revisionary account of the soul, it can easily accommodate these features, and so is more difficult to reject. At the same time, Cebes provides a mechanism that explains why the soul will ultimately be destroyed: being connected to the body puts a strain on it, damaging it over the course of a single life or multiple lives.

As noted earlier, when Socrates restates Cebes' objection (95b–e), he does not mention the parallel argument (phase 1); instead, he begins with Cebes' demand to be shown that the soul is indestructible and immortal (95b–c). In his restatement, Socrates identifies Cebes' central objection as the idea that the soul is destroyed by embodiment: "the very fact of coming into a human body was the start of its [the soul's] perishing, like a disease. On this view, the soul really suffers as it lives this life and eventually, in what is called 'death,' it perishes" (95d1–4). Socrates recognizes that this part of Cebes' objection poses a very serious challenge, one that requires his final argument to address.

10.3 THE FINAL ARGUMENT'S RESPONSE TO CEBES' OBJECTION

Cebes' alternative model shows that Socrates has not yet ruled out a possibility that would explain why the soul is inevitably destroyed. Cebes has not, for example, pointed to some widely recognized feature of the soul that the kinship argument's theory cannot explain or to some feature that the soul has, according to the kinship argument, that it cannot possibly have. Thus Socrates does not need to abandon or change the theory he defended in the kinship argument; instead, he can simply fill it in. His response is designed to meet Cebes' new, stronger demand while showing that the soul is not destroyed by bringing life to the body; on the contrary, bringing life is precisely what ensures its immortality and indestructibility.

The final argument places the soul in a class of things that I call "bringers" (named after "the bringer," τὸ ἐπιφέρον, at 105a4, as discussed in Section 10.5), each of which bring some member of a pair of opposites with them. The argument works by combining general features of bringers with the specific thing the soul is supposed to bring: life. The kinship argument made no mention of the connection between the soul and life. The features it identified the soul as possessing – being unseen, coming to a rest when it inquires itself through itself, naturally being a ruler – are apparently irrelevant to the soul's not being destroyed. By contrast, the final argument identifies precisely the relevant feature that is supposed to be the basis for its being immortal and indestructible: being a bringer of life. The argument says nothing about the soul's other features since these are irrelevant to the argument.

10.4 THE FORMS IN US: 102A–103C

Immediately after Socrates discusses forms, he introduces the immanent forms, which (it will turn out) are brought by bringers to the things that they occupy. Socrates begins by describing "the largeness in Simmias," which he later discusses alongside "largeness itself" (102d). He uses the largeness and smallness in Simmias to describe how an ordinary, perceptible thing – Simmias – is both large and small at the same time. He notes that ordinary objects admit the opposites large and small at the same time, whereas largeness – either the form itself or the form in us – does not admit its opposite. Socrates' discussion here is important for his contrast between forms and ordinary things as well as for the final argument. I argue here that Socrates thinks that once one accepts that there is a form of largeness itself and that some things are large, the existence of an imminent largeness is not a further commitment.

The passage begins with Phaedo, as narrator, speaking in his own voice:

> When these points of his [Socrates] were accepted and it was agreed that each of the forms exists and that other things receive a share of and are named after the forms themselves, I think that he next asked: "So if that's what you are saying, whenever you say that Simmias is larger than Socrates but smaller than Phaedo, don't you mean that at that time both of these, both largeness and smallness, are in Simmias?"
>
> "Yes, I do."
>
> "However," he said, "do you agree that 'Simmias exceeds Socrates' does not express in words as it in fact truly is? For presumably it isn't in Simmias' nature to exceed by this, by being Simmias, but rather by the largeness that he happens to have. And do you agree that, again, he does not exceed Socrates because Socrates is Socrates, but because Socrates has smallness relative to his largeness?"
>
> "True."
>
> "Right, and again that he is not exceeded by Phaedo because Phaedo is Phaedo, but because Phaedo has largeness relative to Simmias' smallness?"
>
> "That's so."
>
> "In that case, this is how Simmias is named both small and large, by being in between the pair of them, offering his smallness to Phaedo's largeness to be exceeded, but providing to Socrates his largeness, which exceeds Socrates' smallness." (102a11–d2)

Socrates provides here a concrete example of how an ordinary object can be rightly called both "large" and "small" at the same time. This example does not have to do with change over time, as was the case in the recollection and kinship arguments (Subsection 5.4.1 and Section 6.3, cf. *Cratylus* 439d–440d) or being *kata* different things, as was the case in the kinship argument (Section 6.3, cf. *Republic* 436d–437e). Instead, this case of the compresence of opposites arises because of how ordinary objects are in relation to (*pros*) one another (cf. *Hippias Major* 285b–d, *Republic* 523b–524e, *Theaetetus* 154c–155c). As noted in Subsections 5.4.1 and 6.3.1, these correspond to the three different ways in which something can undergo opposites, according to the principle of non-opposition in the *Republic* (439b): at different times, *kata* different things, or *pros* different things. By contrast, after the passage just quoted, Socrates says that largeness will never admit of smallness (102d–e). Thus, over the course of the *Phaedo*, Socrates attributes to ordinary objects all three types of compresence of opposites and denies each type of the forms. A given form will not suffer opposites even at different times, *kata* different things, or *pros* different things.

Let us turn to Socrates' introduction here of "the largeness in Simmias." This is a particularly fraught topic, since Aristotle criticizes Plato for thinking that there is a type of largeness that does not exist "in" anything (as discussed in Subsection 5.4.1). Again, it is important to approach the *Phaedo*'s account on its own terms, not through Aristotle's lens. At this stage in the dialogue, Simmias and Cebes have agreed to the existence of forms many times (65d, 74a–b, 76d–77a, 92d–e), and Socrates has defended this claim with his method of hypothesis (100a–101e). Phaedo begins the passage under discussion by saying (in the outer frame of the dialogue) that Socrates and the others agreed that there are forms themselves and that other things receive a share of them. Socrates then says that, "if you say these things" (102b3–4), then when you say that Simmias is larger than Socrates, you are saying that there is a largeness in Simmias. Thus, Socrates thinks that if you are committed to (a) there being the form of largeness and (b) something having a share of this form, then you are committed to (c) there being largeness in this thing. Nonetheless, he treats largeness itself as distinct from largeness in us.[10] When he first mentions them alongside one another, he makes a point of emphasizing that *not only* is largeness itself never willing to be large and small at the same time, *but also* the largeness in us is not willing to do this (102d), which certainly suggests that they are distinct. Moreover, Socrates is emphatic in the kinship argument that the forms themselves are completely unchanging and are not destroyed (e.g. 78c–d, 80a–b). By contrast, the immanent forms either retreat or perish when their opposite approaches (102d–e). The heat in me, which I have when I am hot, perishes when I become cold; by contrast, heat itself will never perish or change in any way. Hence, heat itself must be distinct from the heat in me.[11]

---

[10] Fine 1986 argues that in the *Phaedo* largeness itself could be the same as the largeness in Simmias. If so, this could simplify my interpretation; however, in my view, Devereux 1994 provides decisive arguments against Fine, which I briefly summarize here.

[11] At 106b–c Socrates explicitly says that odd perishes when the even comes to three. Moreover, 106a very strongly suggests that the hot and the cold in things are perishable.

I suggest that we understand this as follows. Largeness itself is what Socrates is looking for when he asks, "what is largeness?" It does not change over time, nor is it destructible, since there is always something that it is to be large and this stays the same. In addition, when something has a share of largeness, there is something about it – something "in it" – that it makes it appropriate to call it "large" in certain situations. It is tricky to identify what this largeness is that is in Simmias, in part because a thing is large only in relation to something else. Suppose that Simmias is six feet tall and Socrates five feet tall. We do not want to say that the largeness in Simmias is his being six feet tall, because six feet tall can also be small, whereas Socrates says that the largeness in Simmias is never willing to be small (102d–e). We might then be tempted to identify the largeness in Simmias as his having a greater height than Socrates. But Simmias would then need a different largeness in him for each person and thing that he is larger than, whereas Socrates only speaks of Simmias having a single largeness in him (102c–d). There is thus much to be said for Sedley's suggestion that we draw on the discussion of largeness in the *Parmenides* (150c–d) (cf. *Hippias Major* 294a–b, *Laches* 192a–b).[12] The proposal is that the largeness in Simmias is his power to exceed. Simmias exercises this power only when he exceeds someone, never when he is exceeded. Being six feet tall gives Simmias' power its specific character, explaining why it is exercised in relation to some people but not others.

Simmias only has a share of largeness when his immanent largeness is appropriately related to someone (or something) else's immanent smallness. By contrast, Socrates treats heat and cold, odd and even, and living and dead as non-relational features. These non-relational features are less complicated: if something has heat in it, it will definitely have a share of the form of heat. Hence, we can think of immanent heat as what it is about something that makes it true that it has a share of the form of heat. I hope that this account provides a useful way to think of immanent forms. But, for the purposes of this chapter, the crucial point is that Socrates thinks that a commitment to the forms themselves and to things' having a share in these forms automatically brings with it a commitment to immanent forms.

Why does Socrates say that this largeness, which can flee or be destroyed, is "in" Simmias, in contrast to this other largeness? I would like to follow a suggestion made by Brett Thompson: Socrates is here, once more, appropriating Anaxagoras.[13] In particular, Socrates seems to be following Anaxagoras' view that if something is rightly called "hot," then it has "the hot" in it. This can be seen as further developing the Anaxagorean model that Socrates began in the autobiography. As David Furley has noted, when Socrates speaks in the autobiography of "having a share of" the

---

[12] Sedley 2018, 211.
[13] Thompson made the suggestion in the *Phaedo* seminar I taught at Humboldt in 2020. My account here has benefitted from our conversations about how best to develop the idea.

forms, he is using the language that Anaxagoras uses when describing ordinary objects as "having a share of" the cosmic stuffs.[14] Socrates' account, like Anaxagoras', explains ordinary objects' features by how they relate to more basic ontological categories (cosmic stuffs or forms). A key difference between their views is that, for Anaxagoras, when something has a share of heat, that heat is *in it*, whereas for Socrates the forms themselves are completely unchanging and only grasped by reasoning, and so cannot be *in* ordinary sensible things. But this leaves Socrates with a question: in virtue of what does an *f*-thing have a share of *f*-ness? In other words, on what grounds can we say that this is hot and that is cold, if heat itself and cold itself are not in it? Immanent forms address this. We can think of it this way: because the forms themselves are unchanging and only grasped by reason, if Plato wants to appropriate Anaxagoras' cosmic stuff model, he needs to divide it into two: every ordinary thing that is *f* has a share of something and has something in it, but these are no longer the same thing.

If this is correct, then there are two different Anaxagorean explanatory models in the *Phaedo*, one modeled on *nous*, the other on ordinary objects' having a share of cosmic stuffs. As discussed in Section 3.4 (and see also Section 7.2), Socrates treats the soul in the *Phaedo* the way Anaxagoras treats *nous*. Anaxagoras says (B12) that if *nous* were not *epi* itself, it would have things in it that thwart it, but instead it is itself *epi* itself, pure and so able to know and rule over all things. I argued that similarly the soul in the *Phaedo* is able to know and rule if it is itself *kata* itself and so pure. When the soul has things poured or mixed into it, it is impure, not *auto kath' hauto*, hindering its ability to know the forms and rule over the body. According to this account, the soul aspires to be like Anaxagoras' *nous*, with nothing mixed into it. By contrast, here in the final argument, *each* of a thing's features corresponds to something that is "in" it, including a thing's proper and natural features. According to the final argument, there is life in the soul and odd in three, but these are not impurities that should be removed. The claim that some souls are impure plays a crucial role in the eschatological account that comes later in the dialogue (see Chapter 11), so Socrates does not simply replace one Anaxagorean model with the other. Instead, they seem to simply exist side by side.

After this lengthy discussion of the immanent forms, let me return to the passage where he introduces them. In it, Socrates emphasizes that it is not in the nature of something like Simmias or Phaedo to be that *by which* things are large or small. This is the causal dative Socrates recently used in his autobiography for what is responsible (*aition*; see Section 9.1). Neither Simmias nor Phaedo is responsible for either's being large or small. Socrates says that instead of Simmias' nature being to exceed, he just "happens" to have largeness; it is *by* this largeness that he is large. If someone put Simmias himself forward as responsible of his being large, one could object that he could just as easily have been responsible for being small, and so, by the same

[14] Furley 1976 and Furley 2002.

10.4 The Forms in Us: 102a–103c

reasoning about opposites that Socrates used earlier (98e–99a, 100e–101c; see Sections 9.3 and 9.5), he should not be identified as responsible for being either large or small. The largeness in him is what makes the difference to whether he is large or small; it is what is truly responsible for Simmias' being large, with no claim on making anything small.

After Socrates' account of how Simmias is both large and small, he further clarifies the difference between Simmias, on the one hand, and the largeness in him and largeness itself, on the other (102d–103a). This is the last place in the dialogue where Socrates contrasts a form with an ordinary thing. He uses himself as an example and says that he is able to admit both opposites, largeness or smallness, whereas the largeness and the smallness in him and largeness and smallness themselves are not able to admit (*dechesthai*) such opposites (102e–103a). Whether Socrates is large or small in relation to something is determined by which he happens to have admitted. This is one of the fundamental features of the ordinary objects that distinguishes them from the forms: they admit opposites, whereas forms do not. It is because ordinary objects admit opposites that it cannot be *by* them that things have their features; instead, it is by the forms that are in them. Even if some ordinary object managed not to be characterized by some opposite – even if it were somehow entirely smooth, in no ways rough – its nature would admit of both. It would not be responsible for its being smooth, but rather would just happen to be that way. But, as we learned in the autobiography, the form of *f*-ness is precisely what is responsible for *f*-things' being *f*. Hence, the forms must not be receptive of opposites – just as Socrates said in the kinship argument (78d).[15] Reflecting on ordinary objects' receptivity to opposites clarifies why forms cannot have such receptivity.

Some of the bringers that Socrates goes on to describe in the next part of the argument are ordinary, perceptible things such as fire and snow, and some not, such as three and soul. Each is unable to receive some specific opposite: cold, heat, even, or death. They are typically taken to be causes (*aitiai*) – called "sophisticated" or "clever" *aitiai* by Vlastos and others. If that were correct, then the account I have just given could not be correct: Socrates' ultimate reason for thinking that forms are not ordinary objects could not be that forms are responsible for ordinary things' having their features, whereas ordinary objects cannot be responsible for this. If fire were a sophisticated cause, then some ordinary objects could be responsible for some of their features. The last step in my account of forms and sensible things will be to argue that Socrates does not think that bringers are responsible and that he has good reasons to think this. But before arguing for this we need a general account of bringers.

---

[15] It might seem like the following should be an option: that forms can admit some opposites, so long as these opposites are irrelevant to what the forms are responsible (*aition*) for. I explain why Socrates does not allow this at the end of the next section.

10.5 THE BRINGERS: 103C–105C

In addition to the forms themselves and the immanent forms, there is a third class of things, which I am calling "bringers." Representative members include fire, snow, three, and fever. The final argument relies on the soul being a bringer. Socrates provides a complicated description of them; I will argue that each part of this description is crucial for the final argument.[16]

After distinguishing fire from the hot and snow from the cold, Socrates notes that fire does not admit cold, nor snow hot (103c–d). Then he says that bringers are always characterized by one member of a pair of opposites (henceforth, simply "an opposite") and do not admit the other member of this pair: fire is always hot and does not admit coldness, and snow always cold and does not admit heat; if heat approaches snow, snow flees or is destroyed, just like the cold in us (103e–104b).[17] Socrates next notes that the bringers have in them the opposite that always characterizes them (104b–c). He refers to this opposite several times as a form (e.g. 104b9, 104d2, 104d9, 105d13): the bringers have in them the immanent forms that Socrates discussed immediately before introducing bringers. Consider the first time one of these opposites is referred to as a form:

> Not only do those opposites evidently not admit one another, but there are also all those things that are not opposites of one another, but always possess the opposites, and they too seem not to admit that form (*idea*), whichever one is opposed to the one inside them; instead, when it attacks, evidently they either perish or retreat. (104b7–c1)

Socrates refers to these opposites that are in them with the term *"idea."* In several other dialogues, Plato uses *"eidos"* and *"idea"* (both translated "form") interchangeably.[18] However, in the *Phaedo*, he seems to have a special usage, which I think Devereux gets exactly right: in one case *"eidos"* fairly clearly refers to both the forms themselves and immanent forms (104c7), but otherwise it is used for the forms themselves, whereas *"idea"* is used exclusively for the immanent forms.[19]

In any event, Socrates is clear in this passage that bringers have an immanent form in them. This is often overlooked or downplayed in the secondary literature,[20] but the textual evidence for it is quite strong. Socrates says again that the bringers have in them the form of an opposite at 104d (quoted later in this section) and at 105a–b he

---

[16] See Sedley 2018, 213–14, for another detailed description of this group.
[17] For a discussion of the idea that things like the "large in us" can flee, see Gallop 1975, 196–9, Sedley 2018.
[18] E.g. *Euthyphro*, ἰδέα: 5d4, 6e1; εἶδος: 6d11. *Republic*, ἰδέα: 596b1; εἶδος 596a6, 597a1.
[19] Devereux 1994, 71, n. 16.
[20] Gallop 1975 mentions this, but then leaves it out when he reconstructs the argument, treating it as if Socrates is simply making a claim about essential predication.

says that what they will not admit is a form (*idea*).[21] Moreover, immediately before the quoted passage, Socrates says that bringers always "merit the same name" (103e3; cf. 103e4) as the form. He gives the example of the number three, which he says merits the same name as the odd.[22] According to his earlier account of the immanent forms, anything correctly called "*f*" should have a form of *f*-ness in it (102c–d). Thus, bringers meriting the same name as the form is one reason for them to have the appropriate immanent form in them.

Scholars often treat the bringers as merely resembling the forms, without having any specific relationship to them that explains why they resemble them.[23] But it seems much more likely that they resemble immanent forms precisely because they always have such forms in them. Immanent forms, in turn, closely resemble the forms themselves because they simply are what it is about something that makes it true that it has a share of a form.[24] The final argument is sometimes interpreted as quite similar to Anselm's ontological argument: it is in the very nature of the soul that it bring life, and so it cannot admit of death, just as for Anselm God is that than which nothing greater can be conceived, and so must exist.[25] According to this sort of interpretation, forms are not needed for the argument at all. Instead, it relies on something like a conceptual connection between the soul and life. Not only do such interpretations ignore the strong evidence that the bringers have forms in them, but when Socrates introduces the hypotheses that there are forms, he says that if you grant these to him, he will use them to show that the soul is immortal (100b). Then, at the end of the final argument Socrates says that to understand the argument as well as humanly possible, they should further analyze the hypotheses (107b).[26] The only hypotheses that Socrates has explicitly identified are that there are forms. He certainly seems to be saying that the argument relies on these hypotheses, which is why they should analyze them further. But if that is right, we should expect the bringers not only to resemble forms – his argument should somehow make use of their existence. My suggestion is that it does so because the bringers have the

---

[21] The repeated use of τήν followed by a genitive at 105a6–b2 is elliptical for τὴν τοῦ ... [X] ἰδέαν, as all translators recognize. It follows the explicit use of this construction at 104c1 (ἡ τοῦ ἀρτίου ἰδέα).

[22] *Pace* Kanayama 2000, 71–2. Kanayama denies this because fever is one of the bringers and so would be able to be called by the name "ill" and would have the form of illness in it. Perhaps Socrates should not have given fever as an example, or perhaps he has a way of making sense of why we should say that fever is ill. But the recently quoted 104b6–c4 passage is clear that this applies to every bringer. Another difficult case is how Socrates is thinking of unit as a bringer of odd. For a discussion of this, see Stone 2018, 55–69.

[23] E.g. Frede 1978, Sedley 2018.

[24] This is true only for the non-relational immanent forms, but Socrates never mentions a bringer of a relational immanent form (and, most importantly, life is a non-relational immanent form), so this complexity can be left aside.

[25] Explicitly in O'Brien 1967, 198, and O'Brien 1968, 104–6, and in a more circumscribed way in Gallop 1975, 200 and 217. See also Kelsey 2004, 31.

[26] For the plural "hypotheses," see Chapter 9, n. 60.

immanent forms in them, and the immanent forms depend for their existence on the forms themselves.

Bringers (1) do not admit one of a pair of opposites, and (2) have the form of the other opposite in them. But bringers also have one other crucial feature. It is controversial how to translate Socrates' first description of this feature – and indeed whether the text needs to be emended. I provide here Sedley and Long's translation and Strachan's text:

> "Now, Cebes," he said, "would they be the following: those that, whatever they occupy, compel it not only to have their own form in each case, but also, invariably, the form of some *opposite* of something as well?"
>
> Ἆρ' οὖν, ἔφη, ὦ Κέβης, τάδε εἴη ἄν, ἃ ὅτι ἂν κατάσχῃ μὴ μόνον ἀναγκάζει τὴν αὑτοῦ ἰδέαν αὐτὸ ἴσχειν, ἀλλὰ καὶ ἐναντίου αὖ τῳ ἀεί τινος; (104d1–3)

I think something like this translation must be right.[27] For understanding the final argument, the key point is that the bringers bring the form of an opposite to whatever they occupy.[28] This is confirmed by how Socrates expands on this principle later:

> Not only does the opposite not admit its opposite, but there is also the thing that brings some opposite to whatever it itself attacks, and this bringer itself never admits the opposite of what is brought. (105a2–5)

This description is what leads to my name "bringer." I chose this name to emphasize what is often minimized in accounts of them: they are not simply things that are always *f*; they also (3) bring *f*-ness to whatever they occupy. They have in them an immanent form and when they occupy something else, that thing, too, comes to have this immanent form in it.

Scholars sometimes claim that Socrates is simply saying that fire is "essentially hot" or the soul "essentially alive."[29] But he never uses such language, and this

---

[27] As Kanayama 2000, 68–9, argues at greater length. Some commentators, such as Rowe 1993 ad loc., prefer "those that, whatever occupies them, compel them not only..." But it is strange to think that there is a special class of entities that are compelled to take on opposites when something occupies them, and Socrates never suggests that this is true for fire, soul, or any other bringer, nor would it play any role in the argument. The more difficult question is how to understand the manuscripts' αὐτῷ. Burnet 1911 (engaging with an earlier debate) suggests it can be understood as [the opposite] "to something," but since Burnet the consensus has been that the text requires some sort of modification. Bluck 1955, Strachan (in Duke et al. 1995), and Sedley and Long 2010 follow Stallbaum's suggestion to replace it with αὖ τῳ, as printed here. This has the virtue that no letters need to be deleted from the manuscript – one simply changes their accentuation, spacing, and breathing marks, which would not have been in Plato's original. The other major option is simply to read τῳ (so Verdenius 1958, Rowe 1993).

[28] People sometimes wonder what snow occupies that leads things to be cold. Denyer 2007 notes that there is ancient evidence for using snow to cool drinks.

[29] O'Brien 1967 and 1968. See also Frede 1978, Sedley 1998, Frede 2011, whose very title is "Das Argument aus den essentiellen Eigenschaften (102a–107d)." Sedley 2009, 146–7, says that they are essentially hot, but also that they are "essential bearers" (147), which is closer to the text – though I wonder whether we should avoid the term "essential" entirely.

obscures the fact that Socrates is talking about something different, and in many ways more specific than an essential feature. A human, according to Aristotle, is essentially alive, but there is nothing that humans occupy such that that thing is then alive.[30] By contrast, Socrates emphasizes that he is talking about the sort of thing that both always has an immanent form in it and brings this immanent form to whatever it occupies. Downplaying this not only leads to misunderstanding the argument, but also makes it difficult to understand Socrates' strategy in responding to Cebes: he is showing why bringing life to the body does not affect the soul in the way Cebes suggests.

In the remainder of this section, I argue that a bringer is not what is responsible (*aition*) or the cause (*aitia*) of any explanandum.[31] Instead, the bringer brings a form, which is the only thing responsible; the only cause (*aitia*) is having a share of this form.[32] This is necessary for my account of Socrates' ultimate reason for thinking that forms cannot be ordinary, perceptible objects: no ordinary object could do the causal–explanatory work that forms do. Some bringers are ordinary objects, so if bringers were causes, then some ordinary, perceptible objects could do this causal–explanatory work. While this is important for my account of forms and ordinary objects, it is not necessary for my overall interpretation of the final argument. If one wishes to maintain that bringers and forms are each responsible (*aition*), then the way in which bringers would be responsible is by bringing, to whatever they occupy, the form of some opposite. On this alternative to my account, the soul, as a bringer, would still have a special relationship with a form, a special relationship in virtue of which it is responsible.

In the autobiography, Socrates repeatedly says that if something is *f* because of the form of *f*-ness, it is so because of nothing other than this form – for example, "what is smaller is smaller because of nothing other than smallness" (101a4–5; cf. 100c–d, 100e–101a, 101c).[33] He never rescinds these claims and he refers back to his hypotheses of forms after his discussion of bringers (107b).[34] As noted earlier, Vlastos famously called bringers "clever *aitiai*," and they are almost always referred to as "subtle" or "clever" causes.[35] But Socrates never says that a bringer is *aition* or an *aitia*, nor does he use causal language to describe what they do. He never says that they "make" (*poiein*)

---

[30] According to Socrates in the *Phaedo*, he is his soul, which simply happens to have human form but could be reincarnated into another animal's body; hence I take it that, according to the theory in the *Phaedo*, Socrates is not essentially human. But what about human – the thing that Socrates happens to be at the moment – is it essentially alive? Socrates does not talk this way, and I worry that such a view does not match the framework he develops here.

[31] For the difference between *aition* and *aitia*, see Section 9.1.

[32] Similarly (without the distinction between *aition* and *aitia*) Denyer 2007, 94–5, and Bailey 2014, 24–6.

[33] See Chapter 9, n. 60.

[34] Bostock 1986, 178, says that Socrates abandons this part of his view without Socrates drawing attention to doing so. My account does not attribute anything so misleading to Socrates.

[35] Vlastos 1969. This does not begin with Vlastos; Burnet 1911 too, for example, calls them causes in his note on 105c2.

things some way, or that things are some way because of them (*dia* with accusative), or "by" them (causal dative). Instead, he says that the bringers bring with them the form of some opposite, which is in them: fire has the form of heat in it; snow has the form of cold in it; and they bring heat and cold to other things.

There is a very tricky grammatical construction at the end of Socrates' discussion of bringers, which is often translated as if it were a causal dative. However, no commentator has defended reading it as a causal dative, commentators' grammatical explanations do not treat it as a causal dative, and Denyer and Bailey have both argued that it is not one.[36] I agree with them, although for my purposes all that is necessary is that it need not be a causal dative and that the broader context suggests that it is not one. Here is my translation of the first two occurrences of the tricky construction:

> For if you should ask me, what is such that, whatever it arises in, in the body, this thing will be hot, I will not give you that safe, ignorant answer, that it is heat, but rather a more ingenious one, based on what we now said, that it is fire. And if asked what is such that, whatever body it arises in, this body will be ill, I will not say that it is illness, but fever. (105b8–c4)[37]

---

[36] So Denyer 2007, 91–3, and Bailey 2014, 24–6. See next note.

[37] εἰ γὰρ ἔροιό με ᾧ ἂν τί ἐν τῷ σώματι ἐγγένηται θερμὸν ἔσται, οὐ τὴν ἀσφαλῆ σοι ἐρῶ ἀπόκρισιν ἐκείνην τὴν ἀμαθῆ, ὅτι ᾧ ἂν θερμότης, ἀλλὰ κομψοτέραν ἐκ τῶν νῦν, ὅτι ᾧ ἂν πῦρ· οὐδὲ ἂν ἔρῃ ᾧ ἂν σώματι τί ἐγγένηται νοσήσει, οὐκ ἐρῶ ὅτι ᾧ ἂν νόσος, ἀλλ' ᾧ ἂν πυρετός.

The interrogative (τί) is embedded within the relative clause (ᾧ ... ἐγγένηται). This construction cannot be translated directly into English, hence the "what is such that" at the beginning of the translation of each question. This translation takes the dative relative ᾧ to be governed by ἐγγένηται. Its antecedent is the omitted subject of the main verb, ἔσται. The ἐν τῷ in Socrates' initial question makes for a somewhat strange question and so Stephanus omits it, but there is no need to do so: Socrates is asking about something (fire) that arises in something else (e.g. the blood, or the brain), which in turn is in the body (so Burnet 1911 and Rowe 1993 ad loc.).

O'Brien 1967 translates it similarly and offers a reasonable explanation for what it means (223–4); and Gallop 1975, 237, in a note (n. 75), also gives a similar "literal translation" (cf. also 204), as does Rowe 1993 ad loc. But most translations (including Gallop 1975) read as if Socrates is saying that fire is that *by which* something is hot (for a list of such translations, see Denyer 2007, 93–4, n. 6). However, the Greek cannot literally mean this (so also Denyer 2007 and Bailey 2014). To think through how such a reading would need to work: note that there would be an omitted τούτῳ in the clause θερμὸν ἔσται, which refers back to the relative ᾧ. Such readings could take the ᾧ to be attracted to the dative, but need not. Second, note that "fire" is the answer to the question "what?" (τί;). Since the interrogative pronoun (τί) is in the same clause as the relative ᾧ, they must refer to different things. Hence, even if this sentence somehow were mentioning something "by which the body will be hot" (τούτῳ θερμὸν ἔσται), whatever this would not be fire, since fire is the referent of τί and this other thing would be the referent of ᾧ. For example, if we take τί as the subject of the ἐγγένηται and ᾧ as its object, ᾧ would be whatever fire arises in. But that does not identify fire as that by which something is hot; instead, whatever fire arises in would be that by which something is hot. Socrates does not want to say that the body is alive by whatever soul arises in. If we took the ᾧ to be a causal dative within the relative clause, then the body would be hot by whatever makes fire arise in the body. Again, this does not identify fire as that by which the body is hot. And Socrates does not want to say that the body is alive by whatever makes the soul arise in the body.

The question that bringers answer is not the original question that *aitiai* were said to answer. *Aitiai*, insofar as they are *aitiai*, answer the "because of what?" question (διὰ τί; e.g. 96a9). Bringers, instead, answer the question "what is such that, whatever it arises in, this thing will be *f*?" Socrates is saying that whatever fire is present in, that thing will be hot. It might be that without fire, something would not be hot. But Socrates is very careful in the autobiography to distinguish the thing that is *aition* from that without which it could never be *aition*. The presence of a bringer of *f* in something is a sufficient condition for that thing being *f*, but that alone does not qualify it as responsible (*aition*).

Since Socrates says that he can answer this question that bringers answer with "that safe, ignorant" answer and this originally was the answer to the "because of what?" question, he might seem to view these two questions as equivalent. Of course, in general one can provide the same answer to many different questions. But Socrates also says, in describing his method of hypothesis, that whatever hypothesis is put forward can be used to answer many different questions: his method involves setting down as true "whatever seems to me to harmonize with the hypothesis *both about cause (aitia) and about everything else*" (100a5–6, emphasis added). Socrates' initial hypothesis, that the form of the beautiful exists, harmonizes with the claim that it is because of this form that all beautiful things are beautiful. But this hypothesis will also harmonize with many other claims that have nothing to do with causes, allowing it to be used to answer other questions, such as the one asked here in the final argument.[38]

Given that Socrates never says that bringers do this causal work and given that he never takes back his claim that anything explained by a form is not explained by anything else, we should conclude that he does not think that a bringer does this causal work. But why not? According to his method of hypothesis, he should put forward whatever theory seems strongest and count as true about *aitia* and everything else whatever seems to harmonize with that theory (100a). He thinks that it harmonizes with his theory that, the *aitia* of x's being *f* is x having a share of *f*-ness. Identifying bringers as *aition* or an *aitia* would be a different theory from the one he has adopted and defended.

We can see why the form theory appeals to Socrates, both intuitively and theoretically. Intuitively, bringers are not what is truly responsible. Instead, bringers bring what's responsible: the immanent forms in them. A bringer is like the accomplice who brought the killer to the scene, rather than the murderer – the one genuinely responsible. If one wants the responsible thing proximate to

---

[38] I argued in the previous chapter (Section 9.8.2) that what makes an answer safe is that one can use this answer without needing to commit to its truth; one acts as if it is true in order to test the hypothesis. That applies equally well here: heat is a "safe" answer to this new question because one can provide it without needing to accept it as correct. What makes an answer "ignorant" is that it requires no substantive knowledge to make such a claim. That is also true for the claim that "whatever heat is present in, that thing will be hot."

the effect, that is the immanent heat in the bringer. If one wants the responsible thing described in full generality, that is the form of heat itself. Neither is the bringer. Furthermore, as discussed in Sections 6.3 and 9.7, ordinary objects are multiform, and so have parts and structural features that are entirely irrelevant to anything they might be responsible for. These parts and structural features make ordinary objects receptive of various opposites. Fire can be beautiful and ugly, equal and unequal, and so on. The relevant feature that fire possesses – heat – is what is responsible for something being hot, rather than fire as such. Any ordinary thing, being multiform – whether a bringer or not – will have many parts and structural features entirely irrelevant to being *f*.

To draw the account together: bringers have an immanent form in them that they bring to something else when they occupy that other thing; when they do so, that thing also comes to have this immanent form in it. The form inside that thing is responsible for its being characterized the same way as the bringer. Fire has heat in it, so when fire comes into iron, that iron becomes hot; strictly speaking, the fire is not responsible for its being hot; instead, the heat is responsible and fire has brought heat to the iron.

10.6 THE FINAL ARGUMENT PROPER: 105C–107A

With the account of bringers in place, Socrates can now explain why bringing life to the body does not destroy the soul, but rather is precisely what ensures that it is immortal and indestructible. Sedley has argued that the final argument should be understood as ending when Socrates reaches his conclusion that the soul is immortal, rather than when he reaches the further conclusion that it is indestructible. Sedley argues this partially on the grounds that Socrates has been asked to show immortality.[39] But Cebes asks Socrates to show that the soul is altogether immortal *and indestructible* (88b); Socrates repeats this request when restating Cebes' challenge (95b–c); he presents arguments for both immortality and imperishability (105c–107a), and he says (in what seems to be the conclusion): "more surely than anything, Cebes, soul is immortal and indestructible, and our souls really will exist in Hades" (106e8–7a1). As we will see, Socrates' argument focuses on immortality because he thinks that the other conclusions follow fairly directly from it, but nonetheless they are part of his main conclusion, not mere corollaries. Socrates' overall strategy is first to show that the soul is immortal, then that anything immortal is indestructible, and so the soul is indestructible, and finally that, as a bringer that is indestructible, the soul must flee somewhere else when death approaches. He takes it for granted that it flees to Hades. His conclusion both meets the cloakmaker objection's more stringent demand (immortal and indestructible) and addresses

---

[39] Sedley 2009, 146–53 and Sedley 2018. Similarly O'Brien 1968, 95.

Cebes' request to be shown that the soul exists *somewhere* after death (70a–b, repeated at 87e–88a), by arguing that it will exist in Hades.

Socrates provides a straightforward argument that the soul is immortal: the soul is a bringer of life; as a bringer of life, it cannot admit death; and if something cannot admit death, then it is immortal; thus the soul is immortal (105d–e). This argument relies on at least two features that Socrates identified in bringers: (1) they do not admit one member from a pair of opposites (in this case death), and (2) they bring the other member (life) to whatever they occupy. (2) is used to identify the soul as a bringer: it brings life to a body (105c). (1) is used to argue that the soul cannot admit death (105d–e).

What does it mean not to admit death? One might worry that a rock could, in some sense, be said not to admit death, and yet one would not want to say that it is immortal.[40] As we have seen, Socrates is committed, in general, to the following: (3) a bringer has in it the immanent form of an opposite, which it brings to whatever it occupies. The soul, unlike a rock, is a bringer of life; this means that it has the immanent form of life in it, and so is alive. Thus it does not admit death because of its special connection to life – unlike a rock. I suspect that in general when Socrates uses the expression "does not admit f" he always means that the thing in question has a feature on a scale that includes f and the opposite of f, so that if something did not admit large, it would need to be either equal or small.[41] But, whether or not this is true in general, Socrates is committed to bringers' always having in them what they bring, and so the soul itself must be alive and so is a living thing that does not admit death.

Dorothea Frede claims that it would be "blatant *petitio* simply to assume that the soul will always be alive."[42] But Socrates certainly is not assuming that the soul, so long as it exists, is alive; instead, Cebes agrees that there is a sort of things, bringers, that always have in them what they bring to something else, and he agrees that the soul is a bringer of life. In fact, it is Cebes, in his cloakmaker objection, who suggests for the first time in the dialogue that the soul is alive. He says that someone could reasonably maintain that "each soul wears out many bodies, especially if it *lives* for many years" (87d7–8, emphasis added). This word for living (βιοῦν) is typically used for the day-to-day activities of one's life rather than living in a biological sense. But in Socrates' reformulation, he switches to the term typically used in biological contexts

---

[40] This concern goes back to Strato (fr. 80 Sharples = Damascius I 438). Denyer 2007, 95, offers a solution similar to my own. So also Ogihara 2018, 199–200.

[41] The immanent form of an opposite does not admit what is opposed to it (102d–e). Thus, if this general claim about what "does not admit f" is correct, immanent forms would need to have a feature on a range that includes f and the opposite of f. While my reading of the final argument does not require this, Socrates does seem committed to the immanent form of f-ness being f (and so to so-called self-predication). He says that Simmias' largeness exceeds (ὑπερέχειν, that is, is larger than) Socrates' smallness (102c–d). If this holds of all immanent forms, then an immanent form of f-ness would be f and not admit the opposite of f.

[42] Frede 1978, 32.

(ζῆν, 95d3), attributing to Cebes the view that the soul suffers as it *lives*.[43] Cebes happily accepts this reformulation (95e). This latter term for "living" is the one used in the final argument (105c–d). All of this said, Socrates never provides an account of what life is, and so what this thing is that is possessed by animals and the soul. Instead, they both happily accept that the soul lives, and Socrates' account of bringers provides theoretical support for this. Socrates suggests at the end of the final argument that they should more fully analyze the hypotheses (107b); the existence of the form of life is the most obvious hypothesis to further analyze. Perhaps Socrates thinks that gaining clarity on what life is will make it clearer why they should accept the conclusion.

Sometimes Socrates is understood as saying that since the soul is a bringer of life, it cannot *be* dead. Then it is claimed that of course it cannot be dead, since after death the soul no longer exists and so has no properties.[44] But Socrates never discusses whether or not a soul can *be* dead; his argument turns on the claim that the soul cannot *admit* death. This is to say that it cannot undergo a process that results in its death. Whether it would exist, if it were dead, is irrelevant. Of course, most things that do not admit an opposite can still be destroyed. By contrast, as we will see, Socrates claims that anything that is immortal (and so cannot admit death) cannot be destroyed.

Socrates concludes that the soul is immortal at 105e, but he does not conclude that it is indestructible until 106e. The page-long gap between these conclusions might suggest that he does not view indestructibility as a straightforward consequence of immortality. But this is not what takes up most of the intervening discussion. Instead, while Socrates' next step seems innocuous, he devotes more time to it than to any other part of the final argument proper (105e–106c). The step is to clarify and then secure Cebes' agreement to the following conditional: if the immortal is indestructible, then, given that the soul is immortal, it too must be indestructible. Before articulating this at 106b, he has Cebes agree to three parallel conditionals (105e–106a), the first of which is: "if the un-even were necessarily indestructible, three would surely be indestructible, wouldn't it?" (105e11–106a1). He goes on to give similar counterfactual conditionals with un-hot and snow and un-cold and fire (106a). Only afterwards does he extend this to the case of the soul. But Socrates nonetheless anticipates an objection: what if someone were to say that when the odd perishes, the even takes its place (106b–c)? Socrates says that they could not respond in this case, because the un-even is not indestructible. However,

---

[43] See the Cambridge Greek Lexicon, s. vv. for this difference in how the terms are used, which is already seen in the Attic orators, including Isocrates. It is a tendency, rather than a strict difference in meaning. For a discussion of this distinction in the *Phaedo*, see Rowett 2021, 106–7. I discuss the importance of the soul's being alive for Plato's various immortality arguments in Ebrey 2022b.

[44] This is another objection that goes back to Strato (fr. 80 Sharples = Damascius I 431).

if the immortal is (unlike the un-even, the un-hot, and the un-cold) indestructible, then this conclusion would hold: that the soul is indestructible.

Why does Socrates articulate and clarify at such length this fairly straightforward conditional? First, doing so clarifies that, although Socrates has spent some time delineating the category of bringers, being indestructible does not apply to the soul insofar as it is a bringer. It applies to the soul as immortal, which most bringers are not. Moreover, Socrates' drawn out reasoning emphasizes that the next step of the argument is about the immortal in general, not about the soul as such. While he anticipates resistance to this conditional, I see no reason to suppose that he is hesitant about it himself. Indeed, this is perhaps the only part of the argument that has not come in for criticism: the conditional that, if the soul is immortal and the immortal is indestructible, then the soul is indestructible.

While contemporary commentators have had concerns about the claim that the immortal is indestructible, Cebes and Socrates treat it as clear, quickly agreeing to it. Socrates begins by saying to Cebes that they need to secure agreement to it[45]; at the end of this part of the argument Socrates says in his own voice: "So because the immortal is also indestructible, surely soul, if it is really immortal, would also be indestructible, wouldn't it?" (106e1–2). As noted earlier, Socrates concludes the argument thus: "more [surely] than anything (παντὸς μᾶλλον), the soul is immortal and indestructible" (106e8–107a1). This follows only if the immortal is indestructible, a claim that Socrates shows no reservations in accepting.

Cebes uses the idea that the immortal is eternal (ἀίδιον) to justify the idea that the immortal is indestructible (106d). He might be thinking that the immortal is indestructible *because* it is eternal. But more likely he thinks that being eternal is a sign that it must be indestructible – if anything, it is eternal because it is indestructible, not vice versa. The reason Cebes thinks that it is especially clear that the immortal is eternal is likely that the gods are a paradigmatic case of something immortal and they are said to exist forever.[46] Socrates highlights this connection between the immortal and the gods when he says: "the god... and the form of life itself, and any other immortal thing there may be, it would be agreed by everyone

---

[45] Both Gallop 1975 and Sedley and Long 2010 translate εἰ... ἡμῖν ὁμολογεῖται at 106c9–10 as "if we secure agreement," but at 72a4 they translate this phrase as "if we agree." I suspect that "if we agree" is also correct for 106c9–10, in which case Socrates' question presupposes that he already accepts it.

[46] In Homer the gods are described as "being always" (αἰὲν ἐόντες, e.g. *Iliad* 1.290, 1.494, 21.518, 24.99) rather than "eternal" (ἀίδιον – see discussion in Long 2019, ch. 1) – at least in part for metrical reasons. In general, "eternal" is applied to divine things, although Thucydides applies it to things that are not divine. Empedocles (B115) and Philolaus (B6) use "eternal" when contrasting the divine with the mortal or human. Diogenes of Apollonia is the only prior extant author to closely link "eternal" and "immortal" (B7 and B8). Interestingly, in B7, Diogenes describes air as "eternal and immortal body," whereas, of course, Socrates is arguing that the *soul* is eternal and immortal. In B8, Diogenes describes air as "great and strong and eternal and immortal and much-knowing" – features, of course, traditionally attributed to the gods.

that they never perish" (106d5–7). The fact that we view the god as never perishing is a sign that in general the immortal is indestructible.

Why does Socrates emphasize that *everyone would agree* that anything immortal will not perish? He may simply be thinking that people would in fact agree to this, whether rightly or wrongly. But it seems more likely that he sees this as something like a conceptual truth, which is why he takes it as clear and thinks that everyone would agree to it. Frede suggests – rightly, I think – that Socrates is implicitly relying on the idea that for a living thing to perish is the same as for it to admit death.[47] As Frede memorably puts it, "whatever way a living being passes out of existence we call that its death, be it a 'natural' one or, e.g., traceless elimination through an atomic bomb. So it is quite inconceivable that to the question 'When did N.N. die?' one would receive the answer, 'He did not die, he simply went out of existence.'"[48] As I understand it, Frede's idea is that for a living thing the process of going out of existence is the same as the process of dying; hence, if a living thing cannot go through the process of dying, it cannot go out of existence.[49]

According to this interpretation, it is the fact that the immortal cannot admit death that underwrites the claim that it is indestructible. I myself find this a plausible idea: that, for living things, going out of existence is simply the same as dying, and so, if a living thing cannot admit death, then it cannot cease to exist. Of course, someone could question this idea, but it strikes me as one of the most plausible ideas in the argument. If one is on the hunt for a premise to doubt, I would be much more inclined to doubt that there is this group of things, bringers, that do not admit the opposite of what they bring, and so to doubt the possibility that the soul is a bringer.

At least since Strato of Lampsacus (the second successor to Aristotle at the Lyceum), the *Phaedo*'s final argument is often thought to rely on some sort of logical fallacy.[50] This seems especially likely if one thinks of the argument as entirely based on "conceptual" connections, somehow similar to Anselm's ontological argument. Instead, it rests on the existence of forms and on a substantive theory of bringers. In my view, there is no logical fallacy in the argument. Once it is admitted that bringers exist and have the features that he describes, and it is admitted that the soul is a bringer, one should grant the conclusion. But Socrates does not think that one should easily grant the premises to him. He says that they should consider the hypotheses more clearly before accepting the conclusion, even if they find them trustworthy (107b).

It seems to me that we should see Socrates as clarifying what he means by "immortal" by connecting it to not admitting death and thereby to being

---

[47] Frede 1978, 31–2; Denyer 2007, 95, agrees. So does Sedley 2009, but he does not think that this is properly part of the argument but rather a "corollary" to it.
[48] Frede 1978, 32.
[49] So also e.g. Sedley 2009, 211. If this idea underwrites the claim that "everything immortal is indestructible," then it relies on everything immortal itself being alive.
[50] Strato, fr. 80 Sharples = Damascius I 431–42.

indestructible. As Alex Long has recently discussed, before Plato the gods are the primary things identified as immortal – Homer often refers to them simply as "the immortals."[51] Moreover, before Plato, not everything called "immortal" was treated as lasting forever. For example, in the Homeric *Hymn to Hermes* cattle belonging to Apollo are called immortal (71) and then later killed and cooked (115–29, 405); these cattle belong to a god, but are not themselves deathless. One might expect philosophers to use "immortal" only for something truly deathless, but Empedocles says that he is now immortal, no longer mortal (B112), and that earlier he was a god who then became mortal (B115) when he was exiled from the gods.[52] Socrates' argument clarifies that in calling the soul "immortal," he is saying that it cannot ever admit death – unlike Apollo's cattle or Empedocles' description of himself.[53]

The final step of the argument is that the soul departs to Hades when death comes to a human (106e). Socrates paved the way for this step when he said that the forms in us can either flee or perish (102d–e). He also noted, when providing his analogous conditionals, that if the un-cold were indestructible, then when cold came to fire, the fire would depart intact (106a). In Socrates' final step, he notes that the same applies for the soul: since the soul is indestructible, when death comes, it must retreat. Socrates does not defend here the claim that it departs to Hades. I take him not to think that this is the controversial part of his view. Already at the beginning of the cyclical argument Cebes happily accepted that if the soul exists after death, it goes to Hades (70c–d).

10.7 THE SOUL AND THE DIVINE AS IMMORTAL

Let us turn to how the final argument fills in the kinship argument's account of the soul (which was discussed in Section 6.4). In arguing that the soul is immortal, Socrates identifies a respect in which its nature is the same as that of the unseen divine, thereby filling in his claim that it is akin to the divine. The most prominently identified members of the unseen are the forms (78c–d), and Socrates claims in many dialogues that the forms themselves are divine (e.g. *Symposium* 211e–212a, *Republic* 500c–d, 611d–612a, *Phaedrus* 249c–d).[54] Nonetheless, it is strange to think of the forms as immortal, and so one might be tempted to think that only the gods, not the forms, are described as immortal in the kinship argument. I will argue that the forms are indeed described as immortal in the kinship argument, and so Socrates is saying that the soul has a characteristic feature of not only the gods, but also of the forms – that is, of the entire divine. Although there is strong evidence that the forms

---

[51] See Long 2019, ch. 1, as well as Ebrey 2022b.
[52] See also the particularly enigmatic Heraclitus B62.
[53] Similarly, in the *Symposium* at 202d–e Socrates says that there is something between mortal and immortal, which means that not everything non-mortal is immortal. The final argument needs a notion of immortality that cuts off that possibility as well.
[54] For a general discussion, see Nightingale 2021, 8–33 and 49–55.

are immortal in the *Phaedo*, I understand the resistance one might feel to this idea. My central claim is that Socrates, in arguing that the soul is immortal, is further clarifying how it is akin to the divine. One could accept this even while denying that the forms are immortal.

Let me begin with the basic evidence that the forms are immortal in the kinship argument. Socrates describes the unseen as immortal (79d, 80b). It is crucial for this argument that the members of the unseen possess all of the features ascribed to it: if the features only applied to some members, the fact that the soul is similar and akin to the unseen would provide very little reason to expect it to be unable to disintegrate, since this would not even necessarily apply to all members of the unseen. Moreover, Socrates first describes the unseen as immortal when identifying it as the object of inquiry, a context where forms are clearly included among "the unseen." In describing what the soul grasps when inquiring itself through itself (αὐτὴ καθ' αὐτήν), Socrates refers to the unseen as "that which is pure, always is, immortal, and holds in the same way" (τὸ καθαρόν τε καὶ ἀεὶ ὂν καὶ ἀθάνατον καὶ ὡσαύτως ἔχον, 79d1–2). This is the first time Socrates uses the word "immortal" in the dialogue. He had already described the forms as pure in the defense speech (66a, 67a–b). And earlier in the kinship argument he had described each form as uniform (μονοειδής, 78d5), a term that he associates with purity in the *Symposium* (211e) and *Republic* (611b–612a). Socrates does not argue that the unseen is immortal, but we can see why it would seem appropriate, since the members of this unseen are pure and they always are. It is only after Socrates describes the unseen as immortal that he calls the unseen "the divine" (80a3). If anything, it is the fact that the unseen is immortal that justifies thinking that it is divine, rather than vice versa.

Socrates is not holding fixed a traditional notion of the divine, but rather expanding it and then arguing that the soul has one feature of the divine: immortality. Santas has given the name "ideal attributes" to the characteristic features that all forms possess.[55] I am suggesting that the final argument shows that the soul has one of the ideal attributes of the forms: immortality. Note that, in the *Sophist*, Plato seems to argue that the forms themselves are alive (248e–249a).[56] Since the *Phaedo* does not provide an account of what life is, it is difficult to know whether he would think that the forms are alive, but if so, they may also be immortal because they are alive and do not admit death.

If all forms are immortal, why does Socrates specifically mention the form of life as immortal (106d)? First, it is the relevant form for the argument: the soul always has a share of this form and brings a share of it to whatever body it occupies. But the form of life also has a special connection to being immortal that the other forms do not have. In general, in the *Phaedo*, Socrates seems committed to what is typically called "self-predication": the form of *f*-ness is itself *f*. As discussed in Subsection

---

[55] Santas 1980.
[56] For a discussion, see Irani 2021.

5.5.2, Socrates generally seems to think there is a difference between the way that the form of *f*-ness is *f* and the way in which other things are *f*. He does not explore in the *Phaedo* how this works, but it is explored in the *Republic*, *Sophist*, and other later dialogues. All forms are good, but the form of the good has a special relation to being good. All forms partake of sameness, but the form of sameness has a special relation to being the same. Similarly, I am suggesting that all forms are immortal, but that the form of life has a special relation to being immortal, since it is alive and so unable to admit death simply by being what life is. The soul, in turn, has a special connection to this form and thereby has a characteristic feature of the divine.

10.8 CONCLUSION

Let me pull together the arc from Cebes' challenge to the final argument. This challenge (69e–70b) asks Socrates to address the fear that the soul is destroyed upon death, to provide some reassurance and conviction, and to show that the soul exists somewhere after the human has died. Socrates addresses this fear in the kinship argument (77d–80b) by identifying three features of the soul that are supposed to show that its nature is related to the unseen, a group that includes the forms and the gods. The members of the unseen are immortal. Socrates argues that, given the soul's kinship with the unseen, one should not fear that it will be dispersed, because its nature makes it unable to disintegrate, or at least close to unable to do so. Cebes' cloakmaker objection (86e–88b) provides a model of the soul that would allow it to have each of the features mentioned in the kinship argument and yet nonetheless be destroyed by the body as it provides life to it. In this objection, Cebes repeats that Socrates should show that the soul exists somewhere after death and, after he concedes that the soul may be reborn many times, makes a new demand: that Socrates should show that the soul is altogether immortal and indestructible – that it entirely possesses these characteristics of the unseen. When Socrates recalls Cebes' objection (95b–e), he starts with this new demand and then identifies Cebes' central challenge as the idea that the soul is ultimately destroyed by its connection to the body. Socrates says that he will closely engage with this objection and that Cebes will be able to use his response to address his concerns. Socrates does this by showing why bringing life to the body does not lead to the soul's destruction; on the contrary, being a bringer of life means that the soul must not admit death, and so must be immortal and indestructible. To argue for this, Socrates provides an account of bringers and the immanent forms that they bring. The soul, as a bringer of life, has a specific relationship to the form of life that guarantees its immortality and so indestructibility. It completely possesses these characteristic features of the divine. Since it cannot be destroyed, it must exist somewhere after death – namely in Hades.

I do not wish to suggest that the final argument exhausts the ways in which the soul is related to the divine. If that were so, we could dispense with the kinship argument once we have the final argument. However, only the kinship argument argues for a broad flexibility in the nature of the soul, which allows it to be more or less form-like. Socrates uses this flexibility in the return to the defense to provide underlying explanations for the ethical claims he made in the defense speech. Although this flexibility is crucial for explaining Socrates' ethical claims, it is precisely this that makes the argument easier to object to in its narrower aim of establishing the soul's continued existence. The final argument provides a tighter argument for this narrower conclusion by focusing on how the soul's status as a bringer of life makes it, in one respect, exactly like the forms. Across many dialogues Plato puts forward the view that there is something divine about every soul (e.g. *Republic* 518e, *Timaeus* 90a) while at the same time maintaining that souls can become more divine (e.g. *Republic* 500c–d, *Phaedrus* 249c–d). The kinship argument identifies two ways in which the nature of the soul allows it to aspire to greater divinity: through inquiry and ruling. The final argument identifies one way in which the nature of every soul is completely divine.

11

The Cosmos and the Afterlife

107c–115a

After the final argument, Socrates describes the differing afterlives of good and bad souls, thereby filling out his claim in the defense speech that good souls fare better than bad ones after death (63b–c).[1] One of the most striking features of this eschatological account is how fully it is integrated into an account of the cosmos. Before the *Phaedo*, eschatological views were sometimes connected to cosmological views, but, as Betegh has noted, no thinker before Plato integrates them so closely.[2] For example, Philolaus, as a Pythagorean, supposedly accepted at least some Pythagorean eschatological beliefs,[3] but there is no evidence that this played a prominent role in his astronomical and cosmological theory.[4]

I provide here a new interpretation of the *Phaedo*'s cosmology, arguing that it draws on and reflects the account of forms and ordinary objects that Socrates presented earlier in the *Phaedo*. The result is a distinctly Platonic account of the cosmos and the afterlife, one that treats the best parts of the cosmos as form-like and the worst parts as the source of flux. In our current embodiment, we live between these two extremes; how we live now determines whether after death we will live in a more form-like or flux-like area; this dwelling, in turn, determines how good or bad our afterlife will be. Since a groundbreaking article by Sedley, the *Phaedo*'s cosmology has typically been seen as at least hinting at a teleological account of the cosmos – the sort that (according to Sedley) Socrates had hoped to find from Anaxagoras.[5] I agree that Socrates is here drawing on his autobiography – including his discussion of Anaxagoras – and that he provides a cosmological account that fits

---

[1] Noted by Karfik 2004, 36.
[2] Betegh 2022.
[3] To what extent is a matter of considerable dispute. See Huffman 1993, 9–12.
[4] I discuss a possible minor role in Section 11.5.2.
[5] Sedley 1990.

with Platonic principles. But I argue that he is not hinting at cosmic teleology.[6] Instead, there are parts of cosmos that are bad and harm the souls that are there, making them worse off; Socrates provides no reason to think that these parts of the cosmos serve any good function. I argue that, since Socrates does not suggest in this cosmology that *nous* or some god is responsible for the cosmos, he avoids needing to explain why the cosmos has these bad things. Similarly, Socrates' account of how souls are harmed in the afterlife does not depend on a decision by some divine judge, but rather this harm is a direct result of these souls' bad character.

Socrates' account not only draws on his autobiography and his theory of forms and ordinary objects, but also on practically every other part of the dialogue, from the opening – which sets up a story about the heroes, gods, and the underworld – through the defense speech, cyclical argument, kinship argument, return to the defense, discussion of misology, and final argument. The return to the defense is of particular importance in his explanation of how souls are benefited and harmed in the afterlife.

In the secondary literature, this section of the dialogue is universally called "the myth," which has led to treating the entirety of Socrates' account as having the same epistemic status. However, Socrates says that he is convinced of some of his claims, and others he says it would be foolish to insist upon, giving different parts very different epistemic statuses. More specifically, Socrates carefully structures his view by: first, stating his central claim about the afterlife (107c–d); second, outlining an account of the journey after death, which he treats as a received view (107d–108a); third, interpreting this received view in light of claims he argued for earlier in the return to the defense (108a–c); fourth, presenting an independent set of claims that he has been convinced of, about the overall structure of the cosmos (108d–110a); fifth and finally, presenting what he calls a *"muthos,"* which is about the surface of the true earth and the underworld (110a–114d). This *muthos* fills in his cosmological picture while explaining how the different environments affect souls' happiness in the afterlife. This is what he says would be foolish to insist upon. The *muthos* takes up more than half of Socrates' account, but it is important to think carefully about how the earlier stages develop the framework within which it operates.

11.1 THE FIRST STAGE – SOCRATES' BASIC COMMITMENT: 107C–D

Socrates' account is introduced with a strong set of claims about the afterlife:

> As it is, however, since the soul is evidently immortal, it could have no means of safety or of escaping evils, other than becoming both as good and as wise as possible. For the soul comes to Hades with nothing other than its education and

---

[6] In Section 9.4 I argued that we should not see Socrates as expecting teleology from Anaxagoras.

nurture, which are said to very greatly benefit or harm one who has died, as soon as his journey there starts. (107c8–d5)[7]

Socrates' recollecting and kinship arguments, along with the return to the defense, provide reasons to expect the soul to retain some wisdom in the afterlife. But they provide no reason to think that the soul has *no means* of safety or escaping evils other than becoming as good and wise as possible, so that nothing other than its education and nurture (τροφή) could benefit or harm it. For example, this means that proper burial provides no safety on one's journey, contrary to traditional religious beliefs.[8] Moreover, it means that Orphic practices of the sort preserved in the gold tablets – or any other religious practices that were supposed to help ensure a good journey to the underworld – can help only to the extent that they effect a soul's education and way of life.[9] This claim about what can affect our afterlife structures the rest of Socrates' account.

Note that Socrates' claim here is about harm, not punishment. Socrates famously argues in the *Gorgias* that appropriate punishment is beneficial (see esp. 477e–481b). By contrast, to harm something is to make it worse. The first stage does not set up a discussion of punishment, but rather of how the soul's condition can harm it after death. As we will see, the gods have some role in benefiting good people, but not in harming them – as one would expect, since Socrates thinks that the gods are only beneficial, never harmful.

11.2 THE SECOND STAGE – THE BARE OUTLINE OF THE JOURNEY: 107D–108A

Socrates next describes the journey to and from the underworld in a strikingly generic way. He does not explicitly endorse this description, and he later modifies some of its steps; nonetheless, it provides a framework for his subsequent claims. We can break it into five steps:

> It is said that, when each person has met his end, [1] the spirit (*daimōn*) of each, to whom he was allotted when alive, undertakes to bring him to a certain place, [2] where the assembled individuals are judged [3] and then must travel to Hades with that guide who has been appointed to take them on their journey there. Once there, [4] the things happen to them that are to happen to them, and they stay for as long as they must, and then [5] another guide escorts them back here again, after many long cycles of time. (107d5–e4)

---

[7] In the other chapters my translations are based on Sedley and Long 2010. In this chapter I have frequently found it necessary to make more significant modifications, sometimes drawing on Gallop 1975 to do so.
[8] For a discussion of how the *Phaedo* fits into this tradition, see Edmonds 2004. Section 12.1 discusses Socrates' attitude toward his own burial.
[9] See Betegh 2022 for how Plato develops and reinterprets Pythagorean and Orphic concerns about retaining one's memory in the afterlife.

Socrates fills in and modifies steps [1]–[3] in the next stage, drawing on the return to the defense to do so. Socrates' *muthos* (stage five) fills in and modifies step [4]. There is no further mention of [5] and it turns out not to apply to some souls, since some never return here – either because of their extreme goodness or badness.

We should probably not understand Socrates' claim that this "is said" as a report that any single person said anything at this high level of generality – at least, we know of no such account. Instead, Plato seems to be abstracting from different accounts, coming up with a general framework. Since this account involves reincarnation, it is not a generic account that fits with all Greek religious views. Similarly, some sort of justice in the afterlife is suggested by the idea that the people will be judged and then guided to where they receive what they must. The idea of justice in the afterlife certainly has pre-Platonic precedent (see esp. Pindar's second *Olympian Ode*, 58–60, Aeschylus' *Suppliants* 226–32, *Eumenides* 267–75), but is not part of all accounts of the afterlife.[10] Plato is selecting and arranging parts of the tradition to provide a framework that he will work within and further modify.

Socrates first uses this framework to criticize Aeschylus' Telephus, who is reported as saying that "a simple 'path' leads to Hades" (108a1).[11] Socrates says that, if this were true, there would be no need for guides; instead, sacrifices and customs suggest that the path has many divisions and forks (108a). This might seem like a trivial point on which to criticize Aeschylus, but it is important to his overall account. Socrates needs the path not to be straightforward or simple to explain why souls are benefited or harmed *as soon as* the journey begins (as claimed in the first stage). It will turn out, in the next stage, that how souls interact with their guides explains how their education and nurture benefit or harm them on the journey, as well as why they arrive at different destinations.

In rejecting Aeschylus' account, Socrates marks his own as different from the sort found in a tragedy.[12] Socrates begins his eschatological accounts in the *Gorgias* (523a) and *Republic* (614b) with references to Homer. By contrasting the *Phaedo*'s account with Aeschylus', Plato yet again makes clear that the *Phaedo* is providing an alternative to tragedy (as argued in Chapter 2). Socrates' eschatology reflects a very different theology and set of values than is typical in tragedy. I argued in Section 2.3 that the *Phaedo* itself belongs to the category of story that is about heroes, gods, daemons, and the underworld, as described in *Republic* II–III. While such a story does not require the presence of daemons and the underworld, it fits naturally, since the *Phaedo* is the story of a hero facing his death. Socrates shows how to properly represent the underworld, daemons, and the soul's journey after death.

---

[10] See Edmonds 2004, 207–11; Svavarsson 2020.
[11] This is typically taken to be from Aeschylus' *Telephus*, but Telephus was also the main character in the *Mysians* and I have not seen any reason to attribute it to one play rather than the other.
[12] Edmonds 2004 discusses journeys to the underworld in comedy, tragedy, and the *Phaedo*.

11.3 THE THIRD STAGE – THE JOURNEY IN LIGHT OF EARLIER COMMITMENTS: 108A–C

This stage uses the idea that souls have different levels of purity (from the defense and return to the defense) to explain why souls are benefited or harmed on their journeys. Good souls are benefited because they are wise enough to know what is good for them and gods will interact with them, since they have pure souls. Bad souls are harmed by their ignorance and impurity.

Socrates begins:

> Now the composed and wise soul follows and is not unaware of what is going on around it. But the soul that is desirous of the body, as I said before [81c–e], is in a flutter for a long time about the body and about the visible region, resists much and suffers much, and is led away by the appointed spirit (*daimōn*) only by force and with difficulty. On arrival at the place where the other souls are... (108a6–b4)

Socrates describes here step [1] of the journey described in the previous stage: in this step, each daemon takes the soul to a place where (in step [2]) each soul is judged.[13] The daemon involved in step [1] is different from the guide who in step [3] takes souls from this place of judgment to their dwelling place. As we will see, in Socrates' fuller account of step [3], pure souls receive gods (not daemons) as guides to their dwelling places and the most unjust souls receive no guide at all. By contrast, every soul is initially guided by its daemon to where souls are judged. Socrates relies in the passage just quoted on his earlier contrast between wise souls and those desirous of the body (e.g. 64d, 68b–c, 80e–81b, 82b–c). The existence of a daemon, set up in the previous stage, allows Socrates to distinguish souls by how they treat their daemon. This is one way the soul's education and nurture benefit it from the very beginning of the journey: the wise soul follows what is superior, whereas the soul desirous of the body resists, bringing about its own suffering.

In the next step of the journey, the bad soul again is responsible for its own suffering. According to step [2] (from the second stage), the souls are judged before they go to Hades. The word I (following Gallop and others) translate as "is judged" (διαδικασαμένους) is translated by Sedley and Long as "is presented in court." However, there are no judges mentioned here, unlike the *Gorgias* and the *Republic*, where divine judges play a crucial role in the eschatology.[14] Instead, in the *Phaedo* the condition of one's soul seems to be directly judged by *everyone* where souls are assembled, and this collective judgment determines who (if anyone) guides the soul to its destination. The impure soul of a murderer or some such person is

---

[13] Sedley and Long's translation says that the wise and composed soul follows "its guide." No guide is mentioned in the Greek; it is not the guide (assigned in step [3]) but rather the daemon (step [1]) that is followed.

[14] I discuss the jurors involved in the underworld punishment in Section 11.5.3, arguing that they are not divine.

"shunned by everyone else: everyone turns away from it, and is unwilling to become either its companion or its guide. The soul wanders alone, in the grip of every deprivation, until certain lengths of time have elapsed, and, when they have gone by, it is by necessity borne into the dwelling suitable for it" (108b7–c2). The collective shunning by everyone – rather than the decision of a few judges – seals these souls' fate. This harm is not actively inflected upon them, but rather is the result of no one's helping them. Contrary to step [3] (in stage two), these souls receive no guide; instead, necessity brings these souls to their dwelling place. Similarly, in the return to the defense Socrates says that the souls of the bad, "necessarily wander around these places [tombs and monuments], paying a penalty [literally: paying justice] for their former way of life, wicked as it was" (81d7–9). The impurity of their souls keeps them around the visible region (81b–d), so that they necessarily pay the penalty, without the need for a judge or other external agent to impose it on them.[15]

In contrast to the way in which murders are shunned, Socrates says that those who pass through life purely and decently meet gods as companions and guides alike, and then dwell in regions appropriate to them (108c). The gods help pure souls, but there is no mention of their harming impure souls. In Subsection 11.5.3 I return to role of the gods in this overall cosmological account. For now, the important thing is that Socrates has set up a central feature of his *muthos* (stage five): there are different regions for souls with different levels of purity.

11.4 THE FOURTH STAGE – CONVICTIONS ABOUT COSMOLOGY: 108D–110A

Socrates describes here the structure of the cosmos and our current place within it, providing the framework for his subsequent discussion of the surface of the earth itself and of the underworld – the two main places where souls dwell after death (the fifth stage). His claims in this stage do not rely on claims from the previous stages, whereas the fifth and final stage draws on all of the previous stages. Socrates reports in the fourth stage that someone (unnamed) has convinced him of two things. The first has to do with the earth not needing support if it has a certain size and location; the second with our dwelling in a hollow in the earth, not on the surface of the earth itself. The second conviction provides the framework for the *Phaedo*'s cosmology, in which the heavens are form-like, whereas the place where we live is influenced by flux that comes up from below.

Interpreters do not normally draw attention to Socrates' claim that he is *convinced* of these claims. It is easy to see why they would rather not, given how unbelievable Socrates' cosmological account is. However, Socrates and Simmias repeat several times that Socrates is convinced of them (108c, 108d, twice in 108e, 109a).

---

[15] For a similar idea, see Reed 2021, 65–67.

11.4 The Fourth Stage – Convictions about Cosmology: 108d–110a

Conviction (πίστις) has been a crucial theme throughout the dialogue: for example, Cebes is difficult to convince (63a), Cebes wishes to be convinced that the soul exists after death (70b), and misology arises from repeatedly being convinced that something is true and then shortly thereafter changing one's mind (90b; cf. Sections 4.1 and 8.2). Socrates does not treat conviction lightly, and so we should take him seriously when he repeatedly emphasizes that he has been convinced.

Socrates says that he will describe his conviction, but that showing that these things "are true seems to me to be too difficult for Glaucus' skill.[16] For one thing, I might not even be able to do so myself, and for another, even if I did have the knowledge, I think that the life left to me, Simmias, isn't enough for the length of the discussion" (108d5–9). Socrates says that he *might* not be able to do so himself and, moreover, that there is not enough time. He does not say that in principle no one could provide adequate arguments for such claims. By contrast, at the end of the stage that he calls a *muthos* (110a–114d), which is about the surface of the earth and the underworld, he says: "now it does not befit a man of intelligence (*nous*) to insist that these things are as I have described them. However, since the soul is evidently immortal, I think that for someone who believes this to be so it is both fitting and worth the risk – for fair is the risk – to insist that either what I have said or something like it is true concerning our souls and their dwelling places" (114d1–6). The things Socrates is convinced of *he* might not be able to show are true, whereas *no one* should insist that these things in the *muthos* are as he described them. Instead, it is worth taking the risk of insisting that it "or something like it" is true. Furthermore, what is worth taking a risk about concerns "our souls and their dwelling places." The *muthos* is where he discusses this; stage four does not mention souls at all or their dwelling places after death. I discuss in Subsection 11.5.4 why Socrates calls this section a "*muthos*." My argument here has nothing to do with meaning of "*muthos*"; I am simply saying that how he describes his conviction and how he describes the part he calls a "*muthos*" make clear that they have very different epistemic statuses.

Let us turn to Socrates' first conviction:

> I've been convinced, first, that if the earth is round and in the middle of the heaven, it has no need of air or of any other such necessity to stop it falling, but the uniformity of the heaven on every side and the equilibrium of the earth itself are enough to hold it in place. For if a thing in equilibrium is put in the middle of something uniform, it will not be able to lean more or less in any direction, but in its uniform state it will stay in place without leaning. (108e4–109a6)

Sedley and Furley have pointed out that Socrates is implicitly referring back to his autobiography, where he said that, because most people confuse the thing responsible (*to aition*) for that without which it could not be responsible (*aition*), one individual puts a vortex around the earth and thus makes it kept stationary by the

---

[16] For the expression "Glaucus' skill," see Clay 1985.

heavens, whereas another props it up with air (99b, discussed in Section 9.5).[17] While the passage quoted here is often taken to show that Socrates thinks the earth is spherical and in the center,[18] he only says that he is convinced of a conditional: "*if* the earth is round and in the middle..." Sometimes one can assert a conditional as a way of asserting its consequent, while highlighting the premise that it relies on. But the reasons Socrates offers in the second sentence strongly support the conditional, while providing no support for the claim that the earth is round and in the middle of the heaven. Only *if* it is round and in the middle will there be uniformity of the heaven on every side. Nonetheless, Sedley says that this is an argument for the earth's spherical shape and position in the center. He says that otherwise Socrates would not be providing a teleological explanation here.[19] He seems to take the reference back to the autobiography to indicate that we should expect such an explanation.[20]

Let me suggest instead that Socrates is saying that the whole enterprise of searching for what holds up the earth, as described in the autobiography, is potentially misguided, since if it is round and in the middle, it does not require anything further to hold it up. Thus these theories do not merely consider the wrong sort of answer, they do not even begin with the right questions. When Socrates describes Anaxagoras' proposal, he draws attention to how the questions come in a certain order. First, he expected Anaxagoras to tell him "whether the earth was flat or round" (97e); then "if he said that it [the earth] was in the center, he would also explain, I thought, that it was better that it should be in the center" (97e–98a). Socrates' conditional shows how, if someone began with these questions, they might never need to investigate what is holding up the earth. Of course, whether the earth is in the center and whether it is spherical might be answered using a teleological theory, but Socrates is not answering those questions here. He is simply saying that if one answered those questions first, there might be no need to find something else to hold the earth in place.

---

[17] Furley 1989, ch. 2, and Sedley 1990. Furley argues that Socrates here draws on Parmenides' description of what is.
[18] e.g. Furley 1989, ch. 2, Sedley 1990, and Karfik 2004.
[19] Sedley 1990, 364.
[20] Sedley further argues that Socrates must be thinking that the earth is spherical, since before this he says that "there is nothing to stop me from saying what sort of form (*idea*) I've been convinced the earth has and describing its regions" (108d9–e2) (Sedley 1990, 365). Sedley interprets "form" here as shape and says that Socrates has promised to say what the shape of the earth is and this is the only place where he might be doing so. But earlier Socrates says he will describe the regions and *nature* of the earth (108c). Perhaps "form" (*idea*) here is used in the sense of nature – the earth's nature is to have many hollows, one of which we live within. In the final argument – directly before this eschatological account – Socrates frequently uses "*idea*" for the immanent forms that can retreat or perish as we change. "*Idea*" does not have such a specific meaning here, but it is worth noting that recently it did not mean mere shape. Alternatively, if "*idea*" does mean shape here, it could simply refer to its having hollows; it need not refer to its overall shape.

11.4 The Fourth Stage – Convictions about Cosmology: 108d–110a

Socrates' considerations in favor of this conditional are abstract and carefully reasoned. Whoever convinced Socrates of these things can engage in such reasoning. This gives this person strong credentials before Socrates introduces his other conviction.

The other conviction is a broad account of our place in the cosmos (109a–110a). The basic claim is that we are living in hollows, unable to see the surface of the true earth. As the sea is to us, so we are to the surface of the true earth. In particular, as things are more decrepit – impure and uglier – in the sea than on land, so things here are more impure and uglier than there. We are deeply misled about the nature of the earth because we think that our position grants us knowledge of how things are, instead of recognizing that it is distorted and myopic. We can see why Socrates would find appealing the idea that we are not recognizing our own ignorance. It is fruitful to compare with the cave in *Republic* VII (514a–517c). Even within the cave – which corresponds to the sensible world – there are things that most people have no inkling of. When the cave dweller turns around and sees the statues and the great fire, he or she is not yet aware of the forms, but still has come to better understand the world. Similarly, most people have no inkling of the surface of the true earth. To comprehend it is not to comprehend the forms, but, as with the statues and the great fire, it brings us one step closer to them.

In the autobiography, Socrates complains that Anaxagoras "assigns responsibility to air, aether, water, and the like, as well as many other absurdities" (98c1–2). They have a place in this account of the cosmos: aether is the pure element in which the celestial bodies are located, and air and water are sediments of aether (109b–c, discussed later in this section). He does not identify any of them as responsible (*aition*) or as that without which the responsible thing could never be responsible – he does not mention *aitia* or *aition* at all in this fourth stage of his account, nor does he use causal language here. Again, Socrates avoids Anaxagoras' mistake; I see no evidence that he is positively providing the sort of causes he had hoped Anaxagoras would provide. In the *muthos*, Socrates will suggest that some things in the cosmos are bad and will assign a distinct cause to them, one in no way connected to goodness or *nous*.

Once we take seriously that Socrates is convinced of this extraordinary account, it is natural to want to know why. But recall that Socrates said that there is not time to show that this is the case and he might not be able to do so (108d). Its emphasis on our ignorance is likely one reason Socrates finds it appealing. I suspect another reason is that it makes the heavens divine and form-like. Socrates says that "the earth itself, however, is pure and is set in the pure heaven in which the celestial bodies are" (109b7–8). According to this account, we live in a hollow in the earth and where we are – as well as the underworld – is not pure. How, then, can the earth itself be pure? It seems that where we live must not count as the earth itself. For example, in his *muthos* he says that the earth itself has gems on it far purer than the ones around us (110d–e); this can only be so if the place where we live does not count as the earth itself. He never uses "the earth itself" to describe where we are or the underworld. "The earth itself" is a celestial entity, pure and heavenly; where we are, in its hollows, is related to the earth itself, but is not part of it.[21] Hesiod's *Theogony* (116–117) makes the earth one of the first gods. If Socrates similarly thinks of the earth as divine (cf. *Timaeus* 40c), we can see why he could be convinced that it must be in heaven, with no part of it in the impure area where we live.

"The x itself" is one of Socrates' regular expressions for forms.[22] Of course, sometimes he uses this construction to identify things that are not forms, but here he identifies the earth itself as *pure*, just as he has identified the forms as pure earlier in the dialogue (67a–b, 79d). The x itself does not have anything else mixed into it, and so is pure. Of course, Socrates has said in the defense speech (65d) and kinship argument (79a–80b) that forms are not visible. Thus the earth itself and the pure heaven cannot be forms; but they are like the forms in some key respects, including being pure, divine, and beautiful. But whereas the forms are entirely pure and beautiful, these celestial entities are only proportionately more beautiful (110d): as we are to the sea, so the earth itself and the heavens are to us. In Socrates' *muthos*, he ends by saying that there is a place better than the true surface of the earth, where the philosophical souls can go (114b–c). This place is entirely pure (cf. 80d–81a), even better than the visible heavens.

In the same way in which things here are large or good because of their relationship with the forms, so other things owe their existence to the heavens. Socrates says that the heavenly bodies are set in aether and that water, mist, and air "are sediments of aether, and they are always flowing together into the hollows of the earth" (109c2–3; cf. Aristotle, *De generatione et corruptione* 2.9–10). These elements come down from the heavens, but the purest element, aether, stays where it is. This explains air and water, but how is our hollow related to the earth itself? And where is fire in this account? And why are things worse here than they are on the true surface of the earth? These questions are answered in Socrates' *muthos*. Let me simply note a small hint here of what is to come. Socrates twice says that water, mist, and air are "flowing together" (συρρεῖν) (109b6, 109c3). While innocuous on its own, in the *muthos* Socrates connects this "flowing" to the Heraclitean idea that things are constantly changing, without any stability. In the context of Heraclitus' views, this verb (ῥεῖν) is normally translated as "flux" rather than "flow." In retrospect, then, we can see Socrates as hinting at the idea that in the hollows of the earth where we live – below the heavens – water, mist, and air are in flux.

Recall that Socrates says that the things that we identify as "just," "holy," "large," and so forth are named after the forms (102b, cf. 78d–e). But what about the things we call "earth" or "heaven"? Instead of these referring to the invisible form of the earth or form of heaven, Socrates may be convinced that they refer to the earth itself

---

[21] For similar ideas, see Kingsley 1995, 106–7, Edmonds 2004, 214–15.
[22] See Section 3.6.

and true heaven in the cosmos. Our earth and heaven are suitably related to these things, but are impure and distorted. It will turn out in the *muthos* that the things around us also have a share of the things on the surface of the earth itself.

Why does Plato have Socrates and Simmias emphasize that Socrates is convinced of these claims? Perhaps to make clear that this stage has a very different status from the *muthos* that comes afterwards. In saying that he is convinced of some things about the cosmos, Socrates is claiming to be in a state that he emphasized, in discussing misology, can be quite dangerous. But since he does not tell others why he is convinced, he mitigates the danger of convincing them. Who convinced Socrates of these things? Obviously, Plato could have said if he had wanted us to know. This may simply be a way for Socrates to distance himself from such views, since in the *Apology* he says that he does not concern himself with cosmological matters (19b–c). But given the Platonic structure described here, if it is supposed to be anyone specific, it seems to me that it must be Plato himself.

11.5 THE FIFTH STAGE – THE *MUTHOS* OF THE OVERWORLD AND THE UNDERWORLD: 110A–114D

Socrates ended the third stage by saying that the soul that lives purely and decently dwells in the region appropriate to it (108c). The fourth stage provided a general account of the structure of the cosmos, but says nothing about souls dwelling anywhere other than the hollows where we live. Socrates then introduces the fifth stage by saying: "for if it's also appropriate to tell a *muthos*, it is worth hearing, Simmias, what the things on the surface of the earth under the heaven are really like" (110a9–b2). This *muthos* ultimately describes not only dwelling in the overworld (110b–111c), but also the underworld (111c–114b). Both of these discussions begin with a physical description of the environment, including its geographic features, and then turn to what life is like there. In doing so, they explain the differences in the inhabitants' quality of life using their physical environments. Subsection 11.5.1 focuses on the environment of the overworld and underworld, arguing that it fills in the Platonic cosmology using causes (*aitiai*) that meet the minimal requirements suggested in the autobiography. Subsection 11.5.2 addresses how this environment in the overworld affects its inhabitants. Subsection 11.5.3 considers life in the underworld and whether there is divine punishment and reward in this eschatological account, and finally Subsection 11.5.4 examines the status of this account as a *muthos*.

11.5.1 Fifth Stage, Part One: The Platonic Cosmology

Socrates' *muthos* provides causal accounts (i) that connect the purity with greater beauty, ultimately explaining why people on the surface of the earth are happier, and (ii) that explain why there is flux in the underworld, which ultimately comes up and influences the hollow where we live. Since he has just reintroduced cosmological topics discussed in the autobiography and referred back to Anaxagoras' views, there is prima facie reason to expect Socrates' causal accounts here to be connected to the search for causes described there. I argue that this is, indeed, the case.

In a pregnant passage describing the surface of the true earth, Socrates (1) extends the ways in which the heavens are form-like, (2) identifies the cause of things on the earth itself being more beautiful than the things here, and (3) explains what brings about the ugliness and unhealthiness around us:

> And likewise the mountains and stones, for their part, have their smoothness, transparency and colors proportionately more beautiful. Moreover, those gems that are treasured here, sardian stones, jaspers, emeralds and everything of the kind, are fragments of them. But there everything is like that, and more beautiful still than our gems. The cause [to aition] of this is that those stones are pure, not eaten up and not damaged either – as the stones in our region have been by decomposition and brine – by things flowing together here, which brings about uglinesses and illnesses in stones, in earth, and in animals and plants too. (110d4–e6)

Note how the precious stones here are *fragments* of those there. Socrates seems to be working with a literal notion of "having a share" (μετέχει), the verb he uses to describe the relationship between forms and ordinary things in the autobiography (100c5). It is as if there were a separate place where Anaxagorean stuffs were pure, whereas our stones simply have a share of those stones. Note also how "flowing together" has returned. Socrates said earlier that water, mist, and air are sediments of aether which flow together (109b–c). Now he says that flowing together brings about ugliness and illnesses in stone, earth, plants, and animals. This flowing leads to the lack of purity, which in turn bring about the lack of health and beauty around us.

Socrates says that being pure is the cause (*to aition*)[23] of the stones there being more beautiful than our stones. This might suggest that purity is responsible for beauty. However, I would suggest instead that purity is responsible for beautiful things being *more* beautiful, because impurities detract from their natural beauty. Gems are beautiful, and so the purer, the more beautiful. Socrates goes on to say that the "earth itself" (100e6–7) is decorated all over with these gems as well as gold, silver, and other such medals. This explains why the greater purity of the heavens make them better: it makes them more beautiful, in turn leading to people's happiness (111a, 111c), as discussed in the next subsection. Later, in describing the underworld, Socrates says that there are rivers of both "purer mud" and "more filthy mud" (111d–e). There is no suggestion that the former is more beautiful than the

---

[23] In Section 9.1 I argued that *"aition"* on its own means responsible, whereas *"aitia"* refers to a more complex fact in virtue of which something is responsible. The expression *"to aition"* is ambiguous: it can either refer to a responsible thing or to the same thing as (the noun) *"aitia."* Since Socrates identifies *"to aition"* here as an overall state of affairs, rather than a particular thing, I take it here to be equivalent to the noun *"aitia."*

11.5 The Fifth Stage – Muthos, Overworld, Underworld: 110a–114d

latter; in fact, he does not describe anything in the underworld as beautiful. Only if mud were naturally beautiful would purer mud be more beautiful.

This account meets Socrates' two restrictions from the autobiography (see Sections 9.3 and 9.5): (i) the same thing cannot be responsible for opposite explananda and (ii) the same explanandum cannot have opposite *aitiai*. Being purer is never responsible for a naturally beautiful thing being uglier – and so the same thing is not responsible for the opposite explanandum. Similarly, being more impure is never an *aitia* for a naturally beautiful thing being more beautiful – and so the opposite is not an *aitia* for the same explanandum. Socrates' *muthos* fits his causal constraints.

Let us turn to Socrates' account of the geography of the underworld (111c–113c). Socrates gives a remarkably long description of this geography, roughly the length of cyclical or the kinship argument. Simply setting his account of the soul's journey into a larger cosmological setting does not seem to justify this length, or its detailed account of how underground rivers flow. I will argue that at least one reason Socrates describes it at such length is because it provides an account of the source of flux in the world.

Socrates first sets up the underworld as a place whose flowing elements can influence where we live. He says that the hollowed regions in the earth – such as where we live – are connected to one another underground and that water flows back and forth as if in mixing bowls (111d). He then describes underground rivers that correspond to three of the four elements: rivers of (hot and cold) water, as well as rivers of fire; and rivers of mud, both purer and filthier (111d–e).[24] Currents of air are mentioned shortly thereafter (112b).

In the account of these rivers, Plato carefully connects the two expressions that he regularly uses for Heraclitean flux: "flow" and "up and down." He uses the verb "to flow" (ῥεῖν) – typically translated "to be in flux" in Heraclitean contexts – twenty-one times here, sometimes as part of compound verbs (περιρρεῖν, συρρεῖν, ἐκρεῖν, and εἰσρεῖν); he also uses related nouns (ῥεῦμα, ῥύαξ) eight times to refer to flowing rivers. On its own, this could simply be because Socrates is describing rivers. But he also uses the expression "up and down," first when saying that "all these things [rivers] are moved up and down (ἄνω καὶ κάτω) as if by a sort of oscillation inside the earth" (111e4–5). He again uses this "up and down" phrase a few lines later, in a key passage where he explains the cause of the rivers' flowing up and down (quoted later in this subsection). In discussing misology, Socrates describes the view that there is nothing sound or true in any thing or argument, but rather all things

---

[24] See Kingsley 1995, ch. 7, for a compelling argument that Socrates' description of the underworld is likely drawn from ancient descriptions of Sicily. Unlike Kingsley, I do not think this provides much evidence that the *Phaedo*'s eschatological account is drawn from an Orphic poem. Instead, Plato could simply be extending what was known about Sicily, widely seen as a gateway to the underworld, to a larger description of the underworld.

turn *up and down* like the waters of the Euripus (90c).²⁵ Socrates describes himself as "up and down" in when he first started to study natural philosophy (96a–b). Across the dialogues this expression is closely associated with Heraclitean flux, as discussed in Section 9.3. Moreover, "flow" was used earlier in the *Phaedo* for Heraclitean flux: in Cebes' cloakmaker objection, Cebes says that it would be reasonable to think that the body is flowing and the soul is constantly reweaving it (87d–e), clearly imagining a sort of Heraclitean flux applying to the body.

Plato's connection between Heraclitus and flowing ultimately derives from Heraclitus' talk of rivers flowing (B12), which is why Socrates refers to rivers flowing when describing Heraclitean flux elsewhere (*Cratylus* 402a, *Theaetetus* 160d–e). Socrates is explaining Heraclitean flow using Heraclitus' example: rivers. The term "up and down" ultimately comes from Heraclitus' fragment B60. Some modern scholars and ancient commentators understand this fragment as an important part of Heraclitus' cosmology.²⁶ But whether or not Heraclitus connected the phrase "up and down" with flow or cosmology, Plato does so here.

At the heart of Socrates' account is an explanation of why these rivers flow up and down. He explains this by describing the largest chasm, which is bored through the whole earth, which he says Homer calls "Tartarus":

> All the rivers flow together into this chasm and flow out of it again. And each river comes to be like the kind of earth through which it flows. The *aitia* of all the streams (ῥεύματα) flowing out from here, and flowing inside, is that this liquid has no base and no foundation. So it oscillates and surges up and down (ἄνω καὶ κάτω), and the air and the wind around the liquid do the same. (112a5–b4)

In the *Cratylus*, the term translated here as "foundation" (βάσις) is used in Socrates' etymology for "stable" (βέβαιος, 437a): stable things have a foundation. Plato opposes stability to flux in the *Cratylus* (e.g. 411 b–c): things that are ever changing have no stability. By contrast, the forms are stable beings. This interrelated set of terms is also in the passage from the misology section mentioned earlier: "they alone have understood that there is nothing sound or stable (βέβαιος) in any thing or argument, but rather all things turn up and down (ἄνω κάτω), exactly as if in the Euripus, and do not stay put for any time" (90c2–6). Here in the *muthos*, Socrates is talking about actual liquids moving up and down because of a lack of stability. The lack of a physical foundation leads things to flow up and down.

Again, we can see how the minimal requirements from the autobiography are met by this proposal: the lack of a foundation would never be an *aitia* for something being stable – and so the opposite thing would not be an *aitia* for this explanandum – nor would a foundation be responsible for something moving back and forth – and so the same thing would not be responsible for opposite explananda.

---

[25] See Pender 2012, 221–2, for this basic connection and some similar ideas, used to reach different conclusions.
[26] Diogenes Laertius 9.8; Betegh 2013, Appendix 1.

11.5 The Fifth Stage – Muthos, Overworld, Underworld: 110a–114d

In identifying the absence of a base as the cause of flux, Socrates makes clear that flux has a cause, but not a divine cause. Gods are responsible only for good things, and so would not be responsible for flux in the world (cf. *Timaeus* 52d–53b). In the *Phaedo*, Socrates provides no reason to think that everything in the cosmos is good or is caused to be better. Some things are less good than they could be because there is flux in the world, caused by the lack of foundation at the center of our earth, as far away from the heavens as possible. Hence not all causes are good: the lack of a foundation is responsible for a bad thing, flux among the elements – which leads to impurity, ugliness, and illnesses.

Recall that water and air are "sediments" of aether, and the more beautiful parts of earth are fragments of the earth itself. But where does fire come from? Socrates says that there are rivers of fire under the earth. He also says that there are "rivers of mud flowing ahead of the lava stream and the lava stream itself" (111e1–2). This is Socrates' only use of "the x itself" locution within the underworld, and the word translated as "the lava stream" (ῥύαξ) derives from the verb flow (*rhein*). The one "x itself" found in the underworld is the flowing thing itself. Could Plato be hinting at Heraclitus' idea of fire as the fundamental principle of the cosmos? Fire is the only element Socrates does not connect to the heavens; he seems to connect it to flux without making it the cause of flux (which is instead the lack of a foundation). I suspect that we are supposed to see this as a sort of corrective to Heraclitus.

After this account of the cause of things flowing up and down, Socrates compares the oscillating air that follows the rivers to pneuma being exhaled and inhaled (112b). Commentators sometimes say that Socrates is claiming that the earth is alive,[27] although Socrates very clearly marks this as an analogy: the *pneuma* oscillates *just like* an animal breathing. There is some reason to think that Heraclitus identified soul with exhalation both for individuals and for the cosmos as a whole,[28] and so Socrates may be adapting and modifying this Heraclitean view as well. In any event, the analogy makes clear that the oscillations are regular and frequent. Socrates then turns to how the oscillations within the earth affect the waters up here, in the hollows, through a process "like people pumping" (112c3). The oscillation of the four elements within the earth leads to the flux of these elements in the hollows where we live and so to impurity here, which in turn leads to ugliness and illnesses.

After describing the pumping that brings rivers up to us from Tartarus, Socrates turns to the four great rivers that structure the underworld (112e–113c) – two sets of opposed pairs. The first is Ocean. According to Homer, Ocean is an ever-flowing river that encircles the earth (*Odyssey* 11.13) and Hades is outside of Ocean (*Odyssey* 10.508–12, 11.13–22). Socrates inverts this structure, making Ocean an ever-flowing, circular river within which are found Tartarus and the land of the dead. The Acheron is opposed to Ocean, flowing in the opposite direction, leading to the

---

[27] Pender 2012 goes furthest in developing such an interpretation.
[28] Betegh 2013.

Acherusian lake, where those who have lived average lives dwell after death (112e–113a). These two rivers mark out the realm of the dead and the journey that most take after death. The other two rivers, Pyriphlegethon and Cocytus, will play a role in the punishment of those who have committed grave but curable offenses.

The overall picture is that the outer surface of the earth itself is pure and relatively free from physical churning, allowing the things there to be more beautiful than here; flux comes from the center, and we find ourselves at the interface, with some beauty coming down from above, but diminished because of the flow coming up from below. This account explains the movement of the elements and the structure of the cosmos in a way that respects Socrates' causal requirements as well as broad Platonic principles. It is a Platonic cosmology.

11.5.2 *Fifth Stage, Part Two: Life in the Overworld*

Why situate one's eschatology within a cosmology? According to the psychological model presented earlier in the *Phaedo*, what one interacts with has a significant effect on one's soul. In the kinship argument, when one's soul grasps things that are wandering, it wanders, and as it grasps things that are stable, it becomes stable (79c–d). The impure souls continue to wander in the place where they are gathered before traveling to their dwelling (108b–c). Similarly, when Socrates began his interest in natural science, he himself was pulled up and down (96b) while considering various ordinary, perceptible objects as candidate causes. Socrates' cosmological account provides souls with radically different environments, dramatically affecting the inhabitants' soul. Being surrounded by much more beautiful things than here leads to souls' being happier. The most unjust are thrown forevermore into Tartarus, the source of all flux, and the next worse spend at least a year in Tartarus and then spend time in the rivers that come from it.

The soul's composition determines both what environment it is drawn to and how it interacts with this environment. According to the kinship argument, the soul is akin to the divine, which is invisible and pure. Because of this kinship, when the pure soul investigates on its own, it departs to what is divine and immortal (79d, 80d–81a; Sections 6.4 and 7.1). When purer souls go to the heavens, they go somewhere that their soul is naturally akin to (80d–81a, cf. 79d, 114c). Socrates suggests that there is a need for guides (108a), and so purer souls do not go to the superior places simply on their own; nonetheless, the guides seem to be taking these souls to where it is fitting for them to be. By contrast, in the return to the defense Socrates says that the impure soul has a "a share of" the corporeal (81c–d). As we have seen, these souls are drawn to their appropriate place by necessity (108b–c).[29]

---

[29] Betegh 2006 provides an insight account of the different pre-Platonic models of the soul. However, he argues that the *Phaedo*'s model of the soul does not relate the soul to the stuffs in the cosmos. I am suggesting that the *Phaedo* does – pure souls go toward what they are akin to and impure souls toward what their impurity is akin to (see Section 7.2).

Already in Homer the environment is an important influence in the afterlife.[30] For the lucky who depart to the Elysian plain, "life is there easiest for humans. There is no snow, no heavy storms or rain, but Ocean always sends gentle breezes of Zephyr to refresh the people there" (*Odyssey* 4.565–8, trans. Wilson). Whereas Homer and Hesiod (*Works and Days*, 170–3) focus on the lack of toil in the afterlife, in Pindar's second *Olympian* (72–4), on the Isle of the Blessed, "flowers of gold are ablaze, some from radiant trees on land, while the water nurtures others; with these they weave garlands for their hands and crowns for their heads" (trans. Race). The beauty here improves people's lives, but in all of these accounts the geography is fundamentally similar to that of where we live – Hesiod places the isles of the blessed "at the end of the earth" (*Works and Days* 168).

By locating the superior afterlife in an entirely different part of the cosmos, Socrates makes the life there superior in ways entirely beyond what is possible where we live.[31] The things on the surface of the earth itself make the humans there happier, wiser, and healthier (111a–c). I noted earlier two environmental features that lead to people's happiness: the things on the earth itself are more beautiful than here (110c–111a) and one can see the celestial bodies as they really are (111c). Socrates also says that one can encounter the gods themselves in the shrines (111b). Supposedly this is possible because the earth itself is purer and in the heavens – and so is also related to the superior geography.

Plato does not seem to be the first to suggest that people live somewhere in the heavens. Philolaus (A20), Anaxagoras (A77), and Herodorus of Heraclea (active in the fifth to fourth century: see Athenaeus 2.57ff.) are all reported to have believed that people live on the moon.[32] Perhaps most importantly – and what I have not seen mentioned in this context – according to our reports of the Pythagorean *acousmata*, the sun and the moon are the isle of the blessed.[33] Assuming that this goes back to the early Pythagorean views (as is generally thought) we can see Socrates as modifying this view: the Pythagoreans are right to think that the better place to go after death is in the heavens, not some far-off part of where we live; but the heavenly isle of the blessed is the earth itself, rather than the sun or the moon. If Philolaus thought that people live on the moon – as Huffman 1993 tentatively accepts – then we can see Socrates adapting his view. According to this testimony (A20), Philolaus thinks that animals and plants on the moon are greater and more beautiful, and that the animals there have fifteen-fold more power, since the day is fifteen times longer.

---

[30] For a fuller examination of how the *Phaedo* engages with these precursors, see Edmonds 2004, 209–18.

[31] Socrates also manages to combine the idea of the Isle of the Blessed with the idea that our soul goes into aether after death, as noted by Edmonds 2004, 211.

[32] Kingsley 1995, 92, notes the connection to Philolaus, as well as to Philolaus' counter-earth, discussed in what follows.

[33] Iamblichus, *On the Pythagorean Life*, 82; the consensus is that Iamblicus is here drawing on a lost work from Aristotle (Burkert 1972, 166 ff.). For a brief discussion, see Huffman 2018, with further references.

By contrast, Socrates says that the earth itself and its gems – rather than the animals – are purer, which makes them proportionately more beautiful (110d), and this is why the people there happier. Socrates' heavenly isle of the blessed provides a clearer explanation of why life there would be happier than here. In fact Philolaus is famous for his counter-earth theory, according to which there is another earth closer to the central fire (A16 and A17); we do not see the central fire; instead, our sun somehow redirects light from it (A19). According to Socrates' account, in our current hollow we do not see the true heaven (109e–110a), whereas on the earth itself we see the heavenly bodies as they really are (111c). Here again, Socrates could be modifying Philolaus' ideas, combining the heavenly isle of the blessed, the people who live on the moon, and the counter-earth theory in a way that fits with his broad commitments. If Socrates is appropriating Philolaus' and Pythagorean views in this way, Socrates would be giving them a very different status than other Pythagorean claims that he has appropriated and reinterpreted, by putting them into a *muthus*.[34]

The description of the true surface of the earth provides a way to understand how amazing the bodiless life of the philosopher must be. After Socrates' description of the underworld, he says that the exceptionally pious dwell on the earth's surface and that those who purify themselves sufficiently with philosophy live without bodies in dwellings fairer still than these, which he says it is not easy to describe (114b–c). It is difficult to understand what life would be like without a body; by describing a vastly superior life than our own and then describing the bodiless life as even better, he makes clear what a significant improvement it must be.

11.5.3 *Fifth Stage, Part Three: The Underworld, Punishment, and the Problem of Evil*

Socrates provides no narrative in his description of the cosmos.[35] There is no fashioning of the world by a demiurge (*Timaeus*); there is no story of an earlier time, when souls were misjudged, which is then fixed by Zeus (*Gorgias*); there is no theogony, as in Hesiod and Orphic poems.[36] Socrates simply describes how things are. As we have seen, the causes that Socrates identifies do not explain the overall structure of the cosmos – they simply explain beauty and flux. Nonetheless, interpreters generally claim that in the *Phaedo* the cosmos is set up for souls in a way that rewards good souls and punishes bad ones.[37]

If the cosmos is set up by a god, then the problem of evil arises: why are there bad things, if a benevolent god is responsible for everything? In the *Republic*, Socrates says that gods are not responsible for everything, but rather only for good things

---

[34] For earlier discussions of how Socrates appropriates Pythagorean ideas, see the Introduction and Sections 1.3, 3.1, 4.3, and 5.1.
[35] As noted by Betegh 2009, 99.
[36] Diotima provides a proper theogony at *Symposium* 202d–204a.
[37] Sedley 1990, Karfik 2004, Pender 2012.

(380b–c). Since the *Timaeus* describes the whole cosmos as created by a god, it addresses the problem of evil (see esp. 42d–e; cf. *Laws* 904a–c). No such explanation is offered in the *Phaedo*. If a god is responsible for the world, why is there Tartarus – this source of flux – at all? There is no reference to Tartarus in the *Timaeus*. If it somehow had to exist, why did the god allow it to influence where we live through these underground rivers? By not offering a creation story, he avoids the need to address such questions. As noted earlier, Socrates carefully describes the geography of the overworld first, without mentioning souls (110b–111a), before explaining how souls are then benefited or harmed by their surroundings (111a–c), and then repeats the same procedure with the underworld (111c–113c, 113d–114b).[38] He provides no reason to think that the geography exists for these effects, as opposed to the souls' finding themselves in this geography and then being appropriately affected.

Recall that at the very beginning of Socrates' account he says that nothing but a soul's education and nurture leads to its benefit or harm. If the gods punish souls, these punishments would be beneficial (cf. *Gorgias* 525b–526b). In their journey to their dwelling place, impure souls are harmed, not by the divine, but by necessity (as discussed in stage three). Such a soul "pays the penalty" (literally: pays justice) by necessity (81d). This is not a divine, beneficial justice, but rather a repercussion of one's way of life that harms one's soul. The *Phaedo* includes nothing like the part of the *Gorgias* where Zeus makes his sons judges whose judgment is as just as possible (524a). The underworld punishments described in the *Phaedo* do not seem to be divine. For those who are incurable, "the fate that belongs to them" (113e5) throws them into Tartarus – no god is implicated in the act. The *Phaedo* does not claim, as the *Gorgias* does, that such people serve as examples that benefit others (525b–c). In the *Phaedo*, when the curable ones who have done great injustice are thrown out of Tartarus, they shout out and call those they have wronged; they "beg and beseech" (ἱκετεύουσι καὶ δέονται, 114a9) them to let them return to the lake. Their evils (τὰ κακά) are only ended if they "persuade" those they have wronged. Why should persuasion determine whether someone escapes evils? Is it not always good to remove evil? Moreover, the person wronged might not be persuaded, even if they should be. The system does not seem just. Socrates says that this punishment is imposed on them by the jurors. The term "beseech" (ἱκετεύειν) occurs only four times in Plato's corpus; once is in the *Apology*, where it is also paired with "beg" to describe what Socrates will *not* do: beg and beseech (34c) his jurors to be lenient on him.[39] He says at length that doing so would be a disgrace, bringing shame on the city; they should not allow such behavior (34d–35b). In the *Phaedo*, the underworld jurors require those who have done wrong to do this bad thing: beg and beseech. Socrates is saying (at 113e–114b) that the only fate worse than being thrown into the source of all flux forever is to be thrown into the source of all flux for a year, be

---

[38] The one exception is at 113a, where souls are briefly mentioned.
[39] For a discussion of the *Phaedo*'s close connection to the *Apology*, see Section 1.4.

thrown into a river in a frightening and savage region (113b–c), and then have to go through what is normally done in the Athenian court system – horror upon horror! Of course, no god would impose such a harmful punishment.

On the true surface of the earth, people are happy and wise and able to interact with the gods in temples and groves. In the underworld, things work in a human way. Socrates says that in the underworld those who have done good deeds receive recognition, each according to their deserts – just as happens here on earth. Similarly, people are "purified" by being punished for their wrongs (113d); there is no need to suppose that this is anything supernatural; the simple act of punishing could be purifying. This purification can be beneficial, just like the purification done in our hollow.

Do these souls get to live on the true earth as a *reward* for living well? If any part of the cosmic order is set up to be good, it would be this. The fact that the gods *guide* souls to this dwelling place (108c) might suggest that this is a reward for their keeping their soul in a good condition. But another possibility is that the gods are good and so simply benefit whomever they can, but – as Socrates said in the defense speech – it is not sanctioned for someone impure to grasp something pure (67b) and one must be purified to dwell with the gods (69c). So the gods' goal is not reward per se – they would happily benefit anyone – but most souls' impurity keeps them from being able to interact with the gods, leading these souls to be harmed by their own impurity. Socrates does say that living in the bodiless dwellings of the philosophers is a "prize" (ἆθλον, 114c9) for those who share of virtue and wisdom in life. But a prize can simply be what is, in fact, a very good thing awaiting those who have lived exceptionally good lives; it need not be offered as a reward.

I argued in Subsection 11.5.1 that Socrates is providing a Platonic version of a natural scientific cosmology. Perhaps Socrates is appropriating and developing the sort of view of justice in Anaximander (B1) and Heraclitus (B94), according to which things in the natural world are governed by justice. If so, justice is served through the ordinary workings of the natural world, but not all of this is divine, beneficial justice: the souls of the unjust will be harmed because of their impurity and desire for the body.

11.5.4 *Fifth Stage, Part Four: Its Status as a* muthos

Why does Socrates describe this last stage as a "*muthos*"?[40] This is a notoriously difficult term in Plato. In Plato it typically refers to a narrative that describes events involving gods or heroes from the past; because it is in the distant past or an

---

[40] See Sections 2.5 and 2.6 for Socrates' description of himself as composing *muthoi* without possessing the art of composing them. Recall that Socrates has recently interpreted his dream as telling him that he should compose *muthoi* (60d–61b). Evidently this is the sort of *muthos* he thinks he should tell.

unknown location, its truth cannot be verified.[41] But, as noted earlier, Socrates does not provide a narrative here. This makes it an unusual *muthos* for Plato, distinguishing it from the other great cosmological myths in Plato: the myth of Er in the *Republic* (614b–621d) is a story of Er traveling around, seeing what it is like after death; the *Statesman*'s myth is a story of what happens when the earth's rotation reverses (268e–274e); the *Timaeus* tells a story of how the craftsman created the cosmos. Given that the *Phaedo* is a story about heroes, gods, daemons, and the underworld (as argued in Chapter 2), one might expect this to be the story of a journey to the underworld.[42] Instead, it describes the environment in which such a journey would take place without describing any particular journey (unlike the myth of Er, *Odyssey* XI, or the story of Orpheus' descent to the underworld). The lack of a narrative makes it more difficult to know how to evaluate this *muthos*. As discussed in Chapter 2, there are norms by which creation *muthoi* are evaluated as well as norms by which *muthoi* about heroes, gods, and the underworld are evaluated. The latter provide some basic constraints for this *muthos* – the gods must be good, the afterlife cannot be presented as simply bad – but do not provide much guidance.

Socrates has not, in his current embodiment, been on the true earth or in the underworld, nor are the details of these accessible through reasoning alone; this seems to be an important reason to call this a *muthos*: anything said about these topics must be speculative, even if working within constraints provided by reason. I suspect that there is at least one further reason to call it a *muthos*. In the *Gorgias*, before Socrates provides his eschatological account, he says:

> Give ear then, as they say, to a very fine account, which you will think is a *muthos*, I suppose, but I think is a *logos*. For the things I am about to say I will say to you as true. (523a1–3)

Socrates implies here that, when someone puts forward a *muthos*, they do not put it forward as true. It would be to misunderstand what someone is doing, in telling a *muthos*, to question its truth. Socrates similarly contrasts *muthos* and *logos* near the beginning of the *Phaedo*: "but, after I had attended to the god, I reflected that the poet, if he is to be a poet, should compose *muthoi* not *logoi*" (61b3–5). My suggestion is that Socrates' description of the true surface of the earth and the underworld is not put forward as true anymore than his description of a *muthos* about the god connecting pleasure and pain at a single tip (60b–c). One would misunderstand this Aesop fable if one were to ask Socrates what his evidence is that pleasure and pain truly were at war, requiring the god to intervene to solve the problem. Nonetheless, that story is meant to reveal a deeper truth about the

---

[41] Brisson 1998, Partenie 2009.
[42] Edmonds 2004 emphasizes that it includes the narrative structure of obstacle, solution, result; while true, this simply means that one could tell a narrative within Socrates' *muthos*, not that Socrates does so.

interconnection between pleasure and pain. Similarly, Socrates' *muthos* here is meant to reveal a deeper truth.

In the *Republic*, Socrates says that we educate our children first with *muthoi* that he describes as false "as a whole," though they have some truth "in them" (377a). This is the deeper truth that children internalize; the censorship in the *Republic* is meant to protect children against internalizing the wrong deeper truths. So too here in the *Phaedo* the *muthos* has something that (Socrates thinks) is true in it. This is why Socrates says, at the end of the *muthos*, that it is worth the risk to think that it or something like it is true, and that one should chant such things to oneself (114d). Doing so will allow one to internalize the truths in it, even if it is false as a whole. What then are these deeper truths supposed to be? At a minimum, the *muthos* fills out how our soul is benefitted and harmed, depending on its education and nurture (stage 1), through substantively different environments that souls will dwell in after death (stage 2), fitting with a Platonic cosmology of which Socrates is convinced (stage 4).

One might be tempted to think that the deeper truth is revealed by an allegorical reading of this natural scientific *muthos*. This would involve seeing some elements of the *muthos* as symbolically representing something different: the heavens would stand in for the forms, and the flowing among the elements would stand in for the broader compresence of opposites that all ordinary objects suffer, and the lack of a physical foundation at the center of the earth would stand in for ordinary objects' lack of (metaphysical) stability. I think such an allegorical reading faces serious textual problems. Recall first that Socrates says he is *convinced* that we live in a hollow, that the earth itself is pure, and that we cannot see the heaven as it truly is from where we are. This is not part of the *muthos* and so would not be part of the allegory. Second, within the *muthos* Socrates says that there is a place where philosophers can dwell entirely without bodies, which is better than the earth itself. If the heavens allegorically represent the forms, then the philosophers would live in a place better than the forms. But this is incompatible with how he described the philosopher's afterlife in the return to the defense (80d–81a).

We can retain at least part of what is appealing about an allegorical reading without taking the *muthos* to be indirectly discussing forms and metaphysical flux. The *muthos* applies basic Platonic concepts within a limited framework where it is easier to understand them: the meaning of "flowing," "stability," and "up and down" are much clearer when applied to physical stuffs that can move around. At the same time, Socrates is not simply applying his basic commitments about flux and purity within the limited sphere of locomotion and stuffs. If it were only that, there would be no reason to think that the flowing brings about ugliness and illnesses to stones, animals, and plants, or that the purity of the gems explains the happiness of the inhabitants (110e–111a). Instead, Socrates seems to be engaged in the natural scientific project of explaining the cosmos and everything around us mostly in terms of stuffs or elements that are rearranged – much as Anaxagoras does. But he provides a distinctly Platonic account of the principles the govern these elements – Platonic accounts of purity and flux – and so a Platonic version of cosmology. Plato thinks that the gods are important to the structure of the cosmos, as is reincarnation and the souls' journey, and so these have an important place in his natural scientific account. Socrates himself is not putting forward this account as true, but it reveals deeper truths about principles of Platonic metaphysics in a way that makes these principles easier to grasp, while at the same time illustrating how Socrates' convictions could be realized within the constraints of the first three stages.

11.6 CODA – AFTER THE *MUTHOS*: 114D–115A

At the very end of the eschatological discussion, Socrates presents a final ethical injunction. The passage is often cited because Socrates mentions pleasures of learning here, making clear that they are good to pursue, unlike bodily pleasures (114d–e). Socrates says that we should develop "temperance, justice, courage, freedom, and truth" (114e5–115a1), since they are the soul's own *kosmos*.[43] The presence of "freedom and truth" is surprising in what is otherwise a list of the traditional virtues. Truth, as we have seen, is the primary goal of the philosopher; it deserves a place alongside the traditional virtues as something good for any soul to possess. In the exchange passage, Socrates contrasted true virtue – which is a purification of bodily affections – with "slavish" virtue – which involves promoting the body's ends. Hence I suggest that "freedom" here is freedom from the body. Socrates discussed earlier how the body enslaves the soul but the soul by nature is ruler (66b–67b, 80a–b, 94a–c). In this coda, Socrates first says that a person should ignore the body's pleasures and its *kosmoi* (adornments). These pleasures enslave a person, putting them in the prison that is the body (82e); instead of this slavery, the soul should adorn itself with freedom.

11.7 CONCLUSION

Socrates' long eschatological and cosmological account is importantly different from those in the *Gorgias*, *Republic*, and *Timaeus*. Unlike in the *Gorgias* and *Republic*, there is no divine judgement that determines all souls' fates. Unlike the *Timaeus*, no god is mentioned as responsible for the overall structure of the cosmos, and there is no claim that it is structured in a way that is best. The *Phaedo*'s account is focused on explaining why it is especially important to purify ourselves now: if we do, we will gain the greatest benefits, and if we do not, we will suffer the greatest harms. These

---

[43] Note that temperance is listed as *part* of the soul's own *kosmos*. Socrates earlier used the adjective "*kosmios*" ("composed, orderly") to describe one aspect of temperance (68c, cf. 83e). But freedom and courage are also part of the soul's *kosmos*. Thus, Socrates is not using the noun "*kosmos*" here in the same way in which he used the adjective "*kosmios*" earlier, *pace* Sedley and Long 2010, 112, n. 67.

benefits and harms come from the environment that the soul finds itself in. These environments are part of a distinctive Platonic cosmology, one that makes the heavens form-like and the center of the underworld the source of flux.

Socrates' overall account also has a complex epistemological status, as is fitting given his warning of misology. Ever since this warning, Socrates has carefully addressed misology while responding to Simmias' and Cebes' objections. I argued that the method of hypothesis aims to address the cause of misology – repeatedly trusting *logoi* and then rejecting them (Subsection 9.8.2). I also argued that Socrates' reply to Simmias' *harmonia* objection applies the method of hypothesis and that this method helps them not become convinced by the final argument too quickly. Socrates' eschatology and cosmology avoid misology in a different way: either by highlighting (stage four) that while he is convinced, he is not explaining why someone else should be convinced, or by highlighting (stage five) that these views are not of the sort that one should insist upon.

12

The Death Scene

115a–118a

Socrates' death is one of the most moving scenes in Greek literature. While it brings some readers to tears, it does not fill them with anguish; there is no despair, no pity. Socrates is not at the mercy of horrible forces; instead, he is in complete control. His death is inspiring and so moving in a very different way from the death of a hero as typically portrayed in tragedies. I argued in Chapter 2 that the *Phaedo* is set up as an alternative to tragedy that shows how a true hero faces death. The dialogue presents the last day of our hero's life very differently from tragic drama: Socrates has spent the day philosophizing with his close companions, offering them support. When it comes to the hour of his death, he is lighthearted and at ease. The scene begins with Socrates making fun of himself for speaking like a tragic hero, saying that he is being called by destiny (115a). This punctures the air of solemnity around a hero's death, emphasizing its insignificance. He says that he will take his own bath so as not to burden the women with the job of washing the corpse (115a), rejecting the ritualistic cleansing of the hero's body after death. When given the opportunity to delay his death, he refuses to do so (116e–117a). He rejects the horribleness of death, as presented in tragedy, not merely in theory but also in action. The dialogue is written so that we come to admire Socrates, but when he scolds his companions for crying (117d–e) we can see if we too fall short of his ideal. I will let the above serve as a reminder of how the death scene fits into the dialogue's overall structure as an alternative to tragedy.

As noted at the beginning of the Chapter 10, the *Phaedo* has a ring composition: in the outermost ring, the opening of the dialogue introduces the topic of Socrates' death as well as Socrates' full group of companions; this group comes back into focus in the death scene. I argued in Section 2.1 that in the opening of the dialogue Socrates refers to many ordinary notions that contrast with the extraordinary alternatives developed later in the dialogue. For example, in the opening Socrates is in an ordinary prison because of the Athenian view that death brings impurity; he goes on to argue that the body is the real prison we should be worried about and that death is our chance to be pure. In this chapter I argue that, just as the opening of the dialogue repeatedly alluded forward, Socrates' death scene repeatedly alludes back to the claims Socrates defended earlier in the dialogue. It does this by showing Socrates exemplifying the extraordinary alternative he developed over the course of the dialogue. Socrates lives in accordance with his views about the soul, courage, temperance, how to act toward the gods, and the correct way to interpret them.

What has dominated scholarship on the death scene, especially in the last thirty years, is Socrates' famous last words: "Crito, we owe a cock to Asclepius. All of you must pay what is owed and not be careless" (118a7–8). It is easy to see the interest: it is enigmatic, suggesting the possibility of a hidden, true message of the dialogue. Given its obscurity and the temptation to project our own desired message back into these words, it is especially important to place them within their context in the death scene and the dialogue as a whole. My procedure will be first to set up constraints within which an interpretation should operate, and then suggest a series of inter-related possibilities that fit within these constraints. Doing so provides the opportunity to review some of the dialogue's major ideas.

12.1 CARE FOR THE SOUL

Washing and properly burying the dead is an important requirement in ancient Greek religious practice. From Homer onward, proper burial is connected to having a safe journey to the afterlife. Socrates has identified each person with their soul (see Section 6.5); he has organized his account of the afterlife around the idea that only the soul's cleanliness – that is, its purity – determines one's fate in the afterlife (see Sections 11.1 and 11.3). Against this backdrop, Socrates takes his own bath in order to save the women the trouble of washing his body, and then strongly admonishes Crito when Crito asks how he would like to be buried (115c). Crito might seem to be making an innocuous mistake in asking Socrates this, rather than how he wishes his body to be buried (115c–116a). But Crito's words are bound not only to a misguided conception of the self, but also to an interconnected faulty conception of how to prepare one's self for the afterlife. It is one's soul, not one's body, that must be cleaned. In admonishing Crito, Socrates is showing that he continues to vigorously maintain his views even after his arguments are over.

Socrates also clarifies his views in an important way here. Socrates' focus in the *Phaedo* on personal purification and contemplation might seem selfish. Plato has Socrates deftly counter that impression at the end of the dialogue, in reply to Crito's asking what the greatest favor is that they can do for Socrates:

> If you take care of yourselves, whatever you do will be a favor to me and mine, and to yourself, even if you don't undertake to do so now. If on the other hand you fail to take care of yourself, and refuse to live by following the trail set by today's conversation and our previous ones, then however many firm undertakings you make now, you won't do any good. (115b2–c1)

Socrates has a long-standing concern that people take care of themselves (see esp. *Apology* 29d–30b, discussed in Section 12.3). Socrates does not say here why taking care of oneself will always benefit others, whereas trying to care for others but not yourself will never lead to any good. But he makes his overall commitment clear; it means that purifying one's soul and contemplating will not come at the expense of others. Socrates here, just as in the *Republic*, rejects the idea that one must choose between caring for oneself and acting properly toward others; on the contrary, one must care for oneself to help others. Socrates has described true courage and temperance in the dialogue (see Subsection 7.3.2), but has not said what is distinctive of true justice. Perhaps we should think of justice as involving care of the soul, as Socrates says in the *Gorgias* (464b–465d; cf. 513e, 521a). This care will lead to conventionally just actions, but justice is to be found in the soul (cf. *Republic* 442d–443e).

Socrates' care for his companions has been clear throughout the dialogue, especially in his discussion of misology. But his care is not limited to them. Soon after the passage just quoted, Socrates' jailor says to him: "I've come to know in other ways too during this time that you're the noblest, kindest, and best man ever to come here" (116c4–6). Socrates' kindness is presented as naturally fitting with his complete dedication to the pursuit of wisdom. Plato provides, in Socrates, a portrait of how caring for oneself goes hand in hand with caring for others.

Why does Socrates say that it is decent of the jailor to cry for him (116d), when shortly thereafter he scolds his companions for crying after he has taken the poison (117d–e)?[1] First, his companions are aspiring philosophers who should recognize the importance of not allowing the body to rule over them. The fact that they stop crying once Socrates scolds them shows that their bodily affections were under their control all along. In telling them to show some resolve (117e), Socrates uses the same verb (καρτερεῖν) that he used to describe true, philosophical courage (82c; cf. Subsection 7.3.2). Another relevant difference is that, as soon as the jailor bursts into tears, he leaves. Socrates says in the *Republic* that if it is impossible not to grieve, then one should be measured in one's response to the pain (603e); the jailor seems to do just this, keeping control of himself and leaving to avoid a public display of grief.

12.2 SOCRATES' TEMPERANCE, COURAGE, AND PIETY

In addition to showing Socrates caring for others, the death scene also shows him living up to the account of temperance and courage he has defended and shows him displaying his special form of piety.

After the jailor leaves, Socrates tells Crito to have someone bring the drug (*pharmakon*, whose meaning is discussed later in this section). Crito says, "I know that others too drink the drug long after the command has come to them, and first have a good dinner and a good deal to drink and, what's more, some have sex with

---

[1] A question raised by Jansen 2013.

whoever they happen to desire" (116e2–5). Socrates yet again makes a philosophical point while living according to his principles: he says that these people think they have something to gain from doing this, whereas he does not, and so will not (116e–117a). He thereby displays temperance derived from broader considerations of what is valuable.

Near the beginning of the dialogue Crito says that, according to the man who will administer the drug, Socrates should keep his conversation as short as possible because "during conversation people get too hot, and one shouldn't combine any overheating with taking the drug. Otherwise, those who do so are sometimes forced to drink two or even three doses" (63d8–e2). Hemlock is an extremely unpleasant poison, often leading to vomiting and convulsions. Socrates says that they should make arrangements for giving two or three doses, if need be (63e) – showing how much more he values philosophy over avoiding physical pain and discomfort. However, it turns out that he only needs one dose. Rather than become overheated, Socrates has been at ease throughout the day, another sign of his temperance. As Gill has noted, the fact that he does not show any of the typical signs of hemlock poisoning is surely another sign of his great composure – some mix of temperance and courage.[2] There is always a question of when reactions become uncontrollable physiological responses. But Plato seems to be suggesting that Socrates' remarkable control over himself extends even this far. He shows this remarkable strength, even while his companions break down, crying for their own loss (117c–d).

Socrates suggests pouring a libation from the drug – an offering to a god. A libation is a type of sacrifice, and just like food sacrifices, it is traditionally understood as being consumed by the god. Typical libations are wine, honey, and olive oil – things that people want to consume. To offer the hemlock as a libation suggests that a god might want this. It is worth noting at this point that Socrates refers to it throughout as a *"pharmakon,"* which means drug.[3] It can be a poison, but more frequently refers to medicine. In fact, a *"pharmakon"* is typically a purgative, that is, a drug meant to purify. Socrates has argued that death will allow the philosopher to finally be pure and so live with the gods. This gives him reason to view the *pharmakon* as good and so something reasonable to offer to a god.

When Socrates is told that he cannot offer a libation, he says a prayer instead: "that the change of dwelling from here to there may be attended by good fortune" (117c2–3).[4] Given that Socrates thinks that the gods are good, only benefit, and are not open to bribes, it is a difficult to see what the point of prayer is for Socrates. Mayhew suggests that, in general for Plato, prayer might be a good thing for members of a community, but that anyone who has Plato's conception of the gods

---

[2] Gill 1973.
[3] Famously discussed in Derrida 1968.
[4] For death as a journey to a new place, see e.g. 67b–c, 67e–68a, 69d–e, 80d, 106e–107a, 107d–108a.

would see no need to pray, because they would recognize that the gods will not do any special favors.[5] But Socrates in the *Phaedo* seems to have this conception of the gods and yet think it worthwhile to pray that his change of dwelling be attended by good fortune. Perhaps Socrates sees prayer as an appropriate way for him to express his hopes while acknowledging his dependence on and subordination to the gods. He said in the defense speech: "the travel now assigned to me comes with good hope, as it does for any other man who considers his thought to have been purified, as it were, and so ready" (67b10–c3). Socrates hopes that his constant devotion to philosophy has left him sufficiently purified to live with the gods. Prayer is a way for him to responding to his uncertainty, while acknowledging his subordination to the gods, as if to say to them: "I hope that I have prepared myself sufficiently to travel to you, but realize that you, rightly, are the one with power and control." In any event, we can see how Socrates – who frequently reinterprets religious practices in the *Phaedo* – could view prayer in such a way.

Socrates says that he has heard that one should meet one's end in a reverent silence (εὐφημία, 117e). As Rowe notes, this reverent silence is typical in approaches the gods, prefacing prayer and some sacrifices. Socrates has argued over the course of the dialogue that he is departing to dwell with the gods (63b–c, 69d–e, 80d–81a, 111b–c, 114c), and so such silence is appropriate. Socrates' attempted libation, his prayer, and his request for reverent silence each show his unusual piety.

12.3 SOCRATES' LAST WORDS

I have argued that throughout the death scene Socrates acts in line with the demanding theories he has developed over the course of the dialogue. With this in mind, let us consider the vexed question of how to understand Socrates' last words:

> By now it was pretty much the parts around his abdomen that were going cold, when he uncovered his head – for it had been covered – and said his last words: "Crito, we owe a cock to Asclepius. You all must give what is owed and not be careless." (118a5–8)

Following the approach of a recent article by Beatriz Bossi, I will begin from broad constraints on how to read the last words and use these to narrow down on possible interpretations.[6]

First, note that Phaedo explicitly draws attention to these being Socrates' last words. If they were not meant to be significant, it is very unlikely that Plato would

---

[5] Mayhew 2008, 16–17.
[6] Bossi 2018. While we reach different conclusions, hers is one of the most levelheaded discussions of this fraught topic. Peterson 2003 notes twenty-one previous interpretations of Socrates' last words. McPherran 2003 usefully divides previous interpretations into four camps.

explicitly note this.[7] Moreover, recall the incredible care that Plato put into crafting the beginning of the dialogue, foreshadowing themes developed in the rest of the dialogue. It is difficult to believe that he did not put equal care into Socrates' last words.

Second, note that these words show Socrates as pious. Whatever the exact importance of this offering to Asclepius, in his final breath Socrates says they should sacrifice to a god.

Third, as Madison has noted, whatever other role they might have, "do not be careless" (μὴ ἀμελήσητε) are incredibly fitting as Socrates' final two words. While perhaps within the sentence these words should be understood as implicitly referring to the cock owed ("do not be careless with the cock that is owed"), they can also be taken as operating on their own, as one of Socrates' central ethical injunctions. Socrates has recently told his followers that what he always says, which is nothing new, is that if you take *care* of yourself (ὑμῶν αὐτῶν ἐπιμελούμενοι), whatever you do will be a favor to me and mine and to yourselves (115b). And immediately after Socrates' final argument, in a passage I discuss later in this section, Socrates says that, since the soul is immortal, the consequences for the soul truly would be dire "if one is careless with it" (εἴ τις αὐτῆς ἀμελήσει, 107c4–5). Hence, in saying that his followers should not be careless, Socrates seems to be saying that they should take care of their themselves – that is, their souls. These references to care for oneself recall the *Apology*, where Socrates says that he will not cease to exhort the Athenians, saying "are you not ashamed that you take care to acquire as much wealth as possible – and reputation and honor – but about wisdom and truth, about how your soul may be in the best possible condition, you take neither care (ἐπιμελῇ) nor thought?" (29d9–e3, trans. Reeve), and, shortly thereafter, "you see, I do nothing else except go around trying to persuade you, both young and old alike, not to care (ἐπιμελεῖσθαι) about your bodies or your money as intensely as about how your soul may be in the best possible condition" (30a7–b2). In the *Phaedo* the related verb (μελετάω) and nouns (μελέτη and μελέτημα) are used for the philosopher's practice for death and being dead (67d, 80e–81a). This practice is fundamentally a way of caring for one's soul.

I have argued that Socrates' dying words are significant, that they show his piety, and that they end with an injunction to take care of oneself. The next question is why Socrates thinks they owe a cock to Asclepius. Asclepius is primarily a god of healing. The most famous reading of Socrates' last words is Nietzsche's: that Socrates is saying that life itself is a disease, of which he has been cured.[8] Glenn Most, in an influential article that revitalized interest in Socrates' last words, argues

---

[7] This speaks against many ancient interpretations, which view this as simply an ordinary debt that Socrates owed.
[8] Nietzsche, *The Gay Science*, Section 340: "This ridiculous and terrible 'last word' means for those who have ears: 'O Crito, life is a disease'" (trans. Kaufmann).

against Nietzsche's reading.[9] We will return to Nietzsche's reading, but it will prove fruitful to begin with Most's.

According to Most, Socrates has had a deathbed vision, in which he sees that Plato has been healed.[10] Like many interpreters, I think there are good reasons to reject the view that Socrates is saying that Plato has been healed.[11] In the rest of the death scene, Socrates has exemplified the views he has argued for over the course of the day. He has emphasized that the philosopher desires nothing other than being dead (64a); indeed, as we have seen, the defense speech is organized around explaining why the philosopher desires to be dead (Sections 3.2 and 3.7), an idea that comes back in the return to the defense (7.1). It is difficult to think of an idea that goes further against the core message of the dialogue than to treat it as a blessing that an aspiring philosopher has avoided death, so that Socrates' last words would emphasize the value of remaining embodied.[12]

Instead, at a minimum this proposed sacrifice seems to be an inversion of ordinary practices and values. A cock to Asclepius is typically offered when one is healed and instead Socrates is, for whatever reason, offering one right before his death.

In rejecting Most's view that Plato has been healed, interpreters have also rejected his view of a deathbed prophecy, although I think there are good reasons to retain this. Socrates says that he has heard that one should meet one's end in reverent silence (117e) and he acts on this until his last words, despite the extreme unpleasantness of the poison. He allowed his head to be covered, and so supposedly thought he had nothing more to say.[13] According to other interpretations, Socrates just happens to think of something at the last moment, before dying. For example, according to Madison, in the moments before death, Socrates realizes that the danger of misology has been averted, and so he thanks Asclepius for helping cure his companions of that.[14] According to Bossi, a "last sudden urge ... seems to have bubbled up" in Socrates, namely pious gratitude and celebration of the modest philosophical triumph of moving his companions to care for their soul.[15] Such a sudden urge does not fit well with the depiction of Socrates throughout the dialogue as

---

[9] Most 1993.
[10] Burger 1984, 13 and 216, makes a similar suggestion.
[11] For arguments against, see Crooks 1998, Madison 2002, Bossi 2018, Patterson 2018; for arguments in favor, Kanayama 2019.
[12] I also agree with Bossi 2018, 75, that it would be crude for Plato to have Socrates, in his dying breath, say that all of Socrates' companions owe Plato a debt. See Section 1.2 for my discussion of why Plato mentions that he was sick.
[13] Gábor Betegh has pointed out to me that there is some reason to think that Eleusinian initiates were covered with a veil and then uncovered, at which point they had some sort of vision of the divine (Burkert 1983, 267–8). Betegh suggests that the whole description of Socrates' death may draw on and rework Eleusinian and Orphic ideas, which are meant to help ensure that one fares well in the afterlife. I am sympathetic to this idea, which I think would fit nicely with my account in this chapter and approach in this book, but do not pursue it here.
[14] Madison 2002, 433.
[15] Bossi 2018, 82–3.

thoughtful and composed in the face of death. He had plenty of time to think of final things to say before taking the drug. He is now enduring its incredibly unpleasant effects. It is difficult to believe that something just happened to occur to him in the midst of his pain and reverent silence.

But a deathbed prophecy explains why Socrates breaks the religious silence before his journey to the gods.[16] Socrates in the *Apology* says that people prophesize most when they are about to die (39c), so the *Apology* prepares us for Socrates' prophesizing right before his death. Deathbed prophecies play an important role at two key places in the *Iliad*: Patroclus' prophecy of Hector's death and Hector's prophecy of Achilles' death (16.843–54, 22.355–60).[17] I argued in Chapter 2 that the *Phaedo* itself is a properly told story about heroes, gods, and the underworld; thus it is fitting for Socrates also to provide a deathbed prophecy – but, of course, a new kind of deathbed prophecy. Earlier in the *Phaedo*, Socrates describes himself as a prophet. His prophecy there seems to come entirely on the basis of argument (84e–85b, as discussed in Section 8.1). Similarly, in the *Apology* Socrates offers a prophecy that is a sort of rational prediction, not on the basis of any special access to the divine (39c–d). But Plato's portrayal of Socrates often does involve some sort of special access to the divine. At the beginning of the *Phaedo* Socrates describes how a dream has been coming to him, which he takes to be a divine messenger (60e–61b). And, of course, Socrates famously has a divine voice that speaks to him (e.g. *Apology* 31c–d, 40a–c). It is entirely in keeping with Plato's general portrayal of Socrates across the dialogues, as well as with the literary structure of the *Phaedo*, for Socrates to be having a deathbed prophecy that provides him with some special, divine insight.

As Most and others have noted, in saying that they *owe* a cock to Asclepius, Socrates suggests that they have already received some benefit from him. This is compatible with Socrates' prophesizing, when straddling the border between embodiment and disembodiment, a universal claim that applies to the past and present as much as the future. This is in fact exactly the sort of content in Socrates' earlier prophecy in the *Phaedo*: he prophesizes a general philosophical truth that applies equally to past, present, and future – namely that the soul is not destroyed upon death. Normally deathbed prophecy has to do with other people's deaths, not only in Homer but also in two examples in Cicero's *De divinatione* (1.23, 1.30). It seems that deathbed prophecies were typically understood in the ancient world as offering an insight into other people's deaths. If Socrates is prophesizing some sort of universal claim about people's death, this could explain why all of his companions owe this sacrifice.

Hence my basic proposal is that Socrates has a prophetic, divine insight confirming that his "good hope" is correct: whoever suitably prepares through

---

[16] Most 1993 refers to it as a "deathbed vision," but I see no evidence in ancient sources that this sort of prophecy comes in a vision.
[17] Cited by Aristotle (fr. 10 Rose).

philosophizing can obtain true wisdom and live with the gods after death (68a–b, 69d–e, 80e–81a). Socrates' companions, as aspiring philosophers, should be grateful for this, as should Socrates, given his life's practice. In short, there is not a hidden message in Socrates' last words, but rather a confirmation of his central message in the dialogue: our souls will exist after death and, if we suitably prepare ourselves, we can live with the divine. Of course, one could accept that this is the main point of Socrates' last words without thinking that it is a sort of divine insight. It might be instead that Socrates simply is confident in these claims and thinks that immediately before his death is the appropriate time to be thankful for this. I think a divine insight better explains the timing of Socrates' last words and why he is now confident enough to think that a sacrifice is appropriate. It also fits with this being the story of a new kind of hero. But any substantive interpretation of Socrates' last words certainly goes well beyond what the text requires.

If Socrates' prophecy confirms his good hope, his companions really should take care of themselves – hence Socrates' final injunction: do not be careless. In fact, exactly this point is made in the other place in the *Phaedo* where Socrates uses this verb for being careless (ἀμελέω), namely directly after the final argument:

> "But, gentlemen," [Socrates] said, "it is right to think *this* much: that if the soul actually is immortal, then it needs to be cared for, not only for the sake of the time in which what we call 'living' goes on, but for the sake of all time; and that now the dangers would really seem to be dreadful, if one is careless with the soul." (107c1–5)

Socrates' deathbed prophecy confirms that the soul in fact is immortal and that the condition of our soul leads to a better or worse afterlife, and so confirms that we must not be careless.

This interpretation explains why a sacrifice to the gods is appropriate, but not one to Asclepius, in particular. That, it turns out, is a problem for which there are at least four plausible solutions. In the end I do not see any decisive reasons to choose one over another – indeed, there may have been more than one reason to sacrifice to Asclepius. In addition to clarifying why this sacrifice would be appropriate, presenting these alternatives provides further opportunity to review some of the dialogue's central ideas.

Recall that Nietzsche's interpretation is that Socrates is saying that life is a disease. According to Most, the notion that life is a disease is unparalleled in Greek literature up to the Neoplatonists, and so it is "inconceivable" that Socrates would be making such a claim here.[18] Nietzsche explicitly disapproves of what he takes Socrates to be saying, and so is a hostile interpreter. Thus it is unfortunate that later interpreters have taken over his way of articulating this sort of interpretation. Socrates thinks that there is life after death, so he certainly would not think that life itself is a disease. If Socrates is treating anything as a disease, it is the soul's embodiment, not life as such.

---

[18] Most 1993, 100–2.

The idea that embodiment is a disease is not merely paralleled in Greek literature; it is paralleled in the *Phaedo* and elsewhere in Plato. When Socrates describes Cebes' view, he says that according to it "the very fact of its [the soul's] coming into a human body was the start of its perishing, like a disease" (95d1–3). Of course, Socrates himself does not think that embodiment destroys the soul, as Cebes' objection suggests. But this objection is effective, in part, because it develops Socrates' idea that the body has deleterious effects on the soul; Cebes simply extends these effects to include the destruction of the soul (cf. Section 10.2). Socrates' own view could easily be that embodiment is a disease, but a non-lethal one. The *Timaeus* shows how embodiment could be seen as a disease. Timaeus contrasts "diseases of the body" (86b1) with "those of the soul that come through the body" (86b2). The latter, Timaeus says, include *anoia* (ignorance) and anything that brings about *anoia*. According to Timaeus, the greatest of the diseases are excessive pleasures and pains (86b); these are diseases of the soul that come through the body, bringing about *anoia* (cf. *Phaedo* 83b–c). Timaeus does not say that embodiment itself is a disease, but he implies it, since he says that embodiment allows the soul to become diseased and that any condition that brings on ignorance should be viewed as a disease (86b). If one prefers, one could say that the body is what allows for psychic diseases, and so by removing the body, one removes what allows for the greatest diseases – for which it is appropriate to sacrifice to Asclepius.

Moreover, Socrates has just referred to the hemlock as a *"pharmakon"* (115a); indeed, this is the only way that the drug is referred to in the dialogue. He has repeatedly identified the body as a source of pollution across the dialogue (66b–67d, 69b–c, 81b–e, 83d–e, 108a–b) and a *pharmakon* is first and foremost something that removes pollution. According to Most, Socrates' references to pollution are religious, not medical; however, this is anachronistic, as Patterson has noted.[19] Discussions of "purification" in medical contexts are not independent of those in religious ones, and so it is very natural for Socrates to think of the purification of the soul as a medical process (cf. *Charmides* 156e–157a).

Of course, this is not a normal reason to sacrifice to Asclepius. But Socrates is sacrificing to the god of healing as he is about to die and he has argued for radical claims throughout the dialogue; we should not expect him to be sacrificing to Asclepius for a normal reason. He has radically reinterpreted religious claims throughout the dialogue (e.g. 67b, 69c–d, 80d, 84e–85b, 107d–114d). In fact, one is hard pressed to find him accepting a standard interpretation of any religious view in the *Phaedo*. If Plato wanted to portray Socrates, in his final breath, as adhering to standard Greek religious views, he would not have had Socrates in the death scene reject the idea that burial is important, offer hemlock to the gods, and then say that he must reach his end in reverent silence. Plato's general strategy is to show that Socrates was a deeply pious person with highly unorthodox views. In any event,

---

[19] Patterson 2018.

Socrates would supposedly reject the standard view that the gods gain some benefit when a sacrifice is made to them. Instead, like the point of his prayer, that of the sacrifice is likely to show their appreciation to Asclepius for the benefit provided, as well as their general subordination to the gods.

Many scholars simply do not want Socrates to be saying anything along the lines that embodiment is a disease or a source of disease, and so they are looking for ways to interpret him differently. One of the guiding ideas of this book is that we should take Socrates seriously when he repeatedly says things that seem radical and perhaps unappealing. Plato has drawn attention to how Socrates' actions are, to the end, in line with the philosophical views he has argued for over the course of the day. He has defended at length in the defense speech the view that the philosopher will never have what he desires so long as he is embodied, and so desires nothing other than being dead (Section 3.7). He argued that he will be able to become more like the divine after death, and can escape the cycle of reincarnation and live for all time among the gods (80d–81a, Section 7.1). We should not shy away from interpreting his dying words in light of this.

Deborah Kamen offers a different reason to sacrifice to Asclepius: Socrates may be viewing Asclepius as the god to sacrifice to when freed from slavery.[20] Socrates has said that the soul is enslaved to the body (66c–d), but that the soul should instead rule over the body (79e–80a, 94b), adorned with freedom (114e–115a); his language of "releasing" (ἀπαλλάττεσθαι) the soul from the body, used throughout the dialogue, is the same as the language used for slaves being released from their masters. The narrator of the dialogue, Phaedo, was a freed slave (see Section 1.1). According to this reading, Socrates says that they owe a cock to Asclepius because they can be freed of their enslavement to the body upon death, so long as they take care of themselves. The main difficulty with this interpretation, as Kamen acknowledges, is that our evidence for making such offerings to Asclepius comes from a century after the *Phaedo* was written. We simply lack evidence from the fifth to fourth centuries of whether any such offerings were made upon acquiring freedom, and if so, to which deity. It is plausible that Asclepius played this role, but we cannot be certain. Kamen's hypothesis is compatible with the interpretation that Socrates is thinking of embodiment as a disease or the source of disease. Either way, Socrates is saying that the soul will continue to exist after death and that a suitably prepared soul can exist separated from the harmful effects of the body.

Let me turn to a third possible reason to sacrifice to Asclepius. In the discussion of misology Socrates says that it is much better for them to assume that they are not healthy than to think that the *logoi* are not healthy (90d–e). Scholars have suggested that Socrates' last words are saying that his companions have been cured of misology.[21] But Socrates never said that they were misologues, only that they should

---

[20] Kamen 2013.
[21] E.g. Madison 2002, Peterson 2003.

be careful not to become misologues (89c). And ensuring that one will avoid misology would require acquiring the craft of *logoi* (90b), which no one could acquire over the course of a single day. However, Socrates also says that *he* should assume that he is not himself healthy, not because he is in danger of misology, but rather because he is in danger of a specific type of motivated reasoning (90e–91c; Subsection 8.2.3). That danger was that Socrates might be deceiving himself into thinking that he is pursuing the truth, when he is really arguing that the soul exists after death because this is a useful thing to believe, independently of its truth. Socrates thought there was a *danger* that he was deceiving himself in this way. But Socrates' deathbed prophecy has revealed that he is not deceiving himself: the soul really does exist after death. And so Socrates' *logos* and his soul are healthy after all. All of Socrates' companions should be thankful for this, and so sacrifice to Asclepius, because it means that Socrates' eagerness did not make him deceive himself and them simultaneously (91c), as he warned it might.

Sera Schwartz suggested to me a new proposal for why Socrates might sacrifice to Asclepius.[22] Asclepius is the son of a god and a human who is said to have brought a human back from the dead – as Socrates notes in the *Republic* (408b–c). According to the traditional story, Zeus punishes Asclepius for violating the boundary between the mortal and the divine. But in the *Republic* Socrates does not suggest that there is anything wrong with violating this boundary – as we would expect, since Plato's dialogues frequently suggest that we should seek to become divine. Socrates, in the *Phaedo*, hopes to escape embodiment and live for all time with the gods, breaking this boundary. Of course, according to the traditional story, Asclepius re-embodied a person, which is not what Socrates wants to happen to him. But if we hold fixed, as Socrates does, that the gods and their children do only good things, then if Asclepius broke down this boundary, he did so for good reason. In any event, we can see why Asclepius could be an apt god to thank if one has a vision and realizes that we can, indeed, transcend the boundary between mortal and divine, coming to dwell with the gods.[23]

If we properly care for the soul, upon death we will be spared the psychic diseases that come through the body, freed from our enslavement to the body, and able to transcend the divide between the mortal and the divine. Socrates turns out not to have deceived himself. A deathbed prophecy could reveal that Socrates was right about each of these things, and so it is difficult to decide why they owe a cock to Asclepius. Again, there may be several reasons. But in any case the broad message is clear. They can be free of the body and have a better life after death, if they suitably

---

[22] In the graduate seminar on the *Phaedo* I taught at Humboldt in 2017–2018.
[23] One could add that in the *Republic* Asclepius is said to heal people precisely in those cases where they are able to keep engaging in their lives' work (405a–408b), as Betegh 2020 notes. Socrates and his companions have dedicated their lives to philosophy, and Socrates' vision reveals that they can continue doing so.

prepare themselves now. In Socrates' final breath, he is trying to get his companions to care for themselves, since he now truly sees the benefit this will bring them.

Socrates first illustrated his approach to interpretation when he interpreted his dream near the beginning of the dialogue (60d–61b, Section 2.6): any interpretation of the gods must yield something true, and actively seeking this truth can lead to new insights. In his final breath, Socrates reinterprets his religious tradition one last time. In producing such obscure last words, Socrates puts his companions – and Plato puts us – in the position of interpreters. And if these words are the result of divine inspiration, he would think that they must also be true. Socrates' last words thus leave us to do the sort of active interpretation that he has done throughout the dialogue.

12.4 CONCLUSION

However one understands Socrates' last words, the death scene shows Socrates facing his death as admirably as possible, entirely in line with the views he has been arguing for over the course of the dialogue. It illustrates how Socrates' theory, though it may seem cold and uncaring, need not be either, even if it is uncompromising. In doing so, it completes Plato's portrait of how the true philosopher faces death.

Bibliography

GREEK TEXTS

Unless otherwise indicated, the text followed is that of the most recent Oxford Classical Text (OCT).

Burnet, J. 1901–7. *Platonis opera*, vols. 2–5. Oxford: Clarendon.
Duke, E. A. et al. 1995. *Platonis opera*, vol. 1: *Tetralogias I–II*. Oxford: Clarendon.
Sharples, R. W. 2011. "Strato of Lampsacus: The Sources, Texts and Translations," in M.-L. Desclos and W. W. Fortenbaugh (eds.), *Strato of Lampsacus: Text, Translation and Discussion*. New Brunswick, NJ: Transaction, 5–229.
Slings, S. R. 2003. *Platonis Respublica*. Oxford: Clarendon.

SECONDARY LITERATURE

Ackrill, J. L. 1973. "Anamnesis in the *Phaedo*: Remarks on 73c–75c," in Edward N. Lee, Alexander P. D. Mourelatos, and Richard M. Rorty (eds.), *Exegesis and Argument: Studies in Greek Philosophy Presented to Gregory Vlastos*. Assen: Van Gorcum, 177–95.
Ademollo, F. 2011. *The Cratylus of Plato: A Commentary*. Cambridge: Cambridge University Press.
   2018. "On Plato's Conception of Change," *Oxford Studies in Ancient Philosophy* 55, 35–83.
Apolloni, D. 1996. "Plato's Affinity Argument for the Immortality of the Soul," *Journal of the History of Philosophy* 34, 5–32.
Annas, J. 1982. "Aristotle on Inefficient Causes," *Philosophical Quarterly* 32, 311–26.
Bailey, D. T. J. 2005. "Logic and Music in Plato's *Phaedo*," *Phronesis* 50, 95–115.
   2014. "Platonic Causes Revisited," *Journal of the History of Philosophy* 52, 15–32.
Balla, C. 2001. "Sailing Away from Antilogic: Plato's *Phaedo* 90b–101e," *Ancient Philosophy* 41, 1–13.
Barnes, J. 1978. "Plato: *Phaedo* by David Gallop," *Canadian Journal of Philosophy* 8, 397–419.
Bedu-Addo, J. T. 1979. "On the Alleged Abandonment of the Good in the *Phaedo*," *Apeiron* 13, 104–14.
   1991. "Sense-Experience and the Argument for Recollection in Plato's *Phaedo*," *Phronesis* 36, 27–60.

Beere, J. 2010. "Philosophy, Virtue, and Immortality in Plato's *Phaedo*," *Boston Area Colloquium in Ancient Philosophy* 26, 253–301.

Benson, H. 2015. *Clitophon's Challenge: Dialectic in Plato's Meno, Phaedo, and Republic*. Oxford: Oxford University Press.

Betegh, G. 2006. "Eschatology and Cosmology: Models and Problems," in M. M. Sassi (ed.), *La costruzione del discorso filosofico nell'età dei presocratici / The Construction of the Philosophical Discourse in the Presocratic Period*. Pisa: Edizioni della Normale, 29–50.

2009. "Tale, Theology, and Teleology in the *Phaedo*," in C. Partenie (ed.), *Plato's Myths*. Cambridge: Cambridge University Press, 77–100.

2013. "On the Physical Aspect of Heraclitus' Psychology (With New Appendices)," in D. Sider and D. Obbink (eds.), *Doctrine and Doxography: Studies on Heraclitus and Pythagoras*. Berlin: De Gruyter, 225–61.

2014. "Pythagoreans, Orphism, and Greek Religion," in C. A. Huffman (ed.), *A History of Pythagoreanism*. Cambridge: Cambridge University Press, 149–66.

2016. "Review of R. Edmonds, *Redefining Ancient Orphism: A Study in Greek Religion*," *Gnomon* 88, 742–5.

2020. "Plato on Illness in the *Phaedo*, the *Republic*, and the *Timaeus*," in C. Jorgenson, F. Karfík, and S. Spinka (eds.), *Plato's Timaeus*. Leiden: Brill, 228–58.

2021a. "The Ingredients of the Soul in Plato's *Timaeus*," in F. Leigh (ed.), *Themes in Plato, Aristotle, and Hellenistic Philosophy: Keeling Lectures 2011–2018*, BICS Supplement 141, 83–104.

2021b. "Thinking with Empedocles: Aristotle on Soul as *Harmonia*," *Oxford Studies in Ancient Philosophy* 59, 1–44.

2022. "Plato on Philosophy and the Mysteries," in D. Ebrey and R. Kraut (eds.), *The Cambridge Companion to Plato*, 2nd ed. Cambridge: Cambridge University Press, 233–67.

unpublished. "Plato and the Origins of the Concept of Body."

Blank, D. L. 1986. "Socrates' Instructions to Cebes: Plato, 'Phaedo' 101de," *Hermes* 114, 146–63.

Blondell, R. 2002. *The Play of Character in Plato's Dialogues*. Cambridge: Cambridge University Press.

Bluck, R. S. 1955. *Plato's Phaedo*. London: Routledge & Kegan Paul.

Bobonich, C. 2002. *Plato's Utopia Recast*. Oxford: Oxford University Press.

Bossi, B. 2018. "Back to the Cock: On Gratitude and Care," in G. Cornelli, T. Robinson, and F. Bravo (eds.), *Plato's Phaedo: Selected Papers from the Eleventh Symposium Platonicum*. Baden Baden: Academia Verlag, 74–83

Bostock, D. 1986. *Plato's Phaedo*. Oxford: Oxford University Press.

Boys-Stones, G. 2004. "Phaedo of Ellis and Plato on the Soul," *Phronesis* 49, 1–23.

Brandwood, L. 1992. "Stylometry and chronology," in R. Kraut (ed.), *The Cambridge Companion to Plato*. Cambridge: Cambridge University Press, 90–120. Reprinted in Ebrey and Kraut 2022a.

Brisson, L. 1998. *Plato the Myth Maker*, trans. G. Naddaf. Chicago, IL: University of Chicago Press.

2019. "Can One Speak of Teleology in Plato?" in E. Keeling and L. Pitteloud (eds.), *Psychology and Ontology in Plato*. Cham: Springer, 109–23.

Broackes, J. 2009. "αὐτὸς καθ' αὑτὸν in the *Clouds*: Was Socrates Himself a Defender of Separable Soul and Separate Forms?" *Classical Quarterly* 59, 46–59.

Brown, E. 2012. "The Unity of the Soul in Plato's *Republic*," in R. Barney, T. Brennan, and C. Brittain (eds.), *Plato and the Divided Self*. Cambridge: Cambridge University Press, 53–73.

Brown, L. 1999. "Being in the *Sophist*: A Syntactical Enquiry," in G. Fine (ed.), *Plato 1: Metaphysics and Epistemology*. Oxford: Oxford University Press, 455–78.
Burger, R. 1984. *The* Phaedo: *A Platonic Labyrinth*. New Haven, CT: Yale University Press.
Burkert, W. 1972. *Lore and Science in Ancient Pythagoreanism*. Cambridge, MA: Harvard University Press.
  1983. *Homo necans: The Anthropology of Ancient Greek Sacrificial Ritual and Myth*. Berkeley: University of California Press.
Burnet, J. 1911. *Plato's* Phaedo. Oxford: Clarendon.
Campbell, I. 2019. *Refutation, Deduction and the Demarcation of Philosophy from Sophistry*. Doctoral dissertation, Princeton University.
Casadesús Bordoy, F. 2013. "On the Origin of the Orphic–Pythagorean Notion of the Immortality of the Soul," in G. Cornelli, R. McKirahan, and C. Macris (eds.), *On Pythagoreanism*. Berlin: De Gruyter, 153–76.
Caston, V. 1997. "Epiphenomenalisms, Ancient and Modern," *Philosophical Review* 106, 309–63.
Clay, D. 1985. "The Art of Glaukos (Plato *Phaedo* 108D4–9)," *American Journal of Philology* 106, 230–6.
Cooper, J. M. 1989. "Greek Philosophers on Euthanasia and Suicide," in B. A. Brody (ed.), *Suicide and Euthanasia: Historical and Contemporary Themes*. Dordrecht: Kluwer Academic Publishers, 24–29.
  2004. *Knowledge, Nature, and the Good: Essays on Ancient Philosophy*. Princeton, NJ: Princeton University Press.
Cooper, J. M. and Hutchinson, D. S. 1997. *Plato: Complete Works*. Indianapolis, IN: Hackett.
Cornford, F. M. 1935. *Plato's Theory of Knowledge: The Theaetetus and Sophist of Plato*. London: Routledge.
Craik, E. M. 2014. *The "Hippocratic" Corpus: Content and Context*. London: Routledge.
Crooks, J. 1998. "Socrates' Last Words: Another Look at an Ancient Riddle," *Classical Quarterly* 48, 117–25.
Crotty, K. 2009. *The Philosopher's Song: The Poets' Influence on Plato*. Lanham, MD: Lexington Books.
Curd, P. *Anaxagoras of Clazomenae: Fragments and Testimonia*. Toronto: Toronto University Press.
Damascius. 2009. *Lectures on the* Phaedo, ed. L. G. Westerink. Wiltshire: Prometheus Trust.
Dancy, R. M. 2004. *Plato's Introduction of Forms*. Cambridge: Cambridge University Press.
Darbo-Peschanski, C. 1999. "Aitia," in S. Settis *I greci: storia, cultura, arte, societa*, vol. 2.2: *Una storia greca: definizione*. Turin: Enaudi, 1063–84.
Delcomminette, S. 2018. "Plato on Hatred of Philosophy," *Review of Metaphysics* 72: 29–51.
Denniston, J. D. 1960. *Greek Prose Style*. Oxford: Oxford University Press.
Denyer, N. 2007. "The *Phaedo*'s Final Argument," in D. Scott (ed.), *Maieusis: Essays in Ancient Philosophy in Honour of Myles Burnyeat*. Oxford: Oxford University Press, 87–96.
Derrida, J. 1968. "La Pharmacie de Platon," *Tel Quel*, 32, 3–48, and 33, 18–59.
Devereux, D. T. 1994. "Separation and Immanence in Plato's Theory of Forms," *Oxford Studies in Ancient Philosophy* 12, 63–90.
Dimas, P. 2003. "Recollecting Forms in the *Phaedo*," *Phronesis* 48, 175–214.
Dixsaut, M. 1991. *Platon, Phédon*. Paris: Flammarion.
Dorter, K. 1982. *Plato's* Phaedo: *An Interpretation*. Toronto: University of Toronto Press.
Ebert, T. 2001. "Why Is Evenus Called a Philosopher at *Phaedo* 61c?" *Classical Quarterly* 51, 423–34.

2004. *Phaidon: Übersetzung und Kommentar*. Göttingen: Vandenhoeck & Ruprecht.
Ebrey, D. 2013. "A New Philosophical Tool in the *Meno*: 86e–87c," *Ancient Philosophy* 33, 75–96
  2014a. "Meno's Paradox in Context," *British Journal for the History of Philosophy* 22, 1–21.
  2014b. "Making Room for Matter: Material Causes in the *Phaedo* and the *Physics*," *Apeiron* 47, 245–65.
  2015. "Why Are There No Conditionals in Aristotle's Logic?" *Journal of the History of Philosophy* 53, 185–205.
  2016. Review of Hugh Benson *Clitophon's Challenge: Dialectic in Plato's* Meno, Phaedo, *and* Republic. *Notre Dame Philosophical Review*.
  2017a. "Plato's *Phaedo*," in Dee Clayman (ed.), *Oxford Bibliographies in Classics*. https://www.oxfordbibliographies.com/view/document/obo-9780195389661/obo-9780195389661-0272.xml.
  2017b. "The Asceticism of the *Phaedo*: Pleasure, Purification, and the Soul's Proper Activity," *Archiv für Geschichte der Philosophie* 99, 1–30.
  2021. "The *Phaedo*'s Final Argument and the Soul's Kinship with the Divine," *Oxford Studies in Ancient Philosophy* 61, 25–62.
  2022a. "The Unfolding Account of Forms in the *Phaedo*," in D. Ebrey and R. Kraut (eds.), *The Cambridge Companion to Plato*, 2nd ed. Cambridge: Cambridge University Press, 268–97.
  2022b. Review of A. Long, *Death and Immortality in Ancient Philosophy*. *Nous*.
  2023. "The *Phaedo* as an Alternative to Tragedy," *Classical Philology* 118.
  unpublished. "Forms and the Origin of Self-Predication."
Ebrey, D. and Kraut, R. (eds.). 2022a. *The Cambridge Companion to Plato*, 2nd ed. Cambridge: Cambridge University Press.
  2022b. "Introduction to the Study of Plato," in D. Ebrey and R. Kraut (eds.), *The Cambridge Companion to Plato*, 2nd ed. Cambridge: Cambridge University Press, 1–38.
Edmonds, R. G. 2004. *Myths of the Underworld Journey: Plato, Aristophanes, and the "Orphic" Gold Tablets*. Cambridge: Cambridge University Press.
Edmonds, R. G. 2013. *Redefining Ancient Orphism: A Study in Greek Religion*. Cambridge: Cambridge University Press.
  2017. "Alcibiades the Profane: Images of the Mysteries," in P. Destrée and Z. Giannopoulou (eds.), *Plato's Symposium: A Critical Guide*. Cambridge: Cambridge University Press, 194–215.
El Murr, D. 2014. "Αὐτὸ καθ' αὑτό : La Genèse et le sens d'un philosophème platonicien," in D. Doucet and I. Koch (eds.), *Autos, idipsum: aspects de l'identité d'Homère à Augustin*. Aix-en-Provence: Presses Universitaires de Provence, 39–56.
Elton, M. 1997. "The Role of the Affinity Argument in the *Phaedo*," *Phronesis* 42, 313–16.
Emde Boas, E. van, A. Rijksbaron, L. Huitink, and M. de Bakker. 2019. *The Cambridge Grammar of Classical Greek*. Cambridge: Cambridge University Press.
Fine, G. 1984. "Separation," *Oxford Studies in Ancient Philosophy* 2, 31–87.
  1986. "Immanence," *Oxford Studies in Ancient Philosophy* 4, 71–97.
Fletcher, E. 2022. "Cosmology and Human Nature in the *Timaeus*," in D. Ebrey and R. Kraut (eds.), *The Cambridge Companion to Plato*, 2nd ed. Cambridge: Cambridge University Press, 468–92.
Franklin, L. 2005. "Recollection and Philosophical Reflection in Plato's *Phaedo*," *Phronesis* 50, 289–314.

Frede, D. 1978. "The Final Proof of the Immortality of the Soul in Plato's *Phaedo* 102a–107a," *Phronesis* 23, 27–41.
  2005. *Platon Phaidon*. Darmstadt: Wissenschaftliche Buchgesellschaft.
  2011. "Das Argument aus den essentiellen Eigenschaften (102a–107d)," in J. Müller (ed.), *Platon, Phaidon*. Berlin: Akademie Verlag, 143–157.
Frede, M. 1980. "The Original Notion of Cause," in M. Schofield, M. Burnyeat, and J. Barnes (eds.), *Doubt and Dogmatism*. Oxford: Oxford University Press, 217–49.
  1988. "Being and Becoming in Plato," *Oxford Studies in Ancient Philosophy* (suppl.), 37–52.
  1992. "Introduction," in *Plato: Protagoras*, trans. S. Lombardo and K. Bell (Indianapolis, IN: Hackett), vii–xxxiv.
Furley, D. J. 1976. "Anaxagoras in Response to Parmenides," *Canadian Journal of Philosophy* (suppl. 2), 61–85.
  1989. *Cosmic Problems*. Cambridge: Cambridge University Press.
  2002. "Anaxagoras, Plato, and Naming of Parts," in R. Caston and D. Graham (eds.), *Presocratic Philosophy: Essays in Honour of Alexander Mourelatos*. Aldershot: Ashgate, 119–26.
Gallop, D. 1975. *Plato: Phaedo*. Oxford: Clarendon.
Gentzler, J. 1991. "συμφωνεῖν in Plato's *Phaedo*," *Phronesis* 36, 265–76.
  1994. "Recollection and the Problem of the Socratic Elenchus," *Proceedings of the Boston Area Colloquium of Ancient Philosophy* 10, 257–95.
Gill, C. 1973. "The Death of Socrates," *Classical Quarterly* 23, 25–8.
Gonzales, F. 2018. "Why the Minotaur is Misology," in G. Cornelli, T. Robinson, and F. Bravo (eds.), *Plato's Phaedo: Selected Papers from the Eleventh Symposium Platonicum*. Baden Baden: Academia Verlag, 90–5.
Gosling, J. C. B. 1965. "Similarity in *Phaedo* 73b seq.," *Phronesis* 10, 151–61.
Gosling, J. C. B. and C. C. W. Taylor. 1982. *The Greeks on Pleasure*. Oxford: Clarendon.
Gulley, N. 1963. *Plato's Theory of Knowledge*. London: Routledge.
Hackforth, R. 1955. *Plato's Phaedo*. Cambridge: Cambridge University Press.
Halliwell, F. S. 1984. "Plato and Aristotle on the Denial of Tragedy," *Proceedings of the Cambridge Philological Society* 30, 49–71.
  1999. "Plato's Repudiation of the Tragic," in M. S. Silk (ed.), *Tragedy and the Tragic: Greek Theatre and Beyond*. Oxford: Clarendon, 332–49.
Hankinson, R. J. 1998. *Cause and Explanation in Ancient Greek Thought*. Oxford: Oxford University Press.
Hobbs, A. 2000. *Plato and the Hero: Courage, Manliness, and the Impersonal Good*. Cambridge: Cambridge University Press.
Horky, P. S. 2013. *Plato and Pythagoreanism*. Oxford: Oxford University Press.
Huffman, C. A. 1993. *Philolaus of Croton: Pythagorean and Presocratic: A Commentary on the Fragments and Testimonia, with Interpretative Essay*. Cambridge: Cambridge University Press.
  2010. "The Pythagorean Conception of the Soul, from Pythagoras to Philolaus," in D. Frede and B. Reis (eds.), *Body and Soul in Ancient Philosophy*. Berlin: de Gruyter, 21–43.
  2018. "Pythagoras," in E. N. Zalta (ed.), *The Stanford Encyclopedia of Philosophy*. https://plato.stanford.edu/archives/win2018/entries/pythagoras.
Hyland, D. A. 1993. "Philosophy and Tragedy in the Platonic Dialogues," in N. Georgopoulos (ed.), *Tragedy and Philosophy*. Oxford: Oxford University Press, 123–38.
Irwin, T. 1977a. *Plato's Moral Theory: The Early and Middle Dialogues*. Oxford: Clarendon.
  1977b. "Plato's Heracliteanism," *Philosophical Quarterly* 27, 1–13.

1983. Review of M. Schofield, M. Burnyeat, and J. Barnes (eds.), *Doubt and Dogmatism: Studies in Hellenistic Epistemology*. Nous 17, 126–34.

1999. "Plato's Theory of Forms," in G. Fine (ed.), *Plato*, vol. 1: *Metaphysics and Epistemology*. Oxford: Oxford University Press, 143–70.

Irani, T. 2017. *Plato on the Value of Philosophy: The Art of Argument in the Gorgias and Phaedrus*. Cambridge: Cambridge University Press.

2021. "Perfect Change in Plato's *Sophist*," Oxford Studies in Ancient Philosophy 60, 45–93.

Iwata, N. 2020. "The Attunement Theory of the Soul in the *Phaedo*," Japan Studies in Classical Antiquity 4, 35–52.

Jansen, S. 2013. "Plato's *Phaedo* as a Pedagogical Drama," Ancient Philosophy 33, 333–52.

Johansen, T. K. 2004. *Plato's Natural Philosophy*. Cambridge: Cambridge University Press.

2017. "The Separation of Soul from Body in Plato's *Phaedo*," Philosophical Inquiry 41, 17–28.

2020. "Plato's Teleology," in J. K. McDonough (ed.), *Teleology: A History*. Oxford: Oxford University Press, 14–38.

Jones, R. and P. Marechal. 2018. "Plato's Guide to Living with Your Body," in J. Sisko (ed.), *Philosophy of Mind in Antiquity*. London: Routledge, 84–100.

Jouanna, J. 1999. *Hippocrates*, trans. M. B. DeBevoise. Baltimore, MD: Johns Hopkins University Press.

Justin, G. 2020. "Opposites and Plato's Principle of Change in the *Phaedo* Cyclical Argument," Journal of the History of Philosophy 58, 423–48.

Kahn, C. H. 1996. *Plato and the Socratic Dialogue*. Cambridge: Cambridge University Press.

2002. "On Platonic Chronology," in J. Annas and C. Rowe (eds.), *New Perspectives on Plato, Modern and Ancient*. Cambridge, MA: Harvard University Press, 93–128.

2004. "A Return to the Theory of the Verb Be and the Concept of Being," Ancient Philosophy 24, 381–405.

Kamen, D. 2013. "The Manumission of Socrates: A Rereading of Plato's *Phaedo*," Classical Antiquity 32, 78–100.

Kamtekar, R. 2016. "The Soul's (After-)Life," Ancient Philosophy 36, 115–32.

Kanayama, Y. 2000. "The Methodology of the Second Voyage and the Proof of the Soul's Indestructibility in Plato's *Phaedo*," Oxford Studies in Ancient Philosophy 18, 41–100.

2019. "Socrates' Humaneness: What His Last Words Meant," Frontiers of Philosophy in China 14, 111–31.

Karfik, F. 2004. *Die Beseelung des Kosmos: Untersuchungen zur Kosmologie, Seelenlehre und Theologie in Platons Phaidon und Timaios*. Munich: K. G. Saur.

Kelsey, S. 2000. "Recollection in the *Phaedo*," Proceedings of the Boston Area Colloquium of Ancient Philosophy 16, 91–121.

2004. "Causation in the *Phaedo*," Pacific Philosophical Quarterly 85, 21–43.

Kingsley, P. 1995. *Ancient Philosophy, Mystery, and Magic: Empedocles and the Pythagorean Tradition*. Oxford: Oxford University Press.

Kurke, L. 2011. *Aesopic Conversations: Popular Tradition, Cultural Dialogue, and the Invention of Greek Prose*. Martin Classical Lectures. Princeton, NJ: Princeton University Press.

Laks, A. 2010. "Plato's 'Truest Tragedy': *Laws* Book 7, 817a–d," in C. Bobonich (ed.), *Plato's Laws: A Critical Guide*. Cambridge: Cambridge University Press, 217–31.

Ledbetter, G. M. 1999. "Reasons and Causes in Plato: The Distinction between αἴτιον and αἰτία," Ancient Philosophy 19, 255–65.

Lee, D. C. 2012. "Drama, Dogmatism, and the Equals Argument in the *Phaedo*," Oxford Studies in Ancient Philosophy 44, 1–39.

Lennox, J. G. 1985. "Plato's Unnatural Teleology," in D. O'Meara (ed.), *Platonic Investigations*. Washington, DC: Catholic University of America Press, 195–218.
Lescher, J. 1999. "Early Interest in Knowledge," in A. A. Long (ed.), *The Cambridge Companion to Early Greek Philosophy*. Cambridge: Cambridge University Press, 1999, 225–49.
Long, A. A. 1968. *Language and Thought in Sophocles: A Study of Abstract Nouns and Poetic Technique*. London: Routledge.
Long, A. G. 2019. *Death and Immortality in Ancient Philosophy*. Cambridge: Cambridge University Press.
Lorenz, H. 2006. *The Brute Within: Appetitive Desire in Plato and Aristotle*. Oxford: Oxford University Press.
  2008. "Plato on the Soul," in G. Fine (ed.), *Oxford Handbook on Plato*. Oxford: Oxford University Press, 243–66.
Loriaux, R. 1969. *Le Phédon de Platon: commentaire et traduction, 1: 57a–84b*. Namur: Presses Universitaires de Namur.
  1975. *Le Phédon de Platon: commentaire et traduction, 2: 84b–118a*. Namur: Presses Universitaires de Namur.
Madison, L. A. 2002. "Have We Been Careless with Socrates' Last Words? A Rereading of the *Phaedo*," *Journal of the History of Philosophy* 40, 421–36.
Mann, W.-G. 2000. *The Discovery of Things: Aristotle's Categories and their Context*. Princeton, NJ: Princeton University Press.
Mayhew, R. 2008. "On Prayer in Plato's *Laws*," *Apeiron* 41, 1–18.
Marechal, P. 2021. "Temperance and Epistemic Purity in Plato's *Phaedo*," *Archiv für Geschichte der Philosophie*.
Martinelli Tempesta, S. 2003. "Sul significato di δεύτερος πλοῦς nel *Fedone* di Platone," in M. Bonazzi and F. Trabattoni (eds.), *Platone e la tradizione platonica: Studi di filosofia antica*. Cisalpino: Milan, 89–125.
McDonough, J. 2020. "Introduction," in J. McDonough (ed.), *Teleology: A History*. Oxford: Oxford University Press, 1–13.
McKirahan, R. D. 2017. "Philolaus on the Soul," in A.-B. Renger and A. Stavru (eds.), *Pythagorean Knowledge from the Ancient to the Modern World: Askēsis – Religion – Science*. Wiesbaden: Harrassowitz, 64–76.
McPherran, M. L. 2003. "Socrates, Crito, and Their Debt to Asclepius," *Ancient Philosophy* 23, 71–92.
McQueen, E. I. and C. J. Rowe. 1989. "Phaedo, Socrates, and the Chronology of the Spartan War with Elis," *Méthexis* 2, 1–18.
Meinwald, C. 1991. *Plato's Parmenides*. Oxford: Oxford University Press.
  2016. *Plato*. London: Routledge.
Menn, S. 1995. *Plato on God as Nous*. Carbondale: Southern Illinois University Press.
  2010. "On Socrates' First Objections to the Physicists (*Phaedo* 95e8–97b7)," *Oxford Studies in Ancient Philosophy* 38, 37–68.
Miller, T. 2015. "Socrates' Warning against Misology (Plato, *Phaedo* 88c–91c)," *Phronesis* 60, 145–79.
Moore, C. 2019. *Calling Philosophers Names: On the Origin of a Discipline*. Princeton, NJ: Princeton University Press.
Morgan, K. A. 2010. "The Voice of Authority: Divination and Plato's *Phaedo*," *Classical Quarterly* 60: 63–81.
  2021. "Paying the Price: Contextualizing Exchange in *Phaedo* 69a–c," *Rhizomata* 8, 239–67.

Moss, J. 2006. "Pleasure and Illusion in Plato," *Philosophy and Phenomenological Research* 73, 503–35.
Most, G. W. 1993. "A Cock for Asclepius," *Classical Quarterly* 43, 96–111.
Mueller, I. 1998. "Platonism and the Study of Nature (*Phaedo* 95e ff.)," in G. Gentzler (ed.), *Method in Ancient Philosophy*. Oxford: Oxford University Press, 67–89.
Nails, D. 2002. *The People of Plato: A Prosopography of Plato and Other Socratics*. Indianapolis, IN: Hackett.
Nehamas, A. 1975. "Plato on the Imperfection of the Sensible World," *American Philosophical Quarterly* 12, 105–17.
  1979. "Self-Predication and Plato's Theory of Forms," *American Philosophical Quarterly* 16, 93–103.
Nietzsche, F. 2015. *Die Geburt der Tragödie aus dem Geiste der Musik: Unzeitgemäße Betrachtungen I–IV: Nachgelassene Schriften 1870–1873*, edited by G. Colli and M. Montinari. Berlin: Deutscher Taschenbuch Verlag.
Nightingale, A. 1995. *Genres in Dialogue: Plato and the Construct of Philosophy*. Cambridge: Cambridge University Press.
  2021. *Philosophy and Religion in Plato's Dialogues*. Cambridge: Cambridge University Press.
Nussbaum, M. 1992. "Tragedy and Self-Sufficiency: Plato and Aristotle on Fear and Pity," in A. Rorty (ed.), *Essays on Aristotle's Poetics*. Princeton, NJ: Princeton University Press, 107–59.
  2001. *The Fragility of Goodness: Luck and Ethics in Greek Tragedy and Philosophy* (rev. ed.). Cambridge: Cambridge University Press.
Obdrzalek, S. 2021. "The Philosopher's Reward: Contemplation and Immortality in Plato's Dialogues," in A. G. Long (ed.), *Immortality in Ancient Philosophy*. Cambridge: Cambridge University Press, 66–92.
O'Brien, D. 1967. "The Last Argument of Plato's *Phaedo*: I," *Classical Quarterly* 17, 189–231.
  1968. "The Last Argument of Plato's *Phaedo*: II," *Classical Quarterly* 18, 95–106.
Ogihara, S. 2018. "Immortality and Eternity: Cebes' Remark at *Phaedo* 106d2–4," in G. Cornelli, T. Robinson, and F. Bravo (eds.), *Plato's* Phaedo: *Selected Papers from the Eleventh Symposium Platonicum*. Baden Baden: Academia Verlag, 199–204.
Olympiodorus. 2009. *Commentary on the* Phaedo, ed. L. G. Westerink. Wiltshire: Prometheus Trust.
Osborne, C. 1995. "Perceiving Particulars and Recollecting the Forms in the *Phaedo*," *Proceedings of the Aristotelian Society* 96, 211–33.
Owen, G. E. L. 1966. "Plato and Parmenides on the Timeless Present," *Monist* 50, 317–40.
Pakaluk, M. 2003. "Degrees of Separation in the *Phaedo*," *Phronesis* 48, 89–115.
Palmer, J. 2021. *The Method of Hypothesis and the Nature of Soul in Plato's* Phaedo. Cambridge: Cambridge University Press.
Partenie, C. 2009. "Introduction," in C. Partenie (ed.), *Plato's Myths*. Cambridge: Cambridge University Press, 1–27.
  2018. "Metaphors of Body and Soul in the *Phaedo* – and Socrates' Last Words," in G. Cornelli, T. Robinson, and F. Bravo (eds.), *Plato's* Phaedo: *Selected Papers from the Eleventh Symposium Platonicum*. Baden Baden: Academia Verlag, 205–9.
Pelling, C. 2019. *Herodotus and the Question Why*. Austin: University of Texas Press.
Pellò, C. 2018. "The Lives of Pythagoras: A Proposal for Reading Pythagorean Metempsychosis," *Rhizomata* 6, 135–56.

Pender, E. 2012. "The Rivers of Tartarus: Plato's Geography of Dying and Coming-Back-to-Life," in C. Collobert (ed.), *Plato and Myth: Studies on the Use and Status of Platonic Myths.* Leiden: Brill, 199–233.

Penner, T. 1987. *The Ascent from Nominalism: Some Existence Arguments in Plato's Middle Dialogues.* Dordrecht: Reidel.

Peterson, S. 2003. "An Authentically Socratic Conclusion in Plato's *Phaedo*: Socrates' Debt to Asclepius," in N. Roshotko (ed.), *Desire, Identity, and Existence: Essays in Honor of Terry Penner.* Edmonton: Academic Printing and Publishing, 33–52.

Price, A. 1995. *Mental Conflict.* London: Routledge.

2009. "Are Plato's Soul-Parts Psychological Subjects?" *Ancient Philosophy* 29, 1–15.

Race, W. 2012. *Pindar, Olympian Odes, Pythian Odes.* Cambridge, MA: Harvard University Press.

Raphael, D. 1960. *The Paradox of Tragedy.* Bloomington: Indiana University Press.

Rashed, M. 2009. "Aristophanes and the Socrates of the *Phaedo*," *Oxford Studies in Ancient Philosophy* 36, 107–36.

Reed, D. 2020. "Deficient Virtue in the *Phaedo*," *Classical Quarterly* 70, 119–30.

2021. "Bodily Desires and Afterlife Punishment in the *Phaedo*," *Oxford Studies in Ancient Philosophy* 59, 45–77.

Reeve, C. D. C. 2002. *The Trials of Socrates: Six Classic Texts.* Indianapolis, IN: Hackett.

Robinson, R. 1953. *Plato's Earlier Dialectic.* Oxford: Clarendon.

Roochnik, D. 1990. *The Tragedy of Reason: Towards a Platonic Conception of Logos.* New York: Routledge.

Rowe, C. J. 1993. *Plato:* Phaedo. Cambridge: Cambridge University Press.

1995. *Plato:* Statesman. Warminster: Aris & Phillips.

1998. *Plato:* Symposium. Warminster: Aris & Phillips.

Rowett, C. 2021. "Pre-Existence, Life after Death, and Atemporal Beings in Plato's *Phaedo*," in A. G. Long (ed.), *Immortality in Ancient Philosophy.* Cambridge: Cambridge University Press, 93–117.

Russell, D. 2005. *Plato on Pleasure and the Good Life.* Oxford: Oxford University Press.

Salles, R. 2018. "Soul as Harmony in *Phaedo* 85E–86D and Stoic Pneumatic Theory," in V. Harte and R. Woolf (eds.), *Rereading Ancient Philosophy: Old Chestnuts and Sacred Cows.* Cambridge: Cambridge University Press, 221–39.

Santas, G. 1980. "The Form of the Good in Plato's *Republic*," *Philosophical Inquiry* 2, 374–403.

Sassi, M. M. 2018. *The Beginnings of Philosophy in Greece,* trans. M. Asuni. Princeton, NJ: Princeton University Press.

Schaffer, J. 2016. "The Metaphysics of Causation," in E. N. Zalta (ed.), *The Stanford Encyclopedia of Philosophy,* https://plato.stanford.edu/archives/spr2022/entries/causation-metaphysics.

Schiefsky, M. J. 2005. *Hippocrates* On Ancient Medicine. Leiden: Brill.

Schofield, M. 2012. "Pythagoreanism: Emerging from the Presocratic Fog: *Metaphysics* A 5," in C. Steele and O. Primavesi (eds.), *Aristotle's* Metaphysics Alpha: *Symposium Aristotelicum.* Oxford: Oxford University Press, 141–60.

Scott, D. 1995. *Recollection and Experience: Plato's Theory of Learning and Its Successors.* Cambridge: Cambridge University Press.

Sedley, D. 1990. "Teleology and Myth in the *Phaedo*," *Proceedings of the Boston Area Colloquium in Ancient Philosophy* 5, 359–83.

1995. "The Dramatis Personae of Plato's *Phaedo*," in T. J. Smiley (ed.), *Philosophical Dialogues: Plato, Hume and Wittgenstein.* Oxford: Oxford University Press, 1–26.

1998. "Platonic Causes," *Phronesis* 43, 114–32.
2006. "Form–Particular Resemblance in Plato's *Phaedo*," *Proceedings of the Aristotelian Society* 106, 311–27.
2007. "Equal Sticks and Stones," in D. Scott (ed.), *Maieusis: Essays in Ancient Philosophy in Honour of Myles Burnyeat.* Oxford: Oxford University Press, 68–86.
2009. "Three Kinds of Platonic Immortality," in D. Frede (ed.), *Body and Soul in Ancient Philosophy.* Berlin: De Gruyter, 145–61.
2012. "Plato's Theory of Change at *Phaedo* 70–71," in R. Patterson, V. Karasmanis, and A. Hermann (eds.), *Presocratics and Plato: Festschrift at Delphi in Honor of Charles Kahn.* Las Vegas, NV: Parmenides, 147–63.
2014. "The Unity of Virtue after the *Protagoras*," in B. Collette-Dučić and S. Delcominette (eds.), *Unité et origine des vertus dans la philosophie ancienne.* Bruxelles: Ousia, 65–90.
2018. "The *Phaedo*'s Final Proof of Immortality," in G. Cornelli, T. Robinson, and F. Bravo (eds.), *Plato's Phaedo: Select Papers from the Eleventh Symposium Platonicum.* Baden Baden: Akademia Verlag, 210–20.
2021. "Socrates' Second Voyage (*Phaedo* 99–101)," in F. Leigh (ed.), *Themes in Plato, Aristotle, and Hellenistic Philosophy: Keeling Lectures 2011–18.* London: Institute of Classical Studies, 47–62.
Sedley, D. and A. A. Long. 2010. *Plato: Meno and Phaedo.* Cambridge: Cambridge University Press.
Sharma, R. 2009. "Socrates' New *Aitia*: Causal and Metaphysical Explanations in Plato's *Phaedo*," *Oxford Studies in Ancient Philosophy* 36, 137–78.
Shorey, P. 1930. *Plato*, Republic, vol. 1: *Books 1–5.* Cambridge, MA: Harvard University Press.
1935. *Plato, Republic*, vol. 2: *Books 6–10.* Cambridge, MA: Harvard University Press.
Silverman, A. 2002. *The Dialectic of Essence: A Study of Plato's Metaphysics.* Princeton, NJ: Princeton University Press.
Stemmer, P. 1992. *Platons Dialektik: Die frühen und mittleren Dialoge.* Berlin: De Gruyter.
Stone, S. 2018. "Μονάς and ψυχή in the *Phaedo*," *Plato Journal*, 18, 55–69.
Svavarsson, S. H. 2009. "Plato on Forms and Conflicting Appearances: The Argument of *Phaedo* 74a9–c6," *Classical Quarterly* 59, 60–74.
2020. "Justice and the Afterlife," in D. Wolfsdorf (ed.), *Early Greek Ethics.* Oxford: Oxford University Press, 593–611.
Szabó, Á. 1978. *The Beginnings of Greek Mathematics.* Dordrecht: D. Reidel.
Taylor, C. C. W. 1983. "The Arguments in the *Phaedo* Concerning the Thesis that the Soul is a *Harmonia*," in J. P. Anton and A. Preus (eds.), *Essays in Ancient Greek Philosophy.* Albany: SUNY Press, 217–31.
Tenkku, J. 1956. *The Evaluation of Pleasure in Plato's Ethics.* Helsinki: Societas Philosophica.
Trabattoni, F. 1988. "La teoria dell'anima-armonia nel *Fedone*," *Elenchos* 9, 53–74.
2011. *Fedone.* Turin: G. Einaudi.
2016. *Essays on Plato's Epistemology.* Leuven: Leuven University Press.
Trivigno, F. 2009. "Paratragedy in Plato's *Gorgias*," *Oxford Studies in Ancient Philosophy* 36, 73–105.
Tuominen, M. 2014. "'Tell Him to Follow Me as Quickly as Possible': Plato's *Phaedo* (60c–63c) on Taking One's Own Life," in M.-L. Honkasalo and M. Tuominen (eds.), *Culture, Suicide, and the Human Condition.* New York: Berghahn Books, 77–104.
Tuozzo, T. 2018. "'Appearing Equal' at *Phaedo* 74B4–C6: An Epistemic Interpretation," *Oxford Studies in Ancient Philosophy* 54, 1–26.

Vasiliou, I. 2012. "From the *Phaedo* to the *Republic*: Plato's Tripartite Soul and the Possibility of Non-philosophical Virtue," in R. Barney, T. Brennan, and C. Brittain (eds.), *Plato and the Divided Self*. Cambridge: Cambridge University Press, 9–32.

Vázquez, D. 2022. "The Last Natural Philosophers in Plato's *Phaedo* 99b2-c6," *Mnemosyne* (published online ahead of print).

Vegetti, M. 1999. "Culpability, Responsibility, Cause: Philosophy, Historiography, and Medicine in the Fifth Century," in A. A. Long (ed.), *The Cambridge Companion to Early Greek Philosophy*. Cambridge: Cambridge University Press, 1999, 271–89.

Verdenius, W. J. 1958. "Notes on Plato's *Phaedo*," *Mnemosyne* 11, 193–243.

Vlastos, G. 1969. "Reasons and Causes in the *Phaedo*," *Philosophical Review* 78, 291–325.

 1991. *Socrates, Ironist and Moral Philosopher*. Ithaca, NY: Cornell University Press.

Warren, J. 2001. "Socratic Suicide," *Journal of Hellenic Studies* 121, 91–106.

Waterfield, R. (trans.). 1998. *Herodotus: The Histories*. Oxford: Oxford University Press.

Weiss, R. 1987. "The Right Exchange: *Phaedo* 69a6–c3," *Ancient Philosophy* 7, 57–66.

White, F. C. 2006. "Socrates, Philosophers and Death: Two Contrasting Arguments in Plato's *Phaedo*," *Classical Quarterly* 56, 445–58.

White, N. P. 1992. "*Plato's Metaphysical Epistemology*," in R. Kraut (ed.), *The Cambridge Companion to Plato*. Cambridge: Cambridge University Press, 277–310.

Wiggins, D. 1986. "Teleology and the Good in Plato's *Phaedo*," *Oxford Studies in Ancient Philosophy* 4, 1–18.

Wilson, E. 2018. *Homer: The Odyssey*. New York: W. W. Norton.

Wolfsdorf, D. 2005. "Αἴτιον and αἰτία in Plato," *Ancient Philosophy* 25, 341–48.

 2008. "The Method ἐξ ὑποθέσεως at *Meno* 86e1–87d8," *Phronesis* 53, 35–64.

Woolf, R. 2000. "Commentary on Kelsey," *Proceedings of the Boston Area Colloquium in Ancient Philosophy* 16, 122–33.

 2004. "The Practice of a Philosopher," *Oxford Studies in Ancient Philosophy* 26, 97–129.

 2007. "Misology and Truth," *Proceedings of the Boston Area Colloquium in Ancient Philosophy* 23, 1–16.

Young, C. 1988. "A Delicacy in Plato's *Phaedo*," *Classical Quarterly* 38, 250–1.

Young, D. 2013. "The Soul as Structure in Plato's *Phaedo*," *Apeiron* 46, 469–98.

Index Locorum

AESCHYLUS
  Eumenides
    267–75   278
  Prometheus Bound
    1013   64
  Suppliants
    226–32   278
ANAXAGORAS
  A77   291
  B12   65–6, 147, 167, 258
ANAXIMANDER
  B1   294
ANTIPHON THE ORATOR
  On the Murder of Herodes
    21, 8   64
ARISTOPHANES
  Clouds
    193–4   64, 66
    264   190, 226
    379–81   226
    1173   190
    1485   98, 190
ARISTOTLE
  De Anima
    I.2   156
    I.4, 407b34–408a5   199
    I.4, 408a7   199
    II.5, 417b23   74
  De Caelo
    I.1   152
  De generatione et corruptione
    II.9–10   284

  Eudemian Ethics
    I.8, 1217b15–16   63
  Fragments
    Fr. 10 Rose   306
  Metaphysics
    A.5, 986a22–b2   97
    A.6   109
    A.9   109
    M.4   109
    M.4, 1078b30–1   63
    M.4–5   109
    M.9   109
    M.9, 1086a32–b5   63
  Nicomachean Ethics
    I.7   156
    II.9, 1109a34–35   227
  Parts of Animals
    I.1   220
  Physics
    II.1–3   220
    II.7–8   220
  Poetics
    5, 1449b12–13   46
    13, 1453a29–30   30
  Politics
    III.13, 1284b19–20   227
  Posterior Analytics
    I.31, 87b37–88a7   74
    II.6   94
  Prior Analytics
    I.23   94
    I.29   94
    I.44   94

Index Locorum

ARISTOTLE (cont.)
  Sophistical Refutations
    5, 167a21–35 . . . 140, 141
ATHENEUS
  2, 57 . . . 291

CICERO
  De divinatione
    1, 23 . . . 306
    1, 30 . . . 306

DAMASCIUS
  I 19 . . . 56
  I 438 . . . 267–8, 270
DEMOCRITUS
  B83 . . . 214
  B118 . . . 214
  B159 . . . 214
DIOGENES LAERTIUS
  2.105 . . . 13
  3.58 . . . 4
  8.4 . . . 102
  9.8 . . . 288
DIOGENES OF APOLLONIA
  B7 . . . 269
  B8 . . . 269

EMPEDOCLES
  B111 . . . 102
  B112 . . . 271
  B115 . . . 269, 271
  B126 . . . 102
  B146 . . . 102
  B147 . . . 102
EUCLID
  Elements
    X.44 . . . 235
    X.47 . . . 235
EURIPIDES
  Ion
    610 . . . 64
  Iphigenia in Aulis
    988–9 . . . 81

GORGIAS
  Encomium of Helen
    6 . . . 210
    15 . . . 210

HERACLITUS
  B12 . . . 288
  B35 . . . 4
  B60 . . . 217, 288
  B62 . . . 271
  B94 . . . 294
HERODOTUS
  Histories
    I 1 . . . 211
    I 4 . . . 211
    II 20, 2–3 . . . 216
    II 30, 12–13 . . . 138
    III 3 . . . 217
    III 139, 1 . . . 210
    III 139–49 . . . 210
    VI 39 . . . 139
HESIOD
  Theogony
    116–117 . . . 284
  Works and Days
    168 . . . 291
    170–3 . . . 291
HIPPOCRATES
  Diseases of Women
    192.11 . . . 64
    205.21 . . . 64
  Epidemics
    6.8.10.1 . . . 64
    8.10.4 . . . 64
  On Acute Diseases
    4.27 . . . 64
  On Affections
    58.2 . . . 65
  On Ancient Medicine
    1 . . . 215
    1.1 . . . 235
    1.3 . . . 236
    6 . . . 235
    13.1 . . . 235
    14.4 . . . 65–6
    15.1 . . . 65–6, 235
    19.3 . . . 215
    20 . . . 215
    20.2 . . . 211
  On Breaths
    15 . . . 216, 233
  On Diseases
    2.29.4 . . . 65–6
    3.17.19 . . . 64, 66
  On Fleshes
    3 . . . 215
  On Fractures
    2.7 . . . 64
  On Regimen
    1.35 . . . 215
    3 . . . 205
    37.7 . . . 64

67	205	PLATO	
On the Nature of Man		Apology	
2.21	65	19b–c	285
On the Sacred Disease		19b–d	99
16	215	20b–c	22
Prognostic		21a–23b	18
12.30	64	22a–c	126
HOMER		23c	22
Hymn to Demeter		25b–e	221
367–9	19	26d	226
480–2	19	26d–e	99
Hymn to Hermes		28b–d	35
71	271	29a–b	24
115–29	271	29d–30b	301
405	271	29d9–e3	304
Iliad		30a7–b2	304
1, 290	269	31c–d	306
1, 494	269	33a–b	22
16, 843–54	306	33b	22
21, 518	269	34a2	16
22, 355–60	306	34c	293
24, 99	269	34d–35b	293
Odyssey		38b7	16
4, 565–8	291	39c	306
10, 508–12	289	39c–d	306
11, 13	289	40a–c	306
11, 13–22	289	40b–c	24
12, 435	139	Charmides	
		155e–158c	133
IAMBLICHUS		156c–157a	308
On the Pythagorean Life		Cratylus	
82	291	386d–e	217
ISOCRATES		389b	73, 124
Against the Sophists		389b5–6	73
12	143	389d	73
		400c	17, 171
PARMENIDES		402a	288
B8	125, 147	404b	164
B8, 3–4	147	411b–c	288
B8, 29–30	147	436c	143
PHILOLAUS		437a	288
A16	292	439a–b	106
A17	292	439d–440d	255
A19	292	Crito	
A20	291	44d	221
A27	198	Euthydemus	
B6	269	280b–281e	26
F6	197	281c–e	78
F6a	197	281d–e	65
PINDAR		290e–293b	44
Olympian Odes		293c–d	140
II, 58–60	278	Euthyphro	
II, 72–4	291	5c–d	126, 230

PLATO (cont.)

5d	72, 231	188e	189
5d4	72, 260	190c	126
6a–c	56	192a–b	257
6d10–11	73	192b–c	178
6d11	72, 260	192c–193e	178
6d–e	119, 230	194d	178
6e	124	199c–d	221
6e1	72, 260	201a	133
6e4–7	73	*Laws*	
11a8	72	765d	144
14e–15a	56	817a–d	30, 35
Gorgias		889b	20, 198
449c–d	126	898a–b	144
454c–455a	188	904a–c	293
464b–465d	221, 301	*Meno*	
465a	126	71e–73a	72
477e–481b	277	72b1	72
480a–b	56	72c7	72
493a–d	51	72c–d	230
495d–497d	48	72c–e	230
497d–500a	85	72d8	72
503e	73	72e5	72
503d–504a	124	81a–86a	26
508e–509a	25	82b–c	26
513e	301	82e	117
521a	301	85c–e	117
523a	278	85e–86b	26
523a1–3	295	86e–87c	234
523a–524a	49	86e4–87a3	234
524a	293	87c–89a	26
525b–c	293	88b	26, 221
525b–526b	293	88b–c	82, 85
Hippias Major		88b–e	78
285b–d	256	88c6	26
287c	230	88c–d	65
287c–d	72	89a	78
287e–289b	73	99b–d	36
289c3	73	100b6	26, 229
289c–d	230	*Parmenides*	
289d	72	129c	217
289d2	73	129d	64
289d4	72	150c–d	257
290a–d	142	*Phaedo*	
294a–b	257	57a	17, 248
294a–e	230	57a–59c	44
296e–297d	230	57a–60a	8
302c5	72	57a–61c	28
Hippias Minor		58a6	32
376a–b	221	58a–c	32
Ion		58b8	32
536e–541e	106	58b–c	14
Laches		58c	56
181b	182	58c3	32
188c	189	58d	21
		58d–e	17

Index Locorum

58e	36, 41	63b–69d	54
58e1–5	31	63b–69e	4, 9, 24, 57, 131
58e3	32, 42	63c	77
58e4	35	63c–69e	43
59a	31, 37	63d–e	15, 58, 163
59b	15, 45	63d8–e2	302
59b9–10	45	63e	57, 302
59b10	16	63e9	4, 77
59b–c	15	63e10	90
59c	36	63e–64a	58, 163
59d	56	64a	2, 32, 36, 43, 54, 59, 162, 305
59d–e	46		
59e6	135	64a–c	58
60a	31, 47	64a–68b	77, 176
60a–b	41	64b	59
60a–61b	9, 13	64b–c	57, 59
60b	97	64c	24, 63, 72, 164
60b–c	31, 47, 295	64c2–8	60
60b3–c7	48	64c–66a	58
60c	51	64d	42, 69, 279
60c–61b	32, 52	64d2	4
60d–61b	43, 294, 311	64d3	51
60e–61a	52	65a–b	175
60e–61b	39, 56, 306	65a–c	75
61a–b	41	65a–66a	101
61b	51	65a–67b	162
61b3–5	295	65a–68b	229
61b–c	9	65b	71
61c	184	65b–c	71
61c6	21	65c	61, 63, 67, 69, 71, 77, 84, 162, 175
61c–62c	9		
61c–63a	55	65c–66a	117, 151
61c–69e	54	65d	2, 110, 123, 128, 231, 256, 284
61d	17, 44, 184		
61d7	19	65d4–5	20
61d–e	17, 200	65d–e	3, 20, 25, 110, 122
61d–62c	54		
61e	17, 51	65d4–e1	71
61e7	19	65e4	75
62b	17, 32, 55–6, 162, 171	65e–66a	2, 33, 62, 74, 175
		66a	63, 67, 71, 73, 145, 272
62b2–6	55		
62c	56	66b	41
62c6	56	66b6–7	75
62c7	57	66b–d	76
62c–e	44, 184	66b–67b	14, 59, 75, 162, 297
62e–63a	21		
62e8–63a3	23	66b–67d	308
63a	5, 41, 44, 90, 188, 281	66b–68b	174, 194
		66c	16, 167, 176, 205
63b	22, 57, 77	66c1	171–2
63b–c	40–1, 56–7, 162–3, 275, 303	66c2–4	158
		66c4	67
63b–64a	248	66c–d	14, 69, 79, 84, 158, 166, 176, 309
63b–68b	170		

330 Index Locorum

PLATO (cont.)
66c–e		69a–c	42, 162–3, 175
66c–67b	61	69a–d	54, 77
66d	70	69a–e	42, 81
66d1	69, 79, 157	69a6–c2	81–2
66d5–6	171	69b1–2	81
66d6–7	76	69b1–4	85
66d7–8	75	69b1–5	82, 84
66d–e	75	69b6–7	80
66e	8	69b7–8	80
66e–67a	84	69b–c	37, 42, 170, 308
66e–67b	33	69b9–c3	85
66e–67c	145	69c	25, 162, 294
66e–67d	71	69c–d	18–19, 42, 58, 86,
66e1–67a1	58		165, 186, 308
66e4–67a1	61	69c–e	37
67a	75	69d–e	39–40, 56,
67a2–3	85, 146		302–3, 307
67a4	75	69e–70b	5, 9, 21, 43–4, 62,
67a5	67		88–9, 101, 128,
67a–b	168		133–4, 164, 179,
67a2–b2	17, 58, 272, 284		184–5, 188, 240,
67b	57		248, 273
67b8	86, 294, 308	69e6–70b4	89
67b–c	75	69e–72d	88
	25, 33, 62, 75,	69e–80b	248
	126, 302	70a	63, 136, 253
67b7–c3	77	70a1	252
67b10–c3	303	70a5–7	91
67b–68b	59	70a7	91
67c–d	32, 62, 85	70a–b	90, 266
67d	47, 84, 304	70b	51, 92, 133–4,
67d12	4		156, 163, 281
67e–68a	302	70b3	252
67e–68b	33, 71, 75	70b4	102
68a9	194	70b10–c2	98
68a–b	8, 33, 62, 84, 126,	70b–80b	103
	307	70c	162, 190
68a9–b1	76	70c–d	271
68b8	4	70c8–d4	92
68b–c	37, 80, 279	70c–72d	9, 88
68b–d	176	70c–107b	9, 24
68b–69a	77–8	70d–71b	48
68b–69e	43, 59, 77, 171	70e–71a	95
68c	42, 79, 82, 170,	71a	94
	177, 297	71a–b	49, 94
68c5	78	71b6	96
68c8–9	78	71c	97
68c9–10	85	71d	94, 97
68c–69a	162	71d–e	94
68d	37, 79, 134	71e	94
68e	176	71e–72a	231
68e–69a	26, 166, 171, 177,	72a	2, 98
	193	72a4	94, 269
68e5–69a4	79	72a6	95
69a	80, 176	72a11–12	98

Index Locorum

331

72a–b	98	74e9–75a2	121
72a–d	49, 98	75a2	124
72c	220	75a–c	121
72c4–5	98	75b1–2	124
72c–d	98	75c	125
72c–73a	231	75c–d	25, 122
72d	44, 98, 101	75c–76e	103
72d4–5	93	75d2–4	73, 122
72e	188	75d3–4	25
72e2–3	26	75d–76d	125
72e–73a	44, 101, 184	76a	119
72e–73b	89	76b	24, 76, 108
72e–77d	9, 43, 88, 100	76b5	4
73a	21, 231	76b8–9	126
73a2	89	76c	102, 119, 122, 176
73a–b	26, 65, 101	76c5	119
73b	101, 106, 119, 125	76c11–12	127
		76c12	158
73c1–3	106	76c–d	96, 125
73c5–6	104	76d7–8	123
73c5–d1	104	76d–e	89, 101, 128, 231
73c–74a	103–4	76d–77a	256
73c–76e	33	76e–77a	201
73d	106	76e–77b	231
73d3	126	76e–77d	103, 128
73d–e	106	77a	128
73e	119, 125	77a–b	21, 101
73e1	105	77a–78a	44
73e–74a	106	77b	128
74a	3, 110, 124	77b3	93
74a5–7	107	77b–c	184
74a9–10	110	77c	44, 128
74a–b	194, 256	77c6–9	93
74a–c	109, 231	77c9–d4	94
74a–d	103, 108	77c–e	90
74b	107, 117	77d	136
74b2	127	77d5	102
74b5–7	113	77d6–7	134
74b6–7	111	77d–e	43, 93, 133, 252–3
74b7–9	111		
74b–c	3, 110	77d7–e3	133
74b–d	117	77d–78a	132
74c	107, 113, 117	77d–80b	88, 273
74c1	112	77d–80d	9, 131
74c6	113	77e	90, 188
74c–d	103	77e5–7	133
74c13–d2	107	78a	24, 133
74d2	105	78a4	4
74d4–7	115	78b	90, 135–6, 253
74d4–8	118	78b–79a	136
74d5–7	123	78b–80b	3–4, 33, 39, 44
74d9–e4	120	78b–84b	4
74d–75b	2, 3, 111, 120	78b–84d	38
74d–75c	103, 118	78c3	91
74e	119	78c6–8	137, 142

PLATO (cont.)

78c–d	25, 40, 135, 231, 256, 271	80d–81a	33, 56, 135, 162–3, 284, 290, 296, 303, 309
78c10–d7	144	80d–84b	10, 21, 44, 56, 131, 135, 162
78d	136, 259		
78d2–3	139	80e–81a	37, 62, 84, 162, 164, 304, 307
78d4	40		
78d5	272	80e–81b	279
78d5–7	144	81a	33, 36, 40, 42, 44, 56, 62, 156–7, 186
78d6	139		
78d7	40, 141		
78d–e	3, 116, 284	81a1	60, 62, 164
78d10–e4	149	81a4–10	165
78e	125	81a5	89
78e2	115	81b	42, 81, 85, 153, 159, 162, 171
79a	2, 136		
79a1–4	151	81b1–2	62
79a7	135	81b5	147
79a9–10	152	81b5–6	168
79a–80b	37, 152, 284	81b–c	146, 164
79b	136, 154, 158	81b1–c2	166
79b1–2	158	81b–d	280
79b9–10	153	81b–e	308
79c	4, 117, 136, 146, 154, 217	81b–82b	165
		81b–84a	70
79c–d	175, 290	81c	167
79d	2, 4, 68, 92, 136, 145–6, 162–4, 217, 272, 284, 290	81c1–2	62
		81c9	147
		81c–d	91, 153, 170, 290
79d1–2	272	81c8–d4	168
79d1–7	154	81c–e	62, 99
79d2	89	81c–82b	93, 97
79d5–6	139	81d	293
79e	158	81d4	167
79e–80a	92, 157, 200, 309	81d7–9	280
80a	135, 164	81d–e	2, 56, 169
80a3	272	81d–82b	56
80a–b	150, 253, 256, 297	81e1–2	169
80b	40, 132, 136, 148, 152, 157–8, 251, 272	81e–82a	169
		81e–82b	169
		82a12	170
80b1	89	82a–b	80, 91, 162
80b4	147	82b	176, 178
80b4–5	149	82b1–3	170
80b9–11	134	82b5–8	170
80b–c	44, 188	82b7	158
80c	135	82b–c	279
80c1	21	82b10–c8	176–7
80c–d	251	82b–83e	171
80d	2, 40, 91, 152, 157, 163, 302, 308	82b–84b	170
		82c	78–9, 84, 181
		82d	154, 162
80d5–8	164	82d–e	17, 32, 56, 193
80d8–9	153	82d9–83e7	171

82e	56, 81, 162, 297, 301	86b–d	251
		86d	196
82e–83b	33, 101, 162, 229	86d2	198
82e–84b	162	86e–88b	4, 21, 44, 88, 185, 248–9, 251, 273
83a	2, 175		
83a–b	117, 171, 175, 188	88b5–6	90
83b	153	87a	20, 91, 254
83b7	173	87b–d	251
83b–c	15, 33, 41, 84, 308	87b–88b	188
83b–d	159	87c4	251
83b–e	175	87c–d	251
83b4–e3	172	87d	63
83c	33	87d3	252
83c2	173	87d7–8	267
83c5	15	87d–e	20, 288
83c7–8	173	87d6–e5	252
83d1	173	87d9–e1	249
83d4–10	181	87d–88a	252
83d6–7	168	87e6	252
83d–e	99, 169, 308	87e–88a	252, 267
83e	78, 162, 178, 297	88a	252
83e5	175	88a8–b6	252–3
83e5–7	176	88b	135, 155, 266
84a2–3	4	88b4	91
84a2–7	178	88b–108c	184
84a8–9	172	88c	44, 185
84a–b	2, 84, 174, 179	88c1–d3	187
84b	40, 62	88c–89a	36, 44
84b3–7	179	88c–89b	10
84c	21, 135	88c–89c	187
84c–85b	186	88c–91c	187
84c–86e	184	88c–95a	184
84c–95a	184	88c–107b	44
84d	41	88e–89a	44
84d7–8	186	89a2–8	189
84d–e	186	89b–c	36, 44
84d–85b	41	89b–91c	45
84d–88c	10	89c	44, 184, 189, 310
84e–85b	39, 53, 306, 308	89c3–4	36
84e3–85a3	186	89c–91c	5, 10, 131
85b	32, 41–2	89d	6, 41, 44, 191
85b–86d	44, 185, 193	89d3–e3	189
85b–88b	44, 131, 184	89d–90e	189
85c7	4	89e–90b	190
85c8	228	90b	5, 91, 239, 281, 310
85c–d	194, 228		
85c1–d4	194	90b–c	21, 44
85e–86a	152	90b4–c6	190
85e–86b	251	90c	217, 239, 288
85e3–86a6	195	90c2–6	288
86b	20	90d	191
86b1	89,	90d–e	309
86b7	198	90d9–e3	191
86b5–c3	196	90e–91c	44, 192, 310

PLATO (cont.)
90e2–91b7	192	95a1–2	243
91a–c	187	95a–b	46
91b–c	23, 41	95b7–8	36, 250
91c	192–3, 310	95b–c	254, 266
91c1–2	193	95b–e	250, 254, 273
91c–d	241	95b–96a	249–50
91c–95a	185, 199	95c1	4, 90, 248
91e–92c	199, 254	95d1	90, 248
91e–95a	5, 131	95d1–3	308
92a7–9	197	95d1–4	254
92a–b	199	95d3	268
92a–c	20	95e	268
92b6	158	95e1	90, 248
92c	191	95e3	250
92c3	243	95e–96a	10
92c6	243	95e–102a	10, 131, 207, 210
92c8	243	95e9–96a3	250
92c–e	46, 200, 243	96a	208, 211
92d	241	96a8–9	209
92d1–2	20, 197, 200	96a9	265
92d7	200, 243	96a–b	288
92d–e	128, 231, 256	96a9–b1	217
92d6–e4	241	96b	290
92e	128	96b2–3	215
92e1–2	20, 201	96b3–5	215
92e–93a	201–3	96b–c	215
92e–95a	200, 243	96b–97b	216
93a	203	96b–101d	18
93a6–7	203	96c	229
93a8–9	203	96c1–8	217
93a–b	202	96c7–8	218
93a–c	243	96c–97b	218
93a–94b	201, 254	96d–e	209, 213, 218
93b	202	96e	218
93b–c	202	96e3	213
93c	202, 244	96e–97a	209
93c9–10	244	96e–99c	2
93c10	243	96e6–97b3	218–19
93d	202	97a–b	79
93d–94b	243	97b–98b	220
93e	202	97c	211
94a	202, 205	97c2	210
94a–b	239	97c2–6	221
94a–c	297	97c4	210
94b	180–1, 309	97c6–7	221
94b1	243	97c–d	210
94b–c	181, 243	97d	221
94b4–c1	203–4	97d1–4	230
94b–e	157, 201–2, 254	97d–e	50
94b–95a	196	97d–98a	209, 225
94c–e	243	97d–98b	210
94c9–e4	204	97d8–98a2	223
94d–e	18	97e	282
94e5	196	97e–98a	209, 282
		98a	225

Index Locorum

98a1–2	230	100e–101b	209
98a7–9	230	100e–101c	214, 218, 244, 259
98a–b	223	101a	213
98b	221	101a1–4	230
98b4–6	221–2	101a4–5	230, 263
98b–c	224	101a–b	214
98b–99c	224	101b	213
98c1–2	283	101b10	210
98c2	209, 225	101b–c	209, 228
98c–d	224	101c	2, 263
98d8	209, 225	101c2–4	230
98e	22	101c4–5	230
98e1–3	212	101c7–d6	238
98e1–5	224	101d	195
98e–99a	259	101d2–3	240
98e5–99a4	224	101d6–8	245
99a4	210	101e	194, 239
99a4–5	225	101e3	246
99a–b	210, 216	102a	44–5, 246, 248
99b	190, 212, 220, 225–6, 282	102a–103c	255
		102a–107b	3, 45, 88, 131, 248
99b3	210	102a–107d	262
99b4	210	102a11–d2	255
99b6	210	102b	116, 284
99b6–c6	226	102b1	71
99c–d	227	102b3–4	256
99c6–d2	228	102b–c	116
99d1	195, 227	102b–d	116
99d–e	101, 228	102b–103a	139
99e–100a	2, 236	102b–103c	232
100a	265	102c	158
100a3–8	237	102c–d	257, 261, 267
100a5–6	265	102d	255–6
100a–101e	5, 256	102d–e	256–7, 267, 271
100a–102a	46	102d–103a	259
100b	230, 237–9, 261	102e	145
100b1–3	25, 74, 229	102e3–5	158
100b5	229	102e–103a	259
100b6	229	103a	96, 184
100b9	90, 248	103b–c	96
100b-e	231	103c	184
100b–101d	244	103c–d	260
100b–101e	3	103c–105c	260
100c	2, 211, 220	103e3	261
100c1–2	242	103e4	261
100c4–6	230	103e–104b	260
100c5	286	104b9	260
100c–d	263	104b–c	260
100d3–6	230	104b6–c4	261
100d5	213	104b7–c1	260
100d–101c	242	104c7	260
100d6–e3	240	104d1–3	262
100e	195	104d2	260
100e6–7	286	104d9	260
100e–101a	230, 263	104e1	261

PLATO (cont.)

105a4	254	108b–c	170, 290
105a2–5	262	108b7–c2	280
105a–b	260	108c	280, 282, 285, 294
105a6–b2	261	108d	280, 283
105b8–c3	264	108d5–9	281
105c	267	108d9–e2	282
105c–d	268	108d–110a	276, 280
105c–107a	266	108d–114c	170
105c–107e	90	108e	91, 280
105d13	260	108e–109a	248
105d–e	267	108e4–109a6	281
105e	268	109a	280
105e–106a	268	109a–110a	283
105e11–106a1	268	109b6	284
105e–106c	268	109b7–8	283
105e–107c	248	109b–c	283, 286
106a	256, 268, 271	109c2–3	284
106b	268	109c3	284
106b–c	256, 268	109e–110a	292
106c9–10	269	110a–114d	276, 281, 285
106d	269, 272	110a9–b2	285
106d5–7	269–70	110b–111a	293
106e	158, 268, 271	110b–111c	285
106e1–2	269	110c–111a	291
106e–107a	302	110d	284, 292
106e8–107a1	266, 269	110d–e	283
107a	46, 91	110d4–e6	286
107a8–b9	239–40	110e–111a	296
107b	23, 25, 46, 76, 91, 128, 201, 241, 261, 263, 268, 270	111a	286
		111a–c	291, 293
		111b	291
107b6–9	245–6	111b–c	303
107b7–9	195	111c	286, 291–2
107c	40, 62	111c–113c	287, 293
107c1–5	307	111c–114b	285
107c2–3	52	111d	287
107c4–5	304	111d–e	286–7
107c–d	40, 276	111e1–2	289
107c8–d5	276–7	111e4–5	287
107c–114c	92	112a	18
107c–115a	5, 10, 131, 248, 275	112a5–b4	288
		112b	217, 227, 287, 289
107d	169	112c3	289
107d–e	2, 93	112e–113a	290
107d5–e4	277	112e–113c	289
107d–108a	276–7, 302	113a	93, 293
107d–108c	97	113b–c	294
107d–114d	308	113c	40
107e–108a	18, 47, 248	113d	294
108a	278, 290	113d–114b	40, 293
108a1	278	113e5	293
108a–b	308	113e–114b	293
108a6–b4	279	114a9	293
108a–c	99, 169, 276, 279	114b–c	284, 292

114c	37, 40, 290, 303	330c–e	124		
114c9	294	330d	72		
114d	47, 91, 296	330d4	72		
114d1–6	281	330d–e	229		
114d4	90, 248	330d9–e1	72		
114d–e	297	332c	230		
114d–115a	297	351b–357e	26, 83		
114e	52	353c–354e	83		
114e–115a	309	356d–357b	221		
114e5–115a1	297	357b–e	78		
115a	36–7, 47, 299, 308	356d	217		
		360d	78		
115a–118a	5, 11, 299	361b	78		
115b	304	*Republic*			
115b–c	180	332d–334a	221		
115b2–c1	300	352d–354a	156		
115b–116a	15	358b	68, 229		
115c	300	358d3	229		
115c4–6	157–8	364b–365a	86		
115c–e	176	367e–368b	23		
115c–116a	248, 300	377a	296		
116a–b	15	377b	39		
116b–d	46	377d–e	38		
116c4–6	301	377d–392c	38		
116d	301	377e–378e	39		
116e	41, 46	379b–c	56		
116e2–5	301–2	379b–380c	39		
116e–117a	37, 42, 183, 299, 302	380b–c	293		
		380c–381e	39		
117c2–3	302	380d	40		
117c–d	34, 41, 302	380d–381e	136		
117d–e	32, 41, 299, 301	380e–381c	40		
117e	301, 303, 305	381b2	40		
118a	42, 44	381e–383c	39		
118a5–8	303	386a–b	40		
118a7–8	11, 300	386b10	40		
Phaedrus		386b–387b	40		
246d–e	132	386c–387b	40		
249c–d	271, 274	387b	39		
270e–271a	148	387b–c	40		
Philebus		387d5–6	40		
19c1–3	227	387d–e	41		
43a	217	387e10–388a3	41		
44c	166	388e–389a	41		
55b	85	389b–d	41		
61b	144	389e1–2	41		
Protagoras		390b–c	41		
319a–320c	49	390c–391e	35		
320d–322d	50	390e–391e	42		
322a3–5	50	392a4–6	47		
329d	72	392a–c	42		
330c	72	392b	42		
330c1	72	405a–408b	310		
330c4–5	72	408b–c	310		
330c–d	230	411d	189		

PLATO (cont.)		614b–621d	295
413b–d	166	616a	40
420c–d	142	*Sophist*	
436b8–9	116, 138	227a–b	153
436c–d	138	230b4–8	138
436d	140	246a–b	152
436d8	138	246e–249d	132
436d–e	138, 140	248e–249a	272
436d–437e	256	252a	144
436e5	141	*Statesman*	
439b	256	268e–274e	295
442d–443e	180, 301	269e	144
443c–e	180	300c1–3	227
443d–e	205	*Symposium*	
454c	144	174d–175b	182
479a–b	114	188a	20, 198
479e	144	189d	50
484c–d	124	189d–193b	50
490a–b	131	202d–e	271
494d–e	132	202d–203a	226
500c–d	271, 274	202d–204a	292
508d	217	202e6–7	226
509d–511e	235	205e	158
510b	235	211a2–4	141
510c	235	211b1	148
511b	245	211e	272
511b–d	246	211e1–3	148
514a–517c	283	211e–212a	271
515e–516a	245	219c–d	183
518e	274	219d	182
523b–524e	256	220d–221b	182
553a–555a	82	223d	31
554a–b	82	*Theaetetus*	
559c	174	154c–155c	256
584a	166	160d–e	288
596a6	260	*Timaeus*	
596b1	260	28a	144
597a1	260	28a–b	124
603e	301	29e–30b	56
604b–606c	31, 35	31b	147
604c	31	34a	144
604d	30	35a–b	132
605c–e	35	40c	284
605d	30–1	41e	127
606b–c	30	42d–e	293
607a2–3	30	43b	217
608d–611b	253	52a	144
611b–612a	148, 272	52a1	139
611c2	148	52d–53b	289
611d–e	155	53c	152
611d–612a	271	63c	168
611e	132	63c–d	168
611e1–2	169	63d–e	169
611e3	169	63e4–6	168
614b	278	69c–71e	205

69d–e	222	STRATO	
79d	155	Fr. 80	267–8, 270
86b	308		
86b1	308	THEOPHRASTUS	
86b2	308	*De sensibus*	
87e–88b	181	1–2	156
90a	132, 274	THUCYDIDES	
92c	147	VI	
PLOTINUS		40, 2, 6	66
6 6.14.13–29	219	VII	
6 6.14–15	219	28, 3, 7	64

Index

Acheron (river), 289
Acherusian lake, 290
Achilles, 35, 37, 306
Adeimantus, 16, 23, 86
Aegina, 16
Aeschines, 15
Aeschylus, 18, 47, 64, 278
   Eumenides, 278
   Mysians, 278 n11
   Prometheus Bound, 64
   Suppliants, 278
   Telephus, 278 n11
Aesop, 13, 28–9, 32, 47, 50–3 and 51 n48, 97, 295; *see also* Socrates, Aesop and
affinity argument; *see Phaedo*, kinship argument
afterlife, 8, 10–11, 18–20, 25, 40, 55–9, 77, 86, 163, 182, 193, 275–80, 290–7, 300, 307; *see also* Hades *and* reincarnation *and* philosophy
aitia/aitiai (noun), 207–31, 213 n20, 215 n28, 221 n40, 233, 235–7, 246–7, 250, 259, 263–5, 283, 285, 287–8; *see also* causes
   in Greek legal context, 209–11
   translation of, 213
aitios/-a/-on (adjective), 208–16, 215 n28, 220, 225, 235, 247, 258, 263–6, 281, 283
   translation of, 213
aition, to, definition of, 210, 215 n27, 286
Alcibiades, 182
Anamnēsis; *see* recollecting
Anaxagoras, 7–8, 10, 18, 65–8 and 65 n23, 98, 145, 167, 207–12, 214, 220–6, 228, 230 n60, 231, 258, 276 n6, 282–3, 291, 296
Anaximander, 294
anoia; *see* ignorance
antilogikoi, 190–1 and 190 n10, 194, 239

Antiphon the Orator, 64
   On the murder of Herodes, 64
Antisthenes, 15
Apollo, 32–3, 39, 42, 53, 186, 271
Apollodorus, 16 n18
Aristippus, 15–16 and 15 n17
Aristippus II, 15 n17
Aristophanes, 21 n37, 50, 66, 98, 226
   Clouds, 21 n37, 66, 98, 190 n10, 226 n50, 226
   Frogs, 21 n37
Aristotle, 30, 31 n9, 46, 63, 74–5, 93, 97, 109–10, 140 n22, 141, 152 n45, 156 n53, 199 n28, 207, 220, 227, 256, 263, 270, 291 n33
   De anima, 156 n53
   De caelo, 152 n45
   Nicomachean Ethics, 156
   Parts of Animals, 220
   Physics, 220
   Poetics, 30, 46
   Posterior Analytics, 93
   Sophistical Refutations, 141
Aristoxenus, 21
asceticism, 5, 17, 22, 162, 174, 182
Asclepius, 11, 17 n21, 300, 303–10, 310 n23
Atheneaus, 291

Betegh, Gábor, 47–50, 102, 152 n45, 196 n18, 275, 305 n13
body; *see also* fear, pain, pleasure, *and* senses
   affections and, 69–70, 80, 85–6, 174–83 and 174 n20, 178 n27, 181 n31, 203–6, 297, 301
   beliefs and, 171–4, 181 n32
   effects on soul and, 162–3, 166, 168, 171, 174–82, 204, 308
   prison and, 17, 32, 56 n5, 162 n2, 171, 297
   slavery to the, 81, 86, 166

body (cont.)
  soul bringing life to, 249, 251–4, 266–7
  visibility and, 153, 157–9
bringers; see forms, bringers of; see also soul

causes, 2–3, 10, 207; see also aitia/aitiai (noun), aitios/-a/-on (adjective), and forms
Cebes, 4–5, 9, 19–27, 36, 46, 55, 62–3, 89–95, 94 n7, 97–8, 104–6, 126, 128, 131, 134–5, 153, 157, 172–3, 176–7, 179, 184, 186–9, 192, 218, 246, 250, 258, 308
  as intellectual, 15
  challenge and; see Phaedo, Cebes' challenge
  cloakmaker objection and; see Phaedo, Cebes' cloakmaker objection
  credulity of, 21
  death of Socrates and, 41
  dialogue writer and, 14–15
  difficult to persuade, 5, 9, 20–1, 23–4, 41, 44, 90, 93, 188, 281
  fear of death and, 43, 80, 93
  forms and, 231, 237, 239, 242, 256
  Heraclitean theories and, 20
  ignorance and, 24
  ignored by Socrates, 241–2
  immortal and, 268–9
  learning and, 101
  logoi and, 189, 252
  opinion of Socrates and, 186
  Orphism and, 13
  Philolaus and, 13, 17, 19, 200
  Pythagoreans and, 13, 19, 27
  shocked by idea of quick death, 9
  Socratic ideas and, 20
  soul and, 51, 62–3, 88–93, 99, 133–4, 136, 153, 155, 157, 160, 165, 167, 185, 200, 251–4, 253 n9, 263, 266–8, 271, 273, 281, 288, 308
  suicide and, 57
  trust (*pistis*) and, 188, 252
chance; see luck
Charmides, 133
Cicero, 306
  On Divination, 306
Cleombrotus, 16
Cocytus (river), 40 n30, 290
comedy, 31 n10, 278 n12; see also Aristophanes
conviction (*pistis*), 23, 89–91, 99, 134, 179, 185, 188, 273, 280–4; see also trust (*pistis*)
cosmology, 7, 215, 223, 226, 233, 236, 275, 280–90, 294, 296–7
courage, 37, 77–86, 79 n42, 81 n46, 122, 133 n6, 163, 170, 174–83, 191–3, 297, 301–2
cowardice, 37, 79–80, 79 n42

Crete, 36
Crito, 11, 15, 31, 36, 41, 44 n33, 47, 58, 157, 163, 300–1, 303
Critobulus, 36, 45 n35
Cyrenaic school, 15

daemons, 47, 226 n51, 278–9
Darius, king, 211
death, 1, 24, 54–64, 60 n9, 72, 77, 88–99, 167, 251–5, 266–71, 299–302; see also Socrates, death of; see also afterlife definition of, 59–63, 164
  desire for; see philosophy
  fear of, 5, 9, 29, 37, 40, 43–4, 46, 53, 80, 86, 90–3, 133–4, 176, 180, 183
  journey after, 47, 276–8, 295, 302 n4, 306
Delos, 32
Delphi, 18
  Oracle at, 18, 52
Democritus, 214
desire, 4, 7, 14, 32, 41, 55–6, 64–5, 67–70, 70 n29, 81, 85–6, 158–9, 165–82, 172 n15, 193, 199, 205
  death and; see philosophy
  truth and; see truth
  wisdom and; see wisdom
dialogues; for individual dialogues, see Plato
  Socratic, 6, 13–15, 24–7, 65, 75, 122–3, 138, 167, 182, 208, 217, 221, 229–30
  transitional, 24–5
Diogenes of Apollonia, 269 n46
Dionysius, 19
divine; see also soul, divine and; and gods
  unseen and, 153–4, 160, 162–4, 196, 200, 251–3, 271–3
doubt, 90–1, 188, 190, 240; see also trust (*pistis*)
drug (*pharmakon*), 31–2, 34, 41, 301–2, 306, 308

Echecrates, 8, 16, 21, 31, 44–6, 53, 184, 188–9, 246–8
elenchus, 24, 126
Eleusinian mysteries, 7–8, 18, 305 n13
Elis, 13
Empedocles, 100–2, 269 n46, 271
epic, 6; see also Homer
Epimetheus, 50
Epistēmē; see knowledge
Euclid
  Elements, 234, 235 n73
Euclides, 15
Euripides, 30 n7, 64
  Antiope, 34 n17
  Ion, 64, 106
Euripus, 190, 288

Euthyphro, 24, 230
Evenus, 9, 21–2

falling short; *see* forms
fear, 4, 55, 67, 69–70, 79–81, 84–5, 88–90, 169, 171–7, 172 n15, 179, 182–3, 188, 204–5; *see also* death, fear of
flux, 11, 20, 73, 217, 227, 252, 275, 280, 284–90, 292–4, 296–8
forms, 1–6, 9–10, 20, 25–6, 54–5, 63, 69–76, 89, 91–2, 100–1, 103, 109–10, 116–17, 119–20, 122–3, 125–8, 130–2, 136–9, 141, 143–7, 150–3, 156, 159, 164, 175, 201, 207, 217, 227–32, 228 n56, 241, 244, 246, 256, 260, 270, 275–6, 284, 296; *see also* justice *and* virtue
   abstract entities and, 3
   Aristotle and, 74, 109
   beauty, form of, 2, 123, 126, 141 n25, 148–9, 214, 230 n60, 237, 239–40, 244, 261 n25, 265
   bringers of, 249, 254, 259–70, 273
   causes and, 3–4, 10, 110, 151, 229–32
   composite, 132, 136–7, 142–4 and 142 n28, 150, 152 n45, 159, 198 n26, 266
   divine and, 5, 154, 271–3
   eidos, definition of, 260
   equality, form of, 2, 103–30, 124 n46, 151, 194, 232
   falling short and, 107, 111, 115, 118–23, 125, 129, 151
   good, form of, 76, 123, 126, 237, 247, 261 n25, 273
   holiness, form of, 72–4, 126, 284
   idea, definition of, 260, 282 n20
   immanent, 249, 255, 261 n24, 263–73
   immortality and, 154, 269 n46, 271–2
   incomposite, 40, 91, 136–7, 142–3 and 142 n28, 150–1, 154, 160
   justice, form of, 2, 4, 69, 72, 74, 78, 124, 126, 146, 284
   largeness, form of, 2, 4, 69, 71, 139, 146, 158, 212, 231, 255–8, 284
   multiform and, 151, 266
   opposites and, 79 n42, 95, 138–42, 145 n33, 149, 197, 214, 219, 225, 228, 231, 232 n64, 244, 249, 254–6, 258–62, 259 n15, 262 n27, 266–7, 296
   ordinary objects and, 3, 25, 74–5, 100, 109–10, 116, 120, 130, 132, 136, 152, 231 n62, 232, 249, 255, 259, 263
   perceptibility and, 74–5, 110, 123, 151–2, 249
   Platonic, 1, 3, 71–5, 72 n31, 100, 108–10, 110 n20, 116, 229, 232
   purity and, 148, 154, 160, 272
   separation of (Plato), 63
   Socratic, 71, 110 n20, 229–32
   uniform and, 148 n40, 148, 150–1, 160, 164, 232, 272
   unseen and, 135, 154, 157, 160, 271
   virtue, form of, 72, 230
Frede, Dorothea, 267, 270
Frede, Michael, 209
Furley, David, 257

Glaucon, 16, 23, 229
gods, 6, 13, 18–19, 25, 29–30, 33, 35–44, 47, 50–3, 55–9, 62, 77, 89, 154, 162 n2, 164, 177, 276, 291–7, 300, 306, 309–10; *see also* Apollo, Asclepius, *and* Zeus
   benevolence of, 39, 42–3, 52, 56–8, 277, 280, 289, 293
   immortality and, 89, 271
   vengeance and, 39, 56–7
good life, concept of, 2, 5, 26, 33; *see also* happiness
Gorgias, 210
   Encomium of Helen, 210
Gosling, Justin, 116

Hades, 18, 36, 40, 43–4, 47, 53, 58, 76, 91–4, 152, 162 n2, 164–5, 168–70, 172, 266, 271, 273, 277, 279, 289
happiness, 8, 162, 174
harmonia, 5, 20, 86, 196–206, 197 n23, 199 n28, 202 n32, 243–4; *see also* Phaedo, Simmias' *harmonia* objection
   composite, 197–200
   definition of, 195
   krasis and, 196
heavens, 11, 226, 280–4, 286, 289–91, 296, 298
Hector, 306
Helen, 210
Heracles, 28, 36–7, 44, 184
Heraclitus, 4 n4, 20, 156 n53, 284, 288–9, 294; *see also* flux
Herakles; *see* Heracles
Hermes, 102
Hermogenes, 16, 73
Herodorus of Heraclea, 291
Herodotus, 138 n17, 210–11
   Histories, 210–11
heroes, 6, 28, 33, 35–43, 47, 276, 294, 306; *see also* Heracles, Odysseus, Socrates, heroism and, *and* Theseus
   Republic and, 40–2
Hesiod, 82
   Theogony, 284
   Works and Days, 291
Hippias, 72
Hippocratic corpus, 7, 64–7 and 64 n20, 65 n23, 66 n26, 198, 205, 211, 215–16 and 215 n27, 233 n67

Hippocratic corpus (cont.)
  Airs, Waters and Places, 215 n27
  Diseases of Women, 64 n21
  Epidemics, 64 n21
  On Acute Diseases, 64
  On Affections, 65 n23
  On Ancient Medicine, 66–7, 145, 198, 211, 215 n27, 215, 227
  On Breaths, 215 n27, 233
  On Diseases, 64, 65 n23, 66
  On Fleshes, 215, 233
  On Fractures, 64
  On Regimen, 64 n21, 205, 215
  On the Art, 215 n28
  On the Nature of Man, 65 n23
  On the Sacred Disease, 215
  Prognostic, 64
Homer, 18, 30, 39, 40 n30, 41, 46, 60 n9, 89, 204, 243, 269 n46, 278, 288–91, 300
  Iliad, 306
  Odyssey, 204–5, 289–91, 295
Homeric hymns
  Hymn to Demeter, 19
  Hymn to Hermes, 271
hypothesis, definition of, 233–7
hypothesis, method of; *see Phaedo*, hypothesis, method of

Iamblichus
  On the Pythagorean Life, 291 n33
ignorance, 24, 65, 171–3, 193, 202, 279, 283, 308
  Socratic acceptance of, 24–5, 207, 217, 229, 283
inequality, 112, 115, 151
initiation practices, 7, 18–19, 86, 165
inquiry, 6, 54–5, 70, 101–2, 123, 130; *see also Phaedo*, hypothesis, method of
  hindrance by body and, 70–1, 75–6
intelligence (*nous*), 10, 26, 47, 66–7, 202, 209 n2, 210–14, 221–6 and 221 n39, 231, 258, 276, 281
intemperance, 79, 83 n49, 177
Isocrates, 143
  Against the Sophists, 143

justice, 85–6, 170, 175, 177, 278, 293–4, 297, 301–4

Kamen, Deborah, 309
knowledge, 8, 75–6, 100–9, 117–22, 125–6, 129, 246; *see also* recollecting *and* wisdom
  imitation and, 106
  prior knowledge principle, 121, 129
  standards and, 106–8, 119, 129

Laches, 178
lamentation, 28, 30–5, 40–1, 43

learning; *see* recollecting, learning and
logos/logoi, 5, 10, 36, 44, 46, 91, 134, 185, 187–92, 194–5, 197 n23, 199–200, 217, 234, 236–44, 295, 298, 309; *see also* misology
Long, Alex, 271
luck (*tuchē*), 16, 28, 32–5, 43

Martinelli Tempesta, Stefano, 227
medicine, ancient, 208, 214, 233–4; *see also* Hippocratic corpus
Megarian school, 15
Meletus, 99
Meno, 72, 230
metaphysics, 24, 54, 297
misanthropy; *see* misology
misology, 5–6, 10, 13–24, 29, 44–7, 53, 91, 131, 184–5, 187, 189–92, 200, 206, 208, 217, 227, 233, 237, 239–43, 247–8, 276, 281, 288, 298, 305, 309
  misanthropy and, 187, 189–90
  Plato first to use term and, 189
moderation; *see* temperance
Most, Glenn, 304–5, 307–8
Musaeus, 86

Nietzsche, Friedrich, 304, 307
nourishment, 179
  body and, 171–2
  soul and, 172 n15
nous; *see* intelligence

objects, ordinary, 3–6, 9, 25, 74–5, 100–1, 116, 121, 130–1, 136, 138, 143, 149–53, 159, 255–9, 263, 275–6, 296; *see also* forms
  composites, 150, 266
  multiform, 151, 266
  opposites and, 132, 259
  perception and, 152
  visibility and, 160
Ocean (river), 289, 291
Odysseus, 204–5
opposites, 3, 6, 9, 48–9, 89, 94–7, 112, 116, 132, 220, 262; *see also* forms, opposites and
Orpheus, 17–18, 19 n30, 86, 295
Orphism, 7–8, 13, 19, 30 n4, 86, 171, 277, 287 n24, 305 n13

pain, 4–5, 15, 29, 31–3, 37, 47–51, 55, 69–71, 77, 81–5, 83 n49, 97, 162 n2, 168, 172 n15, 178–80, 182
  intense, 33, 172–3, 173 n19, 180
Parmenides, 125, 147 n37, 282 n17
Pascal's wager, 193
Patroclus, 306
Penelope, 174, 178

Index

perceptible things; *see* objects, ordinary
Phaedo
   affinity argument; *see* Phaedo, kinship argument
   autobiography (chapter 9), 5–7, 10, 22, 25, 46–7, 53, 71, 74, 79 n42, 91, 98, 101, 110, 131, 184, 200, 207–8, 217, 227, 237, 243, 247, 258–9, 265, 275, 281–3, 285–7
   Cebes' challenge (chapter 4), 58, 88, 90–3, 98, 101, 133, 136, 156, 163–4, 179, 185, 206, 240, 248, 252, 266, 273
   Cebes' cloakmaker objection (chapter 10), 4, 10, 20–1, 89–90, 99, 131, 135, 154, 184–5, 188, 249–51, 254, 266–7, 273, 288
   cyclical argument (chapter 4), 5, 7, 9–10, 21, 48, 56, 88, 90–9, 101–2, 128, 130, 133, 162, 188, 271, 276
   death scene (chapter 12); *see* Socrates, death of
   defense speech (chapter 3), 4, 9–10, 19, 25–6, 39, 42–3, 52, 54, 57–9, 63, 67, 69–71, 75, 77, 83–4, 86–7, 90, 96, 101, 110, 116–17, 122, 126, 128, 131, 134, 145, 151–2, 157, 164–77, 176 n25, 194, 205, 229, 231, 246, 248, 272–4, 284, 294, 303, 309
   eschatological account (chapter 11), 5, 40, 52–3, 91, 97, 99, 131, 170, 185, 248, 258, 275, 282 n20, 285, 287 n24, 295
   exchange passage (chapter 3), 77–8, 81, 83, 85–6, 163, 175, 179–80, 297
   final argument (chapter 10), 23–5, 46, 62–3, 71, 88, 90–3, 96, 100, 110, 116, 131, 158, 160, 185, 201, 227, 232, 239, 241–2, 247, 260–1, 263, 265–6, 268, 270, 272–3, 298, 304, 307
   final immortality argument; *see* Phaedo, final argument
   hypothesis, method of (chapter 9), 5, 10, 20, 45–6, 76, 91, 110, 128, 185, 192, 194–5, 200–1, 207–8, 215, 227–8, 231–46, 256, 265, 298
   interlude, 185–6
   kinship argument (chapter 6), 4–5, 7, 9–10, 21, 39, 42, 44, 58, 62, 71, 75, 88–93, 97, 101–2, 110, 115–17, 131–8, 140, 144–7, 149 n42, 151, 153–9, 184–5, 187–8, 194–6, 198, 200, 206, 217, 231–2, 249–57, 253 n9, 271–3, 284, 290
   misology (chapter 8); *see* misology
   recollecting argument (chapter 5), 9, 25, 33, 43, 71, 73–6, 88–90, 93–4, 96–7, 99–102, 116, 123–4, 128, 133, 139, 151, 175, 188, 199–201, 207, 231, 243, 254–5, 277
   return to the defense (chapter 7), 10, 52, 58, 60, 62, 68–71, 81, 85–6, 91, 97, 101, 117, 131, 140, 146–7, 146 n36, 152–3, 156, 159–60, 162–8, 170, 179, 182, 184, 186, 229, 273, 276–80, 290, 296
   Simmias' *harmonia* objection (chapter 8), 5, 10, 12, 128, 131, 158, 184–5, 188, 193–6, 233, 241, 248, 251–2, 298

Phaedo (individual), 6, 8, 12–17, 21, 27, 31–2, 31 n10, 34, 36–7, 40–2, 44–6, 45 n33, 53, 96, 184, 187–8, 190, 247–8, 255, 309
   background of, 13, 32
   death of Socrates and, 41
   Zopyrus, 14
Philolaus, 6, 13, 17–20, 19 n30, 27, 97, 196–8, 197 n23, 200, 202 n32, 269 n46, 275, 291
Philosophy; *see also* wisdom
   afterlife and, 163–5, 292
   courage and, 43, 179–80, 301
   desire to be dead and, 25–6, 32–3, 36, 43, 53–61, 69, 75–7, 86, 162 n2, 164–5, 170, 176, 194, 304–5, 309
   embodiment and, 8, 14, 25, 33, 55, 59, 62–3, 75–7, 83, 86, 164, 174, 180, 182, 194, 246, 309
   heroic activities and, 6, 43
   luck and, 43
   moderation and, 42
   natural, 6, 98–9, 214, 218, 228, 288
   ordinary people and, 26, 41, 57, 59, 78, 80, 171, 283
   purification and, 25, 57–8, 62, 69, 162 n2, 165, 303
   truth and, 29, 75, 101, 108, 174–5, 179, 193
   virtue and, 26, 37, 55, 59, 77, 175–8, 192
Phlius, 21
Phthia, 35 n22
Pindar, 278, 291
   Olympian Odes, 278, 291
pistis; *see* conviction (*pistis*) *and* trust (*pistis*)
Plato, 12–18, 20, 21 n37, 22, 24, 26, 28–31 and 28 n1, 29 n2, 38–9, 45 n35, 52–3, 55, 56 n5, 63, 66, 68, 74, 76, 82, 100–1, 106, 109, 115, 123–5, 127, 131–2, 138, 140 n22, 143, 145–7, 152 n45, 166–8, 171, 182, 188, 191, 207, 213, 217, 227–8, 233, 253, 256, 258, 271, 275, 278, 285, 294, 301, 303–5, 308, 311; *see also* forms, Platonic; *see also* dialogues
   absence of (*Phaedo*), 15–17
   Apology, 15–16, 18, 22, 24–5, 35, 98, 126, 217, 221, 226, 285, 293, 301, 304, 306
   Charmides, 71, 133, 308
   Cratylus, 16–17, 30, 73, 106, 124, 143, 164 n3, 171, 217, 255, 288
   Crito, 15, 22, 35 n22, 221
   Euthydemus, 15, 26, 44 n33, 140 n22
   Euthyphro, 71–3, 72 n32, 110, 124, 126, 230, 231 n62, 241 n88, 260 n18
   Gorgias, 25, 34, 34 n17, 48–51, 49 n45, 73 n34, 124, 126, 188, 221, 277–9, 292–3, 295, 297, 301
   Hippias Major, 72, 72 n32, 142 n27, 230, 256–7
   Hippias Minor, 221
   Laches, 71, 126, 133 n6, 178, 182, 217, 221, 257
   Laws, 30 n7, 35, 144 n31, 293

346 Index

Plato (cont.)
- Meno, 26, 36 n23, 65, 71–3, 72 n32, 78, 85, 101, 110, 217, 221, 229–30, 231 n62, 234
- Parmenides, 24 n40, 64 n18, 217, 257
- Phaedo; see Phaedo
- Phaedrus, 16, 24 n40, 132, 148, 271, 274
- Philebus, 51, 85, 144 n31, 166, 217, 227–8
- Protagoras, 26, 49–51, 53, 72, 78, 83, 110, 221, 230
- Republic, 8, 16, 23, 24 n40, 26, 28–32, 30 n7, 35, 38–42, 40 n30, 51, 76, 82, 86, 114–16, 124, 131, 138–48, 140 n21, 141 n25, 144 n31, 148 n41, 155–6, 166, 169, 174, 179–80, 189 n8, 205, 220–1, 229, 234, 235 n72, 245–6, 253, 256, 260 n18, 271–4, 278–9, 283, 292, 295–7, 301, 310
- Sophist, 132, 144 n31, 152 n45, 153 n46, 272–3
- Statesman, 144 n31, 227–8, 295
- Symposium, 16 n18, 17, 31 n10, 49–51, 53, 141 n25, 148, 158, 182, 226 n51, 271–2, 271 n53, 292 n36
- Theaetetus, 24 n40, 256, 288
- Timaeus, 124, 127 n54, 132 n1, 144 n31, 152 n45, 155, 168–9, 217, 220, 222, 223 n45, 274, 284, 289, 290 n29, 292–3, 295, 297, 308
- tragedy and, 28–30, 31 n9, 33–5, 37, 42
- pleasure, 4–5, 13–15, 26, 29, 31–3, 37, 41, 47–52, 69–71, 77–86, 83 n49, 97, 162 n2, 166–8, 171–7, 172 n15, 176 n25, 179, 182, 297
  - intense, 33, 172–3, 173 n19
- Plotinus, 219 n34
- poison; see drug (*pharmakon*)
- Presocratics, 155; see also Anaxagoras, Anaximander, Diogenes of Apollonia, Empedocles, Heraclitus, Hippias, Hippocratic corpus, Parmenides, Philolaus, *and* Pythagoreans
  - soul and, 155
- Protagoras, 24, 50, 72
  - *muthos* and, 50
- Pyriphlegethon (river), 290
- Pythagoras, 102
- Pythagoreans, 4 n4, 6–8, 12, 17–23, 19 n30, 21 n37, 27, 30 n4, 88, 97, 99, 102–3, 130, 277 n9, 291–2; see also Empedocles *and* Philolaus
  - *acousmata* and, 7, 18, 23, 291
  - eschatological beliefs and, 17, 275, 292
  - mathematical, 18
  - recollecting and, 128
  - reincarnation and, 97, 102

recollecting, 9, 17, 92, 100–7, 110, 117–22, 125–7, 129, 229; see also Simmias; see also Phaedo, recollecting argument dissimilar things and, 103–7
- falling short and, 108 n15, 121 n43
- learning and, 9, 26, 89, 101, 103, 117, 119 n40, 125, 129, 191, 199–200, 243
- similar things and, 103–8, 108 n15, 118–19, 121
recollection; see recollecting
reincarnation, 2, 7, 10, 33, 49, 56–7, 62, 88, 91, 93, 97, 99, 102–3, 127 n54, 162, 169, 169 n10, 177, 278, 297, 309
- *acousmata* and, 7, 18, 23, 291
- eschatological beliefs and, 17, 275, 292
- mathematical, 18
- Pythagoreans and, 7, 17
- recollecting and, 128
religion (Greek), 17, 19, 52, 186, 277, 300, 308
- purification and, 58, 86
resemblance, 119

Samos, 211
science, natural, 2, 10, 25–6, 99, 207–8, 216–17, 225, 229, 234, 247, 290, 294, 296–7
Sedley, David, 14, 81 n46, 95–6, 111, 126, 257, 266, 275, 281–2
seeming, 112–15
self-predication, 123–4 and 123 n44, 124 n46, 267 n41
senses, 2, 55, 58, 71, 74–5, 86, 101–17, 136, 159, 162 n2, 171, 175, 228
- inquiry and, 76, 101, 118, 229
- knowledge and, 101
sensible things; see objects, ordinary
Sicily, 287 n24
Simmias, 5, 9–10, 12, 14, 17–21, 23–5, 27, 36, 41, 44, 46, 59–61, 71–2, 76, 79, 81, 86, 90–3, 94 n17, 112, 115, 120, 135, 141, 152 n45, 158, 177, 179, 184–202 and 184 n2, 187 n5, 197 n23, 205–6, 208, 212, 228, 233, 239–43, 248, 251, 253–9, 267 n41, 280–1, 285, 298
- as intellectual, 15, 20
- credulity of, 21
- death and, 60
- death of Socrates and, 41
- dialogue writer and, 14–15
- difficult to persuade, 23
- equality and, 103–7, 110, 112–13, 117–22, 124–6, 129, 194
- fear of death and, 93
- forms and, 3, 20, 103, 105, 110, 119, 126, 128, 200–1, 231, 239, 241–2, 256
- *harmonia* objection; see Phaedo, Simmias' *harmonia* objection
- ignorance and, 24
- ignored by Socrates, 241
- knowledge and, 126–7
- largeness and, 158, 212, 255–9, 256 n10
- *logoi* and, 189, 191, 199–200
- methodology of, 194–5, 228, 241 n89

misology and, 21, 200, 243
opinion of Socrates and, 186
Orphism and, 13
Philolaus and, 13, 17, 19–20, 20 n35
philosophers and, 69
Pythagoreans and, 13, 19, 27
recollecting and, 102–17, 108 n15, 126, 129, 199–200, 243
seeming and, 113
senses and, 74
Socratic ideas and, 20
soul and, 90, 93, 101, 103, 128, 162 n1, 185, 195–202, 205, 241, 243, 251
slavery, 6, 13, 37, 53, 69, 79–80, 166, 297, 309–10
Socrates; see dialogues
   Aesop and, 13, 28–9, 32, 47, 52
   Apollo and, 32, 39, 42, 186
   asceticism and, 182
   death of, 5, 11, 13, 15–17, 21–2, 28, 31–2, 34, 36, 41, 43, 45–7, 45 n35, 299, 302–3, 308–9, 311
   eschatology and, 278, 297
   Heracles and, 36–8 and 36 n25, 44, 184, 189
   heroism and, 6, 22, 28–9, 34–8, 36 n25, 41–4, 76, 299
   humility of, 43, 52
   muthos of, 11, 47–51, 51 n48, 53, 276, 278, 280–8, 292, 294–7 and 294 n40
   Phaedo and, 14
   piety of, 42, 52, 186, 301–4, 308
   prophecy and, 185–7, 306–7, 310
   Theseus and, 33–6 and 36 n25, 43
soul, 2, 4–6, 10, 15, 21, 51, 54–65, 60 n9, 67–71, 75, 85–6, 89, 92–5, 97, 101–2, 118, 127, 130–1, 133–46, 140 n21, 152–84, 154 n49, 195–206, 228, 243, 249, 251–5, 258, 266–74, 276–81, 289–90, 292–4, 297–8, 300–1, 307–10; *see also* Simmias; *see also* Cebes
   before birth, 9, 89, 94, 101–3, 119, 122, 254
   body and, 76, 78, 92, 127, 146, 157–60, 162, 164, 167, 170–83, 195–200, 202–6, 241, 249, 252, 254, 266–7, 273, 279, 294, 308–9
   bringers and, 260, 263
   character and, 169
   composite, 198–9, 206
   death and, 1, 4–5, 9, 11, 19 n30, 23–6, 43–4, 58, 61–3 and 61 n12, 68, 76, 88–99, 102–18, 127–8, 130, 132–6, 140, 156, 163, 165, 169, 179, 185–8, 193, 206, 240, 248, 251–3, 253 n9, 267–8, 271, 273, 275, 280, 307, 310
   divine and, 10, 37, 44, 58, 90, 131–2, 153, 157, 271–4
   education and, 279, 293, 296
   fear of unseen and, 168–70
   flexible nature of, 160
   forms and, 4–5, 9–10, 75, 102, 132, 155–6, 172 n15, 271–3
   guides and, 290
   harmonia and, 185, 191, 194–203, 199 n28, 206, 241–3
   immortality and, 4, 8, 10, 21, 26, 37, 68, 76, 89–90, 99, 101, 135, 140, 154–5, 164, 176, 239, 242, 246, 248–54, 261, 266–73, 276, 281, 304, 307
   imperishability and, 4, 9–10, 135, 140, 155, 157, 249–54, 266, 268–9, 273
   intermingled with body, 167
   investigation and, 70, 127, 153–4, 159, 161, 164
   invisibility and, 196
   judgment and, 279
   kinship with the forms and, 155–7, 160, 271–4
   kinship with unseen and, 135–6, 152–3, 164–5, 196, 200, 249, 251–3, 253 n9, 254, 271–3, 290
   krasis and, 196
   multiform and, 148
   purity and, 5, 7, 58, 62, 68, 70, 97, 135, 145, 146 n36, 148, 153–5, 163–71, 175, 180, 258, 279–80, 290, 293–4, 300
   reincarnation and, 7, 9, 88, 93, 99, 102, 158, 164–6, 169–70, 251, 253, 263 n30, 278
   ruling and, 153, 159–61, 196, 202–6, 251–2, 254, 297
   senses and, 153
   separation from the body and, 63, 75, 97
   the visible and, 153, 170
   uniform and, 148
   wisdom and, 102, 127, 130, 136, 154, 156, 160, 163, 277
Stoicism, 33, 207
storytelling, 6, 51–3; *see also* Socrates, *muthos* of
Strato of Lampsacus, 270
Styx, 40 n30
suicide, 17–21, 54–7, 55 n2, 97, 99, 171, 188, 200

Tartarus, 40 n30, 288–9, 293
teleology, 208, 220, 222–4 and 222 n43, 276, 282
Telephus, 47
temperance, 77–86, 83 n49, 163, 170, 175, 177–80, 182, 297, 300–2
Theophrastus, 156 n53
   De Sensibus, 156 n53
Theseus, 28, 32, 36 n25, 36–8, 43
Thompson, Brett, 257
Thucydides, 64, 66 n23, 269 n46
tragedy, 6, 22, 28–31 and 28 n1, 29 n2, 31 n10, 33, 35, 37–40, 42–7, 51, 278; *see also* Aeschylus *and* Euripides
Troy, 210

trust (*pistis*), 5, 46, 184–92, 232–3, 237–40, 252; *see also* conviction (*pistis*)
truth, 4–5, 18, 23–4, 27, 29, 33, 36, 39, 41, 43–4, 53, 55, 57–8, 69, 71, 76, 101, 118, 155, 159, 172, 174–5, 179, 182, 189–91, 191 n13, 193–4, 228, 270, 295–7, 304, 306, 310–11
   acquisition of, 75, 178
   desire for, 75
tuchē; see luck
Tuozzo, Thomas, 114

underworld, 35, 38, 47, 276, 280, 285, 287, 298, 306; *see also* Hades

virtue, 26, 72, 78, 83, 91, 122, 162, 170, 202, 297; *see also* courage, justice, Socrates, piety of, temperance *and* wisdom

wisdom, 5, 8–9, 14, 19, 25–7, 33, 37, 40, 55–6, 58–63, 65, 69–70, 75–8, 80 n44, 81–6 and 81 n46, 83 n49, 88–9, 92, 99, 108, 118, 163, 170, 173–7, 179–80, 182, 192–4, 215, 221, 239, 294, 301, 304; *see also* philosophy *and* soul
   acquisition of, 8, 34, 61, 69–70, 75–6, 246
   currency and, 85
   desire for, 16, 25, 56, 58–9, 61–2, 69, 75, 193, 206
   embodiment and, 75–7, 246
   purification and, 82, 85–7, 165, 175, 179
Wyttenbach's conjecture, 218, 219 n35

Xanthippe, 9, 31, 41, 47

Zeus, 37, 41, 50, 310
Zopyrus, 14

For EU product safety concerns, contact us at Calle de José Abascal, 56–1°, 28003 Madrid, Spain or eugpsr@cambridge.org.

www.ingramcontent.com/pod-product-compliance
Lightning Source LLC
LaVergne TN
LVHW011758060526
838200LV00053B/3623